THE
PENNSYLVANIA
ONE–DAY TRIP
BOOK

To Eleanor Bloch
with loving appreciation

THE PENNSYLVANIA ONE–DAY TRIP BOOK

Jane Ockershausen

MORE THAN
600 SITES BECKON
DAY-TRIPPERS
TO DISCOVER
FOR THEMSELVES
THAT "AMERICA
STARTS HERE"

HOWELL PRESS
Charlottesville, Virginia

ACKNOWLEDGMENTS

I would like to thank Andi Coyle
for her help in planning my itineraries
and routes during the two years I spent
researching Pennsylvania.

Library of Congress Cataloging-in-Publication Data

Ockershausen, Jane.
    The Pennsylvania one-day trip book : more than 600 sites
beckon day-trippers to discover for themselves that "America
starts here" / Jane Ockershausen.
        p.   cm.
    Includes index.
    ISBN 0-939009-88-9
    1. Pennsylvania—Guidebooks.   I. Title.
F147.3.025   1995
917.4804'43—dc20   95-12344
                                                            CIP

Howell Press, Inc., 1713-2D Allied Lane,
    Charlottesville, VA 22903
www.howellpress.com
Printed in the United States of America

Second Printing 2000

Cover and book design by Tom Huestis
Cover photographs:
    A serene Amish scene
    Pittsburgh's skyline a-glitter at night by Andrew A. Wagner
    Illuminated fountains at Longwood Gardens by L. Albee,
        Longwood Gardens

Contents

THE PENNSYLVANIA ONE-DAY TRIP BOOK

═══════════ VALLEYS OF THE SUSQUEHANNA ═══════════

The Keys to the
═══Keystone State═══

T wenty years ago when I began writing the first of my nine
One-Day Trip Books, most American families took one or two
week family trips. In the intervening years, changing vacation
patterns have put a new emphasis on day-tripping and weekend
excursions. My two decades of travel in the Mid-Atlantic region
have taken me to hundreds of historic homes, museums, parks
and other sites. I find that at each spot visitors learn or see something new.

Daytrippers discover why Pennsylvania's motto is "America
Starts Here," as they trace the roots of the country's political,
cultural, industrial and technological advances. This is where
the Declaration of Independence and the Constitution were written. Pennsylvania is also the home of the Liberty Bell and the
site of Lincoln's Gettysburg Address. Here, travelers get a step-
by-step look at the development of America's railroad and canal
system. There are sites that reveal the particulars of the industrial revolution from the first oil well to coal mines and steel
mills. Trips also highlight horticulture, viticulture, agriculture,
astronomy and a host of other academic disciplines.

During my research, I returned again and again to familiar
sites. I found that attractions change, museums expand, new programs are introduced and new information uncovered. I encourage you to revisit spots you toured years ago; even if the
sites remain the same, your experience of them changes because
you see them from a different perspective.

For the past two years, I've criss-crossed Pennsylvania's eight
travel regions. The 310 mile journey across the state takes you
from the East to the Midwest, over the Appalachians through
major cities and into distinctly American small towns. You will
find a state park within 25 miles of any spot you visit. There are
fascinating stories to discover at Drake Well Museum, the Columbus Chapel, French Azilum and Old Economy Village to name
just a few of my favorites. This scenic state has areas of haunting beauty such as the Delaware Water Gap, Pennsylvania Grand
Canyon and Ricketts Glen State Park with its abundance of tum-

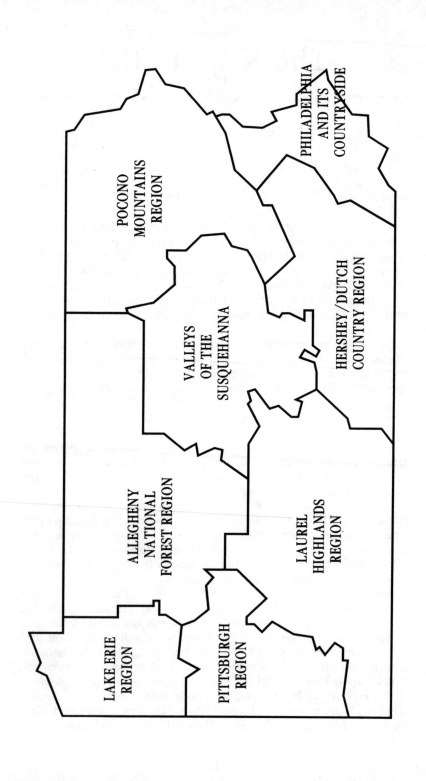

bling waterfalls. The Poconos, the Endless Mountains and the mountains of the Laurel Highlands offer a myriad of recreational options. Longwood Gardens is, in my opinion and in that of many horticultural experts, the finest garden estate in North America. Fallingwater is one of the architectural masterpieces of the 20th century. Philadelphia's Independence National Historical Park is America's most historic square mile.

Even lifelong Pennsylvania residents will find new leisure options among these one-day trips. The Table of Contents contains more than 300 trips which cover roughly 600 places to visit—all of them listed in the Index. In planning your day's itinerary, it's helpful to check all the selections in the geographic region you plan to explore, since many of the attractions can be combined. You should also check the Calendar of Events to see if there are special activities scheduled for the time you plan to visit. Some visitors prefer to schedule trips when there are fewer people, but others enjoy the festivals and fairs that enliven parks and historic sites. If you plan to attend a specific event, call ahead to make sure of its date. Hours of operation often change; so it's always a good idea to call before starting out.

Travelers find day trips appealing because they are an inexpensive way to explore and learn. Many attractions provide lovely picnic areas. Short excursions spaced weekly or monthly throughout the year offer escapes from the winter doldrums, a jump on spring, a wide array of outdoor summer recreation or a fall foliage fling.

No matter when they are taken, these short journeys nourish the spirit and provide shared experiences that are long remembered. This book unlocks the Keystone State for you!

J.O.

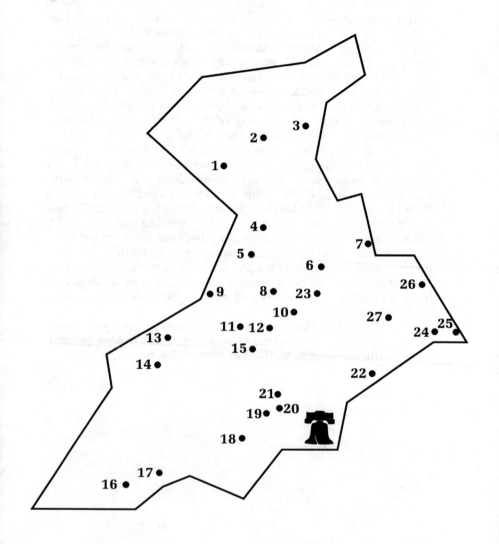

PHILADELPHIA AND ITS COUNTRYSIDE

ALL PHILADELPHIA SITES

1. **Allentown**
   Bridges of Lehigh County
   Dorney Park and Wildwater
   Kingdom
   Lehigh County Historical
   Society Sites

2. **Bethlehem**

3. **Easton**
   Hugh Moore Historical Park
   and Canal Museum

4. **Hilltown**
   Pearl S. Buck House

5. **Worcester**
   Peter Wentz Farmstead and
   Morgan Log House

6. **Doylestown**
   Byers' Choice Christmas
   Gallery
   Fordhook Farm and Henry
   Schmieder Arboretum
   James A. Michener Art
   Museum
   Mercer Mile
   National Shrine of Our Lady
   of Czestochowa

7. **New Hope/Lahaska**
   Bucks County Vineyards and
   Covered Bridges
   New Hope
   Peddler's Village, Carousel
   World and Point Pleasant

8. **Audubon**
   Mill Grove

9. **Pottstown**
   Pottsgrove Manor

10. **Fort Washington**
    Hope Lodge

11. **Chester Springs**
    Historic Yellow Springs

12. **Valley Forge**
    Valley Forge National Historical Park

13. **Glenmore**
    Springton Manor Farm

14. **Coatesville**
    Hibernia Mansion

15. **Paoli**
    Historic Waynesborough
    Wharton Esherick Studio

16. **Kennett Square**
    Longwood Gardens

17. **Chadds Ford**
    Barns-Brinton House and
    Chaddsford Winery
    Brandywine River Museum,
    Chadds Ford and Brandy-
    wine Battlefield Park

18. **Media**
    Colonial Pennsylvania Plan-
    tation and Tyler Arboretum

19. **Merion**
    Barnes Foundation

20. **Havertown**
    The Grange

21. **Gladwyn**
    Woodmont

22. **Andalusia**

23. **Horsham**
    Graeme Park

24. **Fallsington**

25. **Morrisville**
    Pennsbury Manor

26. **Washington Crossing**
    Washington Crossing His-
    toric Park and Bowman's
    Hill Wildflower Preserve

27. **Langhorne**
    Sesame Place

A statue of John Barry, America's first Commodore, stands before Independence Hall, where both the Declaration of Independence and the Constitution were hammered out. (See page 45 for more information.) Photo by Sally Moore

Philadelphia and Its
═══════Countryside═══════

In Philadelphia, the state's largest city, you can explore America's most historic square mile. Here the Declaration of Independence was written, the new nation was born and the U.S. Constitution first heard. Here are the homes and boarding houses where our founders lived, the government buildings where they met, the taverns where they ate, the shops where they worked and nearby the battlefields and winter camps where too many of them died. The Liberty Bell, tangible reminder of our past, invites all who visit to reach out and touch history.

In addition to this unsurpassed historical treasure, Philadelphia offers a range of not-to-be-missed museums including the Philadelphia Museum of Art, the Franklin Institute Science Museum, the University of Pennsylvania Museum of Archeology and Anthropology and the Independence Seaport Museum. Specialized collections can be found at the Rodin, Rosenbach, Norman Rockwell, Mummers and Please Touch Museum.

In Bucks County the bounty continues: history, art, vineyards, recreational options and Sesame Place, a family theme park based on the popular public television show. In addition to Revolutionary War battlesites, history buffs will find General "Mad" Anthony Wayne's family home at Historic Waynesborough, the ruins of a hospital in Historic Yellow Springs where George Washington's troops were treated for yellow fever plus farmsteads reflecting the colonial era such as Peter Wentz Farmstead, Morgan Log House and Graeme Park.

Artists have long frequented this area. There is a school of painting that takes its name from the Brandywine area of Bucks County. Regional artists are exhibited at the Brandywine River Museum and the James A. Michener Art Museum. Audubon created a great deal of his bird studies at his home here, Mill Grove. Pearl Buck, an artist with words, worked from her home, Green Hills Farm. The studio of Wharton Esherick, a less widely known painter, is also in Bucks County. Art being created today is exhibited and sold in New Hope, Historic Yellow Springs and Peddler's Village.

One of the most beautiful spots in all of Pennsylvania is the 350-acre Longwood Gardens. The conservatories, fountains and specialty gardens offer a seasonally changing palette of colors and contrasts.

The Lehigh Valley falls within this region as well. Bethlehem, "America's Christmas City", provides an insightful look at the Moravian sect who founded the community in 1741. The Lehigh County Historical Society has a group of diverse attractions that trace the settlement and development of the region. Breathless fun for the whole family awaits at Dorney Park, home of the world's tallest wooden roller coaster.

PHILADELPHIA

Army-Navy Museum and Marine Corps Memorial Museum

Martial Mementos

Standing on the gun deck of an 18th-century frigate and hearing the sound of water lapping against the ship reinforces the illusion that you have stepped into a time machine. But it is just one of the effective means employed by the **Army-Navy Museum** in the Pemberton House to bring to life the early days of the United States.

A series of lighted maps traces the course of the important naval confrontations of the American Revolution. Visitors can even try their hand at maneuvering for a sea battle in the 1700s. A series of switches enables the operator to move a ship's sails and rudder to position her for battle. A light indicates a successful effort. This is popular with young visitors.

Lighted maps and dioramas trace the major land battles of the Revolution. Militia uniforms reflect how the United States Army developed. Early battle flags and weapons are included in the exhibit. One of the flags is from the First Regiment, the lone infantry regiment from 1784 to 1790.

Just across the cobbled path from Pemberton House is New Hall, which houses the museum of Marine Corps history, completing the military picture. Displays tell the story of Marine action from 1775 to 1783. There is a Memorial Room with an Honor Roll of Marine deaths which rests on sand from Iwo Jima.

Both the Army-Navy Museum and the Marine Corp Memorial Museum are open daily from 9:00 A.M. to 5:00 P.M.

Directions: From I-95 southbound (from points north) take Exit 17. Using the right-hand lanes of the exit, follow the signs for Callowhill Street/Independence Hall. At the bottom of the exit ramp, follow 2nd Street straight ahead to Chestnut Street. Continue a half block past Chestnut Street for the Historic Area Parking Garage on the left. It is best to park your car and walk to all the sites in the Historic District. Start at the Independence National Historical Park Visitors Center, one block away, at 3rd and Chestnut Streets. Here you can pick up an easy-to-follow map of the district and a park schedule. If you are traveling northbound on I-95 (from points south) you will also take Exit 17. Stay in the left lane because you will exit on the left side of I-95. At the exit, stay in the right-hand lane and follow the signs for Independence Hall/Historic Area. Turn left at 6th Street to Chestnut. This will take you through the heart of the Historic District to 2nd Street. Turn right on 2nd Street. The entrance to the Historic Area Parking Garage is on the left.

Atwater Kent Museum

Scope Out the City

Philadelphia brings to life so much of our nation's history that the story of the city itself often gets neglected. If you want to learn how the city got started and how it has grown, the place to visit is the **Atwater Kent Museum**.

The museum is situated in the original home of the Franklin Institute. The building was erected between 1825 and 1826 during the Federal period. Copies of Penn's original plans for the city are in the William Penn room, maps of the city's changing profile are displayed elsewhere. You'll get a brief look at a diverse selection of the city's fire equipment; for a more indepth coverage visit Fireman's Hall (see selection). The exhibit on city police includes old mug books. Annie Cameron, who was wanted in the 1890s for highway robbery, looks like a tough desperado as she stares from the aged pages. The museum's exhibits also include information on the city's gas and water departments.

When Philadelphians celebrated their city's centennial on September 28, 1876, a quarter of a million people turned out for Pennsylvania State Day. Souvenirs of this popular event abound in the museum: flags, fans, medals, games and needlework.

The museum reveals Philadelphia as a transportation center that linked the port with both the Old and the New World. Its collections includes ship models to represent the city's shipbuilding works. There are photographs from Hog Island, the largest shipyard in the world prior to World War I. Philadelphia was also one of the earliest cities in the country to adopt rail transportation. You'll see a model of the 1829 Stephenson's Rocket and Baldwin's eight-wheeled locomotive.

Drawing from its collection of over 70,000 objects, the museum presents changing exhibits on a variety of subjects related to the historical development of the city. For a complete listing of upcoming lectures, tours and workshops call (215) 922-3031.

The Atwater Kent Museum is open at no charge Tuesday through Saturday from 9:30 A.M. to 4:45 P.M. It is closed on Sundays, Mondays and major holidays. A public parking lot is conveniently located next to the museum.

Directions: From I-95 in downtown Philadelphia take the Market Street exit, the Atwater Kent Museum is at 15 South 7th Street between Market and Chestnut Streets.

Balch Institute for Ethnic Studies and Reading Terminal Market

Trace Your Roots

For two centuries many of the immigrants who flocked to the New World landed and settled in Philadelphia, one of America's busiest ports of entry. Like New York, the city is a multi-ethnic community of immigrants. The **Balch Institute**'s collection tells the story of their journey and their past.

This is a spot where virtually every American can find a bit of their family's past. In the museum's lobby a computer lets you key in your cultural heritage and get a print out of when your ethnic groups arrived in Pennsylvania. There is also a list of historical and cultural places to visit to learn more about the contribution of your ethnic group to Philadelphia's development.

Selecting German-American heritage revealed that the first German settlers arrived near Philadelphia on October 6, 1683. They established Germantown and began traditions that endure to this day. By the American Revolution, a third of Pennsylvania's population was German. The print out goes on to list ten spots of interest including the German Society of Philadelphia, the Germantown Historical Society, Historic Rittenhousetown and several churches.

The "Do Your Own Heritage" information sheets also provide restaurants and shopping that expand on the selected ethnic group. There's also a special events sampler. Each ends with a little known fact related to the chosen group. For example, soft pretzels were introduced in Philadelphia by German immigrants. The first recorded soft pretzel maker in the city was Frederick Trefz whose Market Street shop sold pretzels in 1837.

Every visitor to the Balch Institute should take the time to trace their own heritage even if there is not time to explore it in depth. This museum has become the nation's attic with articles revealing the richness and diversity of America's family tree. Some of the items are beautifully crafted quilts and needlework; others are scuffed and worn shoes. Each has a story.

The museum takes up the first floor. The second contains an extensive research library encompassing 80 different cultural groups with 350 newspapers titles on microfilm and 750 archival and photographic collections. Entries are organized by ethnic group and they chronicle the daily life of these diverse groups. The cozy reading room is welcoming. You can research your own genealogy or browse through the fascinating collection, perhaps reading an immigrant's diary or listening to recordings.

The museum and library are open Tuesday through Saturday 10:00 A.M. to 4:00 P.M. A nominal admission is charged.

A perfect complement to your museum visit is a stop at **Reading Terminal Market** where you can partake of an ethnic smorgasbord. Homemade Pennsylvania Dutch, Mexican, Italian, Szechuan, Greek, Chinese, Japanese and Middle Eastern specialties are available at various reasonable and speedy eateries. It's also one of the world's largest traditional farmer's market consisting of vendors selling produce, meat, fish, baked and dairy goods along with a variety of other specialty groceries. For a snack, you can't beat **Bassett's Ice Cream**. The Bassett family is one of two merchants to operate in the market since it first opened its doors to the public on February 22, 1892. Other favorites are the **Famous 4th Street Cookie Company** and **Fisher's Dutch Treats** for hot pretzels made while you watch.

Reminiscent of markets in Paris, Budapest and Stockholm, Reading Terminal Market has been a great market from its earliest days. It is more Old World bazaar than trendy eatery, enjoyed equally by residents and visitors. Eighty businesses, representing at least a dozen countries, operate in this market housed in the historic two-acre former Reading Railroad train shed. The market, conveniently located between City Hall and Independence Historical Park, is open Monday through Saturday from 8:00 A.M. to 6:00 P.M. Closed on Sundays. For more information you can call (215) 922-2317.

Directions: From I-95, if you are traveling north, take I-676 into the city and exit on 6th Street South. For the Balch Institute take 6th Street to Walnut Street and make a right on Wal-

At the Reading Terminal Market, one of the world's largest traditional farmer's markets, more than 80 businesses from over a dozen countries, exemplify Philadelphia's ethnic mix.

nut. Then make another right on 7th Street. The Balch Institute is between Chestnut and Market Streets at 18 South 7th Street. Return to Chestnut Street and turn right on 12th Street; Reading Terminal Market is at 12th and Arch Streets.

Carpenters' Hall and City Tavern

Where to Meet?

A political statement was made in 1774 when the First Continental Congress voted to meet in Carpenters' Hall instead of the State House, now called Independence Hall (see selection), just two blocks up the street.

The moderates wanted to meet in the formal, official government offices of the colony. They hoped to exert more influence at the State House. Joseph Galloway, Speaker of the Pennsylvania Assembly, had aspirations of leading Congress. All of these plans were circumvented when the delegates met at City Tavern on September 5, 1774 and headed as a group to inspect **Carpenters' Hall**.

The craftsmen's guild had not quite finished their work on Carpenters' Hall. It was a handsomely proportioned two-story building. On the ground floor there were two meeting rooms divided by a long hall. The delegates to the First Continental Congress inspected the small bright East Room with its rows of commodious hickory armchairs.

Well-pleased with the hall, the delegates voted to meet for their deliberations in the East Room, over the objection of the moderate contingent. Peyton Randolph of Virginia was chosen to chair the meeting.

The next point of dispute was how to count the delegates' vote: by colony, one vote for each; or by poll, counting heads with a majority winning. There was no correlation between the colony's population and the number of delegates. Massachusetts, with a large population, had four delegates; New Jersey had far fewer residents but one more delegate. Virginia had seven delegates and there were fears that Pennsylvania and Maryland would send additional members to vote on major issues. John Jay of New York proposed that the Congress give each colony one vote as a temporary working arrangement but not as a precedent.

Carpenters' Hall contains exhibits on the carpenters' guild, the oldest trade organization in the country. It is part of Independence National Historical Park (INHP) and opens at no charge 10:00 A.M. to 4:00 P.M. daily.

City Tavern is also part of INHP. If billboards and commercials had been part of 18th-century life, then this tavern would certainly have promoted John Adams's testimonial that this tavern was "the most genteel one in America."

From its opening in 1774, through the next 80 tumultuous years as America found its place in the world, this tavern served the men who made the nation. It was a favorite meeting spot for revolutionaries and businessmen. Paul Revere brought news to tavern patrons on May 20, 1774 that the port of Boston was closed. A larger group gathered at City Tavern and agreed to send a message of sympathy to the people of Boston.

During the American Revolution, the tavern was used by General Washington as his headquarters. Colonial officers lodged here, including Horatio Gates, Benedict Arnold and the Marquis de Lafayette. The British enjoyed the hospitality of City Tavern during their occupation of Philadelphia. Many Tory balls were held here during 1777 and 1778.

This is a reconstruction of the original City Tavern. The first innkeeper, Daniel Smith, was an Englishman who wanted his tavern to resemble those in London. The menu reflects not only colonial but modern tastes.

Directions: From I-95 southbound (from points north) take Exit 17. Using the right-hand lanes of the exit, follow the signs for Callowhill Street/Independence Hall. At the bottom of the exit ramp, follow 2nd Street straight ahead to Chestnut Street. Continue a half block past Chestnut Street for the Historic Area Parking Garage on the left. It is best to park your car and walk to all the sites in the Historic District. Start at the Independence National Historical Park Visitors Center, one block away, at 3rd and Chestnut Streets. Here you can pick up an easy-to-follow map of the district and a park schedule. If you are traveling northbound on I-95 (from points south) you will also take Exit 17. Stay in the left lane because you will exit on the left side of I-95. At the exit, stay in the right-hand lane and follow the signs for Independence Hall/Historic Area. Turn left at 6th Street to Chestnut. This will take you through the heart of the Historic District to 2nd Street. Turn right on 2nd Street. The entrance to the Historic Area Parking Garage is on the left.

Cliveden

Eschew Felicity

A painting by E. L. Henry of the Battle of Germantown hangs at Cliveden on the same walls that still bear traces of the perilous moments in 1777 when the Americans tried valiantly to breach the sturdy stones and defeat the British. You will see reminders of this October 4 confrontation when you tour **Cliveden** (pronounced cliv-den).

Benjamin Chew, who built Cliveden ten years earlier and still owned it, was being held under arrest in New Jersey because of his suspected British sympathies. As Chief Justice of Pennsylvania, he had scrupulously endeavored to uphold the law—British law. This led to his arrest in the summer of 1777 and he did not see his war-ravaged house until the following spring. It was "an absolute wreck, and materials not to be had to keep out the weather". Chew's despair was keenly felt because he had helped design his countryseat. It took four years to build the mid-Georgian $2^{1}/_{2}$ story house. Particularly pleasing to Chew were the five urns that adorn the roof, each on its own ornamental pedestal. These fortunately survived the colonial confrontation.

Another Henry painting you will see when you tour Cliveden is of the Lafayette Reception held in 1825 when the Marquis de

Lafayette returned to America to celebrate the Revolutionary victories. The painting hangs in the front entrance hall and replicates the two portraits and the Tuscan columns that are still there.

In Mrs. Chew's sitting room there is a silhouette of Benjamin Chew. A portrait was painted later from this likeness and it hangs in the parlor. While observing the lavish furnishings look for the names of earlier guests. Their names are not in a guest book but are inscribed on the window panes with a diamond point stylus. The ornate parlor mirrors may have been used to decorate the tent walls when General Howe's junior officers gave an elaborate party, or fete champetre, in his honor before his return to England.

As you move to the second floor you will pass the window that once looked out on the rear court. An 1867-68 addition to the main house has been artistically camouflaged so that visitors do not lose the original ambience. Upstairs the 13-foot high ceilings are reminders of the lavish construction associated with this early era.

Antique lovers and history buffs will appreciate the many fine family heirlooms. Cliveden, with the exception of an 18-year period after the Revolution during which it was owned by a wealthy Irish-American merchant, has always belonged to the Chew family. It was acquired by the National Trust for Historic Preservation from the Chew family in 1972.

You can visit the six-acre Cliveden estate at 6401 Germantown Avenue from April through December on Tuesday through Saturday from 10:00 A.M. until 4:00 P.M. Tours are given on the hour with the last tour at 3:00 P.M. Sunday hours are 1:30 P.M. to 4:30 P.M. (to have a full tour be sure to arrive by 3:15 P.M.). Admission is charged.

Directions: From I-95 take the exit for I-76 west, the Schuylkill Expressway. Take the Expressway to exit 32, Lincoln Drive (it is also marked Germantown-Wissahickon Park). Take Lincoln Drive to Johnson Street. Turn right onto Johnson, go to the fourth traffic light which is Germantown Avenue. Turn left onto Germantown, go one block and turn right onto Cliveden Street. Street parking for Cliveden is available at the end of the first block on Cliveden Street.

Congress Hall and Old City Hall

Seats of Power

On March 4, 1797, America's leaders assembled in the House of Representatives' chamber in **Congress Hall** to watch the inauguration of John Adams as the second President of the United States. George Washington was on hand to facilitate the nation's first transfer of executive power. There is a perhaps apocryphal story about what happened after Adams took the oath of office. Washington was now a private citizen and he motioned for Thomas Jefferson, who was the new Vice President, to precede him from the room. Jefferson hesitated, then stepped in front of George Washington; thus did the nation achieve the transfer of power with dignity and smooth precision.

The young federal government met in Philadelphia, called by some the "capital of the New World," for ten years while the new federal city was built in Washington. The legislative branch used Congress Hall, then called Philadelphia Court House, for its sessions.

The "lower house" met on the lower, first floor chambers. A large dais was added for the Speaker of the House and rows of mahogany desks were built by a Philadelphia cabinetmaker. The county commissioners added a spectator's gallery for those interested in watching the federal government in session.

The upstairs was refitted for the Senate chambers. The senators had their own desks with comfortable leather armchairs. The vice president, who presided over the sessions, sat beneath a canopy in almost "kingly" splendor. The upper floor also had committee and conference rooms and the office of the Secretary of the Senate. All are currently restored.

During the time Congress met here three new states were added to the Union—Vermont in 1791, Kentucky in 1792 and Tennessee in 1796. On May 14, 1800, Congress adjourned to reconvene in the new capital. Philadelphia was no longer the center of the new country.

While government operated from Philadelphia, the judicial branch met in **Old City Hall**. The chamber looks as it did in 1791 when the Supreme Court first met here. Called upon to define the law, but with no power to enforce it, the Supreme Court had initial problems in achieving the respect of the states.

In Chishom vs. Georgia, the court was asked to rule on whether a citizen of one state, in this case South Carolina, could bring a suit against another state, Georgia. The court ruled that it could. Georgia did not even send a lawyer to argue its position.

The Eleventh Amendment to the Constitution reversed this ruling.

Just outside Old City Hall is a colonial watch box. These were used as the city's watchmen made their rounds, keeping their eyes open for fires. The watch boxes contained buckets of water. Each house had to have two buckets of water ready in case the watch sounded the alarm.

Congress Hall and Old City Hall are part of **Independence**

National Historical Park. They have exhibits pertaining to the pivotal events that occurred in their chambers. Both are open at no charge from 9:00 A.M. to 5:00 P.M. daily.

Directions: From I-95 southbound (from points north) take Exit 17. Using the right-hand lanes of the exit, follow the signs for Callowhill Street/Independence Hall. At the bottom of the exit ramp, follow 2nd Street straight ahead to Chestnut Street. Continue a half block past Chestnut Street for the Historic Area Parking Garage on the left. It is best to park your car and walk to all the sites in the Historic District. Start at the Independence National Historical Park Visitors Center, one block away, at 3rd and Chestnut Streets. Here you can pick up an easy-to-follow map of the district and a park schedule. If you are traveling northbound on I-95 (from points south) you will also take Exit 17. Stay in the left lane because you will exit on the left side of I-95. At the exit, stay in the right-hand lane and follow the signs for Independence Hall/Historic Area. Turn left at 6th Street to Chestnut. This will take you through the heart of the Historic District to 2nd Street. Turn right on 2nd Street. The entrance to the Historic Area Parking Garage is on the left.

Declaration House and Betsy Ross House

American Legends

Thomas Jefferson and Betsy Ross are associated with America's fight for independence. Thomas Jefferson is revered as the author of the Declaration of Independence and for his lifetime service in his country's behalf. The second legendary figure may be legendary indeed, since the historical verification of Betsy Ross's contribution is weak.

The **Declaration House**, part of Independence National Historical Park, is where Thomas Jefferson rented rooms during the Second Continental Congress. It was while staying here that Jefferson drafted the Declaration of Independence. These were his second accommodations in the city. The first rooms he rented were too noisy, so he moved to what was then the edge of town and rented two rooms on the second floor from bricklayer Jacob Graff, Jr.

Jefferson attended the regular sessions of the congress in June 1776, then came back to his rooms and worked on a document to express the position of the American colonies regarding British tyranny. There is a short film on Jefferson's labors to bring forth a document that would have the support of the 13 colonies meeting in Philadelphia.

The Graff, or Declaration, House has been completely reconstructed. The only original piece is the lintel in the western window. The bedroom and parlor are replicas of the rooms Jefferson used. An exhibit reveals the sources Jefferson found for some of his statements.

The Declaration House, 7th and Market Streets, is open at no charge 9:00 A.M. to 5:00 P.M. daily.

Did **Betsy Ross** really live in this Philadelphia townhouse? Did she make the first American flag? The Philadelphia Historical Commission disputes both of these claims.

There is some evidence to support the legends that surround Betsy Ross. She did upholstery work for Independence Hall and for various civic leaders, including Benjamin Franklin. She did undoubtedly make flags for the Pennsylvania navy. Many believe that Betsy Ross did make the first American flag. The house on Arch Street that bears her name has a restored upholstery shop where colonial methods and equipment are demonstrated.

Even if Betsy Ross never lived in this house it would be worth a visit. It is an excellent example of in-town living, with a basement kitchen and typical winding staircase. The house is furnished with many pieces that belonged to Betsy Ross.

It was common in the 18th century for both men and women to have a series of matrimonial partners because life expectancy was much shorter than it is today. Betsy Ross had three husbands; the first two died during the Revolutionary War. She is buried with her third husband, John Claypoole, in the Atwater Kent Park next to the Betsy Ross House.

The Betsy Ross House is open at no charge May to October from 9:00 A.M. to 6:00 P.M.; it closes at 5:00 P.M. the rest of the year. The house is at 239 Arch Street.

Directions: From I-95 southbound (from points north) take Exit 17. Using the right-hand lanes of the exit, follow the signs for Callowhill Street/Independence Hall. At the bottom of the exit ramp, follow 2nd Street straight ahead to Chestnut Street. Continue a half block past Chestnut Street for the Historic Area Parking Garage on the left. It is best to park your car and walk to all the sites in the Historic District. Start at the Independence National Historical Park Visitors Center, one block away, at 3rd and Chestnut Streets. Here you can pick up an easy-to-follow map of the district and a park schedule. If you are traveling northbound on I-95 (from points south) you will also take Exit 17. Stay in the left lane because you will exit on the left side of I-95. At the exit, stay in the right-hand lane and follow the signs for Independence Hall/Historic Area. Turn left at 6th Street to Chestnut and drive through the heart of the Historic District to 2nd Street. Turn right on 2nd Street. The entrance to the Historic Area Parking Garage is on the left. The Betsy Ross House, at 239 Arch Street, is also within walking distance of the garage.

Ebenezer Maxwell Mansion

Adams Family Look Alike

The idea of commuting to and from work can be traced to the advent of rapid transportation. By the 1850s one of America's earliest commuter railroad lines linked downtown Philadelphia with rural Germantown. What had been primarily a summer retreat became a year-round green suburb.

One of the prosperous Philadelphia businessmen who built in Germantown was **Ebenezer Maxwell**. His Norman Gothic villa would have made a perfect set for the vintage television series "The Adams Family." The stone house was built of local Wissahickon schist and red sandstone. Following a popular building practice of that day, coal dust was added to darken the mortar; and sand was added to the paint to give texture to the wooden window frames. A gingerbread tower soars over elaborate Flemish cornices. There's a patterned mansard roof and seven different shapes of windows, many of them set with stained glass that contribute to the visual effect.

When the Maxwell house was finished in 1859 it incorporated all the latest conveniences—running water, gaslights, central hot-air heating and even vents to allow the vitiated (used or polluted) air to escape. These new-fangled ideas were viewed with caution. That is why the children's room was heated by a fireplace to avoid any possible ill effects from the new heating system. The "modern" bathroom was put in the servants wing because it too was viewed with skepticism.

New decorating techniques allowed the middle class Maxwells to imitate the homes of the wealthy. Thus, you'll see that the fireplace has marbleized slate and the wallpaper is made to look like marble. The linoleum entrance way was designed to resemble tile, and the wood-graining created a monied appearance. The Maxwells lived here fewer than three years before moving to a house they built next door.

It is hard to imagine how anyone could consider demolishing this wonderful period piece, but it came close to the wrecker's ball. It is fortunate that it was saved because the Maxwell mansion is the only Victorian house museum in the Philadelphia area.

Two time periods are reflected in the interior. The first floor furnishings are of the 1850s and 60s, the second floor, the 1870s and 80s. The rooms appear to be wrapped in brocades, velvets and feathers. The beds are massive and elaborately carved. Ceilings, walls and doors painted in intricate patterns in the 1880s have been carefully restored. From the entrance hall you can see three different floor patterns. The decor assaults the senses.

Though it must have been difficult to live in such a busy decorative environment, it's fascinating to visit. Even the garden continues the dual ambience achieved by the interior. The front-yard captures the landscaping of the early 1850s while the ribbon garden and hemlock arch at the back represents the 1880s. The yard is still enclosed by the original iron fence.

The Ebenezer Maxwell House is open April through December, Thursday through Sunday from 1:00 P.M. to 4:00 P.M. Admission is charged. While you are at the Ebenezer Maxwell Mansion pick up a walking tour map for "Maxwell's Neighbors—The Houses, the Gardens and the People of West Tulpehocken Street and West Walnut Lane." A six-block walk showcases some 40 interesting structures.

Directions: From the center of Philadelphia take Broad Street, Route 611 north to Route 1, Roosevelt Boulevard. Go left for a short way to Route 422, Germantown Avenue. Follow Germantown Avenue into Germantown proper and then go left on Tulpehocken Street to the mansion. You can also take the Schuylkill Expressway, Route 76, west to the Lincoln Drive exit. Follow Lincoln Drive to Harvey Street. Turn right on Harvey Street, and follow Harvey to Greene Street and turn left. The Maxwell Mansion is on the corner at 200 West Tulpehocken Street.

Edgar Allan Poe National Historic Site

Poet of Darkness

"Deep into that darkness peering, long I stood there, wondering, fearing, doubting, dreaming dreams no mortal ever dared to dream before." Allow your imagination free reign and you may see him yet, as you stand inside **Edgar Allan Poe**'s bedroom chamber in the modest Philadelphia house he occupied the year before he published that brooding stanza in "The Raven."

Poe moved to Philadelphia in 1838, but he did not live in the little house on North Seventh Street until 1843. His six years in Philadelphia proved to be the peak period of his literary life and the happiest time in his personal life. Poe wrote 31 short stories during these years. Pay was so minimal, he also worked as a literary critic and magazine editor. On three occasions he tried to establish his own magazine, a life-long goal. The magazines failed each time. Poetry was always his favorite form of expression, but he turned to short stories in order to support his family.

The eight-minute slide presentation at the Poe House acquaints you with the tragedies of the author's life. His mother died of tuberculosis when he was two. His father, an itinerant actor, had already deserted his wife and son. Poe was raised as a foster child by John and Frances Allan, spending the years between six and eleven at boarding school in England. Upon his return to the Allans' home in Richmond, Virginia, Poe enrolled at the University of Virginia. He left college because of gambling debts.

After the death of his foster mother, relations between Poe and John Allan deteriorated. Abandoning hope of reconciliation, the 22-year old Poe moved to Baltimore to live with his aunt, Maria Poe Clemm. He became attracted to Virginia, her young daughter and they married in 1836 when she was just 13.

Maria Poe Clemm managed the household for the newly married couple and subsequently moved to Philadelphia with them. As you tour the unfurnished Poe house, picture the three of them trying to get along on the meager pay Poe was able to earn for his writing. Although they were poor, they entertained the literary and intellectual figures of the day. In the summer they invited guests to share an economical dessert of peaches picked from their own tree. This six-room half-house, so called because it was only one room wide, was the largest they ever shared.

No records exist to tell us how the Poe house was furnished, nor indeed how each room was used. National Park Service researchers make an educated guess as to which room was Poe's study and which were the bedrooms of Poe, his wife and his mother-in-law. A trip to the cellar reminds visitors of Poe's story "The Black Cat."

The Edgar Allan Poe National Historic Site is open 9:00 A.M. to 5:00 P.M. daily except Christmas and New Year's Day. Admission is free.

Directions: From I-95 in Philadelphia traveling southbound, take Independence Hall/Historic Area exit. At the bottom of the exit ramp make a right onto Callowhill Street. Follow Callowhill to 7th Street. Make a right onto 7th and proceed to the corner of Spring Garden and 7th Streets. If you are northbound on I-95 take the Historic Area exit and turn left at the traffic signal at the bottom of the exit ramp onto Delaware Avenue. Take Delaware Avenue about 1.5 miles to Spring Garden Street, make a left and proceed to 7th Street.

Fairmount Park

Fairmount Warrants Superlatives

Fairmount Park's 8,700 acres offer a myriad of recreational opportunities. Its size makes it one of the world's largest city parks.

Its diversity makes it one of Philadelphia's most worthwhile destinations. Within the park there is the **Philadelphia Zoological Gardens**, the **Philadelphia Museum of Art** (see selection), ten historic tour houses and more cherry blossoms than Washington, D.C. can boast.

The greenhouses of the park's **Horticultural Center** supply the plants for the city's public areas. The center, floriferous year round, has special seasonal exhibitions: the Christmas poinsettia show, the pre-Easter spring display and the autumn chrysanthemum spectacular.

The park began in 1812 when five acres were set aside for a Water Works on the Schuylkill River. The park grew and by 1867 it covered more than 2,000 acres. Additional parkland was acquired by the city in 1873 as part of a large area planned for America's first zoo in the park. Many of the plants, whose offspring still grow, were planted by John Penn in 1785, almost 90 years before the animals were added. Animals are presented in a 42-acre natural setting. It is interesting to note the substitution of local plants that bear a resemblance to vegetation found in the animals' home environment. For example, pampas grass is used in place of the African grasses and locust replaces African acacia.

In addition to the art in the Philadelphia Museum of Art, you'll see sculpture throughout the park. There are 200 pieces including works by such world renowned sculptors as Alexander Calder, Auguste Rodin and Frederic Remington.

A major zoo and outstanding art museum are more than enough incentive to warrant a visit to Fairmount Park, but there's more. The park has ten historic and architecturally significant houses that belonged to noted 18th-century Philadelphians. Solitude, on the Zoo grounds, was the home of John Penn, grandson of the colony's founder. Other houses in the park are: Lemon Hill, Mount Pleasant, Laurel Hill, Woodford, Strawberry Mansion, Cedar Grove, Sweetbriar, Hatfield House and the Letitia Street House. Each has its own charm and historic significance.

The Fairmount Park Trolley stops at the houses. You can get a ticket that will allow you to get on and off to visit them. Though all the houses are open, they are not all open on the same schedule. For details call (215) 685-0000.

A popular park feature is the **Japanese House and Garden**. This reconstruction of a 17th-century Japanese scholar's house was given to the city in 1954 by the American-Japan Society. The gardens are designed to be viewed from the house. The landscaping represents in miniature the mountains, rivers, waterfalls and forests of Japan.

Fairmount Park is open year-round; the Horticultural Center is closed on major holidays. Admission is charged for all the historic houses and for the Zoological Park.

Directions: From I-76, take the Schuylkill Expressway and exit at Girard Avenue for the Zoo, or on Montgomery Drive for the other park attractions.

Fireman's Hall and Elfreth's Alley

The Franklin Brigade

Descended in a direct line from the very first fire department in America, **Fireman's Hall** in downtown Philadelphia captures the long and colorful history of firefighting in this country. Benjamin Franklin founded the first fire department on December 7, 1736. This restoration is a descendant of Franklin's Union Fire Company.

Leather buckets, from the colonial days of fire fighting, were supplanted by hand pumpers as you'll see in the story of firefighting that enfolds in the museum exhibits. Probably the oldest piece of rolling stock on display is one of the three fire wagons the Common Council of Philadelphia ordered from England in 1730. It was sold in 1764 to the Middle Ward Fire Department in Germantown, where it was called "Shagrag." Another of the old pieces is a rare 1815 Hand Pump. This old wooden fire wagon looks like it would have been in dire jeopardy if it got anywhere near a fire.

The upstairs displays have as their focal point the colorful stained glass window showing a firefighter saving a young victim from flames. Exhibits give an overview of the rise of the paid department, or salaried firemen. Small models of early equipment are dwarfed by actual pieces of rolling stock. One rather grand piece is the Spider Hose Reel built in 1804. It's as elegant as a gladiator's chariot. The mirrors on each side of the reel look like shining shields and the brass bells and wrought iron lanterns give it more dazzle.

More prosaic tools of the trade hang on the walls. There are firemen's helmets, including a collection from foreign countries; also included is some oversize equipment like the life net that took 14 firemen to hold and a modern asbestos firefighting suit.

A memorial room is dedicated to Philadelphia firefighters who died in the line of duty. The helmets hung above the plaques are scarred, scorched and blackened. If this room reminds visitors of the tragic aspects of firefighting, the mood lifts when they enter the wheelhouse of a fireboat. This wheelhouse replicates that of a fireboat in one of the city's three Marine Fire Fighting Units. Young visitors like taking the helm and steering toward the painting of the Philadelphia skyline. Another recreated area is the living quarters of the firemen, complete with chief's office and sliding pole. Taped reminiscences by firemen recall exciting moments on the job. The human side of firefighting is also brought out during the film shown at Fireman's Hall.

Back downstairs in the old fire hall of the station that was active in the 1870s, there are more large pieces of fire equipment. Many of the wheeled pieces are the traditional firetruck red. You'll see a 1896 red ladder truck, the 1907 pot-bellied Metropolitan Steamer, a 1903 cannon wagon and a 1870 fire wagon hose carriage.

Fireman's Hall, at 147 North Second Street, is owned by the city and there is no admission charge. The museum is open Tuesday through Saturday from 9:00 A.M. to 5:00 P.M. There is a gift shop with a diverse selection of fire-related items.

Just a half a block up the street is another landmark—**Elfreth's Alley**. The 30 houses lining this old town alley were built between 1728 and 1836, making it the oldest residential street in America. The alley was named for Jeremiah Elfreth and was the home and shop for carpenters, printers and other craftsmen. The oldest house, number 122, was built in 1728. At number 126, the 1762 Mantua Maker's House Museum, you will be greeted by a costumed guide. The house is furnished to depict the life of its earliest residents, mantua makers (seamstresses) Sarah Melton and Mary Smith. There is a display of various items made by residents from 1750 to 1800. Included are pottery and pewter and such utilitarian items as the clay roach trap that caught the varmints with molasses. Once a year on the first Saturday and Sunday in June the residents of Elfreth's Alley have an open house and you can tour the privately-owned homes. The little museum is open daily from 10:00 A.M. to 4:00 P.M. A nominal admission is charged.

Directions: From I-95 south take Exit 17 and stay in the left lane of the exit ramp. Follow that straight onto 2nd Street and continue for two blocks. You'll cross Race Street and the Fireman's Hall will be in that block of Race Street. From I-95 north take Exit 16, Washington Avenue, which will put you onto Columbus Boulevard. At the bottom of the ramp take a left at the traffic light and proceed north for four blocks to the museum between Race and Arch Streets.

Fort Mifflin

The Alamo of the Revolution!

Four hundred and fifty men at Fort Mifflin withstood 40 days of bombardment from 94 ships of the British fleet. General

Howe's garrison in Philadelphia needed munitions and supplies before they could pursue General Washington's Continental Army. **Fort Mifflin** and Fort Mercer, straddling the Delaware River, blocked the delivery of these supplies, thus delaying the British.

River traffic was halted by a chevaux-de-frise. This was an obstacle more frequently used to repel cavalry charges. It was simply tree trunks chained together with spiked protrusions.

The British, stuck beneath the forts, began firing on October 11, 1777. After four days the guns were firing every half hour. Except for a brief time on October 22, when British guns turned to aid the Hessian land attack on New Jersey's **Fort Mercer**, the guns remained on the lower, more vulnerable Fort Mifflin. Howe began calling this obstacle to his plans "that cursed little mud fort."

The men manning the fort could be excused if they felt it was cursed. By November 7 only 115 of the fort's 320-man contingent could still man the guns. The men tried to rebuild the fort walls at night but the constant bombardment was reducing the fort to rubble.

By November 13 three of the fort's four blockhouses were destroyed. Only 11 cannon could still be fired. By November 15 the British were firing 1,000 shots every 20 minutes. The chevaux-de-frise was released either by accident or by treachery and it fell to the bottom of the river allowing the British to move into a better position and fire point-blank at the already crumbling fort.

By the afternoon of November 15 the men within the fort were out of ammunition. When night came the 40 defenders still able to walk left the fort. Estimates of American casualties ran as high as 400 men; the British lost only seven lives.

But the British did lose valuable time. When the supply ships finally managed to destroy this small fort, the American army under Washington was beyond Howe's reach and a major confrontation was avoided.

This ended Fort Mifflin's usefulness during the American Revolution. It was rebuilt in the 1800s during Adams's administration. Enlarged during the Civil War, it was used as a prison garrison for deserters, Confederate soldiers, bounty jumpers and political prisoners. The fort conducted executions on what is now the Sunday drill grounds.

Fort Mifflin, which stands on Mud Island, still has its original moat. Some of the walls are from the Revolutionary period. The enlisted men's barracks, underground bomb-proof vaults and fortifications have been restored. On Sunday afternoons, in addition to fort tours, there are militia guard drills and living history programs. A working blacksmith is often on hand to demonstrate how old weapons were made. A museum completes the historical picture of events at Fort Mifflin.

Fort Mifflin is open from April through November on Wednesday through Sunday from 10:00 A.M. to 4:00 P.M. The fort is open to pre-booked tours only during the off-season from December through March. Admission is charged.

Directions: From I-95 if you are traveling south, take Exit 13 and follow the signs for Island Avenue. Make a left at the stop sign and follow the signs to Fort Mifflin. Traveling north on I-95, take Exit 10 for the Philadelphia International Airport. Drive past the airport to the large intersection of Island Avenue and I-291. Make a right at the light. Follow the signs to Fort Mifflin.

Franklin Court

Get in the Spirit

The spirit of Franklin can be felt at **Franklin Court**, part of Independence National Historical Park. The latest in museum technology was employed to create the imaginative and innovative exhibits.

The all underground museum is literally explored from the bottom up. The Franklin Exchange has 22 noted Americans and 26 Europeans you can "telephone" for their opinions of this talented, complex figure. Original quotes from John Adams, Henry Steele Commanger, Jefferson Davis, Ralph Waldo Emerson, Thomas Jefferson, Harry Truman, Mark Twain and George Washington offer interesting insights. Europeans heard from are Lord Byron, Charles Darwin, David Hume, Immanuel Kant, John Keats, Lafayette, D.H. Lawrence and George Sand.

None of these personalities outshines Franklin himself when it comes to wit. His remarks on a wide range of topics appear on projected slides. Franklin's views on women, virtue, money, government and ethics still seem timely. "Franklin on the World Stage" presents a series of miniature figures in a sound and light show depicting Franklin in such settings as before the House of Commons in 1766 and in 1778 before the Court of Versailles.

Next the personal side of Franklin is showcased in the movie, *Portrait of a Family* about his early life and marriage. You'll see how his career affected his family. Franklin's wife died just before he returned to America after representing the fledgling country for a decade in England. He left again to spend eight years representing America's interests in France.

At street level, you discover that the foundation is all that remains of Franklin's home. Not enough documentation survived to support a historically accurate reconstruction. There is a colonial pleasure garden and five Market Square houses, three of which were owned by Franklin. Each house reveals a facet of his life.

Franklin, the builder, is the theme of the center house at 318 Market Street. Explanatory notes let visitors "read" the walls. Plaster, wallpaper, chair rails, chimney and joists all date from the 18th century. Franklin was concerned about fires—in fact, he established the nation's first volunteer fire department—and in his designs he made sure that the joists of one room did not meet those of another. This prevented fires from spreading rapidly from room to room.

Franklin, the printer, is the focus of another house where you'll see a printing press he used to turn out handbills. Franklin's grandson, Benjamin Franklin Bache had an office at 322 Market Street that has been restored. The *Philadelphia Aurora* was published here.

Franklin was the first Postmaster General of the United States and the fourth house is a post office. Letters can be cancelled with the postmark Franklin made famous, "B Free Franklin." A postal museum is a must see stop for stamp collectors. The fifth house is a park sales outlet. Franklin Court is open daily 9:00 A.M. to 5:00 P.M.

Directions: Traveling north on I-95 take I-676 into the city, following the signs for Independence Hall. Turn left on 6th Street and continue down to Market Street, then turn left on Market Street. Franklin Court is between 3rd and 4th Streets.

The Franklin Institute Science Museum

Franklin, Father of American Ingenuity

Benjamin Franklin's political contributions are well chronicled but his scientific discoveries and inventions are less well-known. Franklin introduced numerous plants to America (kale, varieties of barley, Chinese rhubarb and turnips), suggested aerial reconnaissance and bombardment from balloons, developed the lightning rod, made significant discoveries in the field of electricity, established modern ventilation methods, identified the Aurora Borealis as an electrical phenomenon and developed daylight saving time. His inventions were also numerous: the Franklin Stove, bifocal spectacles, flexible catheter, library ladder and a variety of other items.

Franklin made his home in Philadelphia from his early twenties until his death (except the many years he served abroad). It is apt that this city should have a multi-faced, hands-on science museum honoring his inventive spirit. **The Franklin Institute** was founded in 1824. Originally it served as an educational establishment and its innovative curriculum was adopted by the city public school system. The museum and memorial to Benjamin Franklin was established in 1932. The following year Samuel S. Fels donated funds for a planetarium, only the second to be established in the country (Hayden Planetarium in New York was the first).

The memorial and the museum are essentially two separate entities housed together. Congress designated this massive domed hall as the nation's memorial to its most famous native-born scientist and diplomat. Suggesting the Pantheon in Rome, the huge octagonal-shaped dome's floors, walls and columns are made with rare marbles from Portugal, Italy and France. White Seravessa marble was used for the seated figure of Franklin, actually four times bigger than life-size. The hall also contains the country's largest collection of Franklin artifacts.

If Franklin's belongings are exhibited in the memorial hall his spirit is exemplified in the museum. He certainly would have loved the many interactive experiments. In fact, he would recognize some of his own work in the major exhibit on the development of electricity, and delight in the hands-on devices, live demonstration area and video theater with film clips from the 1880s to 1930s. There's an 1800's-era railroad station where you can tap out a message in Morse Code, while push and pull devices demonstrate how magnetic forces work. Storefronts reminiscent of the 1890s and early 1900s showcase electrical household items that simplified daily life. Older visitors particularly enjoy turning the dial on the 1930s radio and picking up Jack Benny, the Mills Brothers and the news—a "live" report on the crash of the Hindenburg.

The museum moves from the past to the future. **The Mandell Futures Center**, with eight permanent exhibits, is the world's first facility devoted exclusively to the science and technology that will affect the next decade. In the Musser Choices Forum special computer keypads at each seat let you vote on science-related topics as you watch the programs. The Futures Center encourages you to work in a weightless environment, test water quality, walk through a huge immune cell, levitate a magnet and follow the flow of chemical messages in the brain. There is a section on careers for the future and cutting edge technology.

Physics comes alive in the interactive mechanics exhibit where 35 stations explore such diverse concepts as leverage, collisions, gravity, energy, vectors and others. Computer terminals provide challenging problems for those who want to explore in greater depth.

Transportation is a re-occurring theme: one exhibit focuses on shipbuilding on the Delaware with ship plans, navigation instruments, models and historical photographs. In the towing tank you can see how waves travel and how a model ship weathers various wave conditions. A computer maritime trade game lets you pick a ship, cargo, and trade route to test your economic savvy. Historical journals and ship logs from the 16th and 17th centuries are programmed into the computer to supply real life situations and outcomes. Another exhibit focuses on communication.

One of the museum's popular exhibits is the **1926 Baldwin locomotive** in the railroad hall. This behemoth—a hundred feet long weighing 350 tons—was hauled through the city's streets in the 1930s and installed before the museum's rear wall was closed. Cases of model trains, engine models and a videodisc of different types of trains in action portray the evolution of the railroad system.

Aviation is another mode of transportation the museum covers. There's an air force jet trainer, hands-on equipment, airplane models and films on flying. A **Wright Brothers Model B flyer** is suspended from the ceiling and there is an extensive collection of Wright memorabilia.

Once in the air, it's an easy transition to celestial bodies. A 30-foot layout of planets shows the earth's position in the galaxy. The Franklin Institute has the largest public observatory in the country with two huge telescopes. Museum staff help visitors recognize distant planets. A smaller telescope allows visitors to view the spectrum of the sun. Another way to experience astronomy is by taking in one of the planetarium shows. Topics range from UFO's to black holes, and there is always the traditional Christmas presentation and seasonal constellation shows.

From outer space to inner space, the museum has exhibits on bioscience, revealing the mysteries of the human body. Dominating this exhibit is a giant walk-through heart that is 220 times larger than a real heart. A stethoscope lets you listen to a heart murmur, then hear a regular heartbeat. A hand pump lets you feel how hard the heart works and red and blue lights show how blood is oxidized. Other parts of the body are also explored in the three interactive videodisc theaters.

A final permanent exhibit is the two-level exploration of the forces that shape and change the earth: plate movement, erosion, weather and the action of man and animals. The institute has its own working weather station and visitors can see how radar and satellites help predict weather patterns.

The museum's **Tuttleman Omniverse Theater** is worth repeat visits, since movies have a new dimension on this four-story screen with 56 speakers. The museum quotes filmmaker Ben

Shedd, who said, "The experience is so strong that the theater itself seems to move and fly." Whether you watch a space craft blast off, see the birth of a star, travel through the human body, fly over the Grand Canal or sink to the ocean depths, these 30- to 40-minute films are guaranteed to thrill.

The Franklin Institute Science Museum is open daily 9:30 A.M. to 5:00 P.M.; the Mandell Futures Center stays open until 9:00 P.M. Tuesday through Sunday. (from September through April on Tuesdays the center closes at 5:00 P.M.) For show times at the Omniverse Theater and Fels Planetarium, call (215) 448-1200. Admission is charged. There are three well-stocked gift shops filled with educational toys, books and science kits. The center also has two restaurants.

Directions: Traveling north on I-95 take Exit 17 and follow I-676 west. Take the Benjamin Franklin Parkway exit. Turn right at the top of the exit ramp, proceed to the first traffic light and make a right turn on the parkway. Turn right at 21st Street; the museum is on your left. The museum's entrance is on 20th Street. From I-76 take Exit 24, Valley Forge onto the Schuylkill Expressway, I-76 east. From the expressway take Exit 38, Central Philadelphia, get to the immediate right to take the first exit on the right which is the Benjamin Franklin Parkway exit. Continue three blocks and museum is on the right between 21st and 20th Streets.

Germantown Mennonite Community

Preserving A Heritage . . . Telling A Story!

On October 25, 1683, lots were drawn for the Germantown settlement in the Pennsylvania colony. The first members of the community were Quakers and Mennonites, and for a time they worshiped together. By 1690, as more Mennonite settlers arrived from Germany, they gradually began meeting on their own. By 1698, they elected their own preacher and deacon. The first Mennonite minister was William Rittenhouse. Philadelphia is noted for its Rittenhouse Square, Rittenhouse Street and Rittenhouse Plaza and it is worth investigating the history of this significant family.

William Rittenhouse came to Germantown from Westphalia, Germany in 1688. His home, at 207 Lincoln Drive in Fairmount Park, is the oldest Mennonite home in the New World. His great-grandson David Rittenhouse, who was born in this house on April 8, 1732, was a noted scientist and a patriot in the American Revolution. The **Rittenhouse Homestead** is open April through October. To arrange a visit, call (215) 438-5711 or write Historic Rittenhouse Town at 206 Lincoln Drive, Philadelphia, PA 19144.

The Mennonite community of Germantown, the first Mennonite congregation in North America, erected a log cabin meetinghouse in 1708. They replaced it with a stone building in 1770. Adjacent to this historic old stone meetinghouse is the Germantown Mennonite Information Center, at 6133 Germantown Avenue. The center has a small museum open Tuesday through Saturday from 10:00 A.M. to NOON and from 1:00 P.M. to 4:00 P.M. with exhibits on the congregation's history.

Just two-and-a-half blocks up Germantown Avenue, #6306, is an old Quaker house open for tours. The house was completed in 1768 as a wedding gift for Germantown tanner John Johnson, Jr. The Johnson home, noted for its interior woodwork, is an excellent example of the style termed Germantown Georgian. During the pre-Civil War period it was one of the stops on the Underground Railroad. Tours can be arranged by calling the Germantown Mennonite Information Center.

The young Johnsons took an active interest in the **Concord School House** located across the street. This one-room schoolhouse was built in 1775 by the residents of upper Germantown. The original schoolmaster's desk and chair are still here, as are other 18th century school items. The schoolhouse at 6309 Germantown Avenue is open April through October. Tours are by appointment only; call (215) 843-0943 A nominal admission is charged.

Directions: From I-95 take the exit for I-76 west, the Schuylkill Expressway. Take the Expressway to Exit 32, Lincoln Drive (it is also marked Germantown-Wissahickon Park). Take Lincoln Drive to Johnson Street and turn right. Take Johnson Street to the fourth traffic light which is Germantown Avenue and turn right. You will see the Germantown Mennonite Information Center on your left.

Historical Society of Pennsylvania and Second Bank of the United States

People and Possessions

The **Historical Society of Pennsylvania** invites you to mentally adjust Benjamin Franklin's bifocals for a fresh perspective as you view their exhibit, "Finding Philadelphia's Past: Visions and Revisions." Various displays in the two galleries, showcasing more than 500 objects, have small drawings of Franklin's glasses. These are reminders to think twice about what you are seeing. You are encouraged to seek new interpretations of past events.

Philadelphia's past is traced from Penn's arrival in 1682. The city is studied during its growth from a commercial seaport and governmental center through upheavals caused by the American

41

Revolution, slavery, the Civil War, the influx of immigrants and the Industrial Revolution. Exhibits reflect changes in work, consumption and leisure during these evolving epochs.

On exhibit are a number of personal items associated with William Penn, Pennsylvania's founder: Bible, chair, family cradle, chest, razor, letters and other documents, plus the wampum belt reputedly given him in friendship by the Lenni Lenape Indians. But it is his portrait that bears a second look. It was painted by a copyist around 1770 of a 1666 portrait. Penn was 22 years old when the study was done and he is shown in armor, identifying him as a member of England's ruling class. Just a year after being painted, Penn joined the Religious Society of Friends. As a Quaker, Penn undoubtedly would not have agreed to be painted in armor.

Significant items in the exhibit include Charles Willson Peale's portrait of Benjamin Franklin, George Washington's desk, James Wilson's first draft of the Constitution and, on a less rarefied plane, the traveling makeup kit of 19th-century actor Edwin Forrest. Some of the items are lighthearted like the doll, one of the earliest in the country, made in 1699 and carried to the New World by Letitia Penn. But other items speak of tragedy, such as the photo of two-year-old Alice, the first African brought to Philadelphia in bondage. The display adds a note that Alice lived to be 116 years old.

After exploring the galleries, step into the **trolley car theater** where you can take any of six video "trips" through turn-of-the-century Philadelphia and its suburban neighborhoods. If you want a taste of your own ethnic heritage and neighborhood, the kiosk in the lobby has free computer listings of dining, cultural and commercial attractions for 19 different ethnic groups.

One of the marvelous lessons this exhibit teaches is that the past is judged at least in part by the articles that reflect it. Sooner or later we, too, will be known for the things we save.

The Historical Society of Pennsylvania's Manuscript and Archives Department is a major repository of Penn family papers. The library has one of the most important genealogical collections in the country with some 20,000 published genealogies, approximately 3,500 more in manuscript form and thousands more on microfilm.

The Historical Society of Pennsylvania is open Tuesday, Thursday, Friday and Saturday from 10:00 A.M. to 5:00 P.M., Wednesday hours are 1:00 P.M. to 9:00 P.M. Admission is charged, with a slight additional fee to use the genealogical library.

The Society exhibits show what people saved. The **Second Bank of the United States** displays portraits of the people themselves. Approximately ten galleries are divided by realm of influence: Declaration and Constitution signers, Constitutional

Congress and Federal government, art and industry, military, diplomatic, financial and local figures of note.

The setting for these "Portraits of the Capital City," is itself of note. The Second Bank of the United States, charted by Congress in 1816, was established like its predecessor to fund a war debt, provide a uniform currency, serve as a government repository and provide credit for private enterprise. Under Nicholas Biddle's direction the bank became one of the world's most influential financial institutions. With Andrew Jackson's election to the presidency a "Banking War" ensued in 1832. Jackson challenged the constitutionality of the bank, objecting to its monopolistic influence on the economy of the country. When the bank's 20-year charter expired, Jackson vetoed its continuation. Fortunately, the imposing Greek Revival building designed by William Strickland in 1818 was adapted for other uses. It served as the Philadelphia Custom House from 1835 to 1935.

The Second Bank Portrait Gallery, part of Independence National Historical Park, is open at no charge daily 9:00 A.M. to 5:00 P.M. It is located on Chestnut Street between 4th and 5th streets.

Directions: From I-95 southbound (from points north) take Exit 17. Using the right-hand lanes of the exit, follow the signs for Callowhill Street/Independence Hall. At the bottom of the exit ramp, follow 2nd Street straight ahead to Chestnut Street. Continue a half block past Chestnut Street for the Historic Area Parking Garage on the left. It is best to park your car and walk to all the sites in the Historic District. Start at the Independence National Historical Park Visitors Center, one block away, at 3rd and Chestnut Streets. Here you can pick up an easy-to-follow map of the district and a park schedule. The Historical Society of Pennsylvania is at 1300 Locust Street, about a ten block walk from the park sites. If you are traveling northbound on I-95 (from points south) you will also take Exit 17. Stay in the left lane because you will exit on the left side of I-95. At the exit, stay in the right-hand lane and follow the signs for Independence Hall/Historic Area. Turn left at 6th Street to Chestnut. This will take you through the heart of the Historic District to 2nd Street. Turn right on 2nd Street. The entrance to the Historic Area Parking Garage is on the left.

Historic Bartram's Garden

This Johnny Seeded More Than Apples

There's a tendency to imagine that during the arduous task of establishing a new country the arts and sciences were ignored in America. But, while they didn't flourish, they did exist.

In 1728, Quaker farmer **John Bartram** purchased a 102-acre farm with a small stone house. From a young age, Bartram was fascinated by plants. Although he had little formal education, Bartram diligently studied botany to further his pursuit of American plant specimens. He taught himself Latin so that he could read the horticultural books that Benjamin Franklin, James Logan and others gave him.

Bartram's interest in American plants was shared by English botanical enthusiasts. Peter Collinson, a prosperous London wool merchant, arranged for John Bartram to provide him an assortment of plants from America. They never met, but Bartram and Collinson corresponded for 35 years. Their letters provide a record of Bartram's expeditions throughout the American wilderness. On his plant quests, Bartram went north as far as New York, south to Florida and west to the Ohio River. Bartram's contacts with English and European botanists were reciprocal; plants were sent both ways. Bartram was responsible for introducing 200 North American species into cultivation here.

Bartram returned from each trip to his Philadelphia farm and planted the seeds, roots and cuttings he gathered. As his collection grew, so did his fame, until in 1765 George III appointed him "Royal Botanist." The noted Swedish botanist, Carl Linnaeus, who developed a system for classifying plants, called Bartram, "the greatest natural botanist in the world."

Following in his father's footsteps quite literally was William, who Bartram called "my little botanist." William accompanied his father on many of his plant exploration forays. In 1765 they went to Florida together. William's interest was intense and he later returned alone and spent four years traveling in the deep south. He wrote of this experience in *Travels*, published in 1791.

William returned to the Schuylkill farm and spent the rest of his life writing and maintaining **America's first botanic garden**. Another of Bartram's nine children, John Jr., organized the garden into a nursery at his father's death. He completed the first sales catalog of American plants.

Purchased as a city park in 1891, Bartram's garden survives. Growing here today you will see descendants of the plants that made horticultural history. One such plant, now extinct in the wild, is the *Franklinia alatamaha* named after Bartram's famous friend. When you walk the garden paths, you follow in the footsteps of George Washington, Thomas Jefferson and numerous noted North American scientists who down through the years have visited and admired Bartram's collection.

You can also tour the 18th-century stone house that John Bartram built around the original portion he acquired with the farm. He labored on the house himself. Above an attic window there is a date stone that reads, "John—Ann Bartram 1731." His stone

44

work can also be observed on a water trough and on the cider mill at the river's edge.

The grounds, at 54th Street and Lindbergh Boulevard, are open daily at no charge during daylight hours year-round. Keep in mind that this is a rustic, 18th-century, native plant garden and not a display garden. There is a nominal fee to tour the house which is open May through October on Wednesday through Sunday from NOON to 4:00 P.M. The house is closed on weekends from November through March.

Directions: From I-76, the Pennsylvania Turnpike, take the Schuylkill Expressway east through Center City. Get off the Expressway at Gray's Ferry, Exit 41. Bear left through the exit light and go over the bridge. Turn right at the next light onto Gray's Ferry Avenue (Marshall Lab/DuPont will be on the right corner). Go over another bridge and turn left onto Paschall Avenue, then turn left at the next light onto 49th Street and follow the trolley tracks. The street name changes to Gray's Avenue and Lindbergh Boulevard. Continue past the sign for 54th Street. Make a sharp left turn into Bartram's Garden just beyond the gas station. The entrance is not visible until after the turn.

Independence Hall and the Liberty Bell Pavilion

Let Freedom Ring

Many historians consider Independence Hall's Assembly Room to be the single-most historic room in the United States. In this room delegates met to debate and sign the Declaration of Independence and to write the Constitution of the United States.

Funds were appropriated for a State House in 1729, but it was 19 years before Alexander Hamilton's designs were fully realized. The State House, later called **Independence Hall**, served as government meeting rooms for the Pennsylvania colony. The ground floor had a large Assembly Room. Unlike other large chambers, it had a door because the legislative body often met in secret sessions.

The Assembly Room has been restored to look as it did when the Second Continental Congress met there. The individual tables that served each colonial delegation are placed in a semicircle before the table where the Declaration of Independence was signed. Few pieces in the room are original. Thomas Jefferson's walking stick has been placed on a table which is believed to have belonged to the Virginia delegation. The original inkstand used by the delegates to sign the Declaration is display on the Speaker's stand.

After Lord Cornwallis surrendered to Washington at Yorktown, the captured colors of the British army were brought to Philadelphia and presented in this room to the state delegations on November 3, 1781.

A chamber on the first floor was used by the Supreme Court of the Province. The court room was in the English tradition and graphically illustrates the term "standing trial." The defendant was forced to stand throughout the trial in a spiked cage-like dock. If dangerous, the defendant would be placed in handcuffs by a blacksmith. Should the defendant be declared innocent, he would have to pay to have the iron cuffs sawed off. Trials were enjoyed by town residents, who watched the proceedings, groaning or applauding at each decision.

Upstairs is the **Long Gallery**, the largest room in colonial Pennsylvania. This was the scene of many balls and banquets. On September 16, 1774, the members of the First Continental Congress gathered here for a sit-down dinner. The legislature of Pennsylvania conducted sessions in part of the Long Gallery, while the Continental Congress met in their Assembly Room below.

The State House was given the name Independence Hall in 1824 when Lafayette was in Philadelphia celebrating the American Revolution victory. While touring the State House Lafayette said, "That is the hall of independence," and so it has been called ever since.

One of the landmarks of the hall has been moved. The one-ton **Liberty Bell** is now in a pavilion directly opposite the hall. This bell was made in England in 1752. After being shipped across the Atlantic, it cracked upon arrival and was recast twice by Pass and Stow, local artisans. Their efforts were successful and the bell hung in the State House steeple for many years. In 1835, John Marshall, Chief Justice of the Supreme Court, died while visiting Philadelphia. The bell was rung for 36 continuous hours and finally cracked. Repairs were attempted in 1846 and it was tested on George Washington's birthday. After three hours it cracked again. From that time on the bell was only a symbol.

The wonderful thing about the Liberty Bell is that it is not roped off, visitors are free to touch this tangible reminder of the turbulent events in our country's past. It is touching to watch the crowds pass by this bell reaching out tentatively, or determinedly, to feel this historic memento.

Before touring Independence Hall, visitors should stop at the **Independence National Historical Park Visitor Center** where a 28-minute film directed by John Huston literally introduces the great leaders who met in Philadelphia in 1774 and 1776. Actors portraying these giants explain the events that took place here.

The hands-on approach at Independence National Historical Park's Liberty Bell lets visitors reach out and touch a visible reminder of the American Revolution.

All of the park's historic buildings are open at no charge daily from 9:00 A.M. to 5:00 P.M.

Directions: From I-95 southbound (from points north) take Exit 17. Using the right-hand lanes of the exit, follow the signs for Callowhill Street/Independence Hall. At the bottom of the exit ramp, follow 2nd Street straight ahead to Chestnut Street. Continue a half block past Chestnut Street for the Historic Area Parking Garage on the left. It is best to park your car and walk to all the sites in the Historic District. Start at the Independence National Historical Park Visitors Center, one block away, at 3rd and Chestnut Streets. Here you can pick up an easy-to-follow map of the district and a park schedule. If you are traveling northbound on I-95 (from points south) you will also take Exit 17. Stay in the left lane because you will exit on the left side of I-95. At the exit, stay in the right-hand lane and follow the signs for Independence Hall/Historic Area. Turn left at 6th Street to Chestnut. This will take you through the heart of the Historic District to 2nd Street. Turn right on 2nd Street. The entrance to the Historic Area Parking Garage is on the left.

Independence Seaport Museum

Chart a Course to Museum's New Berth

On July 4, 1995, the Independence Seaport Museum moved into the innovatively restyled Port of History building at Penn's Landing. This expanded space on the Delaware River is an ideal spot from which to showcase the region's rich maritime heritage.

In 1682, William Penn sailed up the Delaware River aboard the aptly named *Welcome*. Once Penn established his colony, its capital city Philadelphia became one of the leading cities in the colonies and young republic. Its trade routes linked the new world with the old. In 1784, the *Empress of China*, opened trade with China. The Ports of Philadelphia, one of the most active ports in the world, stretch from Trenton, New Jersey to Wilmington, Delaware. The **Independence Seaport Museum** literally has a window on this working waterfront.

Philadelphia's port helped shaped the nation, the U.S. Navy and Marines were founded here. The port served as the nation's first navy yard and first naval academy. For a time in the late 19th and early 20th century, it was the shipbuilding capital of the world.

With Europe at war and the country's neutrality strained, Congress passed the Shipping Act of 1916, expanding the shipping industry. Hog Island in Philadelphia, the largest shipyard in the world, was the most famous of the emergency shipyards: Hog Island alone employed more than 34,000 workers. As a result of the boom, the total number of U.S. shipyard workers jumped from 44,000 to 450,000.

The museum's collections span four centuries of maritime activities in the mid-Atlantic region. State-of-the-art family-oriented interactive exhibit areas draw visitors into the story of the social fabric of an urban port. You'll sense what is was like to steam beneath the Benjamin Franklin Bridge into the harbor. "Coming to America" recreates the era when Philadelphia was a leading entry port for immigrants from Eastern and Central Europe, and Great Britain. You'll have to think about your options in the new world if you, like the incoming immigrants, were confronted by a customs officer. In "Ship via Philadelphia" computers let you participate in world trade, international routing and the details of commerce at this busy port.

"Protecting the Nation" highlights the history of the nation's oldest navy yard. You can step aboard the bridge of the guided missile destroyer, **USS *Lawrence***, and experience the sights and sounds of a general quarters drill. Understand the shift in shipbuilding in the "Wood, Iron & Steel" exhibit. Then finally, focus on the river's recreational appeal in "The Great Outdoors."

In addition to educational programs for school children and organized groups, the museum has a "Workshop on the Water" that teaches traditional wooden boatbuilding techniques. Beginners and seasoned carpenters find their niches in various courses. Call (215) 925-7589 for details on the next series of workshops.

Maritime enthusiasts, naval veterans, genealogists, and those with an interest in America's maritime heritage are welcome to use the resources of one of the nation's finest regional collections of nautical material. The museum's library has more than 12,000 general maritime volumes, hundreds of rare books, manuscripts, charts, thousands of ship plans and more than 25,000 historical photographs.

The Independence Seaport Museum is open daily, 10:00 A.M. to 5:00 P.M. For additional information call (215) 925-5439. The museum has an auditorium where films, lectures, concerts and other special programs are scheduled. There is also a gift shop filled with nautical items.

Directions: From I-76, the Pennsylvania Turnpike, take I-676 (Route 30, the Vine Street Expressway) to immediately before the Benjamin Franklin Bridge. Exit onto Columbus Boulevard and head south to Penn's Landing. The Philadelphia Maritime Museum is at the foot of Walnut Street. From I-95, exit at Columbus Boulevard and head north to Penn's Landing.

John Heinz National Wildlife Refuge at Tinicum

Greenspace in a Concrete Maze

Hiking and wildlife observation await you in the southwest corner of Philadelphia at the **John Heinz National Wildlife Refuge** at Tinicum. The refuge offers ten miles of trails for hiking and bicycling, 288 species of birds (85 of which nest at the refuge) and 75 different species of butterflies to observe and enjoy.

The area protected by the refuge, Tinicum Marsh, was once over 5,700 acres. It extended from the mouth of the Schuylkill River to the mouth of Darby Creek, along the Delaware River. Beginning in the 17th century, Swedish, Dutch and English settlers diked and drained areas of the marsh areas for farmland and pasture. Today, only 250 acres of Tinicum marsh remains.

The refuge's five distinct habitats provide for a variety of wildlife. When entering the refuge, watch to see one of the fields managed as a geese, pheasant and woodcock habitat.

The driveway leads to the refuge's Visitor Contact Station where there is information about trails, current management programs and weekend guided walks. Walking toward the trailhead, you will see a canoe ramp on Darby Creek. If you have a canoe, you can paddle the creek following canoe trail markers that indicate the main channel. The creek leads to the marshes. The terrain gets muddy if you veer off course.

The **East Impoundment Trail** is the most commonly used trail at the refuge. It is a 3.3-mile loop around the 145-acre impoundment with several resting/observation areas along the way. The observation tower, about three-quarters of a mile from the parking lot at the Visitors Contact Station, provides an excellent vantage point from which to spot waterfowl. Be sure to bring binoculars to get a close look at the birds. You're apt to spot egrets and herons throughout the year, shorebirds in August and September and waterfowl in October and November. A lily-like plant known as spatterdock seasonally covers 80-90 percent of the water's surface.

The trails take you past the impoundment, Darby Creek and what remains of **Tinicum Marsh**. This fresh-water tidal marsh experiences a tidal difference of four-to-five feet twice a day. Here amongst the cattails, arrowhead and duck potato are waterfowl, muskrats and other common marsh animals. Two state-endangered species, the red-bellied turtle and the southern leopard frog, reside at the refuge and may be seen either in the impoundment or the marshes.

After stretching along the remnants of an old trolley bed on the south side of the impoundment, the trail leads into the wood-land habitat. Warblers can be sighted in the spring and fall by keen-eyed visitors; they are just one of the songbirds that migrate through the area. Deer, rabbit and fox may also be spotted. A variety of wildflowers may be seen along the paths and trails.

The refuge's trails also follow Darby Creek to the other end of the refuge. There is a parking lot here if you want to start your hike from the other end of the refuge. This is located on Route 420 just south of Prospect Park.

The John Heinz NWR at Tinicum is open daily at no charge from 8:00 A.M. to sunset. For more information call (215) 365-3118. The refuge is also popular with fishermen, although refuge personnel suggest practicing catch and release due to marginal water quality. Anyone 16 years of age or older needs a Pennsylvania fishing license.

Directions: From I-95 north, take the Route 291/Airport exit. At the first light make a left onto Bartram Avenue. At the third light make a left onto 84th Street; at the second light make a left onto Lindbergh Boulevard. The wildlife refuge will be on your right at 86th Street. From I-95 south, take Route 291/Airport exit and use the right fork, exiting on Route 291/Lester. At the light make a right onto Bartram Avenue, then at the first light make a left onto 84th Street. At the second light turn left onto Lindbergh Blvd. If you are traveling on I-76 east, stay in the left lane and follow signs for Route 291 west/I-95 south/Airport. At the light make a right onto Route 291 west and follow signs to I-95 south. Take I-95 south and follow above directions.

Masonic Temple

Architectural Wonders

Every so often you explore a new place, about which you have no preconceived ideas, and it turns out to be a fabulous find. Such is the case with the **Masonic Temple** in Philadelphia. Even its massive exterior is architecturally exciting with majestic turrets and spires rising from the very center of the city.

Some daytrippers miss this unique experience because they are unaware of its accessibility. Many visitors are also uncertain about the exact nature of Freemasonry. The Masonic fraternity began in medieval times as an association of stonemasons and cathedral builders. The Freemasons are open to men of any nationality, religion, creed and political organization. Freemasonry is based on fundamentals of religion held in common by all men. It strives to instill a lofty morality without becoming a religious sect. Although the rituals are secret—just as in any fraternal organization—its meeting places and membership are not.

America's first Mason was Jonathan Belcher, governor of Massachusetts. He joined the fraternal group during a visit to England in 1704. Philadelphia and Boston have long disputed which city had the first Masonic lodge. It is certain that there was a lodge in Philadelphia by 1730, since records indicate Benjamin Franklin became a Mason at a Philadelphia lodge in February, 1730. Other noted Masons from the pages of history include: George Washington, James Monroe, Robert Fulton, Aaron Burr, Thomas Paine, Alexander Hamilton, Robert Livingston, Josiah Witherspoon, Paul Revere, John Hancock and foreign supporters like Von Steuben, De Kalb and Lafayette. Spanning the decades, American presidents have been Masons: Jackson, Polk, Fillmore, Buchanan, Johnson, Garfield, McKinley, Taft, Harding, both Roosevelts and Truman.

Land for the temple in downtown Philadelphia was purchased in 1867. Using a gavel that George Washington had used with Masonic ceremony to lay the cornerstone of the Nation's Capitol on September 18, 1793, the cornerstone of the temple was laid in 1868. A 26-year old Mason James Windrim designed what is described as "one of the greatest works of art ever carried on by Masons in any part of the world." Thirteen thousand Masonic marchers took part in the parade at the temple dedication on September 26, 1873.

The interior is breathtaking from the golden glow of the vast portals of the entrance gate to the ornate interior embellishments of hallways and stairways. Above the grand staircase is a brilliant stained glass window and four large paintings.

Seven lodge halls showcase distinct architectural styles. The **Egyptian Hall**, done in the style of the Nile Valley, is considered the "only perfect specimen of Egyptian architecture in America." Each of the 12 huge columns is a copy of an actual column and all are decorated with authentic cuneiform. Wall murals of domestic scenes were copied from underground chambers of Egypt's Old Empire. The ceiling has a representation of the solar system, with designations for the months copied from the Temple of Rameses at Thebes. Twelve thousand people came to see this room when it opened in January 1889.

Also exotic is the **Oriental Hall**, done in a Moorish or Saracenic style. The room's color and ornamentation are copied from the Alhambra in Granada, Spain. The gilded ceiling has seven thousand ornate panels, while the walls are intricately fashioned with columns, alcoves and ornamental designs.

Two halls exemplify classic Greek design: the **Corinthian** and **Ionic** halls. The columns and capitals in the former are copies of those at the monument of Lysicrates in Athens. The entire ivory, gold and blue chamber overwhelms onlookers with its symmetrical beauty. At one end, the paneled ceiling in the apse, together with the caryatides supporting it, is copied from the Acropolis. A large frieze is painted along the upper walls above the windows. Between the columns in the Ionic Hall are full-length portraits of Past Masonic Grand Masters.

The color scheme shifts dramatically in the **Gothic Hall**, also called the Asylum of Knights Templar. Here the ivory color is dramatized by brilliant scarlet carpet and wall hangings. The regal throne chair is a replica of the Archbishop's throne in Canterbury Cathedral. Gothic characteristics include groins, pointed arches, pinnacles and spires.

The **Norman Hall** reflects Rhenish Romanesque design with scrolled embellishments. Broad arched piers divide the walls into bays; panels between the piers have life-sized figures on a gold-mosaic background. Patterns from ancient Irish and Scandinavian manuscripts are used as decorative designs.

The final hall is the imposing **Italian Renaissance chamber** with two stages of columns in relief, one above the other, around the walls. The high, domed ceiling is in three sections, with the center a circular skylight. Both the walls and ceiling have Masonic emblems.

Descriptions do not do justice to the overpowering grandeur of these magnificent chambers; it is an architectural education just to visit the Masonic Temple. Also educational are the exhibits and collections in the Temple's Byzantine style library and museum. Perhaps the most treasured item is the Masonic Apron that Madame Lafayette embroidered for George Washington. The Marquis presented it to his friend in August 1784. Washington wore the apron when laying the cornerstone of the Capital. The museum also has several letters Washington sent to fellow Masons and Benjamin Franklin's Masonic Sash. These are just a few of the 30,000 items in the collection.

The library has over 70,000 volumes ranging from an incunabulum, a book—or rather two bound together—printed in Basel, Switzerland in 1489, to current Masonic periodicals. Visitors can use the library for research while Pennsylvania Masons can use its circulating service. The archives contain historic documents from renowned Masons as well as prints, daguerreotypes and biographical files.

The Masonic Temple gives tours at no charge Monday through Friday at 10:00 A.M., 11:00 A.M., 1:00 P.M., 2:00 P.M. and 3:00 P.M. On Saturdays only the two morning tours are conducted. Closed Saturdays in July and August. No tours Sundays and major holidays.

Directly across from the Masonic Temple is **City Hall**. An elevator will take you to the roof-top observation deck for a splendid panoramic view of the city.

Directions: From I-95 in Philadelphia take I-676 and exit on Broad Street. Follow that south to City Hall in Penn Square. The Masonic Temple is at One North Broad Street.

Morris Arboretum of the University of Pennsylvania

Around the Horticultural World

One of the main objectives of the American well-to-do has generally been—and still is—to be able to afford the best of Europe.

It was an eclectic, but fashionable, blending of the best of English, Italian and Oriental that John Morris and his sister Lydia assembled at Compton, their baronial Chestnut Hill estate. Now open to the public, the **Morris Arboretum** is a garden of compartments, or special areas, which are enhanced by a selection of outstanding specimen trees—many the largest known representatives of their species.

A splendid range of garden delights is provided by the combination of winding paths and majestic oak allee, formal parterres and spacious English park, a hidden grotto, a Tuscan love temple, a formal rose garden and natural woodland.

Water adds visual appeal within the arboretum. A quiet swan pond mirrors the Tuscan temple on its banks. Thanks to a tercentenary gift to Philadelphia from Ottawa, Canada, the pond now has two mute swans. This scene is a photographic gem which challenges all who try to capture it. From the temple there are stone steps to the water's edge. Leading from the pond to the stream below is a naturalistic waterfall which draws the eye from one garden compartment to another.

Both John and Lydia Morris were conscientious in their desire to achieve authenticity in the gardens they created; no ersatz design was tolerated at Compton. To assure a correct Oriental effect the Morrises brought a Japanese gardener to the estate. They were also interested in the expeditions of plant explorer E. H. Wilson, who brought them rare and exotic plants from the East. One of Wilson's most striking contributions was the Katsura, that stands at the end of the oak allee. The tree's 100-foot canopy makes this another favorite with photographers. The **Katsura** is an impressive artistic subject even in the winter when its boughs are bare.

This is by no means the only special tree to be found at the Morris Arboretum. Other rare specimens include the Siberian and Chinese elms, European weeping birch, Bender oak, blue Atlas cedar, Henry and Trident maples, lace-bark pine and tartar-wing celtis. These are only some of the notable varieties that comprise the collection of over 6,000 labeled and scientifically documented trees and shrubs on the arboretum's 92 public acres.

The arboretum's appeal changes with the seasons. The azalea meadow and magnolia slope offer a spring treat you won't want to miss. The Katsura with its blossom-laden branches is also splendid at this time of year. The meadow, too, is abloom with sunny daffodils. Later in the spring the alpine plants in the rock, or wall, garden below the hilltop where the mansion once stood provide a cascade of blooms.

Summer is the time to see the All-American roses in their parterre setting augmented by balustrade and fountain. In the open garden areas wildflowers still bloom in profusion and the butterfly bushes live up to their name by attracting their winged companions.

As so much of the arboretum is natural woodland, the fall foliage presents an array of color that not even the blooms of spring can equal. Berries, nuts and fruits can be found in abundance. There are even some blooms remaining on the Franklin tree and the Chinese elm. The very last flowers on the grounds are traditionally the common witch hazel.

In winter it is the pattern of the trees that attracts the visitor's attention. Also a pleasure at this time of year is the tropical environment of the indoor **Victorian-style fernery** designed by John Morris.

The Morris Arboretum is listed on the National Register of Historic Places and is the official arboretum for the state. It is open Monday through Friday from 10:00 A.M. to 4:00 P.M. During the summer months it is open weekends from 10:00 A.M. until 5:00 P.M. There are guided tours on weekends at 2:00 P.M., no reservations are needed. There is an admission charge.

Directions: From the Pennsylvania Turnpike, I-276, take Exit 25, Norristown, and drive east on Germantown Avenue, Route 422 about 4^1/$_2$ miles to the Philadelphia city limits. Turn left onto Northwestern Avenue and continue until you can see the entrance on the right.

Mummers Museum

Marching to Their Own Beat

For a very different excursion, drive past the colorful outdoor markets of Washington Avenue to the **Mummers Museum**. Every day is New Year's Eve when you see this evocative reminder of Philadelphia's annual Mummers Parade. You can't miss the museum, it has a bright facade of orange, blue and green tiles. The multi-hued exterior can't compete with the glittering costumes inside. Called "suits" by the Mummers, they cost clubs anywhere from $20,000.00 to $90,000.00.

Most visitors don't know the meaning of the word "mummer." The German word "mumme" means disguise and "mummenkleid" means a fancy dress. From Medieval Europe there are stories of costumed Mummers who silently entered villages to dance and play dice, then left, all without saying a word. Part of the celebration, as it was carried to America by Swedish immigrants, was the firing of guns to welcome the New Year. In the first parades, called New Year's Shooter, each marching group fired a salvo. This practice was banned, as was the equally noisy 19th-century Carnival of Horns.

The **Mummers Parade** became a city-sponsored celebration in 1901 and each year it continues to grow. The parade's sights, sounds and ambience are recreated at this museum. An exhibit designed to suggest a stroll up Broad Street lets you see a selection of suits in the four Mummer divisions: comic, fancy, string band and fancy brigade. Antique mutascopes, also called movie viewers, give you a chance to watch highlights from past parades. Rare photographs capture scenes from parades in the 1880s. On the museum's telephone listening post you can hear old-timers recall parades of their youth.

If you have questions, a handy electronic answering board responds to the 11 most frequent queries. By now you will know what is 2.55 miles long, 69 feet wide, 12 feet high and covered with feathers—the Philadelphia Mummer's Parade. If you'd like to see what you would look like as a Mummer, put your head in the exhibit window and you can be a Mummer. Next, you need to learn how to do the **Philadelphia Strut**; a demonstration display leads you through this distinctive walk that evolved from the Cakewalk. The Strut comes easy with all the music playing at the museum. Youngsters can push buttons to hear what each instrument in the string band sounds like, or they can play them simultaneously. The Hall of Fame presents a 45-minute program featuring the top ten string bands in the previous year's parade.

It is no surprise that the museum is closed on New Year's Day as well as all holidays, Mondays and Sundays during July and August. Hours are 9:30 A.M. to 5:00 P.M. Tuesday through Saturdays, Sunday it opens at NOON. A nominal admission is charged.

Directions: From I-95 take Exit 16 from Philadelphia's Historic area, Washington Avenue is 11 blocks south of Market Street. The Mummers Museum is at 2nd Street and Washington Avenue.

Naval Flagships at Penn's Landing

Anchors Aweigh

You can quite literally stand in the footsteps of history on the deck of the USS *Olympia*. Bronze impressions of Commodore

56

(later Admiral) Dewey's footsteps mark the spot on the bridge where he was standing at 5:40 A.M. on May 1, 1898, when he issued his famous order, "You may fire when you are ready, Gridley." His order marked the start of the Battle of Manila Bay, as well as the beginning of America's status as a world power. The guns that Dewey ordered Captain Gridley to fire were the heaviest battery ever fitted to a ship of this size.

The USS *Olympia* is the sole surviving example of the "New Navy" of the 1880s and 1890s. Flagship of Dewey's Asiatic fleet, she was a protective cruiser that could maintain speeds of 22 knots, considered swift for a ship at that time. It cost $2.9 million to build the *Olympia,* and she was American-designed and built.

Despite her many contributions to American history the Navy was ready in 1955 to scrap this lone survivor of the Spanish-American War. She was no longer of any use and it looked like the "Grand Old Lady," as she was called, was doomed. Then, thanks to a dedicated group of volunteers, The Cruiser Olympia Association, she was painstakingly restored.

When you enter the *Olympia* you will be in the Senior Officers' Mess. The wood paneling and fine old wood furniture provide ample testimony to the diligence of the volunteers who spent endless hours restoring the ship to its original appearance. Before they took over, one could get wet on rainy days five decks below the bridge. You will quickly realize what a complete world existed aboard these cruisers as you view in succession the ship's store, post office, dispensary, operating room, print shop and barber shop which also served as dentist office on alternate days. Be sure to note the ingenious methods employed to berth and feed the crew of 440 men.

On the upper deck of the *Olympia* is the wooden casket used when she sailed from Le Havre on her last mission. In it she carried the body of the unknown soldier of World War I for interment at Arlington National Cemetery. From this deck you look down upon the USS **Becuna** that is anchored beside the *Olympia.* The USS *Becuna* is a guppy-class submarine that saw action in World War II. She was commissioned on May 27, 1944 as the submarine flagship of the Southwest Pacific Fleet under General Douglas MacArthur. The *Becuna* is credited with the destruction of thousands of tons of Japanese naval and merchant ships on her five war patrols.

The submarine is the last of her type on exhibit. She is 308 feet long, and you can explore from the forward torpedo room to the maneuvering and motor room at the opposite end. It is hard to imagine 66 men living in this cramped and confined space. Even the officers' quarters are confining: only the captain has a bunk that resembles a normal size bed. The names of the

16-cylinder engines, Grunt and Groan and Huff and Puff, amuse the kids; but it is the torpedo with cut-aways that really captures visitors' attention. Torpedoes don't look that big when you see them being fired in war movies.

These two symbols of America's nautical past are berthed at Penn's Landing at the foot of Spruce Street on the Delaware River. You can visit from 10:00 A.M. to 6:00 P.M. during the summer months and from 10:00 A.M. to 4:00 P.M. in the fall, winter and spring. Admission is charged. Other historic vessels docked here are the *Gazela* (the largest and oldest wooden square-rigged ship sailing today) and *Jupiter.*

Penn's Landing is the very spot where William Penn first landed in 1682 and it is singularly appropriate that you will also find the Independence Seaport Museum (see selection) at the threshold of the city. The area around the waterfront is burgeoning with shops and restaurants. Across the river is the New Jersey State Aquarium, accessible by ferry.

Directions: From I-76, the Pennsylvania Turnpike, take I-676 (the Vine Street Expressway) to I-95 south. The next exit will be #16 for Columbus Boulevard and Washington Avenue. Stay in the left lane as Exit 16 is the only exit which is from the left lane. At the bottom of the ramp make a left turn and head north on Columbus Boulevard. The next traffic signal will be Lombard Circle. Make a right turn at this light, go around the circle and enter the Penn's Landing Pay Parking lot.

Norman Rockwell Museum

Picture-Perfect America

For a nostalgic look at the past, a visit to the Norman Rockwell Museum is better than perusing the family photograph album. What other artist could so perfectly capture the American family as Rockwell in his series for the Massachusetts Mutual Life Insurance Company? In the display of this amusing series, you'll see moments from your own life—the first hair cut, the first prom dress, backyard picnics, a visit to the doctor, the family dog, fishing with Dad, baby's first steps and traveling aboard. Rockwell said, "I paint life as I would like it to be."

The **Norman Rockwell Museum** has the largest and most complete collection of his work. For background on Rockwell's 50-year career, watch the short slide show on his life and work. Frank Sinatra's moving rendition of "The House I Live In," provides a poignant background to the works of Rockwell.

In 1916, the 22-year-old Rockwell sold his first magazine cover to Curtis Publishing. At the time the popular magazine sold for five cents a copy. The museum has the entire collection of covers that Rockwell did for the *Saturday Evening Post.*

A raft of well-known writers wrote for the magazine. The October 14, 1916 issue, with Rockwell's cover of a typical family evening at the theater, has a story by Ring Lardner. On May 5, 1928 the magazine contained the personal memoirs of Benito Mussolini. By January 27, 1942, the magazine cost ten cents and the cover shows a young couple reading a brochure entitled, "What to do in a Blackout." Rockwell captures a look on their young faces that leaves little doubt that they have their own ideas.

Rockwell not only left us a legacy of our lives, he also vividly captured many of the great political, entertainment and sports figures of the day. You'll see portraits of such diverse celebrities as John F. Kennedy, Gary Cooper, Ronald Reagan and Eddie Arcaro, the well-known jockey. There are Rockwell posters, paintings, lithographs, sketches, movie billboards and commercial advertisements. The museum has recreated Rockwell's studio with a mannequin of the artist hard at work on his front porch. As you view the prodigious output of this artist it will not come as a surprise to learn that he worked seven days a week with only a half day off yearly to celebrate Christmas Day.

The Norman Rockwell Museum is open 10:00 A.M. to 4:00 P.M. daily year-round. It closes for Thanksgiving, Christmas, New Year's Day and Easter. Admission is charged; visitors under 12 are free.

Directions: Traveling north on I-95 take I-676 into Philadelphia and turn left on 6th Street and continue down to Sansom Street. The Norman Rockwell Museum is on the lower level of the Curtis Center at 6th and Sansom Streets, just across the street from Independence Square.

Philadelphia Museum of Art and the Rodin Museum

Rocky Should Have Gone Inside

Sitting imposingly at the end of the Benjamin Franklin Parkway is the **Philadelphia Museum of Art**, one of the world's great art institutions. Chartered in 1876, the museum was a legacy of the Centennial Exposition held that year in Fairmount Park. In the century that has passed since its inception, the museum has grown to encompass over 400,000 works of art, including one of the world's largest and most important collections of European art.

The Museum of American Art at the Pennsylvania Academy of Fine Arts is the nation's first art museum and art school.

In 1995 the museum completed a reinstallation of its European collection and, for the first time, the eighty galleries of European art are exhibited in chronological order. The Philadelphia Museum of Art is also singular because it combines painting, sculpture, prints, drawings, furniture, ceramics, glass, metalworks, costumes, textiles, period interiors and large-scale architectural elements creating a complete look at various periods and styles. This innovative approach was adopted by Fiske Kimball, director from 1925 to 1955, who explained, "The whole pageant of the history of civilization and of art is spread before the visitor, who may travel at ease through space and through time." Kimball's vision is finally gloriously realized.

Highlights of the second floor European galleries include a Romanesque cloister, a Gothic chapel, a 17th-century room from Haarlem and a look at neoclassical and romantic trends in the early 19th century.

The first floor is newly rearranged to offer a look at later 19th-century work ranging from the "official" art of the salons to the offerings of the Impressionist and Post-Impressionist artists. One of the museum's significant works, Cezanne's *Great Bathers*, is the culmination of this section. From there visitors move into the 20th-century galleries. Other outstanding collections include a comprehensive array of rural Pennsylvania German crafts and an exhibit of Shaker furniture. The museum has one of the world's finest collections of **Thomas Eakins's work**.

Free guided tours of the museum are given hourly from 11:00 A.M. to 3:00 P.M. For information on tours given in foreign languages, call (215) 684-7923. For sign language tour information, call (215) 684-7601. Museum hours are Tuesday through Sunday 10:00 A.M. to 5:00 P.M., galleries remain open until 8:45 P.M. on Wednesday. Admission is free on Sunday from 10:00 A.M. to 1:00 P.M.; at other times a fee is charged. There is a well-stocked museum shop on the ground floor as well as temporary shops outside special exhibitions. The museum restaurant is open Tuesday through Sunday 11:45 A.M. to 2:15 P.M. and Wednesday evenings 5:00 P.M. to 7:30 P.M. There is also a cafeteria that is open weekdays from 10:00 A.M. to 3:30 P.M.

Just down the Benjamin Franklin Parkway at 22nd Street is the **Rodin Museum**, administered by the Philadelphia Museum of Art. It's the most complete and arresting array of Rodin's work outside Paris. This collection was amassed by Philadelphia movie magnate Jules E. Mastbaum, who first acquired Rodin's work in 1923. The museum Mastbaum commissioned, but did not live to see completed, showcases 124 of Rodin's sculpture including bronze casts of his greatest work. Brooding over the museum's entrance is **"The Thinker**," certainly one of the world's best known sculptures. Other noted pieces are the heroic "The Burghers of Calais," the lyrical "Eternal Springtime" and "The Gates of Hell," Rodin's culminating work.

It was Rodin's genius to faithfully capture his subjects, he did not follow the tradition of idealizing subjects. This graphic realism gave his work psychological weight, penetrating beyond the mask society imposed on his subjects. No visitor to Philadelphia should miss this outstanding collection, and nearby residents should drop by often to see this outstanding outpouring of one of the greatest sculptors of all time.

The Rodin Museum is open Tuesday through Sunday 10:00 A.M. to 5:00 P.M. Voluntary donations are requested. Guided tours are given on the first and third Saturdays of each month at 1:00 P.M. There is a small museum shop.

Directions: Traveling north on I-95 exit on I-676 west, take I-676 to museum exit, 22nd Street. At the end of the ramp take a right onto 22nd Street and get in the far left lane. At the first traffic light, make a left turn into the middle left lane of the Benjamin Franklin Parkway. Follow parkway up to the museum on the hill; at the parkway traffic circle stay in one of the right lanes and follow signs for Kelly Drive. Once on Kelly Drive you should move to the extreme left lane as you will make a left at the first stop light, which is 25th Street. This will lead to a free parking and the west entrance of the museum. If you are traveling from the west, take I-76 east to Philadelphia, exit at Spring Garden Avenue. Turn left and follow Spring Garden Avenue around past the side of the museum. Go through traffic light and merge in Eakins Oval traffic circle; get in the middle right hand lane of this circle and follow signs for Kelly Drive, then proceed as above.

Please Touch Museum

Learning is Child's Play

A visit to most museums is a frustrating experience for children seven and younger. At this age particularly, children learn best by touching and exploring. Yet in far too many museums intriguing objects are roped off, glassed in or protected by signs that say: Please Do Not Touch!

Philadelphia is fortunate to have the **Please Touch Museum**, the first museum in the nation and the only institution in the Delaware Valley dedicated to providing a high-quality, first museum experience for visitors seven and younger. Responding to a real need, the museum has successfully accomplished its mission of educating and entertaining youngsters. The Please Touch staff believe children learn best by early exploration and direct participation in their environments—in short, "Learning is Child's Play."

The museum stimulates the curiosity and learning of young children with its collections, hands-on exhibits, programs and by encouraging child/adult interaction. The interactive environment stimulates children's imagination, aesthetic appreciation and cognitive skills while appealing to the senses. The museum invites action, independence, discovery and language development. Parents and those with younger visitors are encouraged to serve as teachers and interpreters as children explore the exhibits.

Current exhibits include "Nature's Nursery," "Play in Motion," "Foodtastic Journey," "Building Blocks," "Step into Art" and "Move It." The latter has three areas: John Wanamaker Monorail, SEPTA bus and Kids' Creation. Studio PTM, sponsored by WCAU-TV, places children behind the camera and on stage in a television studio.

The Education Store at the Please Touch Museum has a wide selection of books, games, cassette tapes and toys. Many of the items in the store relate to and reinforce concepts promoted in museum exhibits.

Please Touch Museum is open daily from 9:00 A.M. to 4:30 P.M. It is closed on Thanksgiving, Christmas and New Years. Admission is charged but for the first hour of operation on Sunday morning there is a "Pay-As-You-Wish" contribution admission fee. There must be one adult for every five children.

Directions: Please Touch Museum is at 210 North 21st Street just off the Benjamin Franklin Parkway. From the city center take Arch Street to 22nd Street. Turn right on Race Street and proceed one block east to 21st Street.

Rosenbach Museum & Library

Collectors Nonpareil

For nearly 30 years, from 1928 until their deaths in 1952 and 1953, Dr. A.S.W. Rosenbach and his brother Philip lived in this spacious townhouse on DeLancey Place surrounded by the artistic treasures they collected. The doctor was the world's greatest rare book dealer and Philip a discerning art dealer.

The English, French and American furniture that fill the rooms belonged to the Rosenbach (that's pronounced Rosenback) brothers. Their silver, porcelain, linens, paintings and decorative arts are also part of the decor. The collection includes over 3,000 original drawings and watercolors by Maurice Sendak, the noted children's book author and illustrator. There are prints and drawings by English and French artists of the 18th and 19th centuries including Fragonard, Daumier, Dupre and Blake.

Paintings in the **Rosenbach collection** include works by Thomas Sully, Benjamin West, Bass Otis and Robert Swain Gifford. There are also approximately 500 oil miniatures done in the Dutch, Italian, French, Spanish and English style. One noted miniature is Nicholas Hilliard's portrait of James I. The eclectic sculpture ranges from two Matisse bronze studies to a 15th- century northern Italian figure of Christ.

What attracts scholars from around the world are the 30,000 rare books and 300,000 manuscripts. One pivotal theme of this collection documents America's past. Documents range from Amerigo Vespucci's 1504 book *Mundus Novus* to the typed carbon copy of the Atlantic Charter President Roosevelt signed in 1941. Letters from historical luminaries such as Cortes, Washington, Jefferson, Franklin and Lincoln are exhibited on a rotating and changing basis.

Dr. A.S.W. Rosenbach also concentrated on British and American literary treasures. Among the collection's highlights are a 15th-century illuminated manuscript of *The Canterbury Tales*, Lewis Carroll's own copy of *Alice in Wonderland*, the manuscript of James Joyce's *Ulysses*, manuscripts by Blake, Conrad and Dickens and the working notes for Bram Stoker's *Dracula*. Researchers delving into 20th-century literature find the letters Modernist poet Marianne Moore exchanged with such seminal writers as T.S. Eliot and Ezra Pound profoundly illuminating. The museum also recreates **Moore's Greenwich Village apartment** using her furniture, decorative pieces and books along with her voluminous literary archive.

The Rosenbach Museum gives guided tours Tuesday through Sunday from 11:00 A.M. to 4:00 P.M. The last 75-minute tour is at 2:45 P.M. The museum is closed Mondays, national holidays and the month of August. Admission is charged; seniors and students receive a discount. The research library is only open by appointment; call (215) 732-1600.

Directions: From I-95 take I-676 in downtown Philadelphia and exit on Route 611, Broad Street. Take Broad Street south around City Hall to Spruce Street and turn right. Then make a left on 21st Street and another left on DeLancey Place. The Rosenbach Museum & Library is at 2010 DeLancey Place between 20th and 21st Streets.

Schuylkill Center for Environmental Education

Eco-Tourism

A tranquil oasis of unspoiled natural areas can be found within Philadelphia's city limits at the 300-acre **Schuylkill Center for Environmental Education**. Six miles of trails meander through fields, woodlands and thickets skirting the ponds and streams where visitors see a variety of wildlife. During the fall and winter the bird blinds provide a close look at the feeding stations.

The message at Schuylkill—addressed to young and old—is that we are all the keepers of the earth, and we must understand and learn our role in this important partnership. Environmental education is fostered at the center in a myriad of ways.

Schuylkill calls the family "the ultimate everybody." Weekends are filled with activities geared to families. Guided walks, story telling, workshops and seasonal festivals are just part of the fun. Weekend activities geared especially for children include ex-

ploring nature through sensory experiences, probing the mysteries of animal adaptation or picking a favorite in the bug Olympics.

Young and old can join environmental educators for walks
along the **Widener Trail**, a hard-surfaced level grade wheelchair
accessible trail. This trail skirts a woodland pond and takes you
through a wide variety of habitats. All of the center's interpretative educational buildings are also wheelchair accessible.

Environmental theater is another successful tool in furthering
the center's goal of preserving and improving the natural world
by appreciation, understanding and responsible use of its ecosystems. Theatrical performances pull the audience into the action.
Few visitors refuse to join the skits that are used to trace the cycles of our planet. With the sun as conductor, the audience is
transformed into a chorus of frogs, a thunderous storm or a forest full of animals.

Schuylkill Center is open Monday through Saturday 8:30 A.M.
to 5:00 P.M. On Sunday it opens at 1:00 P.M. The bookstore and
gift shop close daily at 4:30 P.M. Admission is charged. For information regarding special activities call (215) 482-7300.

Directions: From I-76 the Schuylkill Expressway take the Wissahickon exit, cross the Schuylkill River and travel north on
Ridge Avenue. Turn left on Port Royal Avenue, then make a right
on Hagy's Mill Road to the entrance of the Schuylkill Center.

Stenton and La Salle University
Art Museum

Public and Private Art

The stately brick country seat begun in 1723 by James Logan,
William Penn's secretary, hardly looks like an economy move to
modern visitors. But that is indeed what it was. Logan suffered
a series of business failures in the early 1720s, and he decided
to retire to the country while he still had enough capital to establish a workable plantation for his family.

Logan began acquiring land in old Germantown in 1714, while
managing the affairs of the colony in Penn's absence. He eventually had 511 acres and planned to build an inexpensive stone
house. In keeping with his run of bad luck, the quarries failed.
During the next two years, Logan was unable to find any reasonable source of native stones. In 1717, he decided to begin
building his home using bricks. **Stenton**, named after Logan's
father's Scottish village, was finished in 1730.

Although James Logan's economic fortunes suffered, his political fortunes did not. Logan was secretary of the province,

commissioner of property and receiver general, clerk and later president of the Pennsylvania Provincial Council, chief justice for the colony and William Penn's Indian agent.

The brick floor you see in the entrance hall at Stenton was a practical accommodation to the large number of visitors who called on James Logan. Frequently the Lenni-Lanape Indians camped at Stenton while traveling back and forth from Philadelphia.

The elements of Logan's Quaker beliefs are seen in the simplicity of Stenton's design and its furnishings. The room interpreted as Logan's study does not display the one extravagance that Logan enjoyed, his 3,000-book library. It became the nucleus for the Library Company of Philadelphia. Logan was a genuine scholar; in addition to being fluent in seven languages, including Indian dialects, he conducted astronomy and agronomy experiments.

James Logan's son, William, followed in his father's footsteps. He acted as attorney for the Penn family and served on the Provincial Council from 1747 to 1776. He, too, made his mark on Stenton. William added the "old" kitchen and the piazza. His family also contributed some of the finer pieces of furniture. Each room reflects and interprets one of the three generations to live at Stenton from 1730 to 1780, ending with George Logan.

The stone bank barn was added by George Logan, who was intensely interested in agriculture. He turned Stenton into a model farm. His wife, Deborah Norris Logan, transcribed the correspondence of James Logan and William Penn and gained the distinction of being the first woman member of the Historical Society of Pennsylvania.

Stenton is open for tours April into November Tuesday through Saturday from 1:00 P.M. to 4:00 P.M. There is a nominal admission charge.

While in the area stop at **La Salle University Art Museum**, open Tuesday through Friday from 11:00 A.M. until 4:00 P.M. On Sunday, the galleries open at 2:00 P.M. The museum is closed in August. La Salle Art Museum opened in 1976 and boasts a permanent collection of painting and sculpture from the Middle Ages to modern times. Highlights of the collection include work by Provost, Van Cleve, Tintoretto, Bourdon, Ruisdael, Tanner, Raeburn, Lawrence, Robert, West, Eakins, Corot, Degas, Pissarro, Bourdin, Vuillard and Rouault. The museum also has a specialized collection of illustrated and printed Bibles. The art is on display in a series of period rooms in Olney Hall at 20th and Olney Avenue. No admission is charged.

Directions: From I-95 take Schuylkill Expressway, Route 76 north, to Roosevelt Boulevard, Route 1 north, and proceed to second exit on right. Follow exit bearing left to the third traffic light. Beyond this light the road bears left becoming Old Stenton Avenue. At the stop sign, turn right onto Logan Street. At the first traffic light, bear right onto 20th Street and the La Salle campus. Olney Hall and the museum sits back on the right. The entrance to the parking lot is on Olney Avenue at 20th Street.

Thaddeus Kosciuszko National Memorial and the Polish American Cultural Center

Toast of Two Continents

Thaddeus Kosciuszko (pronounced Kos-Choos-Ko) was born February 4, 1746 into an impoverished eastern Polish family. After pursuing military studies in Warsaw and France, he lacked funds to purchase a military commission in Poland. He may also have left Poland because of a doomed love. In 1774, he was injured while attempting to elope with a Polish lord's daughter he was tutoring. Kosciuszko came to America and offered his services to the America cause.

Kosciuszko arrived in Philadelphia a few weeks after the Continental Congress adopted the Declaration of Independence. The 30-year old had training but no experience. Additionally, he was the first foreign volunteer, so it took time before Congress responded to his offer. On October 18, 1776 a resolution was passed that "Thaddeus Kosciuszko, Esq. be appointed an engineer in the service of the United States, with the pay of sixty dollars a month, and the rank of colonel." This began a six-year tour of duty during which he planned and built the fortifications at Saratoga and West Point. At war's end Kosciuszko was promoted to the rank of brigadier general.

On July 15, 1784 Kosciuszko sailed back to Poland and a quiet country life. But by the 1790s, he was actively opposing Czarist Russia's domination of Poland. Kosciuszko drafted the Act of Insurrection, a document reflecting the ideas he had absorbed from America's Declaration of Independence. When Poland adopted a constitution on May 3, 1791, war with Russia ensued. Kosciuszko was made commander of the national armies, but ultimately was seriously wounded in battle, defeated and imprisoned at the Peter-and-Paul Fortress in St. Petersburg.

Only a promise never to return to Poland secured Kosciuszko's release in December 1796. His painful wounds left him partially paralyzed but Kosciuszko traveled to London, via Finland and Sweden, arriving on May 30, 1797. Two weeks later he left on a 61-day journey to America. He arrived in Philadelphia to a hero's welcome. But the then capital city was fighting a lethal yellow fever epidemic, so Kosciuszko visited General Anthony White in New Jersey and General Horatio Gates in New York.

With the cold weather, the mosquitoes died and the threat of yellow fever ended. In November Kosciuszko returned to Philadelphia and rented a small room on the second floor at Mrs. Ann Reif's boarding house at Third and Pine streets. The Polish hero spent the winter reading, also entertaining Thomas Jefferson and other distinguished guests.

Continued concern for Poland prompted him to return to Europe on May 5, 1798. After spending time in Paris he retired to a friend's estate in Switzerland. He died in 1817 after falling from a horse. Before his death he had emancipated all the peasants on his Polish estates. Kosciuszko was buried in the cathedral of Cracow, in his beloved Poland only after his death.

The **Thaddeus Kosciuszko National Memorial**, part of Independence National Historical Park, recreates the room Kosciuszko rented for his last six months in America. Both the second-floor room and the exterior of the house are restored to reflect that time period. In addition to his rented room, exhibits detail Kosciuszko's contributions to the American Revolution, as does a four-minute video. The memorial is open 9:00 A.M. to 5:00 P.M. daily at no charge.

Thaddeus Kosciuszko's valorous exploits are also celebrated at the **Polish American Cultural Center**, as are those of other noted Poles: Queen Jadwiga; Casimir Pulaski, the father of the American cavalry; Nicholas Copernicus, the father of modern astronomy; composers Frederic Chopin and Ignace Paderewski; scientist Marie Curie; novelist Henry Sienkiewicz; religious leader Pope John Paul II and political leader Lech Walesa. There is also a copy of the portrait of Our Lady of Czestochowa (see Shrine selection). Poland's May 3, 1791 constitution is pictured, it was after the drafting of this the world's second oldest democratic constitution that Kosciuszko took command of Poland's national army.

The center has examples of Polish folk art and the music of Chopin fills the air. A modest selection of handicrafts is for sale.

Directions: From I-95 southbound (from points north) take Exit 17. Using the right-hand lanes of the exit, follow the signs for Callowhill Street/Independence Hall. At the bottom of the exit ramp, follow 2nd Street straight ahead to Chestnut Street. Continue a half block past Chestnut Street for the Historic Area Parking Garage on the left. It is best to park your car and walk to all the sites in the Historic District. Start at the Independence National Historical Park Visitors Center, one block away, at 3rd and Chestnut Streets. Here you can pick up an easy-to-follow map of the district and a park schedule. The Polish American Cultural Center is not part of the park, but it is located across the street from park sites on Walnut Street between 3rd and 4th Streets. If you are traveling northbound on I-95 (from points south) you will also take Exit 17. Stay in the left lane because you will exit on the left side of I-95. At the exit, stay in the right-hand lane and follow the signs for Independence Hall/Historic Area. Turn left at 6th Street to Chestnut. This will take you through the heart of the Historic District to 2nd Street. Turn right on 2nd Street. The entrance to the Historic Area Parking Garage is on the left.

Todd House and Bishop White House

Family Life in the City of Brotherly Love

At the time of the American Revolution Philadelphia was one of the largest English-speaking cities in the world. On 48 acres in downtown Philadelphia, the Independence National Historical Park has 40 historic buildings and numerous 18th-century park areas that bring back those by-gone days. The park encompasses government buildings where the nation was organized and initially run, as well as homes such as the Todd and Bishop White houses that reflect the private side of this tumultuous era.

In a perhaps legendary American version of "The Student Prince," the niece of a Haddonfield, New Jersey tavern keeper succeeded where the original heroine failed. Young Dolley Paine, after attracting the admiring attention of the eager soldiers and legislators who frequented her uncle's Indian King Tavern, did succeed in becoming America's First Lady—albeit by a circuitous route. Dolley Paine married John Todd, Jr., a promising young Philadelphia attorney. A year later the Todds moved to the Philadelphia house, now part of Independence National Historic Park.

They lived in the gracious townhouse from 1741 to 1743. During this period Dolley had two children. The Philadelphia yellow fever epidemic was a tragic time for the Todd family. Even though Dolley left the city, one of her children already ill from other causes died, as did her husband who remained in the city. Perhaps a third of the population fled the city; many who stayed perished.

When cold weather killed the mosquitoes the epidemic ended. Dolley returned to the city a widow with a two-year-old son. She had three choices: take in boarders as her own widowed mother had done, open a small shop or marry again. Being young and attractive, she took the last alternative. Aaron Burr introduced her to James Madison and after only a few months they married. Madison had an illustrious career, culminating in the presidency.

69

The **Todd House** is an example of an "end of row" house, a style found predominantly in Pennsylvania, New Jersey and Delaware. It is furnished from exact inventories, representing a middle-class Quaker house in the 18th century. One indication of the era's frugality is the forerunner of the Xerox, a press-like device that created a copy of correspondence. Unfortunately, the copy came out backwards, so a mirror was placed on the desk to enable the copy to be read. The mirror served a secondary function of doubling the candle power, by reflecting the flame.

Bishop William White's house has none of the Quaker sparseness of the Todd House. White's house was built for him in 1786 while he was in London being consecrated the first Protestant Episcopal Bishop of Pennsylvania. The house has a number of floors. At the very top is a loft and below that is the boys' floor where initials are carved into the wood. The third floor is the girls' room, with White's bedroom and library just below. The formal rooms are on the first floor; beneath that is the kitchen area, the scullery, the wine cellar, root cellar and the ice well.

White and his wife, their five children, a cook and coachman filled this large house. The Whites entertained frequently, as Bishop White served as Chaplain of the Continental Congress and of the United States Senate. He lived here for 50 years after his wife died.

This upper class home is quite elegant. The details have been so faithfully recreated that two half-smoked cigars have been added to duplicate those shown in an artistic rendering of the room. Archeological research led to the discovery of silver and crockery in the drain under the house, permitting exact copies of the original pieces.

The Todd House and the Bishop White House are open daily 9:00 A.M. to 4:30 P.M. daily at no charge. As the number of visitors that can be accommodated at the Bishop White House is limited, tickets are required but they can be obtained at the INHP Visitor Center.

Adjacent to the Todd House is a recreated formal colonial garden. This is just one of the gardens that captures the "greene Country Towne" that William Penn foresaw in 1682. Philadelphia was one of America's first cities to be developed according to a plan that included plants. The Pennsylvania Horticultural Society has planted a colonial garden at 325 Walnut Street. Like many gardens in the 1700s, this garden is in three sections: a formal garden, an orchard and the herb and vegetable area. In the formal parterres, or sections, you can see seasonal flowers. There is also a garden on the grounds of the Norris House and the Pemberton House (see Army-Navy Museum selection).

Directions: From I-95 southbound (from points north) take Exit 17. Using the right-hand lanes of the exit, follow the signs for

Callowhill Street/Independence Hall. At the bottom of the exit ramp, follow 2nd Street straight ahead to Chestnut Street. Continue a half block past Chestnut Street for the Historic Area Parking Garage on the left. It is best to park your car and walk to all the sites in the Historic District. Start at the Independence National Historical Park Visitors Center, one block away, at 3rd and Chestnut Streets. Here you can pick up an easy-to-follow map of the district and a park schedule. If you are traveling northbound on I-95 (from points south) you will also take Exit 17. Stay in the left lane because you will exit on the left side of I-95. At the exit, stay in the right-hand lane and follow the signs for Independence Hall/Historic Area. Turn left at 6th Street to Chestnut. This will take you through the heart of the Historic District to 2nd Street. Turn right on 2nd Street. The entrance to the Historic Area Parking Garage is on the left.

United States Mint

No Free Samples

The expression "mint condition" takes on new meaning when you visit the United States Mint in Philadelphia. Watching the shiny coins spill off the assembly line, you find it hard to believe that they are real money. The large presses stamp out as many as 700 coins per minute. Each group of visitors seems to have at least one humorist who inquires about free samples.

The **U.S. Mint** in Philadelphia is the largest of the nation's four operating mints and the fourth to be built here. The original building at 7th and Arch Streets was the first public building erected by the federal government. It was authorized by Congress on April 2, 1792. In 1992, the U.S. Treasurer dedicated a plaque marking the site of the first mint. By the turn of the century only one million coins had been struck. Now, in only one hour, the U.S. Mint can turn out close to $1^1/_2$ million coins. The mint currently makes five denominations for circulation—pennies, nickels, dimes, quarters and some half-dollars. While on the tour you are likely to see at least some part of this money making operation.

The mint covers three city blocks. When you enter, signs direct you upstairs where a welcoming tape introduces you to the mint and gets you started on your self-guided tour. You'll wind around a gallery overlooking the work area below, listen to recorded messages and read the explanatory signs. Although some of the preliminary work is no longer done at this location, you can watch the process from the blanking press, to the annealing and cleaning lines and then to the actual coining. On the last stop, the coins are inspected, counted and bagged.

Along the gallery walls are displays of coins and medals minted over the years. There is a collection of military medals, including the Congressional Medal of Honor. Plaques, marble relics and the first coining press from the 1792 mint remind visitors of the three earlier mints.

A bit of minting lore can be gleaned from the display describing the **Trial of the Pyx**. A pyx is a locked box with a slotted top. It was used to store test coins, which were randomly selected and inserted through the slots. The pyx was opened only in the presence of the assay committee who tested the coins. You'll see an 18th-century pyx which was given to the U.S. Mint by the Master of the Netherlands Mint.

After you complete your gallery-top survey of operations, the self-guided tour continues in the numismatic room on the mezzanine where there is a display of coins and minting equipment. Visitors frequently linger over the case filled with gold coins. Coins and books on coin collecting can be purchased at the gift shop. A machine adjacent to the shop lets visitors make their own Philadelphia mint medal.

The U.S. Mint is open 9:00 A.M. to 4:30 P.M. Monday through Friday from January through April, then resumes these hours from September through December. The mint opens on Saturday in May and June and on a seven day schedule in July and August. For the current schedule call (215) 597-7350. No reservation is required and no admission is charged.

Directions: From downtown Philadelphia take Broad Street north to Market Street. Go around City Hall to Arch Street. The U.S. Mint is located at 5th and Arch Streets. There is street, metered parking around all sides of the mint. There is also a municipal parking lot underground between Market and Arch Streets with entrances on 5th and 6th Streets.

University of Pennsylvania Museum of Archaeology and Anthropology, Academy of Natural Sciences and Wagner Free Institute

Amazing Array of Artifacts

During the 19th century, Philadelphia was extolled as the Athens of the Americas. As the 20th century ends the city still offers a staggering array of cultural treasures. The creative geniuses of the world's finest artists is abundantly evident at the Philadelphia Museum of Art and the Rodin Museum. The Franklin Institute Science Museum is one of the country's leading science museums. (See selections.) The **University of Pennsylvania Museum of Archeology and Anthropology** and the Academy of Natural Sciences are two more world-class facilities. The Wagner Free Institute is a "museum of a museum" with its own venerable history.

The University of Pennsylvania obtained the majority of their items the hard way, sending archaeologists and anthropologists on research and collection expeditions around the world. In its 100 plus-year history, the museum has conducted more than 350 research expeditions and collected more than a million objects, many obtained directly through field excavations or anthropological research. Among the highlights to be found on its three floors of galleries are: the **Lower Egyptian collection** with architectural pieces from the Palace of Merenptah, circa 1200 B.C.; the 12-ton granite Sphinx of Rameses II, circa 1293-1185 B.C.; and the Upper Egyptian gallery pieces, with the crowd pleasing "Egyptian Mummy: Secrets and Science" exhibition. Other famous pieces were collected during the museum's ancient Mesopotamian excavation work, co-sponsored in the 1920s with the British Museum, at the important site of Ur, circa 2600 B.C., in modern day Iraq. Closer both geographically and chronologically are the objects in the **Alaska's Native People** exhibit, featuring significant items from the Inuit, Tlingit and Athapaskan peoples.

The museum is open Tuesday through Saturday 10:00 A.M. to 4:30 P.M. and Sunday from 1:00 P.M. to 5:00 P.M. The museum is closed Monday, holidays and summer Sundays. Admission donation is requested. On mid-September through mid-May weekends at 1:15 P.M. admission includes a galley tour. The museum hosts traveling exhibitions and special events that range from lectures and symposiums to children's programs and musical events. Call (215) 898-4890 for a current schedule.

Some science enthusiasts go back even farther; the world's best dinosaur exhibit can be seen at the **Academy of Natural Sciences**. The Academy was founded by amateur naturalists in 1812, one of whom was Thomas Say, the father of both American Entomology and Conchology (the former studying insects and the latter shells). Other distinguished associates were John James Audubon, Thomas Jefferson, William Bartram, and Charles Darwin (the Academy was the first American scientific organization to recognize the significance of his work). Today the Academy includes a research institution, a 200,000 volume library, an educational center and a museum. It is in the latter capacity that 200,000 visitors annually flock to this significant Philadelphia landmark.

The museum was established to showcase the collections and objects of study of Academy naturalists. Designed primarily for other scientists the collections were occasionally opened to the public. Public lectures were started in 1814 and the Academy's educational programs have grown in number, range and stature from that time. The museum is now "user friendly" to visitors of all ages.

The more than a dozen dinosaurs, including the towering Tyrannosaurus Rex skeleton, are among visitors' favorite exhibits. Also popular are life-like dioramas of North America, Asia and Africa. There is also a **children's nature museum** with live animals and hands-on activities; older visitors can participate in hands-on work in the geology lab.

The Academy of Natural Sciences Museum is open Monday through Friday from 10:00 A.M. to 4:30 P.M.; it closes at 5:00 P.M. on weekends and holidays. Admission is charged. On your way in or out of the museum notice the beautifully figured wood of the princess trees in Logan Square, they are also called Royal Paulownia in honor of Dutch Princess Anna Paulowna.

If the Academy museum was the result of the enthusiasm of a group of natural scientists, the **Wagner Free Institute** is the result of one individual's interest. William Wagner, Philadelphia merchant, philanthropist and amateur scientist, began giving free science lectures to the public at his home in 1847. He illustrated his talks using items from his vast collection of natural science specimens. Wide spread interest in his lectures prompted Wagner to switch the location to the more convenient Municipal Hall and engage a faculty to teach six lectures a week. When the city needed the hall, Wagner began building his own facility and the Wagner Free Institute opened at its present location in 1865.

City Hall designer John McArthur created this Victorian natural science museum now on the National Register of Historic Places. Over the years the Institute has spent its limited budget on research not renovation; consequently the museum looks very much as it did in William Wagner's day. More than 100,000 specimens are exhibited in the same cherry wood cases, books line the original wood cases and the maple floor has achieved a patina of age. Collections include minerals and fossils, stuffed and mounted birds and animals, dinosaur bones and extensive entomological specimens.

The Wagner Free Institute is still free to the public. Hours are Tuesday to Friday 10:00 A.M. to 4:00 P.M. for self-guided tours.

Directions: From I-95, for the University of Pennsylvania Museum of Archaeology and Anthropology, pick up the Schuylkill Expressway, I-76. Exit I-76 at South Street, turn west (away from Center City) over the South Street Bridge. One block over the bridge off Convention Boulevard, turn left. The museum is on South Street, with its main entrance at the corner of 33rd and Spruce Streets. The Academy of Natural Sciences Museum is on Logan Circle at 1900 Benjamin Franklin Parkway; just take the parkway exit off I-676. For the Wagner Free Institute of Science take I-95 to I-676 west. From I-676 take the Broad Street, Route 611 north, exit. Continue on Broad Street to Norris Street and make a left. Take Norris Street to 17th Street and make a left. The museum is one block down at Montgomery Avenue and 17th Street.

Wyck

Rose in Bloom

Old roses and Old World charm are found in abundance at Wyck, home to one Quaker family from 1689 to 1973. The history of **Wyck** dates to 1689 when Hans Millan, a Swiss Mennonite, acquired land on which he built a small house in 1690. After his daughter Catherine married Dirck Jansen a second house, separate from, but aligned with the first, was built in 1736. In 1771, the 1690 house was torn down and a new, large stone house was built. By 1777, when the house was used as a field hospital during the Battle of Germantown, the two dwellings were connected at the second floor level. In 1799, Caspar Wistar Haines visually tied the two houses together into one manor house by applying a coat of white stucco.

Not only is Wyck a National Historic Landmark but it is also a comfortable old home. Nine generations of families, primarily the Wistars and Haines, enjoyed life at Wyck. The original furnishings and decorative pieces are blended in style and period. Over 10,000 objects and 100,000 family documents illustrate the continued family life from the 18th century to 1973.

In 1824, Wyck's interior underwent major renovation when Reuben Haines III asked his friend, architect William Strickland to assist in repairs to the house. He created a suite of sunlit rooms in the Greek Revival style overlooking the south lawn and formal gardens. This series of rooms is beautifully decorated in a comfortable and cheerful style.

A visit to Wyck in late May through mid-June coincides with the peak blooming season of Wyck's historic old roses, planted according to the original garden plan dating from the 1820s. Their form, beauty and especially their fragrance set them apart from the modern hybrid tea roses. A total of 37 different roses flourish in Wyck's box-bordered rose garden. The estate's two-

and-a-half acre grounds also include early outbuildings: a coach house, smokehouse, icehouse and greenhouse.

Wyck, at 6026 Germantown Avenue at the corner of Walnut Lane, is open April through December 15 on Tuesday, Thursday and Saturday from 1:00 P.M. to 4:00 P.M. and year-round by appointment. To arrange a tour call (215) 848-1690. Admission is charged.

Directions: From I-95 take the Vine Street Expressway exit, Route 676. Follow Route 676 until it joins with Route 76 west, the Schuylkill Expressway. Take the Lincoln Drive exit and follow Lincoln Drive to the first traffic light. Turn right onto Rittenhouse Street. Turn left at the second light onto Wissahickon Avenue. Turn right at the first light onto Walnut Lane and follow approximately five blocks up to Germantown Avenue. Wyck is behind a gray fence on your right. Parking is available in a small lot off Walnut Lane or along Germantown Avenue.

COUNTRYSIDE

Andalusia

Southern Charm North of the Mason-Dixon Line

Great river houses with colonnaded porticoes suggest Southern plantations, but some of the finest examples are found north of the Mason-Dixon line. Along the Delaware River in Bucks County are Pennsbury Manor (see selection) and **Andalusia**, perhaps the nation's finest example of 19th-century Greek Revival architecture.

It is not surprising that Andalusia is so highly regarded; it was the work of two of America's most acclaimed architects. The main house was designed in 1806 by Benjamin Latrobe, who made a significant contribution to the architecture of Philadelphia and Washington, D.C. Latrobe designed the Bank of Pennsylvania and the Bank of the U.S., which eventually became the Philadelphia Custom House. He designed the South Wing of the Capitol, and after the British burned this seat of legislative power during the War of 1812, he played a major role in the restoration and rebuilding of the Capitol.

Andalusia was built for the Craig family, prominent Philadelphians who, like so many of their contemporaries, built their country homes on the cool banks of the Delaware River. Their daughter, Jane Craig, married Nicholas Biddle in 1811. When the young couple acquired the house following Mrs. Craig's death,

Andalusia, designed by Benjamin Latrobe, is one of the nation's finest examples of 19th-century Greek Revival architecture.

they hired the noted architect, Thomas U. Walter, to enlarge the house. He designed the Greek Revival additions to the main house. The Gothic "ruin" or grotto along the water's edge and a temple-like billiard room were also added at this time.

These renovations of their summer estate were taking place while Nicholas Biddle, President of the Second Bank of the U.S. and the new nation's most powerful banker, was locked in a struggle for control of the currency with President Andrew Jackson. The battle was a classic confrontation between two strong-minded men, and it led the country into a depression. Jackson removed Federal deposits from the bank and Biddle retaliated by calling in bank loans. This created a series of bank foreclosures and business failures leading to personal bankruptcy on a wide scale.

Throughout this upheaval, Andalusia did not suffer. To this day it is still privately owned by the seventh generation of the Biddle family. It evokes 19th-century elegance without a hint of economic strain. You can easily imagine the Biddles entertaining President John Quincy Adams, Daniel Webster, the Marquis de Lafayette and Joseph Bonaparte, the brother whom Napoleon designated King of Spain.

The grounds are maintained as an English park reflecting the popular landscaping fad of Nicholas Biddle's day. One 20th- cen-

77

tury feature is the **Green Walk,** with its ornamental dwarf evergreens. Nicholas Biddle, in addition to being a financial wizard, was an experimental farmer. Andalusia was the first American estate to stock Guernsey cattle. Like Thomas Jefferson at Monticello, Biddle grew mulberry trees for silkworms.

Visitors enjoy the beauty within and without by appointment only. Groups of four or more can be accommodated. Admission is charged. To plan a tour call Cliveden (see selection) estate at (215) 848-1777 and they will book your visit to Andalusia.

Directions: From I-95 north of Philadelphia take the Academy Road exit. Bear right to Linden Avenue, which crosses above the railroad tracks and exits on to State Road south of Grant Avenue. Turn left and take State Road for about two miles to the white gates of Andalusia on your right.

The Barnes Foundation

Magnificent Obsession

Fine art and the art of landscaping combine at The Barnes Foundation in Merion, a suburb of Philadelphia. A visitor will discover a world of beauty both indoors and out.

The Barnes Foundation has one of the world's finest private collections of Impressionist, Post-Impressionist and Modern paintings. Dr. Albert C. Barnes collected more than 180 Renoirs, 70 works by Cezanne and the largest private collection of Matisse. The work of Manet, Degas, Seurat, Rousseau, Picasso, and Van Gogh are massed from floor to ceiling in a staggering array. Included in the collection are works by old masters such as Titian, Tintoretto, El Greco, Daumier, Delacroix and Corot. Modern painters Soutine, Klee, Miro, Rouault and Modigliani are also represented. Less familiar works from China, Persia, Greece, Egypt, India and Africa as well as American Indian art and a comprehensive selection of antique furniture and wrought-iron objects round out the collection.

Dr. Barnes, a Philadelphia businessman and philanthropist, became interested in Modern art about 1911. His friendship with American painter William Glackens brought him in contact with the Ashcan School painters and introduced him to the work of the French Impressionists. In 1912, Barnes had Glackens travel to Paris and purchase paintings that became the nucleus of the foundation's collection. The concentration on painters like Renoir, Cezanne and Matisse allows viewers a glimpse of the many facets of these artists' creative careers. Barnes once said, "I'm convinced I cannot get too many Renoirs." In 1930, Henri

Matisse visited the Barnes Foundation and created a large mural for the main gallery. The **Matisse mural**, installed in 1933, was viewed as the crowning masterpiece in a collection of masterpieces. Barnes said it was "like a rose window," while the artist declared it "a song that mounts to the vaulted roof."

Nature also sings at The Barnes Foundation, as the grounds leave no doubt that landscaping is also an art. There is a **12-acre arboretum** that contains a collection of more than 290 genera of woody plants. Not all the specimens are from the Northern Hemisphere. Trees from the Orient include the Chinese fringe tree, paperbark maple, Korean boxwood, bee-bee tree, raisin tree and beauty bush. The dove, or handkerchief, tree is an Oriental species rarely found in this country. The best time to see this tree is in early May when the tree looks like it has a bad cold. Beneath the tree the ground is littered with white tissue-like flowers. A visit in late May will let you catch the tree peonies in bloom. During the summer months you can enjoy the rose and rock gardens. The arboretum is open year-round from 9:30 A.M. to 4:00 P.M. Monday through Saturday and from 1:30 P.M. to 4:30 P.M. on Sunday.

The Barnes Foundation opens after extensive renovation in the fall of 1995. Call for times the collection may be viewed, (610) 667-0290

Directions: From downtown Philadelphia take Route 1, the Roosevelt Boulevard across the Schuylkill River. Then go south on Route 1, City Line to Merion. At 54th Street turn right and go up to North Latch's Lane and make a left. The Barnes Foundation is at North Latch's Lane and Lapsley Road.

Barns-Brinton House and Chaddsford Winery

What do vintners buy, half as precious as they sell?

Side-by-side in the picturesque Brandywine Valley are two dissimilar but appealing attractions: the Barns-Brinton House and Chaddsford Winery. They actually have more in common than is immediately apparent because the 18th-century **Barns-Brinton House** was a tavern as well as a home. Although the house no longer offers "ye accommodation of Man and Horse," guides in colonial garb are on hand to welcome guests.

William Barns built his house on the Great Road between Philadelphia and Maryland in 1714, using brick instead of the more common native fieldstone. The house was constructed in the Flemish bond pattern, accented by black headers. On the upper wall at the west gable end, there is a decorative double diamond design in the brickwork. The structure was restored using an early 18th-century floor plan, reflecting its use as a tavern from 1722 to 1731.

You enter the public side of the house through the barroom. Hinges and other hardware are original and are believed to have been done by Barns himself as he was also a blacksmith. It's the cage bar that intrigues most visitors. The wooden grill could be closed and locked at night to protect the tavernkeeper's stock. It leads to speculation that the grill gave rise to the use of the word "bar" to mean a counter from which drinks were served.

Visitors try to guess the purpose of a well-worn hole in the newel post by the narrow winding staircase that leads to the public sleeping quarters. It is called a "distaff hole" because it held the distaff from the spinning wheel so that it could be set up near the window for light.

After William Barns's death in 1731 the house changed owners several times. In 1753, it was purchased by James Brinton and remained in the Brinton family over 100 years. The Chadds Ford Historical Society purchased the building in 1969 and restored and furnished the tavern as a house museum. It is open on weekends May through September from NOON to 6:00 P.M. There is a nominal admission charge.

You leave the house as you entered it, along a walkway lined with beds of medicinal, culinary, ornamental and aromatic herbs. A short walk along a fence-lined path takes you to the adjacent **Chaddsford Winery.**

The winery opened in the summer of 1983. The young couple that own and operate Chaddsford, Eric and Lee Miller, have a background in the industry that far exceeds their years. Eric Miller's parents established New York state's first farm winery, Bernmarl Vineyards. Lee Miller co-authored a book about east coast wineries and helped found the magazine "Wine East." The couple brings both knowledge and enthusiasm to this Chester County winery.

In the remodeled barn visitors learn how grapes are crushed and the juice fermented, barrel-aged and bottled. After touring you can taste the wines made at Chaddsford. At the 1993 Laurel Highlands Wine and Food Festival, in the wine and food matching event, three Chaddsford's wines ranked "excellent."

Tours and tastings are given on Saturday from 10:00 A.M. to 5:30 P.M. and Sunday from NOON to 5:00 P.M. For a weekday tour call (215) 388-6221. The winery is open for tastings and sales during the week from 10:00 A.M. to 5:30 P.M.

Directions: Take I-95 south of Philadelphia to the Wilmington, Delaware area. Exit on Route 52 and continue north about ten miles to the intersection with Route 1. Make a right on Route

1 towards Chadds Ford. In about $1^1/_2$ miles you will see both the Chaddsford Winery and Barns-Brinton House on the right.

Bethlehem

Follow the Star

Each year pilgrims from around the world flock to Bethlehem during the Christmas season. That might seem like an impossible destination for a one-day trip, but not if you head north of Philadelphia to **Bethlehem**, Pennsylvania. This is a town that was named on Christmas Eve back in 1741 when the newly arrived Moravian settlers held their religious services in their Gemein Haus. This community log structure housed both the settlers and their animals (in an adjoining stable). As they sang "Not Jerusalem-lowly Bethlehem 'twas that gave us Christ" their leader Count Zinzendorf, patron of the Moravian Church, suggested that they christen their new town Bethlehem.

The town even has its own Star of Bethlehem, sparkling high above the city from atop South Mountain. The nearly 100-foot high star can be seen for miles. You will see smaller Moravian stars displayed throughout the entire town during the month of December while candles flicker from the windows of houses and public buildings. Special Lanternlight Walking tours are conducted. As you near the old Moravian settlement you will see one of the largest decorated community trees in the country.

By planning at least three weeks ahead you can make the necessary reservations for the hour-long Night Light bus tour, the Old Town Walking tours or Bethlehem by Day tours. These popular annual tours are led by guides dressed in Moravian attire. In the Night Light bus tour, you not only see the sights of this Christmas-bedecked town, you also ride to the top of South Mountain for a view of the valley's twinkling lights. To find out more about these tours call (215) 868-1513.

The city also hosts a Yuletide Market Fair, **Christkindlmarkt**, offering more than two weeks of holiday fun. More than 50 juried crafts people and scores of other retailers sell their unique wares just like they have for centuries in such German towns as Munich, Rothenburg and Nurnberg. Entertainment and a wide variety of food vendors will add to the occasion.

In the Christian Education Building of the Central Moravian Church there is a Moravian putz, which is a German term for "decoration," which has come to be used for Nativity scenes that tell the story of the Christ child. The putz is composed of hand-carved wooden figures, many originally from Germany. Combining these wooden figures with music and narration, the story of the Nativity is told. The story of the Bethlehem settlement is also told.

December, with its special Christmas glow, is the best time to visit this historic town. But it is by no means the only time, as each season has its own appeal. If you prefer warm weather excursions you can wait until August and **Musikfest** with its Moravian crafts, music and food.

Bethlehem, spanning three centuries of history really does not require any special event to warrant a visit. In fact, you might prefer to plan your first trip at an off-time so that you can take in the many attractions of this old town without fighting the additional crowds that predictably accompany the popular annual programs. Whenever you arrive in Bethlehem start your visit at the Visitor Center and pick up a schedule of daily activities and a self-guided walking tour map. Try to see the half-hour orientation film, "City in the Wilderness," as well as "Mission Bethlehem," a 20-minute multi-media presentation on the founding of Bethlehem. Guides costumed in old Moravian dress lead group tours (minimum of five people) through the Moravian community. Call (215) 867-0173 or 868-1513 for information.

The walking tour encompasses 26 sites—probably more than you'll have time to see on a single visit. One stop you won't want to miss is the **Gemein Haus**, the five-story log cabin built in 1741. Constructed without nails from wood and mud plaster, this is the largest log dwelling still standing in the United States. It not only served as a place of worship but also as a dormitory and craft workshop. Today this community house serves as the Moravian Museum where you see examples of early Moravian furniture, needlework, musical instruments, dolls and religious art, plus a typical kitchen and schoolroom. There is also a room furnished as it would have been when Count Zinzendorf stayed at the Gemein Haus. The Gemein Haus, at 66 West Church Street, is open Tuesday through Saturday from 1:00 P.M. to 4:00 P.M. and, like many of Bethlehem's attractions, is closed in January.

Probably the second most significant site to be explored is the 18th-century **Moravian Industrial Quarter** located along the Monocacy Creek, an easy walk from Main Street. In addition to Bethlehem's Christmas connection, the town is associated with one of the country's largest steel corporations—Bethlehem Steel. The town's industrial heritage goes back to the early settlers who developed an industrial complex of 32 craft and trade shops on the banks of Monocacy Creek.

In the **1761 Tannery** you can watch authentically dressed workers demonstrate the art of leather crafting. In its heyday roughly 3,000 hides were tanned annually at this massive plant. You hear a step-by-step description of the tanning operation while gazing down from wooden walkways into the huge vats where the animal hides were soaked. Other early industries are also demonstrated; there is a working model of the 1765 oil mill and the 1762 waterworks. After viewing the small scale models you can visit the reconstructed operating mechanisms of the original waterworks, considered the first municipal works in the American colonies.

The tannery also has a children's discovery room. Youngsters can get in touch with history by trying on old-fashioned costumes, by attempting to communicate using Indian sign language and by guessing the use for various unusual tools. This educational area is open weekends April through December and Tuesday through Sunday during the summer months.

In addition to these pivotal spots, you can visit the **Sun Inn**, circa 1758; the 1810 Federal-style **Goundie House**; the **Kemerer Museum of Decorative Arts**, a townhouse filled with the results of a lifetime search for beauty; and the **Apothecary Museum**, a repository of old medicinal equipment. The latter is open by appointment only. For a glimpse of the Moravians agricultural practices visit **Burnside Plantation**, just off Schoenersville Road. The 1749 farmhouse is being restored and living history makes pre-industrial farm life como alive. Tours are by appointment; call (215) 868-5044.

A change-of-pace place is the **Lost River Caverns** just five miles away in Hellertown, where you can see crystal formations in the caverns, plus a mineral and gem museum.

Directions: From the Northeast Extension of the Pennsylvania Turnpike (I-76), take the Lehigh Valley exit and travel east on Route 22. At the intersection with Route 378, go south to Center City Bethlehem (Historic District) Exit 3 and follow the signs. The Visitors Center is located at 509 Main Street.

Brandywine River Museum, Chadds Ford and Brandywine Battlefield Park

Intoxicating Environment

America's artistic and historic pasts merge in one of the loveliest areas in the Middle Atlantic region at Chadds Ford, the most famous point on the Brandywine River.

This Pennsylvania valley served as the inspirational linchpin of a world-famous group of American artists who painted in a style called "The Brandywine Tradition." The Howard Pyle School of Art, begun during the summer of 1897 in Philadelphia

You can enjoy the source of inspiration for artists of the Brandywine Tradition along riverside trails and then view their work in the 19th-century Hoffman gristmill, now part of the Brandywine River Museum.

PHOTO BY SALLY MOORE

PHOTO FROM BRANDYWINE MUSEUM

by illustrator Howard Pyle, soon moved to this valley, spreading the fame of the area and that of its artists. Today in the 19th-century Hoffman gristmill, itself a work of art, you can see the scope of these artists' accomplishments.

One of the aims of the **Brandywine River Museum** has been to amass a collection of three generations of Wyeths. N.C. Wyeth, patriarch of the family, was a book illustrator and artist. Visitors may be surprised to see colorful paintings he did for some of their old favorites like *Treasure Island* and *Kidnapped*. Paintings by his well-known son, Andrew Wyeth, are represented to such an extent that this is the world's largest museum collection of his work. The work of Jamie Wyeth and other members of the family is also displayed.

The museum galleries, with their old beamed ceilings and pine floors, include a wide range of work by other American painters, sculptors and illustrators. Visitors climb from floor to floor in a striking glass tower with brick terraces that provide a panoramic view of the beckoning Brandywine River. James Michener, popular novelist, regards the Brandywine River Museum as one of the three best-designed museums in the country. A second tower was added in the fall of 1984 with more gallery space, a restaurant and a museum gift shop.

The shop sells framed and unframed reproductions, posters and art books. The Brandywine River Museum is a component of the **Brandywine Conservancy**, an organization that concentrates on improving and managing the environment. Thus, the museum shop also has books on nature and the environment. Available, too, are wildflower seeds that volunteers of the Brandywine Conservancy have collected from the gaily-colored gardens surrounding the museum and from gardens and meadows in the area. With these seeds you can grow your own bluebells, sundrops, black-eyed Susans, New England asters, cardinal flowers and daylilies.

The Brandywine River Museum is open daily, except Christmas, from 9:30 A.M. to 4:30 P.M. Admission is charged. The museum is fully accessible to people with disabilities. For information call (215) 388-2700.

The Conservancy also maintains a mile-long nature trail that starts at the museum and wanders along the riverbank. If you take a walk along the trail in the spring, you'll see a profusion of wildflowers blooming along this woodland path. Elevated crosswalks help avoid the marshy areas; trail markers eschew the Latin botanical names for common-sense pointers. Signs alert you to animal tracks or poisonous plants, like the stinging nettles whose leaf hairs cause a burning sensation when touched. When you hike this trail in warm weather, the river looks especially inviting. If you head upstream to Lenape you can rent a canoe or tube and get a different perspective of the Brandywine River.

The Conservancy's trail leads to John Chad's stone farmhouse, open for a small fee Friday through Sunday from Memorial Day to Labor Day, NOON to 5:00 P.M. On Sunday afternoon bread is baked in the old beehive oven. Chadds Ford was named for this early ferryman and tavern keeper. The two-story springhouse next to Chad's farm was used in the 19th century as a one-room school.

While in the area be sure to stop at **Chadds Ford Village** noted for its crafts. The Chadds Ford Barn Shops, built around an open courtyard, boast an array of artisans. The place for lunch is the Chadds Ford Inn. It has been serving travelers since 1736 when colonists would stop after fording the Brandywine River. Some of Washington's troops dined here before the Battle of Brandywine. For dining times and reservations call (215) 388-7361.

Picnickers can lunch at nearby **Brandywine Battlefield Park**. To put this battlefield into perspective stop first at the Visitors Center to see the 20-minute audio-visual show. General Washington might well have wished for a similar clear picture of what was happening, as he led his men on September 11, 1777. Washington kept receiving conflicting reports on the position of the 15,000 British under General Howe. The 14,000-member American force, although lacking in equipment and experience, still managed to retreat rather than surrender—thus saving the Continental force to fight another day. From this encounter the British moved to their comfortable winter quarters in Philadelphia, while the Americans endured the privations at Valley Forge.

Within the park, the houses used as headquarters by Washington and Lafayette have been restored. Both of these houses belonged to Quakers whose sympathies were with the revolutionary cause. The **Benjamin Ring farm**, General Washington's base, had to be completely rebuilt as the original structure burned to the ground. The spacious farmhouse is again furnished to look as it did in 1777.

The Marquis de Lafayette stayed at the more modest farm of Gideon Gilpin, who later received permission to operate a tavern in recompense for the expenses he incurred during the Battle of Brandywine. A report filed by Gilpin listed as lost such items as 10 cows, 48 sheep, 28 swine, a yoke of oxen, 12 tons of hay, 230 bushels of wheat, 50 pounds of bacon, a history book, a clock and a gun. There are dependencies at the Gilpin farm including a root cellar, barn and carriage house. A shed adjacent to the carriage house contains an original Conestoga wagon. Few people realize that this style of wagon was developed in the upper Brandywine Valley.

Brandywine Battlefield Park is open year-round Tuesday

through Saturday from 9:00 A.M. to 5:00 P.M.; on Sunday it opens at NOON. Admission is charged.

Directions: From I-95 south of Philadelphia, take Route 322 west toward Concordville. Follow Route 322 to the intersection with Route 1; take Route 1 south for approximately five miles. The Brandywine River Museum is located on the left side of Route 1 in Chadds Ford; the Chadds Ford Barn Shops and the Brandywine Battlefield Park will be on the right.

The Bridges of Lehigh County

Covered Bridges and Exotic Animals

Robert James Waller's romantic blockbuster has inspired countless readers to discover the covered bridges on the backroads of their own region. The Lehigh Valley boasts seven picturesque examples, all handily reached on a drive beginning in downtown Allentown.

Begin at Allentown's Center Square, 7th and Hamilton Mall. Head south on 7th Street for two blocks and turn left on Union Street, then go a half block and make a right on Lehigh Street. Take Lehigh to the second traffic light and make a right. You'll still be on Lehigh Street; remain on it through the lights at 8th and 10th Streets. Turn right just past the softball field at Bicentennial Park onto Little Lehigh Parkway. The first covered bridge, **Bogert's Bridge**, will be on your left when you reach the stop sign at the end of the park.

For the next bridge, turn left at the stop sign onto Oxford Drive and then take your first right at Fish Hatchery Road and continue on this to the top of the hill, where you will turn right on Route 29, Cedar Crest Boulevard. Continue on Cedar Crest past the interchanges for Route 309, Route 222 and U.S. 22. After you cross Walbert Avenue (the traffic light after you pass U.S. 22), you'll cross Huckleberry Road at the top of the hill. Continue on Cedar Crest to the bottom of the hill. Before you reach the concrete bridge, make a left onto Iron Bridge Road which takes you to the second covered bridge, **Guth's Bridge**.

For the third in the series, take Lapp Road through Guth's Bridge, then take the first left onto River Road. This takes you to **Wher's Bridge** in Covered Bridge Park in South Whitehall Township.

Turn right, onto Wehrmill Road then make a left at Lime Kiln Road and continue to Route 309; there will be a traffic light and a high school. Make a right on Route 309, and drive a half mile. When you reach the traffic light in Orefield make a left onto Kernsville Road and continue for one mile to Jordan Road, which is the first road on the right past the Iron Bridge. Make a right onto Jordan Road and you will come to **Rex's Bridge**.

Drive through Rex's Bridge and continue for one mile to the junction of Rhueton Hill Road, then bear to the right still on Jordan Road and travel a half mile to **Geiger's Bridge**, the fifth covered bridge.

Backtrack to Rhueton Hill Road and take a hard right, then drive up the hill for 0.2 mile. You will be traveling on a dirt road, continue down the hill and turn right onto Game Preserve Road and go past the entrance to **Trexler Lehigh County Game Preserve**. You may want to make a stop and visit this 1,500 acre exotic animal preserve. When you continue on Game Preserve Road you will travel through Schlicher's Bridge and on to the intersection with Route 309.

For the last bridge, turn right onto Route 309 and continue to the center of Schnecksville. Make a left at the traffic light onto Sand Springs Road. Take Sand Springs to Ironton and make a left onto Mauch Chunk Road (Main Street). Take this to Ballietsville and turn right onto Route 329 and continue to Northampton. At the traffic light in Northampton turn left on Main Street, and continue for two miles to Kreidersville. Continue through the four-way stop intersection and after $3/10$ of a mile, turn right on Covered Bridge Road for **Kreidersville Bridge**.

This completes the circuit, to return to your starting point, backtrack to Route 329 through Northampton, then turn left on Route 145 and head back to Allentown's Center Square. One cautionary note, do not do this route backwards because the signs indicate the route as outlined here. The entire route is approximately 50 miles. It is a popular route for bicyclists who frequently begin at one of the parks and take a portion of the tour.

It's well worth your time to stop at the game preserve, particularly if you are traveling with young children. The preserve was established in 1909 by General Trexler to save threatened animals from extinction. His original collection included North American bison, whitetailed deer and elk, but now the sprawling preserve is also home to more exotic species like zebra and camels.

The Trexler Lehigh County Game Preserve is a combination zoo and wilderness preserve. There is a petting area for youngsters and a nature study exhibit building. The preserve is open 10:00 A.M. to 5:00 P.M. daily from Memorial Day weekend through Labor Day; it is also open on Sundays only in May, September and October.

Admission is charged.

Directions: From I-78 take Hamilton Boulevard exit into Allentown to begin the covered bridge tour route. If you intend to head directly to the game preserve stay on I-78 to the Route 309 north exit.

Bucks County Vineyards and Covered Bridges

Under Arbors and Over Bridges

Even family members who would rather spend their weekends watching the big game, can usually be persuaded to join a wine tasting excursion. There is an increasing fascinating with wines, and while a few enthusiasts still think of American wine in terms of California vintages, vineyards on the East Coast are proliferating.

One of Pennsylvania's first limited wineries is **Buckingham Valley Vineyards**, just a short drive from New Hope. It offers estate bottled vintage varietal wines. This designation is regulated by the Federal government. All, or almost all, the wine labeled "estate bottled" must come from grapes owned or controlled by the winery and it must be grown in designated viticulture areas. If the label reads "Produced and bottled by . . ." it means that particular wine was made with 75 percent of the grapes from the vineyard on the label. On the other hand, if the label says, "Made by . . ." it could mean that as little as 10 percent of the grapes came from the producer's own harvest.

You can take a self-guided tour of Buckingham Valley, Bucks County's first winery, and taste their wines Tuesday through Friday NOON to 6:00 P.M., Saturday 10:00 A.M. to 6:00 P.M. and Sundays NOON to 4:00 P.M. The winery is seven miles north of Newtown in Buckingham. Call (215) 794-7188 for additional information.

Bucks County has three additional wineries you might want to visit: **Peace Valley Winery** (215-249-9058) open Wednesday through Sunday NOON to 6:00 P.M., **Rushland Ridge Vineyards and Winery** (215) 598-0251) open on Saturday from NOON to 6:00 P.M. and Sundays NOON to 4:00 P.M. and **Sand Castle Winery** (215) 294-9181) open daily.

While exploring the countryside, try to take in six of Bucks County's 11 remaining covered bridges. These six are in the New Hope area and can easily be combined with your wine-tasting outing. The covered bridges you will see range from two that were built in 1832 to four constructed during the 1870s. The reason for building bridges with a roof is not definitely known. The most plausible explanation is that the support beams on the sides were protected from the weather. Covered bridges also provided shelter for travelers, shielded animals from their fear of crossing water and kept the snow off important river crossings.

All the covered bridges in Bucks County were made in a lattice-style developed by Ithiel Town in 1820. Be sure to get out of the car and study at least one bridge up close so that you can see the series of overlapping triangles with wooden pegs. No arches or support beams were used by these lattice-work arrangements that supported bridges up to 200-feet long.

You will pass the first of the covered bridges before you reach New Hope. The **Van Sant Bridge** is just off Route 32, River Road. Check your mileage when you reach the Memorial Building for Washington Crossing State Park (see selection). Continue north on Route 32 for 4.4 miles to Lurgan Road, then turn left and go 1.5 miles to Covered Bridge Road, where you turn right and go .6 miles to Van Sant Bridge. It was built over Pidcock Creek in 1875 and is 86 feet long.

Cross over the Van Sant Bridge and drive for one more mile to Aquetong Road where you will turn left and go five miles to Upper York Road. Make a right on Upper York and then an immediate left, and go 2.8 miles to Carvesville, an entire village that is listed on the National Register of Historic Places. In the center of Carvesville turn left for one block and then go right on Pipersville Road. This road changes names twice, first becoming Wismer Road and then Carvesville Road. Take this double-named road for 4.6 miles and you arrive at **Loux Bridge**, the second shortest covered bridge in the county at 60 feet. This hemlock bridge is perfect for photographs, framed as it is by an adjacent waterfall and an old farm.

To reach the next covered bridge continue through Loux Bridge and go five miles until you reach a dead end. At this point make a right onto Dark Hollow Road and continue for one mile to Covered Bridge Road, where you make a right and proceed .6 miles to **Cabin Run Bridge**. This is an 82-foot bridge built in 1871 over Cabin Run Creek.

Backtrack to Dark Hollow Road and take that for 3.2 miles to Cafferty Road. Turn left on Cafferty Road and proceed 8 miles to the **Frankenfield Bridge** over Tinicum Creek. This is one of the longest covered bridges, 130 feet.

For the fifth covered bridge continue up Cafferty Road for .2 miles to Hollow Horn Road and make a right. Proceed 1.3 miles to Headquarters Road and turn right. Go .9 miles to Geigel Hill Road. Turn left on Geigel Hill Road and go .2 miles and you will see the **Erwinna Bridge**, which at 56 feet is the shortest covered bridge in Bucks County.

To see the last covered bridge in this area, return to Geigel Hill Road and proceed .4 miles to River Road, Route 32. Turn left on River Road and go 1.7 miles and make another left on Uhlerstown Road; take that .3 miles for the **Uhlerstown Bridge**. This is the only covered bridge that crosses the Delaware Canal, and the only one that has windows.

Directions: Take I-95 north of Philadelphia and take New Hope exit, Route 32, River Road.

90

Byers' Choice Christmas Gallery

Something to Sing About

The Christmas song that comes to mind when you first see Byers' Choice Carolers is "Joy to the World," for that is what these handcrafted figures create. The business the Byers started in their farm kitchen is now one of the largest manufacturers of Christmas products in the country, selling approximately 500,000 individually made doll-like figures.

From the moment you drive onto the attractively landscaped grounds of **Byers' Choice** and see the bronze statue of gaily romping children you'll feel a sense of festive merriment. At Byers' Choice, it's Christmas all year round, expecially as captured in the gallery's village and countryside scenes. Customs from around the world are revealed by a collection of international Santas and Kids of the World. Village streets are filled with Carolers in a wintry outdoor scene complete with skaters on the frozen millpond. Charles Dickens's "A Christmas Carol" is another Caroler recreation. These gallery scenes showcase both old and new Carolers. You can see the evolution from the earliest figurines to the current dolls.

The Byers family refers to their business as "Joyce's hobby that got out of control." Joyce Byers, an amateur artist with a degree in fashion design, was visiting a London antique shop when she saw a series of porcelain figures that captured the spirit of Dicken's 19th-century England. Returning home, she encountered a set of papier-mache choir figures and the idea of combining the English figures with the choir figures captured her imagination.

Joyce made her figures from materials she had at home. She soon filled her house and those of family and friends with her holiday creations. In the next few years the entire family got involved, spending the autumn making Carolers for craft shows, a display company and select stores. The operation shifted from the kitchen to the garage which was converted to a workshop. By 1981 full-time helpers were hired and the Carolers were incorporated. A video highlights the story of this family business.

Joyce still sculpts all the faces and designs the clothes for the various figures, but 150 workers carry out her vision. From an observation deck you can watch the figures being formed from wire and clay. The faces are made from molds, then individually shaped by the skilled workers and the features hand-painted. All the Carolers share one characteristic, their mouths are open to sing. There are distinct collections: Traditional, Victorian, Skaters, Dickensian figures and the new Nutcracker line, plus other specialty figures.

An extensive collection of Carolers is available in the gift shop. The joy of giving is part of the Byers' story; more than 20 percent of the company profits is distributed by the Byers Foundation to fund primarily local charitable, cultural and historical organizations.

Byers' Choice is open at no charge Monday through Saturday from 10:00 A.M. to 4:00 P.M. Closed during the month of January.

Directions: From I-76 the Pennsylvania Turnpike, take the Eastern extension, I-276, to the Fort Washington exit. Take Route 309 north, then make a right onto Route 202 north at the light in Montgomeryville. Turn left at the second light onto County Line Road. Byers' Choice is a half-mile on the right.

The Colonial Pennsylvania Plantation and The Tyler Arboretum

American Roots

Did you know that houses could be dissected? Through painstaking architectural research at **The Colonial Pennsylvania Plantation** it was possible to trace about 90 percent of the changes at this old farmhouse and uncover its past: when it was first constructed, how the original design was altered and when different rooms were added.

Though the farm was started between 1705 and 1724, it is the 1760s through 1790s that are recreated here. Drop-in visitors occasionally lend a hand with the farm chores—cutting the curd for cheese, carding wool or dipping candles. The staff practices old-fashioned cooking over the fireplace as well as spinning and weaving.

Like the Peter Wentz Farmstead (see selection), this plantation appears as it would have looked during the eras that are recreated. The furnishings and equipment are not preserved in a hands-off museum format, but rather are there to be used. In many cases the furniture, utensils and tools are made right at the farm, using old methods. And the colors of the paint and fabric are bright and unfaded, there is no mellowing with age.

It is interesting to note that although a farm family at that time would have been sufficiently well-off to set aside a room for formal entertaining, the furniture was still more sturdy than comfortable. It wasn't until the Victorian period that seats were upholstered and provided the comfort of springs.

Although this part of Pennsylvania was primarily Quaker and many of the farmers did not leave to fight in the Revolutionary

War, the farms were nevertheless affected by the fighting. A local farmer, Benjamin Hawley, made these entries in his diary:

28 August 1777	"Clear morn, then some Clouds, Draw'd in all the hay."
11 September	"Very hot; finished harrowing the rye; the English Engaged the Americans; the latter defeated with much loss."
12 September	"Cloudy; putting up fences that the American Soldiers (broke) in their retreat."
12 September	"Some Clouds; Some of ye English Soldiers had Sundries to ye value of 8 shillings and did not pay."

The Colonial Pennsylvania Plantation recreates farm life in surprising detail: fields, orchard, kitchen garden, stillroom, root cellar, springhouse and barns. As early as the colonial period Pennsylvania farmers practiced crop rotation. There is likely to be a field of clover or grass interspersed with the major crops of wheat, potatoes, rye and oats. The plantation has instituted a breeding program to develop animals that more closely resemble those of 200 years ago. On a farm this size, records indicate that a family would likely have kept two or three horses, three or four cows, five or six sheep, a sow and boar, plus an assortment of fowl. By visiting at least once during the spring, summer and fall you'll get a picture not only of the daily chores but also of the larger seasonal activities such as planting, shearing and harvesting. The plantation is open on weekends from 10:00 A.M. to 4:00 P.M., April through November. There is an admission fee. The Colonial Pennsylvania Plantation is located within the Ridley Creek State Park. Picnic facilities are available in the park.

Adjacent to Ridley Creek State Park is **The Tyler Arboretum** which has more than 4,000 plants and trees within its 700 acres. Twenty miles of hiking trails give you a chance to see roughly 380 species of native southeastern Pennsylvania plants. Some of the most interesting specimens in the collection are not native to this area. The arboretum is noted for its giant sequoia, which was planted here between 1856 and 1860. It now stands over 65 feet tall and boasts a nine-foot circumference. Camera buffs have a real challenge in capturing this striking beauty. Other unusual trees include the multi-trunked ginkgo, a cedar-of-Lebanon, a tulip tree and a 100-foot tall bald cypress. Specialty areas at The Tyler Arboretum include the pinetum and the fragrant garden for the visually handicapped.

The Tyler Arboretum is open daily at no charge from 8:00 A.M.

Dorney Park, one of America's best traditional amusement parks, has the Hercules, one of the world's tallest wooden roller coasters and the Thunderhawk (shown here), a favorite of coaster enthusiasts.

until dusk. There is a bookstore and gift shop open 9:00 A.M. to 4:00 P.M.

Directions: Take I-95 from the Philadelphia area to Route 476 west, then exit at the Lima-Springfield exit at Route 1. Take Route 1 south to Route 252, exit right toward Newtown Square, continue through first traffic light, pass Rose Tree Park and make a left onto Providence Road. Stay on Providence Road to second four-way stop, and make a left on Cradyville Road into Ridley Creek State Park. At first stop sign turn right and follow the park road to The Colonial Pennsylvania Plantation.

Dorney Park, Wildwater Kingdom and Allentown

Tallest, Steepest, Fastest, Wettest

Dorney Park has run out of superlatives to describe **White Water Landing**, the waterfall plunge ride added in 1993. The park's expansion and improvements have been ongoing since its opening in 1884. **Dorney Park** is not only one of America's oldest, it's also one of the country's best traditional amusement parks. Its popularity is enhanced because it is combined with the top seasonal waterpark in the country. The sprawling 200-acre park boasts three world-class roller coasters, including Hercules, one of the tallest wooden roller coasters in the world. There's also the Pepsi Aquablast. At 701 feet it's the longest elevated water slide in the world and one of 11 in the waterpark. It is indeed a park of superlatives.

If you want to see both Dorney Park and **Wildwater Kingdom**, take the **Cedar Creek Cannonball**, a one-third scale steam train. There's also a smaller train that's been running since 1935, designated for the park's youngest visitors. The TotSpot area features scaled-down adventure rides plus an interactive children's play area. The waterpark has two kiddie areas of its own. The Berenstain Bears, on hand to greet park visitors, seem to have stepped off the page of youngsters' favorite storybooks.

The Bears are not the only group to wander through the park. There's also a strolling Beach Band. Daily performances by a variety of groups are given at the Red Garter Saloon and other venues.

Dorney Park is open on weekends in May and September and daily from Memorial Day to Labor Day. Wildwater Kingdom is open from mid-May through Labor Day and on selected September weekends. Tickets include admission to both the amusement and waterpark; children under three are free. Call (610) 395-3724 for hours, fees and other information.

Dorney Park brings throngs of visitors to Allentown and offers a full day of family fun but there are other nearby attractions that also merit time and attention (see Bethlehem, Lehigh County Historical Society Sites and The Bridges of Lehigh County selections).

History buffs should visit the **Liberty Bell Shrine**. From September, 1777 to June, 1778 the Liberty Bell was hidden in Allentown's Zion Church. A 70-vehicle wagon train, carrying military stores to Bethlehem, spirited the bell from Philadelphia to this refuge. In all, 20 church bells were smuggled out of the city. With the British firmly entrenched in Philadelphia, it was feared the Liberty Bell would be melted down for musket and cannon balls. To mislead the British it was announced that the Liberty Bell was sunk in the Delaware River. After the British evacuated the colonial capital, the Liberty Bell was returned (see Liberty Bell Pavilion selection). It wasn't until 57 years later, during the ceremonies marking the death of Supreme Court Chief Justice John Marshall, that the bell cracked.

Today the shrine contains an exact replica of the bell. A short tape tells the story of its journey to this sanctuary. There's also a 46-foot mural with six scenes depicting events during the American Revolution that impacted this region including the Continental Congress meeting in Philadelphia and the wagon trip to Allentown. Flags, maps, weapons and uniforms are exhibited. The Liberty Bell Shrine is at 622 Hamilton Street. Hours are Monday through Saturday NOON to 4:00 P.M. and Sundays 2:00 P.M. to 4:00 P.M. Admission is free.

Only a block away at Fifth and Court Streets is the **Allentown Art Museum** with a fine collection of paintings and sculpture from Gothic, Renaissance and Baroque masters as well as representative American work from the past two hundred years. Rotating exhibits reveal the best of the fine prints, drawings, photographs and textile collection. There's a Junior Gallery with hands-on art activities and touchable sculpture for young visitors. A Frank Lloyd Wright designed library from the Francis W. Little House is one of the most serene spaces in the museum. Hours are Tuesday through Saturday 10:00 A.M. to 5:00 P.M.; on Sundays it opens at NOON. Admission is charged; no charge for children under 12. There is a museum shop and an art reference library. The latter is open by appointment only. Call (215) 432-4333 for additional information.

Finally, for those with an interest in Native American culture, there is the **Museum of Indian Culture** operated by the Lenni Lenape Historical Society. The museum is located in the Bieber Farmhouse, an 18th-century two and one-half story stone house built by one of the region's early settlers. The story of the Lenape people is told from their own perspective with hands-on exhibits. Three annual ceremonies are held. Each includes crafts, social dancing and a variety of food. The first Sunday in May is the Corn Planting Ceremony; on the second Sunday in August the Roasting Ears of Corn Food Fest takes place. Lastly, there is the Time of Thanksgiving on the second Sunday of October. The public is invited to the special ceremonies held from 1:00 P.M. to 4:00 P.M. The museum is on Fish Hatchery Road between 24th Street and Cedar Crest Boulevard. The museum is open Tuesday through Sunday from 10:00 A.M. to 3:00 P.M. Admission is charged.

Directions: From the Pennsylvania Turnpike NE Extension Lehigh Valley Exit 33, take Route 22 east for $1/4$ mile to Route 309 south. Continue on Route 309 south to Exit 16, and make a left. The Dorney Park/Wildwater Kingdom is just a short distance ahead on the left.

Fallsington

A Capital Contender

After the American Revolution Congress had to choose a site for the nation's capital. One area that was given serious consideration was the "falls" area of the Delaware River. Today much of the quaint village of **Fallsington** is close to the way it was when the legislators weighed its merits as a site for the federal government.

Fallsington grew around a Quaker meetinghouse that was built in 1690. Meetinghouse Square is still the center of town, with three meetinghouses facing each other. William Penn attended the Falls meeting and his home, Pennsbury Manor (see selection), was often used for meetings before an appropriate place to gather was built.

The Quakers kept detailed minutes of their meetings, and these provide a fascinating look at their public and private lives. Records reveal that William Moon was scolded for "marrying his cousin Elizabeth Nutt."

On a guided tour of Fallsington one of the restored historic homes you see is the **Moon-Williamson House**. Samuel Moon, a well-known cabinetmaker and joiner, purchased the log cabin in 1767. A typical colonial log house, it was built in the tradition described as early as 1679 in a traveler's account:

"The house (we stayed in) was made according to the Swedish mode . . . . which are blockhouses, being nothing else than entire trees split through the middle or squared out of the rough, and placed in the form of a square, upon each other, as high as

97

they wish to have the house; the ends of these timbers are let into each other, about a foot from the ends, half on one into half of the other. The whole structure is thus made, without a nail or a spike.

The ceiling and roof do not exhibit much finer work, except among the most careful people, who have the ceiling planked and a glass window. The doors are wide enough, but very low, so that you have to stoop in entering. These houses are quite tight and warm; but the chimney is placed in a corner. My comrade and myself had some deer skins spread upon the floor to lie on . . ."

The restored Moon-Williamson House, one of the oldest houses in Pennsylvania still on its original site, has primitive furniture to reflect the pioneer era. You can imagine their spartan life as you observe the straw mattress and deer skin rugs. The settle table, which converts from bench to table, demonstrates the practice of having a piece of furniture serve more than one function.

The **Burges-Lippincott House**, another restored private home, reflects a later era. It actually reflects several later periods, the 18th-century stone house was built in four stages beginning in 1700 and continuing through 1829. It is noted for its carved front door topped by a glass fan and its interior woodwork, particularly the corner fireplaces and the elegant wall banisters. The rooms, furnished with period pieces, suggest a life style far more comfortable and fashion-conscious than that depicted in the Moon-Williamson House.

Across the street is yet another colonial restoration included on the guided tour, the **Stage Coach Tavern**. This tavern served as a stopping-off place for travelers between Philadelphia and New York from the 1790s until the 1920s when it closed after Prohibition was enacted. The Common Room has a card table ready for play. Clay pipe holders and pewterware tankards stand ready for the evening guests. A private parlor was used for gatherings to discuss town business and politics.

Tours start at the **Gillingham Store** which is now the headquarters of Historic Fallsington, Inc. Guided tours are given from the second Saturday in May until the end of October. Tours are every hour on the hour Monday through Saturday 10:00 A.M. to 4:00 P.M. and Sundays beginning at 1:00 P.M. An introductory slide program provides background information on this remarkably preserved community. You can also obtain a walking tour map and explore Fallsington on your own. On the second Saturday in October during the annual Historic Fallsington Day many of the town's private homes are open for tours.

Directions: From I-95 north of Philadelphia exit on Route 413 toward Bristol. Make a left at the traffic light and go west on

Route 413 to New Falls Road. Make a right and follow New Falls Road into Fallsington.

Fordhook Farm and The Henry Schmieder Arboretum

Giving Nature A Helping Hand

In the rich soil of the Doylestown region W. Atlee Burpee's 60-acre farm was the proving ground for many of the seeds he sold in the company he founded. You can visit or stay overnight at The Inn at Fordhook Farm, then stroll the paths of the Lois Burpee Herb Garden, just one of the specialty gardens at **The Henry Schmieder Arboretum** of Delaware Valley College.

Guests at **Fordhook Farm** stay in the Burpee family's large 18th-century stone house and the adjacent 19th-century carriage house. The public rooms are filled with family albums, pictures and mementoes. The gardens reflect the family's long association with flowering plants. For information on this historical bed and breakfast establishment, call (215) 345-1766.

Delaware Valley College was founded in 1896 as the National Farm School. From the beginning agriculture and horticulture were primary fields of study, but it wasn't until 1966 that the 60-acre arboretum was created and named for one of the college's revered faculty members. In addition to the herb garden, specialty areas include an ornamental grass collection, hedge demonstration area, dwarf conifer collection, rock garden, hosta collection, a woodland walk, vine garden, daylily collection, wetlands area and a 1920s cottage garden. The self-guided tour brochure notes a wide variety of plant specimens found on the campus, as well as in the specialty areas, the greenhouses and a small conservatory which is open to the public at no charge on weekdays from 8:30 A.M. to 4:00 P.M. Brochures can be picked up at the Arboretum office in the greenhouse complex. Spring is the most floriferous time as thousands of bulbs brighten the landscape. Garden enthusiasts can find one of the state's best horticultural research collections in the college's library.

Directions: From I-76, the Pennsylvania Turnpike, take I-276 north around Philadelphia. Take Exit 27, Route 611 north for 11 miles to Doylestown, where you will turn left on Route 202 south, the Norristown/Delaware College exit. Turn left again on New Britain Road, next to Delaware Valley College. For the Schmieder Arboretum follow signs on campus; for Fordhook Farm follow New Britain Road for $1/4$ mile and the entrance is on the left through two stone pillars.

Glencairn Museum and Bryn Athyn Cathedral

A Hint of Europe

On a clear day you can't see forever, but you can see the sky-scrapers and spires of downtown Philadelphia from the tower atop the **Glencairn Museum** in Bryn Athyn. The museum is housed in the castle built between 1928 and 1939 by Raymond Pitcairn, son of the founder of the Pittsburgh Plate Glass Company. From the tower you'll also see majestic **Bryn Athyn Cathedral**, begun in 1913 and dedicated in 1919, which Pitcairn also built.

It is fascinating to learn that to build the cathedral and the castle, Raymond Pitcairn reverted to methods that had proved successful in the Middle Ages. The cathedral, built first, evolved from models, both scale and full-size, that were prepared by the skilled craftsmen who clustered around the foundation of the emerging church in workshops reminiscent of the medieval guilds.

The cathedral is noted for its "softness" which was achieved by avoiding straight lines and right angles through using horizontal curves, vertical bends and slightly bowed lines. The exquisite stained glass windows that filter the sunlight also add to the feeling of softness. Using his collection of medieval glass, Pitcairn had his workers study the work of 12th- and 13th-century European artisans and then create the windows in shops on the cathedral grounds.

When the cathedral was nearly finished, Pitcairn decided to have the workmen stay on in their shops so that he could build a home for his family in a similar style. Glencairn, his beautiful stone castle, now houses Pitcairn's collection of medieval art. Many of the objects were acquired as models during the construction of the cathedral. Pitcairn collected others from around the world. The Great Hall on the first floor has six stained-glass windows reproduced from the Chartres Cathedral. Colors from the windows are picked up in the Oriental rugs scattered throughout the hall. Adjoining the hall is a charming cloister and garden.

Other floors offer treasures from Egypt, the Near East, Greece, Rome, plus medieval collections and American Indian pieces. The master bedroom has been retained as it was when the Pitcairns occupied the house.

The extraordinary nature of this museum makes it a popular destination for scholars, artists and students. Since the museum can only accommodate a limited number of guests, visitors must have reservations. Glencairn is open by appointment. Call (215) 947-9919 or 947-4200 for guided tours Monday through Friday from 9:00 A.M. to 4:00 P.M. It is also open on a walk-in basis on the second Sunday of each month from September to June from 2:00 P.M. to 5:00 P.M. Admission is charged.

Directions: Take I-95 to the Woodhaven exit, travel west on Woodhaven until it ends, then make a left onto Evans Road. At the first light take a right onto Byberry Road. Proceed on Byberry to Huntingdon Pike (that will be seven lights). Take a left onto the Pike and at the first light, Cathedral Road, make a right. The Bryn Athyn Cathedral is located at Cathedral Road and Huntingdon Pike; Glencairn is just beyond at 1001 Cathedral Road.

Graeme Park

Only Surviving Colonial Pennsylvania Governor's Residence

Were they to make a movie of Elizabeth Graeme's life, it would be a two-handkerchief film, for hers was a tragic tale. She was the youngest child of Dr. Thomas Graeme, who traveled to the New World in May 1717 as the personal physician of Sir William Keith, deputy-governor of Penn's colony.

Graeme, a single, twenty-nine year old, lived in the Keith's Philadelphia home where he met and married the governor's step-daughter Ann Diggs. Graeme's career progressed. He became physician of the port of Philadelphia and a judge of the Supreme Court. Meanwhile, Keith's career floundered. After a dispute with the Penn family, Keith was removed from office. He returned to England to raise funds to obtain passage for his family back to England or secure a new appointment. Keith died before realizing either goal.

While in Pennsylvania in 1722, Keith had commissioned a country mansion. He called his estate **Fountain Low** because of the natural springs running through the 1,200 acres, and he established a malt house on his property. Graeme purchased the estate in 1739, remodeling the interior to reflect current English style and taste. He added elaborate paneling, fine marble and imported ceramic delft tiles around the fireplaces.

At Graeme's death in 1772, the estate was inherited by his sole surviving child Elizabeth. Unlike most women in the colonial era, she was well educated with an interest in literary pursuits and a talent for poetry. She hosted some of the country's first literary gatherings and was the only woman to be an informal associate of the Swains of the Schuylkill. This group of budding intellectuals staged what member Benjamin Rush called "attic evenings."

Although of a romantic nature, her own affairs of the heart were tragically unfulfilled. At seventeen she fell in love with William Franklin, the illegitimate son of Benjamin Franklin. Both fathers opposed the match and broke up the relationship. In late 1771, after the death of her mother, while acting as her father's hostess, Elizabeth met Henry Hugh Ferguson, a poor Scottish immigrant ten years her junior. In little over four months she married him, despite her father's disapproval and without his knowledge. The very day she had determined to tell him of her marriage, her father died. Henry then moved into **Graeme Park** with her. They spent only two and a half years together. In 1775 Ferguson traveled to Great Britain. He returned to Philadelphia two years later but remained in the city, working for the British as commissary of prisoners. As a Loyalist, Ferguson was opposed to the American cause. He fled the country after the war and he and Elizabeth never reunited.

Elizabeth's position during the revolution was pitiable. Now in her forties, she remained alone at Graeme Park cut off from family and friends. It is thought she favored the America cause; she contributed food and clothing to the army when it was camped at Whitemarsh (see Hope Lodge selection). Mad Anthony Wayne's troops camped on the grounds of Graeme Park before the Battle of Germantown. Only the intervention of family friends prevented her home from being sold as a spoil of war because of her husband's Tory connections. Most of the contents were sold at public auction. She kept furniture for three rooms and eventually bought back some of the forfeited pieces. In 1791, Elizabeth sold Graeme Park to her brother-in-law. She had been living on less than two hundred dollars a year. The money she received for the house supported her until her death in 1801.

Through all the subsequent owners the original stone exterior built for Keith survived, as did the exquisite details added by Thomas Graeme. The house is an architectural treasure and is presented with only a few pieces of period furniture to focus attention on the details of design and ornamentation. Paint pigments enabled restorers to return the rooms to the colors enjoyed during the years the Graeme family entertained at their country estate. The **Grand Parlor** retains the original 18th-century paint. The Georgian style parlor is the most elaborate room. Portraits of Sir William Keith and members of the Graeme family adorn the walls.

The summer kitchen behind the mansion was reconstructed and a physic garden planted with medicinal and culinary herbs that would have been grown in the 18th century. The Visitor Center is in the 19th-century bank barn, added by the Penrose family, Quakers who farmed the land in the early 1800s. There are exhibits and a video introduction to Graeme Park. The house is open Wednesday through Saturday 9:00 A.M. to 5:00 P.M.; on Sunday it opens at NOON. The last tour begins at 3:30 P.M. Admission is charged. Throughout the year, special events including living history programs are scheduled at Graeme Park; call (215) 343-0965 for details.

Directions: From I-76 take the Willow Grove Interchange and head north on Route 611. At the intersection with County Line Road bear left; Graeme Park is at 859 County Line Road.

The Grange

Changing Grange

During The Grange's 300-year-old history it has had at least ten owners, three names and numerous architectural revisions. It is this layering effect that makes **The Grange** so historically, architecturally and horticulturally interesting.

The present estate is just a small part of the 500 acres claimed in 1682 by Henry Lewis, a Welsh Quaker who was one of the first three European settlers in the area. He named his new home Maen Coch, after his homeland in Wales. The name means Redstone. It is not his house that endures, but a later one built by his son Henry Lewis, Jr., circa 1700. The son's house forms the drawing room of The Grange and the rooms directly above. The part that is now the library and stair hall were added around 1730.

In 1750, the house acquired a new owner, a new name and a new look. Captain John Wilcox named it Clifton Hall, and added a large room for formal entertaining. After only 11 years he sold the property to Charles Cruikshank, a Scot. Cruikshank did not support the American Revolution and left the country when the colonists won the war, selling the estate in 1782 to his daughter's husband, John Ross. Ross helped finance the patriot's cause, an activity that certainly upset his father-in-law. Ross procured clothes, arms and gunpowder for the Continental Army. Like so many who supported the cause of independence he often paid out of his own pocket. Ross renamed his new home, The Grange, after Lafayette's French estate.

Lafayette, Washington and many members of the first cabinet enjoyed the hospitality of John Ross. Entries in Washington's diary refer to visits, such as the one on June 17, 1787: "Went to church. After wch rid 8 miles into the country and dined with Mr. Ross in Chester County. Retd. to town about dusk."

103

Today when you visit you see the house and dependencies so essential to an 18th- and 19th-century gentleman's country home. The estate grounds include ten acres of woodland with a number of record size specimens. One of the last owners of The Grange, Benjamin R. Hoffman of Philadelphia, greatly enhanced the gardens. Blooming from early spring to late fall, boxwood-enclosed terraced beds offer nearly continuous color. Close to the house is a rose garden, an herbal bed with more than 50 different herbs and an old-fashioned knot garden. In the spring daffodils, narcissus and native wildflowers brighten the woodland trails.

The English Gothic appearance of the house is the result of alterations made from 1850 to 1863. It is this period that is reflected in the interior furnishings as well. The property is now owned by the Township of Haverford and operational activities are coordinated by the Friends of The Grange, Inc.

There are guided tours of the mansion, gardens, outbuildings and woodlands from April through October on weekends from 1:00 P.M. to 4:00 P.M. Admission is charged. To arrange a tour at other times or to obtain a schedule of special summer and December evening tours call (610) 446-4958.

Directions: From I-76, take the Schuylkill Expressway from Philadelpia north to U.S. 1. Take U.S. 1 south about four miles to Earlington Road and turn right. Following Grange signs from Earlington, turn right on Bennington Road, then left on Myrtle Avenue. Make a right into The Grange entrance at Warwick Road next to St. James Church, which was once The Grange dairy barn.

Hibernia Mansion, Springton Manor Farm and Historic Waynesborough

Chester County Houses with History

Chester County is part of the Brandywine Valley, where southeastern Pennsylvania meets northern Delaware. Great events took place here, and great men walked, worked and lived on the land. Houses have histories that go back more than 200 years, encompassing sweeping changes.

Hibernia Mansion, a restored 19th-century mansion located north of Coatesville, is on land first deeded in 1765. In the late 1700s a forge was built on the property to convert pig iron into bar iron. In 1821 Charles Brooke purchased the property and developed it into a prosperous iron plantation with two forges, a furnace, rolling mill and grist mill. Brooke also built an imposing house with gardens, orchards and modest dwellings for his workers.

Hibernia House was built in stages; a substantial portion of the house was built by Charles Brooke. The north-side exterior looks as it did in his day. But the house today reflects the rehabilitations and additions made by Colonel Franklin Swayne, a prominent Philadelphia real estate lawyer, who purchased the estate in 1895 as a fox hunting and country retreat.

Swayne added the massive lion heads on the pillar gateposts at the estate's entrance. He bought them on one of his 29 trips to England and they were just one of the English-influenced touches he added to Hibernia. Under Swayne's direction the exterior facade was embellished and servant wings were added.

When Swayne married an English actress, he added a ballroom with a massive fireplace to accommodate a Yule log so they could host an elaborate Christmas party in the English tradition. It never became a tradition at Hibernia as the couple had only one grand party before divorcing.

Much of the furniture in the house belonged to Colonel Swayne, although the house was inherited by his cousin who used it for a family summer house for a time before she sold it to Chester County in 1962. Swayne pieces include most of the wood tables, side pieces, pianos, several rugs, wall decorations, paintings and engravings and most of the sofas and chairs. The Colonel's red hunting jacket hangs in his bedroom. There is a peephole from his wife Dolly's bedroom so she could see guests in the ballroom. It's interesting to speculate as to why she wanted an advance look at her guests. Perhaps she wanted to check on the color of the ladies' gowns or the number of guests who had arrived so that she could time her entrance.

Guided tours are given from Memorial Day weekends to mid-September on Sundays from 1:00 P.M. to 4:00 P.M. Hours may vary so visitors need to call (215) 384-0290 for times and admission charges. In early December, the mansion is decorated to recapture the magic experienced in 1904 at the one grand party held here. Period costumes, chamber music and refreshments add to the festivities.

Hibernia was never a farming plantation, unlike nearby Springton Manor. In the 1730s immigrants from Scotland settled on the land without title of ownership since it was part of an 8,313 acre Penn family manor. The present day **Springton Manor Farm** encompasses one of the thirty-one manor segments found on a 1788 survey. The property passed through several hands before being purchased in 1818 by James McIlvanie, who wanted the land to raise Merino sheep. The present manor house was begun in 1833 and enlarged by George Bartol, who owned it from 1877 until his death in 1917. The house is now rented out for private and public functions. Adjacent to the house is a Victorian garden, gazebo and tiled terrace.

Today Springton Manor Farm operates as a demonstration farm, showing the operation of a small modern Chester County farm, including livestock management and conservation practices. An agricultural exhibit in the barn reveals the development of farm equipment over the years, while a petting zoo delights younger visitors. A catch and release pond lets youngsters try to hook bluegills and bass. Park personnel lead wildflower walks, stream strolls and participatory farm activities.

Springton Manor Farm is open daily year-round from 8:00 A.M. to sunset. The demonstration farm, barn and farm visiting area are open 10:00 A.M. to 4:00 P.M. The farm also has a handicapped-accessible nature trail.

The names of the owners of Hibernia Mansion and Springton Manor Farm are not recognized beyond the borders of Chester County and the Philadelphia area, but **Historic Waynesborough** is noted as the home of Revolutionary War hero Major General Anthony Wayne. The man Theodore Roosevelt called one of the greatest fighting generals in American history led elements of the Pennsylvania Line at Brandywine and Germantown, helped train the army at Valley Forge, went on to fight at Monmouth and led the successful attack on Stony Point. The soubriquet "Mad Anthony" was acquired during the Virginia campaign. Peevish from a leg wound, Wayne ordered punishment for a favorite spy, who had evidently returned to camp drunk. The spy, accustomed to better treatment from Wayne, loudly declared that the general must be "mad." The story was often repeated, and the name came to refer to his dash and impetuosity in battle. After the war, President Washington appointed Wayne the first commander of the Legions of America, as the U.S. Army was first called.

The fieldstone Georgian-style country manor house at Historic Waynesborough interprets the lifestyle of seven generations of Waynes. It was General Wayne's grandfather, Captain Anthony who purchased 380 acres in this Pennsylvania wilderness in 1724. General Wayne's father Isaac built the central portion of the house, while the General's son made some additions. Wayne's military career kept him too busy to spend much time at his family home. The last three generations descended through the female side of the line. The history of the Wayne family is outlined in a slide presentation.

The house has some original Wayne family items, while other pieces represent different generations of Waynes. House tours are given from mid-March through December on Tuesday and Thursday from 10:00 A.M. to 4:00 P.M. and Sunday 1:00 P.M. to 4:00 P.M. Admission is charged.

Directions: From I-76, the Pennsylvania Turnpike, take Exit 23, Route 100 south to Route 30. Head west on Route 30, stay on Route 30 Bypass, not Business 30 as you approach Coatesville. From Route 30 Bypass take Route 82 north for approximately two miles to Cedar Knoll Road, turn left and take that for 1.25 miles to the entrance for Hibernia County Park on the left. For Springton Manor Farm, as you travel west on Route 30 Bypass toward Coatesville, exit at Route 322 north. Travel about four miles and turn right on Springton Road. The farm entrance will be on the right after about 1.25 miles. For Historic Waynesborough go south of the turnpike on Route 100 south. Take Route 30 east to Paoli, then turn right on Route 252 and make a right on Waynesborough Road. The historic property will be on your right.

Historic Yellow Springs

Heal the Body and the Spirit

History and health, art and nature all merge in the tiny village of **Yellow Springs**. The Lenni Lenape and Susquehanna Indians were aware of the medicinal properties of the yellow water that bubbled up from beneath the ground, changing the color of the river banks. Before long the European settlers in nearby Pikeland became aware of the healing qualities of the springs.

By 1721, Philadelphia physicians were sending patients out of the city to Pikeland to "take of the mineral springs." By 1750 the area was a health spa, with roads constructed to carry travelers to the east bank of Pickering Creek where the springs were most active. The first of many taverns, Pritchard's Publick House of Entertainment opened in 1762. The fame of the springs was by this time attracting visitors from as far as the West Indies. As Yellow Springs became more fashionable, the comfortable bathhouses added drawing rooms and fireplaces. Physician Benjamin Rush, who signed the Declaration of Independence for Pennsylvania, promoted the healing properties of the bubbling springs.

In the spring of 1774, Dr. Samuel Kennedy purchased the springs. He served under General Anthony Wayne, whose estate, Waynesborough, was not far away (see selection). Kennedy loaned part of his land to Congress as a hospital for Continental soldiers during the Revolutionary war. The proximity of Yellow Springs was one of the factors that convinced General Washington to make his winter encampment at Valley Forge. In fact, Washington established temporary headquarters at the Yellow Springs Inn after the Battle of Brandywine and the Battle of the Clouds in Malvern.

107

When you visit Historic Yellow Springs you will see the ruins of the only official Revolutionary War hospital constructed with the authorization of the Continental Congress. The hospital remained in use until 1781. General Washington was concerned that his men were contracting smallpox, and he took the progressive step of ordering the men under his command be vaccinated. To reassure the men that the procedure was safe, Washington received one of the first shots administered by Dr. Otto. The unmarked graves around the hospital site are mute testimony to the overwhelming struggle against disease, hunger and the elements fought by the army at Valley Forge.

Once the hospital closed, the village and its spas were restored to their pre-war condition and travelers returned to the healing waters. New buildings were added around 1820. Several still stand including the **George Washington Building**, now the Inn at Yellow Springs, a popular and picturesque restaurant and overnight spot. **The Lincoln Building** is attached by a wooden piazza to the inn. Once called "The Cottage," it now serves as exhibit space for Historic Yellow Springs and other village organizations. The Chester Springs Library, a branch of the Chester County Library system, is located here as well as the offices of Historic Yellow Springs.

The iron springs were the first to be utilized, but over the years a sulphur and a magnesium spring were discovered. New bathhouses were added to serve the growing need. Notable figures joined the crowd seeking the healing waters. Presidents Madison and Monroe visited Yellow Springs as did Henry Clay, Daniel Webster and DeWitt Clinton. Popular entertainers performed at the inn; **Jenny Lind** even had one of the springs named after her. (In a later era, Steve McQueen lived at the inn while filming *The Blob* on location in the area.)

In 1861, the Yellow Springs hospital was reactivated as an army hospital for Civil War soldiers. After the war, the state acquired the spa as an orphanage for children left without parents as a result of the war. In 1876, the hospital was destroyed by fire. It was rebuilt, but burned again in 1964. Today only the fieldstone foundations can be seen.

In 1916 the Pennsylvania Academy of Fine Arts purchased the facilities of Yellow Springs to use as a residential summer school. This first brought the arts to the area. To enhance the scenery for the school's art students, an English landscape artist added an oriental bog garden around the springs.

It wasn't fine arts, but when Good New Production purchased the buildings in 1952 they made two science fiction classics here— *The Blob* and the *4-D Man*. The company also made religious films.

In 1965 the Yellow Springs Association was formed to bring

artistic and cultural programs to the area. In 1974, the village was acquired by its current owners, Historic Yellow Springs, Inc. Today, this charming village offers art, classes, workshops, exhibits, programs and performances. The village, on the National Register of Historic Places, is home to the Chester Springs Studio and Yellow Spring Institute for Contemporary Studies. A restoration of the meadow and wetland is in progress. A path through the wetlands takes you down to the iron, sulfur and magnesium springs. You can peak into the historic spa buildings where the hopeful "took the cure."

The best time to visit the village is during one of the four annual events: the art show, Frolicks, antiques show and the craft festival. Call for details and dates, (610) 827-7414. If you visit in the fall, you are apt to see members of the Pickering Hunt in their scarlet coats following the hounds on their traditional fox hunts.

Not far from Historic Yellow Springs is **Fox Meadow Farm & Winery** which is open for tours and tastings on the weekends from 1:00 P.M. to 5:00 P.M. (Closed February and March) The first French-American hybrid vines were planted here in 1980, and these produce a small amount of award-winning wines. Across from the tasting house a historic red bank barn is filled with tanks and barrels of aging wine.

Fox Meadow Farm was first called the Reis-Pennebecker farm as its first owner was Zachariah Reis who bought the land in 1767. Reis helped build the hospital at Yellow Springs and the powder works on French Creek. After the Battle of the Clouds, General Wayne's two divisions camped on this and the adjoining farm. It was the next owners, the Pennebeckers who built the red barn in 1820 to house their dairy herd. Interested visitors can tour the barn and see the barrels of wine.

Directions: From I-76, the Pennsylvania Turnpike, take Exit 23 and pick up Route 113 north to Chester Springs. Turn right on Yellow Springs Road for the village of Yellow Springs. For Fox Meadow Farm continue on Route 113 past the Yellow Springs turnoff and make a right on Clover Mill Road.

Hope Lodge

Hope Full

Between 1743 and 1748, Samuel Morris, a wealthy Quaker entrepreneur, built **Hope Lodge**, one of the country's finest surviving early Georgian mansions. After Morris's brother Joshua inherited the house he sold it to Philadelphia merchant William

West. The Wests lived at Hope Lodge from 1776 to 1782. Just a year after they moved here, in the fall of 1777, the Continental Army camped in the fields around the house for six weeks after the Battle of Germantown. From this camp the men made their way to Valley Forge. During what was called the Whitemarsh Encampment, George Washington's Surgeon General, John Cochran, used Hope Lodge as his headquarters.

The house received its name from the third owner, Henry Hope, who purchased it as a wedding gift for his ward, James Watmough. The young man named the house in honor of his benefactor, just as years later the family's name was given to the famous diamond. Two generations of Watmoughs lived here before the home was purchased by Jacob Wentz. For nearly a century the Wentz family (relatives of Peter Wentz who owned a nearby farmstead, see selection) farmed the property. Their limited means prevented them from modernizing the house, thus it retained its 18th-century integrity. A development company bought the house in 1921 intending to demolish it. However William and Alice Degn who bought it in 1922, carefully restored its elegant appearance. They added a wing onto the summer kitchen for the cold winter months rather than disturbing the design by installing central heating.

It is the Degn's collection of 18th- and early 19th-century furnishings that fill the rooms. The house reflects two time periods: the Colonial era from 1743 to 1770 when Samuel Morris lived here and the Colonial Revival years, 1922-1953 when the Degns lived at Hope Lodge. An inventory taken at Morris's death aided in the furnishing of the entrance hall, parlor, master bedchamber and various servant areas. Photographs, inventories and interviews have helped curators recreate the parlor, dining room and guest bedroom from the Degn era. The Degns added a rose garden on the south side of the house. Additional flowers and herbs are planted in 18th-century style.

Samuel Morris built his home near his gristmill, now known as **Mather Mill**. The mill was built at the turn of the century (from the 17th to the 18th) by Edward Farmar's heirs who sold it along with 150 acres to Samuel Morris. When Joshua Morris inherited the estate, he sold the house to the Wests and the mill to his son-in-law Isaac Mather. The present mill was built around 1820 by Isaac's son William. The mill was operational until the late 19th century. The exterior is original but the interior has been renovated for meetings, displays and programs.

Hope Lodge is open Tuesday through Saturday from 9:00 A.M. to 5:00 P.M.; on Sunday it opens at NOON. Closed on Monday and holidays except Memorial Day, July 4th and Labor Day. Admission is charged.

Several decades after Samuel Morris built his estate, another colonial Quaker and Philadelphia merchant, Anthony Morris (they were not related) built **The Highlands**. This 32-room Georgian mansion was built on 43 acres overlooking Whitemarsh Valley. The house, designed to provide the Morris family with a refuge from the city's yellow fever epidemics, was finished in 1801. Seven years later financial difficulties led to the sale of The Highlands to Daniel Hitner, who kept the house for only five years before selling it to George Sheaff. It stayed in the Sheaff family for more than a century, finally passing to Caroline Sinkler in 1917, who restored both house and gardens. Her niece, Emily Sinkler Roosevelt and her husband, gave the estate to the state in 1957.

The gardens are a special delight. Caroline Sinkler redefined the formal gardens planted by Anthony Morris. She restored the stone walls built to suggest ruins as well as the grapery and gardener's cottage. During restoration statuary, reflecting pools and specimen trees were added. The Pennsylvania Horticultural Society awarded her a gold medal for her efforts.

The mansion's public rooms can be rented for meetings, receptions and special events. Visitors may enjoy the gardens year around. The house and gardens can be toured Monday through Friday 9:00 A. M. to 4:00 P.M. Admission is charged for tours and appointments are advisable. For additional information, call (215) 641-2687.

Directions: From I-76, the Pennsylvania Turnpike, take Exit 26, the Fort Washington Interchange. Take Pennsylvania Avenue over to the Bethlehem Pike, Old Route 309, and head south for Hope Lodge at 553 Bethlehem Pike. As you head down Bethlehem Pike head west on Route 73, then make a right on Sheaff Lane; The Highlands is on the left at 7001 Sheaff Lane.

Hugh Moore Historical Park and Canal Museum

Hijinks along the Lehigh Canal

Riding the mule-drawn canal boats is the best way to understand what life was like along the canals from the 1820s to the 1930s. Historical interpreters in period dress bring canal days to life during the 45 to 60-minute ride along a $2^1/_2$-mile stretch of the **Lehigh Canal**. The longer $2^1/_2$-hour trip includes a fascinating locking-through maneuver in one of the three restored canal locks. During this procedure the canal boat enters the lock and a valve is opened, raising the water level eight feet in about five minutes, thus allowing the boat to move ahead at this new elevation.

Lehigh Coal and Navigation Company founders Josiah White and Erskine Hazard tamed the turbulent Lehigh River in 1820 by creating a descending navigation system using their own unique "bear trap," or hydrostatic locks. Converted to a two-way navigation system by 1829, it gave the Lehigh Canal the largest carrying capacity of any canal in the country. The Lehigh linked up with the Morris and Delaware Canals to connect this area with New York and Philadelphia. These large metropolitan markets encouraged the development of early industrial parks at power sites along the canal.

One such industrial park was the Abbott Street area which had a dozen manufacturing establishments, employing more than 1,000 workers by 1840. This area, near Lock 47, is now part of the **Hugh Moore Park**. Also part of the park are the ruins of the Glendon Industrial Area and the piers and cables of Change Bridge. Built in 1857, this is the oldest existing bridge using machine-made wire rope. Efforts are now underway to restore the bridge.

When the park was established in the early 60s, restoration work was done on the locktender's house. Now a museum, this house provides an opportunity to step back in time to the days when the locktender and his family lived here. A costumed interpreter is on hand to answer questions.

A second museum, the **Canal Museum**, is located at the juncture of the canal with the Delaware River. This museum is adjacent to the Delaware Canal State Park. From this museum you can see the start of the Delaware Canal and the stone arch entrance to the Morris Canal across the Delaware River in New Jersey. The museum has exhibits on canal life, industries along the canal and the coal mining industry that utilized the canal to transport coal-laden canal boats to America's population centers.

Hugh Moore Historical Park stretches for six miles beside the Lehigh River. The scenic parkland has a three-mile paved bike trail. Bikes can be rented at the Canal Boat boarding area. There is a towpath and river hiking trail plus a picnic and playground area.

The Canal Museum is open year-round Monday through Saturday from 10:00 A.M. to 4:00 P.M. and Sunday 1:00 P.M. to 5:00 P.M. Closed on major holidays. A nominal admission is charged. The Locktender's House Museum is open Memorial Day weekend through Labor Day, Wednesday through Sunday, from NOON to 4:30 P.M. and on weekends in May and September. The canal boat ride charge includes admission to the **Locktender's House Museum**. Boat rides are given Wednesday through Saturday at 11:00 A.M., 1:00 P.M., 2:30 P.M. and 4:00 P.M. On Sunday and on May and September weekends there is no 11:00 A.M. trip. You can also rent boats and bikes during the summer months and on weekends in May and September.

Directions: From I-78 follow the signs to Route 611 north, then turn left at the light onto Berwick Street and continue for 1.1 miles to the end. Turn left onto Glendon Avenue; take the first right into the park. For the Canal Museum take Route 611 north for 1.5 miles off Route I-78. Brown Canal Museum signs direct you to the museum.

James A. Michener Art Museum

"Small Museum with Big Ideas"

The young orphaned James Michener was raised by a financially straitened Doylestown widow. Doylestown natives talk about Henry Mercer (see selection) berating the lad for being on his property by telling him "one day you're going to end up in that (the Doylestown) jail." Little did either of them realize, Michener would indeed end up in the jail, but in a manner neither could have anticipated. (Michener himself has said that although he was Mercer's closest neighbor, they never spoke.)

In 1985, when the Gothic-style county jail closed, the Bucks County Council on the Arts realized it would be the ideal setting for the museum they had long hoped to build. Within the fortress-like walls the prison buildings were demolished. The warden's house, now on the National Register of Historic Buildings and Sites, and the central guardhouse were incorporated in the design. The museum was named for the community's Pulitzer Prize winning-author, James Michener who, with his wife Mari, presided over the opening in September 1988. Three years later an expansion project added a new gallery and art storage space. Within this museum Bucks County artists have a home. The planners and directors have fulfilled their dream of creating "a regional museum where its artistic soul can flourish."

Michener may be a citizen of the world, but his home base is Bucks County. In fact, in 1962 he ran for one of the district's congressional seats. The **Michener Art Museum** has a permanent exhibit showcasing his prolific career, including a specially produced video with Michener. A Doylestown office he maintained for 35 years is now ensconced in the museum complete with desk, files, cabinets and typewriter. He typed all his work, as you will see from the original manuscript for "The Novel." There are copies of some of the more than 40 books Michener wrote plus photographs of him, including one running the bulls at Pamplona. Instilling great pride in local visitors is Michener's Presidential Medal of Freedom. When Michener was asked by a group of writers what he wanted on his epitaph he replied, no doubt jestingly, "Here lies a man who never showed home movies or served vin rose."

From windows beside the Michener exhibit you can look out upon the **sculpture garden** enclosed in the former prison's 25-foot stone walls. A tearoom opens onto a terrace in the garden.

Michener wrote five books on Japanese art, and his first novel *Tales of the South Pacific*, became a classic and a beloved musical comedy favorite when transferred to the Broadway stage. It is therefore highly appropriate to find the Nakashima Reading Room in the museum. Mira Nakashima-Yarnall designed the room as a memorial to her father, George Nakashima, an internationally known woodworker whose studio was in Bucks County. Nakashima believed that all things—trees, stones, water and light—were animated by a divine, creative spirit revealed in the beauty and order that underlie the earth's apparent chaos. Certainly there is beauty, harmony and spiritual peace in this reading room. The floor mats and shoji screens are the backdrop for some of Nakashima's finest pieces of furniture including a Claro walnut free-form table and five claro walnut Conoid lounge chairs.

Gallery space at the Michener Museum will showcase the visual heritage of Bucks County, with selected items on display from the permanent collection from Colonial times to the present. Works are displayed by Edward Redfield, Daniel Garber and Robert Spencer. Redfield was a Pennsylvania Impressionist, one of the leaders in the Pennsylvania School of Landscape Painting. He frequently worked outside in brutally cold weather on his large, dramatic winterscapes. Garber taught at the Pennsylvania Academy for over 40 years and attracted many of his students to the New Hope area. In 1916, six Bucks County artists formed the New Hope Group; among these was Robert Spencer. Michener, a phenomenal art collector himself, is particularly taken with Spencer's renderings of grist mills in the area. The Michener Museum through its exhibits will help define the New Hope circle of Impressionists.

Additionally, the museum will have an ongoing exhibit focusing on selections from the vaults, pieces that range beyond the New Hope style. This small exhibit will change every several months, making frequent visits a must.

The James A. Michener Art Museum is open Tuesday through Friday from 10:00 A.M. to 4:30 P.M. On weekends, hours are 10:00 A.M. to 5:00 P.M. There is an admission charge; however, on Saturdays children under 16 are admitted free until 1:00 P.M.. There is also a museum shop.

Directions: From I-76, take I-276 to Willow Grove, Exit 27. Head north on Route 611 to Doylestown. Make a right turn on Ashland Street then make a right onto South Pine Street. The museum is at 138 South Pine Street.

Lehigh County Historical Society Sites

Nine Local Points of Interest

Lehigh Valley in the foothills of the Pocono Mountains has a history that dates back to the Moravians, the religious group who first settled the region. Bethlehem (see selection) brings the 18th century vibrantly to life; it's a religious Williamsburg similar to Old Salem in North Carolina.

For an overview of the region's history visit the **Lehigh County Museum** in Allentown's Old Courthouse, Hamilton at Fifth Street, headquarters for the Lehigh County Historical Society (LCHS). Exhibits start with the Lenni Lenape Indians who first inhabited the region and extend through the Pennsylvania German settlers and other immigrants to this part of the state. The courthouse also houses the society's Scott Andrew Trexler II Memorial Library with an extensive collection of county, church and census records, genealogies and surveyor's documents. The museum and library are open Monday through Saturday from 10:00 A.M. to 4:00 P.M. and the museum is also open on Sundays 1:00 P.M. to 4:00 P.M.

Allentown's oldest home is the Georgian-style **Trout Hall**, built in 1770 by James Allen, on land given to him by his father William Allen, who founded the city. James Allen was a wealthy Philadelphia lawyer and his father served as mayor of that city as well as chief justice of the state. Trout Hall was planned as a summer retreat, but during the American Revolution it became a refuge for the family while the British occupied Philadelphia. James tried to stay neutral in the conflict, being sympathetic with the patriots but unwilling to support independence. His stand pleased neither side.

Over the years Trout Hall passed out of the hands of the Allen family, becoming over time a boys' preparatory school and the first site of Muhlenberg College. Its exterior has been restored to its earliest appearance and it is furnished with period pieces from the late 1700s. The sideboard in the dining room belonged to one of James Allen's daughters. The house is open April through November on Tuesday through Saturday from NOON to 3:00 P.M. and Sunday 1:00 P.M. to 4:00 P.M. Admission is free to all the Lehigh County Historical sites.

While searching for Lehigh County's seven covered bridges you'll spot barns painted with colorful hex signs.

Another colonial home in the nearby community of Egypt was built even earlier. The **Troxell-Steckel House**, 4229 Reliance Street, dates back to 1756. This house provides an interesting contrast with the Allen property, because it reflects the sturdy medieval architectural style (the walls are $2^1/_2$ feet thick) of rural German farmhouses, rather than the more stately English country homes. Furnishings are from farming families in the late 18th century. An inscription on the 1758 five-plate cast-iron stove reads: "Never Despise Old Age." In the 1875 Swiss bank barn are blacksmithing and carpentry tools as well as an assortment of buggies, sleighs and wagons. This LCHS site is open June through October on weekends from 1:00 P.M. to 4:00 P.M.

Catasauqua boasts a summer home of one of Pennsylvania's signers of the Declaration of Independence. The **Taylor House** at Lehigh and Poplar Streets dates from 1768. The house only served George Taylor for a short period before passing into other hands. It can be toured weekends from 1:00 P.M. to 4:00 P.M. June through October.

In Allentown is the **Victorian townhouse of Frank Buchman**, founder of the Moral Re-Armament Movement. Buchman's parents built this house at 117 North 11th Street in 1894. This rowhouse is furnished with Buchman family pieces and memorabilia from Buchman's world travels. A Lutheran minister, Buchman founded a home for transient boys in Philadelphia. His fight for world peace and moral re-armament made him a world leader. Buchman was decorated by eight foreign governments and was twice nominated for the Nobel Prize.

Noteworthy items displayed at the Buchman house are the Sword of Surrender of the World War II Japanese land armies in China given to Reverend Buchman by Chinese general and former Prime Minister Ho Ying-Chin; a wooden cross made from a four-hundred-year-old Camphor tree given to him by the Mayor of Hiroshima as a symbol of the 1945 atomic blast; and a miner's lamp, a gift from mine workers in Germany's Ruhr. The house is open for tours weekends from 1:00 P.M. to 4:00 P.M.

At the turn-of-the-century, the Lehigh Valley produced 75% of the nation's cement. American Portland Cement originated here and the **Coplay's Saylor Cement Industry Museum**, North 2nd Street, is the only restored industrial site in the country concentrating on cement-making. The museum has nine vertical Schoefer kilns built in 1892. It looks like an industrial Stonehenge. There are also exhibits on the development of the concrete industry. Tours are given weekends 1:00 P.M. to 4:00 P.M. from May through September.

Not far away in Alburtis the anthracite iron industry is explored at the **Lock Ridge Furnace Museum** on Franklin Street. The anthracite iron industry, which began in the Lehigh Valley in 1839, accelerated the area's shift from an agrarian to an industrial economy. Museum exhibits in the former weightmaster's house explain how anthracite iron was made, provide a glimpse of the lives of the Lock Ridge ironworkers and touch on the impact the industry had in the community. Old photographs show how the area looked when the furnaces were operating. Anthracite coal was used as fuel in the production of iron, though later coke replaced it. By 1914 Lock Ridge was the last furnace in the country using anthracite coal. Operation of the furnaces ended in 1921. A walking-tour booklet gives you background on the Lock Ridge Furnaces. The museum is open weekends 1:00 P.M. to 4:00 P.M. May through September. Spring and fall festivals are held on the grounds.

Colonial mills were like today's banks: a farmer's wife would stop at the mill with a bag of wheat, weigh it and sell it to get money to go into town. The **Haines Mill Museum** at 3600 Haines Mill Road in Allentown is one such mill that served the local community for nearly 200 years. The grist mill was built in 1760. After being badly damaged by fire in 1909, it was rebuilt with a water turbine power source. The mill ceased operation in 1956 and now serves as a reminder of its once pivotal role in the life of Allentown. The mill is open weekends May through September from 1:00 P.M. to 4:00 P.M.

The last of the LCHS's sites is the **Claussville One-Room Schoolhouse** on Route 100. Operating from 1893 until 1956, it was the last one-room school in Lehigh County. Its desks, books, and educational aids remind visitors of a simpler era of education. The schoolhouse is open May through September on weekends from 1:00 P.M. to 4:00 P.M.

Directions: From I-78 take Hamilton Boulevard into Allentown to the Lehigh County Historical Museum at 5th Street. Since this is also the headquarters for the LCHS, you can pick up brochures and maps for the other sites under their jurisdiction. For additional information call (215) 435-4664.

Longwood Gardens

America's Premier Garden Estate

If you stopped visitors randomly as they left Longwood Gardens you would undoubtedly hear the same comments repeated again and again. First-time visitors are amazed to discover this perfectly splendid garden accessibly located in America and not in some far-distant country. Longwood seems to induce an evangelical fervor; visitors want to tell everybody they know about its wonders.

Longwood Gardens should be visited during every season to appreciate fully its scope and beauty. A visit during the harsh winter months brings the most solace. Even if you close your eyes and don't partake of the visual splendor in the **four-acre conservatory**, the smell of the delicate blossoms is worth the trip. Suddenly, it's springtime and the snow and slush that may be as near as the other side of the door, seem far away. January's displays, featuring hyacinths and daffodils, advance the calendar three months. The conservatory's great height is utilized by having the large columns entwined with creeping fig and bougainvillea. Hanging plant chandeliers pick up the flower motif of the display. Photography buffs should bring their camera both for floral close-ups and for the breathtaking vista of massed blooms.

Year-round favorites can be enjoyed in this glassed-in garden. There is a special orchid room where displays are changed weekly. Rare specimens are shown in an amazing array seldom duplicated, and certainly not surpassed anywhere. The same can be said for the rose collection where row after row of summer bloomers bask in the winter sun. The conservatory has some unusual specimen like insect-eating plants, air plants and a 400-year-old bonsai. New additions to the conservatory include the **Cascade Garden** featuring exotic jungle plants and waterfalls and the **Mediterranean Garden** with colorful plants that grow in Mediterranean-like climates around the world.

If winter delights visitors by its contrasts, spring at Longwood Gardens is overwhelming because of the sheer scope, size and variety of flowers on display. If you can visit only once, the best time is April or May when both indoors and outdoors are a riot of color.

Along extended walkways there are rows of flower gardens with spring bulbs. A wisteria-topped arbor is particularly appealing in late spring. The walkway leads to the lake where blossom-laden trees are reflected in the still surface of the water. A romantic gazebo provides a perfect focal point for photographers. A wooded trail flanked by azaleas and rhododendrons skirts the lake.

At the far end of the lake there is a special treat: the **Italian Water Garden**. Designed to resemble the garden at the Villa Gamberaia in Florence, Italy, it has numerous blue-tiled pools, each with enchanting fountains. This wonderland of water is only the beginning of the fountains at Longwood.

In front of the conservatory is the **Main Fountain Garden** where you see dozens of large fountain groups. It is during the summer that this fountain area can be enjoyed to its fullest. On Tuesday, Thursday and Saturday evenings there is an illuminated fountain program. It's well worth staying late to catch a performance, for this aquatic extravaganza delights both young and old. The Terrace Restaurant, an indoor-outdoor eatery, stays open on evenings when performances are scheduled. Other shows are presented at the Open Air Theater, one of the few theaters anywhere to boast a ten-foot-high water curtain. Here, too, there are colored fountains used to great effect during many of the musical concerts.

Roses, wildflowers, vegetables and waterlilies are the seasonal pick of the summer months. There are garden walkways with trellised climbing roses, and many of the beds are planned around the rose bushes. Visual delights are also plentiful in the **Hillside Garden** leading to the Chime Tower. Along the banks of a sparkling waterfall ferns grow in profusion. This is another scenic spot from which to take photographs of Longwood.

A special feature much visited in summer is the **Idea Garden**. Here you will see an array of perennials, annuals, vegetables, herbs and fruits plus vines and ground covers you may want to add to your own yard. Like many of the specimens grown at Longwood these could actually discourage some amateur gardeners because everything at Longwood grows bigger and better. Savoy cabbages are bigger than bowling balls; the conservatory delphiniums which come in a staggering assortment of colors are so tall they dwarf most visitors; and the waterlilies have pads that are the size of large truck tires and can support a hundred pounds.

Many hobbyists get quite green with envy when they see the November conservatory display of giant chrysanthemums. The enormous mums—some as big as dinner plates—appear in massed arrays, cascades, baskets and pillars. Fall is also a good time to catch the last big rose display before frost.

Ending the year is the Christmas conservatory display with thousands of poinsettias. Longwood is bedecked with 200,000 colored lights at this festive time of year. Many families have made a visit to Longwood part of their holiday calendars. Of course, the Topiary Garden, with its whimsical collection of shrub creations, can be enjoyed year-round.

If you want to discover how this lovely garden got started stop in the renovated **Peirce-du Pont House**, where the Heritage Display tells the story of Longwood through historic objects and photos. Longwood's acreage was originally purchased from William Penn in 1700 by a Quaker farmer, George Peirce. (One of the earliest battles of the American Revolution, the Battle of Brandywine, was fought within earshot of this property.) Peirce's grandsons turned the land toward horticultural uses when they planted an arboretum of evergreen trees and called it Peirce's Park. In 1906, Pierre Samuel du Pont purchased the land and began developing formal gardens on his new estate. Today there is still a mixture of natural spots and carefully planned garden areas.

Longwood Gardens is open 9:00 A.M. to 6:00 P.M. daily. It remains open on many evenings for special events. During the winter months it closes at 5:00 P.M. The conservatory opens one hour later than the gardens. Fountain performances are given from June through September. Call ahead for the schedule of special events, (610) 388-6741. Admission is charged; on Tuesdays the adult admission is reduced.

Longwood's Terrace Restaurant has two areas, a self-service cafe and a sit-down full-service area. Reservations are recommended for the dining room area during busy seasons and on evenings when special events are held. Call (610) 388-6771.

Directions: From I-95 south of Philadelphia take Route 322 exit west. Follow Route 322 until it intersects with Route 1 at Concordville. Turn left, south, on Route 1 and continue eight miles to the Longwood Gardens entrance. Longwood is three miles northeast of Kennett Square.

Mercer Mile

Written in Concrete

"See Henry Mercer's Three Concrete Extravaganzas" may sound like a huckster's come-on, but Henry Mercer was no sideshow performer. Mercer was a daringly innovative archeologist, anthropologist, historian and ceramist.

Mercer's explorations of the detritus of other civilizations enabled him to spot the "archeology of recent times." This is what he called the spinning wheels, rope machine and salt boxes he spotted at a junk dealer's yard in the spring of 1897, a find which led to the amassing of 60,000 objects that tell the story of work, play and other aspects of daily life in this country before the age of steam.

Mercer not only felt a mission to salvage these fragments of Americana, he also had the daring to house them in an incredible cement castle far more likely to be seen on some English moor than in Doylestown. Mercer designed and built his castle in 1913 without using an architectural blueprint. Like castles of old, Mercer's monument is cold and damp and, during harsh winter storms, it has been known to rain inside the castle walls. Hollywood could easily film a scary movie among the castle's labyrinth of dark passages, twisting staircases, high-vaulted ceilings and absorbing, all-pervasive clutter. Mercer considered himself a writer in the tradition of Edgar Allen Poe and Ambrose Bierce. You see the influence of the macabre as you wander through the assortment of caskets, hearses and gallows.

Skilled artisans still create decorative tiles at Henry Mercer's 1912 Moravian Pottery and Tile Works.

The mood at the **Mercer Museum** changes radically in "A Child's World" where school and play equipment bring to life childhood pastimes of a bygone era. The candy-making display here is just a small example of kitchen-related artifacts to be explored in detail in the rooms on the second floor.

Tools used for more than 50 crafts can be found in four galleries that extend around a central court where other items hang from the high ceiling or are lashed to the railings. A Conestoga wagon and a whale boat are just two of the pieces from the transportation field. As one visitor remarked, "If you can't see it here, it isn't worth looking for."

Henry Mercer was also fascinated with early American redware pottery. Colonial settlers originally made dishes, or trenchers as they were called, out of wood. Later they were made from gray and red clay. After studying the technique Mercer himself began making decorative red clay tiles.

Never one to do anything on a minor scale, he began a factory in 1912 within the cavernous concrete edifice or "extravaganza" that became the **Moravian Pottery and Tile Works**. At first the decorated tiles Mercer produced were used to enhance his home, Fonthill, but it was not long before he was selling them around the world. The tiles grace such haunts of the rich as a Rockefeller home and the casino at Monte Carlo. Mercer's varied designs number approximately 2,000 and include scenes copied from old-fashioned cast-iron stove plates, as well as Indian and medieval motifs. Prices start at $5.00 per tile and extend to $400. A slide show and lecture introduce visitors to the tile works. After that you can take a self-guided tour through the still-operational factory.

There is yet one more Mercer "extravaganza" to be visited—**Fonthill**. This was Mercer's home and the first of the three concrete structures to be built. It's fun to imagine the comments of the Doylestown citizenry who watched the turreted, balconied and pinnacled Fonthill go up. Working with only his own ideas and no architect's drawings, Mercer hired local unskilled laborers to built his house room by room, improvising as he went along. "Ceilings, floors, roofs, everything concrete," he wrote to a friend in 1909. Continuing, "You stand up a lot of posts—throw rails across them—then grass—then heaps of sand—shaped with groined vaults then lay on a lot of tiles upside down & throw on concrete. When that hardens pull away the props & you think you're in the Borgia room at the Vatican."

One might believe that the museum castle would be sufficient to display Mercer's collection but it wasn't. Mercer's five-storied home has endless nooks and galleries filled with memorabilia, as well as walls of tiles. This collection ranges farther afield than that displayed in the museum. It includes artifacts Mercer gathered on his travels around the world. He seems to have kept everything he ever picked up!

It takes at least a day to cover the three Mercer "extravaganzas" and you'll want to wear comfortable walking shoes. All three sites are open daily 10:00 A.M. to 5:00 P.M.; on Sunday they open at NOON. Admission is charged. Reservations are suggested for Fonthill where guided tours are given on the hour. Call (215) 348-9461. The Mercer sites are closed on Thanksgiving, Christmas and New Year's Day.

Directions: From I-95 in Philadelphia take Route 611 north to Doylestown. For the Mercer Museum turn right off Route 611 on Ashland Street and continue to the intersection with Green Street. For Fonthill continue up Ashland and turn left on Pine Street. Take Pine to East Court Street and turn right. Fonthill is on East Court Street on your right. To reach the Moravian Pottery and Tile Works continue up East Court Street to Route 313, turn left and proceed about one-tenth mile to the parking lot on the left.

Mill Grove

Audubon's Inspiration

Only 20 miles from Philadelphia, you can experience the natural beauty that inspired John James Audubon. As you walk the woodland and meadow trails of Mill Grove, the only surviving Audubon house in America, you appreciate why the 19-year-old Audubon was enchanted with the birds of the New World.

In 1789, Audubon's father, using money he brought out of revolution-torn Santo Domingo in the French West Indies, purchased **Mill Grove** as an investment. Audubon was sent from France to work the small lead mine at Mill Grove. John James was the first family member to see the estate, but once the young nature lover saw the abundant bird and wildlife he neglected the mine, spending his days collecting birds and drawing them.

John James Audubon began painting birds while still in France. Like his contemporaries, he depicted birds in a static profile perched on a twig, but once he observed the birds in Pennsylvania his technique changed. He wanted to fill his drawings with the life and movement he observed around Mill Grove. To achieve this effect, he arranged his specimens into real-life attitudes, then completed the painting in a single session.

The 1762 house on this 170-acre estate sits on a high hill overlooking the Perkiomen Creek. From the wide front porch Audubon watched the birds at the small pond and in the nearby woods. Today the house is a museum displaying all the major works of John James Audubon. Highlights include every major work published by Audubon even the double elephant folio for *The Birds of America, 1826-1838.* Audubon did 435 watercolors for this set!

Audubon's wife Lucy Bakewell, who he met while at Mill Grove, gave him her life savings so that he could get his drawings published. At Mill Grove you'll also see a series of murals on Audubon's life and a collection of personal memorabilia. The attic has been restored to a studio and taxidermy room with stuffed birds and small animals informally displayed as they once may have stood during the two years Audubon worked here.

An immediate sense of Audubon and what he called this "blessed spot" is felt strolling the grounds of Mill Grove. More than 175 species of birds and 400 species of flowering plants have been identified at the **Mill Grove Wildlife Sanctuary**. Each season has its special charm and its unique birds in residence. This is the perfect place to banish such remarks as, "I saw a red bird" or "a blue bird" and replace them with correct identifications. At Mill Grove you can become acquainted with the lively, colorful creatures that were the focus of Audubon's life.

Mill Grove is open at no charge Tuesday through Saturday 10:00 A.M. to 4:00 P.M. On Sunday the house opens at 1:00 P.M. The grounds are open daily 7:00 A.M. to dusk. Both grounds and house are closed on Mondays.

Directions: From I-95 take the Schuylkill Expressway west to the Route 202 exit. Head south on Route 202 towards Paoli. After a short distance on Route 202 watch for the sign to the Betzwood Bridge and take that exit. Follow the County Line Expressway for about $1^3/_4$ miles, then take the exit for Trooper and Route 363 north. This exit will immediately follow the Betzwood Bridge crossing of the Schuylkill River. Take Route 363, which will become Trooper Road, to the first traffic light where you will turn left onto Audubon Road. It dead-ends after a mile in front of the Mill Grove entrance on Pawlings Road.

National Shrine of Our Lady of Czestochowa

Queen of the Polish Crown

In 1953 Father Michael Zembrzuski, a Polish Pauline monk, came to America and purchased a tract of land near Doylestown. Two years later a small wooden barn was converted into a chapel and dedicated to Our Lady of Czestochowa. In 1954 an exact copy of the historic painting that hangs in the Polish shrine was made, blessed in the chapel in Czestochowa and was subsequently blessed by Pope John XXIII. It was then shipped to the United States. After traveling for another four years to Polish parishes around the country it was enshrined in the chapel in Doylestown.

Emotions ran high on both sides of the Atlantic as Poland's millennium approached. The Polish nation was consecrated to the Blessed Mother in 1966 during the celebration of the country's one thousand years of Christianity. The Polish clergy in the United States began a drive to build a large Shrine in Doylestown. On October 16, 1966, Archbishop John Krol and President Lyndon B. Johnson dedicated the **National Shrine of Our Lady of Czestochowa**.

The original painting of Our Lady of Czestochowa is one of the world's oldest renditions of the Blessed Virgin. Science dates the painting back to the 5th or 6th century, while legend claims that it was painted by the Evangelist Saint Luke. This pensive depiction of Mary with sorrowful eyes and clouded brow was reputedly painted on a cypress table-top from Mary and Joseph's house in Nazareth.

The sacred painting traveled from Jerusalem through Constantinople to Poland where it eventually came to rest in 1382 in Czestochowa (Chen-sto-hova). The Polish leader, Ladislaus, invited Hungarian monks from the Order of St. Paul the First Hermit to guard the painting.

In 1430, the Pauline Fathers repulsed a devastating attack by bandits who wanted to seize the painting. During this incident the face of the Blessed Virgin was slashed and, despite attempts to repair the damage, the scars are still visible. The Shrine was attacked again in 1655 when the Swedish army laid siege to Czestochowa. For 40 days the prior of the monastery held off the invasion. This heroic defense inspired the Polish people and the following year, King Jan Casimir, made a vow proclaiming the Mother of God to be the "Queen of the Polish Crown." The Shrine of Jasna Gora (as the cathedral in Czestochowa is called) was designated as the "Mount of Victory" and a spiritual capital for the country. Over the years this has become one of the most visited shrines in the world.

Although both the Polish and American shrines sit on a hilltop, the original is of Gothic design while the American is starkly modern. Above the altar is the copy of the painting, while stained glass panels on the side walls tell the story of Christianity in Poland and the United States. The organ that fills the choir loft is one of the largest in the country.

The vestibule is lined with memorial plaques and commemorative urns. The bronze monument to musical virtuoso Ignacy Paderewski actually encases his heart which was not buried with his body. Other memorials honor Polish war heroes. At the base of the shrine is a 200-foot tower with a chapel where pilgrims can light votive candles. There is also a small chapel dedicated to Our Lady of Fatima. The original barn chapel still stands, surrounded by a cemetery where many of those who worked to see the shrine become a reality are buried. Polish veterans are also buried here.

Pauline monks, many from Poland, still live in the monastery on the grounds. Masses are offered daily in English and a Polish mass is said on Sundays at NOON. For information on masses, novenas and special devotions call (215) 345-0600. Polish and American meals are served in the cafeteria on Sundays and by special arrangement. There is also a well-stocked religious gift shop and book store. Many of the items are handcrafted in Poland.

Directions: From I-76 take Exit 24, the I-276 extension of the Pennsylvania Turnpike. From I-276 take Exit 27, Doylestown-Willow Grove and follow Route 611 North, Easton Road, for 12^1/$_2$ miles going past the Doylestown exit toward Easton. Exit at Route 313, Swamp Road, and make a left going west. Go one mile to the second traffic light and make a left, heading south on Ferry Road. The Shrine is two miles down on your right.

New Hope

Old Treasures

Travel back in time on a mule-drawn barge on the historic Delaware canal or the New Hope and Ivyland Railroad to experience a community that dates back to the colonial era. In the early 1900s a group of internationally-known artists moved to New Hope and opened a series of popular galleries and shops.

The charms of **New Hope** include picturesque 18th-century stone houses, narrow streets and alleys lined with quaint row houses, intriguing courtyards, wooded trails and towpath walks. There is also the opportunity to sample the competing transportation alternatives that vied for supremacy in the late 1800s and early 1900s.

The **New Hope Mule Barge Company** lets you travel back in time more than 150 years and experience life along the canal. The Delaware Canal runs parallel to the Delaware River from Easton to Bristol. Construction started in 1827 and was completed in 1832, but engineering and construction problems kept it from opening for two years. It wasn't fully operational until 1840. By 1862 between 2,500 and 3,000 boats traveled on the Delaware Canal passing through 25 lift locks. The canal is now a national heritage corridor, as well as a Pennsylvania State Park.

Trips run on Wednesday, Saturday and Sundays in April and November at 11:30 A.M., 1:00 P.M., 2:00 P.M., 3:00 P.M. and 4:30 P.M. From May through October trips are daily and a 6:00 P.M. tour is added to the schedule. For current prices call (215) 862-2842.

Even if you don't have time to take a barge ride, be sure to walk along the canal towpath to see the old locks and perhaps photograph one of the barges as it travels the still water. If you book one of the two hour rides on one of the few preserved canals in the country, you will pass Revolutionary cottages, artists workshops and colorful gardens. On many of the trips barge musicians and historians entertain passengers.

Another alternative is a half-hour cruise aboard the *General George Washington* on the Delaware River. The big blue pontoon boat departs from Coryell's Ferry, 22 South Main Street, beginning at NOON daily from April through October. For additional information call (215) 862-2050. Coryell's Ferry is located on the river directly behind Gerenser's Exotic Ice Cream store. They make roughly 45 flavors including such offbeat options as Ukrainian rose petal, Jewish malaga, Magyar apricot brandy, Swedish ollaliberry and Oriental green tea.

The noisier iron horse provides a different experience from the slow, tranquil barge rides. Tickets for the **New Hope & Ivyland Railroad** are purchased at the New Hope Station, on W. Bridge Street, where a small exhibit area evokes the early days of locomotive travel. The New Hope line was built between 1889 and 1890 and gradually supplanted the canal as the major carrier to the region.

On the nine-mile journey, fans of old movies may recognize the curved trestle bridge the train crosses as the one used on the matinee serial "Perils of Pauline." The train ride through the countryside gives you an idea why so many artists make their home here. The train travels to Lahaska and back to New Hope. You won't have time to appreciate all this little community offers so plan to return and enjoy the noteworthy collection of shops at Peddler's Village and Carousel World (see selection).

Trains run daily from April through November and on weekends January through March. During December there are Santa rides. Call (215) 862-2332 for updated hours and fares.

Be sure to save some time to browse through the unusual craft and antique shops in New Hope. It's easy to spend hours exploring the hundreds of shops along the tree-lined streets and tucked-away alleys. If you find yourself wishing you could tour the inside of one of the lovely old homes, head over to the 1784 **Parry Mansion** on Cannon Square. Tours of this Museum of Decorative Arts (1775-1900) are given by the New Hope Historical Society, May through October on Friday, Saturday and Sunday from 1:00 P.M. to 5:00 P.M. Admission is charged.

Pick up a schedule for the **Bucks County Playhouse**, located in an old gristmill along the banks of the Delaware River. Celebrity guest artists star in musicals and dramas from the past as well as recent Broadway hits. Call (215) 862-2041 for additional information.

Directions: From I-95 north of Philadelphia take Exit 31, Route 32, the New Hope/Yardley exit. Route 32 becomes Main Street in New Hope.

Pearl S. Buck House

Her Good Earth

In *My Several Worlds* Pearl Buck wrote, "I decided on a region where the landscapes were varied, where farm and industry lived side by side, where sea was near at hand, mountains not far away, and city and countryside were not enemies." It was her Bucks County home she was describing, but it could easily have been the "good earth" of China where she spent her early years.

Throughout her life, Pearl Buck served as a bridge between East and West. The two worlds meet at **Green Hills Farm**, her Pennsylvania home. Pearl Buck and her second husband, publisher Richard Walsh, purchased this 1835 farmhouse with its dependencies and 48 acres during the Depression for $4,100. Pearl Buck legally adopted seven children and cared for many more either at her farm or through her foundation for needy children. In addition, while at Green Hills she found time to write more than 100 novels, children's books and non-fictional work.

A tour of this National Historic Landmark begins in the over-sized kitchen of the rambling old house. The kitchen was added by Miss Buck to accommodate her large brood. Like so much of the house, it is a blend of the old and the new. Modern appliances share space with a Franklin stove, and the large table was the desk her husband used when he was at John Day Publishing Company.

The original kitchen is now the dining room. Miss Buck liked the childproof brick floors because she didn't need to worry about children's spills. The antique Pembroke table that Miss Buck used for morning and midday meals is perfectly at home amid the Chinese porcelains, paintings and pewter that adorn the room.

Four rooms were combined to form the expansive living room and entrance way. The elements that made this farmhouse so appealing to Miss Buck—the stone walls and sturdy wood—are much in evidence in this striking living area. The huge stone fireplace and hand-hewn ceiling beams are balanced, not in size but in eye-appeal, by the artistic treasures of the East. On the console table you'll see the small figure of a 500-year old Buddha. Another treasure is the Tibetan embroidered wall hanging that was a gift from the Dalai Lama.

From the living room the tour goes upstairs to Miss Buck's bedroom which has not one but two fireplaces. In an anteroom, that has become known as the **Treasure Room**, glass cases hold the carved sea-green porcelains, rare fans, inlaid chests and brilliant silk ceremonial robes she collected in China.

In the main library downstairs is the box-like desk Miss Buck used in China when she wrote *The Good Earth*, her Pulitzer Prize winning novel. The Chinese wooden chair looks more decorative than comfortable; its unyielding lines were "good for discipline," according to Miss Buck. Both the library and the adjacent reading room are filled with books. Guides say that no one, not even Miss Buck, was permitted to take books out of the reading room.

Pearl Buck did not use the library as her office, but worked in the attached cottage added in 1938 along with a country kitchen. Here you'll see the typewriter desks she used during 38 prolific years of writing at the farm, as well as some of her sculptures. She sculpted and painted in the cottage loft.

Pearl Buck died at Green Hills on March 6, 1973. Her humanitarian work lives on here through the Pearl S. Buck Foundation. The offices of the headquarters are located on the property. Amerasian children in six Asian countries are supported in keeping with the work Miss Buck began when she founded Welcome House in 1949.

Guided tours are given from March through December on Tuesday through Saturday at 10:30 A.M., 1:30 P.M. and 2:30 P.M. Sunday tours are only in the afternoon. The house is closed on Mondays and major holidays. Admission is charged. For additional information call (215) 249-0100.

Directions: From I-676 in downtown Philadelphia, pick up Broad Street, Route 611, north to Doylestown Bypass. Exit at Dublin. Turn left to Route 313. Continue on Route 313 to the second traffic light in the center of Dublin. Turn left at the light onto Maple Avenue. This changes to Dublin Road after leaving the borough limits. Green Hills Farm is one mile from the intersection on the right.

Peddler's Village, Carousel World and Point Pleasant

Bucks County Bonanza

Peddler's Village is more than a shopping paradise, although with 70 specialty shops it certainly is that. Holiday gifts, presents for hard-to-please recipients and irresistible finds abound at these unique shops. There are no chain stores; here items are personally selected and amazingly eclectic.

The village is the realization of Earl Jamison's dream of creating a community like the one he enjoyed in Carmel, California. In the early 1960s, Jamison, whose family owned a tavern in this area in 1752, purchased a plot of land at the intersection of two Bucks County roads. Jamison converted the chicken barn and coops on his property into the first shops. He went on to create a beautifully landscaped 18th-century village, complete with an old water wheel, gazebo and delightful flower gardens. He moved a 19th-century frame house to the heart of the village and used historic materials in the new buildings.

Even after the shops close, visitors enjoy strolling the village's picturesque paths, often stopping for a meal at one of **Peddler's Village**'s eight restaurants. Jenny's offers classic continental cuisine, while traditional American country fare is served at the Cock 'n Bull. Every Monday night during the winter, Colonial open-hearth cooking is demonstrated and a Colonial menu served in a setting filled with period furniture and Pennsylvania folk art. Downstairs, Peddler's Pub offers soups, hearty sandwiches and brews. Light meals are also served in Hart's Tavern, The Spotted Hog and The Village Cafe. A number of other small eateries are scattered around the village. Several spots have musical entertainment Thursday, Friday and Saturday nights and during Sunday brunch.

The Village's Golden Plough Inn is a well-situated spot from which to explore Bucks County. Its 60 individually decorated guest rooms, many with gas-lit fireplaces and jacuzzis, provide uncommonly fine accommodations. In addition to rooms in the 150-year-old former Buttonwood Inn which Jamison transformed into the Golden Plough Inn, delightful hideaways are available above the shops at various locations around the Village, including the newer section where **Carousel World** is located.

The gift shop, working carousel and **Museum of Carousel Art** delight young and old. The glittering white and gold antique Grand Dentzel Carousel was created in Philadelphia in 1926 and is one of only 60 in the country. It's staggering to realize that each of the 55 wooden animals, representing three major styles and done by eight master carvers, is estimated to be worth between $10,000 and $50,000.

You'll discover more about the three styles of carousel art in the museum at Carousel World. Philadelphia style features realistic, classic carvings that provide an elegant and accurate representation without gems and excess. The Country fair style was done by less significant carvers but exposed thousands of Americans to carousels. Finally, Coney Island style reflected American competitiveness, with flashy decorative touches like gems, sequins and even blinking lights. Coney Island had 24 carousels in its heyday.

The collection was amassed by Carlotte Dinger, who began with the acquisition of a primitive wooden horse, circa 1850. She found her first carousel horse in a Philadelphia antique shop in 1972 and became an instant collector. Her next purchase was 20 more carousel figures. Eventually she amassed one of the world's largest collections and wrote a book on carousels. Together she and Earl Jamison opened this museum complex in 1993.

Horses, the most common carousel animal, were captured in three stances: jumper, prancer and stander. In addition to the various style horses, the museum has a wide range of other carved animals including one of the heaviest ever carved, the 300-pound Looff teddy bear done in 1880. The museum also has a 23-foot-long miniature circus. Visitors are welcomed by the automated clown used to greet ticket-holders to Broadway's "Barnum." There is a fare for the merry-go-round and the museum but would-be collectors can enjoy the gift shop without charge.

One additional shop in the Village also has a museum. The **Heritage Collectors' Museum** has exhibits and sells an amazing array of autographs ranging in price from $15 to over $5,000.

The shops at Peddler's Village are open 10:00 A.M. to 5:30 P.M. Monday through Thursday. On Friday the shops stay open until 9:00 P.M. On Saturday they are open until 6:00 P.M. December through March. The rest of the year shops stay open until 9:00 P.M. on Saturday. Sunday hours are 11:00 A.M. to 5:30 P.M. From mid-November to December 23 village shops stay open until 9:00 P.M. (except Sunday). They are closed on Thanksgiving, Christmas and New Year's Day.

Peddler's Village is well-known for its special events, many now family traditions. That is certainly true of the mid-July Teddy Bear's Picnic, the mid-September through October Scarecrow contest, the mid-November to January Gingerbread House Competition and the Christmas Festival. Call for details (215) 794-4000. For accommodations call the Golden Plough Inn, (215) 794-4004.

Just north of Peddler's Village in **Point Pleasant** is the major base for those interested in riding the Delaware under their own power. Point Pleasant Canoe & Tube outfitters rent canoes, rafts or tubes for the trip downhill. The Delaware has a series of small rapids, but not enough to worry even the faint of heart, just enough to provide an element of excitement. You can even arrange a Pedal and Paddle rate, for a bicycle trip back up the river. The outfitter is open daily from April to October but advance reservations are a must; call (215) 297-8181.

The area around Point Pleasant is quite scenic, be sure to drive through the charming community of Lumberville. Here you'll find a number of bed & breakfasts along the river. For details call the Bucks County Tourist Commission, (215) 345-4552.

Directions: From I-76, take I-276 (Pennsylvania Turnpike Eastbound) to Exit 27, Willow Grove/Doylestown. Take Route 611 north to Doylestown. Follow signs for Route 202 north. Continue on Route 202 until it merges at the intersection with Route 263. Make a left; Peddler's Village is approximately $1^1/_2$ miles ahead, where Routes 202 and 263 split. For Point Pleasant, veer left off of Route 202 before Lahaska, onto Route 413, then make a right on Point Pleasant Pike.

Pennsbury Manor

Hands-On History

Somehow when you read the history books you get the idea that William Penn, proprietor of the Pennsylvania colony, seeking to oversee his great social experiment personally, settled permanently in his domain in the New World. This is far from accurate, although it may have been close to Penn's original intentions.

Instead, Penn returned to England after only two years in his colony, intending to return promptly and bring his family with him. He went back in response to a threat to his land claims, which were based on a charter he received from King Charles II in 1681. From England, William Penn sent regular letters detailing his instructions for his house, gardens and grounds to James Harrison, his steward.

Penn's estate was 26 miles north of Philadelphia on 8,400 acres of land. Although he held title to the land through his land grant from the British king, Penn also acknowledged the rights of the indigenous population. He purchased his land from the native Lenape Indians.

William Penn returned to Pennsylvania in 1699 and in the following spring moved with his second wife to his completed country estate **Pennsbury Manor**. Their son, John, had just been born in Philadelphia. Their stay was to be brief, for after only two years financial problems forced them back to England, this time for good. By the end of his life Penn was in debtor's prison. He considered selling Pennsylvania back to the crown, but his wife wouldn't let him; she wanted it for her children.

Pennsbury Manor had fallen into disrepair and ruin by the time of the American Revolution. By the 20th century no trace of Pennsbury survived above ground. In 1932, ten acres encompassing the ground on which the main house once stood were given to the state by the Charles Warner Company as a memorial to William Penn. A major restoration program restored the Manor House, plantation outbuildings and the landscape to its appearance when William Penn was in residence.

You may notice that the furniture is not like that in the restored homes of Independence National Historical Park. Here the furniture is of an earlier era—the style of Charles II and William and Mary reigns. Some of the pieces were made a hundred years before the American Revolution. Pennsbury Manor has the largest collection of 17th-century furnishings exhibited in the state. The collection reflects the breeding and wealth of the Penn family. Although he was a Quaker, Penn had a taste for gracious living. He never adopted the simple lifestyle typical of most members of his sect.

William Penn's letters to his steward also detailed his plans for the gardens. Skilled gardeners were sent to Pennsbury from England and Scotland. During his first visit to Pennsylvania, 1682 to 1684, Penn wrote to England requesting "a few fruit trees of . . . . Lord Sunderland's . . . . rare collection." Tradition holds that when Penn returned he brought with him 18 rose plants from London. Penn also instructed his gardener to obtain native flowers. The kitchen garden grew large quantities of common vegetables plus specialty crops like artichokes, asparagus and between 10 to 20 types of greens. A wide variety of herbs were also grown for culinary, medicinal and cosmetic purposes. The garden also included apples, plums, pears, cherries, grapes, quince, apricots and a wide variety of berries. The garden today is considerably smaller than it was in Penn's day but it does reflect its style and substance and contains only historically authentic plants. The farm animals are also historically accurate.

Penn's concerns extended to the outbuildings, or dependencies. Today you will see 21 buildings including the icehouse, stone stable, smokehouse, plantation office, wood house and bake and brew house. Historically garbed guides conduct tours of the 43-acre historic site and explain the functions of the buildings. Don't miss the **boathouse** which contains a replica of the barge Penn used for the five hour trip back and forth to Philadelphia.

Pennsbury Manor is open Tuesday through Saturday from 9:00 A.M. to 5:00 P.M.; on Sundays it opens at NOON. Tours take approximately $1^1/_2$ hours. Admission is charged. An audiovisual program in the Visitor Center provides background on this historic property. From April through October on Sunday afternoons from 1:00 P.M. to 4:00 P.M. there are living history programs for families. In the activity room visitors can try writing with a quill pen, carding wool and playing a variety of 17th-century games like ball and cock and drop spindle.

Directions: From I-76, the Pennsylvania Turnpike take Exit 29 to Route 13 north. Then make a right onto Green Lane at the first traffic light. When you reach a dead end make a left onto Radcliffe Street and continue for 4.6 miles (the road changes names twice, becoming Main Street and then Bordentown Road). Make a right onto Pennsbury Memorial Road which leads into the parking lot for Pennsbury Manor.

Peter Wentz Farmstead and Morgan Log House

Everything Old is New Again

Did you ever stop to think that when you visit most historic sites you see the past through the patina of time? The quilt colors are faded, the upholstery frayed, the rugs well-trod and the furniture chipped and worn. This is not the case at the **Peter Wentz Farmstead**; the exception demonstrates how much of the original we do lose over the years. Nothing has aged or dimmed at this colonial farm. Its motto is "As it Was."

A slide presentation at the Reception Center takes you back to the year 1777, thus establishing the correct mood for your tour. The ambience is enhanced by the period dress worn by the guides. You'll quickly discern the difference this approach makes. The main house has shutters so sparkling they appear to be newly painted. Far from having mellowed with age, everything has a crisp brightness. The colors used here are not the subtle Williamsburg shades so popular in our modern colonial-style homes. In fact, the colors and manner of painting on the walls at this farmstead astound visitors. Knowing that visitors wonder whether the bright stripes, spots, diagonals and squiggles are original, the restorers carefully left a small portion untouched as proof that what you see is "As It Was."

What exactly will you see? In the parlor, downstairs hall and upstairs bedroom the wall below the chair rail is painted bright red with a white dots. In the upstairs bedroom this design is fur-

135

ther embellished by the addition of white diamond stripes with commas in the center of each diamond. The wall below the chair rail in the master bedroom is white with black dots, a design also found on an entire wall in the winter kitchen.

It was decided to restore the farmstead to the way it was in 1777 because that was the year the Peter Wentz house had its brush with history. On two occasions, George Washington, who made it a practice whenever possible to avail himself of the hospitality of the grandest home in the area, stayed at this farm. This distinction was fully appreciated and the rooms used by the General have remained structurally intact through the years. One of the rooms has been furnished as **Washington's office**; one of the upstairs chambers served as his bedroom.

Another room at the farm, the winter kitchen, is also closely associated with Washington's visits. The story is told that Washington's fellow officers so feared for their leader's life that his cook was seldom permitted to leave the kitchen. To prevent poisoning, the cook protected the food supplies served to the General both day and night.

The food preparation areas reflect Peter Wentz's German heritage. The dining room has a traditional five-plate heating stove. The tile roof on the beehive bake oven was also a reminder of his native land. The farmstead has a **German kitchen garden**, laid out with a crossed path that forms four raised beds. There are over 100 different seasonal herbs, vegetables and flowers serving a variety of purposes: culinary, medicinal, olfactory and aesthetic. Demonstration crops in the fields and an orchard complete the picture of a prosperous 18th-century farm.

There is an active crafts program on Saturday afternoons that supports the farmstead's goal of keeping the past alive. Costumed volunteers using authentic tools and old-time techniques demonstrate a wide variety of colonial crafts. On a given weekend you'll see such unusual crafts as scherenschnitte (scissor cutting), theorem painting, broom making or fraktur painting. More common crafts include spinning, quilting, weaving, candle making, basketry, carving, block painting and cooking demonstrations using the hearth and beehive oven. For information on craft programs call (215) 584-5104.

The farmstead, considered by the Pennsylvania Travel Industry Advisory Council to be one of the top ten tourist attractions in the state, is open year-round. Hours are Tuesday through Saturday from 10:00 A.M. to 4:00 P.M. On Sunday it opens at 1:00 P.M. The farm is closed Mondays, Thanksgiving and Christmas. In December there are candlelight tours of the house. There is no admission charged, but donations are encouraged with the proceeds going to the furnishing fund.

Just a few blocks from the Wentz Farmstead is an even older

homestead. The **Morgan Log House**, dating back to 1695, was built by Welsh Quaker Edward Morgan, the only surviving son of Sir James Morgan, Fourth and last Baronet of Llantarnum Abbey in Wales.

This splendid example of early architecture is over 90 percent intact. The exterior dressed horizontal logs are chinked with stones laid in a diagonal pattern. All of the paneling and five of the eight interior doors are original. The house is now restored and furnished with period pieces from the Philadelphia Museum of Art and the Deitrich Brothers Collection in addtion to its own collection.

While touring the log house, imagine the Morgans living here with their ten children. Three of the boys inherited 200 acres of the property prior to their marriages. Subsequently, two of the sons left the homestead and moved to Winchester, Virginia. It was here that Joseph and Elizabeth Lloyd Morgan raised their family. Their son Daniel became a Brigadier General in the Revolutionary Army. Their youngest daughter, Sarah Morgan married Squire Boone. They were the parents of Daniel Boone. Other notable Americans are descended from the Morgan family. The Morgan Log House is open April through November on weekends from NOON to 5:00 P.M. It opens year-round by appointment, call (215) 368-2480.

Directions: Take I-76, the Pennsylvania Turnpike NE Extension to the Lansdale exit. Travel east on Sumneytown Pike to Route 363, Valley Forge Road, and make a left. From Valley Forge Road turn left on Route 73 east to the entrance for the Peter Wentz Farmstead. For the Morgan Log House from Valley Forge Road turn left at the sign for the historic property at Snyder Road. Continue several blocks and turn right on Weikel Road. The Morgan Log House is two blocks down on your left.

Pottsgrove Manor

Simply Beautiful

When John Potts, wealthy Pennsylvania ironmaster and founder of Pottstown, completed his early **Georgian-style stone mansion** in the 1750s, it was so spacious and attractive that it drew visitors from as far away as Philadelphia. This 18th-century architectural gem still draws visitors who appreciate its well-preserved condition. The house went through a painstaking restoration, right down to the original paint colors, hardware and furnishings.

Potts built as modern and fine a house as his great wealth allowed. However, in keeping with his Quaker background, "simple and plain" defines the beautiful interior woodwork and finely- made furnishings, mostly of the Queen Anne and Chippendale styles. These are not original to the house but are of the period, matching items listed on Potts's probate inventory.

Your visit begins in the 19th-century kitchen, now a reception room where a slide presentation is given. You then pass through the colonial revival garden and enter the expansive hall where guests were once received. Your tour includes the family's living and working spaces, the newly-discovered slave quarters, John Potts's office and the exhibit areas.

After touring the house, stop by the **museum shop** to browse through the extensive collection of period books and handcrafted reproductions. You can also stroll around the garden, grounds and stop to see the root cellar.

Pottsgrove Manor is open without charge Tuesday through Saturday from 10:00 A.M. to 4:00 P.M. On Sunday it opens at 1:00 P.M. Last tour begins at 3:30 P.M. The house is closed on major holidays. For details on special tours, lectures and events call (610) 326-4014.

Directions: From the I-76 Expressway, west of Philadelphia, exit on Bypass Route 422 west to Pottstown. Exit at Route 100 north; sign will indicate Allentown and Pottstown Business District. Cross over the Schuylkill River and turn right at the first traffic light onto King Street. Pottsgrove Manor is at W. King Street and Route 100, directly across from the Ramada Inn.

Sesame Place

Furry Friends Await in the Neighborhood

If young children were polled, **Sesame Place** would undoubtedly rank as one of their top outings. The "Sesame Street" play park is designed for families with 3 to 15 year-olds, with more enthusiasm generally evinced by the youngest members. The ideal time to make a stop here is while your youngster is still an avid fan of the PBS program because all the familiar characters are on hand—Big Bird, Bert and Ernie, Grover, Cookie Monster, Prairie Dawn, the Count, Elmo, the Honkers and others.

Characters stroll the street of the world's only full-size outdoor replica of the storefronts and building facades seen on the popular television show. Kids become part of a special effects video adventure in the Sesame Studio: dancing on bright lights to play musical tunes, making shadows appear and disappear

At Sesame Place, fans young and old can meet their favorite characters on the only full-sized outdoor replica of the Sesame Street television studio.

and turning their own hand-drawn images into a motion picture. Science exhibits in the studio get children involved with color, motion, sound and light. They generate electricity by pedaling a bicycle.

The slightly more than nine-acre park has more than 50 kid-powered outdoor play activities. Hundreds of yards of cargo netting, connected by 200 feet of suspended net tunnels, create an exciting crawl space. Thousands of colorful plastic balls on a trampoline surface lets kids jump for joy. There's even a huge vinyl cone for youngsters to scale. **Twiddlebug Land**, based on the tiny creatures that live in Bert and Ernie's window flower box, is filled with oversize items designed to shrink visitors to the size of these Lilliputian beings. A 14-foot watering can sprinkles toddlers in a small pool while a seven-foot nozzle on a garden hose squirts tots cavorting in a wave pool.

To call Sesame Place a water park is too limiting, but for many visitors the main appeal is the water rides. **Sesame Island** is surrounded by a winding 1,000 foot inner-tube ride popular with parents and children. There's also a water maze with interactive fountains, water jets and wading areas. Elsewhere there are water flumes and chutes that end in splash pools. These are immensely popular on hot summer days. Bathing suits are required for all water activities.

The park offers daily entertainment ranging from an exotic bird show to Big Bird's Musical Revue. Visitors can get involved in the Sesame Production Company's "Wild Duckie Chase" which gives youngsters a chance to join their furry pals in looking for Ernie's rubber duckie. Visitor's images are mixed with a prerecorded video and appear on the television monitor. The Sesame Players also involve guests in acting out fairy tales and in lively skits. During the summer months there is the Amazing Alphabet Parade as well as special events, programs and concerts. Restaurants and shops are located throughout the park.

Sesame Place opens for weekends in May and by mid-May is open daily 10:00 A.M. to 5:00 P.M. Starting Memorial Day weekend the park stays open until 7:00 P.M. on weekends and by mid-June the later hours extend to weekdays. From about the last weekend in June through August, the park opens from 9:00 A.M. until 8:00 P.M. After Labor Day, the park closes earlier and is open weekends only. For the current schedule call (215) 752-7070. Admission to Sesame Place for a family of four will likely be close to a hundred dollars by the time you park and enjoy a snack. Children under two are free. Call for up-to-date prices.

Directions: From I-95 take the Morrisville Exit 29A/Route 1 North. Continue on Route 1 for just a short distance to the exit for Oxford Valley Road. Sesame Place entrance is on the right at the second traffic light.

Valley Forge National Historical Park

Winter of Their Discontent

A family excursion to Valley Forge National Historical Park provides a splendid opportunity to instill a sense of pride in our
country's past. The story of the bitter winter the young army
spent here in 1777-1778 is a stirring saga of courage, patriotism,
honor and dedication. Exploring this recreated encampment
brings alive the victory at **Valley Forge**.

This victory was not won in battle. At Valley Forge the enemies were starvation, disease and the uncompromising elements.
The road to Valley Forge began in August 1777 when the British
under General Howe landed at the upper end of the Chesapeake
Bay and headed north toward the patriot capital at Philadelphia.
Washington failed to halt the British advance at Brandywine in
September, and again at Germantown in October. With winter
setting in, the British established themselves in Philadelphia and
the Continental Army was forced to seek the cold comfort of Valley Forge 18 miles to the west.

To understand what happened during the six months the army
stayed at Valley Forge, begin at the Visitor Center with the 15-
minute audiovisual program. There are four ways you can explore the park. From mid-April through October you can join a
bus tour that departs from the Visitor Center. The bus's taped
narrative makes this a good way to get an indepth look at the
2,788-acre park. You can spend as much time as you like at the
various stops because you can always catch the next bus. A fee
is charged for these tours. Another option is to rent an audio
tape and drive yourself. Thirdly, if you just want an overview,
use the park map and drive through on your own, stopping to
read the roadside markers at the ten park stops.

A final option is to bring your bicycle and explore the park
along the six-mile cycling trail. The bike trail starts at the Visitor Center and passes all the major points of interest. There are
shorter footpaths for those who enjoy hiking and many miles of
horseback trails. You can enjoy an al fresco meal at any of the
park's picnic areas: Varnum's, Wayne's Woods and Betzwood.

The area near General Varnum's Quarters is the **Grand Parade**
grounds where General von Steuben, formerly of the general staff
of Frederick the Great of Prussia, transformed the ragtag Continental Army into an effective fighting force. One of the major
problems the army faced prior to Valley Forge was the lack of a
standard training manual. Although soldiers did have minimal
training it was from a variety of field manuals. Thus, coordinated battle movements were all but impossible to achieve.

Living history at Muhlenberg Brigade brings to life George Washington's 1777–1778 military encampment at Valley Forge.

PHOTO BY SALLY MOORE

Benjamin Franklin sent Baron von Steuben from Paris with his personal recommendation to see if he could be of assistance to the Continental Army. Franklin's idea proved to be invaluable, since within six months the Baron produced a well-trained army. Von Steuben's work was all the more remarkable when seen against the formidable obstacles he overcame: he spoke little English, the men were weary from long marches and unsuccessful campaigns; they were poorly fed and inadequately clothed and housed. At one point there were 4,000 men listed as unfit for duty. Baron von Steuben labored day and night to overcome these obstacles, and part of the victory at Valley Forge can be attributed to his perseverance and skill.

If you visit during the summer months, you will see authentically clad soldiers demonstrating various aspects of military life at the Muhlenberg Brigade. Visitors should plan to spend some time at the **Isaac Potts House**, used by General Washington as his headquarters. This fieldstone building has been restored to look as it did when Washington was in residence. At the Visitor Center there is a field tent used by Washington when he first arrived at Valley Forge and chose to share the rough field conditions his soldiers were experiencing.

In addition to the redoubts, reconstructed fortifications, artillery park and other officers' quarters there are two privately operated sites within this park. The first is the **Washington Memorial Chapel** which tells the story of the founding of our country in 13 stained-glass windows. During the summer, tours are conducted of the chapel and bell tower. The chapel's carillon was purchased in 1926 with money collected from the original 13 states. The second site, next to the chapel, is the **Valley Forge Historical Society Museum** with a fine collection of Revolutionary memorabilia. A nominal admission fee is charged.

Valley Forge is a marvelous spot to visit at any time of year. You might want to plan your first visit for the summer months when living history reenactments bring the camp dramatically to life. But a winter's visit captures the real spirit of Valley Forge. You will appreciate the army's accomplishments more fully on a bitter cold day when there is snow on the ground and a stiff wind blowing across the elevated plain. On President's Day weekend, there are hundreds of young Boy Scouts camping "under the same circumstances" as the Revolutionary soldiers. Spring is a delight because the park's 1,000 pink and white dogwood trees are in bloom and in the fall the bright foliage adds color. The park is open year-round from 9:00 A.M. to 5:00 P.M., except on Christmas Day.

Headquartered in Valley Forge in a park-like setting near the National Historical Park is **Freedoms Foundation**. The mood is set before you even arrive. A good distance from the entrance you can see the American flag made especially for the Foundation. Its bold red and white stripes extend for 60 feet. Also larger than life is the nine-foot bronze statue of a kneeling George Washington looking out over Valley Forge.

The Foundation has an **Independence Garden** designed around bricks and stones from the homes of all 56 signers of the Declaration of Independence. Although 12 signers had their homes burned to the ground, five signers were captured and imprisoned and nine gave their lives, not one signer defected to the British cause. It seems highly appropriate that the non-denominational chapel nearby is called Faith of Our Fathers Chapel. It has a stained-glass window duplicating the one in the chapel of the Capitol in Washington, D.C.

The exhibits in the Henry Knox Building honor the 3,414 recipients of the nation's highest military decoration, the Medal of Honor. A 52-acre Medal of Honor grove provides an contemplative natural setting.

The Freedoms Foundation at Valley Forge is open by appointment only and a nominal admission is charged. To make reservations to tour call (215) 933-8825 or write Freedoms Foundation at Valley Forge, Valley Forge, PA 19481.

Directions: Take the Schuylkill Expressway, I-76, west to Exit 24, the Valley Forge exit. Take Route 202 south to Route 422 west, then exit on the Route 23 west exit. Follow Route 23 west through the park and through Valley Forge Village. Freedoms Foundation is on your right at the top of the hill.

Washington Crossing Historic Park and Bowman's Hill Wildflower Preserve

A Christmas to Remember

Washington crossed the Delaware in defeat. His men were beaten in battle, their clothes were in tatters and their stomachs were empty. Nobody—certainly not the celebrating Hessians—thought they would recross the ice-clogged river. The Hessian commander, Colonel Rall, was so confident and so disdainful of the ragtag Continental force that he didn't even read an intelligence report about Washington's imminent attack. Rall's arrogance cost him his life and his men the battle.

You can retrace the tumultuous events of December 25, 1776, when you visit **Washington Crossing Historic Park**. At the Visitor Center and Memorial Building, the best place to start your visit, you'll see a 30-minute movie on the historic events that occurred here. The Memorial Building has a copy of the huge painting by Emanuel Leutz of Washington Crossing the Delaware.

As you discover when you visit the Durham Boat House and see the cargo boats used to transport the 2,400 men who finally made it across the river, the famous painting probably erred in the depiction of the boat. Although all types of boats were used, it is doubtful that Washington crossed in a boat like the one shown in the painting. Additionally, Washington's standing pose, although typical of the artistic style of the 1840s, is unlikely to have been assumed during the hazardous crossing complicated by a blinding snowstorm and virtually iced-over water.

Within the park you see the house from which Washington planned his unexpected about face, and the inn where he took Christmas dinner before his heroic crossing. The **Thompson-Neely House**, whose oldest stone section was constructed in 1702, was used by Washington's staff for conferences. They met in the kitchen as it was the warmest room in the house. Guides dressed in 18th-century garb answer questions about the period furniture and the colonial artifacts on display in the building. Before leaving this section of the park, be sure to visit the grist-mill. During the summer months it is open for guided tours.

Authenically garbed guides escort visitors through McKonkey Ferry Inn, or Old Ferry Inn as it is also called, where Washington ate his Christmas dinner. A novel way to spend Christmas day, is to visit the park for the annual reenactment of the crossing. On the weekend of George Washington's birthday, hot gingerbread is served at the Thompson-Neely House.

In the upper section of the park, commanding the hilltop from which sentries once kept watch, is the Bowman's Hill Tower. An extensive renovation program made it possible to reopen the tower. Beneath this frequently photographed tower is the 100-acre wildflower preserve dedicated to the brave Revolutionary soldiers serving under Washington who once camped here.

There are 26 trails and habitat areas in **Bowman's Hill Wildflower Preserve**. The best time to visit is April and May, but during the summer months the field flowers are also colorful. Each season has its own appeal. A self-guiding trail map and a monthly blooming list is available at the Wildflower Preserve headquarters. The garden outside this building displays plants suitable for backyard gardens in this part of the state. Altogether there are more than 1,000 different kinds of native trees, shrubs, vines and wildflowers preserved in the park. There is a pond for flowering aquatic plants and a bog for those requiring a swampy terrain.

Washington Crossing Historic Park is open Monday through Saturday from 9:00 A.M. to 5:00 P.M. On Sunday it opens at NOON. There is a nominal admission fee for some of the historic buildings.

Directions: From I-95 north of Philadelphia take the Yardley Interchange. Signs will direct you north on Route 532 to Route 32. Washington Crossing Historic Park is located on both sides of Route 32.

Wharton Esherick Studio

Visionary Artist

Wharton Esherick, a native Philadelphian, studied art at the Philadelphia Museum School of Industrial Art and the Pennsylvania Academy of Fine Arts. In 1913 he left the city, finding his artistic vision better inspired by the countryside around his stone farmhouse near Paoli.

The wooded hills proved to be a source of material as well as inspiration. It was here Esherick had what he called his "conversation with wood." In 1929 he began carving decorative wooden frames for his paintings. Esherick next worked on woodcuts and then wooden sculpture. His innovative pieces gained him a reputation in the front ranks of modern American sculptors.

Esherick was not satisfied with art for its own sake but sought to make it part of life's practical side by designing sculptured furniture and furnishings. This aspect of his work received its first national/international exposure at the 1940 New York World's Fair when he was asked to design a room. Esherick's room, called "A Pennsylvania Hill House," was designed around the furnishings Esherick had available in his studio. The room's most prominent feature was the studio's oak spiral stair. The flowing lines were also picked up in **Esherick's five-sided table**. This room is now recreated at the studio, although some pieces are missing and others are not in the same arrangement as in the America at Home pavilion.

Esherick worked for 40 years building and decorating his studio. Every aspect reflects his attention: the wooden coat pegs are carved as caricatures of the workmen who helped him build this visionary place.

Wharton Esherick died in May, 1970, but his studio still retains the look of a working environment. On display are more than 200 examples of his paintings, prints, woodcuts, sculpture, furniture and utensils. There are no signs and no museum-like displays.

Because of the size of the studio, reservations are needed for the one-hour guided tour of this National Historic Landmark site. Tours are given March through December from 10:00 A.M. to 5:00 P.M. on Saturdays and from 1:00 P.M. to 5:00 P.M. on Sundays. Admission is charged. Call (610) 644-5822 or write The Wharton Esherick Studio, Box 595, Paoli, PA 19301.

Directions: From I-76, the Pennsylvania Turnpike, take Exit 24, the Valley Forge exit. Take the first right after the tollbooth onto Route 23 west. Take Route 23 west through Valley Forge Park. Turn left at the light onto Route 252 south. Go one mile, then turn right and go through the covered bridge. Continue 2.5 miles. Before overpass, turn right onto Diamond Rock Road (Octagonal School House at intersection). At the top of the hill, turn right onto Horseshoe Trail. The Wharton Esherick Studio driveway is $1/10$ th mile on the right.

Woodmont

Religious Retreat

Woodmont, a 32-room French Gothic mansion, is located on a 73-acre estate in Gladwyne on the Philadelphia Main Line. The house sits on the highest point in Montgomery County and overlooks the bend in the Schuylkill River and the town of Conshohocken.

William Price designed this chateau of granite shist and limestone with a multi-spired roof of Spanish tile for Alan Wood, Jr. who founded a local steel company. Three years after **Woodmont** was finished in 1892 at a cost of one million dollars, Wood sold it to his nephew, Richard Wood. The next owner, J. Hector McNeal, a corporation lawyer and noted horseman, modernized the house when he acquired it in 1929.

Mrs. McNeal was an admirer of Father Divine and his Peace Mission Movement and wanted the estate to belong to his mission church. At her death in 1952, the estate was purchased by the Palace Mission Church for $75,000. A year of extensive labor restored the chateau to its former opulence, so that it was once again "one of the most magnificent estates in Pennsylvania."

Free tours of the house are given by enthusiastic and ardent followers of Father Divine. His widow, Mother Divine, still lives at Woodmont and greets many guests on Sundays during open house. Visitors are expected to come modestly and appropriately dressed; this excludes shorts for both men and women.

It is absolutely fascinating to tour the first floor of this three-story manor house. Craftsmen from Italy did the interior and exterior wood and stone carvings. Massive bronze doors lead from the vestibule into the aptly named great hall. The 45-foot high ceiling has flying buttresses, and the dovetail wedges under the gallery are in matching oak. Limestone for the massive stone fireplace was imported from Caen, France.

The dining room is an outstanding feature of this Victorian home. The McNeals completely refurbished it by importing the interior of Pope Innocence II's chapel from Avignon, France. The oak panelled walls with niches display various figurines of the saints. The mantel of the fireplace resembles an organ front. The massive carved-oak table, chairs and servers enhance the room. They are the only furniture remaining from the McNeal residency.

The grounds of Woodmont are landscaped with a maze of formal and terraced gardens, rock and wildflower gardens, orchards and vegetable gardens. The swimming pool makes an attractive focal point on the sweeping front greensward. Father Divine is buried in a mausoleum adjacent to the manor house. Its great bronze door is noted for its beauty.

Woodmont is open Sundays from 1:00 P.M. to 5:00 P.M. Guides give free tours April through October.

Directions: From I-76, the Pennsylvania Turnpike, take I-276 the Philadelphia Expressway and exit at Route 23 east, Conshohocken State Road. Turn left at the traffic light at Spring Mill Road, continue on this to Woodmont Road, which is opposite the Philadelphia Country Club. At the bottom of the hill, turn right through double iron gates on to the estate.

147

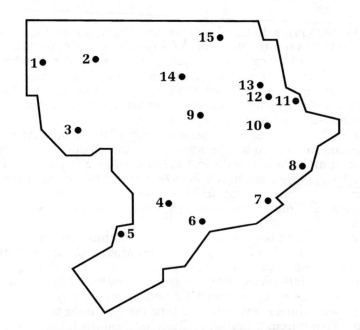

POCONO MOUNTAINS REGION

1. **Troy**
   Bradford County Heritage
   Museum

2. **Towanda**
   French Azilum

3. **Eagles Mere**
   Eagles Mere and Ricketts
   Glen State Park

4. **Weatherly**
   Eckley Miners' Village

5. **Ashland**
   Ashland's Pioneer Tunnel
   Coal Mine and Steam
   Lokie

6. **Jim Thorpe/Lehighton**
   Jim Thorpe and Asa Packer
   Mansion
   Mauch Chunk Lake Park and
   Lehigh Gorge State Park
   Pocono Museum Unlimited

7. **Stroudsburg**
   Quiet Valley Living Historical Farm

8. **Bushkill**
   Bushkill Falls
   Delaware Water Gap Na-
   tional Recreation Area

9. **Scranton**
   Houdini Museum
   Pennsylvania Anthracite
   Museum and Lackawanna
   Coal Mine Tour
   Steamtown National Historic
   Site

10. **Hawley**
    Lake Wallenpaupack

11. **Lackawaxen**
    Zane Grey Museum and
    Roebling's Delaware
    Aqueduct

12. **White Mills**
    Dorflinger Glass Museum
    and Dorflinger-Suydam
    Wildlife Sanctuary

13. **Honesdale**
    Stourbridge Lion and Stour-
    bridge Rail Excursions

14. **Nicholson**
    Nicholson Bridge

15. **Starrucca**
    Starrucca Viaduct

Pocono Mountains
Region

T he nation's industrial heritage and the state's premier recreational area are found in the Poconos. The somber story revealed at the Pennsylvania Anthracite Heritage Museum really hits home when you go down into the Lackawanna Coal Mine or Ashland's Pioneer Tunnel Coal Mine. To complete the picture, Eckley Miners' Village provides an authentic look at the daily life of miners who worked the region's hard coal.

Transportation was crucial to the region's industrial development. The railroad story is presented at Steamtown National Historic Site on the site of an old railroad yard. Trains are once again running on the old tracks, rekindling the romance of the rails. For a glimpse of railroad magnate Asa Packer's opulent home, visit the town of Jim Thorpe. The mansion overlooks this quaint Victorian community, once second only to Niagara Falls as the most popular tourist destination in the country. It is a delightful discovery.

Hiking, biking and whitewater activity can be enjoyed in abundance in the area around Jim Thorpe and in the rest of the Pocono Mountains. Pennsylvania's section of the Appalachian Trail winds through the scenic splendor of the Delaware Water Gap. There is quiet water at Lake Wallenpaupack and dramatic tumbling water at Bushkill Falls. A walk through Ricketts Glen State Park in the region's Endless Mountains takes hikers past 25 waterfalls. In this mountain area, Eagles Mere is another popular resort from the Victorian era.

One of the most intriguing stories in the state is told at French Azilum. Few Pennsylvanians realize that a community of aristocrats, who fled the slaughter following the French Revolution, settled along the Susquehanna River miles from civilization.

This is a region with four seasons of outdoor fun. Sports options span the calendar with top-notch winter skiing and exciting summertime whitewater rafting. From spring through autumn there is horseback riding, canoeing, hiking and mountain biking.

Ashland's Pioneer Tunnel Coal Mine and Steam Lokie

Cold Coal Mining Blues

At its peak in the late 1800s and early 1900s the Pioneer Tunnel in Ashland produced 400 tons of coal a day. Small cars carried the miners deep into the bowels of the earth, into the damp, chill depths of the anthracite coal mines in Mahanoy Mountain. On most mornings, the miners entered the inky depths before sunup and spent the day in a dim, carbide-lit tunnel hacking away at the deeply embedded coal, as much as 500 feet below the surface.

What was once a tedious, dangerous ordeal is now a fascinating experience, thanks to a group of public-spirited volunteers in Ashland who reopened **Pioneer Tunnel**. Their efforts give you an in-depth look at a real mine. The volunteers timbered up the entire mine, including the first 100 to 200 feet that caved in when the mine was dynamited shut in 1931. Like the early miners, you are taken into the mine on old mine cars, with guides who were themselves experienced miners. There is no need for safety concerns as the mine is inspected daily. Even when in operation, the mine had an excellent safety record, since no miner ever died in Pioneer Tunnel.

Once inside, you'll walk down the gangways, or tunnels. The guides explain what was involved in mining coal in this adit mine. Adit means that the tunnel was driven into the rock horizontally at right angles to the coal seam. You'll be able to peer down lighted shafts that lead from one level to the next more than 200 feet below. With a little imagination you can picture the miners, each carrying 250 pounds of gear, struggling along the steep inclines.

The tour takes about 35 minutes. As you leave the cold depths, the guides turn off the lights for just a minute so that you can experience the inky blackness of the subterranean shafts. The temperature stays at about 50 degrees year-round, so be sure to bring a sweater or jacket.

After your trip down into the mine you can board a **steam lokie** for another kind of ride. The lokie is an old-fashioned narrow-gauge, steam locomotive called the Henry Clay that once hauled coal cars. It takes you on a 30-minute, three-quarter-mile trip along Mahanoy Mountain and the site of an old strip mine. Mammoth Vein was an immensely thick vein of anthracite coal that pushed its way to the earth's surface. The coal was simply scooped up by huge steam shovels. The 250-foot-high wall of solid rock left by the strip mining extends to the west as far as

150

you can see. It gives mute testimony to the harmful effects of strip mining.

There is yet another example of mining you'll see on your train ride. Mahanoy Mountain also has its "bootleg" coal hole. During the Depression, men defied the dangers and the law to obtain coal to heat their homes or to sell for much needed cash. From the highest point on your ride, you have a panoramic view of Ashland, which looks like a toy town at the foot of the mountain.

Ashland's Pioneer Tunnel Coal Mine and Steam Lokie is open daily from Memorial Day through Labor Day, 10:00 A.M. to 6:00 P.M. It is open weekends only May, September and October. Admission is charged. There is a picnic area and playground equipment adjacent to the tunnel. The offices at Pioneer Tunnel are patterned after a colliery office. There is a snack bar and gift shop which sells interesting items made of anthracite coal.

While in the area you should also stop at the **Museum of Anthracite Mining at Ashland**, 17th and Pine streets. Photographs, models, graphics and actual equipment show how coal was located and extracted and give a glimpse of the miner's way of life. The museum is open Tuesday through Saturday from 9:00 A.M. to 5:00 P.M. and Sundays from NOON to 6:00 P.M.

Directions: From I-76, the Pennsylvania Turnpike, take the Reading exit, I-276 north. From Reading continue north on Route 61 to Ashland; the tunnel will be on your left. You can also reach Route 61 via I-81 or I-78. From I-80 take I-81 south and follow above directions.

Bradford County Heritage Museum

History, Hardware and Hardwood

Wilmer Wilcox's hobby reveals Bradford County's past. Wilcox, a Canton dairy farmer, started collecting farm tools and equipment around 1950. His goal was to memorialize the life of area farmers with memorabilia representing their work, homes, businesses and leisure activities.

In 1990, the **Bradford County Heritage Association** was formed to establish a home for Wilcox's collection at Alparon Park in Troy. Volunteers built the museum and local residents added their own antique items to the museum's collection. Since the museum opened in 1992, the community support has been so enthusiastic, that in less than two years the museum's size is being doubled to showcase additional large farm equipment.

In the main exhibit hall large pieces of farm equipment fill the center of the room, while along the wall there are six additional room areas. The bedroom area has a rope bed, cradle and dresses from bygone eras such as the 1894 wedding dress and the 1923 prom dress. Utensils in the kitchen reveal that each chore had its own tool. There is a cast-iron pot scrubber, apple peeler, butter churn, pie safe and pots and pans. Various shops are exhibited on a rotating basis: a fully equipped carpenter's, tinsmith's and blacksmith's shop, a doctor's office and an old store. One room contains a wealth of memorabilia on the Grange, a brotherhood of farmers.

Tools hang on the walls and from the ceilings, while other collections fill standing cases. There are model tractors and equipment, ladies' assessories, an array of China shaving mugs and old bottles.

The museum is open mid-April through October on Friday, Saturday and Sunday from 10:00 A.M. to 4:00 P.M. It is also open on Memorial Day, July 4 and Labor Day. Admission is charged. In late April a Maple Festival is celebrated and the museum sells maple syrup throughout the year. The Troy Fair is held every July and the museum is open daily during fair week.

Handcrafted items are plentiful at the local fair, but one craft item you can buy year-round is handmade, hardwood baskets from **Bradford Basket Company**, a short distance up the road from the museum. The outlet store is in the greenhouse on the left immediately past the wood store. When you visit you can watch the baskets being made in the shop. During the half-hour tour you'll also see logs sliced. The maple wood baskets are made in 23 styles with trim in seven colors. The shop is open Monday through Saturday 9:00 A.M. to 4:00 P.M. To order by phone call (800) 231-9972.

If you want to fill your basket and enjoy a picnic, head to the nearby **Mt. Pisgah State Park** in the Endless Mountain region. The 1,302-acre park extends along Mill Creek at the base of the 2,260 foot Mt. Pisgah. There is a network of trails in the park. The Nature Trail is a short mile-long trail on the shore of Stephen Foster Lake (named in honor of this former local resident). Watch for beaver dams and muskrat lodges as you hike along the lake. You may also spot wood ducks, mallards and hawks. The fairly level two-mile Oh! Susanna Trail also winds around the southern shore of the lake. The two-mile Ridge Trail is only for the hearty because, though it starts out level, it has some steep sections and is a strenuous workout. The lake is popular with fishermen and boaters, and boat rentals are available in the summer. There is a pool for swimming, a playground and picnic area. Winter sports include snowmobiling, ice skating, cross country skiing and ice fishing.

Directions: From I-81 take Route 6 west to Troy, turn north on

Route 14 for less than a mile and you will see the museum in the park on your left. For Mt. Pisgah State Park, head east on Route 6 and turn left on Steam Hollow Road. Head north for two miles to the park.

Bushkill Falls

The Niagara of Pennsylvania

Older generations generally resist innovative suggestions of the young. So it was when fourth-generation Charles E. Peters recommended to his elders that they charge visitors admission to see the waterfalls on the family property in the Pocono Mountains. His older relatives doubted that anyone "would pay to see a waterfall," but nevertheless gave him a grudging go-ahead.

Charles fixed up the trail, built a shelter and fashioned a bridge over the falls to high ground. When he opened his "Niagara of Pennsylvania" to tourists, he charged an admission of ten cents. That was more than 90 years ago. Admission is still being charged and appreciative crowds are still coming.

Billed originally as "A Delightful One-Day Auto Trip," **Bushkill Falls** is that and more: 300 acres of mountain scenery, eight waterfalls and several trails. The falls are on two streams. Little Bushkill Creek originates in the Pocono Mountains highlands of Pike County. Pond Run rises in the lakes owned by Unity Resort and tumbles down three of the falls before joining Little Bushkill Creek just beyond the Lower Gorge. The longest trail is two miles and takes two hours to hike, but it gives you a chance to see each of the distinctly different falls. The series of three Bridal Veil Falls can only be seen on this hike.

Most visitors choose the 45-to 60-minute hike. Along this walk there is a view of both the top and bottom of the main falls and the Lower Gorge Falls, Laurel Glen Falls and the Upper Gorge Falls. A short detour off this trail affords a look at Pennell Falls. If you are in a hurry, or are not up to a long climb, you can take a 15-minute walk to the main falls. At 100 feet this is the most spectacular of the eight falls at Bushkill. From the top of the first falls to the bottom of the lower gorge is a drop of about 300 feet.

Either before or after your hike, take the time to explore the wildlife exhibit featuring 80 mounted birds and animals native to Pennsylvania and the Pocono Mountains. If you stop at the exhibit before your hike, the displays will identify the wildlife you may encounter: red squirrels, chipmunks, snowshoe rabbits, muskrats, woodchucks and beavers.

Picnic tables are available and there is a snack shop. Even if you pack a lunch, consider indulging in dessert at the old-fashioned ice cream parlor. Craft shops, miniature golf, fishing and paddleboats provide additional diversions if you want to make a day of it. If you plan to hike be sure to wear comfortable walking shoes. Bushkill Falls is open April through November from 9:00 A.M. to dusk.

Directions: Bushkill Falls is off I-80 at Exit 52. Take Route 209 north to Bushkill. You can also take the Pennsylvania Turnpike Northeast Extension from the Philadelphia area and proceed north to Exit 33, Route 22. Take Route 22 east, then Route 33 north and connect with I-80 east.

Delaware Water Gap Trolley and National Recreation Area

Delight at the End of the Line

Delaware Water Gap was once the end of the line for resort-going Philadelphians who traveled by trolley to this vacation spot in the Pocono Mountains. The ride took almost ten hours and required six transfers—now you get on the trolley after you arrive.

Trolley tours cover the scenic and historic high points of the lower portion of the **Delaware Water Gap National Recreation Area**. You ride beside the steep, stony Delaware River to the town of Delaware Water Gap in what was, during the 1800s, the third largest resort area in the country.

When the European settlers entered this area, they encountered the Shawnee Indians. Indian relics and artifacts have been recovered by archeological teams working along the river. Today, however, the name Shawnee is more closely associated with a resort offering year-round sports in a Victorian atmosphere.

Many well-known entertainment figures have been frequent guests at Shawnee. You'll hear about them on your trolley trip which boards at the depot on Route 611 in the center of the town of Delaware Water Gap. Older visitors will remember band leader Fred Waring; he lived here from 1940 until his death in late 1984. Waring did his broadcasts from the local playhouse, as did old-time radio favorites Fibber McGee and Molly. The trolley passes Waring's workshop from which he published music. Jackie Gleason came to Shawnee years before he made Ralph Kramdon a familiar figure in homes across the U.S. "Diamond" Jim Brady built the Castle Inn for the famous dancer of the 1920s, Irene Castle. A later generation may be nonplussed by such dated trivia, but they perk up when the home of Captain Kangaroo's sidekick, Mr. Greenjeans, is pointed out.

154

Scenic Silver Thread Falls is just one of the attractions in the Delaware Water Gap Natural Recreation Area.

History goes back much farther as the trolley passes through the lower portion of the Delaware Water Gap National Recreation Area. There are still remnants of the original home of Louis Depue, the first white settler in this part of Pennsylvania. Later in the colonial period, Benjamin Franklin commandeered a home at Shawnee to use as a base from which to subdue the local Indians. The stable for this early fort serves as the gatehouse at Fred Waring's house.

Nature lovers get a good bit of geological lore. The trolley stops at the Point of the Gap where you can clearly see how the Kittatinny Ridge developed from a great upfold in the earth's crust. Over millions of years the water cut a gap through the rocky ridge leaving tilted layers visible on the rocky surface. This ridge at Point of the Gap was once 20,000-feet high. The tail end of the giant Wisconsin glacier came down through the Delaware Water Gap.

The Delaware Water Gap can also be explored on the miles of hiking trails and by water. There are canoe launching sites within the recreation area. A bit farther north but still within the area is **Dingmans Falls**. You can see two waterfalls on an easy half-mile hiking trail. The Visitor Center has an audio-visual program and exhibits on the natural world of the Pocono Mountains. The center is open from late April through the end of October.

One other area of interest within the park is the century-old **Millbrook Village**. This is not simply a town that has been restored, but rather a representative look at American life in this mountainous area in the mid-1800s. Old homes, from rustic log cabins to comfortable farmhouses, are complemented by commercial concerns: a general store, gristmill, blacksmith shop and shoemaker's shop. There is also a school, church and cemetery to help draw you into the past.

The roughly one-hour-long **Delaware Water Gap Trolley** runs on the half-hour beginning at 9:30 A.M. and continues throughout the day. There are also twilight tours at 6:00 P.M. and 7:00 P.M. Even on warm days you may need a sweater or jacket in late afternoon because it gets cool in the tree-shrouded gorge. A fare is charged. For additional information call (717) 476-0010.

Directions: From the Pennsylvania Turnpike Northeast Extension take Exit 33, Route 22 east. From Route 22 pick up Route 33 north to I-80 east. Take I-80 to Exit 53. From the exit continue straight into the town of Delaware Water Gap. At the light you'll see the Water Gap Trolley depot. It is about an hour farther to the Dingmans Falls area. Return to I-80 west and continue to Exit 52. Follow Route 209 north to Dingmans Falls. At the blinking light in the town of Dingmans Ferry turn left and follow the signs.

Dorflinger Glass Museum and Dorflinger-Suydam Wildlife Sanctuary

Glass Class

The reasons for visiting **Dorflinger Glass Museum** are crystal clear. First, items in the collection are works of art. Second, you will learn how to discern high quality glass. Third, there is an exciting array of contemporary glass items for sale in the museum shop. Finally, the natural setting is striking.

Christian Dorflinger's immigrant success story epitomizes the American Dream. At age ten, he was apprenticed to his uncle in the Alsace region of France. There he learned the fundamentals of glassmaking. When his widowed mother brought him and his four siblings to the United States, Dorflinger obtained a job in a glass factory in New Jersey. While working there Dorflinger designed a glass chimney for oil-burning lamps. He soon realized its marketing potential and opened his own factory in Brooklyn. In less than 17 years, at the age of 35, he had built an industrial complex of three factories. The effort required to achieve this success left him in poor health and Dorflinger sold two of his plants, placed the third in his brother's hands and retired to a farmhouse in White Mills.

A summer at this bucolic farm was a tonic that restored his health. Dorflinger's renewed energy prompted him to clear some of his land and establish a glass factory and cutting shop. By the early 1900s Dorflinger employed 650 workers, not only creating his own distinctive pieces but also making blanks, high-quality uncut glass, for cutting shops throughout the United States.

The Dorflinger name was an indication of the highest quality glass. Dorflinger glass was purchased and used by such distinguished people as Queen Victoria, the Prince of Wales, the Vanderbilts, Goulds and customers of Tiffany's and Gorham's. Dorflinger tableware was used by eight American presidents from Lincoln to Wilson. The White Mills factory was affected by wartime shortages of essential ingredients, a decline in the demand for cut glass and the coming of Prohibition which further decreased demand for wine and table service pieces. After Christian Dorflinger's death in 1915, his sons continued the business for four years before closing the factory in 1919.

The Dorflinger Glass Museum is the only museum is the country dealing exclusively with cut glass. It has the largest collection of Dorflinger glass on display in the country. Most of the 600 pieces displayed were cut, engraved, etched, gilded, enameled or colored at White Mills, but a few items date to the New York years.

Dorflinger glass is recognized by its quality—it has a high lead content that causes it to refract light—and by its shapes and patterns. There are no identifying marks on the glass—they originally had tiny paper labels. Factory records, catalogs and pattern books detail the various glass pieces produced at White Mills.

The natural light streaming in the museum's windows is reflected off the gleaming glass making the hollow diamond pattern glitter as much as the gemstone. One of the museum's most historic commissions was cut in 1861, in the Brooklyn Factory, for Mary Todd Lincoln. She ordered a $1,500 set of glasses while refurbishing the White House. An array of styles is represented including the single-etched flower in the Kalana line, the Art Nouveau pieces and the glowing colors of the Venetian Reproductions line.

Although the museum gift shop does not sell any Dorflinger glass, it does have an extensive array of artistic glass objects: vases, paperweights, ornaments, window hangings, jewelry and bibelots. Books on collectible glass are also sold. An adjoining room has changing art exhibits. The Dorflinger Glass Museum is open from mid-May through October Wednesday through Saturday from 10:00 A.M. to 4:00 P.M. On Sunday it opens at 1:00 P.M. Admission is charged.

The museum is in Christian Dorflinger's 19th-century farmhouse. The surrounding 600 acres make up **Dorflinger-Suydam Wildlife Sanctuary**. The sanctuary was established by Dorothy Grant Suydam, the widow of Christian's grandson Frederick Dorflinger Suydam. There are almost six miles of interlocking trails meandering through the fields and forest. A half-mile trail circles the six-acre lake and a self-guiding trail map identifies the flora and fauna. Bird watchers should bring binoculars as the area is a haven for bluebirds, bobolinks, finches, swallows and many other species.

From late June through August you can enjoy the Wildflower Art and Music Festival. There are Saturday concerts at 6:00 P.M. in the Wildflower Theater. It's BYOC (that's bring your own chair) or blanket, so you can comfortably listen to the music al fresco. Patrons also enjoy bringing a picnic supper on concert days. For information or tickets to the festival call (717) 253-1185.

Directions: From I-84 take Exit 8, the Blooming Grove Exit, and head east on Route 402. At the intersection with Route 6 turn left and head west through Hawley. Halfway between Hawley and Honesdale on Route 6, you'll enter White Mills. At the village's only blinking yellow light, turn right onto Elizabeth Street and go up a steep hill for .6 mile to the stop sign. Continue through the intersection and go .10 mile to the sanctuary entrance.

Eagles Mere and Ricketts Glen State Park

Soaring Success

Eagles Mere Lake has, for nearly a century, been a vacation mecca for harried city dwellers from Philadelphia, New York, Baltimore, Washington, D.C. and elsewhere. This is an old-fashioned resort that has no glitzy rides or frenetic boardwalk. The pleasures here are quieter: birdwatching, fishing and wading in the comfortable 70-to-80 degree water. Bear in mind though that there is no public beach along the lake; access is through the shore-side rental cottages and inns. Laurel Path winds around the crystal-clear mountaintop lake. A network of trails leads into the mountains where there are waterfalls, streams and spectacular vistas.

The village of **Eagles Mere** reflects the Victorian era with gaslights, quaint shops and a community green. The shops themselves were built at the turn-of-the-century and their owners carefully retain their old world charm. There are specialty shops and antique galleries. The Village Shoppes are open weekends only January through June and September through December; during July and August they are open Wednesday through Sunday. Throughout the year there are arts and crafts festivals and antique show as well as musical performances, theatrical events and slide lectures; call (717) 525-3503 for the schedule.

While you can find waterfalls in the Eagles Mere area they are not as numerous or as striking as those in **Ricketts Glen State Park**, one of the most scenic spots in the state. There are 22 named waterfalls in the park. In the Glens Natural Area, a Registered National Natural Landmark, a series of trails parallels the two branches of Kitchen Creek with ten falls on the stream flowing through Ganoga Glen and eight on the branch through Glen Leigh. The 94-foot Ganoga Falls is the highest but each has its unique appeal. The half-mile Evergreen Trail provides a good vantage point from which to see the final series of falls after the two branches merge at Waters Meet then flow through the heavily forested Ricketts Glen. The towering trees are over 500 years-old; rings on fallen trees indicate that some reach back over 900 years.

This is just one section of the 13,050-acre park. In all there are 20 miles of hiking trails, which are also used for cross-country skiing in the winter, and a five-mile network of bridle trails. Boating (there is a boat rental concession), fishing and swimming are available at Lake Jean. Roughly 9,000 acres of the park is open for hunting and adjacent state game lands are to the west and north. Within the park there are 120 tent and trailer campsites, plus ten family cabins. Call (717) 477-5675 for information on Ricketts Glen State Park.

Directions: From I-80 take Exit 34, Route 42 north to Eagles Mere. For Ricketts Glen State Park from I-80 take Exit 35, Route 487 north to Red Rock, then head east on Route 118. Parking for the Evergreen Trail is directly off Route 118. For the Lake Jean portion of the park continue north on Route 487, (the road is quite steep) to the park entrance.

Eckley Miners' Village

Picture Perfect Evocation of the Past

Several Pennsylvania coal mines take visitors down into their inky depths (see Lackawanna Coal Mine Tour and Tour Ed Mine selections). But that is only part of the story. For the rest of the story, visit **Eckley Miners' Village**. Here in the heart of the anthracite region, surrounded by black-silt ponds and strip-mining pits, is an authentic "patch town" settled in 1853. Some houses are still occupied by retired miners, miners' widows and children.

Arthur H. Lewis in his *Lament of the Molly Maguires* described these towns: "A patch was a cluster of a few dozen company houses along a crooked, unpaved street, built within the shadow of a towering colliery." Eckley's turn-of-the-century appearance prompted Hollywood producers to shoot the Sean Connery movie "The Molly Maguires" on location at this Pennsylvania site in 1968. The few elements that were missing were rebuilt by Paramount. When Eckley was operational there were several breakers in the village. None survived, so Paramount added a large coal breaker. The house exteriors were restored to their 19th-century look. They were painted red because in 1853 that was the cheapest color paint. Imitation siding was added to duplicate the original and overhead wires were run beneath the ground. The film company spent three million dollars in the area.

At the conclusion of the filming, the Hazleton Chamber of Commerce bought the town from the Huss Coal Company. In 1971, they donated it to the Pennsylvania Historical and Museum Commission, it is now a National Register District. Eckley Miners' Village is much the same as it was in the 1870s. It's approximately the same size, with 58 buildings on 150 acres. Only a few homes on Main Street were taken down and almost all the structures that remain are original. After the turn-of-the-century Eckley, like other patch towns, declined because of the switch to strip mining that required fewer laborers. Eckley is the only patch town in the state preserved in its original condition.

The Visitor Center has a 15-minute video on the history of the region's coal industry with special attention to the activity at Eckley. At its peak in the late 1870s, Eckley had 1500 people living here; almost all were immigrants. In the video you hear the voices of miners. They speak of "leaving the light behind" and "the dark maze" in which they earned their living. They also noted that they "could, by our own carelessness, bring our work down upon us."

Exhibits in the Visitor Center provide the first glimpse of the worker's home life. Sunday was the day of rest, but most miners and their families walked three miles to church. The guided tour takes you into the Catholic Church of the Immaculate Conception built in 1861. Today only the altar is original to the interior church. The other elements, looking more like the 1920s than pre-Civil War, were obtained from various churches in the region. But all are typical of a patch town church.

The original founders of the village were all Protestants. St. James Episcopal Church, completed in 1859, was moved to the village from White Haven. It is of the same period as the church it replaced, and one of two Protestant churches in Eckley. The houses nearest this church were those of the mine managers. At the very end of the street, off by itself in a clump of trees, is mine owner Richard Sharpe's Gothic Revival house.

The tenant houses on the back street are in blocks of two houses each. These double dwellings had three rooms, two bedrooms and a kitchen. These were for the lowest level of laborers. On Main Street (now the sole-surviving street) the double house had four rooms. Behind each house was a small garden area where families could grow vegetables. A **demonstration miner's garden** is planted each spring. Only the mine managers had single family dwellings. Unmarried men boarded in the crowded family houses of fellow immigrants.

The houses changed as the village became established. To their basic house, miners added a summer kitchen, then a shed and sometimes a passageway connecting the house with the kitchen. On the inside, the walls changed from board-and-batten to a newspaper-and-calendar covering. Eventually the walls were painted. The floor covering improved as well—from a bare floor, to burlap bags, rag rugs, linoleum and finally actual rugs.

When you take a guided tour you can go in one of the double houses. One side is set up to suggest the 1870s while the other shows the same family 20 years later. The first side reflects the economic conditions of the immigrants who spent all their money just to get to America. There was little left to furnish their new home. The miners even had to purchase their own tools, including the dynamite they used to extract the coal. Although they mined coal, their stoves were wood-burning so they could cut their own fuel. Otherwise they had to buy coal. The bedrooms had trundle beds and the children frequently slept on the floor on bags filled with straw. The family often ate in shifts, with the wife arising at 4:00 A.M. to fix breakfast for her husband before he began his shift, usually at 6:00 A.M.

Twenty years later the walls are painted and hung with framed religious pictures. There are gaslights, a sewing machine, real chairs, dishes and plates and a coalburning stove. There are also glass windows and a better quality furnishings. Behind this portion of the house is a summer kitchen.

The village also has a **company store** that now serves as a museum as well as a gift shop. Workers could easily get in debt at the company store by paying in scrip. This made it difficult for them to move from one job to another. Along Main Street you'll also see the Eckley Social and Sports Club, added in the 1940s. The mine owners did not allow the sale of alcohol at Eckley Village, but they did not forbid the consumption of it. More than one householder grew grapes in his garden and made wine; others distilled liquor in their home stills. There is also a **doctor's office** with exhibits on medicine used in these company towns. The workers paid 50 to 75 cents a month to the doctor, who did not charge by the visit. The medical exhibits include surgical tools, an 1860 amputation kit, an operating table, medical kit, books and photographs.

Eckley Miners' Village is open Monday through Saturday 9:00 A.M. to 5:00 P.M. and Sunday NOON to 5:00 P.M. Closed holidays except Memorial Day, July 4th and Labor Day. Admission is charged. Guided tours are given daily in the summer months and on weekends in late spring and early fall. Call for schedule, (717) 636-2070 or 2071.

Directions: From I-76, the Pennsylvania Turnpike, take the Northeast Extension to Exit 35 (Poconos). Get on I-80 west. From I-80 traveling west, take Exit 40 (White Haven). Turn left onto Route 940 west. Continue for approximately 6 miles to Freeland. Turn left at Mike Stower's Coal and Oil Company and go three miles to Eckley Miners' Village (this road has no route number or name, but there is a sign for Eckley). If you are traveling east on I-80 take Exit 39 (Hazleton). Turn right onto Route 309 south. Follow this to the first traffic light. Turn left at the light and go up a mountain, straight through Freeland, past the Ford Dealer to Mike Stower's Coal & Oil. Turn right and go 3 miles to Eckley. If you are heading north on Route 81, take Exit 41 (West Hazleton). Follow signs to Route 93 south. Follow Route 93 past the Penn State campus to the Hazleton Beltway. The Forest Hill Inn is on your left at this intersection. Turn left at the light onto Hazleton Beltway. Follow this road to the first traffic light. Turn right onto Route 309 south. Proceed approximately 1 mile to the first traffic light. Turn left at McDonalds to Route 940. Follow

Route 940 for approximately 5 miles. Look for directional sign; the road to Eckley bears to the right. Follow for approximately 2 miles to the end. At the T, turn right, go one mile to Eckley.

French Azilum

Quasi-Aristocratic French Court in Exile

One of the most remarkable stories in all of Pennsylvania is told at **French Azilum**. Few realize before visiting this historic site that in 1793 French aristocrats fleeing the excesses of the Reign of Terror settled along the Susquehanna River. Legend has it that they built a home for Marie Antoinette and her two children, not knowing until a year passed that these tragic figures had failed to make good their escape.

Azilum, meant a place of refuge, and that was what these citizens sought. Those fleeing the upheaval in post-revolutionary France were joined by others escaping the slave uprising in the French colony of Santo Domingo (Haiti). Lafayette's brother-in-law, General Louis de Noallies, was instrumental in promoting this plan. He offered the refugees hospitality at his home in Philadelphia while they arranged transportation to Azilum.

The American promoters were Robert Morris, financier for the colonies during the American Revolution; Stephen Girard, banker and wealthy Philadelphia merchant; and John Nicholson, Comptroller General of Pennsylvania. While sympathetic to the plight of the French, these businessmen also saw an economic opportunity. They purchased a 2,400-acre tract covering the whole valley. Three hundred acres on a horseshoe bend of the meandering Susquehanna River were laid out in a town plot. The plan included a two-acre market square, and 413 half-acre lots which were sold to the French settlers. By the spring of 1784 there were approximately 50 rough-hewn log cabins.

You can't help wondering what the noblemen and titled ladies from Paris were thinking as they traveled the overland trail from Philadelphia to Wilkes Barre, then poled their way up the Susquehanna on Durham boats or in dugout canoes to their new home. The group's leader was Antoine Omer Talon, Chief Justice of the criminal court of France under Louis XVI and head of the royal secret service.

The approximately 250 refugees remained in this isolated setting for ten years. During that time Azilum was expanded under the supervision of Aristide Dupetit-Thouars (for whom the town of Dushore is named). A school, chapel, gristmill, shops, inns and a distillery were added. Although the two-story log cabins were crude, many of the refugees made additions to lend a touch of beauty to their spartan existence. Some cabins were wallpapered, others had glass windows, shutters and porches.

One residence stood out from the rest. **La Grande Maison** was reputedly built for Queen Marie Antoinette. This two-story log house was 84-feet long and 60-feet wide with small-paned windows and eight fireplaces. Talon, who oversaw the building of this house, lived in it for several years. The refugees also entertained Talleyrand and Louis Philippe (who later became king) in this wilderness showplace.

Economic reversals signaled the demise of this colony. The American founders Morris and Nicholson went bankrupt. Money that had been funneling in from French sources also dried up. By the late 1790s, settlers began leaving for more temperate climates. Many had feared to expose themselves to scrutiny from agents of the revolutionary government who, for years after the revolution, hunted the fleeing aristocrats. The republicans wanted to eradicate the French noble class, including the children, so the aristocracy could never be re-established. But after nearly a decade, many emigres felt it was safe to relocate in such southern cities as Charleston, Savannah and New Orleans. Some even returned to Santo Domingo and France after Napoleon promised amnesty. Only a few families stayed in Pennsylvania and even they eventually moved from Azilum, helping to found other communities. Not one structure built by the French refugees remains.

Several rustic cabins have been moved to the site to give visitors an idea of what it was once like. There are also traces of the old road. The millrace and millstone can still be seen on one of the former land plots. The spring that supplied water for "La Grande Maison" still flows. But despite the loss of the original buildings, you can get a sense of what it was once like. When you look across the empty expanses toward the river, the view is much the same as it was for the lonely exiles. The sense of the frontier is not lost because civilization does not intrude on this out-of-the-way site.

When you visit Azilum you will see the **LaPorte House** built in 1836 by John LaPorte, son of one of the colony's founders. The house reveals its French heritage in the delicately painted ceilings and interior decor such as the hand-stenciling in the gold parlor. Victorian furnishings fill the room.

French Azilum is open Wednesday through Sunday during the summer months from 11:00 A.M. to 4:30 P.M. It is open on weekends in May, September and October, through the second weekend. The last tour is given at 4:00 P.M. Admission includes an hourly guided tour of the LaPorte. Be at the front door five minutes before the hour. You are welcome to wander the Azilum site. Several of the reconstructed log cabins have exhibits on the

French colony, including artifacts uncovered during archeological digs. Other cabins are used for blacksmithing, weaving and dying demonstrations. There is a nature trail along the river. For additional information call (717) 265-3376.

If you continue east on Route 6 past the turn for French Azilum you will come to a cliff-side overlook on what was once the old Sullivan Trail. A bronze marker at the Marie Antoinette Lookout, with a view of the broad plain on which the colony was located, tells the story of French Azilum. There are several turnouts overlooking the Susquehanna River. The **Wyalusing Rocks Lookout** is particularly picturesque with rocky outcroppings jutting from the cliff. Native Americans following the Warrior Path, a centuries-old Indian highway linking the Six Nations tribes in New York with the Catawba in the Carolinas, stopped at these rocks.

Continuing on into town you can stop for a meal or even stay overnight at the delightful Victorian **Wyalusing Hotel** (111 Main Street). The hotel opened in 1860 and was built by J. Morgan Brown, called the "Gingerbread Man" for the profusion of delicately cut wood and intricate facades on the houses he designed. For what was originally called the Brown Hotel, he outdid himself adding Mississippi Riverboat porches and scores of decorative touches. Call (717) 746-1204 for additional information.

Directions: From I-80 take I-180 north toward Williamsport, then pick up Route 220 north to Towanda. From Towanda take Route 6 east. Make a right turn on Route 187 south to Durell, then take State Road 8076 to French Azilum. Watch for signs. From I-81 north of Scranton take Route 6 west to Wyalusing.

Houdini Museum

Unlock the Mystery

Legendary performers never die. The magic they create lives in the memory of their audience and in films that capture them at their peak. **Harry Houdini** literally created magic and two enthusiastic fans want to be sure that he is remembered. Performers and magicians themselves, Dorothy Dietrich and John Bravo, although not related to the famed magician, have amassed an astonishing collection of Houdini photographs, film clips, personal belongings and other memorabilia.

Three rooms of a private home have been transformed into exhibit space. Photographs in one room cover the major periods of Houdini's life. He was born Eric Weiss on March 24, 1874, in Budapest, Hungary. The museum has family photographs, showing his father, the Rabbi Samuel Weiss, and his mother and brother; the latter also became a performer and magician. Houdini claimed he began performing as a trapeze performer when he was eight. His growing ability to extricate himself from manacles changed the focus of his act and he was soon called the "**Handcuff King**," while his developing magical skills earned him the soubriquet "Master of Mystery." Paying homage to the great French magician Robert Houdin, he changed his name to Harry Houdini.

The second room has huge billboards that enticed audiences to view Houdini's mystifying stunts. In Pittsburgh, 20,000 people stood on the sidewalk and street to watch Houdini escape from a straitjacket while hanging 50 feet in the air. A second Pittsburgh stunt attracted twice that many fans. On that occasion he was chained and shackled before jumping from a bridge. In Scranton, where only Houdini and Will Rogers could sell out the theater for an entire week, he successfully escaped from a filled beer barrel on February 26, 1915. There are also pieces of furniture from Houdini's New York brownstone on 113th Street. One of Houdini's cabinets contain tools such as his lock-picking device.

In the third room, visitors watch a slide presentation on Houdini's life and famous escapes. Monitors also show Hollywood's version of Houdini's life, a movie that had almost all the vital facts wrong. Clips from five films that Houdini made are shown at the museum. He also wrote several books about magic, including a volume on handcuff secrets. His books and his lectures exposed charlatans, phonies and tricksters.

Houdini died on October 31, 1926. Houdini, his wife Beatrice and several of their associates had made a pact that whoever died first would try to contact the others. Beatrice held seances for ten years as a test to see if she could contact Houdini—she never succeeded.

The Houdini Museum, 1433 North Main Avenue, is open 9:00 A.M. to 10:00 P.M. by appointment only. Call (717) 342-5555. Tours take approximately two hours. Admission is charged.

Directions: From I-81 take Exit 56 and go left for two miles on Main Avenue. There is a parking lot in the rear. Off the Scranton Expressway, take the Main Avenue exit east for $3/_4$-mile to the Houdini Museum.

Jim Thorpe and Asa Packer Mansion

Peaks and Valleys

Peaks and valleys describe both the scenery and the fate of Jim Thorpe, the town and the man for whom it was named. The original 1815 settlement along the Lehigh River was called Coalville. The Lehigh Coal and Navigation Company soon began operating here, shipping coal from mountain mines on the Lehigh and Delaware canals.

Before long the community's name was changed to **Mauch Chunk**, Indian for Bear Mountain. Its image was perceived as forward-looking with the development of the country's first railroad in 1827. This gravity-powered railroad was abandoned in 1870 when Asa Packer's Lehigh Valley Railroad steam trains took over the job of transporting coal. The Switchback Railroad (see Pocono Museum Unlimited selection) became a phenomenally popular tourist attraction. Between 1874 and 1933, it was the nation's second most popular tourist destination, surpassed only by Niagara Falls. Crowds flocked to the 18-mile long gravity railroad to race down the mountain at dizzying speeds approaching 60-miles-per hour.

Asa Packer arrived in Mauch Chunk in 1833 with little money but lots of ambition. Local legend claims he walked from Mystic, Connecticut where he was born to Mauch Chunk. If so, it is no wonder he envisioned a railroad route to the east. He quickly realized that transporting anthracite coal to eastern markets was the key to prosperity. First, he built canal boats to haul the coal but soon founded the Lehigh Valley Railroad. This brought him great wealth. By 1879, Packer was worth $54^1/_2$ million dollars. He was the third wealthiest man in the country, surpassed only by Cornelius Vanderbilt and George Pullman. Packer became a philanthropist who helped his town and state. He founded Lehigh University.

The **Asa Packer Mansion**, built in 1861 for $14,000, reflected his success. This Italianate-style mansion was the largest and most expensive house in town. At the front of the house, two wide porches with carved fretwork overlook the town (now the Old Mauch Chunk National Historic District). The original design was changed somewhat in 1877 when $85,000 was spent remodeling the house.

Tours of the mansion start in the library and office where Asa Packer and his secretary worked. The ornate wooden desk and chair are reputedly from the estate of Robert E. Lee. Equally ornate is a blue-glass chandelier that won a prize at the 1876 Centennial Exposition in Philadelphia. The room seems to burst with competing patterns: the wallpaper is in an intricate floral pattern, as is the red carpet beneath the desk. The wooden mantle and bookcases are also carved in a decorative manner.

From the office, you pass through the main hallway. It took 16 artisans 18 months to carve the 1,000 rosettes, each a slightly different design. Next you'll see the west parlor, which extends the entire depth of the house. The 1877 remodeling was done before the Packers hosted a huge 50th wedding anniversary party. The opulent pink velvet draperies, hand sewn with gold thread, were added for that occasion. They complement the Victorian rosewood furniture. The crystal chandelier with its buttons-and-bows design is a copy of one featured in the movie *Gone With the Wind*.

The ladies' parlor, or sitting room, is another room with competing patterns: the carpet, wallpaper, carved Hondorus mahogany doorways and trim and furnishings all vie for attention. The American Emprise-style table was a 50th wedding anniversary gift from Queen Victoria.

The dining room has a hand-carved Hondorus mahogany ceiling and built-in china cabinets. The shelves are filled with decorative china and crystal. The north wall is dominated by exquisite stained glass windows added in 1885. You'll see additional china and stemware in the butler's pantry. The kitchen was considered quite modern for the time, with nearly eye-level ovens that were coal burning and self cleaning. There was also an icebox. The settler's bench belonged to Asa Packer's father and dates back to the late 1700s.

Upstairs are the family and guest bedrooms. Asa Parker died in 1879 at age 74. His daughter Mary Packer Cummings lived in this house until her death in 1912 and you will see her bedroom suite. In the hallway are family portraits of Asa and his wife as well as their children: Harry, Robert, Lucy and Mary. When Mary died she deeded the house and furnishings to the Borough of Mauch Chunk. The house needed no restoration and it has survived as you see it today, reflecting the years the Packers lived here, 1861 to 1912.

The Asa Packer Mansion is open April through May on weekends and daily June through October from NOON until 4:15 P.M. Admission is charged. Reservations are not a must but on busy summer weekends or during the fall foliage period they are advisable; call (717) 325-3229.

Adjacent to the mansion is the **Harry Packer Mansion** (717-325-8566), now a bed & breakfast. Harry Packer was Asa and Sarah's youngest son. Like his father he was a director of the Lehigh Valley Railroad. He was also an Associate Judge of Carbon County. Harry had a drinking problem and died at age 34. This 18-room house was a wedding gift from his father when he married Mary Augusta Lockhart in 1872. Period furniture fills the rooms. Tours are given Sunday, Monday, Thursday and Friday on the hour from NOON to 4:00 P.M.

Asa Packer was not the only one who built a fortune from the railroad. Many local entrepreneurs became wealthy from their involvement in coal, lumber and transportation. Between 1860 and 1890 a number of these town leaders built imposing homes.

Broadway, the main street, became known as **Millionaires Row**. Strictly speaking, most of these nouveau riche were not actually millionaires, it just seemed that way to Mauch Chunk's working class. Walking up Broadway you can see over 30 of these old homes. They are included in the booklet "A Walking Tour of Historic Jim Thorpe," available at the Tourist Welcoming Center in the 1888 New Jersey Central Railroad Station. You will see the station on the right just as you enter the town. Broadway also boasts quite a host of quaint shops, galleries and restaurants.

Another not-to-be-missed site is **St. Mark's Episcopal Church**, which was heavily endowed by the Packer family. From 1867 to 1869, architect Richard Upjohn built this rural Gothic church into the granite hillside. It was built 40 feet above street level because of frequent flooding. Harold E. Dickson's *A Hundred Pennsylvania Buildings* mentions this church as one of the state's most unique buildings.

It is astonishing to see the array of art treasures within the church. The church has lovely Tiffany windows, Minton tile floors and a reredos (ornamental wall behind the altar). The altar itself is copied from St. George's Chapel in Windsor, England and is a memorial to Asa Packer who was a vestryman of St. Mark's for 44 years. The choir stalls and clergy chairs are hand-carved butternut wood given to the church in memory of Harry Packer. The pipe organ was donated by Mary Packer Cummings as a memorial to the rector of the parish. A number of the church bells were given in memory of Mary Packer Cummings. The nine bell chime is the second heaviest bell in the nation. (The heaviest is in Notre Dame Cathedral in South Bend, Indiana.)

The **baptistry** is one of the loveliest areas of the church. The angel ceiling is done in 24 karat gold, while the font is made of a solid block of white marble. The gold candleholders are designed in flowerlike patterns and the great brass gas standards flanking the font represent the flames of the Holy Spirit.

Tours of the church are given daily June through October and on weekends in April and May. The church doors are kept locked while tours are in progress, but a sign on the door will indicate when the next tour will be given. A donation is requested. Concerts are given in the church's Great Hall.

Up Race Street from St. Mark's is a group of houses called "Stone Row." Originally there were 16 houses here known as "Packer's Row." The street got its name from the race, or water channel, that ran down the center of the street to the mill. The race still runs beneath the street's pavement but the railroad station now stands in place of the mill. The row houses Packer built for his engineers and foremen may have been copied from Elfreth's Alley (see selection) in Philadelphia. The houses along

Stone Row are now shops, boutiques and eateries. Other town landmarks included on the walking tour are the courthouse, the old jail, library and the opera house. For details on touring **Jim Thorpe** call the Pocono Mountains Vacation Bureau at (800) 762-6667.

Mauch Chunck experienced an economic decline along with the 1920s decline of the coal industry. Town leaders decided to merge three nearby towns—Mauch Chunk, Upper Mauch Chunk and East Mauch Chunk. The widow of Native American athlete Jim Thorpe, contacted the community and suggested that her husband be buried there in exchange for the town being named in his honor. His 20-ton granite mausoleum is along Route 903 on the east side of town.

Jim Thorpe won gold medals in the pentathlon and decathlon at the 1912 Olympic games in Stockholm, Sweden. King Gustav, when presenting the medals said, "Sir, you are the greatest athlete in the world." The Olympic committee stripped Thorpe of his medals after they learned that he had played one season of professional baseball in North Carolina at $60 per month. Although he played professional sports, by the time he died in 1953 he was destitute. When the state of Oklahoma would not help his widow establish a memorial she contacted Mauch Chunk and the connection was forged.

Directions: From I-76, the Pennsylvania Turnpike, take Turnpike NE Extension to the Mahoning Interchange. Turn right and travel south on Route 209 to Jim Thorpe.

Lake Wallenpaupack

State's Third Largest Manmade Lake

In 1924, the Pennsylvania Power and Light Company embarked on a major hydroelectric project that created a 15-mile long lake. Its 52 miles of shoreline offer numerous recreational opportunities.

The story of the lake's construction is told at PP&L Visitor Center at the head of the lake outside Hawley. A covered lake-side pavilion has audiovisual exhibits on the **Wallenpaupack** project and information on the indigenous wildlife. Under a protective shelter there is a Indian canoe found along the Wallenpaupack River. The PP&L Center sits beside the dam, and an overlook is on the dam's opposite side. A short distance south of this center is the Pocono Mountains Vacation Bureau Information Center with brochures and maps on the region's recreational, shopping, dining and overnight options. Near the information center is the public beach. Docked beside the beach is the *Spirit of Paupack*, an excursion boat that runs hourly cruises during the summer months, as well as a sunset cruise and a dinner cruise; call (717) 857-1251 for details. Wallenpaupack Scenic Boat Tours provide excursions aboard a 30-foot pontoon boat, call (717) 226-6211 for additional information.

Driving up the southern shore of the lake from the interstate on Route 507 you will notice it is more commercial than the northern shore. There are more motels, condominiums and developments. One of the newest and most popular restaurants on Lake Wallenpaupack is Ehrhardt's Lakeside. Diners enjoy the view from the picture windows as well as the tasty cooking. The family has operated the adjacent Silver Birches Lakeside Resort for more than 50 years. The restaurant is one mile south of the intersection with Route 6, which leads into Hawley.

In the Hawley area there is another scenic restaurant, Old Mill Stream, with two decks overlooking a tumbling waterfall. To reach this eatery turn at Castle Antiques and Reproductions, located in the oldest and largest bluestone building in the country.

Heading around the northern side of the lake on Route 590, you'll reach **Shuman Point Natural Area** and **Beech House Creek Wildlife Refuge**. The former is a 250-acre undeveloped wooded area with three miles of hiking trails and two miles of shoreline for fishing. The Blue Trail parallels the shoreline and provides an opportunity to see waterfowl as well as woodland birds. Adjacent to Shuman Point is the 60-acre wildlife refuge that also has trails. Wildlife is abundant and you're apt to spot beaver, ducks, herons and hawks.

Continuing on the northern side, down near the narrow foot of the lake is **Lacawac Sanctuary**, a private wooded sanctuary on Lake Lacawac. This lake is described as "one of the least disturbed natural lakes in Northeastern United States." Natural and cultural walks of this National Natural Landmark and Historic Site are given on summer Saturday mornings or on specially scheduled sanctuary walks; call (717) 689-9494 for current schedule. There is a one-mile self-guided loop trail that extends from the parking lot to a Lake Wallenpaupack overlook. The sanctuary offers a series of programs and workshops.

At the very tip of the lake is the **Ledgedale Natural Area**, a 100-acre woodland tract with hiking tails. The area gets its name from the profusion of glacier boulders and rock ledges. This too is an area where wildlife abounds. To reach this take Route 507, then turn onto Ledgedale Road and follow the signs.

Swimming is just one of the water-related activities popular with visitors at Lake Wallenpaupack. The lake is also a renown fishing spot and boating mecca. Along the shores there are four

171

camping areas. During the winter months options include ice skating and ice fishing on the lake and snowmobiling on the various trails.

Directions: From I-84 take Exit 6, Route 507 to Route 6 and turn left. The public beach and information center will be on your left in approximately one mile.

Mauch Chunk Lake Park and Lehigh Gorge State Park

A Destination for all Seasons

The spectacular scenery of the southwest region of the Pocono Mountains around Jim Thorpe (see selection) can be appreciated while enjoying a wide range of recreational activities. Hikers, bikers and skiers flock to the wide-open countryside, clear lakes and rugged mountains. The waterways can be enjoyed by swimmers, rafters and canoers.

Mauch Chunk Lake Park in Jim Thorpe and the nearby Lehigh Gorge State Park are ideal for sports enthusiasts of all ages, levels of expertise and interests. There is also the Delaware & Lehigh Canal Heritage Corridor that bikers and hikers can enjoy.

The area, with dozens of Colorado-style trails, is recognized as one of the best in the east for mountain biking. Blue Mountain Sports & Wear (800-599-4421), 34 Susquehanna Street (across the park from the railroad station in Jim Thorpe) offers everything you need to enjoy a mountain bike experience. They rent well-maintained mountain bikes, provide transportation to trailheads and offer advice and maps for the best trail for varying skills. They also rent other sports equipment (from snowshoes to tents and rowboats) and sell a wide range of sporting goods.

One of the area's most popular trails begins in the 2,300-acre Mauch Chunk Lake Park. The 11-to-18 mile Switchback Trail (length depends on whether you do the upper and lower track) is ideal for beginners and intermediates. The ride takes between $1^1/_2$ to 3 hours. The trail follows the old Switchback Gravity Railroad track linking Summit Hill and Jim Thorpe (see Pocono Museums Unlimited and Asa Packer selections). It starts at the railroad station in downtown Jim Thorpe, climbs up to Summit Hill where there is a marvelous view of the Lehigh River and Gorge, then descends on the "Wagon Road." This descent is considered advanced because of the washed-out, rocky terrain. Novice bikers may want to walk down the hill until they pass the Packer mansions.

In all there are nine trails that either begin or end in Jim Thorpe (two others begin in Mauch Chunk Lake Park). Another easy bike trip is along the Lehigh Canal, a length of between $8^1/_2$ and 13 miles. This has the advantage of being level and smooth, ideal for families. At the other end of the spectrum is the ten mile Mauch Chunk Ridge trail with rolling and hilly terrain and a single-track descent. Advanced riders can anticipate spending two hours on this trail.

One of the most scenic trails is the **Lehigh Gorge Trail**, a rails-to-trails route that extends for 60 miles along what is, for the most part, a level railroad grade that parallels the Lehigh River. You can access this trail from the Glen Onoko Area on Coalport Road in Jim Thorpe. This is the southern end of the 4,548-acre park that extends to the Francis E. Walter Dam, a distance of 30 miles. The route takes hikers and bikers through the river's deep gorge, past steep walls and dense vegetation. You'll pass rocky escarpments and, if you trek inland at all, there are scenic waterfalls on the streams that feed the Lehigh River. The river and streams are popular with fishermen.

Mountain bikers are not the only sports enthusiasts who flock to the area; there are also great white-water adventures. The Class III rapids challenge rafters, kayakers and canoers. The boating season is mid-March through June but varying conditions may affect these dates. There are four commercial outfitters operating in the **Lehigh Gorge State Park**: Whitewater Challengers (717) 443-9532, Pocono Whitewater Adventures (717) 325-3656, they also rent mountain bikes and offer guided mountain bike treks), Jim Thorpe River Adventures (717) 325-2570 and Whitewater Rafting Adventures (717) 722-0285. Much calmer water awaits at Mauch Chunk Lake Park where you can rent canoes, kayaks and rowboats at the Camp Store (717) 325-4408 or 325-4421.

This is a spot for all seasons. During the winter both parks open trails for cross-country skiing and a section of the trail at Lehigh Gorge State Park is open to snowmobiles. Carbon County has three ski resorts: Blue Mountain (215) 826-7700 in Palmerton and Big Boulder (717) 722-0100 and Jack Frost (717) 443-8425 in Blakeslee. The spring Laurel Blossom Festival celebrates the abundant state flower. In mid-June the area hosts the east's oldest mountain bike festival. Autumn foliage is a big draw. The view from overlooks like the 1662-foot elevation at Flagstaff Park, just outside Jim Thorpe on Route 209, attracts visitors back year after year. (This was once an amusement park with a night-club, Ballroom in the Sky; the Dorsey Brothers got their start playing there.)

If you want to enjoy the scenery in a less participatory manner, take **Audubon's Auto Tour** and discover why this noted naturalist was attracted to the region. The approximately 53-mile drive, which can be accessed in Jim Thorpe or several other communities, takes between three and eight hours depending on the number of side trips you choose to include. Audubon traveled to Mauch Chunk in the fall of 1829 and this drive traces his route through the area.

You can stop at the Visitors Welcome Center in the New Jersey Central Railroad Station on the right just as you reach the outskirts of Jim Thorpe and pick up information on all the recreational, historical and other options in Jim Thorpe and Carbon County (717) 325-3673.

Directions: From I-76, the Pennsylvania Turnpike, take the Notheast Extension to the Mahoning Interchange. Turn right on Route 209 and head south to Jim Thorpe. From I-81 traveling south take Route 44 to Jim Thorpe; if you are traveling north exit at Route 209 east.

Nicholson Bridge, Mormon Monument and Starrucca Viaduct

Engineering and Environment

The Endless Mountains has natural and manmade wonders. You can take a meandering drive that winds past a half dozen of these special spots. Start your drive in Nicholson with a look at the Tunkhannock Viaduct, or **Nicholson Bridge**.

The American College of Engineers lists this as "the Ninth Wonder of the Modern World" and it is listed on the National Register of Historic Places. It was built between 1912 and 1915 by the Delaware, Lackawanna & Western Railroad as a cut-off to reduce rail mileage, eliminate curves, reduce the grade and cut running time. The railroad did not want to transport the dynamite needed to build the bridge on their own lines so it was shipped on the Lehigh Railroad and then brought in by horse and wagon.

Building this towering span 240 feet above the Tunkhannock Creek Valley was an engineering feat. Concrete piers were sunk into the ground to depths of 138 feet. Towers of concrete were poured from a tramway at the top, bucket by bucket. Concrete— 4,509,000 cubic feet—was used to construct the bridge. The arches are reinforced with steel making the bridge virtually indestructible. Like the Pyramids of Egypt it should endure for millennia.

Writing of the Nicholson Bridge in *Hoosier Holiday*, Theodore Drieser said, "a thing colossal and impressive—those arches! How really beautiful they were. How symmetrically planned!

*Roman aqueducts were the model for the 1848 Starrucca
Viaduct, which ranks as one of the most beautiful bridges in the
country.*

And the smaller arches above, how delicate and lightsomely graceful! It is odd to stand in the presence of so great a thing in the making and realize that you are looking at one of the true wonders of the world."

For the next spot of interest, a natural wonder, take the back roads. Head north on Route 11 to Hop Bottom, then north on Route 167 to Brooklyn, where you will take Township Road 2024 to Dimock. Turn right, north on Route 29 to hike the nature trails at **Woodbourne Forest and Wildlife Sanctuary**. This hemlock and hardwood forest looks as it did when the area was called Penn's Woods and the entire northeastern portion of the country was forested. The sanctuary trails pass glacial ponds with floating bog-islands, alder swamps, second-growth woods and open fields. The woods abound with wildlife and wildflowers. On Saturdays in May, naturalists lead walks to spot migrating birds; call (717) 278-3384 for details.

If it's a weekend, the next stop should be **Old Mill Village** in New Milford (if you are driving from the Sanctuary take Route 29 north, then Route 706 east). Old craft buildings were moved to form this village around the site of Bellknap's Mill Pond and Sawmill which operated on Meylert Creek in the 1830s. When the village hosts special events, craftsmen again practice their age-old arts. You might see a blacksmith, harness maker, cobbler, spinner, weaver, soap maker, chair caner and other artisans. The village has a general store, covered bridge, shingle mill and exhibit area. There are 26 buildings on the $42^1/_2$ acre site. Some have been rebuilt using old materials but many were moved to this site. Across Meylert Creek there is a nature trail. For a schedule of Old Mill Village's special events call (717) 465-3448 or 465-9050. On days when an event is planned the village is open NOON to 5:00 P.M.

The next point of interest is the roadside **Mormon Monument** just past Hickory Grove. Two markers and a statue explain what Joseph Smith, founder of the Church of Jesus Christ of Latter-Day Saints, did while living in this area. Smith and his wife Emma Hale purchased a 13-acre farm just 100 feet west of the marker. They lived in a three-room cottage built by Emma's brother while Smith translated *The Book of Mormon*. The Smiths moved to Ohio in 1831.

Continuing on Route 171 to Lanesboro, you will see another impressive bridge, the **Starrucca Viaduct**. Built in 1848, this National Historic Civil Engineering Landmark is considered one of the most beautiful bridges built in America. The Erie Railroad needed to bridge the 1,000-foot gap over the Starrucca Creek ravine. Their choices were either to construct a huge fill for their tracks or to build a towering bridge. Using Roman aqueducts as his example, civil engineer Julius Adams designed the Starrucca

Viaduct. Be sure to get off the main road and drive up under the bridge for a close look at this amazing structure.

A good spot for lunch or early dinner is the Starrucca House. This Erie Railroad station, now on the National Register of Historic Places, has been newly renovated with shops, a bar and a restaurant.

Continue east on Route 171 to Thompson for the **Florence Shelly Preserve of the Nature Conservancy**. The refuge is a mile north of town. For the entrance turn right on Little Ireland Road. Self-guided trails wind through the 357-acre wetlands. Over a hundred species of birds have been sighted in the preserve. Two distinctive features are Plews Swamp, a boreal bog, and Wiers Pond, a ten-acre glacial pond that local folklore claims is bottomless. A boardwalk begins at the parking lot and extends through the hemlock forest to a marsh overlook.

Wildflowers abound at the nature preserve, but they are also featured at **Wildflower Pottery** in Thompson. Potter Sharon DiGennaro, partner Veronica White, and friends converted an old Model-T Ford showroom into a working pottery studio and shop. Functional yet fascinating stoneware and earthenware bowls, pitchers, mugs, crocks and other items fill the shelves. You can step into the back room and watch the potters and their interns at work. Shop hours are Friday through Monday from 10:00 A.M. to 6:00 P.M. Tuesday through Thursday by appointment or by chance, (717) 727-3113. While in Thompson you can stop at the picturesque Jefferson Inn for lunch, dinner or overnight accommodations; call (717) 727-2625. It's been open since 1871.

Directions: From I-81 take Exit 64, Route 92 west to Nicholson. The Nicholson Bridge can be seen from Route 92. Continue on Route 92 south to Route 6 west to Tunkhannock. Turn right on Route 29 north to Woodbourne Sanctuary north of Dimock. Continue north to the village of Montrose. From Montrose take Route 706 east to New Milford for Old Mill Village. For the Mormon Monument get back on I-81 and go north one exit, taking Route 171 east. The Starrucca Viaduct, Florence Shelly Preserve and Wildflower Pottery are all handy to Route 171 and each is well marked.

Pennsylvania Anthracite Heritage Museum and Lackawanna Coal Mine Tour

Hard Life in Coal Times

In McDade Park, the **Pennsylvania Anthracite Heritage Museum** and the Lackawanna Coal Mine Tour combine to provide an understanding of the rigors of the coal industry that dominated the northeastern part of the state for more than a century. You will see what the miner's life was like above and below ground.

Using photographs, oral history, artifacts, machinery and tools, the museum tells the story of the men, women and children who immigrated to this hard-coal region of Pennsylvania from more than 24 countries. The museum staff found the stories behind the objects they display and share them with the visitor.

The first exhibits focus on the ethnic roots of the region's settlers. The Irish and Welsh were among the first to arrive. Scranton still has the largest settlement of Welsh outside Wales. The faces in the large photo murals make the exhibits more personal, particularly when you see the faces of the six- and seven-year-olds. In John Spargo's 1906 book, *The Bitter Cry of the Children*, he writes: "I once stood in a breaker for half an hour and tried to do the work a 12-year old boy was doing day after day, for ten hours at a shift . . . I tried to pick out the pieces of slate from the hurrying stream of coal . . . my hands were bruised and cut in a few minutes. I was covered from head to foot with coal dust and for many hours afterwards I was expectorating some of the small particles of anthracite I had swallowed."

You'll discover that the International Correspondence School got started helping miners get certified. The certificates on display reveal the country of origin of the workers. This ethnic diversity is also reflected in the multiple languages used for signs. The immigrant workers sought comfort in their church and their taverns. Both are represented at this museum. The story of John Mitchell, John Lewis and the formation of the United Mine Workers union is another theme. Nor are the women forgotten, since women's work in the home, the textile industries and the community is covered.

The exhibits not only examine coal mining but also the iron and steel industry in this region. While in the area be sure to stop in downtown Scranton and see the remains of four massive stone blast furnace stacks of the **Lackawanna Iron and Coal Company**. Built between 1848 and 1857, these furnaces were part of the second largest iron producer in the country. The Scranton Iron Furnaces are in a park-like setting at 159 Cedar Avenue within walking distance of Steamtown National Historic Site (see selection).

The Pennsylvania Anthracite Heritage Museum is open Monday through Saturday 9:00 A.M. to 5:00 P.M. and Sunday NOON to 5:00 P.M. Closed holidays except Memorial Day, July 4 and Labor Day. Admission is charged. The museum has an extensive library and archives for those doing research. Please call ahead (717) 463-4804 for an appointment to use these resources. There is also a museum shop.

Children prepare for their journey 300 feet into the depths of the Lackawanna Coal Mine, an award-winning tour called "The Most Amazing Hour You Can Spend in Pennsylvania."

Once you have this overview, you're ready to get a more tactile sense of the hard-coal industry by taking the **Lackawanna Coal Mine Tour**. This anthracite mine was operational from 1862 to 1931, then reopened in the summer of 1937. Portions of the mine remained in use until 1966. In 1985, it opened as a window on mining's past, offering a nationally award-winning experience that is billed as "The Most Amazing Hour You Can Spend In Pennsylvania."

A mine car takes visitors 300 feet into the bowels of West Mountain along Slope #190. At this depth it would be like having a 25-story building overhead. The horizontal shaft travels through three different veins of hard coal. The miners worked in 20 by 30-foot chambers extracting the coal. They moved from one chamber to the next, slowly working their way up the shaft. They left timbers and pillars of coal to support the chambers as they finished. Every five feet they would put in a supporting timber. Sometimes before a mine section was closed, the workers would engage in "robbing out" the mine, which meant they went back and extracted the pillars of coal. This often created sink holes, resulting in mine subsidence. The miner's had a saying, "When timbers are talking, you best start walking."

This room and pillar method was used in Europe and the immigrant miners continued the practice. Many miners were given a free passage from their European homes to this region by the mining company, then were never paid enough for them to move on to something better. The mine companies usually had three men in a chamber, a miner and two laborers. The miner had to pay for his own tools and dynamite and out of the 60 cents he earned for each car of coal he loaded, he had to pay his laborers. It worked out to roughly 21 cents an hour for the miner and 18 cents for the workers. They worked 12 hour days, 6 days a week. The miner paid 3 to 4 dollars a month to rent a company house and also a 10 to 15 percent mark up on items at the company store.

While in the mine you will see the tools used by the miners and the various improvements in mining equipment as it became more mechanized. Before mechanization, mules pulled the filled cars to the tracks where the same cars that carried the workers down the shaft would carry the coal out. The mules were blindfolded and brought down in the car—and never again saw the light of day. While the average mule lived 25 years, the mining mules averaged only seven. There are plans to rebuild the mule stables in the mine.

If a miner didn't fill three cars of coal a day he could be docked or fired, so a miner's chamber assignment was important. One of the more difficult assignments was in chambers with low coal. These low seams had to be mined either on one's hands and knees, or sometimes from a prone position. Even with rubber knee pads, the miners would be soaking wet all day. This led to devastating health problems such as rheumatism. It also was hard to meet a quota when mining these "monkey veins." While down in the Lackawanna Coal Mine you will see examples of this low coal mining.

The Lackawanna Coal Mine Tour is given from 10:00 A.M. to 4:30 P.M. from April through November except on Easter and Thanksgiving. Admission is charged. A jacket is advisable since you will be in the mine for approximately an hour. There are exhibits in the Shifting Shanty, a gift shop with handcrafted jewelry made from anthracite coal. There's a refreshment area. Call (800) 238-7245 for additional information.

Four properties are linked as Pennsylvania's Anthracite Heritage Museum Complex: the Pennsylvania Anthracite Heritage Museum, Scranton Iron Furnaces, Eckley Miners' Village (see selection) and Museum of Anthracite Mining (see selection). A 75-mile drive encompassing all four takes you through the heart of the hard-coal mining region that fueled America's Industrial Revolution. Covering all of these sites will give you a better understanding of the region and its significance.

Directions: From I-76 take the Northeast Extension of the Pennsylvania Turnpike to the Keyser Avenue exit in Taylor. Turn right on Keyser Avenue and proceed three miles to McDade Park. The Pennsylvania Anthracite Heritage Museum and the Lackawanna Coal Mine are in the park.

Pocono Museum Unlimited

Make Trails to these Rails

"I've Been Working on the Railroad," should have been the theme of the enthusiastic volunteers who spent $7^1/_2$ years building the "Land of Steam" train display at the **Pocono Museum Unlimited** in Lehighton. It is one of the country's biggest operating model railroads.

Size alone—it's 117 by 33 feet—doesn't account for this O-scale model train's fascination. Sixteen trains traverse more than 2,000 feet of track, chugging through bucolic country settings and bustling city streets. Periodically, there is a thunderstorm with lightning, thunder and rain falling into a fish-stocked lake. Three waterfalls cool the air and over 12,000 hand-planted trees create a wooded effect. As the trains approach the city, they pass cars, trucks and buses on the highway. Some of the cars are parked at the drive-in movie where a film flickers on the screen. The layout has shopping malls, apartment buildings, churches, housing developments, industrial parks and factories complete with puffing smokestacks.

The model railroad combines sight with sound: shrieks of delight echo from the 16 operating amusement park rides, the freeway resounds with honking horns, church bells chime and jackhammers reverberate through the factories. All of this is augmented by the "oohs" and "ahs" of visitors. One area that invariably causes comments is the reptile zoo with live snakes and lizards.

Every 45 minutes, a new sound and light show begins, which changes the scene from day to night and includes a convincing thunderstorm. The last program begins at 4:15 P.M. The final section of the layout is on a larger scale with an engine pulling two cars on a #1-Gauge train line.

Pocono Museum Unlimited was established to showcase the more than 125 trains in Rev. Joseph Kean's collection. Another complete layout that belonged to Father Kean is exhibited on the second floor of the **Hooven Building** across from the Railroad Station in Historic Jim Thorpe (see selection).

Pocono Museum Unlimited is open 10:00 A.M. to 5:00 P.M. daily (closed Tuesday) from May through Labor Day. From September through the first week of January, the museum opens at NOON. From the second week of January through April, it is only open weekends and Mondays, still from NOON to 5:00 P.M. Admission is charged.

The Model Train Exhibit at the Hooven Building in Jim Thorpe is open weekdays NOON to 5:00 P.M. and weekends 10:00 A.M. to 5:00 P.M. From November to June, it is only open on weekends NOON to 5:00 P.M. The last show each operating day begins at 4:30 P.M.

Admission is charged.

The Hooven's Model Train Exhibit intriques model railroaders, but Jim Thorpe is interesting for fans of both little and big railroads. The Switchback Railroad began hauling coal from the anthracite mine in Summit Hill in May 1827, making it the second oldest working railroad in the country and the first of any significance in the state. Coal was hauled nine miles to the Lehigh Canal in Mauch Chunk, now the town of Jim Thorpe.

Gravity powered the coal-laden cars down the single railroad track, while mules pulled the empty cars back up to the mine. Eventually two inclined planes and a figure 8 track provided more continuous service. By 1872, the state's network of railroads reached the coal mines and began direct hauling to the markets, so the gravity switchback was converted to a tourist attraction. It attracted considerable attention. After his ride, Thomas Edison was asked about changing the power source to electricity. He responded that he would not change a thing. For a time, only Niagara Falls was a bigger attraction for American travelers. The Depression curtailed travel and the railroad closed. The tracks were sold for scrap metal in 1937. Reconstruction of the railroad did not begin until 1986, although it had been proposed on numerous occasion prior to that time. Restoration efforts are now under way.

Excursion trains from the Jim Thorpe Railroad Station are run by **Yesterday's Trains Today**. There are three excursions: 40-minute, 8-mile runs; 105-minute, 18-mile trips to Lake Hauto and $2^1/_2$-hour trips to the Hometown trestle, plus dinner runs and special event trains like Fall Foliage, Christmas and Easter Bunny Rides.

Directions: From I-80, take the Pennsylvania Turnpike Northeast Extension south (if you are on I-78 take this north) to the Mahoning Valley Exit 34. Take Route 209 south three miles to Route 443 west. Take that for two miles and Pocono Museum Unlimited will be on your right. To reach Jim Thorpe, take Route

443 east. Just before the Lehighton McCall Bridge, turn left on Route 209 south. When you enter Jim Thorpe, the visitors parking for the Railroad Station Visitor Center will be on your right.

Quiet Valley Living Historical Farm

Be It Ever So Humble

Do you regret the demise of the extended family, when several generations customarily lived close together? If so, visit **Quiet Valley Living Historical Farm** and experience this forgotten way of life. Authentically-clad guides represent four generations as they recreate life on this self-sufficient homestead from 1765 to 1913.

You'll be introduced to Johan Peter Zepper, a Lutheran from the Palatinate, who brought his family to the New World. Their sea voyage was beset with hardship; there was little food or water and disease was rampant. Only one child, their daughter Catherine, survived. Once the Zeppers arrived in Pennsylvania they had to walk more than a hundred miles to claim their land in the foothills of the Pocono Mountains.

The family expanded in 1777. John Ludwig Meyer, a German soldier impressed into combat in the New World, was wounded, captured and imprisoned in Philadelphia after the Battle of Trenton. When the Americans learned he was not a willing combatant, he was released and he stayed in Pennsylvania earning his living as a circuit tailor. His route brought him to the Zepper farm where he not only stayed the night, he stayed a lifetime. He married Catherine and raised his own family on this farm.

There are 14 buildings at Quiet Valley but the farmhouse, a typical Pennsylvania Dutch "grossdawdy house" is certainly one of the most interesting. You might encounter the "great-grandmother" of the family in the upstairs bedroom talking about the problem of keeping warm on the old farm. Gran imparts a good bit of folk wisdom in her rural Scotch-Irish dialect. When a youngster in the crowd gets fidgety she advises the young mother to put honey on the thumb and forefinger of each hand and then give the young lad a feather. When she demonstrates this method, she always gets a big laugh. Sitting in her rocking chair with a gourd hearing aid and a corn-cob pipe, she looks right at home.

Another room of the main house that intrigues visitors is the upstairs parlor. One of the women who married into the family in the 1890s was dismayed by the lack of privacy at Quiet Valley. In order to "keep her down on the farm," the great-grandmother gave up her bedroom and converted it into an upstairs parlor for the young bride. However, this room was an after-thought. Its floor is built on top of the slanted roof. The effect is that of an amusement park fun house.

The dissatisfied bride also requested and got a "modern" kitchen. She had a new iron range and a dry sink. But the heart of the house was still the cellar kitchen. In it is the wooden yoke used for hauling water or milk by adding buckets to its hooks. There is speculation that this gave rise to the expression "letting you off the hook" since it was such a relief when the filled buckets were removed.

As you wander around the farm from the smokehouse to the ice-house to the old barn, you'll see a variety of farm animals under foot. Sheep, ducks and chickens delight youngsters, who also enjoy the hay jump in the barn.

Each day food is prepared, animals tended and farm chores done as they would have been in the 18th and 19th centuries. Throughout the season farm staff make baskets, brooms, candles and other useful articles. In May, the Farm Animal Frolic is held with special events including sheep shearing, pony rides, and the chance to pet the baby farm animals. In December the farm hosts an "Old Time Christmas" with carol singing, a live barn-yard nativity, stories and refreshments. Call (717) 992-6161 for additional information. Quiet Valley is open from June 20 to Labor Day from 9:30 A.M. to 5:30 P.M. On Sunday the farm opens at 1:00 P.M. Admission is charged.

Directions: From I-80 west take Exit 46S onto Route 209. Continue on Route 209 west and make a right at Shafer's School House Road and follow the signs for $1^{1}/_{2}$ miles to farm. From I-80 east, Exit 46S will take you south on Route 33 to second Syndersville exit, where you will turn left on Manor Drive and follow signs for $2^{1}/_{2}$ miles to Quiet Valley.

Steamtown National Historic Site

Starlight Express Meets the National Park Service

Anytime a museum collection comes under the auspices of the National Park Service good things happen. This is certainly true of the private train collection purchased from Nelson Blount, a Vermont millionaire and brought to Scranton's abandoned Delaware, Lackawanna and Western Railroad Yard by a private non-profit group who called their attraction Steamtown USA. These steam locomotives and rail cars became the nucleus of **Steamtown National Historic Site**.

The goal at this still-evolving site is to tell the history of steam

184

railroading between 1850 and 1950. During that century steam railroads powered the industrial growth of the country. Track mileage expanded from 9,021 miles in 1850 to a peak of 252,845 miles in 1920. In 1850 there were 20,000 railroad workers in America; by 1950 there were 3.6 million.

This is the story told at the restored railroad yard of the DL&W. The core complex includes two restored sections of the roundhouse. When the railroad was operational this is where locomotives were stored and serviced. A small section, three small stalls and an office, date back to 1902, while 13 (out of 46 that were once active) larger stalls date from 1937. Each stall has a track leading to a work bay which accommodates one or two locomotives. The tracks lead from the bay to the turntable, a bridge-like structure around which the roundhouse is built. Other pie-shaped wedges surrounding the turntable are built to resemble the old roundhouse. These rebuilt sections serve as Visitor Center, Technology Museum, History Museum, Theater and Oil House.

The Visitor Center provides site orientation and schedules for the train excursions, daily tours and special programs. The train rides are popular and you should make advance reservations; call (717) 961-2035. You will need to arrive at Steamtown at least 30 minutes before your train excursion. There is a $2^1/_2$- hour excursion 13 miles southeast to the village of Moscow. Park rangers also lead walking tours of the roundhouse and locomotive shop tours that let you see rolling stock in various stages of refurbishing and restoration.

Steamtown has approximately 29 steam locomotives and 86 cars. One of the most well-know is Union Pacific's "Big Boy." Weighing more than a million pounds, this is one of the largest steam locomotives ever built. Originally there were 25 of these locomotives; this is one of eight that have survived. The oldest engine in the collection is the 1887 Union Pacific RR #737.

The **Technology Museum** has a state-of-the-art HO-scale model of the Delaware, Lackawanna and Western Railroad yard during its heyday in the 1930s. Exhibits detail the industrial technology of railroading. You'll see how steam locomotives were made. Across the turntable is the **History Museum** which not only delves into the story of how railroading developed but also focuses on the people who developed, owned and worked for the railroads. A film on America's steam railroading heritage is shown in the theater. The **Oil House**, where lubricating oil was kept in underground reserves, will have exhibits about its use in 1912 when it was built as well as the Steamtown Volunteer Association Bookstore.

Steamtown National Historic Site is open daily year-round 9:00 A.M. to 5:00 P.M. It is closed on Thanksgiving, Christmas and New Years Day. There is no admission fee but there is a charge for the long rail excursion.

Directions: From I-76 take the Pennsylvania Turnpike Northeast Extension to Exit 37, Wyoming Valley, to I-81 north. Take I-81 to Exit 53, Central Scranton Expressway. Follow this expressway to the third traffic signal, turn left and go $1^1/_2$ blocks. You will pass the Steamtown Mall entrance and the Scranton Parking Authority lot. The park entrance is off Lackawanna Avenue.

Stourbridge Lion and Stourbridge Rail Excursions

A Roaring Start

A full-scale replica of the Stourbridge Lion, the first locomotive to run on commercial track in the United States, is the feature exhibit at the **Wayne County Historical Society Museum** in Honesdale.

The museum is in the 1860 offices of the Delaware & Hudson Canal Company. The canal began outside this office and extended 108 miles to Kingston, New York. Also originating here was the canal company's gravity railroad that hauled coal from the mines at Carbondale, Pennsylvania. In 1827, D&H began considering the feasibility of using steam locomotives to haul coal from the mines to the canal. The company sent Horatio Allen to England to evaluate their steam engines. He was impressed and purchased an engine, the **Stourbridge Lion**, and rails. The engine, named for the huge lion's head painted on the front of the boiler, made its first historic run on August 8, 1829. Pieces of the original engine are on exhibit at the Smithsonian in Washington, D.C. Although this first run proved the idea was sound, the Stourbridge Lion was too heavy for the tracks and never made another run.

The Stourbridge Lion prototype was the work horse; the show horse was D&H's passenger gravity car. The museum has an original 1920s passenger car. All the hand-carved decorations and hand-stenciled trim have been painstakingly restored. It was more luxurious than most subsequent passenger cars with elegantly upholstered seats, wooden shutters, inlaid wooden panels and intricate decorative touches.

It's easy to visualize life on the Delaware & Hudson Canal after visiting this museum because the story is told with strong visuals: eight large panels on the wall provide highlights, photographs fill in details and a 30-minute movie covers the construction and operation of the canal. The D&H Canal Company was the first million-dollar company in the country.

186

Museum exhibits on the lower level include: Indian artifacts discovered locally, household items that were found in frontier homes, flags and weapons from military engagements and printing equipment. Back upstairs there is a research library for genealogical research on Wayne County residents. Here, too, is a glass exhibit. If you've visited the Dorflinger Glass Museum (see selection) you should be able to recognize these distinctive pieces. The process of glassmaking is explained and locally-made glass is featured. The quality of the sand in the valley was particularly suited to fine glassmaking. At one time there were 28 glass cutting shops in the county.

Adjacent to the museum and open at visitor's request is the **Jason Torrey Land Office**. Torrey was the region's first big land owner and his surveying equipment and maps are on exhibit. Furniture made by Alanson Blood, who arrived in Wayne County in 1828, is displayed. Paintings by Honesdale native Jennie Brownscombe are exhibited here.

The museum is open from 1:00 P.M. to 4:00 P.M. on Monday, Wednesday, Friday and Saturday from January through March. During April and May it also opens on Tuesday and Thursday. From June through September the museum opens at 10:00 A.M. and from July through Labor Day Sunday hours are NOON to 5:00 P.M. Closed major holidays. Admission is charged for the museum and library.

Down the street from the museum at the Wayne County Chamber of Commerce, 742 Main Street, you can purchase tickets for the **Stourbridge Rail Excursions**. They offer a wide variety of excursion trips to Hawley and Lackawaxen; call (800) 433-9008. Theme rides include Fall Foliage, Great Train Robbery, Concert in the Park, dinner theater and holiday oriented trips.

While in Honesdale you can take a $1^1/_2$ mile self-guided walking tour of the town. Maps are available at the museum, highlighting 28 points of interest.

Directions: From I-84 take Exit 8, and head north on Route 402. At the intersection with Route 6, drive west to Honesdale. The museum is at 810 Main Street. There is parking directly behind the museum.

Zane Grey Museum and Roebling's Delaware Aqueduct

Creative Minds

Writers who visit the Zane Grey Museum are apt to think they are working in the wrong genre when they learn Grey made somewhere in the neighborhood of 37 million dollars from his books. While the country was suffering through the Great Depression, he purchased and refitted Kaiser Wilhelm's private yacht. But Grey suffered from his own demons and frequently isolated himself from his family because of severe depressions. He sought the desert when the dark moods came on him, because its beauty and vastness restored his good temper.

Grey is more interesting than his fictional characters. It's a treat to wander through rooms where he wrote and relaxed, seeing his belongings and hearing about his amazing accomplishments.

Zane Grey was born in 1872 in Zanesville, Ohio, founded by his great-grandfather. His father was a dentist and his mother an admirer of Queen Victoria. She named her son, Pearl Zane Grey, because pearl was the color Queen Victoria wore. The athletic young boy went on to study dentistry at the University of Pennsylvania on a baseball scholarship. After graduating he changed his first name and played semi-professional baseball from 1896 to 1902. The museum has photographs and memorabilia from these early years, including his baseball shoes, dentistry tools and fishing rods. His monogrammed sheepskin jacket hangs on the hatrack with a collection of hats.

From 1898 to 1904, while still playing ball, Grey practiced dentistry in New York. But "Doc," as he was called, yearned to write. In 1900, he met a 17-year-old New York City girl studying to become an English teacher, Lina Elise Roth. Even before they married they moved to Lackawaxen with his mother and sister. In 1905 they married and her inheritance provided the capital for them to set up housekeeping in Lackawaxen along the banks of the Delaware River. Here Grey could pursue his two loves—writing and fishing. He wrote fictional and fishing magazine features. His wife gave him $150 to pay for for the publishing of his first novel, *Betty Zane*. His first success came in 1910 with *Heritage of the Desert*, followed in 1912 by *Riders of the Purple Sage*. The latter sold over a million copies and was one of the most widely read novels ever written about the American west. Grey was called the "Father of the Western Novel" with 85 novels in this genre, translated into 23 foreign languages and made into 104 movies. Grey himself was a Hollywood producer. He also wrote books on fishing and travel.

Fishing was another of Grey's great passions. He set ten world deep-sea fishing records. In 1930, when he was 58-years-old he caught a 1,040-pound blue marlin off the coast of New Zealand with a rod and reel, the first person to bring in a fish that size. Legend has it that it weighed even more but parts were eaten by sharks while it was being hauled to shore. There are those that say this inspired Hemingway's *The Old Man and the Sea*.

The home of "Western" author Zane Grey sits along the bank of the Delaware River at Lackawaxen.

Zane Grey lived in the Lackawaxen area 14 years, four of them in the house that now serves as a museum. It had been his brother Romer's house, but Zane purchased and enlarged it. Stylized Native American drawings are painted on a border along the upper wall of the museum's two rooms. Grey and his family moved to Altadena, California in 1918. He never sold this house and Zane and his wife returned for a visit in 1929. Grey died of heart failure at age 67 in 1939.

The Zane Grey Museum is open daily 10:00 A.M. to 4:30 P.M. from Memorial Day weekend through Labor Day and on weekends only in mid-April through May and September through October. Call for hours of operation (717) 685-4871. There is no admission but donations are welcomed. Twenty-minute guided tours are given every half hour.

Virtually within sight of the Zane Grey House is **Roebling's Delaware Aqueduct.** The conflicting needs of two local industries prompted the construction of this aqueduct. From the late 1700s, lumber companies floated rafts of timber down the Delaware River

189

to the shipyards of Philadelphia and Trenton. Beginning in the 1820s, with the completion of the Delaware and Hudson Canal, coal mines filled canal boats and crossed the Delaware from Lackawaxen to the New York shore. Such cross traffic resulted inevitably in collisions, fistfights, claims and lawsuits.

In 1847, the canal directors sought a solution to the problem of cross traffic by hiring John Roebling to build an aqueduct that would carry the canal over the river. This Prussian-born civil engineer immigrated to America in 1831 and built two suspension bridges in western Pennsylvania. This type of span used fewer piers, enabling the log rafts to float unimpeded. Roebling built four aqueducts for the Delaware and Hudson Canal. The largest and the only one still standing, is the Delaware Aqueduct at Lackawaxen, which was ready for traffic in April 1849. It was used until the canal ceased operations in 1898. Later it was turned into a highway toll bridge. Vehicles can still cross this span, and on the New York side there is a Visitor Center in the old **Toll House**. The center has diagrams, maps and photographs dealing with this project. The Toll House is open 9:30 A.M. to 5:30 P.M. Memorial Day to Labor Day and weekends in September and October.

The Delaware Aqueduct is the nation's oldest surviving wire-suspension bridge. It still has its suspension cables and masonry piers. Known locally as Roebling Bridge, it is a National Historic Landmark and is listed by the Historic American Engineering Record. Several decades after it was built, John Roebling and his son built the bridge for which they are remembered, the Brooklyn Bridge. John Roebling died in July 1869 of tetanus while building the New York span.

This part of the river is part of the Upper Delaware Scenic and Recreational River system administered by the National Park Service, which administers both the Zane Grey Museum and the Toll House at the Roebling Bridge. A variety of recreation opportunities encourage visitors to get out on the river. There are outfitters who supply canoes, kayaks and inner tubes. Most of the river is Class I, meaning it moves and has a few ripples but no difficult passages. Only Skinners Falls Rapids above Narrowsburg is challenging. There is swimming in the river, but it is moving water and caution should be observed. Footwear should be worn as protection against the rocky bottom. The Delaware is popular with fishermen. The catch includes trout, bass, walleye, fallfish and American eels. In late spring, American shad spawn in the Upper Delaware.

A charming bed and breakfast, the Roebling Inn is a neighbor of the Zane Grey Museum. Also nearby is the Lackawaxen House, an excellent dining spot. The Bridge Restaurant is adjacent to the Toll House on the New York side. Just off the interstate before heading toward Lackawaxen you can detour to stop at **Grey Towers National Historic Landmark**. This striking stone mansion was the home of Gifford Pinchot, whose distinguished career included serving as the first Chief of the Forest Service and the Governor of Pennsylvania. Pinchot is considered the founder of American conservation.

Grey Towers, overlooking the Delaware River, was Pinchot's summer retreat. Designed in the French chateauesque-mode in 1885, this estate was decorated and enlarged by Pinchot's wife Cornelia. She also took an interest in the gardens that surround the house. Walkways lead past patios, ponds, a playhouse and an office area. Grey Towers is open daily Memorial Day weekend to Labor Day from 10:00 A.M. to 4:00 P.M. Tours are given on the hour.

Directions: From I-84 take Exit 10, Milford, and head west on Route 6. At the intersection of Route 590/434 turn right and continue on these until they split. Follow Route 590 north to Lackawaxen and the Zane Grey Museum. Grey Towers is on Route 6, just two miles east of Exit 10 interchange.

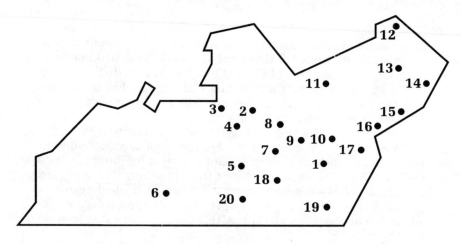

HERSHEY/DUTCH COUNTRY REGION

1. **Lancaster**
   (All Lancaster Area Sites)

2. **Harrisburg**
   (All Harrisburg Area Sites)

3. **Hershey**

4. **Cornwall**
   Cornwall Iron Furnace

5. **York**
   Harley-Davidson Museum &
   Factory Tour and U.S.
   Weightlifting Federation
   Hall of Fame
   Wolfgang Candy and
   Brown's Orchards
   York Historic District

6. **Gettysburg**
   Gettysburg National Military
   Park and Eisenhower Na-
   tional Historic Site
   Jennie Wade House and Lin-
   coln Room Museum
   Land of Little Horses
   Lincoln Train Museum and
   Gettysburg Railroad

7. **Mount Joy**
   Groff's Farm and Bube's
   Brewery

8. **Kleinfeltersville**
   Middle Creek Wildlife
   Management Area

9. **Lititz**

10. **Ephrata**
    Ephrata Cloister

11. **Womelsdorf**
    Conrad Weiser Homestead

12. **Kempton**
    Hawk Mountain

13. **Boyertown**
    Boyertown Museum of His-
    toric Vehicles

14. **Douglassville**
    Merritt Museums

15. **Elverson**
    Hopewell Furnace

16. **Intercourse**
    People's Place and Amish
    Farms

17. **Strasburg**
    Railroad Museum of Penn-
    sylvania, Toy Train Mu-
    seum, Choo Choo Barn
    and Gast Classic Motor-
    cars
    Strasburg Rail Road

18. **Columbia**
    National Association of
    Watch and Clock Collec-
    tors Museum and Wright's
    Ferry Mansion

19. **Quarryville**
    Robert Fulton Birthplace

20. **Airville**
    Indian Steps Museum

Hershey/Dutch Country ═══Region═══

The rolling fields of central Pennsylvania offer a microcosm of the state. Indian Steps Museum reaches back to the region's earliest inhabitants. The Hans Herr House, Conrad Weiser Homestead, Fort Hunter Mansion and the Daniel Boone Homestead reflect colonial settlement.

York was the nation's first capital. When the members of the Continental Congress fled the British occupation of Philadelphia during the American Revolution, they met in York. In Lancaster you can visit Wheatland, the home of the nation's 15th president, James Buchanan. Early industry can be explored at the Cornwall Iron Furnace and Hopewell Furnace.

Gettysburg is the site of one of the great battles that did so much to turn the tide in the Civil War. The story of Lincoln's journey to Gettysburg and the background on his remarks at the Gettysburg National Cemetery is told at the National Military Park, Lincoln Room Museum and Lincoln Train Museum.

Distinct religious communities have long followed their own interpretation of Biblical injunctions. In the 1740s Ephrata Cloister, built in a European medieval architectual style, was a spartan settlement for Seventh-Day Baptists. Mennonites and Amish who settled in this area more than a century ago still adhere to their religious practices. Their farms and horse-drawn buggies are an integral part of the Lancaster scene. Questions about these religious groups are answered at the People's Place.

Transportation is a big story in this region. At the Railroad Museum of Pennsylvania trains made, or run, in the state are highlighted. Model trains are featured at two nearby sites. Strasburg Railroad offers excursion rides on steam trains. The birthplace of Robert Fulton, who is credited with inventing the steam boat, is nearby. Automobiles are featured at Gast Classic Motorcars and the Boyertown Museum of Historic Vehicles.

Family play comes in great variety in this region from the crowd-pleasing Land of Little Horses to the thrills of Hersheypark in "Chocolatetown USA" where the street lights are shaped like candy "kisses."

Finally, near the region's center looms Harrisburg, the seat of state government. There is not a state capitol building in the country that surpasses this magnificent (and newly restored) building.

LANCASTER

Folk Craft Center, Bird-in-Hand Farmer's Market and Weavertown One-Room Schoolhouse

Crafts Teach About Past

The line between real and recreated has become so blurred travelers sometimes have trouble recognizing the difference. One indignant tourist demanded that Lancaster area tourism information personnel fire a bearded gentlemen working the farm down the road because he didn't want his picture taken. They mistakenly believed it was a recreation of early Americana. Instead it was an Amish farmer working his own fields who wanted to retain his privacy. (The Amish religion strictly prohibits the taking of photographs.) The Amish dress in an Old World manner and their presence in the Lancaster area creates the illusion of stepping back in time. The covered buggies, the immaculate farms that eschew electric wires, the plain-colored dress, the bonnets and hats are all part of 20th-century lifestyle for the Plain People of this area.

The lifestyle and crafts of the region's Amish, Mennonites and Pennsylvania Dutch are captured in the photographs of Mel Horst at his **Folk Craft Center** in Witmer. Your visit starts in the center's auditorium, designed in the style of an Old Order Mennonite meetinghouse, where a 12-minute slide show is presented. Be sure to notice the Declaration of Independence on the wall; it's one of only two surviving copies printed in German for Pennsylvanians.

Even the staircases are rich in history. As you leave the auditorium you'll take the staircase used by females at the Lutheran meetinghouse from which the stairs were taken. The stairs used by males is opposite. Note the 1822 Valentine at the top of the stairs. It's paper cut to look like lace, an art form called Scherenschnitte.

The stairs lead to an exhibit gallery overlooking the extensive array of objects in the Great Hall. If your grandparents kept every-

Mel Horst's Folk Craft Center in Witmer presents the lifestyle and crafts of the region's Amish, Mennonites and Pennsylvania Dutch.

thing they and their forebears used, cleaned it up and organized it by use, it would look like this exhibit. The tools of the trade for butchering, lumbering, ironmaking, farming, printing, photography and household chores are displayed. Broom making, quilting and pinprick embroidery are among the folk arts you'll see.

As you leave the hall, you'll see folk art created by local artists. An interesting array of crafted work is for sale in the gift shop and the adjacent country store. Behind the museum are three gardens: an herb garden, dyeing garden and four-square garden. The latter adopts the German practice of sectioning off gardens with walkways between each area.

During the summer and fall, the Folk Craft Center has various special events, including quilt tours. Visitors view Folk Center founder and owner Mel Horst's private collection of antique quilts. Refreshments are served while Mr. Horst regales attendees with the history of various quilts. Mr. Horst also entertains in the guise of his humorous alter-ego, Jakey Budderschnip, at the Center's **Old Time Music Festival**.

The Folk Craft Center Museum is open 9:30 A.M. to 5:00 P.M. Monday through Saturday from April through mid-November. Sunday hours are 11:00 A.M. to 4:00 P.M. Hours may be abbreviated in the spring and fall, call (717) 397-3609 for current times and a listing of special events. Admission is charged.

Just down the road is the **Bird-in-Hand Farmer's Market** where you can obtain fresh vegetables and fruits, preserves, jams and jellies, homemade baked goods and candy; and handcrafted items like quilts, leather goods and engraved wooden signs. The market, on Route 896, is open 8:30 A.M. to 5:30 P.M. Wednesday through Saturday from July through October. From April through June, and during November, the market is open Wednesday, Friday and Saturday. At other times of the year, it is only open on Friday and Saturday.

The Folk Craft Center and Farmer's Market give you an idea of the pursuits of the adults—what they are producing, how they work and the crafts they still practice. If you want a glimpse of what the children are doing, visit the **Weavertown One-Room Schoolhouse**. Classes for Amish children were held in this school, built in 1877, until May, 1969. At one time there were 396 schools of this type. The Amish still operate approximately 100 one-room schools in Lancaster County.

The nearly 95-year-old Weavertown school still has its original wooden desks, blackboards and school bell. Students from grades one to eight attended this school. Life-size animated mannequins recreate a typical school day circa 1930. There are even potatoes baking on top of the pot-bellied stove for the children's lunch.

The Weavertown One-Room Schoolhouse is open daily from Easter weekend through Thanksgiving weekend from 10:00 A.M. to 5:00 P.M. During the summer months, it opens an hour earlier. A nominal admission is charged.

There is so much to do in the Lancaster area that visitors often extend their stay. If you are staying overnight in the area and would like accommodations that offer the comfortable country decor of a B&B, with the privacy and modern conveniences of a motel, consider the Country Living Motor Inn just west of Mt. Sidney Road on Route 340, the Old Philadelphia Pike. The inn has rocking chairs on the front porch and antiques in the lobby. There is an Amish school across a field from the inn and horse-drawn buggies clip-clop along the highway. Call (717) 295-7295 for additional information.

Directions: From I-76, the Pennsylvania Turnpike traveling east, take Exit 20, Route 72 south. Pick up Route 30 around Lancaster. At the intersection with Route 340 drive east. The Folk Craft Center is at 441 Mt. Sidney Road off Route 340 just west of Smoketown. For the Bird-in-Hand Farmer's Market continue on Route 340. The market is at the intersection with Maple Avenue. The Weavertown One-Room Schoolhouse is on Route 340 between Bird-in-Hand and Intercourse. From I-76 for this site take Exit 21, Route 222 south until you intersect Route 30 east.

Historic Rock Ford Plantation and Hans Herr House

Windows to the Past

Historic Rock Ford Plantation in Lancaster is a quiet 18th-century oasis virtually unchanged from the time Edward Hand, physician, war hero and close friend of George Washington, lived here.

Edward Hand rose to the rank of Adjutant General during the American Revolution. You see his field desk in the parlor when you tour the house. In the dining room, there's a copy of the famous Gilbert Stuart portrait of George Washington. When Washington visited Hand, he was able to relax in his own specially-built chair made to accommodate his six-foot, four-inch frame. A dinner invitation from President George Washington is also displayed.

The Hand family lived in the gracious 1794 Georgian-style brick mansion in the latter years of the 18th century. The house still has the original floors and fixtures. In some rooms the paint on the walls is more than 200 years old. Costumed guides point out a window pane in the dining room on which two of the Hand children, John and Sarah, scratched their names. One reason for its remarkable condition is that Rock Ford remained in the Hand family through the years. Records kept by the family made it possible to furnish the house with period antiques conforming to Hand's own inventory.

During the spring and summer the plantation's garden is a delight. Since Edward Hand was Irish, his garden eschews the formality of the elaborate British boxwood garden. This Irish country garden is full of delphiniums, columbines, lilies, coral bells, daisies, zinnias, snapdragons and marigolds.

On the site of the original barn is an 18th-century stone barn housing the **Kauffman Collection of Pennsylvania Folk Arts and Crafts** featuring over 400 examples of fraktur, pewter, copper, tin, glassware, firearms and furniture typical of southeastern Pennsylvania artisans and craftsmen from 1750 to 1850.

Historic Rock Ford is open April through October on Tuesday through Saturday from 10:00 A.M. to 4:00 P.M., on Sundays it opens at NOON. Special candlelight tours are offered in December. Call (717) 392-7223 for additional information.

The **Hans Herr House** is the earliest surviving dwelling in Lancaster County and the oldest Mennonite meetinghouse in America. Hans Herr and a small group of Mennonites came to Pennsylvania in 1710 in response to William Penn's call for settlers. Herr was 71 years old at the time, yet he undertook the ardors of the journey to escape religious persecution in the Palatinate.

The medieval-looking sandstone house you see was built by Hans Herr's son Christian. The date of construction, 1719, can be clearly seen on the door lintel along with Christian's initials, CHHR. This two-story house has a cellar that extends beneath one-third of the house. The windows of the underground room open to the outside to allow some air circulation in this cold storage area.

The Herr House is laid out according to a standard Germanic floor plan. The furniture is sparse and plain and represents items found listed on Christian Herr's 1749 inventory. It is interesting to see the way in which the huge "kas," or wardrobe, can be taken apart almost like a tinker toy. The house has a masonry heating stove and a cellar door that closes by itself which prevented small children from falling down the steep stairway.

Before you explore the house stop at the Visitor Center where exhibits provide background information on the Mennonites and the Herr family. There is also a shed with an exhibit on Mennonite rural life, a blacksmith's shop and period Pennsylvania German raised bed gardens.

The Hans Herr House is open April through December Monday through Saturday from 9:00 A.M. to 4:00 P.M. It is closed on

Sundays. You can visit by appointment only January through March; call (717) 464-4438. The first Saturday in August is Hans Herr House Heritage Day with demonstrations of 18th and 19th century crafts. The first Saturday in October is the Apple Harvest Festival called **Snitz Fest**; Christmas Candlelight Tours are held the first Friday and Saturday evenings in December.

Directions: From I-76, the Pennsylvania Turnpike, take Exit 21, Route 222 to Lancaster. Rock Ford Plantation is located in Lancaster County Park, just off Route 222 on Rock Ford Road. The Hans Herr House is off Route 222 on Hans Herr Drive near the town of Willow Street.

Lancaster

Lowdown on Downtown

Lancaster County abounds with enticing destinations that lure visitors into the countryside but the downtown district has other must see spots: The Heritage Center of Lancaster County, Central Market, Newseum, Steinman Park and the Charles Demuth House and Garden.

The Heritage Center of Lancaster County is appropriately situated in the heart of downtown Lancaster at Penn Square in the old city hall and Masonic Lodge, both circa the mid-1790s. This is a repository of three centuries of treasures crafted by regional artisans from home furnishings to fine art and folk art.

Displays by artisans who have lived or worked in and around Lancaster include tall clocks, cabinets, cases, quilts, coverlets, samplers, silver, pewter, copperware, printed works, Pennsylvania long rifles (what many call the Kentucky rifle was actually made in Lancaster County), homemade toys, baskets, kitchen utensils, fraktur, woodenware, weather vanes and an authentic Masonic Lodge meeting room. Younger visitors enjoy the **Hands-on-Heritage** museum classroom with seven interactive learning stations. Activities include a mock archaeological dig in a sandbox. Children can capture a glimpse of the immigrant experience through packing a trunk and fashioning quilt patterns.

The Heritage Center of Lancaster County is open at no charge year-round Tuesday through Saturday from 10:00 A.M. to 4:00 P.M. Don't miss the center's gift shop with its interesting array of handcrafted items.

The Heritage Center's next door neighbor is the **Central Market**, the nation's oldest publicly-owned, continuously-operated (since the 1730s) farmers market. You're likely to be more impressed with the staggering array of products and handicrafts than with the fact the market is on the National Register of Historic Places. Amish and Mennonite farm families bring their wares to the market each morning; the fruits, vegetables and meat are always fresh and the baked goods, preserves, pickled items are all tempting. The market has more than 80 stands. Hours are Tuesday and Friday from 6:00 A.M. to 4:30 P.M. and Saturday from 6:00 A.M. to 2:00 P.M.

Another downtown point of interest is the Lancaster Newspapers' **Newseum**, a block long self-guided series of window exhibits explaining how, when and why newspapers have served the local community. You'll see one of the earliest iron printing presses among the more than 25 pieces of equipment, each carefully labeled as to its use. You'll see a variety of paper sizes, and a row of front pages with historic headlines. For news-in-the-making there is a moving message bar with current stories, sports scores and weather. Twenty four black pylons present the history of printing and that of Lancaster's three papers. The display ends with a photo pyramid capturing current and historic happenings. The Newseum, at 28 South Queen Street, is dramatically lit at night.

Newspapers are also an integral part of **Steinman Park**, one block over at 20 West King Street. Flanking the entrance of Steinman Park is a captivating bronze statue of a gentlemen reading a paper. A close look shows that it is the first issue of the Lancaster Sunday News from September 1923. Two more bronzed but readable papers rest on the bench: a copy of the Intelligencer-Journal story on the 1979 Three-Mile Island nuclear accident and the Lancaster New Era story heralding man's first steps on the moon in July 1969. The park's fountain and 20-foot high waterwall makes a delightful spot to enjoy lunch al fresco with some of the tasty items selected at Central Market; there are even tables and benches. If you want a more elegant dining spot, cross the street to Windows on Steinman Park, noted for its French cuisine.

Having perused the work of regional artists at the Heritage Center, it is particularly meaningful to drop by the **Charles Demuth House and Gardens** at the rear of 120 East King Street. Demuth, Lancaster's most renowned artist, spent most of his life here, although as a young man he did spend a brief time in Paris as part of the "avant garde scene" absorbing the cubist influence. Demuth, who was in frail health most of his life, worked in a small second story studio overlooking the garden. Today the second floor parlor is an art gallery. The house has been restored to its early 20th century appearance to reflect the years Demuth lived and painted here. Next door is the still-operational **Demuth Tobacco Shop**. Founded in 1770, it is the oldest tobacco shop in the country. The shop has an exhibit of firemens' antique parade hats and helmets. The Victorian garden has been restored to look as it did when tended by Demuth's mother, Augusta. It is in bloom from April through November.

All these spots and more are on the **Historic Lancaster Walking Tour**. Costumed guides regale you with anecdotes and history as you pass more than 50 locations in the old town district, where the colorful history reaches from the colonial era to contemporary days. Ninety minute tours are given daily from April through October, Monday through Saturday at 10:00 A.M. and 1:30 P.M. and Sundays and holidays at 1:30 P.M. For more details call (717) 392-1776 or stop by the Historic Lancaster Walking Tour headquarters at 100 South Queen Street.

Directions: From I-76, the Pennsylvania Turnpike, take Exit 21, Route 222. Proceed south on Route 222 into downtown Lancaster, where it becomes a one-way street, Prince Street. Make a left on King Street for Penn Square and the sites surrounding this central landmark.

Landis Valley Museum and Hands-on House

Sowing Seeds of the Past

It might be stretching the truth to claim that **Henry and George Landis** collected one of just about every item found in a house or barn on a typical late 19th-century farm. But the mixture of meticulously collected items, and painstakingly recreated settings in which they would have been found, gives visitors a complete picture of rural life in southeastern Pennsylvania. It is the country's largest museum of Pennsylvania German rural heritage. The magazine *Early American Life* rates it as one of the "20 Best Places To See Historic America."

The place to start is the Visitor Center where old photographs introduce you to the Landis brothers, who are responsible for this microcosm of life as it once was. From May through October in special exhibit buildings, costumed workers bring the past to life through displays and demonstrations. In the spinning and weaving barns artisans demonstrate various looms. Curious visitors will see such arcane tools as a flax breaker, walking wheel, heckling comb and scrutching board. On certain days at the **Pottery Shop**, you can watch skilled craftsmen at work and see examples of Pennsylvania redware pottery and other styles. A Lancaster house, circa 1800, has been moved here and restored as a seamstress's house. Another shop presents the skills of the printer and harness maker.

The Conestoga wagon is the most well-known vehicle in the transportation building amid other wagons, sleds and carriages. Contrary to popular thinking, Conestogas were not used by the pioneers on their westward trek. They used a similar wagon called a prairie schooner. The Conestoga wagon was a freight hauler. Its sloping bed had no place for passengers, and the only place for the driver to sit was the lazy board on the wagon's side. These wagon drivers were hard-living men. Many smoked potent cigars, now called stogies. Another expression that is said to have originated with the passenger wagons heading west is, "I'll be there with bells on." If your wagon got mired in the mud, broke an axle or needed help getting back on the road, it was customary to give the wagon driver who came to your aid your wagon bells. Thus, being there with bells on meant arriving without a hitch or problem.

Near the transportation building is the **Gun Shop** with its collection of Pennsylvania and other vintage weapons. Here you'll discover the origin of several other American expressions, "lock, stock and barrel" once referred to a craftsmen who made all parts of a rifle. When the gunsmith demonstrates the tricky procedure used to load a flintlock rifle he explains that when powder was put in the flash pan it would occasionally spark and not fire—this was called "a flash in the pan." Also, guns would sometimes go off "half-cocked" before the rifleman was ready.

In all there are 15 historical buildings including a tavern, an 1850s hotel that still serves food mid-spring through mid-fall and a farmstead with barns, animals and gardens. The farm animals are breeds of sheep, poultry and horses that would have been found here in the 19th century. The landscape, orchards, kitchen gardens and dyer's example garden are also authentic with the correct historical plant material. The Landis brothers' home has been restored to its appearance in the late 1800s. You start exploring this old farmstead in the kitchen. Notice the tulip-shaped container on top the old iron stove. Water was put in this container to add moisture to the air. As you move into the family room, you'll see wallpaper that was hung over hundred years ago. The parlor is vintage Victorian from the horsehair furniture to the pump organ.

The Landis brothers might have shopped at the **country store** you'll see at this museum. The store's shelves are fully stocked and there is a post office in the corner with letters in the mail slots. Like most country stores of its day, there is a pot-bellied stove to warm the customers. Set up in front of the stove, is a checkers game the regulars would have enjoyed as they caught up on local news. Although you can't buy any of the intriguing items in stock, you can shop at the Weathervane Gift shop for handcrafted items and an extensive collection of books on crafts, antiques and history.

There's so much to see that you will want to allow ample time to explore this farm community. Landis Valley Museum is open Tuesday through Saturday from 9:00 A.M. to 5:00 P.M. On Sundays it opens at NOON. Closed on Mondays and most holidays. Admission is charged. Call (717) 569-0401 for additional information.

Across the street in the 1902 **Pierce Landis House**, leased from the Landis Valley Museum, is the **Hands-on House**. In the Victorian farmhouse children from two to ten discover they can learn from their play. Since 1987 adults and children have had fun in the eight participatory exhibit areas.

The home-like atmosphere makes young children instantly comfortable. The emphasis on touching, movement and playing encourages young visitors to get involved. There are eight rooms, divided equally upstairs and down. Downstairs has a building area with Legos, bricks and blocks. Youngsters can be a city planner, carpenter or brick layer. In another area they work on an assembly line, learning sequencing at the **Whatcha-Ma-Giggle Company** with its time clock, manager's desk, and post office. Children enjoy donning aprons and goggles for this pseudo-factory project. Upstairs they can shop at the corner grocery store, learning how to select products before checking out on a real cash register. This museum is not high-tech (there are no video games or computers) but it engages its young visitors in a host of activities. Each room has layered activities so that there is something for each age level. Also upstairs is an exhibit about how the body grows and one that uses light as an art medium. Hands-on House has a unique form of advertising, since its young patrons almost always have their faces painted before leaving.

From mid-June to mid-September the Hands-on House is open Monday through Thursday and Saturday 10:00 A.M. to 5:00 P.M., Friday 10:00 A.M. to 8:00 P.M., Sunday NOON to 5:00 P.M. From mid-September to mid-June hours are Tuesday through Thursday and Saturday 11:00 A.M. to 4:00 P.M., Friday 11:00 A.M. to 8:00 P.M., Sunday NOON to 5:00 P.M. Admission is charged. For additional information call (717) 569-KIDS. Hands-on House is at 2380 Kissel Hill Road.

Directions: From I-76, the Pennsylvania Turnpike, if you are traveling west take Exit 21, Route 222. Proceed south on Route 222 to the Oregon Pike exit. Continue south on Oregon Pike, Route 272. The Landis Valley Museum will be on your right. Traveling east on I-76 take Exit 19 onto Route 283 south which eventually joins Route 30. At Lancaster, exit off Route 30 at Route 272 north, Oregon Pike, and travel two miles north. At the fourth stop light turn left and go two blocks to the museum entrance.

Wheatland

Country Residence of 15th President

The scene had all the elements of a Hollywood historical drama: the elderly politician in short-sleeves, the folksy porch in the June heat, then the unexpected news—at long last, the party nomination to run for the presidency! It all happened just that way in June of 1856 when, after three unsuccessful bids, James Buchanan finally got the Democratic nomination. He was Pennsylvania's first, and thus far, only president. His home is much the same as it was back on that eventful day when he delivered his acceptance speech from his front porch.

Buchanan once said that he "never intended to enter politics ... but as a distraction from a great grief which happened at Lancaster when I was a young man ... I accepted a nomination." He was talking about his broken engagement to Anne C. Coleman, who died shortly after they became estranged. This unhappy experience resulted in Buchanan's remaining a bachelor—the only one to ever become president. His niece, Harriet Lane, served as his official hostess both at **Wheatland** and while he was in the White House.

Although Buchanan may have entered politics reluctantly, he went on to devote 42 years to public service in various capacities. His list of titles is formidable: he served in Congress as representative and senator from Pennsylvania, he was Jackson's Minister to Russia, Polk's Secretary of State and Pierce's Minister to Great Britain.

The lavish Victorian ambience of Wheatland reflects Buchanan's years of travel and diplomacy. Some of the decorative pieces were gifts from heads of state. The 200-pound fishbowl was a gift from the Japanese Mikado when trade was inaugurated between the United States and Japan. A message from Queen Victoria commemorates the completion of the Trans-Atlantic Cable. Signed portraits of the Queen and Prince Albert recall Buchanan's years as Minister to Great Britain.

Many of the furnishings represent the White House years. On the large formal dining table, built specifically for Wheatland and never removed, is the French porcelain used by Buchanan in the White House. Be sure to note the unusual wine rinsers used by dinner guests to rinse their glasses when changing wines.

After exploring the house, step out on the famous porch and imagine Buchanan's emotions on that long-ago day. The estate has a garden and several outbuildings. Don't miss the carriage house where Buchanan's old Germantown wagon is exhibited.

Wheatland is open daily April through November from 10:00 A.M. to 4:14 P.M. Admission is charged.

Directions: From I-76, the Pennsylvania Turnpike, traveling west take Exit 22, Route 222 south, then take Route 30 west to the Harrisburg Pike exit. Head south on Harrisburg Pike to Presidents Avenue, turn right and head south to Route 23, Marietta Avenue, and turn right. Wheatland is 20 yards on the left at 1120 Marietta Avenue. If you are traveling east on I-76 take Exit 19, Route 283 south to Route 30 west and take that to the Harrisburg Pike exit.

HARRISBURG

Fort Hunter Mansion and Park

Susquehanna Bluff

In 1754, during the French and Indian War, the British undertook defensive measures to protect their Pennsylvania settlements from hostile Indians. Small forts were erected along the Susquehanna River north from Harris Ferry (now Harrisburg) to Sunbury. On a bend of the river at a settlement called Hunter's Mill, Fort Hunter was built. Hunter's Mill, a grist and sawmill, was operated by Samuel Hunter, who settled the land in 1725.

Fort Hunter offered a commanding view of the Susquehanna River as it approached Harris Ferry. A 10-by-14-foot log blockhouse protected the fort's alarm station and supply depot. The stockade was patrolled by local farmers who served as volunteer soldiers. Pennsylvania did not have the resources to provide for the citizen soldiers and the colonial government issued instructions on January 26, 1756, stating: "As the Province is at present in want of Arms and Blankets, if any of the men . . . . will find themselves with these articles, they shall receive half a dollar for the use of their gun and half a dollar for the use of a blanket."

In 1787, the Indian threat was removed and the fort fell into ruins. The property, including the mills, was acquired by Captain Archibald McAllister, one of George Washington's Revolutionary officers. McAllister developed the property, establishing a prosperous village with mills, country store, blacksmith's shop, school, artisans' shops, a distillery and tavern.

In 1870 Daniel Dick Boas purchased McAllister's property. When Boas died, his daughter Helen and her husband John W. Reily inherited the estate and it remained in the Reily family for half a century. It was a Reily niece, Margaret Wister Meigs, who established the foundation that preserves this historic site as a public trust.

The Federal-style mansion, open for tours, was built in 1814 by Archibald McAllister. He incorporated in his design the more modest house he had constructed in 1786. (The rear wooden portion was added by Boas in 1870.) Today the house is furnished with 19th-century pieces; roughly 80 percent belonged to the Reily family with a few McAllister pieces. Visitors might be relieved that the lifestyle of the last residents John and Helen Reily isn't faithfully captured. They were great pet fanciers and had about 25 dogs, an orangutan and several parrots in the house, plus peacocks on the lawn. You can see Helen Reily's Victorian and Edwardian clothes and accessories in the upstairs gallery, guest room closet and in the galleries of the Centennial Barn. Children's toys, including a doll house, toy soldiers, tea set and books are exhibited in the upstairs playroom. The summer kitchen represents the 1890s but in most of the rooms pieces range from the 1820s to the early 1900s. To fully appreciate the house be sure to see the ten-minute slide program on the history of the family before your tour.

Include time to explore the grounds; a walking tour guide highlights 14 points of interest. Between the house and gardens is the icehouse, where blocks of ice from the river were stored to refrigerate food during the summer months. There is an herb garden and boxwood allee. On the sprawling grounds are 300 year old buttonwood trees, also called sycamores, that are the oldest in the state.

Several buildings are in the process of being restored. Currently the tavern, springhouse and blacksmith shop can only be seen from the exterior. The **1876 Centennial Barn**, combining Gothic Revival with German bank barn style, was used for the once thriving Reily dairy farm. Now it has gallery space and conference facilities. The park acreage has a meandering river walk trail and another that parallels the Pennsylvania Canal. The canal enhanced the property's value when it opened in 1833. This waterway linked Columbia to the mouth of the Juniata River some 43 miles away. A 20-minute walk leads to the McAllister Cemetery where Archibald McAllister and his wife are buried along with many of their descendants. Notice the use of both head- and foot-stones, so that each grave site is carefully delineated. Legend has it that McAllister was partial to snakes, and never wanted any killed on his land. At his death, according to local tales, all the snakes in the area congregated on his grave. And to this day there are snakes around Archibald's grave.

The Fort Hunter grounds also have picnic tables, grills and play equipment. Fort Hunter is open May through November

Tuesday through Saturday from 10:00 A.M. to 4:30 P.M. On Sundays it opens at NOON. December hours are NOON to 7:00 P.M. One-hour tours are given on a walk-in basis. Admission is charged. Call (717) 599-5751.

Directions: From I-81, exit on North Front Street. Fort Hunter Mansion and Park is 1.5 miles north of I-81 at 5300 North Front Street.

Harrisburg's Museums and Parks

Stately Pleasures

The **State Museum of Pennsylvania** is part of the Capitol Complex, directly across the street from the government operational center (see State Capitol selection). The modern six-story museum showcases the history, culture and heritage of the Commonwealth. A commanding statue of founder William Penn gazes across the grand Memorial Hall as you enter the museum. Here too you'll see Penn's original 1681 charter from King Charles granting him land in the New World in settlement of a debt the King owed to Admiral Penn, William's father.

Also on the first floor is a recreated street from the early colonial era with storefronts and modest dwellings such as the summer kitchen that evokes the everyday life of the settlers. The four floors of exhibits include archaeological artifacts, anthropology, geology, furniture, decorative arts, animal dioramas and stuffed specimens, armaments, industrial and technological innovations and a fine arts gallery. If you are traveling with children see how many of the state's official symbols you can spot: the seal, coat of arm, flag, beverage (milk), fish (brook trout), flower (mountain laurel), bird (ruffed grouse), conservation plant (crown vetch), insect (firefly), tree (hemlock), dog (great Dane), animal (whitetail deer). The museum also has a planetarium. There is a nominal charge for the weekend afternoon shows; reserved shows are given on Tuesday through Friday and on Saturday mornings. Call (717) 772-6997 for tickets. For those doing genealogical research there are 22 stories of archives. A museum shop has an array of educational and crafted items.

The State Museum of Pennsylvania in the William Penn Memorial Building is open at no charge Tuesday through Saturday 9:00 A.M. to 5:00 P.M. On Sundays it opens at NOON. Closed on holidays except Memorial and Labor Days.

Just up the street at Strawberry Square, North Third and Walnut Street, is the **Museum of Scientific Discovery**. The idea of including a hands-on scientific learning center in an upscale in-town mall is certainly innovative and proving quite popular. Children love the participatory exhibits, imaginative demonstrations and hands-on workshops that unveil the mysteries of energy, engineering, electricity, mathematics, aerodynamics and a multitude of other disciplines. A clear hit is the 1942 **link trainer**, a real-life flight simulator that you can sit in, just as pilots once did to learn how to fly. There are daily supervised demonstrations of the simulator. The museum also has the largest electrostatic generator in the state. The **Dino Lab** in the **Hall of Geology** features a skeleton of the Late Triassic dinosaur, Coelophysis. The skeletal remains are still embedded in a huge block of stone excavated in New Mexico. You can watch paleontological technicians work with this skeleton and other fossil vertebrates, many of which have been entombed for some 225 million years. There are over 100 hands-on exhibits that shed light on 21 scientific concepts.

The Museum of Scientific Discovery is open Tuesday through Saturday from 10:00 A.M. to 6:00 P.M. and Sunday NOON to 5:00 P.M. Admission is charged.

Harrisburg has more than 20 park areas but four deserve special mention and inclusion on day-tripping forays. **Riverfront Park** is a four-and-a-half block stretch along the eastern shore of the Susquehanna River from Shipoke (see the John Harris/ Simon Cameron Mansion selection), south of Center City, north to the city line. Riverfront offers river vistas, a restored sunken English garden in the 1200 block of North Front Street, a parcourse trail and contemporary three-dimensional sculpture.

Reservoir Park is the city's largest park and a popular recreational spot with tennis and basketball courts, a playground area and a historic bandshell for the frequent outdoor concerts held here. The antique-styled street-lighted lanes lead to a restored 1898 mansion that contains exhibit and gallery space. In 1991 gardens, fountains and pavilions were added to the park as were a series of Victorian buildings that now serve as an art colony. It's fun to browse through the shops at the **Village of Reservoir Park**.

Another picturesque park is **Italian Lake** in the Riverside neighborhood. In the 1930s the swampy terrain was transformed into a lovely formal garden surrounding a man-made lake. Concerts are performed here during July and August on Sunday at 7:00 P.M. Photographers are attracted to the Japanese bridge across the lake and the *Dance of the Eternal Spring*, a sculpture that stands in the center of the southern lake.

The park with the highest visibility and most visitors is **City Island** across the Susquehanna River from City Center. At night Walnut Street Bridge, now exclusively a pedestrian walkway, and the island shops are outlined in thousands of lights creating a much photographed nighttime focal spot. The more than 60-acre island is the home stadium of the AA Montreal Expos minor league affiliate, the Harrisburg Senators. There is also an extensive sports complex with volleyball courts, playing field and jogging trail. This park also has a collection of shops, the Riverside Village Park, designed with an 1840s canal village theme. It also has eateries and souvenir shops. Authentic paddle-wheel riverboats depart from City Island; there is a City Island Railroad that takes visitors on an island trip. Riding stables provide an alternative means of exploring the island. During the summer months visitors enjoy the beach and swimming area and the miniature golf course.

Directions: From I-76, the Pennsylvania Turnpike, take I-83 into Harrisburg, take the Second Street exit and go straight at traffic light to Second Street. Take Second Street north to Market Street and turn right on Market Street. Make your first left at Court Street, behind the Hilton Hotel, and you will find parking for Strawberry Square and the Museum of Scientific Discovery. For the State Museum of Pennsylvania take Market Street down to Third Street.

John Harris/Simon Cameron Mansion

Encapsulated History

If a single house can be said to encompass the history of a city, that claim can be creditably made for the **John Harris/Simon Cameron Mansion**. The house was built by the first settler in the Harrisburg area, then enlarged by the founder of the city, modernized in the 19th century by its most influential political leader and now serves as the home of the Historical Society of Dauphin County. Touring the mansion not only fills you in on two hundred years of Harrisburg history, it also acquaints you with colorful legends and gives you a chance to see period furniture and art.

John Harris was sent to central Pennsylvania by the Penn family to mediate the problems between English settlers and the Indians. In 1705 Harris established a trading post along the banks of the Susquehanna River. His post included storehouses for trading goods, barns for crops and animals, residential buildings, slave quarters and, it is thought, a tavern. Harris also farmed. In fact, he was considered the first to introduce the plough on the banks of the Susquehanna.

By 1740 Harris began building a stone mansion above his first settlement along the river. Two rooms of this early structure are incorporated into the present house (they were used by subsequent owners as an office and a library). At his death, Harris owned 3,000 acres that stretched on both sides of the Susquehanna.

There's a lithograph in the mansion's front room depicting a time when John Harris's negotiating skills failed. According to the legend, which became important enough in local lore to warrant an early 19th-century painting of the alleged incident, a band of intoxicated Indians, returning from the south, stopped at Harris' trading post and demanded rum. He refused to give it to them and they carried him to a nearby mulberry tree and prepared to burn him to death. There are a number of versions about how he won his freedom. One story maintains he was freed when his black slave, Hercules, sought help from friendly Shawnees, who rescued Harris. Some versions of the story embellish Hercules's role in Harris's rescue, others eliminate him completely.

All the stories agree that he was indeed saved and lived until 1748 when his estate passed to his son John Harris, Jr. At Harris's death the faithful Hercules was freed, and John Harris, at his request, was buried under the mulberry tree. Instead of working with the Indians, his son John Harris, Jr. embarked on a policy of expansion hoping to drive the remaining Indians from their land.

With the outbreak of the French and Indian War, Harris Jr. stockaded the trading post complex and cut gunports into the mansion walls. Although no troops were ever stationed at the post, it was called Fort Harris. After the war ended in 1763, John Harris, Jr. added a new wing and stone barn to the mansion. Several decades later in 1785 Harris, Jr. and his son-in-law William Maclay laid out the city of Harrisburg.

Several families inhabited the mansion between the Harris years. In 1863 it was sold to Simon Cameron, for whom the house is also named. Cameron was a controversial state politician, who served as Lincoln's Secretary of War—he threw his support to Lincoln during the Republican convention of 1859 in return for a cabinet position. Cameron's support for the policy of arming slaves to fight their former masters cost him his position within a year.

Even though short, his tenure served Harrisburg since Cameron designated the city the staging and supply center for the Union Army. This brought hundreds of miles of railroad lines into the city and insured Harrisburg's position as a transportation center. After the war the city grew as steel and coal industries flourished.

Simon Cameron purchased the Harris Mansion when he returned from serving as the U.S. Minister to Russia. Lincoln appointed him to that far-flung post so that Cameron could escape a Senate investigation of his one year tenure as Secretary of War. Cameron extensively remodeled the mansion, adding a Grand Drawing Room, a new formal dining room, breakfast room and extra bedrooms. Interior refurbishing was in the Italianate style, with high ceilings, bay windows and ornate plaster trim. To achieve the high ceiling look, Cameron had the floors on the first level lowered by three feet.

The last private owners of the house were Richard and Margaret Haldeman, grandson and granddaughter-in-law of Simon Cameron. He modernized the house and redecorated it in the Colonial Revival style, though he did choose an art deco look for the bathroom.

The mansion was used as office space from 1935 to 1940 and in 1941 it became the headquarters of the Historical Society of Dauphin County. Only a few Harris family pieces are displayed in the furnished downstairs rooms; most are period pieces relating to the Camerons and Haldemans. Upstairs you'll find period rooms, gallery space and a small collection of toys including doll houses, toy soldiers, baby carriages, cradles and other play things. There is also a collection of case clocks and music boxes, along with items related to Dauphin County history.

The John Harris/Simon Cameron Mansion is listed in the National Register of Historic Places and is bounded by the Susquehanna River and Riverfront Park and Second and Washington Streets. The mansion borders on the **Shipoke National Register Historic District**, a delightful area to explore as the streets are lined with attractive rowhouses. The district also boasts one of Harrisburg's most popular restaurants, Au Jour Le Jour, on Race and Conoy Streets. This tiny little bistro is a delightful lunch or dinner spot.

The John Harris/Simon Cameron Mansion is open Monday through Friday 11:00 A.M. until 3:00 P.M. Tours are given hourly. Tours are also given on the second and fourth Sundays from 1:00 P.M. until 4:00 P.M. Admission is charged.

Directions: From I-76, the Pennsylvania Turnpike, take I-83 north into Harrisburg. Exit on Second Street, get in the left lane, go through the light and make the second left onto Washington Street. Take the first right past River Street into the mansion's grounds. The John Harris/Simon Cameron Mansion is at 219 S. Front Street.

State Capitol Building

Pride of Place

Exploring the statehouse the Smithsonian Institution calls the finest in the nation brings to mind Coleridge's words, "In Xanadu did Kubla Khan a stately pleasure-dome decree ..." To Penn-

211

The Harrisburg Capitol, an architectural and artistic treasure, is unquestionably one of the most glorious state houses in the nation.

sylvanians it also brings a stirring sense of pride. Not since Theodore Roosevelt dedicated the building on October 4, 1906 has the statehouse looked this good. A costly and painstaking restoration project has insured that the gold once again glitters, the stained glass shines, the murals are vibrant and the chambers and halls are returned to their original appearance.

This architectural and artistic treasure cost four million to build. Another nine million was spent to enhance and furnish the 633 rooms spread out on four floors. The crowning feature of this classic Italian Renaissance-style building is the **great dome**, inspired by St. Peter's in Rome. The Rotunda staircase copies the one in the Paris Opera House. The rooms are a glorious mingling of styles: French in the Senate, Italian in the House, and English in the Governor's Reception Room.

Capitol architect Joseph M. Huston envisioned his accomplishment as "a palace of art." He selected Edwin Austin Abbey to create the brilliant murals that so impress visitors. Abbey created five murals in the Hall of the House, including the huge work *The Apotheosis of Pennsylvania* that hangs behind the Speaker's rostrum. Abbey painted 35 distinguished Pennsylvanians who appear to have stepped from the pages of history to witness the establishment of the colony. Depicted are William Penn, Benjamin Franklin, Robert Morris and a host of other intellectual, spiritual, military and industrial leaders. Flanking this great work are depictions of Penn's treaty with the Indians and a reading of the Declaration of Independence. On the center ceiling, against a celestial background, Abbey painted 24 maidens representing the passage of the hours. On the back wall of the House chamber is Abbey's vision of *The Camp of the American Army at Valley Forge*. The **Rotunda** is enhanced with Abbey's allegorical paintings.

The 24 deeply-hued stained-glass windows in the Chamber and House were done by William B. Van Ingen. Each of these opalescent works of art is framed by 22-karat gold leaf. Van Ingen also created 14 vaulted murals for the House corridor. When you walk through the corridors and rotunda be sure to notice the art at your feet—the Capitol may well have the most distinctive floor of any American public building. The floor contains 419 mosaics formed from Mercer tiles (see the Moravian Pottery and Tile Works selection) crafted by Henry Chapman Mercer of Doylestown.

One of the most attractive rooms is the Greek Ionic styled Supreme and Superior Court Chamber where Violet Oakley masterfully created 16 panels outlining the evolution of law. Van Ingen did the stained glass dome. Four huge chandeliers hang from the ceiling. Twenty years before she did the court chamber, Violet Oakley designed the murals in the **Governor's Reception Room**. The room suggests an English Baronial Hall. Originally it was planned as an office suite for the Speaker of the House, but the governor decided that it would be helpful for him to have an office close to the legislative chambers and so it has served from its earliest days.

Everywhere you look is another treasure. On the main floor of the rotunda are 352 historic flags and banners carried by Pennsylvania regiments throughout our nation's conflicts. Tucked in corners and elsewhere are 202 wooden cabinet clocks.

Be sure to notice the heroic statues by George Grey Barnard that flank the Capitol's main entrance. The one-ton bronze doors are enhanced by intricate relief work. At the rear entrance of the Capitol, a neo-classical East Wing was added in 1987 with offices and conference rooms. This functional space highlighted by a skylit **Little Rotunda** with a mini-dome blends felicitously with the Capitol. The new wing is fronted by a hemicycle plaza lit by a 12-foot candelabra and dancing fountain.

The Capitol is open daily from 9:00 A. M. to 4:00 P.M. Be sure to stop at the Information Desk and pick up a brochure that will direct your attention to the various points of interest. With prior planning you can also arrange to tour the **Governor's Residence**, 2035 North Front Street. Tours of this stately Georgian mansion on the Susquehanna River can be arranged by calling (717) 787-

1192. The house is furnished with Pennsylvania antiques and art. In the spring be sure to see the landscaped grounds and gardens.

Directions: From I-76, the Pennsylvania Turnpike, take I-83 into downtown Harrisburg. Exit on Front Street for the downtown area and make a right on Walnut Street. The State Capitol Complex is on Third Street between North Street and Walnut Street.

PENNSYLVANIA DUTCH COUNTRY

Boyertown Museum of Historic Vehicles and the Pagoda

A Variety of Ways to Go

Southeastern Pennsylvania was a pivotal transportation spot in the early days of the automobile industry. In the early 1900s, approximately 20 manufacturers established companies in the area. The first was Charles Duryea who, backed by Reading industrialist Herbert Sternberg, turned out "scientific" automobiles at his Reading factory. The town of Fleetwood was noted for the custom-designed Fleetwood auto bodies it produced for three decades. The name survives even today as a top-of-the-line Cadillac.

The area's transportation history goes back even further. In 1872 Jeremiah Sweinhart opened a factory making farm and delivery vehicles, carriages and sleighs. Later known as the Boyertown Carriage Works, the factory grew to become the Boyertown Auto Body Works, one of the country's best independent truck body builders until it closed in 1990. There could be no more appropriate location for the **Boyertown Museum of Historic Vehicles**.

The museum has more than 100 vehicles made in southeastern Pennsylvania. Powered by steam, electric, internal combustion, horse and pedals, they span the gamut of early transportation options. These are not luxurious vehicles, nor were they owned by celebrities; here are the working vehicles made in the area. For example, an 1872 doctor's buggy is just one of approximately 20 carriages exhibited. There are surreys, buggies, traps, wagons and, for use in snowy weather, sleighs. A 1910 Pleasure Trap, the forerunner of the station wagon, was used to pick up passengers at the train station.

A Conestoga wagon designed in Berks County in 1827 trans-

214

ported iron ore. Farmers in Lancaster, a landlocked agricultural center with no river to aid in the transportation of its produce, adopted the Conestoga wagons to transport the harvest. There are other farm vehicles including 19 wagons.

James Hill was a mechanical experimenter in Fleetwood. He built a steam engine to power his early horseless carriage. You will see that he later converted the engine to a two-cylinder gasoline-powered engine. There are those that believe this is America's oldest existing auto. Another product of an automotive pioneer is the 1907 Duryea **Buggyaut**. It's engine is mounted in a cradle in a system of power transmission which works without gear or drive mechanism. Like the earlier 1904 Duryea Phaeton, also exhibited, one model was produced per week. Ford soon revolutionized the industry by adapting Duryea's assembled auto techniques to mass production on an assembly line.

Another Reading automobile manufacturer, former GM vice-president George Daniels and partner Neff Parrish, began production in 1915 of what they advertised as America's "most distinguished automobile." You can see the elegant Daniels cars in the museum. Other Reading-built cars on exhibit are the Dile, the air-cooled Middleby and the Boss streamer. Reading was also a major bicycle production center. Around 1900, approximately 100,000 were being produced annually.

While the emphasis is on significant vehicles from the past, there is a section that focuses on cars of the future. Exhibits trace more than 90 years of electric vehicle development. Both early electric production models and recent prototypes are displayed. There are also license plates, vehicle building tools, automotive art, children's vehicles and a few unusual items from afar such as the intricately painted Sicilian cart.

The Boyertown Museum of Historic Vehicles in open weekdays 9:00 A.M. to 4:00 P.M. and weekends 10:00 A.M. to 4:00 P.M. It is closed on Monday. Admission is charged. The museum's library contains an extensive collection of books, periodicals and photographs on local vehicles and their builders.

Reading's most unusual architectural site, the **Pagoda**, sits atop Mt. Penn. It is reached by Duryea Drive, the mountain road named for the automobile pioneer who used it to test his new cars. The Pagoda was built in the early 1900s by Mt. Penn quarry owner William Witman. Concerned that his business was destroying the beauty of the mountain, he decided to close the quarry and build a mountain top resort. He built it in the style of a Japanese Shogun Dynasty castle. The six-story red brick and tile "resort" opened in 1908. Guests entered through a Japanese temple gateway. Unfortunately, there was no suitable access road to the resort and it never succeeded. In 1911, Witman sold the Pagoda to a local merchant who donated it to the city.

Time, weather and fire took its toll and by 1969 the Pagoda was badly in need of restoration. The Pagoda Skyline group undertook the project. The only Japanese pagoda east of California is again open. Visitors can climb the majestic oak staircase, or take the elevator, to the observation deck for a panoramic view of Reading. On a clear day you can see for 60 miles. There are some changing exhibits within the pagoda, but most of the interior space is used for offices. There is also a **Bonzai Island**, an oriental garden with stone lantern, gazebo and bridge. Nature trails wind down Mt. Penn.

Directions: From I-76, the Pennsylvania Turnpike, take Exit 24, King of Prussia. Travel south on Route 202 for a half mile to pick up the Pottstown Expressway, Route 422 west. At Pottstown take Route 100 north. Continue 7 miles to Route 73, the Boyertown exit. Make a left and head west on Route 73 to the center of town (the 4th traffic light) to Route 562 and turn left. The museum will be on the left in $1^1/_2$ blocks at 28 Warwick Street. Traveling eastbound on the turnpike (I-76), take Exit 22, Morgantown, and head north on I-176 to Route 422. Follow Route 422 east to Route 100 at Pottstown and follow directions above.

To reach the Pagoda from Business 422, cross the Penn Street Bridge and immediately turn right onto S. Second Street. Go one block and turn left onto Franklin Street and follow to 13th Street and Hill Road. At the light, take the second left and drive up the hill. Make your first right onto Walnut Street and second right onto Duryea Drive and follow the winding road up Mt. Penn to the Pagoda.

Conrad Weiser Homestead and Koziar's Christmas Village

Settlers and Indians

When Conrad Weiser was a young boy his family emigrated to New York from Germany. Growing up in the New York colony the youngster became fascinated with the Iroquois Indians who also considered this area their home. His interest and friendship with the Indians deepened when he spent the winter of 1712-1713 as the adopted son of the Iroquois Chief Quahant in the Schoharie Valley. This experience proved invaluable to him as Pennsylvania's "ambassador" to the Iroquois Indian nation.

In 1729, **Conrad Weiser**, his wife and children moved south joining a group of Germans from the Schoharie who settled at the foot of Eagle Peak in the Tulpehocken Valley of Pennsylvania. He built a one-room cabin for his family with an upstairs sleeping attic. In 1751, he added a second room to accommodate his family (of the 14 children he fathered, 7 survived). This rustic homestead is now a museum filled with period pieces reflecting the simple life on the frontier during America's earliest years, 1750-1800.

With the help of his large family Weiser operated a farm, which eventually included 800 acres and a tannery. He also served as the colony's liaison with the Indians. Weiser was highly regarded for his skills in communicating with the Indians and his grasp of Indian affairs. Working with James Logan, the Pennsylvania Provincial Secretary, he helped formulate and carry out a policy that maintained peace with the Iroquois.

Today on 26 acres of this once extensive holding you can visit the graves of Weiser, his wife and several of their children. Legend adds that Indians are also buried here reflecting the harmony of Weiser's long years of peaceful coexistence. Near Conrad Weiser's grave you'll see a statue of his Iroquois friend, Shikellamy, who was responsible for overseeing the Lenape Indians in the Susquehanna River Valley.

A Visitor Center provides background information on the contributions of Conrad Weiser to early American history. You can visit Wednesday through Saturday from 9:00 A.M. to 5:00 P.M. On Sunday the homestead opens at NOON. Although the house is closed on Monday and Tuesday, the grounds are open daily from 9:00 A.M. to 8:00 P.M. for picnicking and recreation use. Admission is charged.

From the Conrad Weiser Homestead you can extend your outing by heading either north to a very different attraction, **Koziar's Christmas Village** in Bernville. This is a night-time only display of what *Display World Magazine* called "The Best Outdoor Christmas Display in the World."

Talk about enthusiasm, the Koziar family certainly had it in abundance when it comes to decorating. In 1948, William M. Koziar began stringing lights on his house and farm buildings to the delight of his wife, Grace, and their four children. Each year he added more lights until the barns, walkways, trees and lake-front house sparkled and glittered. Family members have constructed elaborate decorations that they adorned with lights—there are now approximately 500,000 lights.

It takes about an hour and a half to see everything, including more than ten glass-enclosed buildings such as the toy shop, Santa's post office, Bavarian shop and a display concentrating on how Christmas is celebrated in other countries plus another with ornately decorated trees. A model train winds through a miniature town in the refreshment barn. A wide variety of ornaments, decorations and gifts can be purchased.

Koziar's is on the Pennsylvania Travel Council's list of Top 10

Pennsylvania Attractions. It is open weekends in October from 7:30 P.M. to 9:30 P.M. In November it opens at 5:30 P.M. and adds Friday nights. From Thanksgiving through New Year's Day is it open daily 6:00 P.M. to 9:00 P.M. and weekends 5:00 P.M. to 9:30 P.M. Admission is charged.

Directions: From I-76, the Pennsylvania Turnpike, take Exit 22, Reading/Morgantown. Take Route I-176 north to Route 422. Go west on Route 422 to the Conrad Weiser Homestead at Womelsdorf. For Koziar's Christmas Village from Womelsdorf take Route 422 west to Route 419 north, then in one mile turn right on Christmas Village Road. The twinkling lights can be seen at a distance. If you want to go directly to Koziar's follow above directions from turnpike but do not take Route 422 west, instead follow the signs for Allentown (Routes 222,183 and 61). Stay on this four-lane highway for .5 mile and get off at the first exit, Route 183. Take Route 183 to the traffic light and turn left on Route 183 north. Continue on this for 13 miles then make a left on Robesonia Road, the next right will be Christmas Village Road and this will take you to the village.

Cornwall Iron Furnace and Mt. Hope Estate

A Blast From the Past

Think about any contemporary commercial corridor and you'll picture ubiquitous fast-food chains. Fast forward a century an imagine that only one survives, that is the analogy you should make when you visit **Cornwall Iron Furnace**. Cornwall was the first iron furnace in this part of Pennsylvania, with passing years it became one of many.

Now it is, again, one of the few. Nowhere else in the United States, and few places in the world, has an iron furnace as well preserved as Cornwall. What you have at Hopewell and Curtin Village are reconstructed iron furnaces; the village at Hopewell is preserved not reconstructed. Robert Vogel of the Smithsonian Institution, in speaking of the restoration of iron-working sites says, ". . . there are two sites of transcendent significance, noteworthy as a consequence of their being true survivals from important periods in American ironworking. These are the Cornwall and Sloss Furnace sites." (The later is a 19th century Alabama furnace.) Vogel continues, ". . . I doubt that elsewhere in the world is there a 19th century iron furnace complex with the degree of historical integrity to be found at Cornwall, where it has been estimated that fully 95% of the fabric is original."

Remarkably, the entire iron-making complex at Cornwall survived intact, providing the visitor an authentic look at 19th century iron-making. Cornwall produced bars of "pig" iron as well as cast-iron products. Pig iron was sent to nearby forges for further refining.

Cornwall was built in 1742 by Peter Grubb to utilize the deposits in the Cornwall Ore Banks, once the greatest known deposit of iron in the country. It was the seventh furnace in the colony but the first in the area. In 1856-57, the furnace was extensively renovated by the Coleman family who then owned the complex (they also owned Hopewell Forge and Colebrook and Elizabeth furnaces). By 1883 the Cornwall Iron Furnace was obsolete and went out of blast.

As you walk through the complex, a guide will explain the complex process by which iron was separated from the ore taken from the nearby pit mines. First the iron was heated by charcoal in the core of the furnace to the melting point. It took an acre of wood *per day* to make the charcoal used in the furnace. One acre of forest equalled 21 cords of wood. The bulk of the work force was involved in making charcoal for the furnace. Each year Cornwall schedules a **charcoal making demonstration**. The Visitor Center is situated in one of the charcoal storage rooms. There were four other equally large storage areas.

Every hour charcoal, iron ore and limestone were added to the furnace. The 32-foot-tall furnace was built beside a hill to make it easier for the workers to load the materials into the furnace. Every 12 hours molten iron was removed from the bottom of the furnace, while slag and waste material were removed at 30 to 60 minute intervals. At its peak the furnace employed 60 men and boys and used 46 horses and mules. It may surprise visitors to learn that for the first couple of generations roughly a third of the workers were black slaves who were the property of the furnace owner.

After you peer 32 feet down to its base, metaphorically looking into the mouth of the furnace, you will discover its lungs. Oxygen needed to keep the fire burning was blown in at the base of the furnace. When Cornwall was first built, air was pumped in using large bellows powered by a water wheel. Later, blowing tubs were added. At first they were powered by the water wheel, but eventually by steam engine. (Note the difference if you visit Hopewell, which is water powered.) Furnace heat was then recycled to create more steam.

This process was hot, noisy and filled the air with charcoal dust and sulphur fumes. The roar of the furnace could be heard throughout the village and its glare created an unholy glow. Both owner and workers lived near the furnace. When you visit Cornwall you can see (but not tour) the owner's house, the mines where the ore was extracted and the miners' and workers' sturdy stone houses.

During the Revolutionary War, some ironmasters became gunfounders. That was the case at Cornwall where 42 cannons were cast. During the Civil War gunblocks were cast at Cornwall, but these did not prove successful. A defective cannon still sits in the casting area. It's in this area you'll discover why they call it pig iron. The molten ore was channeled into sand troughs that reminded workers of a row of hungry pigs lined up beside their mother for lunch.

Cornwall Iron Furnace is open daily Tuesday through Saturday from 9:00 A.M. to 5:00 P.M. On Sundays, it opens at NOON. It is open Memorial, Independence and Labor Days. Admission is charged.

Be sure to visit nearby **Mt. Hope Estate and Winery**, which was originally the site of Mt. Hope Furnace and part of the estate owned by the Grubbs who built Cornwall. This will give you a chance to tour the period rooms on the first floor of an early ironmaster's opulent house. The first ten-room portion of the house was built in 1800. Daisy Grubb, the last family member to inhabit the mansion, added 22 rooms and gave the house a Victorian look. You can tour the mansion's first floor and sample the Mount Hope wines daily from July through October and on weekends year round.

Each December, Mt. Hope evokes the era of Charles Dickens. Victorian decorations fill the house: lacy ribbons cascading down the stairwell and festive wreaths and garlands. Each tree-bedecked room becomes a stage where beguiling tales from Charles Dickens are told. There are carols, charades and parlor games.

The Dickens celebration is one of many special events at Mt. Hope Winery, for schedule details and admission prices call (717) 665-7021. The most well-known is the **Pennsylvania Renaissance Faire** held weekends and Mondays August through Labor Day and weekends only until early October. Twenty-five acres at Mt. Hope are transformed into 16th century England with jousters, conjurers, storytellers, jugglers and jesters. Entertainment is continuous on a replica of Shakespeare's Globe Theatre and 11 other stages. Skilled artisans offer an array of crafts seldom found at other fairs.

There are three other wineries in Lancaster County. **Lancaster County Winery** at 799 Rawlinsville Road in Willow Street, (717) 464-3555, is open Monday through Saturday from 10:00 A.M. to 4:00 P.M. and Sundays 1:00 P.M. to 4:00 P.M. **Nissley Vineyards & Winery Estate** in Bainbridge is open Monday through Saturday from 10:00 A.M. to 5:00 P.M. and Sundays 1:00 P.M. to 4:00 P.M. For more information call (717) 426-3514. **Twin Brook Winery** at 5697 Strasburg Road in Gap is open April through December for sales, tastings and tours on Monday through Saturday from 10:00 A.M. to 7:00 P.M. and Sundays NOON to 5:00 P.M. From January through March the winery is open Tuesday through Saturday from NOON to 6:00 P.M., Sunday hours remain the same. Call (717) 442-4915.

Directions: From I-76, the Pennsylvania Turnpike, take the Lebanon/Lancaster Interchange and proceed north on Route 72. At the traffic signal at Quentin, turn right onto Route 419 north. Follow signs 1.7 miles to the Cornwall Iron Furnace on Rexmont Road at Boyd Street. For Mt. Hope Estate take Exit 20 from I-76, Route 72 south. Mt. Hope is .5 mile from the turnpike.

Ephrata Cloister

A Disciplined Life

Visit **Ephrata Cloister** and enter another era and another continent. The 11 surviving cloister buildings are medieval in design and European in origin. More than 250 years after the community was founded, it still retains an aura of harmony and otherworldliness. At dusk, or on a cold gray day, the atmosphere of austerity and simplicity is most keenly felt.

Life in the colonies was hard for all newcomers, but the members of Conrad Beissel's Ephrata sect were not content to merely suffer the normal hardships of settlement in William Penn's tolerant colony. Beissel's society strove to discipline themselves still more. The sparse nature of their furnishings attest to their philosophy of self-denial. As you tour the **Saron**, or sisters' house, notice the narrow corridors. These reminded the community of the "straight and narrow path of virtue and humility." The low doors were constant reminders to members of their vows of humility. Wooden benches with wooden "pillows" kept the notion of self-denial in their mind even as they slept. Members went to bed at 9:00 P.M., then were awakened at midnight for nightly prayers.

The brothers' quarters, **Bethania**, was torn down in 1908. A group of married householders were also part of the sect. At its height, the community numbered about 300.

Members toiled in the fields growing the food necessary for their survival. Eating, like sleeping, was carefully governed by this religious group. Special dietary restrictions were imposed so that the members could purify their voices and perform the hymns written by Beissel in the proper fashion.

Conrad Beissel was one of America's first composers, he wrote a number of hymns extolling the tenets of ascetic self-denial. Using the calligraphic art of **Frakturschriften**, the sisterhood created hand-illuminated song books. The calligraphy on display at the Visitor Center is as elaborated as today's laserprints. Illuminated books were a special art form practiced at the cloister.

A slide show at the Visitor Center reveals the daily life of this otherworldly sect. After your orientation, guides wearing the white garb of Ephrata members escort you through the sisters' house, the austere chapel and the householder's modest dwelling. After these stops, you are on your own to explore the alms and bake house, Beissel's log cabin, the print and weaver's shop, a solitary cabin and the old graveyard where many of the original members of the society are buried.

Ephrata Cloister is open Monday through Saturday from 9:00 A.M. to 5:00 P.M., on Sunday it opens at NOON. Admission is charged.

Ephrata also has another fascinating spot associated with a religious group—the **Selfhelp Crafts of the World Shop** is operated by the Mennonite Central Committee, a relief and service agency of the Mennonite and Brethren in Christ churches in North America. This is a not-to-be-missed spot for bargain hunters and devotees of handcrafted work. Crafts and art objects from 37 countries are represented and the work is often better than you can ferret out even if you visit the country of origin.

Missionaries who work in these countries encourage the very best craftsmen to pursue their art and improve their economic lot. More than 30,000 low-income artisans have benefited from this enterprise. In addition to the delightful array of crafts on sale there is also a one-of-a-kind ethnic folk art gallery with exhibited pieces.

Try to visit around lunch time because the Nav Jiwan (New Life) Tea Room each week features the food from a different country. Exotic cuisine from Sri Lanka, Laos, Ethiopia, Nigeria, Lesotho and a host of other countries is expertly prepared. The shop sells ingredients used for these weekly specialties so that interested diners can try them at home. The tea room also serves fresh muffins and an assortment of teas for breakfast from 9:00 A.M. to 11:00 A.M. and lunch from 11:00 A.M. to 4:00 P.M.

Directions: From I-76, the Pennsylvania Turnpike, take Exit 21, the Reading Interchange. Go south on Route 222 to Ephrata. The cloister is at 632 West Main Street in Ephrata. The Selfhelp Crafts Shop is at 240 N. Reading Road (Route 272 north) in Ephrata. There is also a smaller shop at 2713 Old Philadelphia Pike (Route 340) in nearby Bird-in-Hand just east of Lancaster.

Gettysburg National Military Park and Eisenhower National Historic Site

Three Days that Broke the South

History was made at Gettysburg—and notable historic figures have traveled to this rural Pennsylvania town to reflect on that past. You should do likewise!

The North Carolina State Monument at Gettysburg National Military Park is the work of world-famous sculptor Gutzon Borglum, who did the granite faces on Mount Rushmore.

The conflict between the Southern forces under General Robert E. Lee and the Northern Army of the Potomac under General George Meade cost more American lives than any other single battle in our history. The battle at Gettysburg was the turning point of the Civil War.

Gettysburg National Military Park has been called the world's largest outdoor open-air museum. An estimated 1,320 markers and monuments tell the story of three tumultuous days in July 1863. The scope of this historic park is daunting; it's important to understand the significance of what you see. It isn't enough to trudge along the fields and woodlands of Gettysburg; you need to people the countryside in your mind with the young men and gallant leaders who fought here.

The Visitor Center's electric map orientation program provides background on the battle fought here, as does the free movie shown at the adjacent **Cyclorama Center**. For a small admission fee you can also see the sound and light program in the circular auditorium built to display the 356-foot cyclorama painted in 1881 by Paul Philoppoteaux. This is one of only three of these once popular cycloramas still on view in the country.

Once you have a basic understanding, you're ready to tour the battlefield. Park maps have a well-marked auto tour route that takes between two and three hours to explore. Be sure to stop along the way and follow one of the foot trails as they encourage a more direct involvement since you literally follow in the footsteps of the soldiers who fought and fell here. Park roads are open 6:00 A.M. until 10:00 P.M. Bikes are welcome on the roads. For an alternative method of exploring there are also horse trails. The Visitor Center is open 8:00 A.M. to 5:00 P.M. and the Cyclorama from 8:30 A.M. to 5:00 P.M.

Just a few short months after the July encounter, on November 19, 1863, Abraham Lincoln came to Gettysburg for the dedication of the Soldier's National Cemetery. Lincoln's brief two-minute address after the two-hour main speech is the perfect example of less is more. His simple message of national purpose still speaks to the heart of our country's pride. The **Soldier's National Monument** was the first of many memorials built at Gettysburg; it stands near the spot where Lincoln stood to deliver the Gettysburg Address.

Another president, Franklin Delano Roosevelt, was on hand in 1938 for the 75th anniversary of the Battle of Gettysburg. He dedicated the **Eternal Light Peace Memorial**.

Gettysburg, once so battle-scarred and bloodied, was quiet rolling farmland both before and again after the battle. The area around Gettysburg is still farmland. One farm in particular draws visitor's attention, the farmhouse of Dwight and Mamie Eisenhower, and is now the **Eisenhower National Historic Site**.

The Eisenhower's farm was built in the 1840s and acquired by them in 1950. This 189-acre farm on the edge of the Gettysburg battlefield was the only home Dwight David Eisenhower ever owned.

When Eisenhower became NATO Commander and spent two years in Paris, Mamie spend her time planning the major reconstruction of their farm. The new modified Georgian farmhouse incorporated the south portion of the old house in its design. The new house had 18 rooms and eight baths. When it was completed in 1955, the farmhouse became the summer White House during Eisenhower's second term. After Ike's first heart attack in late 1955 he recuperated at his new home. When he left office on January 20, 1961, he retired to this haven and spent his last years here.

One of the nice things about visiting this farm is that it really does seem like a home. You'll get no museum feeling when you tour. Homey touches abound—like Ike's faded blue rocker and much-used easel. There are seven of his oil studies on an upstairs wall. Mamie, too, had her pictures: family photographic portraits are framed and massed on the grand piano, indicating her close family ties. The open door in Mamie's pink and green bedroom and the General's robe and slippers on the bed where he often napped give an illusion that the Eisenhowers have just stepped out and will soon be coming home.

One can imagine such distinguished guests as Winston Churchill, Charles de Gaulle, Nikita Krushchev and Jawaharlal Nehru getting a genuine look at real life in America while visiting the Eisenhowers at Gettysburg. A warm and friendly atmosphere still makes itself felt here.

Tickets to the farm can be obtained at the Eisenhower Information Center, located in the Gettysburg National Military Park Visitor Center. Buses transport visitors from the center to the farm for a nominal fee.

Directions: From I-76, the Pennsylvania Turnpike, take Exit 17, Route 15, south to Gettysburg. Once in Gettysburg follow the signs to the Gettysburg National Military Park Visitor Center.

Groff's Farm and Bube's Brewery

Taste Treats

Sometimes dining establishments are more than restaurants, they are not to be missed destinations. Two such spots beckon in the Mount Joy section of Lancaster County: **Groff's Farm and Bube's Brewery**.

If you don't want to leave the area without a true taste of Pennsylvania Dutch life, experience it done to perfection at the award-winning **Groff's Farm Restaurant**, where world-renowned cookbook author and chef Betty Groff presents the best of this regional cuisine. The late food guru James Beard called her farm restaurant "one of the steadfast outposts of true Americana." He heralded her cooking as "a wonderful example of how great American food can be."

In the early 1960s Mennonite housewife Betty Groff, with the help of her husband Abe, converted several rooms of their 1756 farmhouse into a restaurant to give visitors a taste of authentic Pennsylvania Dutch cuisine. The cooking was not the only thing that was home style. Betty used her wedding china and crystal which meant she only had dishes for 36. That would hardly suffice today since diners from around the world seek out this rural restaurant. It hasn't lost its homey ambience. Betty is the hostess and she, or her husband, personally greet and chat with their delighted clientele.

From her kitchen to yours is possible now that two of Betty Groff's four best-selling cookbooks are available at bookstores and at the restaurant: Betty Groff's *Country Goodness Cookbook* and Betty Groff's *Up-Home Down-Home Cookbook*. Executive chef, Charlie Groff, Betty and Abe's son, continues the tradition of preparing the restaurant's trademark chicken Stolzfus, a tasty creamed chicken served over pastry points. The delicious vegetables are all locally grown during the seasons. Many are served with another house specialty, browned butter. Unlike some Lancaster area Pennsylvania Dutch establishments, Groff's diners are elegantly served at individual tables either family-style or a la carte.

Groff's Farm is open Tuesday through Saturday for lunch from 11:30 A.M. to 1:30 P.M. Dinner is at two seatings: 5:00 P.M. and 7:30 P.M. Tuesday through Friday and 5:00 P.M. and 8:00 P.M. on Saturday. Reservations are required for dinner and suggested for lunch; call (717) 653-2048.

The Groffs also own and operate nearby (it's just $4^1/_2$ miles from the farm) **Cameron Estate Inn and Restaurant**, situated in the imposing country home of Simon Cameron, President Lincoln's first Secretary of War. This farmland was worked by Cameron's grandfather and his great-grandfather. In Simon's later years he acquired this property as a link with his past. The mansion he purchased was built in 1805 by Dr. John Watson, a great-grandfather of President McKinley. It's a rural retreat tucked away on 15 wooded acres behind **Donegal Presbyterian Church**. In the churchyard are plaques commemorating the tree under which the congregation gathered in 1777 to pledge their allegiance to the new country. Most of the inn's 18 rooms are filled with reproductions of fine Early American pieces. Many rooms boast a working fireplace. Here the restaurant features French and American country cuisine. For accommodations and reservations call (717) 653-1773.

Lancaster was known as the Munich of the New World during the 1800s because of the high-quality beer brewed by German immigrants in the area. **Bube's Brewery** is the only one of the many breweries still standing. It also has the distinction of being the only intact brewery from this period in the country. Although it is not currently operational, plans are on the drawing board to reactivate it. You can still tour the plant daily from Memorial Day to Labor Day, 10:00 A.M. to 5:00 P.M.

You'll learn about Bavarian immigrant Alois Bube who came to America in 1869 to avoid the military draft. He found work in one of the Lancaster breweries. In 1876, he bought the property that would come to bear his name for $4,250. Thirteen years later, Bube built a large brewery and the Central House Hotel, digging large vaults under the brewery and hotel. On the brewery tour, you'll descend 43 feet into these aging vaults and passages (some were used to hide escaping slaves, as part of the Underground Railroad). If you dine at Bube's Brewery, the cost of the tour is refunded.

There are three restaurants, each uniquely appealing. The most unusual is the **Catacombs**, situated below ground in the brewery's caves that once held great oaken casks. The arched ceiling and niched stone walls with glowing candles provide the proper ambience for the authentic medieval feasts held here on festive occasions. Also on the lower level, in the brewery's original bottling plant, is the moderately-priced **Bottling Works Restaurant** with light meals and weekend entertainment. If you want a more romantic, leisurely dinner make a reservation at Alois's, the upstairs portion of the establishment. The six course meal warrants rave notices and the Victorian ambience of the parlor and small dining rooms is delightful. Reservations are requested for all three restaurants, (717) 653-2056.

If you are traveling from the Lancaster area to Reading, stop halfway at **Ed Stoudt's Black Angus Restaurant** and **Stoudt's Microbrewery** (it's just one mile north of the Pennsylvania Turnpike on Route 272). There are weekend brewery tours and a brewery store where you can purchase these award-winning beers. The microbrewed beers made here were awarded four medals at the 11th Annual Great American Beer Festival in Denver. On Sundays, the **Black Angus Antique Mall** has hundreds of dealers on hand from 8:00 A.M. to 5:00 P.M. During the summer months, there is a 10-weekend long **Bavarian Summer Festival** in the Brewery Hall. In late November and early December, the Antique Hall becomes a "**Christkindlesmarkt**," like the huge market fairs held in Nurnberg, Germany in the 18th and 19th centuries. For more information you can call (215) 484-4385.

Directions: From I-76, the Pennsylvania Turnpike, take Route 222 south to Route 30 west. When Route 30 intersects Route 283, take that west to Route 230 west which will take you into Mount Joy. When you reach Mount Joy, go a half block past the first traffic light and bear left at the "Y" in the road onto Route 772 west, Marietta Avenue. Continue on Route 772 for four blocks and make a left onto Pinkerton Road. Groff's Farm is one mile up the road on the left. Bube's Brewery is one block off Route 230, Main Street, at 102 N. Market Street.

Harley-Davidson Museum & Factory Tour and U.S. Weightlifting Federation Hall of Fame

H.O.G. Heaven

You don't have to ride Harleys or own a motorcycle to be fascinated by the tour of the **Harley-Davidson factory**. In this day of limited plant access, it's a real experience to get on the assembly line floor and watch the smooth operation as motorcycles are put together from the frame to the finished cycle.

This is the only place in the world where Harley-Davidsons are assembled. The company's corporate headquarters is in Milwaukee, Wisconsin and the plant outside Milwaukee makes the engines. But it is at the York facility that three shifts turn out approximately 380 bikes a day. It is interesting to note how many employees wear Harley t-shirts. There seems to be a strong esprit de corps at the plant.

There are two assembly lines and they operate very differently. One line uses a three-person team approach with the workers traveling along with a bike. There are 15 different operations involved in putting together an individual motorcycle. Starting with a bare frame the bike moves down the line, spending about $3^1/_4$ minutes at each of the 15 stations. In 49 minutes the bike is assembled. This line makes between 105 and 110 cycles a day.

The other line, called the **jelly bean line**, makes a wide variety of models in various colors at 77 stations. It takes approximately $2^1/_2$ hours to make a bike on this line and one comes off the line every $2^1/_2$ minutes. These are bigger bikes with more parts. The smaller cycles have about 850 parts, while the bigger models use about 1,250 parts. Approximately 50 percent of the components—with the exception of the engines, transmissions and fiberglass parts—are made at the York plant. On your tour of the factory floor you'll see various parts being formed, like the exhaust pipes that are bent into different configurations.

When a motorcycle comes off the line, test riders run it to make sure it meets specifications. If a cycle has a problem it is taken to the "hospital area" where it is carefully checked before being retested.

Roughly 70,000 people take the free factory tour each year. There are a few safety restrictions to keep in mind. First, no one under 12 is permitted on the factory floor. There are no cameras permitted and no sandals or open-toed shoes.

Adjacent to the plant is the **Harley-Davidson Museum**. Antique motorcycles go back to 1903 and trace the history of America's premier motorcycle manufacturer. Posters highlight the decade-by-decade changes made by Harley-Davidson. There are World War II army bikes that sold for $25 after the war. There are also police bikes, the 1988 Super Bowl half-time all white metal bike and others owned by celebrities like Malcolm Forbes. Just outside the doors of the museum is an area where cameras are permitted. You can sit astride one of the jazzy motorcycles and have your photograph taken. There is also a small gift shop.

Harley-Davidson plant tours are given Monday through Friday from 10:00 A.M. to 2:00 P.M. Museum tours only are given Monday through Friday at 12:30 P.M. and Saturday at 10:00 A.M., 11:00 A.M., 1:00 P.M. and 2:00 P.M. No plant or museum tours are given on major holidays or on Saturdays prior to Monday holidays. Tours may be cancelled so call before visiting, (717) 848-1177.

Nearby is the **U.S. Weightlifting Federation Hall of Fame**. In the 1930s, York was called "Muscletown USA." This distinction occurred because York was the home of Bob Hoffman, the "Father of World Weightlifting." Young athletes came to work with Hoffman, who coached World Championship and Olympic teams and was instrumental in the evolution of iron sports. The Hall of Fame tells the story of his career. It also focuses on three arenas of action: weight lifting, bodybuilding and powerlifting. The exhibits trace weight lifting back to its earliest days, the time of the "Iron Men." Professional and circus strongmen performed crowd-pleasing stunts like bar bending, horseshoe breaking as well as lifting cumbersome and weighty objects. Later the sport of weight lifting was more standardized as it became an Olympic competition. One section has on display trophies, awards and a championship belt awarded individual competition winners. Another gallery has photographs, life casts and other exhibits celebrating those who have been awarded the **Mr. America** title. This is just part of the bodybuilding story recounted here. The final area of competition is powerlifting which got its start in York in 1964. The men and women who have excelled in this relatively new arena are honored.

The USWF Hall of Fame is open Monday through Saturday from 10:00 A.M. to 3:30 P.M. There is no charge for the self-guided tour.

Directions: From I-83, take Exit 9E and travel one mile east on Route 30. Signs will indicate the Harley-Davidson plant on the left. The USWF Hall of Fame is also off I-83, take Exit 11. Turn left, which will take you over the interstate. Then turn left on Board Road; it is $^1/_4$ mile to the Hall of Fame.

Hawk Mountain

Raptor Rapture

Have you ever experienced raptor rapture? You will if you go to Kittatinny Ridge and the 2,200-acre **Hawk Mountain Sanctuary**. It's a thrilling sight to see birds of prey on the wing, riding the wind.

At least 16 species of raptors, more commonly known as birds of prey, can be spotted over Hawk Mountain from mid-August through November. The species you see on a particular visit will vary. During September you are likely to sight ospreys, bald eagles and broad-winged hawks. The biggest sightings are is usually mid-month when thousands of medium-sized soaring hawks ride the warm air currents. October brings the greatest variety of hawks. You may spot a sharp-shinned hawk, red-shouldered hawk, Northern harrier, Cooper's hawk or rough-legged hawk. As October ends you may well catch sight of the striking golden eagle riding the cold winds. A chance to see this magnificent bird with its seven-foot wingspan is worth braving the cold weather.

If you feel that half the thrill would be lost because you would not be able to identify the various species, then stop first at the sanctuary's Visitor Center to see its collection of mounted birds of prey and to browse through the books. When you're ready to tackle the slopes, you have two options—the South Lookout and the North Lookout. The former is the easier climb; the trail is only three-quarters of a mile. If you are really out of shape don't try for the North Lookout, it's a 45-minute hike and involves scaling a few rocky areas. Amateur hikers in sneakers can manage it with effort.

Once you reach the top, it's worth the climb. From massive sandstone blocks you gaze over a magnificent 70-mile view. Many of the birds of prey actually fly beneath you. Between

20,000 and 25,000 birds are logged in a season and on a "hot" day you may see hundreds, even thousands, of raptors. On a few occasions during broad-winged hawk migrations they have counted more than 10,000 raptors. Ironically, a "hot" day usually occurs during cold weather when a front rolls down from Canada. A phone call to Hawk Mountain Sanctuary, (215) 756-6961 after sunset August 15 through December 15, can give you current flight updates plus local weather forecasts. It is well to keep in mind that even when there is not a cold front coming through, it is cold on the lookouts, so dress warmly. In addition to the lookouts, there are five miles of hiking trails open sunrise to sunset. During the spring and fall there are guided hikes.

Bird watching requires patience. Be prepared to spend some time waiting. As you wait, there are other wonders to observe. Beneath South Lookout you can see the **River of Rocks** which dates from the Silurian Period, between 408 and 438 million years ago. These sandstone boulders wind along the valley floor like a river; water flows not over, but under, them. You may also spot deer in the valley below, but most of the time you will be scanning the sky. Be sure to bring binoculars so you can zero in on the birds once you spot them. Novices get help from more experienced birders who usually are quick to identify the various raptors. In fact, on weekends Hawk Mountain can get quite crowded and regulars try to plan their visits for less frequented weekdays.

Visitors to Hawk Mountain are the beneficiaries of the raptors' practice of daytime migration. (Some birds fly at night using a system of celestial navigation.) Raptors follow the mountain ridges and great kettles of broad-winged hawks soar together on the thermals, the warm air currents that allow the birds to glide from ridge to ridge. Hawk Mountain is the southern ridge of this system.

Hawk Mountain has been a sanctuary for migratory birds of prey since 1934. It is the oldest refuge offering this protection. Prior to 1934 hunters, not bird watchers, lined the top of Kittatinny Ridge. Surprisingly, it was not the government that ended the carnage but Hawk Mountain Sanctuary, a privately-maintained association. The sanctuary is supported by the minimal admission and by annual memberships. There is a small bookstore and restrooms. Picnic lunches are often enjoyed on the mountain lookouts. Bring an apple or snack even if you don't plan to picnic so that you can munch while you wait. The Visitor Center at Hawk Mountain Sanctuary is open 9:00 A.M. to 5:00 P.M. daily.

On weekends in the spring and fall the sanctuary has interpretive programs. Two live raptors, a hawk and an owl, are introduced in the 30-minute "Raptors Alive" program given in the amphitheater four times daily on fall weekends and three times during the spring. The adaptations of these predators of the air are discussed. A slide presentation on identifying northeastern raptors in flight is presented at the Visitor Center. As you scan the sky it is hard to imagine how hawk counters keep track of the birds they sight from the sanctuary's lookouts.

While in the area take a steam train ride on the **Wanamaker, Kempton and Southern Bell Rail Road.** It has trains and a trolley that meander along the scenic Hawk Mountain Line from Kempton to Wanamaker, a 40-minute, $6^1/_2$ mile roundtrip. There's time enough to alight and have a picnic at **Fuhruman's Grove**, explore the nature trails or browse through an antique shop.

The WK&S runs March through June on weekends from 1:00 P.M. to 5:00 P.M. From September through November, when most bird watchers are in the area, the weekend hours are 1:00 P.M. to 4:30 P.M. For additional information and fares, call (215) 756-6469 or (215) 437-1239.

Directions: Take the Northeast Extension of the Pennsylvania Turnpike; when it intersects I-78, take that west to Route 143. Take Route 143 four miles to Hawk Mountain Road, signs will point the way to the sanctuary. The WK&S, or Hawk Mountain Line, is just five miles south on Route 143 in Kempton.

Hershey

How Sweet It Is!

Does the word Hershey conjure up the marvelous taste of chocolate? After a visit to **Hershey**, it will call up many more pleasant associations.

The first impression you are likely to get in Hershey *is* the rich scent of chocolate which with the slightest breeze, wafts through the community. Next you'll be visually stimulated by the town's unique street lights and street signs. Where else in America could you see candy-kiss shaped lights? Few families can resist a candid shot of these street lights or of the street signs at the junction of Chocolate Avenue and Cocoa Avenue.

You grasp the scope of the chocolate business and have a chance to enjoy a variety of chocolate treats at Hershey's information center, Chocolate World Visitor Center. This is a good first stop because **Hersheypark** is adjacent to the center and the town's other attractions are accessible by tram and shuttle bus from here. **Chocolate World** is open at no charge from 9:00 A.M. to 4:45 P.M. (6:45 P.M. during the summer months). If the kids are in a hurry to get to the rides in Hersheypark you can assure them that at Chocolate World they also have a ride. This ride guides visitors through the world of chocolate from its beginnings on the cocoa plantations of South America to the finished product made at Hershey. Old-timers may remember the tours of the plant itself, which so overwhelmed visitors with the smell from vats of chocolate that it was hours before anyone could taste a sample. There is no such sensory overload on this ride, and you may well want to stop at the boutiques, restaurants and shops for a taste of the company product. Chocolate can be purchased from a single kiss to a ten-pound Hershey bar.

One of the big advantages of this well-laid-out town is that since one parking lot serves all the points of interest, families can split up and follow their individual bents. Older kids can head immediately for Hersheypark. Keep in mind that the easily located **Kissing Tower** inside the park is a good place to plan a rendezvous. Flower fanciers in the family can meander through **Hershey Gardens**.

If a national committee had won their campaign Milton Hershey would have contributed to yet another garden in Washington, D.C. In 1936, he was asked to donate a million dollars toward the establishment of a National Rosarium. He chose instead to develop a garden more or less in his own backyard. Pennsylvanians can be glad he did because the results are striking. It is worth a trip to Hershey just to see the gardens, particularly in early summer and fall when the roses are at their peak. Although the gardens have many specialty areas, roses are the primary focus. Roses are featured in the All-American Rose Avenue, the Old-Fashioned Rose Garden and in Mrs. Hershey's personal rose garden.

Other plants are certainly not neglected at Hershey Gardens. Spring arrives in a burst of color provided by tens of thousands of daffodils and tulips plus brilliant azalea and rhododendron bushes. Mid-summer is brightened by 400 day lily varieties and fall by 4,000 chrysanthemums. Tours of the garden include the Japanese, Italian and English Formal Gardens. America's past is captured in the Colonial Garden and the Herb Garden.

If you come to Hershey particularly to see the flowers, then extend your pleasure by strolling through the grounds of The Hotel Hershey on the hilltop above Hershey Gardens. The hotel's formal gardens are attractive and your day can be capped by lunch in the elegant Hotel Hershey's circular dining room overlooking the gardens.

To balance the day's outing for youngsters stop at the **Hershey Museum** before taking them to the rides at Hersheypark. This museum presents exhibits from the earliest inhabitants on the North America continent to the collectibles of this generation. There are crude utensils from prehistoric people, intricately crafted Indian baskets, beaded Eskimo clothes, memorabilia from the wars in which America has been involved, a Conestoga wagon and the household belongings that have furnished our homes through the centuries. The collection of Pennsylvania-German artifacts is one of the largest in existence. Another exhibit describes the accomplishments of founder Milton Hershey. Admission is charged. Hours are 10:00 A.M. to 5:00 P.M. During the summer the museum stays open until 6:00 P.M.

The most well-known attraction in Hershey, aside from chocolate, is Hersheypark. A redevelopment campaign was initiated in 1971 and today it ranks among America's top theme parks. Animal fanciers enjoy the park's **ZooAmerica** which has plants and animals from the five natural regions of North America.

Obviously you can't cover everything in a day, but with the varied attractions at Hershey you can plan an outing that will please everyone in the family.

Directions: From I-76, the Pennsylvania Turnpike, take Exit 19 at Harrisburg. I-283 north to Route 322 and follow that east to Hershey. From I-82 take Exit 21 and follow Route 743 south to Hershey. Also use Exit 28 of I-81 and go south on Route 743. You can use Exit 27 and take Route 39 east to Hershey.

Hopewell Furnace, St. Peters Village and Daniel Boone Homestead

Triple Treat

Hopewell Furnace does for the travel buff what John Jakes's novel *North and South* did for the historical novel buff—it presents a rarely captured look at a paternalistic iron plantation. Like the Hollywood movie sets of the plantations of the Old South, Hopewell looks a lot cleaner now than it did in the 1770s. From the late 18th century until 1883, the furnace ran day and night, filling the air with smoke and coating the village with ash and cinders.

Now the dust is long settled. You can see an idealized, picture-perfect iron-making community, operating as it did between 1820 and 1840. It's interesting to compare the small houses of the iron workers (still planted with their kitchen gardens) with the comparative luxury of the ironmaster's home, the Big House. Like their counterparts in the South, the ironmasters were community leaders. In fact, James Wilson and George Ross, both ironmasters and brothers-in-law of Hopewell's founder Mark Bird, were members of the Continental Congress and signers of the Declaration of Independence. Another Pennsylvania signer, George Taylor, was the ironmaster at Durham Furnace.

When you arrive at this National Historic Site, managed by

Restored stone buildings and reconstructed wooden ones at Hopewell Village National Historic Site provide an authentic glimpse of the social, cultural, economic and industrial life in this early American ironmaking community.

NATIONAL PARK SERVICE PHOTO, RICHARD FREAR

the National Park Service, you will begin your exploration at the Visitor Center where an easy-to-follow ten-minute orientation slide program provides an idea of how an iron furnace operated. This will, in turn, give you a greater appreciation of what you will see on your self-guided walking tour.

Many of the 17 stops on your tour route are concerned with the iron-making process. Hundreds of acres of timber had to be cut annually to make charcoal for the furnace. The massive iron furnace was the linchpin of the village. You'll see the cast house where the molten iron was formed into armaments for the Continental Army and such utilitarian products as stoves, sash weights and cookware. Taped messages will help you understand the process as you follow the step-by-step procedure on your tour route.

The voices of those bygone days, heard on taped recordings, reveal intriguing details about daily life and concerns. Some villagers have serious problems: one worries about child labor, while a widow laments the hardship of her life.

Although interesting year-round, it is in the summer that Hopewell is most alive. During June, July and August the living history program presents authentically clad blacksmiths, cooks, moulders, seamstresses, an office clerk and teacher as well as other craftspeople who talk about their lives and demonstrate their skills. Hopewell Furnace is open daily from 9:00 A.M. to 5:00 P.M. except Thanksgiving, Christmas and New Year's Day. Hopewell is accessible to the handicapped.

Adjacent to this historical site is a natural one—**French Creek State Park** where you can enjoy a picnic lunch. This 7,339-acre park, with its three lakes, offers a variety of activities. Hiking, fishing, swimming and camping are popular in pleasant weather. During the winter months you can ski, sled, toboggan, skate or ice fish.

Another nearby attraction is **St. Peters Village**, a picturesque Victorian village where you can enjoy lunch, hike along French Creek and browse through well-stocked boutiques. While having lunch on the outdoor patio of the Inn at St. Peters you can watch the French Creek Falls, which drop 155 feet in less than half a mile.

One additional historic site easily combined with a visit to Hopewell is the **Daniel Boone Homestead**. It was in this untamed part of Pennsylvania that Daniel Boone was born and lived until he was 16. In the woods around his home he learned to hunt and trap. Only the foundations remain of the log cabin Daniel Boone called home. A two-story stone house built in the late 18th century has been furnished to recreate rural life in this part of Pennsylvania. It is interesting to compare this independent rural life with that of the iron workers at nearby Hopewell.

The Boone cabin is now furnished to tell the story of the three families who lived on this land in the 18th century—the Boone,

Maugridge and DeTurk families. Through these families both English and Germanic rural traditions are encompassed as the fascinating story of the settlement of this part of the state is told.

The homestead has a working blacksmith's shop. Daniel Boone's father practiced this trade and as a young boy Daniel learned how to fix his own rifle and musket. Additional outbuildings including the smokehouse, barn, Bertolet log house, bake oven and sawmill. The Visitor Center provides orientation and an extensive collection of publications on sale related to Boone and Pennsylvania colonial history. Tours and historical programs are presented year-round.

There are trails extending through part of the homestead's 579 acres of rolling countryside. The area around the farm is a game sanctuary where deer, raccoon, rabbits, pheasants and quail can occasionally be spotted, just as it could when young Daniel learned to hunt.

On the grounds there is also a picnic area, lake and overnight camping, both indoor and outdoor, for organized youth groups. Admission is charged to the historic area. For additional information call (215) 582-4900.

Directions: From I-76, the Pennsylvania Turnpike, take Exit 22 at Morgantown and pick up Route 10. At Route 10 turn left, south, for $1/4$ mile into Morgantown. In Morgantown turn left, east on Route 23 and go five miles to the intersection with Route 345. Then take a left, north, on Route 345. This leads into Hopewell Furnace, which is only ten miles from the turnpike. Follow the above directions for St. Peters Village and continue on Route 23, then make a left on Route 8 and go north to the village. For the Daniel Boone Homestead you will also take Exit 22 at Morgantown, then bear left at the McDonalds. Proceed to the intersection and make a right, then very shortly, bear right again on Route 176, north. Follow Route 176 until you see a sign for Pottstown. This will take you to Route 422 east. Continue for approximately four miles to the highway division. Stay in the left lane and proceed through a traffic light. Watch for a blue and gold historic marker. Make a left turn and cross over the divided highway. This is the Daniel Boone Road and it leads into the homestead.

Indian Steps Museum

Steps in Time

When the first settlers arrived at Jamestown, Virginia, in April 1607 they did not build homes and plant crops. Under pressure because they feared the London Company would abandon them if they failed to discover riches in the New World, they spent the spring and summer in a fruitless search for gold. Had it not been for Captain John Smith who supervised the construction of crude cabins and wisely began trading with the local Powhatan Indians, the colony very likely would have failed.

After a time the Indians in the area had so reduced their own supply of surplus food they refused to trade and Smith had to find new sources. In 1608 he sailed up the Potomac River searching for new trade opportunities and gold. He went as far as the Susquehanna River where he encountered the Susquehannock Indians, taller and more warlike than the Virginia Powhatans.

The Susquehannocks and other tribes who used the river for their north-south migrations often hunted, fished, traded and fought along the river bank. The last Indians to inhabit this area, the Shawnees, left in 1765.

The **Indian Steps Museum** derives its name from the footholds, or steps, the Indians carved into the rocky river bank. The steps, unfortunately are now covered by water. Arrows, spearheads, stone axes and other artifacts left by the thousands of Indians who traversed this area have been found along the shores of the Susquehanna River.

In the early 1900s John Edward Vandersloot, a local attorney, acquired 9.6 acres along the Susquehanna River. While preparing the ground for his garden he uncovered arrowheads, spears, tomahawks, stone tools and pottery shards. The artifacts introduced him to a hobby he would pursue for the remainder of his life.

Both house and hobby continued to grow. In 1908, the first floor of the house was built; it was followed by the second and third floor and, finally, a tower was added in 1912. The two massive fireplaces, winding stone steps and stained glass windows all make this a far-from-ordinary museum. The museum contains artifacts from the Susquehanna Indians and fossils found in this area.

Like all collectors, Vandersloot had to find a place to display his finds. He had a great portion of his collection, some 10,000 relics, embedded in the wall and floor of the **Kiva**, a round room. There are no artifacts embedded in any other part of the interior; however, some of the findings are in the form of a spider web, a wasp nest and a turkey on the exterior walls.

On the grounds which yielded this amazing array of artifacts are picnic tables and a riverside hiking trail. The grounds support an abundant bird and animal population, as well as 70 species of trees. If you visit Indian Steps during fishing season you will notice that there are some great fishing spots along the trail. Boats are also available from a nearby boat yard and, if you choose, you can reach Indian Steps by boat. The museum has its own dock. Campers can stop at the convenient **Otter Creek Recreation Area**, located about a mile upstream at its confluence with the Susquehanna River.

The Indian Steps Museum is open at no charge, but donations are solicited to help maintain this unusual site. The museum is open April 15 through October 15 on Thursday and Friday from 10:00 A.M. to 4:00 P.M. on weekends and holidays hours are 11:00 A.M. to 6:00 P.M. Special entertainment is scheduled on Sunday afternoons during the summer months.

Directions: From I-83 south of York take the Queen Street exit, Route 74 south. Continue on Route 74 through Spry, then Dallastown and Red Lion. Once through the square in Red Lion take Burkholder Road to New Bridgeville. Proceed straight through the intersection; Burkholder Road becomes Route 425. Continue on Route 425 for eight miles to Museum Road. Take Museum Road for $1^1/_4$ miles to Indian Steps Museum.

Jennie Wade House and The Lincoln Room Museum

Rooms with History

The big story at Gettysburg is told on the battlefield, but there are other stories, sidebars to the main action. One tragic story is revealed at the **Jennie Wade House**. At the time of the battle this was the McClellan home.

Just a few days before the battle Jennie Wade's sister Georgiana McClellan gave birth to her first child. On the morning of July 3, 1863, 20-year-old Jennie was helping in her sister's house by baking bread for the Union soldiers. The house tour begins in the McClellan kitchen, restored to its mid-19th-century appearance.

The mini-ball that struck Jennie in the back was not the first fired into the house. An hour earlier, a bullet fired through the parlor window, struck the bedpost where the recuperating Georgiana McClellan lay and fell to the pillow beside her head. By the end of the battle all the windows on the north side of the house were destroyed by gunfire. Jennie was the only family member hit, and the only civilian in Gettysburg to be killed.

Jennie Wade never received a message sent her from childhood sweetheart Jack Skelly. He sent a message with Wesley Culp, a local boy who joined the Confederate Army. When Corporal Skelly, who was serving with the 87th Pennsylvania Volunteer Infantry, was wounded while fighting in Virginia, his path

239

crossed that of his friend Culp. But Culp was one of the 51,000 military casualties of the Gettysburg battle and the romantic message was never delivered. Perhaps this mishap accounts for the superstition that has arisen at the Jennie Wade House. Unmarried girls are advised to put a finger through the bullet hole, this will insure that they receive a marriage proposal before the year ends. Testimonials attesting to this hang on the door, including a letter dated July 4, 1926.

After visitors hear the story of Jennie Wade's death from a holographic figure in the kitchen, they view the parlor, then continue to the second-floor bedrooms. During the battle an artillery shell landed on the roof. Its trajectory broke down the wall between the two sides of this double-occupancy house. Union soldiers enlarged the hole made by the shell and carried Jennie Wade's body upstairs and through the adjoining house to the McClellan cellar. The tour follows this route to the subterranean room.

Jennie's family maintained a vigil beside her body from 8:45 A.M. on July 3 until 1:00 A.M. the next morning. She was buried in a temporary grave in the garden at 5:00 P.M. on the 4th. She is now interred in the town cemetery that gave Cemetery Hill its name.

When you leave the basement, you'll pass through the gift shop stocked with souvenir items, then enter **Olde Town**. Here you'll see storefronts and mannequins to suggest the shops in Gettysburg during the tumultuous days in July 1863. The Jennie Wade House is open daily. Hours in the summer are 9:00 A.M. to 9:00 P.M., otherwise it is open until 5:00 P.M. Admission is charged.

There are several other museums on the same street as the Jennie Wade House. Across the street is the **Hall of Presidents**, with life-size mannequins of all the Chief Executives. Brief taped messages from each tell the pivotal events of their administration. Mannequins of the president's wives show them in their inaugural gowns. Beside this is the **Soldier's National Museum** with ten dioramas depicting Civil War battles.

The **Lincoln Room Museum**, on Lincoln Square in the heart of Gettysburg, is another pivotal room that figured in our country's history. When President Lincoln took the train from Washington to Gettysburg to deliver a short address following the main speaker at the dedication of the National Cemetery, he stayed overnight at Judge David Wills's house. The bedroom is furnished to look just as it did during Lincoln's visit.

A ten-minute sound-and-light program in the room Lincoln used, takes you step-by-step through the events of Lincoln's stay. You'll learn that after Lincoln arrived at the Wills's house a crowd gathered in the square beneath the bedroom window. Lincoln opened the window and talked to the throng. He even asked the band to play "Dixie".

As you sit and listen to these events unfold, few can resist the pull of the past. For this is the very room in which Lincoln sat pondering the text he had begun in the White House for his Gettysburg Address. In the room adjacent to the Lincoln bedroom there are exhibits on his visit and copies of the five drafts that Lincoln made of his address. One of the five copies was the one Lincoln began writing at the White House and finished at the Wills's House.

The Lincoln Room Museum is open during the summer season from 9:00 A.M. to 7:00 P.M., closing at 8:00 P.M. Friday and Saturday. The museum closes at 5:00 P.M. in the off-season. Admission is charged.

Directions: From I-76, the Pennsylvania Turnpike, take Exit 17, Route 15 south to Gettysburg. From I-81, take Exit 6, Route 30 east to Gettysburg. From Route 15 turn left on Carlisle Street, which will become Baltimore Street, bear left on Route 97 and the Jennie Wade House will be on your left. Coming into town on Route 30, turn right on Baltimore Street. The Lincoln Room Museum is on Lincoln Square in the heart of town on Baltimore Street.

Land of Little Horses

A Breed Apart

When this Pennsylvania farm celebrates the birth of a healthy seven-pound, thirteen-inch baby it isn't at all what you'd expect. The congratulations are likely to be for the latest horse born at the **Land of Little Horses**. For Tony Garulo, the ex-sea captain who launched this highly successful attraction, life took an unexpected turn when he visited Argentina and learned about Falabella horses.

Garulo began frequenting the breeding farm of Julio Cesar Falabella and learned that the miniaturization program had been carried on by the Falabella family since the 1860s. One of the early Falabella favorites was a stallion called Napoleon. Short and stocky, this miniature marvel was only 20 inches high and weighed 70 pounds, but he sired many foals and is related to a number of the horses at the Gettysburg farm. Napoleon lived to the age of 42, quite a respectable record for a horse of any size.

The downbreeding achieved by Senor Falabella kept the horses proportionally correct, just far smaller than the norm. If you take a picture of a **Falabella horse** with nothing beside it to

The miniature Falabella horses at the Land of Little Horses cap-tivate young and old.

indicate size it looks the same as a full-size horse. Other miniaturizers have bred horses with oversize heads and short, stubby legs.

When Garulo ended his maritime career in 1971 he brought 51 of the Falabella horses to Gettysburg. He had an exclusive agreement to be the only Falabella representative in North America. This is still the largest herd of Falabella miniature horses in the country. In 1993 the Land of Little Horses was purchased by Sandy and Ray Hawkins.

From the farm's earliest days, it has captivated the public. The horses delight young and old. They range from poodle-size to that of a Great Dane, and come in a variety of breeds and colors: appaloosas, English trotters, Clydesdales, Arabians, pintos and palominos. Some are part quarterhorse and part thoroughbred.

The horses appear to be natural performers. They have been bred for disposition and are tame and gentle, although some of the stallions may nibble a bit. Like their full-sized counterparts, different breeds excel at different activities. There are jumpers and those that dance and respond to commands as you will see if you catch one of the four shows presented daily in the 700-seat arena.

There is always at least one of these gentle horses for young visitors to ride. The horses can carry no more than 80 pounds and there is an additional charge for rides. The Clydesdales pull a tiny wagon. There are other farm animals to be seen as well as a **carriage museum**.

If you think it would be fun to own one of these miniature horses, you're right. You would have to own 12 miniatures before you'd require the amount of feed necessary for one standard-size horse. Numerous well-known personalities have owned Falabellas: Princess Grace of Monaco, Lord Mountbatten, Charles de Gaulle, Jacqueline Kennedy Onassis, Frank Sinatra, the Queen of England and the Dutch royal family. There is a sizeable waiting list for these horses because demand is high. So is the price!

You can see the miniature horses at the Land of Little Horses from April through the end of October. Hours are 10:00 A.M. to 5:00 P.M. daily; during the summer months the farm stays open until 6:00 P.M. Shows are at 11:00 A.M., 1:00 P.M., 3:00 P.M. and 5:00 P.M. from Memorial Day through Labor Day. In the spring and fall there is no 5:00 P.M. performance. Admission is charged and rides are extra. There is an extensive gift shop and tables are available for picnics.

Directions: From I-76, the Pennsylvania Turnpike, take Exit 17, Route 15 south to Gettysburg. About three miles west of Gettysburg on Route 30 you will see a large sign directing you to the farm.

Lincoln Train Museum and Gettysburg Railroad

Steam into the Past

The train never moves but yet it covers the distance between Washington, D.C. and Gettysburg in 12 minutes. Seated in the 1863 **Lincoln Train**, you take a simulated journey with President Lincoln and his traveling party to the dedication of the National Cemetery on the site of the bloodiest battle of the Civil War.

A screen at the front of the car reveals the Civil War countryside with soldiers occasionally straggling along beside the tracks. The soundtrack recreates conversations that might have occurred during this historic journey. You can hear the train whistle and clatter as it seems to bounce and sway along the tracks. Once the president arrived in Gettysburg, he went to the home of his host Judge David Wills (see Lincoln Room Museum selection).

This museum also has the only complete Civil War military railroad layout. A six-minute program reveals details about the first military use of the railroad. Armies and supplies were moved by rail from one battlefield to another. Many of the war's tactical campaigns involved destroying these vital rail links. Colorful dioramas reveal the various roles played by the railroad during the war. Details are also provided about the **Underground Railroad**, which was not a railroad at all but an escape route for slaves fleeing the South. Children enjoy the toy train collection with numerous operating layouts. There are also over 1,000 trains collected from around the world.

The Lincoln Train Museum, 200 Steinwehr Avenue, is open during the summer from 9:00 A.M. to 9:00 P.M. In the spring and fall the museum closes at 5:00 P.M. Admission is charged.

To literally ride the rails, climb aboard one of **Gettysburg Railroad**'s steam trains. Trains leave the downtown station, just a block from where Lincoln disembarked, then travel past the first-day battlefield into the scenic countryside. There are special event excursions, such as the **Civil War Train Raid** and Lincoln Train plus holiday runs. There are also 50-mile dinner trips and Fall Foliage excursions. The regular trip is an $1^1/_2$ hour, 16-mile round trip that runs on weekends in the spring and fall and on select weekdays in the summer. For details on the schedule and fare call (717) 334-6932.

This really is a ride through history, because the Gettysburg Railroad can be traced back to April 1864 when South Mountain Iron Company was incorporated. Included in the original holdings of this company were the 1770 Pine Grove Furnace and the Laurel Forge plus 20,000 acres of ore and timber land.

Although a railroad line headed into Gettysburg at the time of the Civil War, this line connecting the area with the Cumberland Valley Rail Road in eastern Carlisle was not built until 1868. Over the years the line from Gettysburg north was owned by a variety of railroad companies, including Conrail. It is now a short-line railroad.

Directions: From I-76, the Pennsylvania Turnpike, take Exit 17, Route 15 south to Gettysburg. From I-81, take Exit 6, Route 30 east to Gettysburg. The Lincoln Train Museum is on Business Route 15 south, also called Steinwehr Avenue, across the street from the National Park Service Visitor Center. The Gettysburg Railroad station is at 106 N. Washington Street. This is one block west and one block north of Lincoln Square.

Lititz

Birthplace of the American Pretzel

Few destinations offer the diversity of **Lititz**, the quintessential American hometown of yesteryear. What other Main Street offers the sound of music and the scent of chocolate? It's also one of the only spots where you can learn how to twist a pretzel.

The town was established in 1756 on land donated to the Moravian Congregation. It was named in honor of the barony of Lititz in Bohemia where King Podiebrad offered sanctuary to the persecuted Moravians, or Unitas Fratrum, as they were also called. The oldest Protestant denomination, Unitas Fratrum, was established in 1467, 60 years before the Reformation. Followers of John Hus, Czech theologian and martyr, broke away from the Catholic Church.

The center of community life in Lititz, as in any Moravian town, was the church. The church you see when you visit was built in 1786 and it's flanked by the Sisters' and Brethren's Houses. Located next to the Brethren's House is the archives and museum that house an outstanding collection of old musical instruments.

Music was an integral part of the Moravian service. Thus it is not surprising to discover that the Moravians were an important musical force in colonial America. They were the first musical educators; they made many of the first instruments and wrote a substantial number of the religious compositions of the 18th century. They also composed the first chamber music in this country.

The tradition of the trombone choir is closely associated with Moravian music, and so you will see an excellent selection of brass instruments in the church's exhibit. The oldest brass instrument in the Lititz collection is a hunting horn, made in France in 1750, likely the prize possession of one of the early settlers. Another room has woodwind and stringed instruments. It is a marvel that so many of these old pieces survived. They were located, restored, researched and put on display by a dedicated couple, George and Julia Keehn. They, with the able assistance of the late R.M. Shank, are largely responsible for making this museum a reality. Tours of this unique museum can be arranged by calling the church office at (717) 626-8515.

Directly across the street from the church, the **Johannes Mueller House** gives you a glimpse of how German settlers in Lititz lived in the 18th century. The main portion of this seven-room house was built in 1792 by Johannes Mueller, a printer and dyer of linen. He lived here with his wife, their four children and his three apprentices. This house has been furnished with antique pieces donated by the residents of Lititz, many of which were actually made by early settlers.

Directly adjacent to the Johannes Mueller House is the **Lititz Museum**, where visitors can see an illustrated history of the area and displays of local interest. One room contains the furnishings which belonged to well-known resident, General John Augustus Sutter, whose elegant two-story brick home just up the street at 19th E. Main Street now serves as the offices for Farmers First Bank.

The most unusual pieces in the museum are two inlaid wooden clocks made by local craftsman, Rudolph Carpenter. His hobby was making complex inlaid wooden furniture. During the colonial period furniture made out of solid wood was taxed while that made of multiple kinds of wood was not. Evidently the wood was often stained or painted to make detection difficult. Wood was used for a great many household items including toys. On the second floor of the Mueller house you can see a wooden "slinky" dog, wooden perpetual motion ducks and a two-sided wooden puzzle.

The Johannes Mueller House and the Lititz Museum are open May through October Monday through Saturday from 10:00 A.M. to 4:00 P.M. At other times you can visit by appointment by writing to the Lititz Historical Foundation, 137 East Main Street, Lititz, PA 17543. An admission is charged.

Family roots are important to James E. Hess. He used old maps to find old homesteads and graveyards as he researched his family's Lancaster County ties. This research instilled in Hess an interest in old maps that resulted in the creation of the world's first museum devoted to antique maps. **Hess's Heritage Map Museum** has maps from 1493 to 1875. The collection includes the first map showing the United States' East Coast, the first map of Florida and the first map to show the name of America.

In addition to the museum's gallery displays, there is also a retail shop with hundreds of old maps. The museum, at 55 N. Water Street, is open Monday through Saturday from 10:00 A.M. to 5:00 P.M.

A block from the Johannes Mueller house is a popular favorite with Lititz visitors, the **Sturgis Pretzel House**. You can't miss this establishment at 219 E. Main Street because it has an oversized pretzel hanging outside the entrance. Billed as the birthplace of the American pretzel industry, this small bakery dates back to 1784. Years later in 1861, a weary traveler stopped at the bakery, and when he was given food, returned the favor by sharing the recipe for German hard pretzels with the baker. When the baker did not try the new idea, his apprentice, Julius Sturgis, decided to experiment and the American craze for pretzels began.

The bakery is still making soft pretzels by hand and baking them in the original 200-year old ovens, but hard pretzels are made by machines, which turn out 125 a minute. During tours each visitor is encouraged to try to form a pretzel. Excited amateurs quickly learn the knack of rolling, crossing and shaping, but no beginner can equal the speed of longtime workers who can do 40 pretzels a minute. After the tour, few can resist buying some of these tasty snacks. The horse and buggy pretzels are a popular item that make a fun addition to parties and lunch boxes. Tours are given Monday through Saturday from 9:00 A.M. to 5:00 P.M. The bakery is closed on Sunday. A nominal admission is charged. Appropriately, your ticket is a pretzel; just don't eat it before you get inside.

Follow your nose a few blocks to the **Wilbur Chocolate Company** where another tasty Lititz treat is made. All phases of the candy industry—manufacturing, processing, packaging and advertising—are displayed. There is an extensive exhibit of old candy making equipment and more than 150 china and porcelain chocolate pots. There are also hundreds of wood and metal candy containers. For young visitors more interested in content than containers, they sell a wide range of candy. You can watch workers hand-dip chocolates and purchase up-to-date supplies for your own kitchen. Wilbur's Factory Candy Outlet is open at no charge Monday through Saturday from 10:00 A.M. to 5:00 P.M., closed on Sundays.

Pretzels and chocolates can augment a picnic lunch in **Lititz Springs Park**, noted as the site of the nation's first community-wide Fourth of July celebration in 1818. At the 25th celebration, floating candles were added to the festival. Now the **Fairyland of Candles Festival** has more than 5,000 candles that line and float along the stream that flows through the park. Festival events include an outdoor concert, **Queen of Candles Pageant** and a fireworks finale.

If you would rather try the local restaurants you can get a sandwich and ice cream treats at the Sundae Best just across Klein Street from Wilbur's. On the square in Lititz you can enjoy lunch at the General Sutter Inn, built and operated by the Moravians as a stage-coach stop.

Directions: From I-76, the Pennsylvania Turnpike, take Exit 21 and head south to Ephrata on Route 222. Continue past Ephrata to the intersection with Route 772. Make a right on Route 772 into Lititz, where Route 772 becomes Main Street.

Merritt Museums

It's Dolling

In the Lilliputian world created in **Mary Merritt's Doll Museum**, childhood lasts forever. From a collection of 5,000, there are 2,500 prize dolls on exhibit. The "little people" in this collection, which ranks as one of the largest and finest in the country, include every type of doll imaginable. There are rag dolls, china dolls, bonnet dolls, pumpkin heads, wax figures, French bisque dolls, German jointed figures, mechanical dolls and even paper cutouts. Some of the dolls are named for their creators: Greiner, Joel Ellis and Schoenhut.

Among the oldest dolls in the collection were those made during Queen Anne's reign, 1665 to 1714. These wooden dolls are elaborately dressed in silk, brocade and lace. Less ornate are the peddler dolls made during the 1700s and 1800s, often called Notion Nannies because they were dressed like English peddler women holding their wares in trays and baskets.

Dolls were not just playthings. In China they used doctor's dolls for women patients to indicate their areas of distress. Some mannequins straddled the line between plaything and fashion model; this was true of the lovely French fashion dolls. Women admired them for their fashion forecast, while children treasured them for their beauty. Milliner's models that demonstrated the latest fashions were popular in England and the United States in the early 1800s.

What's a doll without a house to call its own? To eliminate that dilemma, the museum has more than 50 complete doll houses on display. The oldest is a three-story Queen Anne cabinet filled with period furniture. There are also more than 40 miniature period rooms including a grand French ballroom and a simple Pennsylvania Dutch barn. These provide an amazingly accurate picture of the times they reflect. They are complete down to the smallest piece of decorative art and household accoutrements. The museum also has an extensive collection of doll dishes.

Then there are the toys. One whole section is devoted to transportation. You'll see shelves filled with trains, wagons, fire engines, boats and carriages. Balance toys, pull toys, whittled hobo art, playing cards and hobbyhorses are on display. If, after a visit to the full-size reproduction of a mid-19th-century Philadelphia toy shop, you feel the urge to acquire an antique toy or doll, stop at the museum gift shop.

Adjacent to the doll museum is the **Museum of Early Childhood and the Pennsylvania Dutch**. This museum also reaches into the past and brings alive an earlier era through household items, toys and arts. There is an 18th-century frontier kitchen with its dining area and bedroom section and a collection of period clothes. Indian pottery and baskets also reflect an earlier era. The gift shop has collectibles and a selection of more than 100,000 old postcards.

The Merritt Museums are open Monday through Saturday from 10:00 A.M. to 5:00 P.M. On Sundays and holidays they open at 1:00 P.M. The museums are closed on major holidays. A nominal admission covers both museums.

Directions: From I-76, the Pennsylvania Turnpike, take Exit 23, Route 100 north. At Pottstown turn left off of Route 100 onto Route 422. The Merritt Museums are halfway between Pottstown and Reading on Route 422 near Douglassville.

Middle Creek Wildlife Management Area

Birds of a Feather Flock Together

It's certainly improvisational theater at the "staging" of tundra swans at **Middle Creek Wildlife Management Area**. From early January to the peak period in late February and early March, the swans preen and posture—they stretch their wings, which can have a four-to-five-foot span, and crane their graceful necks. These feathered performers are not silent; their mellow, rich bugling calls fill the air.

It's a mystery why the swans gather here during their spring migration to the Arctic Circle's tundra, but do not stop on their return trip. Bird enthusiasts and curious travelers are grateful to have a once-a-year chance to see between 5,000 and 8,000 of these majestic birds. The swans rest for several weeks before resuming their journey, sometimes traveling in flocks of several hundred, a truly spectacular sight when they are on the wing.

Tundra swans, formerly known as whistling swans, can weigh

as much as twenty pounds. They are remarkably graceful when flying or swimming, but are quite ungainly on shore or as they prepare to take off or land. Wherever they are, they are a captivating and enthralling sight.

The swan's call is often mistaken for that of the Canada goose, another bird found in great numbers at Middle Creek. Unlike the migratory swans, there is a resident population of approximately 5,000 Canada geese. Nesting islands have been built on the 400-acre shallow water lake for the Canada geese. Nesting devices for mallards and wood ducks can be seen around the 70-acres of impounded ponds and dikes. Most of the migrating waterfowl (other than tundra swans) visit Middle Creek during October and November and again in March and April. Another excellent time to visit is in May and June when the young goslings and ducklings are plentiful.

There are nine miles of hiking trails in the wildlife management area. Be sure to bring binoculars for a close look at the wildlife. **Willow Point Trail**, one of the better short trails, is a half-mile flat walk to a lake-side vista overlooking the propagation area, a 756-acre sanctuary where the public is excluded and nature is left to unfold without interference. **Millstone Trail** will take you along a mountain crest to an old millstone quarry, and there is a short 250-yard loop portion of Millstone that is a **Braille trail** with signs for the visually impaired. Trail maps are available in the Visitor Center which also has displays on the wide variety of birds to be seen in this management area. The center is open March through November on Tuesday through Saturday from 8:00 A.M. to 4:00 P.M. and Sundays NOON to 5:00 P.M. When the center is closed, portable facilities are available spring, summer and fall. Fishing and hunting are permitted in designated regions, including a trout stream accessible to wheelchair-bound fishermen. There are four picnic areas. You are welcome to enjoy a meal al fresco, but don't feed the waterfowl. There is a $100 fine for feeding these wild birds. It is important that they do not become dependent on people to feed them.

Middle Creek hosts a wildlife art show the second weekend in August and a decoy and wildfowl show the weekend after Labor Day. There are evening programs at the Visitor Center at selected times April through September. For additional details call (717) 733-1512.

Directions: From I-76 east, the Pennsylvania Turnpike, take Exit 20, Route 72 north for about four to five miles to Route 419 east. Follow Route 419 for roughly seven miles to Route 897 in Schaefferstown. Take Route 897 for about two miles to Kleinfeltersville. Turn right at Hopeland Road; the Visitor Center will be about two miles on your right. Traveling west on I-76 take Route 272 north for three miles, then at the traffic light turn left on Route 897. Head north on Route 897 for about 14 miles to Kleinfeltersville, and turn left on Hopeland Road.

National Association of Watch and Clock Collectors Museum and Wright's Ferry Mansion

The White Rabbit's Favorite Spot

"It's about time"; "You'll have the time of your life"; "Time out" ... It's hard not to think in cliches when you visit the **National Association of Watch and Clock Collectors (NAWCC) Museum** and see the amazing diversity of timepieces housed here. The museum has one of the most comprehensive collections of its kind in the world with more than 8,000 items representing four centuries of horological developments. The majority of visitors to the museum are not collectors, although some actually join the organization before they leave.

Appropriately, as you enter the museum you punch in on an old time clock. Within the museum's well-organized galleries you will see a display of American clocks from 1700 to 1900. The clocks reflect the change from brass to wood to spring movements. They show that old case clocks were often masterpieces of the cabinetmaker's art. You can also see the component parts of a typical eight-day tall clock. Many displays have audio-explanations activated by a touch of a button.

Some of these early clocks were called **"wag-on-the-wall"** clocks. This was a clock without a case. It was a more economical time-piece, but few children could resist tampering with the hanging weights. The habit of calling tall timepieces "grandfather" clocks was inspired by the lyrics of an old song.

There is a striking musical mahogany tall clock crafted by Martin Shreiner of Lancaster. His clock runs eight days, plays seven tunes on a nest of eight bells, has a center sweep-second, calendar and moonphase.

The **Sidney Advertising Clock**, made in 1890, is intriguing because every five minutes it presents three different ads. A story goes that this concept was put to good use by an enterprising father, Alonzo Stubbs, who had seven marriageable daughters. He bought an advertising clock for his parlor where his daughters entertained their beaus. The father's first message said: "Let those love now who never loved before, and those who always loved now love the more." His next placard was more practical: "Gas bills are getting higher." The third restored a romantic

The National Association of Watch and Clock Collectors Museum has one of the world's most comprehensive and fascinating collections of timepieces.

mood but the fourth was definitely a warning; "Long courtships cost money and are a great waste of time." The fifth left little doubt of the clock's purpose:

> "Let us then be up and doing
> With a heart for any fate;
> Let's have done with endless wooing
> And propose or emigrate."

By the end of two weeks all seven daughters were engaged.

Another direct-action clock can be found in the collection of alarm clocks. You can't ignore the wake up message of the "Tugaslugabed." A large coiled spring is attached to a string which when tied to your toe will literally pull you awake. The clock does give an eight-second warning, but if the slumberer does not awake the clock spring delivers "a savage yank to the toe."

Also on display are novelty clocks. One is a copy of Grant Wood's American Gothic painting. It's called the "wandering eye clock" and creates an eerie sensation that is definitely not to everyone's taste. Other novelties include wagging tails and tongues, bobbing dolls and talking clocks.

Displays range from some of the earliest timepieces to some of the most current. The antikythera, the world's oldest known time mechanism, believed to have been made around 87 B.C., was recovered from a Roman ship at the bottom of the Aegean Sea. It shows the position of sun, moon, stars and major constellations. Other early timepieces include the clepsydra, or water clock, candle clocks and sundials. In the **Old Time Shop** you can see cases filled with watches that you might have purchased at a jewelers between 1890 and 1910. Another window on the past overlooks a watchmaker's bench. The museum has over 6,000 watches.

Other timepieces that deserve close attention are the Engle Clock, which took 20 years to craft and was called the "8th Wonder of the World," the Farcot conical pendulum statue clock, the Tiffany globe clock and the sophisticated atomic clock. There is so much to see that you are likely to spend far more time than you anticipate. You may find yourself agreeing with the mosaic motto inscribed at the entrance—*Tempus Vitam Regit—Time Rules Life.*

The museum has a well-stocked library on horology and is open Tuesday through Saturday from 9:00 A.M. to 4:00 P.M. From May through September it is also open on Sunday from NOON to 4:00 P.M. It is closed Mondays and holidays. Admission is charged.

Just a few blocks away is the beautifully restored **Wright's Ferry Mansion.** Massachusetts had Abigail Adams and Maryland had Margaret Brent, but Pennsylvania had its own inspirational woman, Susanna Wright. When she was 29 years old, Susanna purchased 100 acres of land along the Susquehanna River and became known as "the bluestocking of the Susquehanna."

One of her hopes in coming to this virtually uninhabited area was to be instrumental in Christianizing the Native Americans. She learned the Shawnah dialect in order to achieve her goal. She operated a ferry on the Susquehanna and the settlement formerly called Shawnahtown became known as Wright's Ferry. Susanna served as the prothonatary, drawing up documents and writing letters for the other settlers in the area. She also practiced medicine; one of the upstairs rooms of the mansion contains drying herbs and plants she would have used. She wrote poetry and kept up a spirited correspondence with many of the country's leading thinkers. She was a particular favorite of Benjamin Franklin and they exchanged ideas and advice.

The mansion was built for Susanna Wright in 1738 and reflects her Quaker heritage as well as her links with England and Philadelphia. The house has been singled out as "the best effort to achieve an exact recreation of 18th-century reality." It has one of the finest collections in the country of Pennsylvania furnishings and accessories made before 1750. The pieces have been chosen because of their historical significance and their architectural purity.

Susanna Wright's austerity can be seen in the curtainless windows and the bare scrubbed floors, but she also had an exquisite artistic sense and a love of beauty. You can see this in the silk quilt and bedcurtains in her room which enhance the only known example of a Philadelphia Queen Anne high post bed.

Susanna Wright was interested in establishing a silk industry in Pennsylvania and had more than 1,500 silk worms. The quality of the silk she produced was so good that Queen Charlotte of England wore a dress made from Susquehanna silk, presented to her by Benjamin Franklin, at George III's birthday celebration.

Wright's Ferry Mansion is a special place that reflects a special lady. When you visit you come away with a new appreciation for a woman who few remember today but who was a generation ahead of her time. Wright's Ferry Mansion is open May through October on tuesday, Wednesday, Friday and Saturday from 10:00 A.M. to 3:00 P.M. Admission is charged.

Directions: From I-76, the Pennsylvania Turnpike, take Exit 21. Travel south on Route 222 to Lancaster, then proceed west on Route 30 to Columbia. Take Route 441, N. Third Street, into Columbia. Turn left at Poplar Street for the NAWCC Museum which is located on the right at 514 Poplar Street. For Wright's Ferry Mansion take Poplar Street down to Second Street and proceed to 38 Second Street. You will see the restored home on your right.

People's Place and Amish Farms

God's Green Earth

Pilots say Lancaster County can be recognized from the air because of its neatly laid-out farms. As you drive through the area, the feeling of returning to a simpler era is enhanced by the county's extensive Amish and Mennonite population, which numbers nearly 60,000 (around 15 percent of the county's population) of which about 8,000 are church members of the Old Order Amish, just one of 20 different Amish and Mennonite groups.

The natural curiosity of visitors and the Amish desire to protect their privacy and maintain their way of life can conflict. For example, the Amish believe that taking photographs violates the biblical injunction against graven images, so it is extremely discourteous and disrespectful to try to photograph the Amish even with telephoto lenses.

One way to gain an understanding of the lifestyle, beliefs and heritage of the Amish and Mennonites is at The **People's Place** in Intercourse. This creative museum shows a three-screen, 25-minute documentary film, "Who Are the Amish?" The movie offers far more that just factual background, it presents the spirit and feelings of the "plain people" who are caught between seeking perfection and humility. One of the most satisfying features of the film is that a tourist's voice is heard asking all the questions that visitors have but wouldn't think of voicing. If you have a question that isn't answered, you can query the knowledgeable staff at a "question and answer" session following the film.

This people-to-people interpretative center also offers "an adventure into another world." Here eight issues are addressed revealing the tensions between the Amish and the mainstream, or English, world, as the Amish call it. One issue, the sense of time, is explored with a question box that reads: "Most Americans despise it, while most Amish choose it." Do you know what it is? You will if you visit The People's Place.

The feeling box has 14 items to touch and identify. As part of the transportation display you can sit in the front seat of a buggy and operate the signal indicators. A collection of summer and winter hats for men plus a group of women's bonnets leads to an area where youngsters may try on typical Amish clothes. Children may also want to sit in the small schoolroom and try a page of work; lessons are given for grades one to eight. Other issues covered are mutual aid and barnraisings, social security and government aid, energy use and the important question of peace. The exhibit concludes with a collection of folk art.

The People's Place is open Monday through Saturday, hours are 9:30 A.M. to 9:30 P.M. Memorial Day through Labor Day, the remainder of the year it closes at 5:30 P.M. Admission is charged.

There is a **Book and Craft Shoppe** and **The Old Country Store** which specializes in quilts and fabrics. Just behind The People's Place is a collection of craft shops called the **Kitchen Kettle**

On snowy days in Lancaster County sleighs and sleds may replace the traditional Amish horse-drawn buggy.

Village. Amish buggy tours begin here and take visitors around the town of Intercourse or out on the country roads.

When you leave The People's Place, drive along Route 772, you'll share this road with numerous horse and buggies. This gives you a chance to test your new knowledge of the Amish; see if you can spot the differences between the Amish farms and their neighbors'. Many of the Amish farms have produce and craft stands where you can purchase homemade delicacies popular in this area.

Adding another dimension to your visit is a chance to tour an Amish farm. There are two farmsteads open to visitors: **The Amish Farm and House** and The Amish Village. The Amish Farm and House has a typical Pennsylvania-German stone farm house. You'll be given a conducted tour through the house after which you can explore the farm on your own. This look at a typical Old Order Amish home makes you appreciate the difficulties involved in living without electricity, telephones and automobiles. The Amish Farm and House opens daily at 8:30 A.M., winter closing 4:00 P.M., spring and fall 5:00 P.M. and during the summer months at 6:00 P.M. Admission is charged. The farm is six miles east of Lancaster on Route 30 at 2395 Lincoln Highway East.

At **The Amish Village** on Route 896 in Strasburg there is a guided tour of a typical Old Order Amish farmhouse that dates back to 1840. You can visit a one-room schoolhouse, a blacksmith's shop, windmill and water wheel and an operational smokehouse where visitors can purchase locally made cookies, tomato jelly, shoofly pies and other regional specialties. The village is open daily 9:00 A.M. to 5:00 P.M. spring, summer and fall; 10:00 A.M. to 4:00 P.M. in December and weekends during the winter months, weather permitting. Admission is charged.

For urban and suburban dwellers the idea of a farm vacation is becoming increasingly popular. The Pennsylvania Dutch Convention and Visitors Bureau (717-299-8901) has a listing of farms where you stay and take part in the unique lifestyle of farm families. You can help milk cows, feed the livestock, ride horses, catch fish, bale hay, round up cattle or simply watch the action from porch rockers. One of the delights of these vacations is the hearty country breakfast that is usually served every morning except Sundays. The Pennsylvania Farm Vacation Association has a statewide booklet the offers even wider choices. You can obtain it by writing the PA Department of Agriculture, Market Development, 2301 North Cameron Street, Harrisburg, PA 17110-9408.

After visiting one of these farms, you'll be ready to enjoy a hearty farm meal at a family Pennsylvania Dutch restaurant. You can try some of the "sweets and sours" that traditionally accompany the meal. The entree usually includes three meats and an assortment of vegetables served with homemade breads and followed by an appetizing selection of desserts (don't miss the shoofly pie). Stop at the Pennsylvania Dutch Visitors Bureau at 1799 Hempstead Road and pick up brochures for the family-style restaurants in Lancaster. It is safe to choose at random because all are highly regarded.

Directions: Take I-83 to York and then take Route 30 east to Lancaster.

Railroad Museum of Pennsylvania, Toy Train Museum, Choo Choo Barn and Gast Classic Motorcars

Transportation Hub

Transportation buffs delight in the variety of railroad museums in and around Strasburg. There's also the bonus of a first class antique car collection. The **Railroad Museum of Pennsylvania**, the state's official railroad museum, has one of the largest and most significant collections of historic locomotive power and rolling stock in the world.

Even if you only have a casual interest in transportation, you'll find yourself becoming excited when you see vintage passenger trains from the heyday of rail transit. Trains range from colorful Civil War era steam locomotives to massive 250-ton steam and electric engines. The museum covers all the railroads constructed or run in the state.

Interpreters are on hand during the summer months, and on weekends at other times of the year, to share with visitors stories of the early days of railroading in Pennsylvania. You'll get an engineer's view of how a steam locomotive operated or hear a retired ticket agent talk about his job in a recreated turn-of-the-century passenger depot—**Steinman Station** has a waiting room, ticket office and a baggage room that now serves as a mini-theater. A look at lavish private cars and damask covered, silver-laden tables in the dining cars reflects the era when rail travel was *the* way to go. These exhibits provide a starting point for the interpretation of the golden age of the railroad. Another interpretative program focuses on the danger, sweat and grueling work required on heavy freight trains.

There are 24 locomotives and passenger cars in the museum's enormous Rolling Stock Hall. Seeing all the trains under one roof is an impressive sight; represented here are many of the oldest and most important locomotives and rail cars in the country. There's a second floor balcony spanning the width of the building that provides a great overlook. You'll also want to gain the perspective of the pit which is one flight of stairs below the hall. From this vantage point you can view the underside of a locomotive.

You can climb aboard some of the trains and peer into others through special viewing cases. Children enjoy the chance to get behind the throttle of a locomotive and pretend to be an engineer.

The oldest locomotive in the collection is the **Tahoe**, the Virginia and Truckee Railroad's #20. Although this locomotive, built in 1875, never ran in Pennsylvania, it was built by the largest and most successful of all steam locomotive builders, the Baldwin Locomotive Works of Philadelphia. In 20 years the company built over 500 locomotives. This engine weighs $49^{1}/_{2}$ tons and looks huge until you compare it with the 200-ton engine in the outdoor collection, which includes over 40 locomotives and cars.

Another famous engine is the **John Bull** locomotive replica built in 1939. It actually looks more like the original, than the actual John Bull (now in the Smithsonian display in Washington, D.C.) which changed over the years. The smokestack on the replica and the color are true to the original 1831 design. The John Bull was the first continuously successful locomotive used in the U.S.

There is an entire train of ornate Victorian cars from the gay nineties. You can see baggage cars, a postal car and several passenger day coaches. The oldest passenger car is the 1855 Cumberland Valley Car built in Chambersburg. It is thought to be the third oldest piece of passenger equipment in the country. It was in regular service for more than 30 years, then continued in work service until 1909.

The **1913 Pullman Lotus Club Restaurant-Sleeper** is a standardized steel car with ten sleeping sections, later reduced to eight, plus a kitchen and dining area. The original open platform was enclosed when the car was rebuilt in 1936. After this glimpse of regular passenger cars, take a look at the Western Maryland Business Car #203, built for the president of the railroad. Cars like these were used by industry executives before the days of private jets.

The **Rolling Stock Hall** also has exhibit cases on the side walls filled with old railroad station signs, direction posts and surveying and excavation equipment. Exhibited are old horsedrawn and early motorized vehicles, mail carts and railroad office furniture.

At the entrance of the hall is an oversize bronze statue of Alexander Johnston Cassatt, seventh president of the Pennsylvania Railroad. This statue stood in Penn Station before the station was leveled in the 1960s. A portrait of Cassatt, the brother of artist Mary Cassatt, by John Singer Sargent is just one of the collection that includes 12 of the past 14 Pennsylvania Railroad presidents. These paintings are hung on a rotating basis in an exhibit that includes furnishings from the Board Room at Philadelphia's Broad Street Station. The museum has an extensive collection of railroad art, including calendar art, illustrations of 1930s and 40s passenger car interiors and watercolors of Pennsylvania railroad stations.

At the back of the Rolling Stock Hall are massive doors that lead to the Yard, where scores of additional locomotives and cars are displayed. The Yard is open to visitors on certain days during the summer season; for safety reasons it is not open more frequently. If you're able to schedule a visit when the Yard is open, you're apt to see ongoing restoration and preservation work being done out on the tracks.

The Railroad Museum of Pennsylvania has an outstanding library and archive facility with more than 6,000 volumes and 120,000 photographs. Visits to the library/archives may be arranged by writing or calling: P.O. Box 15, Strasburg, PA 17579; (717) 687-8628.

The museum is open Monday through Saturday from 9:00 A.M. to 5:00 P.M. and Sunday NOON to 5:00 P.M. It is closed on Mondays from November through April Admission is charged.

Across the street from the Railroad Museum of Pennsylvania is **Strasburg Rail Road** where you can actually take a 45-minute ride on a steam train (see selection). Just down the street is the **Choo Choo Barn**, where you can get a miniaturized view of railroading. There are 15 operating trains on a 1700 square foot model railroad display that has 130 animated scenes. For more than 30 years this model railroad layout has been growing. It is a collector's delight with fireman fighting a smoking blaze, a circus with ten animated figures in the big tent, a Memorial Day parade, an Amish barn raising, a zoo and a myriad of other surprises. Connected to the Choo Choo Barn is a well-stocked hobby shop. Exhibits are open daily 10:00 A.M. to 5:00 P.M.; during the summer months it stays open until 6:00 P.M. Admission is charged.

Railroading in miniature is also on view at the nearby **Toy Train Museum** on Paradise Lane. Here you'll see display cases filled with antique locomotives, literally hundreds of toy tinplate trains representing locomotives and cars from the 1880s to the present. There are also five extensive operating layouts. The museum is open April through October daily from 10:00 A.M. to 5:00 P.M. In May, November and December it is open weekends only. Admission is charged.

Finally, if cars are your weakness then you'll want to see the 50 cars displayed at **Gast Classic Motorcars Exhibit**. They have both the first and last MG to come off the assembly line. This is also your chance to see the beautifully designed and lovingly made Tucker. After seeing this car be sure to watch the movie by the same name. If you visit during December, you'll see decorative trees perfectly color coordinated to match the nearby cars. The exhibit rotates so if you want to see a specific car be sure to call ahead. Gast is open daily, from June through September; hours are 9:00 A.M. to 9:00 P.M. From October through May it stays open until 9:00 P.M. on Friday and Saturday evenings, while closing Sunday through Thursday at 5:00 P.M. For more information call (717) 687-9500. The admission price is comparable to an evening movie rate, but car buffs will certainly want to check out this museum, ranked as one of the ten best among the approximately 230 automobile museums across the country. Don't miss the gift shop with its array of automobile related merchandise.

Directions: From the Pennsylvania Turnpike, I-76, take Exit 21, Route 222 south to Lancaster. From Lancaster take Route 30 east to Route 896 south. At Strasburg turn left on Route 741 for the Railroad Museum of Pennsylvania and the Choo Choo Barn.

For the Toy Train Museum turn left off Route 741 onto Paradise Lane; the museum will be on your right. Gast Classic Motorcars is on Route 896 just north of Strasburg.

Robert Fulton Birthplace

Master of all Trades

Visiting homes associated with figures from the pages of history fills in the blanks. Take Robert Fulton, for example. He's well known as the inventor of the steamboat, although there was an extensive litigation disputing his claim to originality and his monopoly of the steamboat service. His patents were improvements on basic ideas of both American and European steamship designs. It was, however, unquestionably Fulton who developed the steamboat into a commercially successful venture.

At **Fulton's Lancaster County birthplace** you'll get to know the man behind the legend. Fulton was a Renaissance man who combined a lifelong love of art with a talent for scientific endeavors. During his youthful years in Lancaster, his family moved from this stone house in the country when he was only a few years old. At an early age, Fulton showed artistic promise. He visited local gunshops and designed firearms and drew designs for the etchings engraved on them. Fulton also drew political and military caricatures and painted tavern signs.

When he was 17, the handsome and charming Robert Fulton moved to Philadelphia and studied art. He began painting the miniatures for which he became noted; his tiny portraits were among the finest in the country. His talent brought him in contact with the leading families in the state. With political and social contacts to assist him, Fulton headed to London for more training at the London Academy of Art, under the direction of American-born painter Benjamin West. Fulton's personal appeal and ability made him popular with the leading figures in London. He was befriended by two men: the Duke of Bridgewater, who was deeply involved with canal research, and Lord Stanhope, an inventor and engineer. These associations brought out Fulton's own scientific bent. He patented devices for marble-sawing, flax-spinning, rope twisting and a double inclined canal-boat plane. A move to Paris brought Fulton to the attention of a fellow countrymen, Joel Barlow, who became his main financial supporter. Fulton's interest expanded to torpedoes, submarines and steam navigation.

After a 20 year sojourn in England and Europe, Fulton returned to the United States in the fall of 1806 and built the *Cler-*

mont, his famous steamboat. It was dubbed **Fulton's Folly** until its inaugural trip on the Hudson on August 17, 1807. People lined the river banks expecting to see the new-fangled boat sink. After its success, Fulton supervised the building of 17 steamboats, a torpedo boat and several ferryboats. His financial partner in these endeavors was Robert Livingston, the American minister to France. The day after the *Clermont's* successful voyage, Fulton became engaged to Livingston's cousin, Harriet. Fulton only lived eight more years, dying at the age of 49 on February 24, 1815.

The Robert Fulton Birthplace was once part of a commercial hamlet that grew up around a stop on the Peach Bottom Railroad, later called the Lancaster, Oxford and Southern Railroad— known locally as the Little, Old and Slow. Although only a few buildings remain, there were once tobacco and grain warehouses, a creamery, butcher shop, country store, post office, doctor's office and other businesses. The Fulton's three-story fieldstone house is within a hundred feet of the railroad tracks.

Visitors can tour the first floor of the Fulton birthplace modestly furnished with period pieces. An exhibit room provides a chance to see several miniatures done by Robert Fulton as well as a model of the *Clermont*. The Robert Fulton Birthplace is open Memorial Day to Labor Day Saturday 11:00 A.M. to 4:00 P.M. and Sunday 1:00 P.M. to 5:00 P.M. A nominal admission is charged. There is an herb garden behind the house.

Directions: From I-76, the Pennsylvania Turnpike, take Exit 22, Route 222 south of Lancaster. The Robert Fulton Birthplace is on Route 222 just north on Goshen on the left.

Strasburg Rail Road

Ride the Rails to Paradise

How can you resist a trip to Paradise? Steam trains departing daily from **Strasburg Rail Road**, the nation's oldest short-line railroad, travel to a quiet picnic spot in Paradise. This is an ideal getaway for the extended family; grandparents can regale the younger generation with tales of traveling on the network of rails that crisscrossed America. It is also a chance to experience an authentic operational railroad in contrast to the cars that carry crowds around most of the large theme parks.

Alas, you can't stay in Paradise. The 45-minute round trip takes you through the picturesque Lancaster farmland. From the train's windows you glimpse straw-hatted Amish farmers working the fields with horse, and mule-drawn plows. The somber clothes of the Amish hang neatly on the wash line outside the immaculate white farmhouse. Black buggies sit in front of barns. The entire experience provides a sense of slipping into a time warp. A more with-it look, is sported by the younger Amish members who have taken to using in-line skates as a method of transportation.

At Strasburg Rail Road there are reminders of the past wherever you look. Trains depart from a 1892 Victorian railroad station. Adding to its visual appeal is an old water tower and several pieces from the line's rolling stock. The entire panorama seems designed for a period movie, and indeed several of the railroad cars have been used in films. An open observation car and several others made a colorful backdrop in the movie *Hello Dolly*. One of the world's oldest standard-gauge coach, called the **Willow Brook**, shared billing with Elizabeth Taylor in *Raintree County*.

You can climb aboard several of these interesting old cars, including the private coach of the president of Reading Railroad, that once epitomized traveling elegance. With its separate sitting, dining and sleeping areas the car cost $100,000 to build in 1916. Designer touches include cut-glass ceiling lamps, lace-curtained windows and mahogany paneling inlaid with rosewood. There are those who claim that Harry Truman used this car in his famous 1948 whistle-stop campaign across the country.

Preservationists restored the cars in the Strasburg collection to the way they looked in the late 1800s. They have puffer-belly engines, plush seats, inlaid wood paneling, kerosene lamps and potbellied stoves. When you ride aboard one of these coaches, the conductor will move down the aisle punching your ticket. He'll also answer your questions and tell stories about the early days of rail travel. If you want you can disembark for a picnic, but you have to bring it with you.

It's easier and more in keeping with the train theme to eat at the nearby Red Caboose, a local restaurant located in an actual dining car. There are rooms available in cabooses for overnight guests. Each converted caboose has either regular or bunk beds plus a fully equipped, though tiny, bathroom. There are even television sets hidden in the potbellied stoves. Call (717) 687-6646 for details.

If time remains be sure to explore Strasburg's Main Street, part of the town's National Historic District. This street was once part of the Conestoga Highway, the first westward route from Philadelphia. The district has at least a dozen log houses; the **Christopher Spech House** dates back to 1764. Other historic buildings date from the 18th and 19th centuries. On a hot day there's no better place for a treat than the **Strasburg Country Store and Creamery** where old-fashioned ice cream is served at an 1890 soda fountain.

The Strasburg Rail Road is open daily from mid-March through November. It is closed on Thanksgiving. There are special Santa Claus runs the first two weekends in December. Call (717) 687-7522 for current steam train schedule.

Directions: From I-83 take Exit 24 in York. From York take Route 30 east through Lancaster and turn right on Route 896 to Strasburg.

Wolfgang Candy and Brown's Orchard

Country Crafts

Since 1921, the Wolfgang family has been making candy. Their headquarters, **Das Sweeten Haus Center**, is redolent with the sweet smell of success. A 29-minute video talks about four generations contributions to the business. The video also explains how Wolfgang makes its candy. Animated displays and candy-making equipment add additional details. Candy collectibles are displayed including Bavarian porcelain chocolate pots, wooden sugar molds and glass candy containers.

September through Easter from 8:30 A.M. to 3:30 P.M. you can watch while hand-dipped chocolate candy is made in the center kitchen. If you call ahead, you can arrange a plant tour, (800) 248-4273. The center has a retail outlet and a soda fountain where you can enjoy ice cream cones, sundaes and milkshakes. The center is open at no charge Monday through Friday from 8:00 A.M. to 4:30 P.M. and Saturday until 4:00 P.M.

South of York is another family business, **Brown's Orchards and Farm Market**. The Browns purchased a 40-acre orchard in 1948 and began selling apples at a small roadside stand beside their poultry farm. Now they have 180 acres and a farmer's market selling a wide array of produce, fresh baked goods (they're well-known for their fruit pies), handcrafted items and country collectibles.

Brown's Orchards Farm Market is open Monday through Thursday 8:00 A.M. to 8:00 P.M., Friday until 9:00 P.M., Saturday until 7:00 P.M. and Sunday 11:00 A.M. to 6:00 P.M. During the summer weekday hours are 8:00 A.M. until 9:00 P.M., Saturday until 8:00 P.M. and Sunday 11:00 A.M. to 7:00 P.M. Closed major holidays.

There are two other spots where you can watch goods being made; one is big business while the other the shop of skilled artists. Just west of York in Hanover is **Utz Quality Food, Inc**. A glass-enclosed observation gallery gives visitors a view onto the 500,000 square foot plant floor. Close-circuit TV monitors and audio programs detail the potato chip production process from beginning to end. On the walls are displays outlining the company's history. The observation gallery is open weekdays 8:00

A.M. to 4:00 P.M. The plant does not always go into production on Fridays. Visitors have to climb steps and there is no wheelchair ramp. Just down the road is an outlet store, stocked fresh daily, where you can purchase company products.

David and Carol Klein weave Jacquard coverlets, table runners, place mats, ingrain carpet and yard goods of museum quality. Their work is sold at **Family Heir-Loom Weavers** in Red Lion. These skilled crafters are often called upon for historic restoration projects. They have worked on homes belonging to Abraham Lincoln, Mark Twain, Martin van Buren and numerous other historic properties. Their shop is open weekdays 9:00 A.M. to 4:00 P.M. and Saturday by appointment or chance. Call (717) 246-2431.

While you are out and about in this area, stop for lunch or dinner at the **Glen Rock Mill Inn**. The history of this establishment goes back to 1837 when William Heathcoat built a woolen mill on the foundation of an abandoned sawmill. You could hear the sound of the water-powered sawmill all over Glen Rock, the town Heathcoat founded.

Today at the Glen Rock Mill Inn original foundation stones from the sawmill are used in the restaurant. In one dining room, water from an old race falls over Heathcoat's "inspirational rock." The mantle over the rock is made from one of the counter tops in the mill's sales room. The restaurant is open daily from 11:00 A.M. to 10:00 P.M. The mill is also a bed & breakfast with 14 rooms; call (717) 235-5918 for details.

Directions: From I-83 traveling south take Exit 10, which puts you on North George Street. Turn left on E. 4th Avenue, Wolfgang Candy is at 50 E. 4th Avenue in North York. Traveling north on I-83 take the I-83 bypass to Exit 9W, then turn left at signal light onto N. George Street and proceed to 4th Avenue and turn left. For Brown's Orchards Farm Market traveling south on I-83 take Exit 3. Go to the top of the ramp and bear sharply right. Travel one block to the stop sign, turn left and continue $1^1/_2$ miles. Traveling north on I-83 take Exit 2, Route 216 west to the intersection of Main Street (Route 111) and turn right. For the Utz plant take Exit 9, and head west on Route 30. At the intersection with Route 94 turn left and head south. Then make a right on Clearview Road and a left on High Street. The plant is at 900 High Street. For the Utz Outlet Store get back on Clearview road, cross Route 94 and the store will be on your right. For Family Heir-Loom Weavers from I-83 take Exit 4, Route 74 to Dallastown. In Dallastown take S. Duke Street for $1^1/_2$ miles, then turn right on Meadowview Drive. The showroom and shop are at 775 Meadowview Drive in Red Lion. For Glen Rock Mill Inn from I-83 traveling south take Exit 2, Glen Rock exit. At the bottom of the ramp make a right onto Route 216 west. At the end of the road (approximately one mile) make a left onto Main Street heading south. Make an immediate right onto Church Street. Follow Church Street down the big hill to the center of town. Glen Rock Mill Inn is diagonally across the intersection on the right.

York Historic District

Briefly Capital

To many people's surprise, especially Philadelphians, York was the nation's first capital. When the British captured Philadelphia in 1777, Congress was forced to flee the city. They traveled 88 miles to York, prudently putting the Susquehanna River between themselves and the British. Congress reconvened in the York courthouse and drafted the Articles of Confederation, which, when adopted, served as the nation's first constitution.

History comes alive at the **York County Colonial Court House** with a three-dimensional dramatic narrative. Actors give voice to the words of John Adams, John Hancock, Thomas Paine, Samuel Adams, Philip Livingston, Francis Lightfoot Lee, Charles Carroll, Gouverneur Morris and many other significant figures of the day are heard. The courthouse has been restored to look as it did when the Continental Congress met here from September 30, 1777 to June 27, 1778. Time appears to stand still when you look at the rare tall case clock that marked the course of time for these patriots who proclaimed the formation of the United States of America. Copies of the documents associated with American liberties—the Articles of Confederation, Declaration of Independence and the Constitution—are on display. The courthouse is located at 205 W. Market Street.

It was also in York that George Washington came perilously close to losing the command of the Continental Army. General Horatio Gates, hero of the Battle of Saratoga, was headquartered in York during 1778 while Washington stayed with the army at Valley Forge. Congress, either because of proximity or the spell of Saratoga, appointed Gates to the position of President of the War Board. General Thomas Conway then attempted to secure the command of the Continental Army for Gates. The Conway Cabal was thwarted by the Marquis de Lafayette, who realized that a plot was afoot while attending a dinner party at the Gates house. His timely toast to Washington as Commander-in-chief is credited with scotching the plot.

The Gates House, at 167 Market Street, is across Pershing Street from the courthouse. It contains period pieces representing the

The 1741 German half-timbered Golden Plough Tavern is the oldest surviving structure in York. It contains a fine collection of William and Mary period furnishings.

---

furnishings popular in this southcentral Pennsylvania region in the 18th century. Attached to this historic old home is the **Golden Plough Tavern**. This half-timbered tavern with a pitched roof is worth visiting as it is one of the few buildings in the country constructed in a medieval style. Behind the tavern you'll see the **Barnett Bob Log House** typical of the homes of German settlers who frequented the tavern after it was built in 1741.

The **Historical Society of York County Museum** at 250 E. Market Street has recreated a life-size village square. You can stroll down the "**Street of Shops**" and look into store windows replete with toys, apothecary jars and other necessities of a bygone era. Costumed mannequins also add to the sense of "history come alive." In addition the museum has a Revolutionary War collection plus weapons and uniforms from the country's Second War of Independence in 1812.

The attractions of Historic York are open Monday through Saturday from 10:00 A.M. to 4:00 P.M. and on Sunday from 1:00 to 5:00 P.M.

There is much more to see in the York area so you may want to stop at the York County Visitor Center just outside the city on Route 30 to obtain additional information.

Directions: From I-76, the Pennsylvania Turnpike, take I-83 exit. Travel south on I-83 to York. Take the Market Street exit for the historic attractions.

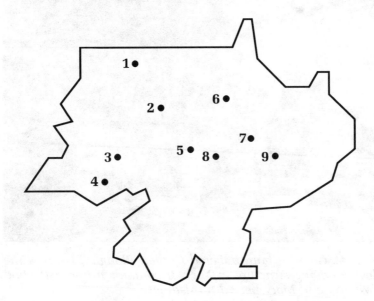

VALLEYS OF THE SUSQUEHANNA

1. **Hyner**
   Hyner View State Park

2. **Lock Haven**
   Heisey Museum and Lock
   Haven

3. **Bellefonte/Centre Hall**
   Bellefonte Walking Tour
   Curtin Village
   Penn's Cave

4. **State College/Boalsburg**
   Columbus Chapel and Boal
   Mansion Museum
   Penn State Museums
   Pennsylvania Military
   Museum and Boalsburg
   Shaver's Creek Environ-
   mental Center/Stone Valley
   Recreation Area

5. **Woodward**
   Woodward Cave

6. **Williamsport**
   Little League Baseball
   Museum
   Millionaires' Row

7. **Lewisburg**
   Packwood House Museum
   Slifer House Museum and
   West Shore Rail Excursions

8. **Mifflinburg**
   Mifflinburg Buggy Museum

9. **Northumberland**
   Joseph Priestly House and
   Fort Augustus

Valleys of the
——————Susquehanna——————

Think Currier and Ives, or Norman Rockwell and you're apt to conjure up scenes like those you'll discover along the main streets and back roads of the Susquehanna River Valley. Fortunes were made in the mill towns along this river. All but the smallest towns boast a collection of impressive Victorian mansions. In the 1880s there were reputedly more millionaires in Williamsport than any other town in America. Many of their homes survive along "Millionaires' Row." Fascinating walking tours of historic districts can also be taken in Lock Haven, Bellefonte and Boalsburg.

Boalsburg has one of the state's most amazing sites, the Columbus Chapel, North America's closest tie to Christopher Columbus. The story of this chapel and adjacent Boal Mansion is linked with a score of famous individuals. The roots of the solemn Memorial Day commemoration can be traced to Boalsburg. You can also get a comprehensive look at the state's servicemen and women at the Pennsylvania Military Museum.

Natural attractions range from exploring the depths of Penn's Cave and Woodward Cave to the hang gliding heights of Hyner View State Park. This region is sometimes called Lion Country, but not because of any natural predators. (The area's Visitor Center once received a phone call from a Georgia farmer who wanted to sell them his aging herd of horses. When asked why he thought they might be interested, he replied, "To feed your lions.") The name refers to Penn State's mascot, the Nittany Lion. The University offers educational experiences galore even if you have only a few hours to spend at any of the six museums on campus.

Two additional museums in the region should not be missed. The Mifflinburg Buggy Museum, in what was once called "Buggy Town," is an intriquing time tunnel to the past. The hands-on Little League Museum, in the town where the League was born, delights ballplayers and fans of all ages.

Bellefonte Walking Tour

Home of Seven State Governors

The Treaty of Stanwix in 1769 opened the center of the Pennsylvania colony for settlement. Griffith Gibbon was one of the first to purchase land from the local Indians. The following year, surveyors laid out a settlement along the steep hills. In 1785, William Lamb purchased 750 acres and settlers came to Lamb's Crossing, the community that grew on the banks of Spring Creek.

The surveyors found a natural spring, the third largest spring in the state, that contributed to the settlement's development. In the mid-1790s, the town of Big Spring, as it was then called, was visited by French statesman Charles Maurice Talleyrand, who was impressed by its "beautiful fountain," and ever after the town was called **Bellefonte**.

The beautiful in-town Talleyrand Park also reminds visitors of the diplomat's visit. Flowering gardens, sculpture garden, gazebo, a stream-side oasis of natural greenery adds a touch of Europe to this Pennsylvania community.

The Bellefonte Historical & Cultural Association publishes a *Historical Walking Tour of Bellefonte* that lists 45 points of interest. Tour maps are available at the 1889 Pennsylvania Railroad Station in Talleyrand Park, now the headquarters of the Bellefonte Area Chamber of Commerce, Stop 1 on the tour. The **Bush House Hotel**, Stop 3, was one of the first hotels in the country to have electric lights. Stop 5 and 5A are **Talleyrand Park** and the **George Grey Barnard Sculpture Garden**.

Bellefonte is the home of seven state governors, a record unmatched by any community in the country. Five served as Pennsylvania governor: William Bigler (1852-1855), William F. Packer (1858-1861), Andrew Gregg Curtin (1861-1867), James A. Beaver (1887-1891) and Daniel H. Hastings (1895-1899). John Bigler was Governor of California from 1852 to 1856 and Robert J. Walker was Territorial Governor of Kansas in 1857. Only a few of the homes of these prominent Bellefonte residents still stand.

Andrew Gregg Curtin's Tuscan Revival house at 120 West High Street is Stop 10. Curtin had the distinction of being the first Republican governor of the state. He achieved fame after the first Battle of Bull Run, when the Pennsylvania Reserves that he sent to help the Union cause saved Washington, D.C. from Confederate capture. The lavish house built by John Lane in the 1840s was acquired more than forty years later by Governor Hastings. He remodeled the house (Stop 21), adding porticos and windows to resemble the old State Capitol in Harrisburg.

From the mid-1860s to the 1960s, visitors to Bellefonte stayed at the **Brockerhoff Hotel**, a Gothic Revival-influenced building on the southwest side of Allegheny Street, now a senior citizens residence (Stop 11). Henry Brockerhoff was a clerk in Napoleon's army who was shipwrecked and taken to Philadelphia. From there he made his way to Bellefonte. A statue of Andrew Gregg Curtin stands in front of the **Centre County Courthouse**, first constructed in 1805-06 (Stop 12).

"After the Ball is Over" was first sung at **Bellefonte's German Opera House** (Stop 15) and music may again fill the hall when the Bellefonte Music Theater opens. Architects and builders must have been singing "Anything Goes" while constructing the eclectic Crider Exchange Building (Stop 18), a unique 1889 structure with a fishscale tin facade.

An historical museum and library now fills the rooms of the **Georgian Miles-Humes House** (Stop 20), built in 1815 by John Miles, son of Philadelphia mayor Colonel Samuel Miles who founded Milesburg. Noted American sculptor, George Gray Barnard (for whom the sculpture garden is named) was born at the farmhouse at 113 East Linn Street (Stop 24). He carved the flanking pieces at the main entrance of the State Capitol.

Big Spring, the source of the town's water and its original name is Stop 41. This spring still supplies a daily flow of 11,500,000 gallons of water. The spring was given to Bellefonte by Mayor William F. Reynolds on October 1, 1879 for $1.00.

There are numerous other interesting spots along the way and the walking tour brochure has details on each one. While this walk is enjoyable in any season, for five days in early December the private and public buildings in Bellefonte are decorated to recreate the town's Victorian past. Another popular time to visit is the third weekend in August when the Arts and Crafts Fair is held. Close to a hundred jurored exhibitors demonstrate and sell their wares. For more information about Historic Bellefonte or specific dates and details on special events call (814) 355-2761.

Directions: From I-80 take Exit 23 Route 220 south to Milesburg, then bear left on Route 144/150 to Bellefonte.

Columbus Chapel and Boal Mansion Museum

America's Most Tangible Link to Christopher Columbus

A veritable wealth of historical treasures are hidden away on a wooded estate outside Boalsburg. Here you will find **Columbus Chapel** with family heirlooms dating back to the 1400s. One of the chapel's prized possessions is a silver reliquary containing two pieces of the True Cross. The pieces, part of the Left Arm of the Cross (the name for the upper left side), were detached in 1817 by the Bishop of Leon and presented to the Columbus family for their family chapel.

What puzzles visitors is why and how the Columbus Family Chapel was transported from a castle in Spain to a stone chapel in Pennsylvania. Theodore Davis Boal, whose family built the Boal Mansion and in whose honor the town was named, married Mathilde Denis de Lagarde. Her mother's sister, Victoria, married Don Diego Columbus. He was a direct descendant of Christopher Columbus and inherited the family chapel, its relics and heirlooms.

Victoria Columbus never had children and her husband predeceased her, so at her death she left part of her estate to her niece Mathilde Boal. In 1909 the Boals transported the entrance door and interior of the Columbus Family Chapel, along with all its contents to their Boalsburg home. It's thrilling to see the admiral's desk that Columbus took with him on his voyages. It is a trunk-like container that could be securely locked to protect its contents. The desk is studded with gilt cockleshells, emblematic of St. James of Compostella, a saint much admired by Christopher Columbus. Also associated with Columbus's voyages are the small painted wooden crosses he slipped onto pikestaffs and planted on the beaches of islands claimed in the name of Isabella and Ferdinand. There are also carved wooden miniature statues of saints that fit in the cramped space of a ship's chapel.

Columbus family relics and heirlooms fill the chapel. The great family escutcheon hangs on the railing of the choir loft, while fine Spanish linen and lace drape the altar. There are paintings, silver altar pieces and brocade vestments, including a maniple that is over 500 years old.

A small room off the chapel contains the Columbus family tree; actually it would be helpful if it also contained a Boal family tree, as there are enticing links to a great many historic figures besides Columbus. Marriage ties the family to Simon Bolivar; Jacques Denis de Trobriand, a decorated and devoted officer of Napoleon Bonaparte; the Denys family for whom the Denis Islands and Trobriand Islands were named and St. Bernard of Menthon, who founded the hospices on the Alpine passes of Switzerland.

Within the **Boal Mansion Museum** you will see reminders of some of these illustrious individuals. The first Boal to settle in America was David, who emigrated from Northern Ireland in the latter part of the 18th century. David Boal served in the Revolutionary army, then settled in Pennsylvania. A small stone house was built for him on this site in 1789. His son, David, built an extensive addition to the house in 1798. It was in David the younger's honor that the village was named Boalsburg.

Theodore Davis Boal, David the younger's great-grandson, followed in his family's martial tradition (the first Pennsylvanian to volunteer for the Spanish-American War was George Boal Thompson) by raising and equipping a mounted machine-gun troop in the Mexican War of 1916. Boal's machine guns mounted on Ford trucks, one of the earliest examples of motorized armaments of this type in the country, were used in an expedition against General Pancho Villa.

Pierre Denis de Lagarde Boal, son of Theodore Davis Boal, served in the French cavalry and the Lafayette Flying Corps during World War I. Later he was Ambassador to Bolivia. It was Pierre Boal who established a museum on the estate that contained family heirlooms. Visitors can see a large collection of weapons and armor from Europe, Asia and America plus old-fashioned conveyances like the traveling coach of David Boal the younger and other family carriages and sleighs.

The house is filled with original furnishings and family memorabilia. The guides tell fascinating stories about the subjects of the portraits you see hanging in the ornate rooms. The house has been home to nine generations of Boals.

The Boal Mansion Museum is open May through October daily except Tuesdays. Tours are available from 1:30 P.M. to 5:00 P.M. in the spring and fall, 10:00 A.M. to 5:00 P.M. during the summer months. For additional information, or to arrange group tours, call (814) 466-6210. Admission is charged.

Directions: From I-80 take Route 220 south to Martha Furnace then head east on Route 322, which becomes the Mt. Nittany Expressway. Take the Route 45 exit which becomes Main Street in Historic Boalsburg. The Boal Mansion Museum is on Old Route 322 across from the Pennsylvania Military Museum (see selection).

Curtin Village

Ironing Out the Wrinkles of Time

The earliest surveyors to canvas the primeval forests of central Pennsylvania discovered rich iron deposits, the highest quality ore found up to that time in the country. By 1829 nineteen iron furnaces, rolling mills and forges operated in the Bald Eagle Valley. One of these was Eagle Iron Works, founded by Roland Curtin between 1807 and 1809. His forge and furnace were the nucleus of **Curtin Village**, an iron producing center from 1810 until 1921.

At its height the Curtin iron plantation covered 30,000 acres and included a charcoal-fired furnace, rolling mill, forge, 67 houses for workers, the ironmaster's mansion, numerous sheds

Ride the Bellefonte Historic Railroad to Curtin Village, a vital Pennsylvania iron producing center from 1810 to 1921.

PHOTO BY MICHAEL BEZILLA

and outbuildings, a boarding house, school, general store, post office, railroad station and carpenter's shop. Curtin Village was only one of the workers' villages spread out on Roland Curtin's land holdings. At each location of a furnace, forge or rolling mill there was a cluster of houses, or village, for the workers at that facility. You do not need to image what it was like on this iron plantation in the 1800s; it has been faithfully recreated allowing you to experience the social, cultural, political, economic and industrial aspects of this self-sufficient community. The village you see today served the workers at the Eagle Forge and the **Pleasant Furnace**.

When you visit Curtin Village you can explore Pleasant Furnace, built by Roland Curtin's sons in 1848 to replace the original Eagle Furnace. This was the last operating charcoal-fired, cold-air blast furnace in the country but it was destroyed by fire in 1921. The facility you see today was rebuilt during the 1970s. The Pleasant Furnace complex includes a water-powered blast house, charging house, flume, casting rooms and tapping shed. How each of these contribute to the production of iron is explained by easy-to-understand display boards.

Iron plantations of the north are often compared with agricultural plantations of the south, but an important distinction is that the slave labor of the southern plantations could not leave, while the early iron workers frequently traveled from one furnace to another to improve their economic lot. In its heyday the Eagle Iron Works employed approximately a hundred workers, most of whom had large families. It is not unrealistic to estimate an ironwork's population at between 400 and 500 individuals. Work is underway to recreate the village area and you can explore a restored iron worker's log cabin that has been assembled using material from several original homes. This spartan cabin, circa 1825, has only one room and a sleeping loft. Skilled workers had more elaborate framed houses.

In sharp contrast to this pared-down existence is the ironmaster's mansion, the architectural and cultural centerpiece of Curtin Village. This three-story Federal-style stuccoed mansion was built in a park-like setting in 1830. Ten of the 15 rooms in the mansion are filled with period furniture and a few family pieces. Each room has a fireplace and each mantle is a different design. Your tour begins in the imposing entrance hall. In the old days only invited guests would get beyond this hallway. It's a surprise to see venetian blinds but they were popular even in this pre-Civil War era. There are nine bedrooms; four on the third floor are not included on tours. The Curtin sons (including future Governor Andrew Craig Curtin) slept in the upstairs bedrooms. One of the cradles in the upstairs bedroom belonged to the Curtins.

Curtin Village is open Memorial Day to Labor Day Wednesday through Saturday from 10:00 A.M. to 4:00 P.M. and Sunday from 1:00 P.M. to 5:00 P.M. Admission is charged. The tour of the mansion and village takes approximately an hour and a half, and the last tour leaves one hour before closing.

Throughout the year a variety of special events are hosted by Curtin Village beginning with the season opening on Memorial Day. There is generally a special event planned each month. Favorites include the mid-October Apple Butter Day and Christmas at Curtin.

The best way to get to Curtin Village on weekends is by taking the **Bellefonte Historic Railroad** from the restored Pennsylvania Railroad Station in Bellefonte (see Bellefonte Walking Tour selection). Curtin Village is one of several destinations that you can visit on these scenic train excursions. The other spots are **Sayers Dam** where passengers can disembark for a picnic before returning to Bellefonte, **Lemont** at the base of Mt. Nittany where you can stroll past a number of intriguing gift shops and **Julian**, noted for its gliderport where sailplanes have set world endurance records riding the Appalachian air currents. For details on these trips and their dinner trains, fall foliage runs and Santa Claus Express call (814) 355-0311.

Directions: From I-80 take Exit 23 and head north for two miles on Route 150. Turn right at the sign for Curtin Village.

Heisey Museum and Lock Haven

Unlocking the Past

The history of the Heisey house is intrinsically linked with that of Lock Haven. Settlers arrived in the area in the early 1770s, but threats of Indian uprisings forced them to flee for a five year period. It wasn't until 1831 that the town of Lock Haven was laid out. Two years later, Dr. John Henderson built a federal brick farmhouse, now encompassed by the **Heisey Museum**. The house, however, has been extensively enlarged and remodeled over the years.

Jerry Church, the founder of **Lock Haven**, lived in this house when it was used as a tavern. He named his town Lock Haven, because it was the location of the last lock of the Pennsylvania Canal and he felt it was a safe haven. There was a canal lock on both sides of the river; the one in town is located near the museum. A little more than a decade after the town was established, a lumber boom created great wealth in the community. Timber magnates built elaborate homes along Water Street, which became known as mansion row. During the height of the boom there were nine sawmills and three planing mills in and around Lock Haven.

An impressive number of these estates still stand in the **Water Street Historic District**. The Heisey house is the only mansion open for tours, but before you explore it in depth take a drive or stroll along Water Street. The president of Lock Haven University, founded in 1870, lives in the elaborate **Colonial Revival house** on the north side of West Water Street between Mill and First Streets. A large columned portico, modillioned (that's an ornamental bracket usually used in a series that is located under the cornice) cornice and flanking porches enhance this well-maintained house.

The **Spanish Colonial Revival** at 47 West Water Street is quite different. This is one of only two surveyed examples of this design in Lock Haven. Distinguishing features include a low-pitched roof with broad eaves, first floor front casement windows set under a round-head arch with ornamental accents and windows of varying sizes.

Representing **Georgian Revival** and **Neo-Classical Revival** styles is the Grant estate at 104 West Water Street. From the former period are the gabled dormers, modillions on raking cornice and projecting eaves, elliptical windows and two-story semi-circular projecting bay. The Greek Ionic columns, rectangular transom and flanking sidelights are from the latter period.

At 118 West Water Street you'll see a **Second Empire** masterpiece. Outstanding features include the exterior decoration on the windows, an ornate front porch and a four-story tower. Colonel William Simpson restyled this house by putting frame over its brick exterior, an understandable choice given the fact that he was one of the town leaders responsible for the development of the lumber industry in what was called the City of Locks.

There are other impressive homes on West Main and West Church Streets. Lock Haven is also noted for its outstanding array of architecturally interesting churches. There are 350 buildings within the National Register Historic District.

The **Gothic Revival style Heisey House**, 362 East Water Street, is Lock Haven's oldest brick building. The Victorian Gothic Revival look, complete with gables and vergeboard (decorative trim at the roof edge) was achieved in an extensive remodeling in 1865. The interior represents life in Lock Haven in the mid-Victorian period more than 125 years ago. You can tour the house museum Monday through Friday from 10:00 A.M. to 4:00 P.M. and at other times by appointment, call (717) 748-7254.

The Heisey Museum is the main office of the Clinton County Historical Society. The society's collection of Native American artifacts and Central Pennsylvania pottery is exhibited at the museum. The versatility and creativity of potters working in this area between 1835 and 1920 is reflected in the collection, which includes redware, glazed crocks, jugs and urns.

The remains of several Indian villages were discovered along the Susquehanna River. One that is on the National Register, the **Memorial Park Site**, is on East Water Street along the south bank of the river, next to the Piper Airport. From these villages archaeologists have uncovered stone tools, points, sinkers, beads and pottery fragments.

In the Ice House on the museum grounds there is a collection of artifacts associated with the Pennsylvania Canal, including a canal lock replica. The West Branch of the canal, linking Lock Haven with other parts of the state, opened in 1834. Most of the lumber was not shipped out by canal but by railroad.

The former Lock Haven Station of the Beech Creek and Clearfield Railroad is in nearby Castanea just across Bald Eagle Creek from Lock Haven. This station has also been acquired by the Clinton County Historical Society and houses the **Clinton Central Model Railroad Club**'s layout of model trains and railroad memorabilia. While the train station does not currently open at scheduled times, it does have model train shows several times a year.

Just 5.2 miles north of Lock Haven is the remains of yet another local industry—the **Farrandsville Iron Furnace**. Once one of six furnaces in the county, it's one of only two that have survived (the other is on state forest land and is difficult to access). Farrandsville, listed on the National Register of Historic Places, was one of the first and largest hot-blast iron furnaces in the country. Every week it turned out roughly 50 tons of high quality pig iron.

One last local business needs to be mentioned, **Piper Aircraft Corporation** which operated in Lock Haven from 1937 to 1984. A museum recalls the glory days of this aircraft company noted for its Piper Cub as well as its series of planes bearing Indian names—Aztec, Cherokee, Cheyenne, Comanche, Navajo. Restored aircraft, models, photographs and memorabilia fill Hanger #1 at William T. Piper Memorial Airport. It's open daily 10:00 A.M. to 4:00 P.M. Wednesday it closes at 3:00 P.M. and Saturday at 2:00 P.M. Closed on Sundays.

Directions: From I-80 take Exit 26, Route 220 north to Lock Haven.

Hyner View State Park

A Great Spot to Hang Around

A stone overlook built in the 1930s by the Civilian Conservation Corps gives visitors a spectacular panoramic view of the

278

west branch of the Susquehanna River. It's quite a spectacle to watch hang gliding enthusiasts launch themselves from this 2,100-foot precipice. Expert gliders have been wafted on wind currents well into West Virginia, roughly a nine hour trip. Gliders congregate from March through October.

Both **Hyner View State Park** and **Hyner Run State Park** are located in the heart of the 276,764-acre Sproul State Forest. Within this forest are numerous hiking and snowmobiling trails as well as scenic overlooks and state forest roads.

Hyner Run State Park occupies a small valley created by Hyner Run. The park's 180 acres are generally level, although there are steep mountains on both sides. Brook and brown trout are found in abundance in Hyner Run. While these are stocked, the upper reaches boast native brook trout. Fly fishermen test their skill on the right branch of **Young Womans Creek**, only a short distance from the park.

While hunting is prohibited within the park, thousands of surrounding acres of public land lure both small and big game hunters as well as trappers and dog trainers. Game includes deer, bear, turkey and grouse. Other wildlife in the area include bobcat, red and gray fox, coyote and raccoon. Hunters should always be aware that hikers and other sports enthusiasts are enjoying the same terrain.

Hyner Run State Park is the eastern trailhead for the 50-mile **Donut Hole Trail System** enjoyed by backpackers. The **Log Road Hollow**, recommended for moderate to experienced hikers, leads out of the state park area. A shorter 0.4 mile trail, the **Twin Valley Nature Trail**, has 11 points of interest encompassing the geological, biological and cultural history of the area. Between 1860 and 1900 this area was an active lumbering territory. White pine and hemlock were cut and carried out of the valley by logging locomotives. As you walk this trail you'll see a logging railroad bed.

The park is also the trailhead for the 64-mile **Hyner Mountain Snowmobile Trail**. Snowmobiles are not permitted in either the state park or state forest during the antlerless deer season. There is also an ice skating area.

A 30-site camping area is open year-round. A seven-acre picnic area has 172 picnic tables. There is a children's play area between the camp grounds and the swimming pool (open from Memorial Day weekend to Labor Day). If you want additional information on Hyner Run State Park call (717) 923-0257.

Directions: From I-80 take Exit 26, Route 220 north. At Lock Haven pick up Route 120 north to Hyner. Hyner Run State Park is three miles north of Hyner on Hyner Run Road. Hyner View State Park entrance road is also accessed from Hyner Run Road.

Joseph Priestly House and Fort Augusta

Founder of Modern Chemistry

Have you ever read someone's name on a signpost and, while you can't remember the particulars, you know this was an important person? Just such a reaction occurs for many travelers when they spot the sign for the **Joseph Priestly House**: the name is familiar but they can't recall the reason for Priestly's fame.

This never happens if the travelers are scientists, particularly chemists, because for them the Joseph Priestly House is virtually a shrine. This preeminent Englishman is considered the father of modern chemistry. He discovered oxygen and described eight new gases. The last decade of Priestly's life was spent in the laboratory of this Northumberland house.

The exhibits and brief orientation tape at the Visitor Center only hit the highlights of Priestly's illustrious but controversial career. Priestly emigrated from England to America in search of political and religious sanctuary. Priestly was born in 1733 to a family of Dissenters, nonconformers to the Church of England. Religion was one of the pivotal thrusts of Priestly's life, and he studied for the ministry. His theological studies led him to Unitarianism and he made significant contributions to the development of that religious group.

Priestly was a secular humanist and a strong exponent of personal liberty. He supported the American and French Revolutions. His espousal of the latter led anti-French rioters to burn his house, laboratory and library in England.

Priestly, his wife Mary and their three sons departed England for America in 1794. First he established himself in New York, but ran into political difficulties on this side of the Atlantic as well, this time due to his support for Jefferson over Adams. (Their support was mutual; Jefferson felt Priestly was the quintessential intellect of enlightenment.) Priestly preached for a time in Philadelphia, then moved to Northumberland, Pennsylvania. Only about 100 settlers lived in this frontier community when he began building his country estate overlooking the Susquehanna River. Priestly's sons had worked to establish a colony for English Dissenters in this part of Pennsylvania, but the plan was never realized.

Priestly's wife died two years before the Federal-style manor house was finished. Tragedy struck again just before the house was completed when his 18-year-old son, with whom he had a close relationship, died of a fever. With only three sons surviving and his daughter still in England, Priestly did not need a home appropriate for entertaining and he changed the nature of the downstairs rooms. The dining room became a land speculation office, where Unitarian services were held. The parlor was converted to a work space overflowing with over two thousand books, scientific equipment, maps and a daybed where he slept. He relaxed by playing chess and checkers and by taking walks and gardening. The laboratory, the first scientific laboratory in the country, was in a wing off the parlor with a passageway providing easy access. Although Priestly isolated oxygen in an experiment while he was still in England, a replica of the apparatus he used is in the laboratory.

Both the dining room and parlor are in the process of being restored to suggest their appearance during Priestly's ten years in Northumberland. This was a productive decade for him. He identified carbon monoxide as a distinct "air" and wrote more than 30 scientific papers plus more than a dozen religious volumes. He also developed an academic curriculum; so impressive were his scholastic recommendations that Thomas Jefferson sought his advice concerning the establishment of the University of Virginia. Joseph Priestly died here on February 6, 1804.

Priestly's estate home was a re-creation of an English gentlemen's with a house, barn complex and outbuildings enclosed by a fence. Long range goals are to restore the landscaping and some of the outbuildings of this complex.

On July 31 and August 1, 1874 chemists from 15 states, District of Columbia, Canada and England met at the Priestly House to celebrate his discovery of oxygen. The meeting led to the establishment of the American Chemical Society. A century later in 1974, the American Chemical Society met here to mark their founding.

The Joseph Priestly House is open Tuesday through Saturday 9:00 A.M. to 5:00 P.M.; on Sunday it opens at NOON. Closed on Monday and holidays except Memorial Day, July 4 and Labor Day. Admission is charged.

Roughly 40 years before Priestly settled in the Susquehanna Valley, during the tumultuous time when the French and British were vying for control of this region, forts were built.

One of England's strongholds during the French and Indian War was **Fort Augusta**, built near the former Indian village of Shamokin, where the Susquehanna divides into branches.

In January, 1756, the Indians of the Six Nations requested the British build Fort Augusta. Work began that summer and the 200-foot log fort was finished the following winter. The fort never came under siege but its existence held the Susquehanna Valley for Britain. The formidable presence of the fort protected the surrounding area. In 1772 Sunbury was established near Fort Augusta as the county seat of Northumberland County. The fort's magazine was used as the jail. The magazine and well are the only elements of the fort that survived.

During the America Revolution, Colonel Samuel Hunter directed the activities of the county militia from his residence in the commandant's quarters of the fort. When the fort deteriorated, Hunter continued to reside here and eventually the house became his property. It was passed through his descendants until 1848 when the log house burned. Colonel Hunter's grandson, Captain Samuel Hunter built the **Hunter House** that stands today.

The Northumberland County Historical Society is headquartered in the house. Museum exhibits in the house include artifacts uncovered during archaeological digs and reminders of the Native Americans' long presence in this region. There is a historical and genealogical library at Hunter House.

The Hunter House is open Monday, Wednesday, Friday and Saturday from 1:00 P.M. to 4:00 P.M. The research facilities are open concurrently except on Saturday.

Directions: From I-80 take Route 147 south to Northumberland. The Joseph Priestly House is at 472 Priestly Avenue, one block south of Route 11. For Fort Augusta continue south on Route 147 to Sunbury.

Little League Baseball Museum

A Hit with Visitors

The days are long past when children have to be cajoled to visit a museum. With hands-on exhibits, interactive computers and state-of-the-arts effects, museums are as entertaining as the theater. But some are undoubtedly more appealing to young visitors than others, and right at the top of the list is the **Peter J. McGovern Little League Baseball Museum**, the only sports museum concentrating on a child's game.

Little League is more than a game, it is an avocational pursuit of more than $2^1/_2$ million children and roughly 750,000 adults in more than 80 countries. Two-thirds of all Major League Baseball players started in Little League.

When you enter the lobby, you expect to hear the shout, "Play ball!" The lobby's photographic mural, one of the largest in the world, recreates **Lamade Stadium**. This is where the Little League World Series is played. (After your tour you can walk behind the museum and see the stadium. Consider returning during the last full week before Labor Day to watch the series. Tickets for the grandstand are distributed without charge beginning in January, but the expansive grassy hillside provides an excellent vantage point.) To see where Little League is played around the world, check out the lobby's fiber-optic map.

The first exhibit room tells the story of Little League's founding in Williamsport in 1939. The uniform and equipment for the first three teams cost $35.00. From the beginning the teams had corporate sponsors. Although Little League is used as a generic term, it does apply to a specific organization to which teams belong. It is one of only three organizations incorporated under the federal government. (The other two with federal charters are the Boy Scouts and the Red Cross.) Five display cases present a timeline of Little League's development. Throughout the day baseball related movies are shown in the museum's small theater, including such classics as *Who's on First*, and *Casey at the Bat*.

Your self-guided tour will take you downstairs to the interactive exhibits that emphasize Little League's leadership role in promoting player safety. One example is the batting helmet developed by Little League. The importance of nutrition and the dangers of drugs and alcohol are stressed. Orel Hershiser, pro-baseball player, advises kids how to deal with peer pressure. A computer video lets young visitors make choices while attending a video party about whether or not to drink and overindulge.

Next is the basics room with exhibits on how baseball and softball equipment is made. Little League was instrumental in creating the aluminum bat, which was more economical than the wood. A hands-on question board about Little League and an oversize coach's manual gets youngsters involved with the exhibits. It's the next room where interaction is most keenly enjoyed, because the play ball room lets you practice batting and pitching. There's no radar gun so it isn't how fast you pitch, but how accurate. A video replay helps you evaluate your performance. The only limit to the number of times you can test your skill is the number of visitors waiting.

The showcase room highlights Little League's divisions, from Tee-Ball to Big League softball and baseball. Visitors young and old like to look at the baseball cards of major league players who played Little League such as Steve Garvey, Rick Wise, Keith Hernadez, Mike Schmidt, Noel Regan, Rollie Fingers and Tom Seaver.

Back upstairs there's the impressive **Hall of Excellence** and **Gallery of Achievement**. All of the honorees were involved in Little League and include individuals from a wide spectrum of high profile achievements: Tom Seaver, Bill Bradley, Dan Quayle, Mike Schmidt, Nolan Ryan, Tom Selleck, Kareem Abdul Jaber, George Will and Hale Irwin. Finally, there's the **World Series Room** with photographs of each championship team, plus video highlights of the World Series games.

The Peter J. McGovern Little League Museum is open Memorial Day through Labor Day Monday through Saturday 9:00 A.M. to 7:00 P.M., Sunday it opens at NOON. The remainder of the year the museum closes at 5:00 P.M. Admission is charged. The museum has a gift shop with a variety of Little League memorabilia. Quite a number of the items are priced for young patrons' budgets.

In downtown Williamsport the **Children's Discovery Workshop** encourages hands-on participation by children 3 to 11, with the active encouragement of their parents. Exhibit themes change three times a year. Science is the focus from April to September; during October and November, the theme is playhouse theater, while exploration of the mind is featured from December through March.

Certain elements remain constant, like the popular construction elements piled on the floor: tubes, wheels, disks, blocks and Legos. Easels with paper rolls encourage the young artist. Stuffie, an oversize puppet, teaches how the body and its internal organs work (see Pittsburgh Children's Museum selection). There are climbing areas and other sections designed to encourage a visitor's imagination including the ice cream parlor, bank office, television studio and the hospital and dental section.

The museum is open September through May, Tuesday through Friday and Sundays 1:00 P.M. to 5:00 P.M., Saturdays it opens at 11:00 A.M. From June through August, Tuesday through Saturday hours are 10:00 A.M. to 4:00 P.M.; on Sunday it opens at 1:00 P.M. Admission is charged.

One more spot that young children love is **Clyde Peelings's Reptiland**, south of the Little League Museum on Route 15. Youngsters "ooh" and "aah" at the cobras, crocodiles, pythons, vipers and other reptiles exhibited within this tropical garden setting. Five daily shows give visitors a chance to see, touch and learn about reptiles. Reptiland is open daily 9:00 A.M. to 7:00 P.M. May through September and 10:00 A.M. to 5:00 P.M. the rest of the year. Admission is charged.

Directions: From I-80 take Exit 30B Route 15 north toward Williamsport for 18 miles. You will see the Little League Museum before you reach the outskirts of Williamsport. For Children's Discovery Workshop continue north on Route 15 and cross the Market Street Bridge into Williamsport. Turn left on Fourth Street; the museum is on the 2nd floor of the Williamsport YMCA at 343 West Fourth Street and the corner of Elmira Street. Reptiland is six miles north of I-80 on Route 15.

Mifflinburg Buggy Museum

Time Stands Still

It wasn't geography, natural resources or any other particular factor that accounted for Mifflinburg's emergence as "The Buggy

Town." In the mid-1800s several buggy works began operating along with the town's two tanneries, two breweries and two potteries. America's population was becoming more mobile and affordable transportation was needed, so the buggy business in Mifflinburg flourished. Between 1890 and 1920 Mifflinburg had 50 separate buggy works, selling their products up and down the East Coast. In 1910 Mifflinburg companies turned out approximately 5,000 vehicles, more horse-drawn vehicles than any other town its size in the country.

The shops and ancillary structures of one of these companies survives as a microcosm of the past. The **William A. Heiss Coach Shop** operated from 1885 to 1920, while the family lived in the adjacent house. There were two children, and one of the sons lived in this house until 1944. Almost all of the furniture now in the house belonged to the family. Curios, photographs and household items give the impression that the family has only temporarily departed. The kitchen has its original appliances including a cookstove, home-made refrigerator and crank-washer. The house reflects a modest life style. The parlor has some Victorian touches but the furnishings are more utilitarian than decorative. Upstairs in the master bedroom, Anna Smith Heiss's nurse uniform hangs from a hook on the wall.

After a look at the private side of the Heiss's life at the turn of the century, walk over to the buggy shop for a step-by-step look at buggy making. Here again all the tools, supplies, equipment and work in progress suggest a mere temporary absence. There's even a 1912 Excelsior Seat and Body Company calendar on the wall, plus notes on ordering supplies. When you enter the shop you'll see a double forge where, on special occasions, there are blacksmith demonstrations. During your visit you'll see how flat iron was bent to form tires, while another tool shrinks the tire. The wood on the wheel often shrank as it weathered so the steel tire had to be exactly fitted. Belts and pulleys operate much of the equipment. This is one of only six or seven 19th century shops in the entire country that have survived intact, and it is the only buggy and carriage works to survive.

In the back room you'll see vehicle bodies that were shipped to Heiss. He then made additional parts and assembled the vehicles. In 1915, Heiss put in his own New Holland gasoline engine to run the belts and pulleys in his shop. His original blueprint can be seen drawn in chalk on the wall. The last supply of dashboards that Heiss received are still leaning against the wall awaiting use, indicating that his was not a planned retirement. In fact, the shop was closed without advance notice (and no records exist to explain why it closed). Heiss was still buying supplies up until the time the shop ceased operating.

In the rear of the shop there is a completed Heiss buggy with a standard piano box design, which simply meant it was open-sided. This is just one of several buggies and vehicles displayed in the shop. Signs indicate that Heiss rented both buggies and bicycles to traveling salesmen who came in by train.

Still more vehicles can be seen on the shop's second floor including a collection of sleighs. The paint and trimming departments are on this level. Heiss made his own paints and you can see boxes of pigment. He would put 15 coats of varnish on each vehicle, rubbing it down with pumice between coats. Mrs. Heiss did much of the upholstery work. A cupboard is well-stocked with supplies like carriage knobs, springs, wood and leather.

Across the street from the shop is a buggy showroom, or repository, where additional locally-made vehicles and other carriages and sleighs are exhibited.

The Mifflinburg Buggy Museum, on the National Register of Historic Places, is open May through mid-September Thursday through Sunday 1:00 P.M. to 5:00 P.M. Admission is charged. The parking lot is on Quarry Road next to the repository and the sign reads Jerome E. "Red" McGraw Parking Area. The Heiss House is at 523 Green Street, and the buggy shop is behind the house. Once a year, on Memorial Day weekend, the entire town celebrates **Buggy Days** with crafts, buggy rides, demonstrations and regional food. A special **Mifflinburg Christkindl Market** is held on Market Street Thursday through Saturday the week after Thanksgiving.

While in Mifflinburg, pick up a walking tour brochure and explore the historic district of this quaint community. There are several interesting craft shops in town and two antique shops. Those interested in crafts will also want to head approximately three miles out of Mifflinburg toward Middleburg on Route 104 and visit the **Penns Creek Pottery**. In an old mill beside Penns Creek, Bill Lynch creates distinctive pottery. His shop also sells unique handcrafted items from other skilled artisans. The gallery is open Monday through Saturday from 10:00 A.M. to 5:00 P.M.

Just up the road from Penns Creek Pottery on the other side of Route 104 is the entrance for **Walnut Acres Organic Farm**, considered the grandfather of the natural foods movement. This internationally known organic farm, which has been operational since 1946, sells vegetables and grains. Their shops not only sell their own locally produced organic products but a wide variety of health foods, cookbooks and kitchen products. They preserve and can a large quantity of items at their plant. Tours of this facility are given weekdays at 9:30 A.M. and 11:00 A.M. and 1:00 P.M. The farm store is open Monday through Saturday from 9:00 A.M. to 5:00 P.M. and Sunday NOON to 5:00 P.M. Lunch is served Monday to Saturday from 11:00 A.M. to 2:00 P.M. It is closed on major holdiays. At Walnut Acres you can also fish in Penns Creek and enjoy the hiking trails. If you would like to obtain a free catalog call (800) 433-3998.

Directions: From I-80 take Exit 30 south, Route 15 to Lewisburg. Then turn right on Route 45 to Mifflinburg and follow the signs. You'll turn left from Chestnut Street, onto 5th Street to Green Street where you will turn right for the Heiss House and the Mifflingburg Buggy Museum. For Penns Creek Pottery and Walnut Acres continue on Route 45 past Mifflinburg and turn left on Route 104 and head south to the tiny village of Penns Creek.

Packwood House Museum

Meet a Delightful Character

Edith Fetherston captured her unique vision in her paintings and in her house. Wandering through the home she shared with her devoted husband John, you can't help wishing that you could have met and talked with this fascinating woman, a Lewisburg native. Touring the **Packwood House Museum** is the next best thing.

Edith Hedges Kelly was born on the first day of summer in 1885. Her mother was an accomplished artist and her father an agent for the Pennsylvania Railroad. Edith studied languages at Bucknell University, learning French, German, Spanish and Russian. She was teaching languages when she married John Turney Fetherston in 1917. He was an engineer, inventor, lecturer and self-made millionaire.

After she married, Edith became involved in the two great interests of her life—gardening and painting. Studying art only briefly, she developed her own style and technique. She had a one-woman show at a New York gallery and was exhibited in several shows. When the Fetherstons moved to Lewisburg, Edith founded the Central Pennsylvania Artists Association.

When John retired, they purchased Edith's parents' Market Street house in Lewisburg. Eventually they also acquired property that had been a log tavern and then a hotel, returning it to a single dwelling. John envisioned their house becoming a museum, showcasing Edith's paintings and their collection of furniture, Americana, Parisian fashions, fine china and glassware.

The guided house tour reveals 26 areas of interest. The rooms were arranged by Edith in a deliberately eclectic manner, whimsically juxtaposing cultures and artistic periods. The garden reflects Edith's fascination with the Orient, an influence that is apparent throughout the house.

The mid-1800s Tavern Room is one of the 27 rooms in the Pack-wood House Museum created by Edith Fetherston, a brilliant Lewisburg artist.

From the garden oasis, replete with bronze statuary, visitors enter the house through the garden room. Next is the dining room where treasures include the Tiffany bowl on the table beneath the Tiffany-style hanging light. There's also a painting that Edith's mother did of her own mother. All of the paintings with gold labels were done by Edith. Those in the hallway reflect her love of orchids. She merged color and form with imaginative images creating a myriad of different renderings of these delicate flowers.

At the top of the steps are photographs of Alfie, her pet rooster. Edith was born in the Year of the Rooster and this was a popular theme in her paintings. The first bedroom also served as her correspondence room. There's a mini-gallery room that was used for art and botanical meetings. Several pieces of interest are found in the third floor study including the desk used by the commanding general at Bull Run, a Lewisburg painted chair and a Tiffany lamp. Edith's bedroom has a short wave radio. After her arthritis became debilitating Edith installed an elevator, which got stuck the first time she rode in it. She immediately added a telephone, portable commode and made sure the elevator was always stocked with food and water.

Returning to the second floor you'll see her painting studio and a wardrobe room with brilliant scarves from Parisian designers like Jean Patou, Pierre Balmain, Yves Saint Laurent as well as shoes, hats, gloves and gowns. Here too is John's bedroom with his sleigh bed facing the wall so that he could wake up and see her painting.

Back on the first floor is the kitchen area with several cases of their glassware and china. Here also is John's study filled with his favorite paintings and books. Finally, in the oldest portion of the house, the area that once served as a tavern, there's an extensive collection of old furniture and Americana. Intriguing pieces include a harvester's ring, a canteen that is literally worn on the upper arm to keep the hands free, an example of tramp art and a 1779 painted cabinet.

The Packwood House Museum is open Tuesday through Friday 10:00 A.M. to 5:00 P.M., Saturday 1:00 P.M. to 5:00 P.M. and Sunday 2:00 P.M. to 5:00 P.M. Admission is charged. Tours are arranged at the Tour Center next door to the Packwood House. While there be sure to look at the exhibits, the gallery and the well-stocked museum shop.

Directions: From I-80 take Exit 30, Route 15, seven miles south to Lewisburg. Once in town, Route 15 becomes Derr Drive. Turn left on Market Street and continue to North Water Street directly before the bridge that crosses the Susquehanna River. The Packwood House Tour Center is at 15 North Water Street.

Penn's Cave and Woodward Cave

America's Only All Water Cavern

"You've seen one cavern, you've seen them all," travelers are apt to remark. But that is far from true. Take Penn's Cave where the mile-long tour is taken by motorboat. Penn's Cave is a unique all-water limestone cavern.

It's estimated that the cave was formed roughly 30 million years ago. The cavern floor was once the bed of a shallow sea. Water from an immense spring dissolved the limestone rock and formed a cavern. This spring still flows into the cavern providing an aquatic route through the darkened chambers. Guides, equipped with electric spotlights, illuminate the unusual geological formations. Nature has sculpted gigantic columns, dripping pillars, immense cascades and water-dampened flowstone.

James Poe, a relative of poet Edgar Allen Poe, was the first white man to own Penn's Cave. Records indicate that his farm was surveyed in 1773. The cave was first discovered by European settlers in 1795 when Reverend James Martin, pastor of the area's first Presbyterian congregation, found an entrance to a dry section of the cave in the farm's orchard. Early explorers found arrowheads, pottery and beads from Indians who had frequented the cave. The cave's name is derived from John Penn's Creek, honoring William Penn's nephew, that originates in the cavern.

It wasn't until 1860 that two young men explored the water filled portions of Penn's Cave. Before their journey, no one realized that the water in the relatively dry section came from the same stream as the water at the main entrance to the cave. The first trip through the cave also revealed that the two parts of the cave were connected.

By 1885, the cave's owners, Jesse and Samuel Long, built a boat and started tours through the cave. They also built the **Penn's Cave Hotel** which is still standing. Both the cave and the building are on the National Register of Historic Places.

Penn's Cave is also a wildlife sanctuary. As you walk down to the cave entrance, accessible via a steep flight of stairs, you'll see a collection of animals and birds. To get a bird's eye view of the rolling farmland and forested mountain slopes, stop at Penn's Cave Airpark and arrange an airplane tour.

Penn's Cave is open 9:00 A.M. to 5:00 P.M. throughout the year. During the summer months it stays open until 7:00 P.M. and in December it is open weekends only from 11:00 A.M. to 4:00 P.M. It is closed on Thanksgiving, Christmas Day and from January until mid-February. Admission is charged; call (814) 364-1664 for current prices.

As you drive toward State College it seems whenever you see a Penn's Cave sign very shortly you'll see one for **Woodward Cave**. They are not far from each other in Centre County. The 400-million-year old Woodward is one of the largest, if not the largest, live cavern in the state. The half-mile walk through the cavern goes through five huge rooms on two levels.

When Pine Creek ran high, it flowed through this cavern, so before it could be open to tours the creek had to be diverted and accumulated clay removed. It took three years to complete this work and the cave, named for Pennsylvania Senator Woodward, opened in 1926.

During the clean-up evidence was found indicating that Native American ceremonials were held in the cave. Legend claims that **Red Panther**, son of Seneca Chief Mountain River, was buried in the cave after being struck by lightning for cutting down a sacred beech tree. Local lore also speaks of a band of robbers who used the cavernous rooms over a century ago.

The rooms are so big that some private organizations have held banquets and other functions in the cave. There is no problem, even for the claustrophobic, in touring this cave as the passageways are wide and flat. One interesting formation in the first room, called the ballroom, is certainly appropriate for Lion country—it's a clearly recognizable profile of a majestic lion.

The third of the massive cave rooms, 150 feet beneath the ground, has massive stalactites (remember these are the ones that hold tight to the ceiling). Stalagmites extend up from the floor, and in the fourth chamber, you'll see one of the largest example in the country. Roughly two million years old, it's 14 feet high and weighs about 50 tons. This formation is unusual because it stands in the middle of the chamber. There is also a gigantic seven tier long clump of cave bananas—a form of stalactite.

From mid-May through Labor Day, Woodward Cave is open daily from 9:00 A.M. to 7:00 P.M. From mid-March to mid-May and from Labor Day to mid-November hours are 10:00 A.M. to 5:00 P.M. Admission is charged. There is also a 19-acre campgrounds with electric and non-electric sites. For camping information call (814) 349-9800.

Directions: From I-80 take Exit 24 at Bellefonte. Take Route 26 south to Pleasant Gap. Continue south on Route 144 to Centre Hall and then take Route 192 five miles east for Penn's Cave. You can also take Exit 25 off I-80. Take Route 64 southeast to just past Lamar, then at Nittany take Route 445 south to Madisonburg and turn right on Route 192 for Penn's Cave. Woodward Cave is 22 miles east of State College on Route 45. Turn at the Woodward Inn and follow the signs to the entrance for the right turn into Woodward Cave and Campground.

Penn State Museums

University Appeal

What better spot to find intriguing and educational museums than on a university campus? At Penn State's University Park campus there are six museums of varying size and subject matter. The most impressive is the **Palmer Museum of Art**.

Penn State's transformed art museum, designed by Charles W. Moore in association with Arbonies King Vlock, opened in 1993 and is itself a work of art. It is truly a signature building created by a major architect. The building's dramatic entrance loggia flanked by monumental bronze lion's paws is an inviting public space.

The theatrical museum lobby is lit by tall stepped windows with center panels of blue glass suggesting a cathedral. Nine of the ten new galleries showcase a permanent collection that encompasses 35 centuries of painting, sculpture, ceramics and works on paper from the United States, Europe, Asia, Africa and South America. There is also a wonderfully relaxing outdoor sculpture garden. Before leaving, visit the museum shop which offers a distinctive collection of books, jewelry, art objects and other items. The museum, located on Curtin Road, is open at no charge Tuesday through Saturday 10:00 A.M. to 4:30 P.M., and Sunday from NOON to 4:00 P.M.

Just down Curtin Road from the museum is the **Nittany Lion Shrine**, with Heinze Warnecke's 1942 limestone sculpture of Penn State's mascot. Art enthusiasts will also find exhibits at the **Kern Graduate Building**, the **Zoller Gallery** in the Visual Arts Building, the **Hetzel Union Galleries** and **Paul Robeson Cultural Center**.

For Native American art and culture, visit the **Matson Museum of Anthropology**. As diverse as the study of anthropology itself, exhibits cover biological anthropology, archaeology, cultural anthropology and linguistics. Casts of bones from fossilized remains illustrate the evolution of primate species including mankind. The museum's collection shows that man's artistic and technological development varies among cultures. The Mesoamerican galleries have pre-Columbian artifacts from the Teotihuacan region of Mexico. There's even a life-size Central American farm house. Artifacts from prehistoric cultures in North America are also exhibited. The **DeForest Collection** has folk pottery from cultures worldwide. The museum is open without charge during the fall and spring semesters, weekdays 9:00 A.M. to 4:00 P.M., Saturday until NOON and Sundays 1:00 P.M. to 3:00 P.M.

Artifacts extracted from the earth tell the story of man's passage, but the **Earth and Mineral Sciences Museum and Art**

In 1942 Heinze Warnecke created Pennsylvania's State University's limestone Nittany Lion Shrine.

Gallery features the earth's building blocks: minerals, gems and fossils. The museum has more than 22,000 specimens including fine minerals such as microcline crystals, azurite and "velvet" malachite. Push-button devices demonstrate the electrical, optical and physical properties of minerals as well as certain oddities they possess. The museum boasts the country's most extensive collection of paintings and sculpture about Pennsylvania's mining industry. There are also more than 100 mine safety lamps and other scientific equipment. Hours are Monday through Friday 9:00 A.M. to 5:00 P.M. There is no charge.

One quarter million insects and related arthropods are exhibited at the **Frost Entomological Museum**. Although the collection concentrates on Pennsylvania, other areas are represented. Exhibits include live and mounted specimens. Hours are weekdays 9:00 A.M. to NOON and 1:30 P.M. to 4:30 P.M.

The National Cable Television Center and Museum has the nation's only collection of documents, publications, personal papers and taped history on the cable industry. You'll learn about industry pioneers and see videos of cable programming. The story of this grass-roots programming is told from 1940s to the present. Hours are Tuesday, Wednesday and Thursday 1:00 P.M. to 5:00 P.M.

Sports enthusiasts can visit the **Football Hall of Fame** in the Greenberg Sports Complex for exhibits on Penn State's Nittany Lions. Uniforms, photographs of former football teams and former players and the Heisman Trophy are exhibited. During the academic year hours are weekdays 8:30 A.M. to 4:30 P.M. and weekends 11:00 A.M. to 3:00 P.M.

While you are on campus, make a point of stopping at the creamery on Curtin Avenue. The ice cream is delicious, a favorite of students and local residents.

Directions: From I-80 take Exit 24, and follow Route 26, East College Avenue, south into State College. From I-76, the Pennsylvania Turnpike, take Exit 19, Harrisburg East, and follow I-283 it will briefly become I-83 before intersecting I-81. (If you are traveling on I-76 from the west take Exit 16, and head north on I-81.) Take I-81 west to Route 322/22 west exit. Take Route 322 west through Lewistown to Penn State exit, Park Avenue.

The Palmer Museum of Art is on Curtin Road. The Museum of Anthropology is in the Carpenter Building in the western corner of the campus. The Earth and Mineral Sciences Museum is at 112 Steidle Building on Pollock Road. Frost Entomological Museum is on Curtin Road, 102 Patterson Building. The National Cable Television Center and Museum is in the Sparks Building; use the Fraser Road entrance, Level B. The Football Hall of Fame is in the Greenberg Sports Complex on McKean Road.

Visitors' parking is provided for a nominal fee weekdays until 9:00 P.M. on the central campus and until 5:00 P.M. in other areas. Metered and permit parking is available close to most locations. Free parking is available after 5:00 P.M. weekdays, west of Atherton street and east of Shortlidge Road, except the Eisenhower Parking Deck. Most parking areas are available without charge on weekends, except where signs indicate special restrictions. Parking permits and parking assistance are available at parking kiosks, Monday through Friday from 7:00 A.M. to 9:00 P.M. Parking rules are enforced and violators are prosecuted.

Pennsylvania Military Museum and Boalsburg

Citizen Soldiers

Memorial Day was first commemorated in Boalsburg in 1864. Boalsburg claims the earliest and most continuous observation because military graves in the Boalsburg cemetery have been decorated every year since that first occasion. The event is now accompanied by community picnics and parades.

The Pennsylvania Military Museum reflects Boalsburg's military assocation. The museum tells the story of the men and women from this state who served in the country's armed forces from colonial days through eight major conflicts as well as more recent engagements.

The formation and involvement of military units associated with the Commonwealth is described and the uniforms, weapons and equipment displayed. The museum was an outgrowth of the 28th Division Officers' Club formed in France at the end of World War I. Colonel Theodore Boal invited fellow officers to his home where they dedicated a memorial to deceased comrades. Each year members of the 28th Division returned and added tablets in the long fieldstone wall erected above the bank of a stream. On both stream banks monuments honored slain officers and individual units within the Division. In 1931 what was called the "Shrine of the 28th Division" was purchased by the state, which added a monument to the memorial park's founder Colonel Boal.

The museum building was designed to suggest a defensive military position but it does not copy any specific fortification. Displays extend back to artifacts from the French and Indian War. During this conflict the state's first military act was passed on November 25, 1755 (although the act was rejected by King George III), followed two days later by an act providing money to undertake defense by raising a regiment of paid troops. Dioramas bring back pivotal encounters in the Revolutionary War and the War of 1812. There are uniforms and equipment from the Mexican War and the Civil War.

A highlight of the museum tour for most visitors is the walk through a World War I battlefield, complete with uniformed "soldiers," weapons, equipment, realistic looking trenches and the sounds and sights of battle from the eerie crack of rifle fire to the simulated artillery flashes.

The Pennsylvania Military Museum is open Tuesday through Saturday from 9:00 A.M. to 5:00 P.M.; on Sunday it opens at NOON. It is open on Memorial Day, July 4th and Labor Day but is closed on other holidays. Admission is charged.

Be sure to save some time to stroll along Boalsburg's Main Street, a Pennsylvania Brigadoon. Time seems to have stopped in the early 19th century. The log and native stone homes and shops that line the street look just as they did when the town was a stagecoach stop. On the village square **Duffy's Tavern** still serves patrons as it has since 1819. Antiques add to the ambience of this historic dining establishment, open daily for lunch from 11:30 A.M. to 2:00 P.M. and dinner from 5:00 P.M. to 10:00 P.M., Sunday 4:00 P.M. to 9:00 P.M. For reservations call (814) 466-6241.

The village's bed and breakfasts are linked with its history.

The **Victorian Summer House B&B**, (814) 466-3304, was the home of Emma Hunter-Stuart, one of the founders of the first Memorial Day. This charmingly decorated house on the village square has a wrap-around porch where visitors can sit and enjoy the town's ambience. Down the street is the **Springfield House Bed & Breakfast**, (814) 466-6290, which still retains the village's original name. An assortment of quaint shops line the street. At the end of East Main Street is the **Boalsburg Heritage Museum** located in the 1825 home of the local tanner. Museum hours are Tuesday, Thursday, Saturday and Sunday from 2:00 P.M. to 4:00 P.M. If you're visiting on a Tuesday from mid-June through October don't miss the **Boalsburg Farmers Market** where you can purchase fresh produce, homemade baked goods, jams, jellies, plants and other specialty items.

Directions: From I-80 take Route 220 south to Martha Furnace, then head east on Route 322, which becomes the Mt. Nittany Expressway. Take the Route 45 exit off the Expressway, this becomes Main Street in Historic Boalsburg.

Shaver's Creek Environmental Center and Stone Valley Recreation Area

Taking Nature's Temperature

Raptors indicate the health of the environment. Since they are at the top of the food chain, birds of prey signal to the observant the levels of toxicity in the environment. In the late 1950s and early 60s, Rachel Carsen noticed that only mature bald eagles were heading south. Eagles were not reproducing because of DDT accumulation. This observation led to regulations designed to protect us all from the dangers of DDT.

Visitors learn about raptors at **Shaver's Creek Raptor Center**, one of only a few spots in central Pennsylvania licensed to conduct educational programs with permanently injured birds of prey. Programs are given on weekends in the spring and fall and during the summer months. Roughly half the birds at the center were hit by cars, some flew into electrical wires, while a few were deliberately and illegally hurt by hunters and farmers. The staff, with help from State College veterinarians at the Animal Medical Hospital, treat the birds and restore them to their proper weight and strength, then release them back to the wild. If the birds are permanently incapacitated they remain at the center. There are now 12 species at the raptor center including a turkey vulture, red-tailed hawk, golden eagle and several varieties of owls. In an average year the center cares for approximately 200 wild birds. Rare barn owls are captively bred and released annually.

The Raptor Center is just one part of the **Shaver's Creek Environmental Center**. For a broader understanding of the center's work, stop at the exhibit room, housed in a wood-and-stone lodge built by the Civilian Conservation Corp in 1939. The exhibit room encourages hands-on involvement: there is a touch and feel table, movable displays, an electric quiz board, natural history puzzles and live specimens.

Staff, members of the faculty from Penn State's School of Hotel, Restaurant and Recreation Management, present environmental programs to increase visitors' understanding and appreciation of their natural surroundings. There are seasonal discovery walks, summer camp programs for children and teens, family science and nature studies, Native American craft and game programs and diverse workshops. From mid-February through March when the sap begins to run, groups of visitors participate in the harvesting and refining of maple sap into sweet syrup. For information on special programs call (814) 863-2000 or 667-4324.

Horatio's Natural History Bookstore and Gift Shop has books for children and adults plus a wide variety of nature-related items. Wildlife prints, bird-call tapes, animal models, bird feeders, jewelry and handcrafted items are available.

An extensive 25-mile trail system offers access to 1,000 acres of hemlock and oak woodlands, meandering streams, open meadows and cattail marshes within the ridges and valleys of central Pennsylvania. In front of the nature center you'll see herb, bee, butterfly and hummingbird gardens. There is also an information kiosk with an oversize map of the Stone Valley trails. For a nominal cost you can pick-up a checklist of the birds or wildflowers you're likely to encounter. The **Black Walnut Trail** takes you past a beaver dam, while the Lake Trail winds along Stone Valley Lake, as does part of the **Point Trail Loop**. The **Iron Stone Trail** reveals remnants of a 19th-century iron industry. The trails are used for cross-country skiing in the winter.

Shaver's Creek Environmental Center is located within the 700-acre **Stone Valley Recreation Area**, offering year-round recreational fun. There is boating and fishing on the 72-acre lake. Boat rentals are available from March through October at the boathouse and the Mineral Industries Day-Use area. Sailing and canoe lessons are given at the boathouse. Fishermen try their luck catching rainbow trout, bass and pickerel. Cabins can be rented year-round. During the winter there is sledding, skating and skiing (both ski and skate gear can be rented and ski lessons are available). For additional information on these recreation options, plus moonlight canoe trips, skating parties, hayrides and other seasonal events call (814) 863-0762.

Directions: From I-76, the Pennsylvania Turnpike, head west on Route 522/22 to just south of Water Street and turn right on Route 305 to Mooresville. The west entrance is just 2.9 miles from Mooresville on State Route 1029. From I-80 take Exit 24, Route 26 south. Follow Route 26 through State College. Make a right off Route 26 on State Route 1029. The east entrance is 1.7 miles from that intersection.

Slifer House Museum and West Shore Rail Excursions

(Delta) Place in Time

When Colonel Eli Slifer purchased **Delta Place**, its history already extended back a century. The land was hunting grounds for the nomadic Muncy-Minsi (or Wolfe) tribe of the Lenni-Lenape. Indian remains were found when work was done on Colonel Slifer's land near the mouth of Buffalo Creek. The first patent on the land was issued in 1769 and is now displayed in the museum.

Eli Slifer, orphaned at 13, walked with his brother from their home in Chester County to the Lewisburg settlement. Although apprenticed to the hatting trade, Eli's interest was soon captured by the canal boats along the Susquehanna. By 1840 he was involved in building canal boats—an undertaking that also built his fortune as the business grew to employ over a hundred men. When Slifer acquired the Delta Place property, he tore down the existing house and hired Philadelphia architect Samuel Sloan to design the Victorian mansion that you see today.

Sloan's ornate three-story villa, one of the few he designed that have survived, was featured in Sloan's book, *Homestead Architecture*, and in the fashionable *Godey's Lady's Book* of 1862. The crowning exterior feature was the cupola. From its imposing heights one could see the river and countryside. Large windows on the first floor opened out on a veranda that extended around three sides of the house. Each room on the first and second floor had a white marble fireplace.

Eli Slifer's commitment to the anti-slavery cause prompted him to join the Whig party in 1848. He was soon actively involved in politics and was elected to the state legislature in 1849, for the first of five consecutive terms. Slifer next served as state treasurer, a position he held for three non-consecutive terms. In 1860 Governor Andrew Curtin appointed Slifer as Secretary of the Commonwealth, a position second only to governor. As a reward for his service to Curtin during the Civil War, Slifer was given the use of a naval vessel to visit Europe in 1871.

The library table was purchased by Eli Slifer in Florence during his trip abroad. For the most part the house is furnished with Victorian period pieces, wherever possible duplicating items on the auction inventory list made after Slifer's death in 1888. Since Slifer was a member of the German Dunkard religion, his house was furnished in a more austere style than some Victorian properties. The estate is still surrounded by its original grounds and they look remarkably like they did in Slifer's day.

Following the Slifer years, the house was acquired by the Evangelical Association. They established a home for the aged. The house was expanded and an orphanage and hospital built. The story of this activity at Delta Place is also included in the exhibits at **Slifer House Museum**.

The house and Victorian gardens are open daily April through December from 1:00 P.M. to 4:00 P.M. Tours last approximately 30 minutes. From January through March the house is open weekdays only. There is a nominal admission. During the spring and summer there are concerts on the grounds; these move inside during the fall. Seasonal decorations and period music are part of the December celebration.

Maintaining the period ambience is West Shore Rail Excursions which offers rides aboard Victorian rail cars. Trips leave from Delta Place Station along tracks of the former Reading Railroad. The **Lewisburg and Buffalo Creek Railroad** excursions take you south to Lewisburg and Bucknell University, then the trains parallel the Susquehanna River with the cliffs of the Buffalo Mountains in the distance. At the village of Winfield the train is turned for the return trip. The 14-mile trip takes 90 minutes. From June through October West Shore Railroad runs a two-and-a-half hour trip on Sunday afternoons that goes to Mifflinburg. For current times and fares call (717) 524-4337. There are a number of specialty trips including dinner trains, champagne sunset dinner trains, holiday rides, murder mystery trips and others.

Across Route 15 from Delta Place Station is popular **Country Cupboard** complex. The Baylor family opened this restaurant and gift shop in 1973, on a far smaller scale than you see today. Now the shop extends over an acre and includes a wide variety of regional handicrafts and food specialty items.

Located adjacent to Country Cupboard is the Susquehanna Valley Visitors Bureau where you can pick up literature on the attractions and visitor oriented properties in the region.

Directions: From I-80 take Exit 30, Route 15 south toward Lewisburg. Five miles south on Route 15 you will find Delta

Place, Country Cupboard and the Susquehanna Valley Visitors Bureau. One mile north of the city, you will see the Slifer House on your left on the grounds of the Lewisburg United Methodist Homes, across from the Evangelical Community Hospital and Plaza 15 shopping center.

Williamsport's Millionaires' Row

Enjoy the High Life

You can dine, stay overnight and tour the sumptuous mansions of Williamsport's lumber barons. This town along the Susquehanna was, for a time, the lumber capital of the world with more than 30 sawmills in operation. The Susquehanna Boom stretched seven-miles along the river with 400 chain-linked stone and timber cribs reaching diagonally from shore to shore. This floating fence caught logs as they went down river. The logs were sorted, cut at the sawmill and shipped around the world. Enough lumber was cut here to build 900,000 homes.

Lumbering brought wealth to Williamsport, and by the late 1800s the town had more millionaires than any community its size in the country. The town's 18 millionaires vied for the distinction of building a lavish house along Fourth Street from the 400 to the 1000 block—more millionaires' lived on this street than any other in the world. It was Peter Herdic who made sure this street became a stately residential avenue. He purchased a large tract of farmland and divided it into lots. A condition of purchase for the lots along Fourth Street was that the house was 20 to 30 feet from the street. Herdic was the first to build, and his **Eber Culver-designed Italian Villa**-style house was one of the town's show spots. A massive restoration effort returned the house to its former glory and today it is an elegant restaurant. The four lower porches have Egyptian Lotus columns, with grooves and leaf-like outward curls on the lower portion. The flat overhanging roof has carved bracketed eaves and the house is crowned by a large square cupola (reached inside by a carved mahogany staircase that curves up three floors). The house is painted a soft pink with white trim. The **Peter Herdic House**, 407 West Fourth Street, serves lunch weekdays 11:00 A.M. to 2:00 P.M. and dinner 5:00 P.M. to 10:00 P.M. Monday through Saturday. Reservations can be made by calling (717) 322-0165.

Next door is the **Snyder House Victorian Bed and Breakfast**, at 411, built in 1890 as a wedding present for Fannie and Lemuel Ulman. It too was designed by Culver about 30 years after the Hedric mansion. Here the influence is late Victorian with a tower and intricate stained-glass windows. For information on accommodations call (717) 494-0835 or 326-0411.

Continuing down Millionaires' Row at 522 West Fourth Street, you'll see one of the fine **Queen Anne homes** designed by Eber Culver. Built for Hiram Rhoads in the late 1880s, the house features the steep gables and multiform porches associated with this style. It is also noted for the stained glass on the front door. Rhoads introduced the telephone to this area; it was only the second exchange in the state (Erie was first). These two communities had the telephone before larger cities like Philadelphia and Pittsburgh.

There are several attractive churches along West Fourth Street, including the **First Baptist Church** built on a swampy lot given to the congregation by Peter Herdic. He was not a member but wanted to help his wife's church. The deed stipulated that it was to be a "first-rate" house of worship. The church that stands today is a Romanesque style building of native mountain stone.

Herdic also donated land for the **Church of the Annunciation** (in all he provided land for five Williamsport churches). The Romanesque church that stands today was begun in 1886 with supporting groups of buttresses and crowning towers. A steeple was planned but when the scaffolding collapsed and four workers died, the tower was capped and a cross placed at the top. Forty-three stained glass windows add a glow to the interior.

Across from this Catholic church is the **Rowly House**, at 707, one of the most magnificent of the Culver Queen Anne mansions along Millionaires' Row. This ornate three-story brick mansion is now the residence of the Sisters of the Immaculate Heart of Mary.

There are two spots along West Fourth Street to obtain information on the area. The first is the **Lycoming County Tourist Promotion Agency** at 848. The house was once the rectory for the Trinity Episcopal Church. The downstairs provides tourist information and a period room. Hours are weekdays 10:00 A.M. to 2:00 P.M., or you can call (800) 358-9900. Just next door is the **Lycoming County Historical Museum**, providing a comprehensive look at the region's history. There is a frontier room that shows you what it was like to live here in 1769. The importance of the **West Branch Canal**, constructed in 1834, is highlighted. If you are confused about how the Susquehanna Boom operated, exhibits here will explain its operation in detail. One of the museum's most popular collections is the Shempp model train exhibit with 300 models, including 12 one-of-a-kind models. In addition to exhibits that tell the story of the development of Williamsport and Lycoming County, there is a library and archives. You can visit Tuesday through Friday 9:30 A.M. to 4:00 P.M. On Saturday it opens at 11:00 A.M. and Sunday at NOON (Sunday hours are only May through October). Admission is charged.

An excellent way to explore Millionaires' Row is by boarding the **Herdic Trolley**. These hour long narrated tours run Tuesday, Thursday and Saturday throughout the day from Memorial Day to Labor Day. Tickets are available at the Trolley Gazebo just in front of the Sheraton Inn, 100 Pine Street. There is a nominal charge for this ride through history.

A different kind of ride is available aboard the *Hiawatha*, a replica of a paddlewheel riverboat like those that once plied the Susquehanna. The narrated cruise, that sails from Susquehanna State Park, acquaints visitors with the Susquehannock Indians, who lived along the riverbanks for hundreds of years before the European settlers arrived. You'll also see remnants of the cribs built for the Susquehanna Boom. The small piles of stones that extend out of the water at regular intervals like miniature islands were part of the floating fence. You'll hear stories about the logging camps and the lumberjacks, the jam crackers who broke up the congestion at the boom, and the millhands of Williamsport who worked hard and relaxed hard in the town's saloons.

Hour-long *Hiawatha* cruises run four times a day Tuesday through Saturday during the summer months and three times on Sunday. In May, September and October cruises are given on weekends. Call for exact times and rates, (717) 321-1206 or (800) 358-9900.

Another dining treat in Williamsport is the **Thomas Lightfoot Inn**, 2887 South Reach Road, a charming historic spot offering lunch and dinner, as well as overnight accommodations in a 1792 plantation. The land was settled by Thomas Updergraff, a Quaker Friend of surveyor Thomas Lightfoot. He and his descendants farmed this land for 162 years from 1792 to 1954. Over the years the house became an inn on the West Branch of the Pennsylvania Canal as well as a stop on the Underground Railroad. The cellar of this house is converted to an English Pub serving the public Friday and Saturday nights. For information on the restaurant and the five guest rooms call (717) 326-6396.

Another bed and breakfast spot in the heart of Williamsport's historic district is the **Reighard House** at 1323 East Third Street, (717) 326-3593. This Victorian mansion was built in 1905 and has six guest rooms. On West Third Street stop by the **Old Jail Center** to see more than 45 artisans and craftsmen whose shops are located in a restored 1868 stone prison. Historic displays vie for attention with the varied merchandise. You can't miss it because just outside on the corner of this unique shopping plaza sits a mannequin in a jail cell. Carved on the entrance doors is a wooden policeman wearing an old-fashioned long coat.

Directions: From I-80 take Route 15 north 20 miles to Williamsport. Route 15N and Route 220S intersect, Route 15N

302

will be a right-hand split; you want to remain on Route 220 south. For Millionaires' Row take Maynard Street exit off Route 220 and follow to West Fourth Street. For *Hiawatha* remain on Route 220 south until the Reach Road exit, turn right off the exit and follow signs for *Hiawatha*.

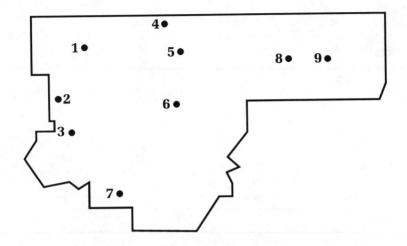

ALLEGHENY NATIONAL FOREST REGION

1. **Warren**
   Warren County Historical Society
   Allegheny National Forest
   Kinzua Dam and Allegheny
   Federal Fish Hatchery

2. **Tionesta**
   Flying W Ranch and Tionesta
   Lake

3. **Cooksburg**
   Cook Forest State Park
   Sawmill Center for the Arts
   and Cook Forest Art
   Center Museum

4. **Bradford**
   Penn Brad Oil Museum

5. **Mount Jewett**
   Kinzua Bridge State Park and
   Knox, Kane, Kinzua Rail-
   road

6. **Saint Marys**
   Elk View Scenic Drive
   Straub Brewery

7. **Punxsutawney**

8. **Galeton**
   Pennsylvania Lumber Mu-
   seum and Surrounding
   State Parks

9. **Wellsboro**
   Grand Canyon of Pennsylvania

Allegheny National
═══Forest Region═══

Three-fifths of Pennsylvania is still forest and an impressive segment of that can be found in the Allegheny National Forest region. The rugged terrain and hard winters kept settlers in the Susquehanna Valley from moving northwest into this area, so it remains a pristine wilderness enjoyed by outdoor enthusiasts.

Hunters stalk big game, more abundant here than anywhere else in the state. The magnificent elk, however, may not be shot except by photographers. The region is home to one of only two elk herds east of the Mississippi River. Another protected animal is the popular weather prognosticator, Punxsutawney Phil. The home of the famous groundhog is in the center of the town whose name he bears. He attracts visitors from around the world and receives almost as much mail as Santa Claus.

Not all the animals in the region are wild; outside Tionesta is the Flying W Ranch, one of the only dude ranches in the East. Tionesta and Pine Creek challenge trout fishermen and the state record muskie was caught at Kinzua Dam.

Horseback riders, hikers and whitewater buffs find unparalleled delights exploring the Pennsylvania Grand Canyon. The 50-mile gorge cut by Pine Creek reaches an impressive height of 1,000 feet within Leonard Harrison and Colton Point state parks.

Specific attractions reflect the vocational interests of the region's residents—Penn-Brad Oil Museum and Pennsylvania Lumber Museum—and avocational—Straub Brewery.

Allegheny National Forest

State's Only National Forest and National Scenic Byway

Sprawling across four counties and spanning more than a half million acres, the **Allegheny National Forest** is a recreational and scenic treasure. Tree-covered mountains, lush valleys, crystal-clear lakes and fast-moving rivers are the backdrop for hiking, all-terrain vehicle trails, riding, camping, hunting, boating, fishing, swimming, cross-country skiing and snowmobiling.

Several of the roughly 180 miles of hiking trails within the forest are part of the National Trails System. **North Country National Scenic Trail**, the longest trail in the forest, has 86.7 blue-blazed miles of trail. If it is ever fully completed it will encompass 3,200 miles and link the Appalachian Trail in Vermont with the Lewis and Clark Trail in North Dakota. The off-white-blazed **Johnnycake Trail** is far shorter, taking hikers to scenic Handsome Lake campground. Two additional trails are national recreation trails: **Black Cherry** offers an easy walk for all ages in the lower loop area of the Twin Lakes campgrounds, while **Tracy Ridge** runs along a ridge top before intersecting with the North Country and Johnnycake Trails. Additionally, there are more than ten interpretative trails, including the 1.1 mile Longhouse Interpretative Trail accessible from the Longhouse National Scenic Byway, a 29-mile driving loop around the southern arm of the Allegheny Reservoir.

Along this driving route are two information centers. The Kinzua Point Information Center (see Kinzua Dam selection) sits at the intersection of Longhouse Scenic Drive and Route 59. This center operates seasonally from Memorial Day through Labor Day daily from 9:00 A.M. to 5:30 P.M. Visitors are also warmly welcomed at the Bradford Ranger District Center at the junction of Route 59 and 321 south. It is open weekdays year-round from 7:00 A.M. to 4:30 P.M. and during summer months weekends from 9:00 A.M. to 5:00 P.M. Both spots have interpretative exhibits and an array of nature-related books in addition to trail maps and informative brochures on the Allegheny National Forest. Along the scenic byway there are two developed overlooks with picnic areas, two swimming beaches, three campgrounds, three boat launches, a full-service marina, a bank fishing area that is handicapped accessible and numerous trail entry points.

Also on the Longhouse National Scenic Byway is the **Old Powerhouse**, a historical site now in the process of being restored. There are over 5,000 oil and gas wells on national forest land and this powerhouse interprets both of these industries. The Cooper Bessemer engine in the powerhouse was used to drive 27 rod lines connected to oil and gas jacks located between 25 feet to 2 miles away. The engine, band wheel, numerous rod lines and pump jacks are still in place. Plans are underway to add interpretive bulletin boards and displays (an operational powerhouse can be seen at Drake Well, see selection).

The entire Allegheny National Forest area is scenically splendid but a few spots deserve special mention. **Rimrock Overlook** has a spectacular view of the Kinzua Dam. Paved walks lead to a rocky promontory and a natural stone stairway leads through a narrow rock crevasse to the base of the huge rocks. Another excellent vantage point is **Jake's Rocks**, where there are three automobile overlooks and two that are easily reached by foot. While bird watching is popular throughout the forest it is particularly rewarding at **Buzzard Swamp** and **Owl's Nest**, located in the southern portion of the forest.

While the scenery is always noteworthy, it becomes spectacular in late-September when the fall foliage begins to turn, peaking in mid-October. It also has a special appeal in mid-June when the mountain laurel blooms.

Directions: From I-79 take Route 6 east to Warren County. Route 59 east, just outside of Warren, leads to the reservoir and a variety of outdoor activities. From Route 6, take Route 62 just below Warren—it is a very scenic drive along the nationally designated Allegheny Wild and Scenic River. From I-80 take Exit 8, Route 66 north or Exit 13, Route 36/899 north onto the national forest.

Cook Forest State Park

Gary Cooper's Favorite Getaway

Daniel Day-Lewis loped through North Carolina during the filming of *Last of the Mohicans*, Pittsburgh starred in *Striking Distance* and Mount Rushmore provided the gripping climax of *North by Northwest*. But predating these is the 1946 Cecil B. Demille cult favorite *The Unconquered*. Star Gary Cooper was impressed with the primeval forest in which the film was shot. Various points in **Cook Forest State Park** were incorporated into the movie including Seneca Point, Forest Drive and Clarington.

A pivotal scene in the movie was shot at the Cook Forest Riding Academy, operated at the time by Bill Kuhns who supplied the horses for the film. DeMille hired Native Americans from a reservation in New York, but this attempt at realism failed when the director discovered that his Indians couldn't ride bareback—they kept falling off the horses. Kuhns contacted some of his local cronies, and with the help of Paramount's make-up experts they became Indians for the princely fee of $10 a day.

Cooper's interest in the area was certainly warranted, since the woods have remained unspoiled from well before William Penn founded his colony. In Penn's day the area was called the Black Forest. Nearly one-third of Cook Forest is virgin white pine and hemlock, one of the largest and finest stands in the eastern United States. This stand, called the **Forest Cathedral**, is marked as a National Natural Landmark. Some of the trees are over 350 years old and tower skyward more than 200 feet. To hike through this stand, take the 1.2 mile **Longfellow Trail** at the Log Cabin Inn Nature Center, along the Cooksburg-Vowinckel Road. At the start of this trail you'll see the Memorial Fountain dedicated to the visionary nature enthusiasts who raised the money to purchase this state park land. Longfellow is just one of 17 trails. Approximately 30 miles of hiking is available in the park.

The 1.1 mile Birch Trail leads to a picnic shelter. **Liggett Trail** is another ideal family hike as its two mile distance covers flat terrain and it ends at a playground and picnic area at the Information Building on Tom's Run Road. Rhododendron grows abundantly along Hemlock and Rhododendron trails. These are only a few of the options. For detailed information on all the trails stop at the park office or various area businesses.

Three of these trails are designated for cross-country skiing (others are also suitable as are some of the park roadways). Twenty miles of trails are set aside for snowmobiling. There is a sledding area at Ridge Camp and another beside the skating pond. The lighted outdoor ice skating pond beside the Clarion River is open daily at no charge during the winter months.

There are 4.5 miles of riding trails in the park. Horses can be obtained at the four riding stables adjacent to the park. One of these stables is the **Cook Forest Riding Academy** that proved so helpful during the 1940s filming. It's still run by the Kuhns family; call (814) 927-8391. At Pine Crest you can take one to three-hour-rides on one of their four deep-woods trails; call (814) 752-2375.

Pine Crest also runs down-river canoe float trips from 9-mile/3-hour trips to 38-mile overnight adventures. Other outfits that run trips include the Cook Forest Canoe Livery, where options extend from 90-minute to two-day trips (814) 744-8094; Belltown Canoe Rental also rents tubes, (814) 752-2561; the Pale Whale Canoe Fleet handles both canoes and tubes (814) 744-8300. Canoeing on the Clarion River in Cook Forest is an experience the entire family can enjoy since the rapids are small and the passing riverbank is scenic. Fishermen may want to jump out and try their luck. Along the Clarion River at Cooksburg the rocks have Native American carvings authenticated by experts from the Carnegie Mellon Museum. One rock shows a horse, rider and tree.

To get a panoramic view of the Clarion River Valley hike or drive to **Seneca Point**, named for the Seneca Indians who frequented this area and featured in the DeMille movie. This boulder-laden overlook is located next to the 70-foot Fire Tower. Seneca Trail also leads to this overlook.

There are numerous private waterparks in Cook Forest, the only state park in Pennsylvania that has private commercial activities within the park. The park itself has a pool located adjacent to the Sawmill Center for the Arts (see selection).

If you want to extend your one-day trip for a weekend or a week call (800) 348-9393 to obtain information on accommodations. Within the park there are 226 class A tent and trailer sites plus 24 rustic cabins and two group tenting areas. There are also a selection of private campgrounds and cabin rental companies in the area. The **Gateway Lodge and Cabins** is listed as one of the ten best country inns in the United States. The lodge bedrooms are furnished with Early American pieces and the front porch was featured in *Innsider Magazine*. When it is too cold for the porch, visitors gather around the weathered stone fireplace in the lounge. For more information call (800) 843-6862; if you are outside the state call (814) 744-8017.

Directions: From I-80 take Exit 13, Brookville exit, and go north on Route 36 for about 16 miles. Gateway Lodge is on Route 36 on the right side of the road just $^1/_4$ mile south of the Cooksburg Bridge.

Elk View Scenic Drive

Watching Wapiti

Unlike many county names, Elk County means just that—it and neighboring Cameron County are home to close to 225 free-roaming elk. Locals and visitors take part in a full-scale game of "I Spy" as they take **Elk View Drive** through the towns of Saint Marys and Benezette trying to spot the state's largest game animal. As you park beside the fields on Winslow Hill, a car may pass with the news that elk have been spotted just ahead, or down the road a few miles, and off you go in pursuit of a glimpse of these striking animals.

If you're lucky you might spot a royal or imperial bull. The former has 12 point antlers, while the latter, patriarch of the herd, has an impressive 14 points. During a 1990s elk survey, spotters saw 25 branched-antler bulls and 12 spike bulls, yearlings with only a single spike between 10 and 24 inches in length. Racks on older bucks may extend four to five feet in length.

The Native Americans called the native elk "wapiti," which meant white deer. They were once plentiful throughout Pennsylvania. By the mid-1900s most had disappeared, although a small herd survived in Elk County. In 1867 the last native Pennsylvania Eastern elk was killed near Ridgway. Between 1913 and 1926 the Pennsylvania game Commission released 177 Rocky

Scenic drives provide frequent glimpses of Pennsylvania's largest game animal; close to 225 free-roaming elk are found in this region.

Mountain elk. Other states in the Northeast also experimented with elk releases but less successfully than Pennsylvania. The Keystone State's herd has remained healthy and it has become a popular tourist attraction particularly in the autumn breeding season when the elk put on their best show.

In September and October you can hear bulls bugling to attract cows to their harem. Often other bulls challenge the bugling male and these aggressive opponents face-off, pushing, shoving and sometimes joining antlers until the weaker bull breaks off the confrontation and trots away. Bugling is exciting to hear. It's best described as a low bellow that ascends to a high note that the bull elk holds until he runs out of breath. The bellowing elk call is followed by guttural grunts. Cows occasionally bugle but they are more likely to communicate by barking and grunting. Calves make a sharp squealing sound. Visitors are more likely to spot elk grazing, though they also feed off of trees and bushes. Although they seem to move slowly, almost majestically, elk can run 30 miles per hour for short distances and can trot for miles at a time. Elk ranges cover between 150 and 200 square miles. Roughly 78 miles of the herd's range is within the Elk and Moshannon State Forest and state game lands. There are hiking trails in these public areas. Eight scenic driving tours are outlined in an "Autumn in the Alleghenies" booklet available from the Allegheny National Forest at 222 Liberty Street, Warren, PA 16365 (814-723-5150) or the Elk Co. Rec/Tourism Co., P.O. Box 35, Ridgway, PA 15853 (814-772-5502).

One of the most popular routes is the Elk View scenic Drive tour that heads south from Saint Marys on State Route 255 to Weedville, then east on State Route 555 to Benezette. There are fields in the tiny community of **Benezette** where elk congregate; but be sure to respect private property. The only shooting permitted is with a camera; the elk herd is protected by law. From Benezette take a detour up **Winslow Hill**, one of the favorite areas with locals. To continue on the Elk View Drive loop return to State Route 555 and head toward Driftwood in Cameron County, then take State Route 120 north to Emporium and west to Saint Marys. Elk are often sighted near the airport in Saint Marys.

Directions: From I-76 or I-80 take Route 219 north to Ridgway then take Route 120 east to Saint Marys.

Flying W Ranch and Tionesta Lake

Find the Old West in the East

Adjacent to the lush, sprawling 500,000-acre Allegheny National Forest is the **Flying W Ranch**, the largest dude ranch in the east. This ranch has all the necessary ingredients: plenty of horses, forested mountain trails, an assortment of horse riding options including pack trips, an annual rodeo, hayrides, cottages, bunkhouse and a restaurant. You don't need to ride like Annie Oakley or Wild Bill Hickok to enjoy the trail rides. The cowboys, who look like extras from every western movie you've ever seen, gear the rides to the skill of the riders.

The Weller family ranch has been operating since 1965; originally it was a cattle ranch. Such is the popularity of the Flying W that you need to make advance reservations for riding and staying overnight as early as possible. Call (814) 463-7663. You can bring your own horse or use theirs. The ranch operates April through November. The International Professional Rodeo Association sanctioned rodeo takes place on the fourth weekend in July.

The Flying W is just north of the Allegheny National Forest's **Tionesta Lake** area. A Visitor Center near the lake acquaints you with the multiple recreational options available. Trails skirt the lake and head into a forest that is a small reminder of the six million acres once covering the Allegheny Plateau that extends across Pennsylvania and New York. Two thousand acres survive, with huge 400-year-old hemlocks and 300-year-old beeches. It is easy to imagine the Iroquois Indians traveling through this virgin forest and settlers clearing land for their farms. There is a long 1.1 mile trail that takes about an hour to hike, and a short 0.25 mile trail that can be covered in 15 minutes. More than 68 species of birds have been sighted in this scenic area. Around Tionesta Lake you can hike the Mill Race Trail, the Dam Site Trail, Plantation Trail and Summit Trail.

Trail maps are available at the Visitor Center where you can also see photographs of the dam construction, completed in 1940, that created this roughly 6⅓-mile lake. You can stop at the dam tower and overlook to see the dam from 1:00 P.M. to 3:00 P.M. on Sundays, Memorial Day to Labor Day, and on holiday Mondays. There is an on-going slide presentation in the tower.

Recreational options include several campgrounds with tent and trailer sites. There is even a rent-a-tent program for those who want to try this recreational option before investing in the necessary equipment; call (814) 755-3512. There are two boat launches one at the dam site area and the other at Nebraska Access Area. Canoes can be rented at the Visitor Center and local marinas rent craft. There is a beach on the bank of Tionesta Creek and, although there is no beach, swimming is permitted on the lake at your own risk. Swimmers need to beware of submerged stumps, logs and rocks which are prevalent near the shore. Tionesta Lake is a popular fishing spot, with muskie being the most frequent catch followed by bass, perch and crappie. The fall is an ideal time to picnic at one of the lake overlooks, while winter sports enthusiasts can enjoy ice fishing and cross-country skiing.

Directions: From I-80 take Route 8 to Oil City, then head east on Route 62 to Tionesta. Just north of the town take Route 666 to Kellettville and the Flying W Ranch. To reach Tionesta Lake from town take Route 36 south about a half mile.

Grand Canyon of Pennsylvania

AKA Pine Creek Gorge

Don't think in terms of the canyons of the west for this is no steep, rocky canyon. The **Grand Canyon of Pennsylvania** is a

50-mile gorge through the densely forested northcentral mountains. As the glaciers melted, a dam of gravel, sand and clay changed the flow of Pine Creek from a northeasterly direction to a southern flow. This new creek path carved out the canyon.

State parks provide access to this scenic area, designated as a National Natural Landmark by the National Park Service. Across the canyon from each other are the 585-acre **Leonard Harrison State Park** on the eastern rim and the 368-acre Colton Point Sate Park on the western rim.

Hiking is a major draw at Leonard Harrison State Park. There are two major trails: **Turkey Path Trail** that descends one mile to the bottom of Pine Creek Gorge and **Overlook Trail** that leads to a scenic view of the southern portion of the gorge. Turkey Path Trail, while not a long hike, does follow a steep and narrow path. After you pass the halfway point on your way to the canyon floor you will see a scenic waterfall along Little Four-Mile Run. The .6 mile loop Overlook Trail heads in the opposite direction for a completely different view of the canyon. These trails can be hazardous and it is important to wear appropriate hiking shoes and stay on the trail. The elevation at the canyon rim is roughly 1,830 feet. Avoid the temptation of climbing out on rocky overhangs for a better view.

Leonard Harrison State Park has picnicking and camping facilities. A Visitor Center at the main overlook orients you to the park and its wildlife.

Across the rim is the smaller **Colton Point State Park** with additional hiking trails. **Turkey Path** leads one mile down to Pine Creek which, when flowing slowly, can be crossed. The trail continues up to the overlook at Leonard Harrison (the trail up and down is easier on the east rim). The trails at Colton Point connect with the 30-mile long **West Rim Trail** in Tioga State Forest. The northern end of this trail is one-mile south of Route 6, on Colton Road near Ansonia. The southern end is on Route 414, two miles south of Blackwell.

The **Barbour Rock Trail** also heads out from Colton Road, through Pine Creek Gorge Natural Area. A mile hike leads to a canyon overlook. At the overlook this trail intercepts the West Rim Trail. Combining the state parks, state forests and other natural areas, the state owns 300,000 acres of the Pennsylvania Grand Canyon. This is the largest wilderness area between New York and Chicago.

An entirely different vantage point is provided when you use horsepower instead of footpower. **Mountain Trail Horse Center** offers everything from half-day rides to five-day camping trips. You'll get a chance to travel deep into the forests where cars and all-terrain vehicles never venture. These trail rides are adventurous. Some of the rides follow logging roads and mountain trails, others with more advanced riders blaze their own path, bushwacking their way through the rugged terrain. All the trips are escorted and guides report that sometimes beginners do better than those who think they know all about riding. By the end of a full day of trail riding, participants have earned the right to sit around a campfire enjoying the Indian legends and the guide's tall tales. For information on the half-day, day-long and overnight trips, call (717) 376-5561.

If you want to get out into the wilderness but the trail rides are too adventurous, consider the wagon rides that Mountain Trail Horse Center runs through the Pine Creek Canyon. Rides range from two to four hours. Some are planned with picnics and others at sunset. They also arrange combination packages that include horseback riding with rafting or canoeing on Pine Creek. There's a ride and ski package that lets participants cross-country ski.

Another adventurous way to explore Pennsylvania's Grand Canyon is by rafting or canoeing down Pine Creek. The Iroquois called Pine Creek, "Tiadaghton" or River of Pines. Pine Creek combines moderate whitewater with long quiet stretches that pass through breathtaking scenery. Pine Creek is part of the state's Wild & Scenic Rivers System and is under consideration for federal designation. The best way to see this free-flowing river is by raft or canoe.

Pine Creek Outfitters have literally written the book on the area. Chuck Dillon who, with his wife Susan, owns and runs the company, has written *Pennsylvania's Grand Canyon: A Natural & Human History*, the definitive book about the canyon. Dillon has also produced maps, trail guides, hiking manuals and regional natural history articles. In addition to guided trips, the Dillons rent rafts, canoes, bicycles and other equipment. They provide help in trip planning as well as logistical support.

There are four major sections of Pine Creek. The "Upper Pine" is a scenic ten mile section of the river from Watrous to Ansonia. This part of the river is excellent for novice canoeists or family trips. The "Canyon" portion of the river, a roughly 18-mile stretch from Ansonia to Blackwell, has some Class II/III rapids and is recommended for rafting and those with canoeing proficiency. The "Middle Gorge" extends for 12 miles from Blackwell to Slate Run. It has a few Class II rapids but is an easy run. The deepest part of the gorge is the "Lower Gorge," the 15 miles from Slate Run to Waterville. Pine Creek Outfitters provide information on the river conditions Monday through Friday from 8:00 A.M. to 5:00 P.M. and on weekends from 1:00 P.M. to 5:00 P.M. Call (717) 724-3003.

Pine Creek Outfitters runs one day guided canyon float trips. You can also check with Pine Creek Outfitters about mountain bike rentals and accessible trails, including the nearby **Pine**

Creek Rail-Trail that opened in 1995. Fishing, camping, hiking and cross-country skiing are also popular options. They operate combination packages with Mountain Trail Horse Center. Both companies also have packages that include dining and/or lodging at Cedar Run Inn, a country inn that has been open since 1891. For information on the Inn call (717) 353-6241.

Directions: From I-80 heading west, take Exit 31, I-180 north to Williamsport. Pick up Route 15 north to Mansfield, then Route 6 west to Wellsboro. Traveling east on I-80 take Exit 26, Route 220 north to Williamsport. Take Route 287 north to Wellsboro. From Wellsboro, take Route 660 west to Leonard Harrison State Park. For Colton State Park, follow Route 6 west toward Ansonia, turn left on Colton Road (the signs for the park are small, so watch carefully).

Kinzua Bridge State Park and the Knox, Kane, Kinzua Railroad

Eighth Wonder of the World

Ninety-four days after work started on May 10, 1882, a 40-man crew built the world's highest railroad viaduct over the valley of Kinzua Creek. The creek's defile was 2,000 feet wide and 300 feet deep. The alternative presented to General Thomas L. Kane, who was attempting to connect the coal, timber and oil riches of northwestern Pennsylvania with markets via a railroad, was to build eight additional miles of track over the steep and wooded slopes of the ravine.

Instead Kane decided to build what is now a National Historic Civil Engineering Landmark. The first viaduct was 301 feet high, 2,053 long and swayed so much that rail cars had to travel across it at no more than five miles an hour. Trains vibrated as they crossed and a strong wind set the bridge in motion. In 1900, the bridge was replaced with a new steel structure designed to handle heavier locomotives and to withstand wind stress but otherwise having no structural changes from the original. Octave Chanute was an engineer on both bridges. Currently it is the second highest railroad viaduct in the country and the fourth highest in the world.

During the summer months the **Knox, Kane, Kinzua Railroad** has daily steam-powered train excursions that cross the trestle bridge. As the only train that runs across the bridge, it crosses, then circles and returns. There are pedestrian walkways on both sides of the train tracks; it is a thrilling experience to walk to the center of the bridge and view the deep chasm of the Allegheny Mountains. You are advised not to be on the bridge when the train arrives at noon.

Trains depart Marienville for a 97-mile round-trip to Kinzua Bridge, or you can board at Kane for the 33-mile round-trip. To obtain a current schedule, prices and tickets call (814) 837-8621 or (717) 334-6932. You can also arrange for a box lunch. Normal schedule is a daily run Tuesday through Sunday in July and August with extended weekends in June, September and fall foliage runs in October.

Excursions have been popular since the bridge was first constructed. Trains ran from Buffalo and Pittsburgh and raised enough money to offset the $167,000 cost of the viaduct. According to local legend, there's another rich lode awaiting the treasure hunter who finds the $40,000 in gold hidden by bank robbers in glass containers and buried within sight of the viaduct. Keep your eyes open as you hike **Aspen Trail** that winds from the overlook to the valley below.

Recreational options in this 316-acre park include picnicking and hiking. From the fall archery deer season through March hunting, trapping and dog training are enjoyed in the park. There is no hunting from the bridge itself. This is a day-use park and it closes at dusk.

Just about a mile down the Kinzua Valley, although it's farther by automobile, is **Silverside Inn**, a gracious Victorian estate built in 1889 by Elisha Kent Kane, the third son of General Thomas Kane who built the Kinzua Bridge and founded the nearby city of Kane. This inn, on 2,000 acres, offers visitors a quiet but luxurious stay in antique-filled rooms. They will even pick you up at the Kinzua Bridge if you want to arrive by train. For details on weekend packages call (814) 778-5991. In Kane itself the **1896 Kane Manor Country Inn** gives you the chance to stay in the second home of General Thomas L. Kane. His grandson Elisha Kent Kane II opened the home as a restaurant and guest house in the 1930s and it has been a popular spot ever since; call (814) 837-6522 for additional information.

Finally, you can visit the grave of General Kane at the **Thomas L. Kane Memorial Chapel**. This stone chapel is an exact copy of a Presbyterian church Kane saw on a trip to England in 1844. He had it built between 1876 and 1879. A legacy from his aunt provided funds for the stained glass windows. While Kane was living in Philadelphia, he became close friends with Jesse Little, a devout Mormon. Kane became interested in the Mormons and traveled with them when they were expelled from Ohio and sent west. Kane also met with Brigham Young as an emissary from President Buchanan during the 1858 conflict over the Mormon practice of bigamy. Kane's intervention helped prevent bloodshed. The chapel is an historic site of the Church of Jesus

Christ of Latter-day Saints and has memorabilia on Kane's life. A genealogical library is available to interested visitors. The chapel is open Tuesday through Saturday from 9:00 A.M. to 5:00 P.M. and on Sunday from 1:00 P.M. to 5:00 P.M.

Directions: From I-79 head west on Route 6 to Mount Jewett. Kinzua Bridge State Park is four miles north on State Route 3011. To reach Kane continue on Route 6 to the town and make a left turn on Chestnut Street; the chapel will be on your right.

Kinzua Dam and Allegheny Federal Fish Hatchery

Dam Good

It is a double boon when a costly engineering project serves the community in multiple ways, and such is the case with the **Kinzua Dam**. Completed in 1965, Kinzua proved its worth in 1972 after Tropical Storm Agnes by preventing an estimated $247 million in flood damages. Since opening the dam has reputedly saved in excess of $323 million. By water release it maintains the quality and quantity of water for domestic, industrial and recreational use plus maintaining navigable routes for barge traffic on the Allegheny and upper Ohio Rivers. The dam also provides hydroelectric power to the region. This process is explained at the **Big Bend Visitor Center**, at Big Bend Overlook just east of Warren. This is a good spot for photographers to capture the imposing dam which rises 179 feet from the streambed.

For daytrippers, it's the recreational opportunities presented by the vast 25-mile Allegheny Reservoir that are of interest. The nearly 100 miles of forested shoreline are protected acreage, partly within the Allegheny National Forest (see selection). On the upper New York portion of the dam the shoreline is within the Allegany State Park and the reservation of the Seneca Nation of Indians.

Three miles from the dam on Route 59 is the **Kinzua-Wolf Run Marina**, (814) 726-1650, where you can rent a canoe, pontoon boat or small craft, with or without motor, and get out on the water. The best way to enjoy this 12,000-acre elongated lake is from the water as there is no waterside auto route. Another option is to take a 45-minute narrated paddlewheel cruise aboard the *Kinzua Queen*. Tours depart hourly from the marina dock from 1:00 to 6:00 P.M. For those with their own boats, there are six launch areas within the National Forest. There are also two beaches on the lake and several picnic areas.

The **Allegheny Reservoir** is one of the state's best fishing areas. For information on fishing conditions, call the Fishing Hotline, (814) 726-0164. The state record walleye and northern pike were caught here, as well as trophy smallmouth bass, muskellunge and brown trout. For a preview of fish that will eventually fill the state waters, stop at the **Federal Fish Hatchery** where they rear over one million finger-sized lake trout each year. This hatchery near the dam is accessible by traveling Hemlock Road from Warren's east side; you can not reach it from Route 59. Hours are 9:00 A.M. to 3:00 P.M.

Directions: From I-79 take Route 6 east to Warren, then Route 59 east to the Kinzua Dam. From I-80 take Route 8 north to just past Franklin, then pick up Route 62 north to Warren and go east on Route 59.

Penn-Brad Oil Museum

Barkers, Yellow Dogs and Go-Devils

The **Penn-Brad Oil Museum** has the only operational, completely accurate 1890-style 72 feet-high wooden oil rig in the country. You get a glimpse of life in the northwestern Pennsylvania oil fields watching museum staff, with years of experience in the oil field, run this standard rig.

In 1859, the world's first well drilled expressly for oil began operation in Titusville (see Drake Well Museum selection). A little more than a decade later, in 1871, oil was discovered around Bradford. By 1947 there were between 400 to 500 drilling rigs running in the Bradford Field. Some wells had an initial flow of 800 barrels per day. The price quickly dropped from the $20 a barrel that Drake got in 1859 to between $1.39 to $2.62 per barrel in the 1930s and 40s.

The western part of Pennsylvania is rich in oil and gas; nearly half of the state's 67 counties have wells. Throughout the United States there are roughly 10,000 small independent oil and gas producers; approximately 600 of these operate in Pennsylvania. A "miracle molecule," distinct to Pennsylvania grade paraffin base oil, supplies 15 to 20 percent of the country's lubricating requirements. This oil has a unique light green color as opposed to the chocolate syrup consistency of most crude oil. Bradford has the distinction of being the first billion-dollar oil field.

Rigs, like the one you see in the museum, were found in backyards and throughout the wooded mountainsides. To help the men see while drilling at night, they had yellow-painted cast-iron jugs, rather like a teapot with two spouts. Crude oil filled the jugs and soft rope served as wicks; when they were lit the spouts glowed like a dog's eyes. Locals say that the lights from the "yellow dogs" blinked along the mountain slopes like lanterns on the riggings of a massive fleet of sailing vessels. There's still a yellow dog hanging in the museum's rig.

The first thing you'll notice on your museum tour is the huge four-cylinder Buffalo drilling engine, a 1920s substitution for the earlier steam engine and boiler. A belt was put around the fly-wheel pulley of the engine to operate the small Roots blower you see on the floor beside the engine. Whenever a fire was needed, an air draft was sent through a pipe to the forge on the derrick floor.

As you walk through the belt hall to the derrick floor, notice the large wooden band wheel with different sections. Ropes lead from the wheel to the derrick floor. At the back of the derrick floor are the large Bull wheels, used in "running the tools," that is lowering and pulling them from the well. Next to this is the lazy bench where the men ate their lunch and whittled. You'll see sizeable tin lunch buckets in the museum's collection. Locals say the men knew their wives were angry with them when they packed their lunch and left out forks and other utensils.

There were two sources of heat on the derrick floor, the derrick stove and the forge used to heat the drilling bits. A crane lifted the heavier equipment out of the forge and into the slack tub for tempering.

The main drilling controls of the rig, a grooved derrick pulley also called a telegraph wheel, are connected to the engine by a wire attached to what was called a headache post. This stalwart support was underneath the walking beam, a long overhead pine beam, which sometimes during drilling pulled loose from its saddle and fell. The headache post stopped its fall and saved those drilling beneath from a massive headache.

The walking beam was held up by another massive timber called appropriately, the Samson post. The exterior sections of the derrick are made up of legs, girts and sway braces.

Finally, a barker let well owners and operators know from a distance whether the well was running or shut down. The barker fit over the exhaust of steam-pumping engines. Each barker had an individual sound or bark.

Within the museum are photographs depicting oil operations and the roughnecks who worked them, mining tools and an Emery horse-drawn steam fire engine used in the 1875 independent oil producers fight with Standard Oil Company. Guides regale visitors with fascinating stories about working on the oil rigs.

The Penn-Brad Oil Museum is open Memorial Day to Labor Day Monday through Saturday 10:00 A.M. to 4:00 P.M. and Sunday NOON to 5:00 P.M.

There were three principle economic livelihoods in this part of northwestern Pennsylvania: oil, timber and farming. The Penn-Brad offers a look at the first, the Pennsylvania Lumber Museum (see selection) the second and **Crook Farm** the third. The Bradford Landmark Society has assembled various elements of rural life on the grounds of Crook Farm. The 1800s farmhouse is furnished simply and there are numerous outbuildings including a blacksmith's shop, carpenter's shed, barn and an 1853 one-room schoolhouse that has been moved to this bucolic setting. The best time to visit is for the annual **Crook Farm Fair**, the weekend before Labor Day weekend, when there are more than 75 artist and craft exhibitors, old time craft demonstrations, a children's carnival, entertainment, tours and down-home cooking. At other times the farm opens Tuesday through Friday afternoons (1:00 P.M. to 4:00 P.M.) from May through September.

Directions: From I-80 take Exit 16, Route 219 north, to Custer City and the museum will be on the right, three miles south of Bradford. For Crook Farm continue on Route 219 to Bradford and take the Foster Brook exit, then turn right, then right at the light.

Pennsylvania Lumber Museum and Surrounding State Parks

TIM . . . BER!

The magnificent forest of the northcentral highlands of Pennsylvania brought settlers in the 19th century and travelers in the 20th century. Over a hundred years ago lumber was wealth, and an essential ingredient in the growth of the nation. Two of the largest sawmills in the world were located close to the site of the **Pennsylvania Lumber Museum**.

On part of the museum's 160 timbered acres you'll see a reconstructed logging camp. The woodworkers, nicknamed woodhicks, were housed in rustic bunkhouses near the work site. The foreman attempted to get maximum effort from the between 20-to-60 man crew, while maintaining morale and discipline. It was a hard existence. The men worked from first light to last light for a daily wage of $1.50 to $3.00. There were no refreshing showers at the end of the day to wash away the grime since the camps had no bathing facilities. Before 1910 the men worked 11 hour shifts, six days a week, without regard for weather conditions. The next decade they worked ten hour shifts and, after 1920, eight hour shifts, five days a week.

Just as it helps to start your visit to this part of Penn's Woods at the Lumber Museum, it's best to begin at the Visitor Center. Amid the hundreds of artifacts, you can see actual trunks of the various trees harvested by the loggers: black birch, northern red oak, sugar maple, red maple among others. There is a model of an up-down sawmill and one of a tanning operation, while a diorama depicts rafting the lumber down river. If time permits, before exploring the grounds see the film on the logging industry.

There is a lot more to see on the grounds; in the engine house there is a 70-ton Shay built in 1912 for a West Virginian railroad. Ephram Shay designed this gear-driven, steam-powered logging locomotive in 1880. He owned a Michigan sawmill and needed a locomotive that could run on steep-graded, crudely laid light rail track. There were 3,000 Shays produced from 1878 to 1945.

Nearby is a loader shed which has a Barnhart log loader with a rotating cab, stationary boom, cable and pulley. Logs were raised by the cable, then swung by the boom to the log car. This method was far more efficient than hand-loading the railroad cars by 12-man crews with cant hooks and peavies (points used when handling logs in the river and rolling them on a landing). The log cars on display at the museum have the large wheels necessary when the Barnhart loader was used.

There is also an operational steam-powered circular sawmill on the museum grounds. Mills like this could be found across north-central Pennsylvania during the later part of the 19th century. The mills typically sawed 12 to 15 thousand board feet each day. Beside the mill is a one-acre sawmill pond.

Manpower was assisted by horsepower, with a 60-man logging crew, there would be between 25 and 35 horses, so the museum has a stable. The tools used by the workers had to be repaired on-sight at the filer's shack and blacksmith-carpenter's shop. At the former, the men sharpened their axes at a grinding wheel at night or on Sunday. The camp's sawfiler worked on the crosscut saws and sharpened about 12 saws a day. His daily wage was $2.00.

In addition to the weathered wooden bunkhouse, the logging camp has a kitchen and mess hall. The mess tent was always the first to be put up at a new logging camp. The cook earned one of the highest wages, about $3.50 a day in 1909. Loggers did not pay for their lodging or their meals, which were substantial. Breakfast included hot biscuits, steak, eggs, fried potatoes, oatmeal, cake, donuts, prunes or other fruit and coffee. There was also a laundry shed, but clothes as well as bodies were infrequently washed.

A **1936 Civilian Conservation Corps Cabin** has also been moved to the museum grounds. It is one of eight cabins built by the corps as part of their work in the Susquehannock Forest District. During the Depression the CCC planted more than 200 million trees in forests throughout the country, constructed and improved thousands of miles of forest roads and trails, established hiking trails and undertook a variety of other civic improvements. Within the visitor center there is an exhibit on the C C C which includes uniforms and a camp bed.

The Pennsylvania Lumber Museum is open April through November, Monday through Saturday 9:00 A.M. to 4:30 P.M. On Sunday it opens at 10:00 A.M.. Admission is charged. There is a nature trail, picnic area and seasonal gift shop.

For the past 20 years over the 4th of July weekend the museum hosts the **Bark Peelers' Convention**. Demonstrations during this two-day event include log skidding, hewing, shingle-making, blacksmithing, broom making, woodhick skills and lathe turning. The sawmill also operates. There is spirited competition involving tobacco spitting, birling, frog jumping, fiddling and staying atop a greased pole. There's music, food and crafts. Call (814) 435-2652 for details. Throughout the year the museum holds classes and workshops.

Within a half hour drive of the museum are several state parks and the orange-blazed **Susquehannock Hiking Trail** that winds through 85 miles of the Appalachian Mountain wilderness linking old railroad grades, logging trails, roads and fire trails.

Across the highway from the museum is **Ski Denton** with 20 slopes and trails, four lifts, night skiing, a ski school and cabins. Two secluded beginners trails and the steepest ski slope (66 degrees) in the east make this ideal for all levels of skiers. Call (814) 435-2115 for information. A number of the state parks in the county offer cross country skiing.

One of the seven parks is **Ole Bull State Park**, named after Old Bornemann Bull, a famous Norwegian violinist who was so impressed with Potter County during his 1850s tour that he attempted to bring a colony of his countrymen to the area in 1852. Just behind the present park office he tried to build a wooden "castle" but hardship and misadventures caused the group to move west into Michigan and Wisconsin. Before emigrating to this country, Bull had established the National Theater in Bergen, his hometown. His writer and stage manager was Henrik Ibsen, who it is believe modeled Peer Gynt after Ole Bull.

Ole Bull State Park reflects both focus points of the Pennsylvania Lumber Museum. The lumber industry prospered in this area, called the Black Forest because of its dense tree cover, with two railroads hauling logs to nearby sawmills. The state purchased the parkland in the 1920s when the lumbering interests moved elsewhere. In the 1930s the CCC enlarged the park and built several stone park buildings.

During the summer months a park environmental interpreter leads guided walks and conduct programs. The **Daugherty Loop Trail**, which takes between $1^1/_2$ and 2 hours to hike, combines old logging trails and railroad grades through dense forests and past steep rock-strewn ridges. The park has an abundance of wildlife and many species of plants, in a variety of habitats: streams, wetlands, pine plantation and hardwood forests.

Recreational options at the park include picnicking, camping and swimming along Kettle Creek. There is a 150-foot guarded sandy beach open Thursday through Monday from Memorial Day to Labor Day from 11:00 A.M. to 7:00 P.M. The creek also appeals to anglers who like to catch the brook, brown and rainbow trout found here and in Ole Bull Run. Areas outside the park are available for hunting and trapping.

Twenty miles down Route 144 off State Route 4001 within the Sproul State Forest (and along the same stream that flows through Ole Bull) is the 1,626 acre **Kettle Creek State Park**. Boating and fishing is popular on the 167-acre Kettle Creek Reservoir. There are numerous hiking trails and a 15-mile equestrian trail. Camping, picnicking, hunting, swimming, sledding, tobogganing, ice fishing, ice skating, snowmobiling and cross-country skiing are all available at different times of the year.

There are two state parks closer to Coudersport—Lyman Run and Cherry Springs. The former is just 15 miles east of Coudersport and seven miles west of Galeton. Water activities are the main thrust of this 595-acre park as it has a 40-acre lake, with a 300-foot sandy beach. **Cherry Springs** is named for the park's large stands of native black cherry trees. From the park's fire tower you can get a panoramic view of this forested mountain area. Each year in early August the park hosts a Woodsmen's Show with horse-pull competitions and tractor pulls. For information call (814) 435-2907. Of note: Elliot Ness, the FBI Untouchable, started a paper watermarking business in Coudersport when he retired.

Directions: From I-80 traveling west, take I-180 to Williamsport then north on Route 15 to Mansfield and west on Route 6 past Galeton to the Pennsylvania Lumber Museum. Travel east on I-80 exit on Route 219 and take that north to Route 6 and head east eleven miles past Coudersport. For Ole Bull State Park continue on Route 6 to Galeton and take Route 144 south for 18 miles to the park. From Coudersport take Route 44 south then make a right on Route 144. For Lyman Run State Park take Rock Run Road off Route 6. For Cherry Springs State Park take Route 44 south off Route 6 at Sweden Valley.

Punxsutawney

Weather Capital of the World

Bill Murray's movie hit *Groundhog Day* capitalized on, and enhanced, the popularity of Pennsylvania's world-renowned weather prognosticator but it didn't explain how such a phenomenon began.

Seasonal forecasting goes back to the early days of Christianity. In Europe on Candlemas Day the clergy blessed and distributed candles to their flock. Legend proclaimed:

> *If Candlemas be fair and bright*
> *Come, Winter, have another flight;*
> *If Candlemas brings clouds and rain,*
> *Go, Winter, and come not again.*

Roman legions encountered this superstition in Scotland and carried it to the German territories who adapted it into a belief that if the hedgehog cast a shadow on Candlemas Day there would be six more weeks of bad weather, or a second winter.

The Germans who settled Pennsylvania found a profusion of groundhogs, resembling European hedgehogs, and adapted the legend to this new weather predictor. The first **Groundhog Day in Punxsutawney** is believed to have been on February 2, 1886 and it wasn't long before 19th-century farmers were reciting, "Groundhog Day—Half your hay."

It is apparent that Punxsutawney has taken the groundhog to its heart, though that's not to say that the local hunters don't occasionally fricassee a few. The legendary weather forecaster **Punxsutawney Phil** has a tidy and highly visible home in the heart of town. He lives in a glass-enclosed natural habitat in the library of the town's Mahoning East Civic Center next to Barclay Park. You can peer in the window of this Groundhog Zoo, or step inside the children's section of the library for another glimpse of Phil. Members of the Groundhog Club's Inner Circle are often available to bring Phil out to greet visitors. The park also has two delightful groundhog statues. Punxsutawney Phil gets almost as much mail as Santa Claus, and folks across the country have become members of the **Groundhog Club** simply by paying a nominal annual fee. The address is: 124 West Mahoning Street, Punxsutawney, PA 15767. For more information call (800) 752-PHIL or (814) 938-7700.

The annual February 2nd trek to **Gobbler's Knob** began shortly after the Groundhog Club was formed in 1899. This imaginative group began the rituals that are followed to this day. Thousands flock to this frigid hill at sunrise to see the furry forecaster. It seems those responsible for the hoopla have gauged the mood of their audience and it is all done with great fun and good spirits. While there are certainly groundhog souvenirs to be had, the event has not become overly commercial and retains its small-town appeal. Gobbler's Knob is just outside town off Woodland Avenue. Celebrations are not limited to winter. In June there's a **Groundhog Festival**, during which Phil partakes of a magic elixir that insures his longevity.

Punxsutawney's history and groundhog memories and myths are detailed in the **Bennis House Museum**. In 1903, noted architect Stanford White combined Victorian style with Renaissance architecture to build this charming house at 401 West Mahoning Street. Seven display rooms are filled with artifacts reflecting the history of the area back to its earliest inhabitants. The museum has a genealogy room open on Thursdays or by appointment. Call (814) 938-2555. The museum is noted for its photography collection which includes 33,000 negatives taken from the 1890s to the 1930s. There is also an interesting mining and railroad exhibit. While at the museum pick up a walking tour handout on the eleven historic and architectural homes of interest along Mahoning Street. The museum is open Wednesdays and Sundays from May to November.

Both east and west of Punxsutawney there are interesting diversions. Just 14 miles southeast is **Smicksburg**. This tiny 1827 village is the home to the largest Amish settlement in western Pennsylvania, approximately 200 families. Drive carefully on these winding roads because you frequently come over a hill to discover a slow moving buggy directly ahead. Local wares are sold in the town's specialty shops. It's a good place to buy quilts, leather goods, blacksmith wares and homemade chocolate, cheese and even spices like homemade vanilla. The town is also home to **Windgate Vineyards**, an award-winning winery with tours and tastings.

Roughly 25 miles west of Punxsutawney outside Grampian you'll discover **Bilger's Rocks**, a fascinating 300-million-year-old sandstone formation with caves, massive cliffs, passageways and other unusual features. Trails off the parking lot let you stroll into this unique geological terrain, called rock city, that covers 20 acres. One of the formations is a 500-ton boulder balanced perfectly on a smaller stone.

For additional information on the Punxsutawney area contact the Magic Forest Travel Bureau, RR 5, Box 47, Brookville, PA 1525. You can also call (800) 348-9393 or (814) 849-5197.

Directions: From I-80 take Exit 17, Route 119 south to Punxsutawney. Or you can take Exit 13 off I-80, then take Route 36 south for approximately 20 miles. For Smicksburg continue south on Route 119 and turn right on Route 210, then turn right on Route 954. For Bilger's Rocks in Grampian take Route 36 south out of Punxsutawney, then Route 219 northeast to Grampian. The Rocks are four miles north of town.

Sawmill Center for the Arts and Cook Forest Art Center Museum

Where Vision Becomes Reality

At the sylvan center of Cook Forest State Park, the multi-faceted **Sawmill Center for the Arts** teaches, exhibits, sells and entertains. This creative environment was the dream of Verna Leith who in 1974 founded this institution for the instruction of traditional crafts.

More than 125 classes are offered, some just one day others two or three days, some a week long. Subjects include wood-carving, basketry, photography, weaving, quilting, painting, spinning, chair caning, dulcimer-making and playing, rug-hooking, leaf printing and even clown workshops. The Sawmill Center has an intensive summer dance camp, a children's drama workshop and **Nuthole**, an eight week craft program for youngsters 6 to 14. The center is associated with Elderhostel, a program for senior students that ranges across the United States and 40 countries around the world.

Western Pennsylvania is known as the "**Black Cherry Capitol of the World**." An outstanding collection of black cherry wood carvings are displayed at the Sawmill Craft Market Site 2, also known as the museum. Individual pieces are for sale, including turned black cherry wood Christmas ornaments. The museum area has a craft studio, art gallery, children's discovery area and a Christmas corner. Artfully created work by 250 artisans is sold at the Craft Market, adjacent to the Sawmill Theater. These two facilities offer the most extensive array of handcrafted work in this part of the state.

In 1981 a theater was added to this artistic complex, though the current hexagon-shaped, open-sided building was built three years later. Theater groups from Northwestern Pennsylvania and Clarion University present Broadway musicals and a broad range of drama, both classics and current favorites. Performances are customarily given Thursday through Saturday at 8:00 P.M.

To obtain current class listings and a theater schedule call (814) 744-9670 year-round, or 927-6655 from May through September. Sawmill also hosts a series of annual events including an **Herb Festival** in early June, a **Summerfest** in mid-August with a special Quilts in the Forest segment and **September's Great Dulcimer Roundup**. The Cook Forest Art Center Museum is open daily year-round from 10:00 A.M. to 5:00 P.M.

Directions: From I-80 take Exit 13, Brookville, and go north on Route 36 for roughly 20 miles. The Sawmill Center for the Arts will be on your right.

Straub Brewery

Brewing Legends

Masterbrewer Tom Straub explains the presence of seven breweries in the small St. Marys community in one word—Germans. He said, "The story goes 'did they build the brewery and then the church or the church and then the brewery.'" German Catholic immigrants settled the town in the 1840s, and locals swear that it was the brewery that was built first.

Nineteen-year-old Peter Straub, came to Pennsylvania in 1869 from Felldorf, Wurttemberg, Germany, settling first in what is now Pittsburgh's North Side, then moving to St. Marys in 1872. A brewer's apprentice and cooper, he worked at several breweries before purchasing his father-in-law's brewery and operating it as **Benzinger Spring Brewery**. At Peter's death in 1912 the operation continued as **Peter Straub Sons Brewery**. Like the other establishments in town it ran during Prohibition producing "near beer." Some say other brews were hidden in an underground "federal room." Customers supplied their own yeast to the near beer to make home-brew.

Straub Brewery is owned by Peter Straub's linear descendants. While it is one of the smallest commercial breweries in the country, it is among the top 30 breweries. Workers admit that Anheuser-Busch, Miller and Coors spill more beer than Straub produces—the big three account for 81 percent of the beer marketed. Straub brews daily during the summer and three or four times a week in the winter, producing roughly 27,000 barrels annually.

Visitors (children under 12 are not permitted on the tours) are welcome to tour the brewery from 9:00 A.M. to NOON. If you're driving from a good distance, call ahead because it is possible they won't be brewing or bottling. Because it is a small operation, with only 20 full-time employees, they only run one shift. The brewery operation starts at 4:00 A.M., sometimes earlier. In the brewery entrance hall you'll see some of the tools Peter Straub used as he traveled around the state repairing wooden barrels.

Straub beer is an all natural, all-grain beer with no salt, sugar, syrup or preservatives added. It's the beer for health conscious consumers, but since there are no preservatives it does have a shorter shelf life. Recommended consumption is within three months. The packaging date is noted on each bottle.

Straub has been brewing beer for over 120 years by much the same process and you can watch each step if you time your visit right.

To test the process, stop at the **Eternal Tap**, weekdays 8:30 A.M. to 5:00 and Saturday until 4:00 P.M. The tap is open to anyone over 21. You can stop in, even if you don't tour the brewery, and help yourself to a draft or two. The only thing that's asked of you is that you wash your glass. There are a number of breweries with tasting rooms, but this is the only one with an open-door policy hospitality room. Of course, it's not fancy, it's just a tap jutting out of the brick wall just off the brewery floor. In fact, you may be joined by brewery workers who often stop for a brew during their breaks. There are no tables and no pretzels but the tap is endless, and eternal, it's as old as the brewery. You can also purchase Straub beer and a variety of logo-imprinted items from the Brewery's gift shop.

Directions: From I-80 take the Dubois exit and go north on Route 255 to St. Marys. The brewery is on Sorg Street, just a half mile from downtown St. Marys, directly off Brussells Street (Route 120 east toward Emporium).

Warren County Historical Society

Christmas, Clocks and Historic Blocks

Walk along the tree-lined streets of Warren, and you'll stroll into the past. The **Warren County Historical Society** has prepared a self-guided walking tour that gives you an opportunity to appreciate the fine old homes in Warren's National Register Historic District. The town was laid out in 1795, and named in honor of General Joseph Warren, killed at the Battle of Bunker Hill.

Connected to Pittsburgh via steamboats on the Allegheny River, the town thrived in the lumber era and by 1883 was connected to diverse markets via the railroad. This proved economically significant when oil was discovered just to the east in Titusville. In the early 1900s there were 13 oil refineries within a six-mile radius of Warren.

One of the town's old homes serves as the headquarters for the historical society and it can be toured Monday through Friday from 9:00 A.M. to 5:00 P.M. An old-fashioned general store from the town of Tidioute, once owned by Julius Bourquin, is inside. There are also period rooms and a geneology reference library.

One of the most fascinating buildings in town is The Historic Library Theatre, built in 1883 by local industrialist Thomas Struthers. First used a library hall (the original book-filled shelves can still be seen), it was tranformed in 1919 into a vaudeville theater, then a movie house. It now is an active summer playhouse. For a schedule of performances call (814) 723-7231. The theater is at 304 Third Avenue.

Just around the corner at 110 Liberty Street is a branch of the **America's First Christmas Store**, whose main store is located in the heart of Smethport. A full range of collectibles, ornaments, music boxes, outdoor holiday displays and gift items are available at both stores.

If you want an even more extensive array of music boxes and clocks head for the **Van Dorn's Clock Shop** on Main Street in nearby Sugar Grove, open 9:00 A.M. to 5:00 P.M. Tuesday through Saturday. John and Mary Lou Van Dorn began collecting clocks on their honeymoon and opened a shop in their home nine years ago. They have an amazing collection, most of which are for sale. A few special items are merely on exhibit, like the painting of a clock tower alongside a river. The clock in the picture keeps time and plays music. They have a stock of approximately 250 new and antique clocks, the largest selection in this half of the state. One small room is devoted almost entirely to their almost 400 music boxes and pendelum clocks. It's hard not to be tempted by this collection. They also do clock repair; call (814) 489-3929. Interested visitors can request a tour of their intriquingly decorated Victorian home.

Directions: From I-79 take Route 6 east to Warren, from I-80 take Route 8 north to just past Franklin, then pick up Route 62 north to Warren.

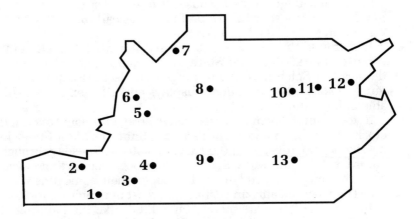

LAUREL HIGHLANDS REGION

1. **Point Marion**
   Friendship Hill National
   Historic Site

2. **Brownsville**
   Nemacolin Castle

3. **Farmington**
   Laurel Caverns
   Fort Necessity National Bat-
   tlefield and The Mount
   Washington Tavern

4. **Ohiopyle**
   Fallingwater
   Ohiopyle State Park and
   White-water Rafting

5. **Greensburg**
   Hanna's Town

6. **Harrison City**
   Bushy Run Battlefield

7. **Ligonier/Laughlintown**
   Idlewild Park
   Fort Ligonier
   Compass Inn Museum

8. **Johnstown**
   Johnstown Flood Museum
   Johnstown Flood National
   Memorial and Historic
   St. Michael
   Johnstown Inclined Plane
   and James Wolfe Sculp-
   ture Trail

9. **Somerset**
   Somerset Historical Center
   and Georgian Place

10. **Cresson**
    Allegheny Portage Railroad
    National Historic Site

11. **Altoona**
    Altoona Railroaders Memor-
    ial Museum and Horseshoe
    Curve National Historic
    Landmark
    Baker Mansion
    Benzel's Pretzel Factory and
    Family Parks
    Fort Roberdeau National
    Historic Landmark

12. **Huntington**
    East Broad Top Railroad,
    Rockhill Trolley Museum
    and Lake Raystown
    Lincoln Caverns
    Swigart Museum

13. **Bedford**
    Old Bedford Village and Fort
    Bedford Museum
    Shawnee State Park and
    Gravity Hill

Laurel
Highlands

Fallingwater, whitewater and the story of flooding water are all found nestled in the foothills of the Allegheny Mountains. The home Frank Lloyd Wright designed for Pittsburgh industrialist Edgar J. Kaufmann cantilevers over a rushing mountain waterfall. It's one of the architectural masterpieces of the 20th century. In nearby Ohiopyle State Park the Youghiogheny River has some of the best whitewater rafting in the east. For quiet water the region offers the 118-mile-long Raystown Lake, one of the longest lakes in the state.

Many of Kaufman's follow industrialists vacationed in the mountains. Andrew Carnegie, Henry Clay Frick and Andrew Mellon belonged to the South Fork Fishing and Hunting Club located on a reservoir above Johnstown. When heavy rains crumbled the reservoir dam one of America's greatest natural disasters ensued—the Johnstown Flood.

Railroading is another major story of this region. One of the country's first rail experiments was the Allegheny Portage Railroad, now an intriquing National Historic Site. Presenting an overview of the railroad story is the updated Altoona Railroaders Memorial Museum. Photographers flock to the Horseshoe Curve National Historic Landmark to capture trains negotiating the hairpin turn. If you want to see it first hand take a National Park Service excursion on Amtrak's Pennsylvanian.

The region's military history goes back to one of the colonial era's first struggles, the French and Indian War. That story is told at Fort Necessity, Fort Roberdeau, Fort Ligonier and Fort Bedford Museum. To get a sense of how people lived in this area during that tumultuous time visit Old Bedford Village and the Somerset Historical Center.

Allegheny Portage Railroad

Transportation Marvel

City and state rivalry is nothing new. Shortly after the Revolutionary War, Philadelphia, New York and Baltimore were vying with each other. The merchants of each city clamored for links with the raw materials and markets of the west. By the 1820s, New York had the Erie Canal and Maryland was pushing for the Chesapeake & Ohio Canal. If Pennsylvania did not create a link to the west, her port city would not be able to remain competitive. On July 4, 1826, ground was broken for the Main Line Canal at Harrisburg. It would be two more years before President John Quincy Adams turned over the ground for the beginning of the C&O Canal (on the same day that Declaration of Independence signer Charles Carroll heralded the beginning of the Baltimore & Ohio Railroad).

The Pennsylvania Main Line ran from Philadelphia to Pittsburgh with a combination of 82 miles of railroad track and 276 miles of canals. One 36-mile stretch over the Allegheny Mountains confounded engineers, until they devised a unique portage railroad to negotiate the extremely steep grade between Hollidaysburg and Johnstown.

Most visitors at the National Park Service's **Allegheny Portage Railroad** are not clear about how a portage railroad functions. Canal boat passengers and goods were moved to railroad cars and towed by a stationary steam engine up a series of five inclined planes, then lowered down another series of five steps on the other side. Eventually sectional packet boats enabled the entire boat to be loaded onto the railroad for portage.

To get a clearer picture about how this works, watch the 20-minute film at the park's Visitor Center. Exhibits and models also provide details on the construction and operation of this short-lived railroad. Visitors to the park have a real sense of learning about something new—albeit vanished. Quotes on the center's walls recall portage journeys taken more than a hundred years earlier. Charles Dickens wrote in 1842, ". . . It was very pretty traveling thus at a rapid pace along the heights of the mountain in a keen wind, to look down into a valley full of light and softness and catching glimpses through the treetops . . . and we riding onward high above them like a whirlwind." A gentleman named Woodruff wrote, "This was one of the awful, fearful, dangerous, exciting, affecting, grand, sublime and interesting day's journeys I ever took in my life." This trepidation seems excessive for a trip that covered only four miles per hour as it climbed the inclines.

The portage railroad was obsolete within a few years and the railroad lines were taken up when it was abandoned in 1857;

no train survives to demonstrate the antiquated method. But a one-eighth mile walk along a raised boardwalk brings you to an overlook where you can see Incline 6, and a section of reconstructed track provides a glimpse of what it once looked like.

Stones, called sleepers, were quarried at spots you can see along the boardwalk and were used for the railroad ties. There are still hundreds of sleepers where the tracks once ran. Also visible from the overlook is the **Skew Arch Bridge**, about a third of a mile down the track. This uniquely constructed bridge is turned, or twisted. It was built in this manner to allow a wagon road to cross the railroad without adjusting its straight course up the mountain. If you walk down the hill you can walk across the bridge.

Next, you should investigate **Engine House 6**, built over the foundations of the original. Interactive exhibits provide answers to questions about the technical side of the railroad's operation. A large engine and pulley system replicates the original, although when it was operational there were two engines. Originally hemp rope was used to pull the cars, the rope only lasted for a season and a half. At the suggestion of John Augustus Roebling, who later designed the Brooklyn Bridge, wire was substituted for rope. Exhibits show how the water brake and other safety devices worked, while newspaper accounts reveal details of the accidents that occurred along this line.

The trains ran up and through the building then along level track to the next incline. You can follow the path of the tracks on the other side for roughly $3/4$ mile along the Summit Level toward Incline 5; this will give you the chance to see numerous stone ties.

Before you begin this walk, take the time to stop in the **Lemon House**, where Sam Lemon and his family lived and operated a tavern during the 1830s and 40s. The barroom and parlor have period pieces from the latter decade, while the dining room uses reproductions so that it can be used for special programs. Two trails lead from the Lemon House area. One takes you to the Summit Picnic area while the other is a mile-and-a-half nature trail. Many of the trails and train beds in the 1500-acre park are used for ski trails.

On summer Saturday nights programs are held in the park amphitheater. These range from historical and nature talks to musical performances. During the summer months the rangers lead hikes, demonstrate the art of stonecutting and give daily talks about life along the portage railroad.

The Allegheny Portage Railroad National Historic Site is open at no charge daily 9:00 A.M. to 6:00 P.M. Memorial Day to Labor Day, closing at 5:00 P.M. the remainder of the year. It is closed on Christmas Day.

Directions: From I-76, the Pennsylvania Turnpike take Exit 6, Route 22 west toward Altoona. Ten miles east of Ebensburg take the Gallitzin exit; the park entrance is directly off Route 22. From I-80 take Exit 23, Route 220 south to Altoona, then head west on Route 22 to the Gallitzin exit.

Altoona Railroaders Memorial Museum and Horseshoe Curve National Historic Landmark

Tracks through Time

Altoona was once the greatest railroad town in the world with the largest railroad shops. The work force numbered 17,000 and their labors created the world's largest railroad and corporate entity. Altoona is the spot to tell the story of this accomplishment and that objective is achieved at the **Altoona Railroaders Memorial Museum**.

The museum began in the 1970s when a group of volunteers began collecting stories and railroad artifacts from local residents. Most railroad museums focus on the evolution of the technology of railroading and big pieces of rolling stock, but the goal of the people-oriented Altoona museum has always been to tell the historical, cultural and social story of the men and women who built and ran the railroad—not the owners but the workers. The railroad influenced every aspect of its workers' lives and that influence is traced in this memorial museum.

The railroad schedule even determined when the women did the washing. Fewer trains ran on Mondays, since they were in the shop undergoing repairs, so Mondays were the only day the coal dust wouldn't ruin the wash. Discover what is was like for families when the men traveled the rails or when the family breadwinner was furloughed. At the museum you'll learn what it was really like living in a railroad town, from its preindustrial early days through the transition from steam to diesel and ultimately to other forms of transportation that again changed the focus of the community.

The museum's new quarters is the Master Mechanics Building, just part of this incredible complex that was the heart and soul of the **Pennsylvania Railroad**. Rolling stock still stands in the yard in front of this building and yard lights shine day and night. Signs indicate where various shops stood on this 217-acre complex. A viewing platform lets you watch trains pass on what was once the Pennsylvania Railroad's main line and one of the busiest sections of railroad in America.

The foyer of the Master Mechanics Building has stage-set style vignettes that bring Altoona's heyday to life. Appropriately, the front of a locomotive seems to be chugging into the lobby itself. Scenes depict the workers who rebuilt 150 locomotive a month and built roughly 6,783 steam and electric locomotives during the complex's 100 years of operation.

Entering the museum you'll get an identification card that will encourage active participation and decision making as you explore. Exhibits do not have to be covered sequentially; each, while part of the larger story, tells an entire story unto itself.

To partake of daily life step up on the cutaway porch of a middle-class railroad worker, whose life ran on a schedule dictated by the shop whistle. You can hear dialogue between family members and radio programs of the era. The house's decor changes every few months to reflect the ethnic contributions of the German, Italian, African American and other groups that settled in Altoona. The town was considered a one-class city. Altoona really didn't experience a surge of immigrants as it developed into Railroad City; even in its peak years it had 90 percent native-born inhabitants.

Pennsylvania Railroad set the standards for the world, their testing laboratory maintained the highest efficiency and safety records. The Altoona lab was the most advanced, productive test lab in the world and it carefully checked every aspect of the railroad from the heavy equipment to squeezing oranges to get the most juice for the dining cars. In one year the chemical lab ran an impressive 66,000 tests and the physical lab more than doubled that with 194,000 tests.

In the museum's testing lab you'll see stacks of oranges as well as a light bulb testing room. You can insert your hand into a glove box to check insulation and experiment on computer simulators. You'll experience the sensations of rail travel amid the luxury of an elegant dining car. The private rail car of steel magnate Charles Schwab is now in the process of being restored after a devastating fire.

The museum's state-of-the-art exhibits include touch-screen videos, recorded oral histories and task simulators. The Altoona Railroaders Memorial Museum is open daily May through October 10:00 A.M. to 6:00 P.M. From November through April hours are 10:00 A.M. to 5:00 P.M. It is closed Mondays. Admission is charged. Before exploring the museum be sure to see the introductory theater presentation on the birth, complexity and significance of the Pennsylvania Railroad and the people who made it run.

One story told at the museum is about the building of the **Horseshoe Curve**. There is an award-winning documentary film, photographs and exhibits. After exploring the museum take a drive to see this National Historic Landmark. The Horseshoe Curve solved the problem of the steep Allegheny Mountains (an

Horseshoe Curve is a railroad engineering marvel that circumvents the steep Allegheny Mountains. You can watch trains traveling around the "Amphitheater of the Alleghenies" or enjoy the trip yourself.

earlier solution had been the Allegheny Portage Railroad, see selection). The curve, designed by Pennsylvania Railroad Chief Engineer J. Edgar Thomson, connects one side of the valley to the other, circumventing the steepest point in the Alleghenies.

This engineering marvel was built by 450 Irish workers using hand picks, drills, black powder, shovels, horses and mules. They filled in the ravine between the ridge and carved the railroad bed out of the mountainside creating a new grade around the contour of the mountain.

Looking at the model in the Horseshoe Curve Visitor Center of the area before the curve was built, one can only marvel at Thomson's vision. In the more than 140 years since the Horseshoe Curve opened in 1854, it has never been altered and it's still one of the most congested railroad areas in the country. Roughly 50 trains traverse the curve daily, and the Visitor Center has a timetable so that you can monitor their appearance around the **"Amphitheater of the Alleghenies."** During the latter part of the week there is usually a train every 15 minutes; early in the week many of the trains are in the yards being loaded or unloaded.

You take a single-track funicular up the steep hill to track elevation to watch the trains pass. Alternatively, you can reach the hilltop by climbing 194 steps. Either way it's a thrill to watch the trains a mere 30-to-40 feet away. You'll definitely want your camera. One of the first diesel locomotives is exhibited beside the active track.

There is a Visitor Center and gift shop at Horseshoe Curve National Historic Landmark. The only charge is for the funicular. Be sure to watch the short film, "Birth of the Curve." Hours are daily May through October 9:30 A.M. to 7:00 P.M. November through April 10:00 A.M. to 4:30 P.M. Closed on Mondays.

Railroad buffs will want to continue on to nearby Allegheny Portage Railroad National Historic Site just 15 minutes away (see selection). After all this background you'll really appreciate the chance to climb aboard **AMTRAK's Pennsylvanian** for a train ride from Altoona to Johnstown. The National Park Service narrates this excursion from early June through mid-October. For schedules and rates call (814) 946-1100 in Altoona and (814) 535-3313 in Johnstown.

Directions: From I-76, the Pennsylvania Turnpike, take Exit 11, Route 220 north to Altoona. From Route 220 take the 17th Street exit into downtown Altoona, turning right onto Ninth Avenue at Station Mall. The museum is located adjacent to Station Mall at Ninth Avenue and 13th Street. To reach Horseshoe Curve National Historic Landmark follow the Heritage Route Trail signs. Take Ninth Avenue to 17th Street and turn left, then make a right on Sixth Avenue and take that to Burgoon Road, then turn right. Turn left on Beale Avenue and right on 40th Street. Horseshoe Curve is on State Route 4008. Heritage Route will continue to the Allegheny Portage Railroad National Historic Site.

Baker Mansion

Baker's Rise to Prominence

Elias Baker, owner of Alleghany [sic] Furnace, was a leading ironmaster in Blair County, an area that in 1855 had 14 iron furnaces, 12 forges, 7 foundries and one rolling mill. This was one of the nation's leading iron producers, a significant cog in America's industrial growth.

The ironmaster was truly master of his village, supplying his furnace workers and foundrymen with housing, a place to purchase provisions and medical care. **Baker's Alleghany Furnace** was the second built in the county. It was put into blast in 1811 and acquired by Baker (and his cousin Roland Diller) in 1836. Baker became sole owner eight years later.

Baker's furnace turned out 200 tons of pig iron each month, with prices ranging from $23 to $33 per ton. Taking advantage

337

of the Pennsylvania Canal and the Allegheny Portage Railroad (see selection), Baker shipped his iron west.

In 1844 when Baker acquired sole ownership of the furnace, he also contracted Baltimore architect Robert Carey Long, Jr. to build a grand house. Four years later the house was finished at a cost of $75,000—a princely sum in that era! Local settlers called the house **Baker's Folly**.

Baker's imposing mansion was designed in the then-popular Greek Revival style and built from local limestone, with lead used to seal the joints between the stone blocks. Alleghany Furnace supplied the iron used for the window sills, exterior moldings and the bases and capitals of the columns. The interior featured Italian marble fireplaces and black walnut woodwork. Built before the city of Altoona was founded, nothing in the region compared with this stately edifice.

Moving into the new house was Elias, his wife Hetty, their second son Sylvester and Anna, the daughter who was born after their move to Blair County. Their oldest son Woods moved to Philadelphia, and was killed in an 1852 steamboat boiler explosion on the Hudson River just two-and-half weeks after his daughter Louise's birth (she was the Baker's only grandchild).

Sylvester ran Alleghany Furnace for twenty years after his father's death in December 1864. By 1884, the furnace was unable to compete with the iron and steel plants in Pittsburgh and other large cities. Sylvester's later years were spent in real estate, selling portions of the family's 5,000 acres for residential development. With the 1914 death of Anna, the last family member, the mansion was closed. It was leased by the Blair County Historical Society in 1922 and purchased in 1941. The grounds containing the furnace stack and office were purchased by the Altoona Woman's Club.

The Baker Mansion's four floors and 28 rooms are filled with period furniture and historic collections. All the rooms on the first floor provide a glimpse of the Baker years. But it is in the formal double parlor that the lavish life style of Elias Baker is most dramatically apparent. You'll see the elaborate 33 piece suite of hand-carved dark oak furniture he imported from Belgium in 1854. The furniture sat in a warehouse in New York for several years because Baker couldn't afford the additional expense of shipping it to Blair County. The heavy red velvet upholstery and scagliola (imitation marble) pillars are indicative of the Victorian era. Across the hall, the single parlor is also decorated in the Victorian mode. Here, too, many of the pieces remain from the Baker years. This room also has a heating stove made at Alleghany Furnace. The dining room was designed to provide elegant and efficient service for the Bakers. Meals were sent up from the kitchen by a dumbwaiter and servants could be contacted through a system of speaking tubes. In 1862 the 13 loyal northern governors met around the wooden Logan House table, which stands in the center of the room, to pledge support for Lincoln and the Union cause. At the end of the reception hall, opposite the dining room is Elias Baker's office with his original desk and double-lock safe.

Upstairs only Elias and Hetty's master bedroom is fully furnished with the original bed, dresser, washstand and carpet. Unlike most rooms of the day, you'll see two built-in closets. The bathroom was also ahead of its time, although water had to be carried in by servants until plumbing was installed around 1900. Most of the second floor chambers are exhibit rooms. The **Lincoln Room** has displays about the pivotal northern governors' Logan House conference September 24, 1862. Regional history exhibits are also here. Military artifacts are in the war veterans room and the Synder Room has medical exhibits. The third floor has a furnished servant's bedchamber (which most of the rooms would have originally been), Sylvester's chemistry study, a nursery with antique toys and the Blair County Historical Society's library and archival and genealogical files. There is an additional nominal fee for using the research materials.

Visitors exit through the basement which has a fully restored and well-stocked kitchen, as well as the bake room, cold cellar and pantry area. Exhibit areas include local education, collections on rocks, minerals and the iron industry plus displays that trace the development of the Allegheny Portage Railroad and the Pennsylvania Railroad. An excellent series of photographs captures railroad lines, bridges and terminals. The pictures were taken for the 1893 Columbia Exposition in Chicago.

The Baker Mansion is open weekends in mid-April, May, September and October from 1:00 P.M. to 4:30 P.M. It is open daily from June through Labor Day, except for Mondays and holidays. Tours take an hour with the last tour beginning at 3:30 P.M. Admission is charged. For additional information call (814) 942-3916.

Directions: From I-76, the Pennsylvania Turnpike, take Exit 11, Route 220 north to Altoona. Exit at Plank Road, and make a left onto Plank Road. Proceed to Logan Boulevard and make a left, watch for the Baker Mansion sign in about a mile on the right. From I-80, Exit 23, at Milesburg, follow Route 220 south to Logan Boulevard in Altoona and watch for signs.

Benzel's Pretzel Factory and Family Parks

Tasty Tour

Here's a tour where you can pick up more than knowledge. Few visitors leave **Benzel's Pretzel Factory** empty-handed. Even if you aren't buying for your neighborhood, and many out-of-town-ers get requests from family and friends, stop at the outlet store and watch the short video on the pretzel making process and the Benzel factory. They give free samples and you can buy over-size bags of all varieties of pretzels for undersize prices.

Windows overlook the production area where Benzel's makes five million pretzels daily. Video cameras throughout the work space capture the process for visitors. Founder Adolph Benzel came to America in the late 1800s with his family recipe for pretzels. He worked for other bakers before settling in Altoona where on November 18, 1911, he opened his own pretzel busi-ness. It's always been a family business: the modern factory you see on your visit was opened by Adolph's grandsons in 1981.

It's a 40-minute process from raw dough to pretzel. Visitors are fascinated by the extruder which molds and cuts the dough into distinctive pretzel shape. The new method is quite a time saver over the first years when 20 employees hand-twisted the dough. Benzel's pretzels are baked more slowly than others re-sulting in a lighter pretzel.

Benzel's Pretzel Factory is open Monday through Thursday 9:00 A.M. to 5:00 P.M., Friday until 6:00 P.M., and Saturday until 1:00 P.M. For additional information call (814) 942-5062. To or-der by mail call (800) 344-GIFT.

The Altoona area has another factory that appeals to families. **James Industries Inc.** makes **Slinky Toys** and they too have an outlet store. They also produce Slinky construction toys: Tower-ifics, Form-a-tions and Ringa-majigs, plus a wide variety of items sure to interest children.

The slinky was invented by the husband of James Industry's President Betty M. James. Engineer Richard James was on a naval vessel trial run when a tortion spring fell to the floor and bounced back and forth. This provided the inspiration for the popular toy first sold in 1945. Because Slinky is a toy you need to play with in order to discover its appeal, it was not an im-mediate hit. The days of sitting on the shelves ended when Philadelphia's Gimbels allowed the toy to be demonstrated on the end of one of their counters. The entire stock of 400 Slinkys sold in 90 minutes, and the rest is toy history.

On your way into the James Industry Outlet shop you can see part of the production plant through a high mesh fence. Safety precautions prevent the company from taking visitors on plant tours. The shop is open weekdays 9:00 A.M. to 5:00 P.M. and in December Monday through Saturday 10:00 A.M. to 6:00 P.M.

The Altoona area also has two family parks, **Lakemont Park** on the outskirts of town and Bland's Park in nearby Tipton. Lakemont is the 15th oldest amusement park in the country and has the world's oldest roller coaster. You can ride all day on Lakemont

Park's 30 rides, including coasters, waterslides, bumper cars and paddle boats. There's also a go-kart slick track. There is an additional fee for the mini-golf, state-of-the-art go-karts and aquamania boats. The park is open daily from mid-June through late August and weekends after Memorial Day and in September. For more details, and a schedule of special events, call (814) 949-PARK.

North of Altoona in Tipton is **Bland's Park**. Here, too, you'll find rides galore, including some for the very young. There are coasters, carousels, bumper cars, live ponies and a miniature golf course. A free concert series is presented during the summer months. The park has two speedway tracks. The first is a 960-feet go-kart track with 20 vehicles, three of them two-seater family cars. The second 500-foot track is for licensed drivers. The park is open daily, except Mondays from early June through Labor Day and on weekends in May and September. For more details on the park call (814) 684-3538.

Directions: From I-76, the Pennsylvania Turnpike, take Exit 11, Route 220 to Altoona. Exit off Route 220 on 6th Avenue, Route 764. Benzel's Pretzel Factory is at 5200 Sixth Avenue. From I-80, Exit 23, at Milesburg, follow Route 220 south to Altoona. The James Industries factory is on Beaver Street in Hollidaysburg. Hollidaysburg is on Route 22 just southeast of Altoona. Turn off Business Route 22 onto Newry Street, go two blocks and turn right onto Beaver Street. Continue three blocks for the toy outlet. Lakemont Park is on Route 220 in Altoona south of the city. Bland's Park is north of Altoona on Route 220.

Bushy Run Battlefield

Pontiac's War Battleground

In October 1758, thirteen Indian nations and the governors of Pennsylvania and New Jersey signed the **Treaty of Easton**, agreeing that the Ohio Indians would sever their alliance with France and would withdraw to west of the Alleghenies, and that the lands in the west were to be Indian territory. But the British did not withdraw from this western region. Instead they sent troops to occupy former French forts and on the site of Fort Duquesne erected **Fort Pitt**, their largest and most elaborate fortress in North America.

The Native Americans, sought as allies during the French and Indian War, were obstacles to settlement once that conflict was resolved. The British stopped selling the Native Americans gun powder, lead and alcohol. Tribal members used their munitions not only in conflict but also in hunting, from which they maintained their livelihood, so to be deprived of them was a severe blow. The westward expansion of European settlers threatened the hunting grounds and spread diseases such as smallpox throughout the tribes.

These provocations prompted Pontiac, an Ottawa war chief, to unite the Great Lakes tribes and attack **Fort Detroit** on May 8, 1763. Thus began a Native American war for independence, driving some settlers back east and prompting others to seek sanctuary in frontier forts such as Fort Pitt. Initially the British command did not take this threat seriously, but within two months nine forts were captured, another was abandoned and Fort Detroit and Fort Pitt were under siege. In a not often-reported effort to undermine the Native American threat, Captain Simeon Ecuyer, head of the 125-man garrison at Fort Pitt, employed germ warfare against the Delaware and Shawnee laying siege to the fort. He gave the warriors infected blankets and handkerchiefs from the fort's hospital.

Fearing conditions on the western frontier, General Amherst, in command of the British forces in North America, sent Henry Bouquet with troops from three regiments to resupply Fort Pitt. Bouquet left Carlisle, Pennsylvania on July 18 and reached Fort Ligonier (see selection) on August 2. Trying to increase the speed of his march, as it had been over a month since any report had been heard from Fort Pitt, Bouquet abandoned the barrels and wagon train, repacked the flour into bags and loaded them on 340 pack animals. Without the heavier equipment, he was able to take a less-traveled route in hopes of avoiding a surprise attack. But on August 5, near **Bushy Run**, the column was attacked by as few as 95 warriors (although Simon Ecoyer at Fort Pitt estimated the attacking force at 400). The warriors had terminated their siege of Fort Pitt to attack the fort's reinforcements. During the attack Bouquet's men suffered 50 casualties and were forced to retreat. With nightfall, Bouquet used the flour bags to create a fortification. Feigning a retreat the next morning, the British were able to catch the Native Americans in a deadly cross-fire and force them to retreat. With more than a quarter of his troops killed or wounded, Bouquet continued his march to reprovision the fort, covering the remaining 26 miles in four days.

Bouquet's ability to withstand and turn the tide of the Native American attack and his successful provision of Fort Pitt were significant contributions to British victory in **Pontiac's War**. Bouquet continued westward into Ohio and the Native Americans ceased their struggle and returned their hostages. Two hundred and six Pennsylvania and Virginia settlers were turned over, later the Shawnees released another hundred captives. This victory opened the west for further colonial expansion.

When you visit this battlefield, use your imagination to populate the undulating hills with troops. Take a guided **Edge Hill Battle Trail** tour to retrace the course of the battle. You can also pick up a trail map for the **Flour Sak [sic] Battle Discovery Trail** and the **Iroquois Nature Trail**.

The Visitor Center has exhibits that provide additional details about Pontiac's War and an electric map gives the positions and progression of the battle that occurred here.

Bushy Run Battlefield is open Wednesday through Saturday from 9:00 A.M. to 5:00 P.M. On Sunday the Visitor Center opens at NOON. Closed Monday, Tuesday and holidays except Memorial Day, July 4th and Labor Day. A nominal admission is charged. Flags, maps, munitions and other artifacts fill the display cases.

Directions: From the east and south take I-76, the Pennsylvania Turnpike, to Exit 8. Follow signs for Toll 66 north and take that to the Greensburg-Harrison City exit; go left off the exit onto Old Route 66 north, to Route 993 west and turn onto Route 993 west for approximately three miles. From the west and north take I-76 to Exit 6, follow Route 22 east for approximately ten miles to Greensburg exit. Follow signs for Old Route 66 south and take that to Route 993 west.

Compass Inn Museum

Don't Lose Your Way

Since 1799 when Philip Freeman built a log house, travelers have stopped at this roadside rest. Foot travelers and drovers with small wagons were the first customers. In 1820, Robert Armor added the stone portion as a stagecoach stop along the turnpike.

Guides at the **Compass Inn Museum** share a wealth of stories about the people who passed through here, the tools and other articles they used and the things they accomplished. When you enter the inn you'll see the common room, where travelers drank and shared news. It was customary to put toast in mugs so that it would absorb the sediment from the crudely-made alcohol. When drinking a person's health you would drink down to the toast and from this practice we get the term "toast." Two other expressions become clear in the inn's reconstructed cookhouse. Upper crust is derived from the fact that the lower portion of the bread became sooty as it baked, so preferred guests were given the top part of the bread. Since the dirty portion was caked with soot, it was called cake. "Let them eat cake" did not refer to pastry but rather to the dirty part of the bread.

343

Although documentation does not confirm their visit, it is thought that Henry Clay and Zachary Taylor stopped at this inn. At overnight stops like this, space was rented rather than rooms or beds. The beds were shared by as many customers who could squeeze onto the mattresses. The rest of the travelers slept on the floor. The third floor was reserved for the family; Robert Armor, his wife and ten children.

The inn closed in 1862, with the advent of the canal and railroads. The property stayed in the family until 1966. A few original family furnishings still occupy the rooms such as the cradle, highchair and reading lamp in the ladies' parlor. Other pieces are of the period. For a time after the inn closed, the common room served as a general store.

On the museum grounds there is a barn filled with tools of various trades and vehicles like sleighs, a Conestoga wagon and stagecoach. A blacksmith often works in the museum's shop, where they have an intriguing **ox cradle**. Unlike horses, ox are unable to stand on three legs, so to shoe an ox they needed to be lifted off the ground—not an easy operation.

The third weekend in June, July and August, the museum sponsors living history days when skilled craftsmen demonstrate 18th and 19th century crafts. During these living history weekends, food is prepared in the beehive oven and visitors are invited to observe household tasks like dipping candles or making lye soap.

Compass Inn Museum is open May through October on Tuesday through Saturday from 11:00 A.M. to 4:00 P.M.; on Sundays it opens at NOON. Admission is charged. There are also weekend candlelight tours, November through mid-December. Call (412) 238-4983 for the schedule.

Directions: From I-76 take Donegal exit and head north on Route 711, toward Ligonier, to the intersection with Route 30. Turn right and head east on Route 30. The Compass Inn will be on your right in Laughlintown.

East Broad Top Railroad, Rockhill Trolley Museum and Lake Raystown

Getting Around

Ride the only narrow-gauge railroad in the eastern United States still operating at its original site, climb aboard an antique streetcar for a rural trip on a urban transportation link and sail on a paddle wheel cruise boat—all these options are available in Huntington County to the west of Altoona.

Four major seams of coal lay beneath the ground in this part of Pennsylvania. Much of the population of the Broad Top area depended on coal for their livelihood. The **East Broad Top Railroad** carried coal and other raw materials in and out of the region. When the railroad closed in 1956 the trains, track, yard and shop were left intact. In August 1960, this National Historic Landmark began operating excursions.

Your visit includes a guided walking tour of the rail yard and roundhouse, a chance to see the repair shops and the **Orbisonia Station** and a 50-minute narrated ride on EBT's steam-powered trains. Much of the countryside in the picturesque Aughwick Valley has not changed since the heyday of the bituminous bonanza almost a century ago. Passengers are welcome to disembark at **Colgate Grove**, where the locomotives turn for their return trip, and enjoy a picnic lunch before returning on a later train.

From Memorial Day weekend through mid-October Saturdays through Tuesdays the East Broad Top Railroad offers three daily train trips and four guided walks. For current prices and times call (814) 447-3011. Railroad buffs may also want to stop by the **Hunt Tower Transportation Museum** in Huntington, the only signal tower converted to a railroading museum. The tower stands beside the tracks where Amtrak and Conrail trains still run.

Across the street from East Broad Top is the **Rockhill Trolley Museum**, open from Memorial Day through mid-October from 10:30 A.M. to 4:30 P.M. Rockhill has more than 20 trolleys and interurban cars in their collection. Here, too, you can ride the rails on the **Shade Gap Electric Railway** aboard one of the 15 operational trolleys, including cars from Johnston, Philadelphia, Harrisburg and Scranton.

Trolleys have three unique features: they run on railroad tracks, they are powered by electricity and they almost always run on time. Trolleys obtain their power from a trolley wire suspended high in the air above the track. Electrical current is transferred to the trolley by a sliding contact "shoe" at the end of a long trolley pole on the roof of the car. Within the city, trolleys were often called streetcars, while high speed trolleys connecting cities were called interurbans. When trolleys were combined and run by a single motorman they were called rapid transit trains. When the train ran underground, it was a subway; when it was above the streets it was an elevated train. The peak year for trolleys was 1918 when it was the fifth largest industry in the country.

An all-volunteer organization founded the Rockhill Trolley Museum in 1962, and you can frequently see members at work in the restoration shop rebuilding historic trolleys. There is also a museum shop. The nominal admission includes unlimited rides on the trolley. If you walk down the track a short way you'll

Steam-powered trains take visitors on a round-trip over the oldest narrow-gauge in America at the East Broad Top Railroad.

---

see the ruin of Rockhill Furnace. You can also see the old coke ovens out behind the second carbarn.

To the east of Orbisonia and the south of Huntington, you can experience another enjoyable mode of transportation, an old paddlewheel excursion boat. The *Proud Mary* sails on the 118-mile long **Raystown Lake**. The lake with its serpentine shoreline was constructed between 1968 and 1978 by the U.S. Army Corps of Engineers. It was built for flood control but now serves as one of the most popular recreational lakes in the state for swimming, boating and fishing. The lake has more than a dozen freshwater species including lake trout, muskellunge, northern pike and several varieties of bass.

Lake Raystown Resort and Lodge has a marina from which the *Proud Mary* departs daily and a waterpark with slides, an inner-tube ride and a children's activity pool. For information on the resort call (814) 658-3500 or (800) 628-4262.

There are hiking and biking trails at various points around the lake particularly in the **Rothrock State Forest** and **Trough Creek State Park**. The latter is noted for the balanced rock, a geological wonder. Called an erosion remnant, the huge sandstone boulder seems precariously balanced on the edge of a cliff, but it has stood thus poised for centuries. Trough Creek State Park also has an ice mine. This is not a real mine, although it was perhaps a prospect hole dug by an early miner. Today it serves as an airduct for escaping cold air trapped in the rock mass above the short opening. From spring into the summer months ice forms in this hole as warm moist air freezes at the mine mouth. **Terrace Mountain Trail** winds from Lake Raystown Resort along the lake's shore and through the edge of the state forest and Trough Creek State Park.

Directions: From I-76, the Pennsylvania Turnpike, Exit 13, Fort Littleton, take Route 522 north to Orbisonia. East Broad Top and Rockhill are just east of Route 522 on Route 994 in the small community of Rockhill Furnace.

Fallingwater

Mr. Wright Can't Be Wrong

One of the world's most architecturally innovative buildings nestles amid towering trees in the Laurel Highlands at Mill Run. Frank Lloyd Wright believed in organic architecture and incorporated the natural environment in his design of **Fallingwater**. Cantilevered out over the rushing mountain waterfall, the house appears to grow from the earth as naturally as the trees around which the rooms are angled. Huge boulders are used for the flooring and fireplace. The windows capture the sound of the falling water. Wright, himself, claimed, "I think you can hear the waterfall when you look at its design."

Fallingwater was designed in 1936 as a summer weekend retreat for Pittsburgh department store owner Edgar J. Kaufmann, whose son studied architecture at Wright's workshop in Taliesin, Arizona. The house took a year to build and the contractor who carried out the work was aghast at the design. He was reluctant to remove the supports and would do so only under Wright's personal supervision. Architectural historian Henry Russell Hitchcock writes: "A house over a waterfall sounds like a poet's dream. A house cantilevered over a waterfall is rather the realized dream of an engineer." Fallingwater combines those dreams into a stunning reality.

The story of the gushing flow of creativity that led to the architect's first drawings may be somewhat exaggerated but it is probably close to accurate. Wright was at his Wisconsin studio and had not started his plans for Kaufmann's house when he received word that his client was en route from Milwaukee having just concluded a business meeting in Chicago. Wright's apprentice Edgar Tafel recalls a burst of creativity, "Pencils being used up as fast as we could sharpen them when broken." By the time Kaufmann arrived not only the outline but the name of the house was established.

Hour long tours of the house begin in the oversize living room-dining room. Huge boulders were used for the floor and the magnificent fireplace. The sandstone brings the outside in, as do the

Frank Lloyd Wright's architectural masterpiece Fallingwater enhances the beauty of its Laurel Highlands setting.

walls of windows designed to capture the sound of the falling water. There's even an opening in the floor space, leading to steps down to Bear Run. Since much of the simple, Wright-designed furniture is built in, there is a great feeling of spaciousness. In contrast, some of the upstairs rooms are quite intimate, and the narrow hallways suggest the enclosed space of a cave. The rooms are still filled with Kaufmann family decorative pieces: rugs, lamps, paintings and sculpture. Although Frederick Gutheim has called this the "quintessential house museum" you do not peer at the rooms from roped off doorways, you can walk around in the rooms.

Fallingwater is designed on three levels with stone separating the reinforced concrete trays that form each section. These levels have extended terraces that jut out over the tumbling water.

Frank Lloyd Wright also designed a private home for his cousin, newspaper-publisher Richard Lloyd Jones, which typically for Wright went 50 percent over budget and leaked. Jones's wife commented, "Well, this is what we get for leaving a work of art out in the rain."

Guided tours of Fallingwater are conducted from April to mid-November from 10:00 A.M. to 4:00 P.M. Tuesday through Sunday. In the winter, tours are only on weekends from 11:00 A.M. to 3:00 P.M. Reservations are strongly recommended, especially for weekends; call (412) 329-8501. Children under nine cannot tour the house, but there is a supervised Child Care Center for the young. Admission is charged. The exhibit center has displays covering Frank Lloyd Wright's stellar career. Fallingwater has a restaurant that serves lunch.

The Western Pennsylvania Conservancy owns and operates Fallingwater as well as the **Bear Run Nature Preserve** just a half mile north on Route 381. This 4,000-acre preserve has 20 miles of hiking trails; they're also used for cross-country skiing in the winter.

Directions: From the Pennsylvania Turnpike, I-76, take Exit 9, Donegal, and head east on Route 31 to Route 381/711, which takes you to Mill Run and the entrance to Fallingwater.

Fort Ligonier

The British Flag Still Flies

There was a time when the Americans were not fighting against the British, they were fighting with them. The enemies in this early North American conflict were the French and Native Americans. George Washington, who later played a pivotal role in the war for independence, was a colonel in the Virginia Provincial forces in service to King George II. The colonial powers were vying for control of the vast inland basin of this new empire.

In 1758, the British launched attacks against three of France's largest forts: Fortress Louisbourg in Novia Scotia, Fort Ticonderoga in New York and Fort Duquesne at the Forks of the Ohio. General John Forbes approached the task of taking Fort Duquesne by cutting a passage across the Alleghenies—the

Forbes Road. Along this route a series of fortifications were built to provide provisions and a safe haven for troops traveling to and from Fort Duquesne.

Fort Ligonier was one of these outposts. Originally it was named after the site of an old Delaware Indian village, Loyalhanna. In September 1758, 1,500 men under Colonel James Burd built this square fort with bastions and a wooden outer retrenchment, an uncommon addition. On October 12th, Burd and his command withstood an attack by a combined force of French and Native Americans emanating from Fort Duquesne. (This event is commemorated annually as **Fort Ligonier Days**, on the weekend nearest the 12th.) Forbes's army moved west from Raystown (later Fort Bedford, see selection). George Washington and his men, who had suffered defeat at Fort Necessity (see selection), also joined the force gathering at Loyalhanna.

On November 18, 1758 General Forbes led 2,500 men out of Loyalhanna to Fort Duquesne. The French had suffered reverses during the autumn, culminating in the **Treaty of Easton**. Although they were not a party to this treaty, it cost them most of their Native American allies (see Bushy Run Battlefield selection). With Forbes on the march, the French abandoned and burned Fort Duquesne.

Forbes, who was dying of a wasting disease, reported to Secretary of State William Pitt that he had renamed the French fort Pittsburgh, in his honor. He also renamed Loyalhanna, Fort Ligonier for Sir John Ligonier, Commander-in-Chief of military forces and Raystown.

From 1758 to 1766, Fort Ligonier served as a vital link in the supply line to the west and, though attacked, it was never taken. During Pontiac's War in 1763, the fort was attacked twice and under siege for two months before Colonel Henry Bouquet's men broke through the Indian lines. It was between Fort Ligonier and Fort Pitt that Bouquet fought the decisive battle at Bushy Run (see selection). Fort Ligonier was retired from military service in 1766, although it was used by settlers in the area during Lord Dunmore's Indian War of 1774 and again by the Pennsylvania militia during the American Revolution. But by 1800 no aboveground trace of the fort was in evidence.

But it's back in evidence today. A full-scale reconstruction stands on the same commanding hilltop as the original fort. The sharpened wooden pickets of the retrenchment provide a photographic point of interest as you approach the fort. Before exploring the fort, stop at the Visitor Center to see the exhibits and film on Fort Ligonier and the French and Indian War. The film covers the military, political and social ramifications of the war in the colonies and Europe.

One portion of the museum focuses on history and another on

both military and civilian life during the colonial era with emphasis on fine and decorative arts. There is a drawing room in the Georgian style one would have seen in Field Marshall John Louis Ligonier's London residence. Hanging here is an original Joshua Reynolds portrait painted of Ligonier in 1760. When the fort was decommissioned in 1766, Arthur St. Clair was appointed civil commandant and he built an estate several miles from the fort. The log parlor, exhibited in the museum, is the only portion of **St. Clair's Hermitage** that survived. It is furnished with 18th- and 19th-century English and American pieces, several belonging to the St. Clair family. There is a portrait of St. Clair over the mantle as well as silhouettes of Arthur and Phoebe St. Clair. Arthur St. Clair was a major general in the Continental Army during the war for independence. He later served in Congress and was Governor of the Northwest Territory from 1788 to 1802.

Fort Ligonier is a complete reconstruction of the original, with the surrounding retrenchment and gun batteries providing an outer circle of defense. The palisade or stockade provides an inner defensive picket wall around the interior buildings. Formed of tree trunks, these walls could stop musket balls but offered no protection against artillery.

The placement of the interior buildings was determined by an archeological dig. The dig yielded approximately 125,000 artifacts. Officers and the ranks ate, drank and lived on vastly different levels as you'll see in the officers' mess and sleeping quarters and in the soldiers' barracks. Soldiers originally slept in tents around the fort, but, in 1763, barracks were added housing 30 to 40 soldiers, two to a bunk.

Each of the fort's structures is filled with articles that may once have been stocked. The quartermaster's storehouse has a wide array: clothing, tents, packsaddles, blankets, kettles, cooking utensils, arms, gunflint and assorted equipment. All supplies were dearly come by on the frontier, even the flags. Garrison flags were flown only on Sundays from 11:00 A.M. to 1:00 P.M. Today the Union flag, like the original, still flies. History buffs may observe that the cross of St. Patrick of Ireland is not part of this Union flag. That is because Ireland did not become part of Great Britain until four decades after Fort Ligonier played its part in history.

Another vitally important part of the fort was the armory, which originally served as the powder magazine. When the underground magazine was added in 1759, weapons were stored in the heavy-timbered old powder magazine. The underground structure was added because military engineer Harry Gordon felt the entire fort endangered by the above ground magazine: enemy mortar fire could explode the magazine and lay waste to the fort.

The east side of the fort and half the north and south have an additional line of defense, a horizontal log wall that, unlike the palisade wall, could withstand an artillery bombardment. Its basketwork construction was filled with stones and earth offering protection from cannon shot.

The fort's hospital was originally on Ligonier's Main Street, but it is interpreted in what was part of the storehouse. A surgeon's chest displays implements used in the 18th century such as the bone saws, amputating knives, skull drills and blistering irons. The only anesthesia was rum or whiskey; many died not from their wounds but from the surgeon's knife.

General supplies were stored at the quartermasters but food supplies were kept at the commissary. The daily ration for the soldiers was customarily a pound of flour, a pound of salt pork or beef, butter and rice or dried peas. A diet this delinquent in fresh vegetables and fruit often led to malnutrition and scurvy.

Outside the fort's main gate is a reconstruction of the hut the ailing General John Forbes requested. Like other high-ranking officers, Forbes traveled with his own supplies, servants and aides. The hut contains tableware, linens, chests and furnishings to suggest those he used while headquartered here. To get a sense of what it was like when the fort was fully garrisoned visit during Fort Ligonier Days in October; call (412) 238-9701 for dates and details.

Fort Ligonier is open daily April through October from 9:00 A.M. to 5:00 P.M. Admission is charged.

Directions: From I-76, the Pennsylvania Turnpike, traveling west take Exit 10, Somerset and follow Route 601 north to the intersection with Route 30. Take Route 30 west to Ligonier and Fort Ligonier will be on your right. Traveling east on the Turnpike, take Exit 9, Donegal, and head north on Route 711 to the intersection with Route 30. Fort Ligonier is just beyond the intersection.

Fort Necessity National Battlefield and The Mount Washington Tavern

Washington's First Campaign

George Washington experienced a crucible at **Fort Necessity**. As a result of the action here, some accused Washington of assassination, while others proclaimed him a hero. This was Washington's first military engagement and the only one he ever fought in which he had to surrender. It was Washington's men who fired the shots that are thought to have been the first in the conflict that led to the Seven Years' War in Europe. The experience Washington gained during the French and Indian War, as it was called in the colonies, influenced the decision to appoint him commander-in-chief of the Revolutionary forces.

At the age of 21, George Washington was sent by Virginia Governor Robert Dinwiddie to lead an expedition into the Ohio Valley to warn the French against intruding into what the English viewed as their territory. Young Washington was picked because he had done surveying in the disputed territory and because his older brother, Lawrence, was a major stockholder along with Dinwiddie in the Ohio Company of Virginia. This venture, begun in 1747, brought the English and French into direct competition for the rich fur trade and land in the Ohio Valley.

Washington first traveled to Fort LeBouef (see selection) in November 1753 on a diplomatic mission to convince the French to withdraw. When this proved ineffective, a military force was assembled. Volunteers were promised land in the Ohio Valley. Troops were under the command of Colonel Joshua Fry and Lieutenant Colonel Washington, who at Fry's death in Wills Creek (present day Cumberland, Maryland) was put in charge and promoted to colonel.

As they proceeded from Wills Creek toward Fort Duquesne, Washington and his force of 150 men cleared a path through the forested region. After approximately four weeks they had covered 50 miles and were in the Great Meadows area when they received word from Indian scouts that a company of 33 French soldiers was five miles away.

Washington led a party of 40 soldiers and surprised the French at dawn. In the first military skirmish of his career, Washington was victorious. The French leader, Ensign Jumonville and nine others in his party were killed; within 15 minutes the French surrendered. One member of the French party escaped and walked barefooted to Fort Duquesne. He reported Washington failed to order a cease fire when the French called out they were on a diplomatic, rather than a military, mission.

Neither Washington, nor any of his men, had heard this appeal. The yells of the Indians, the cries of the wounded and the noise of the battle may well have obscured the plea, if indeed it was made. This brief encounter was the start of the war that ended with the English acquiring full claim to all the French land in North America.

Washington returned to Great Meadows after the Jumonville incident and built a fort "of necessity" in case the French returned with a larger force. Washington continued to have his men build the road west. Little more than a month later, in early July 1754, a large French force did appear, led by Jumonville's brother. The French attacked Fort Necessity. Even though Washington had been reinforced by Captain McKay and his Independent Corp of Regulars from South Carolina, the British were still outnumbered. Washington's force was able to hold them off for eight hours but then surrendered. In the terms Washington signed there was a statement he was responsible for the assassination of Jumonville. Washington and the British officers later stated the French word l'assassin was incorrectly translated and he believed the document read the killing or death of Jumonville in action. This signed statement by George Washington was used to discredit the English in Europe.

The Visitor Center has a slide presentation on the dramatic events in this opening chapter of the French and Indian War. The location of Jumonville Glen is marked and Fort Necessity has been reconstructed. The fort is unbelievably small, making it difficult to believe that it is indeed the exact size of the fortification Washington fought so hard to defend on July 3, 1754. But extensive archeological excavation proved that this was indeed the size of the original fort.

A year later, General Edward Braddock followed the road Washington had cut through the forest, although eventually he turned north toward modern day Pittsburgh while Washington's route veered west toward modern day Brownsville. When Braddock was mortally wounded at the **Battle of the Monongahela** on July 9, 1755, General Washington, who was leading the retreat, was instrumental in removing the suffering Braddock from the battlefield. Four days later Washington read the burial service at Braddock's grave, just a mile west of Fort Necessity. He was buried in the middle of the road, in hopes that the Indians would not find his grave. A monument stands near the site of his burial.

In 1770 George Washington returned to survey this area. He had purchased 234.5 acres around Great Meadows for $120.00 in 1770. This was only a portion of the 200,000 acres of frontier land that Washington owned. As early as 1784, Washington recommended the land as an excellent spot for an inn, a claim he would repeat several times before he died in 1799. It was not until 1827 or 1828 that the **Mount Washington Tavern** was built along the National Road which ran in front of the property. Today the tavern is part of Fort Necessity National Battlefield. It has been restored to appear as it did when it was one of the most famous and lively inns on the National Road. Outside there is a Conestoga wagon. The public room, parlor, kitchen and upstairs bedroom have been furnished to suggest the tavern's heyday. In the dining room there is a display on the National Road and its many inns.

Fort Necessity National Battlefield is open daily during daylight hours and the Visitor Center and tavern are open from 8:30

A.M. to 5:00 P.M. The park is closed on Christmas Day. A nominal admission is charged.

Directions: From I-76, the Pennsylvania Turnpike, take Exit 8, New Stanton and follow Route 119 south to Uniontown. In Uniontown Route 119 and Route 40 will become the same road for a short distance. Remain on Route 40 for approximately 11 miles past Uniontown; the park entrance will be on your right.

Fort Roberdeau National Historic Landmark

Get the Lead Out

To paraphrase the old axiom, through the woods and over the meadows to great-great-great-grandfather's fort we go. Actually when you come to the open farmland, you're apt to think you've missed the fort, but keep driving through the pastoral landscape and you'll see a directional sign that will take you to the fort in the valley.

Fort Roberdeau was a military fort for two years, 1778 to 1780. The stockade and cabins were built in 1778 initially as a central depot for ordnance and ammunition for Bedford County (far larger in those days than now, it was eventually subdivided into five counties). The fort strategically located was near the Juniata River and the main east/west Native American trail, the Kitanning Path. It was also near the north/south Warriors Path. Rangers were dispatched from the fort to patrol the Native American trails, gathering information on the tribe's activities.

It became apparent during the early stages of the American Revolution that the colonial cause would not succeed unless the fledgling nation found a source of lead for their bullets. To meet this need, lead was mined in New York, Virginia, Missouri and at **Sinking Stream Valley, Pennsylvania**. Another primary purpose of the fort was to protect the lead mining operations in Sinking Stream Valley.

Brigadier General Daniel Roberdeau, seeking a solution to the lead shortage, took a leave of absence from the Continental Congress to find a source of lead. He found it in the Sinking Stream Valley where lead had been crudely smelted during the French and Indian Wars. The lead was used even earlier by the Native Americans, who smelted the ore over their camp fires.

Roberdeau's mining efforts were disrupted by Indians and Tories, so this wealthy merchant built a fort to protect this vital war effort. Local militia from Cumberland and Bedford counties not only helped construct the fort, but also manned it, along with **Fort Standing Stone**, near Huntington. It is thought that be-

355

tween 60 and 200 men were stationed at these two forts. Lead ingots smelted at Fort Roberdeau traveled to the east on the Juniata and Susquehanna Rivers. Soldiers would then melt the lead a second time to make their own bullets because each rifle was different.

Fort Roberdeau, as you see from the reconstruction, was not built like most forts with the logs placed vertically. Logs could not be secured in the limestone ground, there was not enough topsoil to dig a trench, stand the logs and then backfill. Instead, the logs were placed horizontally. The fort's defenses included four double fortified four-pounder cannons. It was never attacked and provided a place of safety for lead miners, soldiers and settlers.

The reconstruction of this significant fort was a 1976 Blair County Bicentennial Project. Within the fort are cabins that served as officers' quarters and soldiers' barracks. Fort officers included Major Robert Cluggage, Captain Thomas Cluggage and Captain John Lane. The militia elected their officers during this period, and Robert Cluggage also served as the District Justice. Their quarters have camp beds, tables and chairs. A replica of a map from 1770 rests on the table. It looks more comfortable than the bunks that served the twelve men in the barracks cabin. The thin "tick", or mattress, filled with hay or straw, did little to soften the plank bunks. There is also a rebuilt hut that housed the lead miners. Records indicate that among the miners were British deserters and prisoners of war who had knowledge of smelting.

The lead smelter looks like it is ready to begin operation. In front of the furnace are bins for lead ore and wood. The smelter was essentially a furnace where the ore was heated to 600 degrees. The molten lead was collected at the bottom of the smelter in the form of ingots which could then be melted and cast into bullets, grapeshot or cannonballs. Next to the smelter was the blacksmith's shed, where miner's tools and weapons were repaired. The blacksmith was needed to make hooks, hinges, nails and horseshoes. There was also a storehouse with provisions: food, blankets, uniforms and weapons. Powder and shot was stored in the powder magazine. Research indicates that the reconstructed magazine was built where the original stood. The magazine was off to the side of the stairway entrance, since bullets cannot turn a corner.

Once a month from June through September the fort holds **Militia Musters**, 18th-century garrison encampments that provide a look at what it would have been like when Fort Roberdeau was operational. Also in late July the fort hosts **Revolutionary War Days** featuring a military field camp, weapons and artillery demonstrations, crafts, English country dancing, traders' tents, children's games and colonial food.

The Fort Roberdeau site includes 47 acres with five nature trails through field, forest, pond and stream habitats. An eight-minute video on the fort and smelting process is shown in the 1858 Pennsylvania bank barn that serves as a Visitor Center and museum shop. The upper level of the barn is used for 18th-century dances, concerts and summer theater performances. On the hill above is White Oak Hall, a conference and public meeting hall.

On the north side of the fort, there is a farmhouse that will eventually have exhibits on farming and daily life in the 1830s to 1860s. The stream that flows north of the fort sinks into the ground directly behind the farmhouse. There is an archeology area being worked beside the farmhouse.

Fort Roberdeau is open from mid-May through early October, Tuesday through Saturday 11:00 A.M. to 5:00 P.M. On Sunday it opens at 1:00 P.M. A nominal admission is charged. Call (814) 946-0048 for additional information.

Directions: From I-76, the Pennsylvania Turnpike, take Route 220 north to Altoona; from I-80 take Route 220 south. Take the Bellwood exit, follow signs to Route 1013 and turn right. This will lead you directly into the fort parking lot. If you are traveling from Altoona you can take a more scenic route by traveling north on Route 220 and taking Kettle Road, Route 1013, that winds along Sinking Stream.

Friendship Hill National Historic Site

Gallatin's Getaway

The orphaned young aristocrat Albert Gallatin, influenced by the ideas of freedom promulgated in the New World, left his native Switzerland a few weeks before his 19th birthday. He landed in Massachusetts in 1780.

An acquaintance with Monsieur Savary, a Frenchman, prompted Gallatin to leave Boston, where he had been teaching French at Harvard, and travel to Philadelphia. Both Gallatin and Savary became involved in land speculation. Gallatin, having no money to put up for his half-shares of the 120,000 acres they purchased, was responsible for giving his personal attention to the land's development. He also paid a percentage when he reached in 21st birthday and received his inheritance. So in 1784, Gallatin, with a small exploration party, crossed the Alleghenies and established a temporary base along the Monogahela River in Fayette County, Pennsylvania.

Gallatin's forays in the area brought him to a high bluff overlooking the Ohio River. He chose that spot to build his western Pennsylvania home, **Friendship Hill**. Gallatin's dream was to create New Geneva, a community of European immigrants on the wilderness frontier. In 1796, he and his partners built a glass factory, the first of its kind west of the Allegheny Mountains. By 1800 they also had a sawmill, gun factory, gristmill and general store along the river.

Long before he began building his community he began building his personal estate. Work on Gallatin's two-story brick house started in 1789, the year he married and brought his wife, Sophia Allegre of Richmond, Virginia to his rural property. Sophia died just five months after their wedding.

Gallatin was not highly successful as either a land speculator or a farmer, but he quickly became a community leader. In September, 1788 he was chosen to attend a conference on revising the United States Constitution, which Pennsylvania ratified the previous December. In 1789–90 Gallatin served on another convention to revise the state constitution. In 1790, he was elected to the State legislature, serving three terms before being elected to the United States Senate. Since he was a few months shy of being a citizen for nine years, he was denied the senatorial seat.

Gallatin returned to Friendship Hill in 1794 with his second wife, Hannah Nicholson of New York. Four years later to accommodate his growing family (though only three of his six children survived infancy) Gallatin added the frame addition to the house. His arrival in western Pennsylvania coincided with a spirited uprising in opposition to the whiskey tax imposed by Alexander Hamilton's excise tax of 1791. Disgruntled farmers combined to stage angry military skirmishes that terrorized revenue officers. Gallatin, while not supporting the tax, argued for peaceful submission to the law. His reasoned advice helped prevent civil war, but Hamilton tried to prove that Gallatin was the chief instigator of the **Whiskey Rebellion**.

His return to a rustic life was brief; deeply grateful for having been spared a civil conflict, western Pennsylvanians elected Gallitin to Congress. He served in the House for three terms, 1795-1801. Gallatin believed in fiscal accountability. He thought that "a country, like a household, should live within its means and avoid debt." He devised a system whereby the executive branch would report to the legislative branch on its expenditures. Gallatin served as Secretary of the Treasury under Jefferson and Madison, from 1801 to 1814, holding the office longer than any other man in American history. It was Gallatin who arranged for the financing of the **Louisiana Purchase** and the **Lewis and Clark expedition**. He also greatly reduced the national debt, although this progress was halted with the expenses associated with the War of 1812.

For the next decade, Gallatin's contribution was on the international scene and again he was unable to spend any time at his Pennsylvania estate. President Madison sent Gallatin to Russia in 1813 in response to a Russian offer to mediate the conflict between America and England. He next served on the commission that negotiated the **Treaty of Ghent** which ended the War of 1812. For the next seven years, Gallatin was minister to France.

He returned to Friendship Hill in 1823, to enjoy a new stone addition his son had added at his direction while he was in Europe. During this interlude at his estate Gallatin entertained Lafayette during his 1825 tour of the United States. Gallatin wrote that his famous guest "encumbered. . . . my house with a prodigious crowd." Later that year Gallatin left Friendship Hill.

Gallatin served briefly in 1826 as Ambassador to the Court of St. James, then retired from public service and moved to New York.

He became president of a bank, help found the University of the City of New York and wrote a highly regarded study of the American Indians. Finding he was not able to return to his Pennsylvania estate, Gallatin sold it in 1832. Gallatin died at the age of 88 on August 12, 1849.

Friendship Hill is furnished only with memories and mementoes. There is a room full of items belonging to, or associated with, Albert Gallatin. A time line reviews his life and a portrait comes to life. We hear Gallatin's words seemingly coming from his portrait. Rangers conduct 25 minute exterior and interior tours of Friendship Hill three times daily during the summer. You can call ahead to check times, (412) 725-9190. There are also regularly scheduled special programs that deal with different aspects of Gallatin's life and times.

Friendship Hill is open at no charge daily 8:30 A.M. to 5:00 P.M. If there is not a scheduled tour, you can use a 40-minute compact disk audio tour at no charge. If you have additional time to explore, pick up a map of the park's eight miles of trails. There is also a picnic area.

Directions: From I-79 take Route 21 west to Masontown, then Route 166 south to New Geneva. Continue one mile south to the entrance for Friendship Hill.

Hanna's Town

Country Justice

In 1773 when Westmoreland County was created, Robert Hanna, a Bedford County Justice, moved to this frontier area. He became a justice in this southwestern Pennsylvania county and his home served as the courthouse. Hanna planned a town on his tract of land. According to his agreement with purchasers, within two years owners of his lots had to build an eighteen-foot-square house.

No printed record survives of this developing town but journal entries indicate between 20 and 30 homes were built. Even as settlers began building in this new town, the land was so vigorously contested by Virginia and Pennsylvania that they nearly had a border war. A permanent boundary giving the land to Pennsylvania was finally agreed upon on April 1, 1784.

By this time **Hanna's Town** had suffered greatly in the Revolutionary struggle. Residents got involved in the struggle for independence early in the conflict. On May 16, 1775 there was a gathering in Hanna's Town to discuss England's violation of the rights of the colonists in Massachusetts Bay. Participants issued the "Hanna's Town Resolves," stating that the people of Westmoreland County, though loyal to the British crown, would resist the tyrannical acts of the British parliament. As part of this resolve regiments were formed to resist the imposition of legislation like the Stamp Acts.

Many of the men of Hanna's Town left to fight in the Colonial Army; others protected the frontier. The threat of Indian attack necessitated the building of a stockade in 1774. After it fell into disrepair another fort was built during the Revolutionary War period.

The safety of the fort proved necessary when on Saturday, July 13, 1782 a Seneca raiding party along with British officers and troops from the British Indian Department at Fort Niagara, sacked and burned Hanna's Town. Local residents working in the field spotted the raiders in time to warn the town and all the inhabitants sought refuge in the fort. Twelve-year-old Peggy Shaw was wounded trying to rescue an even younger child and died several weeks after the attack.

The fort and two houses were all that remained standing after the raid. Hanna's Town was rebuilt and served as the county seat until 1786 when the court moved to Greensburg. In a matter of years, Hanna's Town reverted to farmland.

Archaeological investigations of this colonial community began in 1969. The field work pinpointed the location of 12 areas of occupation and recovered more than a million artifacts. A stockade fort, Robert Hanna's house (set up to look like court is in session) and the one-room jail have been reconstructed. There is also a wagon shed with a Conestoga wagon. The historical society moved the **Klingensmith House** to this site. It represents an early German-style log house built around 1800. A field museum exhibits archaeological artifacts. Outside the jail, which now serves as a gift shop, is a pillory and whipping post. There is also an herb garden. The road that separates reconstructed buildings from the fort was originally the Forbes Road, used by military troops traveling to Pittsburgh (see Bushy Run Battlefield selection). Visitors are welcome Memorial Day through Labor Day, Tuesday through Sunday from 1:00 P.M. to 5:00 P.M. During May, September and October it is open on weekends only.

Directions: From I-76 take Exit 8, New Stanton and follow Route 119 north through Greensburg. Hanna's Town is three miles north between Route 119 and Route 819.

Idlewild Park

Forested Highlands Favorite Family Fun Spot

America's fourth oldest operating amusement park began in 1878 when William Darlington permitted Judge Thomas Mellon, owner of the Ligonier Valley Railroad to use his 350-acre **Idlewild** estate for "picnic purposes or pleasures grounds." But Darlington stipulated "no timber or other trees are to be cut or injured." The concern for the natural beauty of the setting has continued throughout the park's history and accounts for the claim that this is the most beautiful theme park in America.

The **Ligonier Valley Railroad**, originally a narrow gauge operation, carried coal from Ligonier to Latrobe, where it connected with the Pennsylvania Railroad's main line. As originally developed the park had picnic grounds on both sides of the tracks, an artificial lake and a large hall. The first building at the park was the train depot, once the smallest full- service depot in the country. It now serves as a Guest Services office.

The park's success prompted the railroad to convert to standard gauge and offer direct service to Idlewild from Pittsburgh. The crowds were so great on the Fourth of July in 1890 that according to published reports "the tops of the [railroad] coaches were covered with boys."

During the 1890s the park was primarily used for picnicking and such recreational activities as boating, fishing, tennis and ball playing. One of the first rides was the merry-go-round added about 1894. A new carousel was added two years later and the pavilion in which it was placed houses the park's current carousel.

In 1931 the Idlewild Management Company, directed by C.C. Macdonald and Richard Mellon (son of park founder Judge Mellon), took control of the park and began to add new amusement rides and make substantial improvements. Macdonald had 35 years of experience in a variety of recreational parks. In 1925 he introduced the country's first kiddieland in a San Antonio, Texas park. By 1951 the Macdonald family had bought out the Mellons and were sole owners. They continued to make improvements and in 1956 added **Story Book Forest**. What started as a collection of 15 life-size displays of famous nursery rhymes, today has over 40 attractions and still retains live characters that help bring age-old fables to life.

In 1983, Kennywood Park Corporation assumed control of Idlewild Park and began adding new focal points including a children's participatory area, a substantial waterpark, new kiddieland and perhaps the park's most beloved area, **Mister Rogers' Neighborhood of Make-Believe**. Fred Rogers, a resident of nearby Latrobe, remembered the park from his childhood and suggested the concept of recreating his PBS kingdom utilizing animated figures. Rogers wrote the script, provided the voices of the characters and acted as a creative consultant. Full-size brass and wood replicas of the trolley on his television show transport enthusiastic families through this delightfully familiar neighborhood.

Idlewild Park is open Tuesday through Sunday from the first weekend in June through the last weekend in August; it opens on weekends in mid-May and on holiday Mondays. Park gates open at 10:00 A.M. A single admission fee includes all park areas and activities. Swimsuits are required in the pool and on water rides. There is live entertainment in the park and various eateries, shops and games of skill.

After the park closes in September the **Ligonier Highland Games** are held on the grounds. This one-day event includes massed band parades, Scottish music and dancing, athletic events, genealogy booths, crafts and food.

Directions: From I-76 take Exit 9, Donegal and head north on Route 711 and then take Route 30 west to Idlewild Park. You can also use Exit 7 or 8 off the turnpike.

Johnstown Flood Museum

Disastrous Consequences

Watching the 1989 Academy Award broadcast, it was exciting to hear that the year's Best Documentary Short Subject was a Pennsylvania entry, the **Johnstown Flood Museum**'s 26-minute film. Using still photographs of flood victims and damaged property, plus special effects, the movie recreates the fury of the wall of death that decimated Johnstown.

This is one of the worst natural—although aided by human

error—disasters in the nation's history. It was also one of the first stories to rivet the attention of the nation and the world. For nine days the front pages of the *New York Times* featured reports on the flood. The *Pittsburgh Commercial Gazette* had to curtail the size of its pages, otherwise it would have run out of paper. Relief assistance was provided by 16 foreign countries, when combined with domestic contributions, a total of $3,742,818.78 was collected.

The Johnstown Flood Museum offers scientific explanations of how the flood occurred, with easy to understand state-of-the-art physics charts detailing the path and movement of the water. A 24-foot relief map with fiber optic animation and sound effects reconstructs the dam and the valley giving a visual sense of the flood path. The first floor's focal point is a three dimensional wall of wreckage that dramatically captures the carnage.

There are striking before and after photographs of Johnstown, plus cases filled with items salvaged after the flood. There is a quilt that was used as a rescue rope to pull survivors through a shattered window. The pile of debris beneath the stone bridge covered 30 acres; four square miles of Johnstown were completely destroyed. The path of destruction eliminated 1,600 homes and 280 businesses.

The flood occurred on a Friday and by the following Wednesday 67-year old Clara Barton arrived in Johnstown with 50 men and women from the newly organized **American Red Cross**. It was their first major relief effort. Clara Barton stayed for five months distributing clothing and supplies and helping people get a new foothold on life. Local factories still standing resumed operation in some cases within the week, but many inhabitants lived in mud and debris for months. It took between 7,000 and 10,000 laborers to clear the wreckage. One in three victims were never identified, 99 entire families were lost, 396 children under age ten died, and 568 lost one or both parents. It was well into July before a day went by without discovering additional bodies, and the last victim's body wasn't recovered until 1911. There were 124 women and 198 men widowed. Photographs and enlarged news stories capture the tragedy.

The Johnstown Flood Museum, in the old Carnegie Library, is open May through October Sunday through Thursday from 10:00 A.M. to 5:00 P.M.; on Friday and Saturday it stays open until 7:00 P.M. From November through April it closes at 5:00 P.M. daily. Admission is charged.

The best way to gain a thorough understanding of this disaster is to start at the Johnstown Flood National Memorial (see selection), then drive through St. Michael's Historic District stopping at the South Forks Fishing & Hunting Clubhouse, and to put it in perspective end at the Johnstown Flood Museum.

Directions: From I-76, the Pennsylvania Turnpike, take the Somerset Exit and head north on Route 219 to Johnstown. Near Johnstown, take the Route 56 Expressway into the city. Once in the city, you will turn right on Walnut Street and right on Washington Street. The Flood Museum is on the corner.

Johnstown Flood National Memorial and Historic St. Michael

Deadly Memorial Day

It's not surprising that many thought it was the end of the world. First, heavy rain caused the Little Conemaugh River, by which Johnstown stood, to rise roughly a foot an hour, flooding the streets of the city. Around 4:00 P.M. on the chilly, wet Memorial Day, the people in Johnstown heard a rumble that grew to a "roar of thunder." After years of worrying that the spring rains might cause the **South Fork Dam** 14 miles upstream to break, it finally happened. Twenty million tons of water raced down the narrow valley at speeds up to 40 mph. The wall of water averaged a height of 35 feet and carried with it a tower of wreckage. Preceding the cresting water was a violent wind, that independently destroyed smaller buildings. Hanging over the wave was what survivors called a "death mist," a black cloud of smoke and steam. Those who had reached high ground said the wave "snapped off trees like pipestems," and "crushed houses like eggshells."

The disaster was compounded by several factors. One was that miles of barbed wire from the wire works above Johnstown was swept up and became part of the debris. Many who tried to escape the water became entangled in the wire. It took only ten minutes for the cresting water to cut a path of destruction through Johnstown. After the wave crest a 20-foot current continued to pour through the city decimating still more buildings, locomotives and trees. Tons of debris continued to pile up in front of the stone railroad bridge. A 45-acre mass was eventually piled up against the bridge, held by the current and the barbed wire. This mountain of debris, soaked with kerosene and other flammable liquids from leaking tank cars, was perhaps ignited by live coals in floating stoves, burning with "all the fury of hell", claimed at least 80 victims.

In all over 2,200 people died and there was $17 million in property damage in one of America's worst disasters. It wasn't totally a natural disaster. Although nature played a role, there was also human error and neglect on the part of the South Fork Fishing and Hunting Club. To gain a perspective on why Johnstown suffered this horrendous fate, visit the **Johnstown Flood National Memorial**. This site is situated where the flood began. The park Visitor Center overlooks the remnants of the South Fork Dam which held back the waters of Lake Conemaugh. The center stands in front of the restored Victorian house owned by Elias J. Unger, the last president of the South Fork Fishing and Hunting Club. Only the exterior is restored to reflect the era, the interior serves as park offices.

The 35-minute award-winning film *Black Friday* shown at the Visitor Center is the most emotionally gripping film you're likely to see at any national park site. Given the nature of the disaster, the scenes of the flood victims may be too frightening for young viewers. It is presented as an eerie and haunting ghost story.

At the Visitor Center you can see 1880s photographs taken of South Fork Fishing and Hunting Club members. Johnstown residents called the group, "the Bosses' Club." Pittsburgh industrialists like Andrew Mellon, Henry Clay Frick, and Andrew Carnegie were among the 60 elite members of the club who owned the South Fork Dam and Lake Conemaugh. The 72-foot high dam, in its day possibly the world's largest earthen dam, was built in 1853 to create a reservoir for the Pennsylvania Mainline Canal, which was obsolete by the time the project was completed. For a time the dam and lake were owned by the Pennsylvania Railroad, then a Congressman from Altoona, and finally in 1879 they were purchased by the sporting club. In July 1862, a break in the dam drained the lake but no damage was done because the water level was low. The club repaired and rebuilt the dam without consulting an engineer, lowering the breast of the dam three feet to allow carriages to cross. Businesses in Johnstown, including the Cambria Iron Works, expressed concern about the weakness of the dam, but club officials scoffed at the concept of danger. No club member was found legally responsible for the dam breaking and the courts considered the disaster more of a "visitation of providence."

During the summer months the National Park Service presents costumed programs highlighting many elements of the disaster from life at the club to relief efforts afterward. When staff is sufficient, rangers lead guided walks around the dam site. After visiting the National Park Memorial, drive into the 1889 Historic District of St. Michael and see the clubhouse (now undergoing restoration) with its wide front porch that once overlooked the lake. Docked outside the clubhouse were two steam yachts, four sailboats and 50 rowboats. Each club member and his family could stay two weeks at the clubhouse. Many members built homes along the lake shore, and quite a number still stand in the historic district. Today the clubhouse contains a restaurant and gift shop.

The Johnstown Flood National Memorial is open at no charge 9:00 A.M. to 6:00 P.M. daily from Memorial Day to Labor Day. It closes at 5:00 P.M. the rest of the year. It is closed on major holidays. Each Memorial Day weekend there is a poignant presentation **"Tales of the Great Flood"** that tells survivors' stories. More than two thousand luminaries line the abutments of the dam. For more about the Johnstown Flood, particularly the relief efforts, stop at the **Johnstown Flood Museum** in downtown Johnstown. It is worth including both of these sites as they present different elements of the story (see selection).

Directions: From I-76, the Pennsylvania Turnpike, take Exit 10 and pick up Route 219 north of Johnstown to the Saint Michael/Sidman exit. Head east on Route 869, $1^1/_2$ miles to Lake Road and make a left, continue for $1^1/_2$ miles and the Johnstown Flood National Memorial Visitor Center will be on your right. You can pass through the Historic District in St. Michael before reaching Lake Road.

Johnstown Inclined Plane and James Wolfe Sculpture Trail

View from the Top

The Guinness Book of Records claims the **Johnstown Inclined Plane** is "the steepest vehicular inclined plane in the world." This incline, built in 1891, is also one of the five last vehicular incline planes in the United States. Riders, with or without their cars, travel up Yoder Hill on a 71.9 percent grade to an overlook with a commanding view of the Conemaugh Valley. A newspaper advertisement in the 1930s read, "Up, Up, Up! 900 Feet into Scenic Paradise!" (Actually, it is only 896.5 feet long.)

This was not merely a recreational ascent, it provided dependable transportation for commuters from the hilltop community of Westmont to the city below. The flood of May 31, 1889 (see Johnstown Flood Museum selection) led to the construction of the inclined plane. After that devastating calamity, the community looked to the hills for safer living conditions.

Cambria Iron Company, at the time of the flood one of the four largest steel producers in the country, began selling lots on 600 acres above the flat fields of the city. The town was first called **Tip Top**, but soon changed to **Westmont**. It was laid out by Charles R. Miller, the landscape architect who laid out Grand View Cemetery. Essential to the success of this town atop Yoder

Hill was a link to the city below, and the only feasible means of transportation was thought to be an inclined plane as a steep and rugged roadway would be impassable in bad weather.

It is not surprising that this idea occurred to town developers because in 1834 the Allegheny Portage Railroad (see selection) linked Johnstown and Hollidaysburg. This railroad used a series of ten inclined planes to cross the mountains. Gravity inclines were used by industrial companies to transport loads from mines and quarries. In 1890, there were 11 inclined planes in Allegheny County.

Work began on the incline, designed by Samuel Diescher of Pittsburgh, on May 1, 1890. The Johnstown Incline had two cars, that counterbalanced each other. As one rose, the other was lowered. This was economically advantageous because it only used one power source. Originally the cars had two decks with the passengers below vehicles and horses. This proved an unpopular arrangement. By 1921 they were rebuilt as a single-deck car. On opening day, June 1, 1891, six hundred passengers and 30 wagons and teams traveled the inclined plane. After only two months an average of 1,300 passengers and teams used the incline each day. It cost five cents a trip, but residents of Westmont could buy a monthly book for one dollar covering 122 trips. While passengers loved the convenience, horses did not take to the experience. More than one horse was killed when it jumped over the side and fell to the rocks below. The passenger safety record is near perfect—in all the years of operation there has been only one fatality and that was due to carelessness and had nothing to do with the operation of the incline. (A driver was crushed when he removed the safety blocks from under the wheels of his vehicle and his truck pinned him against the gate of the descending car.)

Passenger decline and deteriorating equipment led to the sale of the incline to the city of Westmont. There was even talk of abandoning it all together in favor of bus service. In 1936, the incline proved its worth once more by transporting 4,000 people from the 18-foot deep waters of the flooded city. When rumors began that a massive dam had broken, panicked individuals climbed up the steep hill alongside the track. This tragedy in which 14 lives were lost and damage was close to forty-five million dollars proved the necessity of having the incline. A federal grant provided financial assistance for repairs.

During World War II there was a ban on picture taking from the top of the incline because of a fear of flashing cameras above the miles of defense production. The incline's popularity increased as gas rationing limited automobile travel. Bankruptcy again loomed in 1953 and the community of Westmont's operating budget was disproportionly spent subsidizing the incline,

The 1891 Johnstown Inclined Plane is the world's steepest ve-hicular inclined plane.

accounting for 21% of the budget. On January 31, 1962 the in-cline took its last run under Westmont ownership. But it was soon taken over by the Cambria County Tourist Council and it resumed operation on July 4, 1962. The incline proved its worth after Johnstown's third major flood on July 20, 1977 when wa-ter again washed out roads and devastated the city. In 1983, the incline changed hands again, coming under the jurisdiction of the Cambria County Transit Authority.

The inclined plane is now brilliantly lit by 114-track and 104-car lights. Its significance is recognized by an inclusion on the National Register of Historic Places and a Regional Historic Mechanical Engineering Landmark. In 1983, a major restoration project restored the incline, revealing the ingenuity and craftsmanship of the original design while incorporating new mechanical improvements behind-the-scenes.

At the top of the incline there is a Visitors Center with exhibits, brochures, maps and a knowledgeable tourism representative to help you plan your Johnstown visit. The view from the observation deck and the **Incline Station Restaurant and Pub** is particularly enjoyable at sunset. Across from the center flies one of the largest free-flying American flags in the country, measuring 30 by 60 feet.

At the bottom you can walk the 1.4 mile **James Wolfe Sculpture Trail**, the first nature trail in the country to incorporate steel sculptures. Wolfe was commissioned by the Johnstown Flood Centennial Committee to honor the city's steel heritage with ten pieces; eight are located along the trail. On the trail you will also pass a spring and pond as well as a striking rock strata. Wolfe's ninth and largest work is on the hillside below the observation deck; another of his pieces can be seen on Walnut Street in downtown Johnstown opposite the Bethlehem Steel offices. Opposite the sculpture trail on the other side of the incline is the 1.4 mile **South Trail** that runs parallel to Stonycreek River. For the rugged hiker, there's the 2.5 mile steep-graded **Poverty Trail**, built by coal miners and steel workers during a period of underemployment in the steel mills.

If you take your car to the top of the incline be sure to drive into Westmont. Along Luzerne Street you will see the longest continuous stand of American elms east of the Mississippi. The elms meet above the street creating a cathedral-arch effect that is striking.

Westmont's designer was also responsible for Grandview Cemetery. The first internment at the one-hundred acre cemetery was in 1887. Many of the 2,209 victims of the Johnstown Flood of 1889 are buried here (see Johnstown Flood National Memorial selection). The bodies of 777 unidentified dead are buried in the "Unknown Plot." The cemetery is one of the largest in the state.

If you ride the inclined plane Friday or Saturday night you can see a changing array of laser light sculptures that light up the sky. Regulars insist you can feel the lights change as you move up the incline. The observation deck is also an ideal vantage point.

The inclined plane operates daily from 6:30 A.M. on weekdays, from 7:30 A.M. on Saturday and 9:00 A.M. on Sunday. It closes at 10:00 P.M. The fare is nominal. Parking is available at the top and bottom of the incline, or you can take your car on the incline. There is a gift shop at the top of the incline.

Directions: From I-76, the Pennsylvania Turnpike, take the Somerset exit and head north on Route 219 to Johnstown. Once in the city Route 56 and 403 pass by the bottom of the incline. The top is accessible from Route 271.

Laurel Caverns

Spelunking, Rappelling, Climbing, Fossil Hunting

There's good and bad news when it comes to **Laurel Caverns**, but the bad news is actually good news for adventurous explorers. Laurel Caverns, the 16th longest cave in the country and Pennsylvania's largest, lacks the delicate formations seen in many other caves. This may seem disadvantageous but it actually makes available a wide array of activities that are impossible when fragile stalactites and stalagmites need to be protected.

Not that preservation isn't important. Here more than at many caverns little has been done to change the natural elements in the cavern. The 2.3 miles of passageways are often narrow and steep and the footing is uneven. Many sections of the cavern, laid out like a maze, remain unlighted and visitors carry their own illumination even on the regular 45-to-55 minute guided tours which include the lighted-developed portion and a brief excursion into the undeveloped section by candlelight. In both you will see distinctive catacombs and natural sculpturing. You can also explore on your own, equipped with a light and cave map, for two to three hour excursions. You'll need to bring your own light with back-up batteries (size D flashlights are the minimum light permitted and a second back-up light is strongly recommended). If this is slightly too adventurous, with advance reservations you can arrange a guided spelunking trip through the undeveloped cavern.

Any size group can arrange rappelling and climbing sessions. Within the cave there is a fifty-foot high cliff used for the former and two high stone walls, 18 and 25 feet high, for the latter. Another different but less athletic option is fossil hunting as groups of ten or more can take a 30-minute walk and collect fossils. A variety of brachiopods, blastoids, crinoids, pelecypods, bryozoans, gastropods, trilobites and rugose corals are found in the caverns.

These fossils are reminders of species found in southwestern Pennsylvania more than 300 million years ago when much of the area lay beneath a shallow sea. Over eons the limestone base of this sea was buried beneath layers of rock. The pressure of continental drift pushed the plates into parallel ripples that were slowly pushed higher and higher. During the Mesozoic era there were Appalachian peaks over five miles high, and the mountain ranges continued for thousands of miles. One of those ripples is Chestnut Ridge in which Laurel Caverns is found. When you visit the caverns you can explore in depth the geological factors that led to the formation of the caverns. Scout groups can arrange one-day seminars focusing on the geological aspects of the cave as well as do badge work on other cavern options like spelunking and rappelling.

A popular feature of the cave tours is the sound and light show that ends the tour. The colored lights let you "see" Handel's *Messiah*. The lights change with the pitch and intensity of the music, rather like the giant keyboard in *Close Encounters of the Third Kind*.

Laurel Caverns is open daily from 9:00 A.M. to 5:00 P.M. from May through October and on weekends in March, April and November. The cave is always a cool 52 degrees so a jacket is advisable. Reservations are required for some of the special programs, call (412) 438-3003. There is camping, picnicking and even an underground miniature golf course.

Directions: From I-79 take the Waynesburg exit and head west on Route 21 to Uniontown, then take Route 40 east to the mountain top turnoff for Laurel Caverns. From I-76 take Exit 8 and head south on Route 119 to Uniontown, then pick up Route 40.

Lincoln Caverns, Whisper Rocks and Indian Caverns

Rock of Ages

Pennsylvania has just under 1,000 mapped caves. Of these nine are open to the public. Four are in relatively close proximity in Raystown County, at the center of the state. Each offers unique features, but if you want to feel adventurous don't miss Lincoln Caverns. Unlike most of the others, here you won't find passageways wide enough to permit vehicular access. Instead the walkways are narrow and sometimes tight. This makes the experience closer to that felt by true spelunkers who frequent the non-commercial caves. Just as Lincoln offers more for the adventurous, it also may be more than the claustrophobic can tolerate, nor is it for the infirm. It takes a degree of agility to negotiate the steep, wet steps within Lincoln Caverns and those leading to Whisper Rocks.

The words cave and cavern are often used interchangeably. A cavern is actually a connected system of caves. A cave is a natural opening in the ground extending into the earth beyond the zone of light. It is also sufficiently large to permit a person to crawl or walk within. Deposits of calcite in the cave system form speleothems, or cave formations, the most common being stalactites and stalagmites. An easy way to remember which extends up and which hangs down is that stalactites hold tight to the ceiling. Lincoln Caverns and Whisper Rocks are noted for their outstanding formations. In addition to these dramatic formations you'll also see cave pearls, formed by minerals crystalizing in small beads on the wall, and soda straws, the precursor of all stalactites. There are even some helictites that grow straight out from the wall.

Highway construction crews on Route 22 discovered Lincoln Caverns in May 1930. The farmer who owned the land opened the caves to the public 13 months later. By 1932 the caverns were acquired under a lease/purchase agreement by Myron Dunlavy, Sr. and it is now run by his granddaughter Ann Dunlavy Molosky.

One of Ann's main thrusts is education. This is the only cavern in the state offering classroom programs on caves and cave life through a study guide on speleology. Lincoln Caverns also hosts **Geology Badge Day for the Scouts**. The last four weekends in October the theme shifts from education to entertainment with a **"Ghosts and Goblins Tour."** It's a haunted house beneath the earth.

One admission covers both Lincoln Caverns and Whisper Rocks. One hour tours are given every few minutes during the summer and on the half-hour in the spring and fall. From Memorial Day to Labor Day the caverns are open daily 9:00 A.M. to 7:00 P.M. In April, May, September, October and November the caverns close at 5:00 P.M. The temperature in the caverns is always close to 52 degrees so a sweater or jacket is advisable. There is a well-stocked gift shop, picnic facilities (snacks are sold during the summer months) and nature trails.

The unique feature of nearby **Indian Caverns** is indicated by its name. This cavern has tangible reminders of the Indians who used it as a winter shelter, council chamber and burial ground. A massive stone within the caverns has Native American picture writing done by the Mohawks. Totem drawings include a profile of an Indian chief, tepee, peace pipe, turtle and other symbols. There are also three cases filled with Indian artifacts unearthed in the cave including arrowheads, tomahawk heads, fishing sinks, scrapers, skinning knives, burial beads, peace pipes, building and digging tools. A stone toy called a chunkee, used by young boys to test their skill at shooting, is also displayed. The chunkee was rolled and the Indian boys tried to shoot their arrows through the hole in the stone.

A popular area in the cavern is **Grotto of Wah Wah Taysee**, an Indian term for fire flies. When the lights are dimmed the radium in the cave causes a greenish glow to appear. Indian Caverns is also noted for its large cascade and flowstone.

Indian Caverns is open daily during the summer from 9:00 A.M. to 6:00 P.M. It closes at 4:00 P.M. in May, September and October and is open weekends only November through March 9:00 A.M. to 4:00 P.M. Admission is charged. The cave has wide concrete passageways making it easy for visitors of all ages.

Directions: From I-76, the Pennsylvania Turnpike, traveling west, take the Ft. Littleton exit. Drive north on Route 522, then west on Route 22 three miles past Huntingdon to Lincoln Caverns. Traveling east on I-76, take the Bedford exit and head north on Route 220 then east on Route 22 to Lincoln Caverns. From I-80 take Milesburg Exit 23, south on Route 220, then south on Route 453 to Waterstreet. Make a left on Route 22 and travel east for seven miles to Lincoln Caverns.

For Indian Caverns traveling east or west on I-76 take Route 22 to Waterstreet, then Route 45 to Indian Caverns (it's 11 miles east of Tyrone). From I-00 take Route 220 south to Bald Eagle, then turn left on Route 350 and head south to Indian Caverns in Spruce Creek.

Nemacolin Castle

Gateway to the West

There was a time when people in Brownsville felt that "Pittsburgh might amount to something if it weren't so close to Brownsville." That was in the town's heyday in the early 1800s when the community on the banks of the Monongahela River was the place to reprovision for the trek west. From Maryland, the **Nemacolin Trail**, named for a local Native American leader who charted the route for the English, went over the mountains and ended at the Monongahela River. The National Road, charted in 1806 followed much of the route of the earlier trail. Those not choosing to go overland, bought or built flatboats to continue their journey by river.

The first trading post in Brownsville was opened in 1786 by Jacob Bowman and his partner Colonel Elliot. Bowman, like many of those he supplied, traveled west from Hagerstown, Maryland. He knew the need to resupply in order to continue into the wilderness and he ordered the first wagon load of trade goods that traveled over the mountains. Pulled by four horses, the wagon carried 2,000 pounds of supplies. The round trip from Hagerstown took a month.

In 1789, after Bowman had been in Brownsville three years, he built the oldest portion of **Nemacolin Castle**. His trading post had one room below and one above that served as the Bowman home. Five years after this trading post was established, Colonel Elliot was killed by Indians and Bowman became the sole owner.

As he shipped more and more goods over the mountains, Bowman realized that he would make more money if he manufactured the goods in Brownsville. He started a nail factory and paper mill, and was involved in machine parts manufacturing, boat building and shipping. In 1795, George Washington appointed Bowman as Brownsville's first postmaster. The trading post served as the post office until 1829. In 1812, Bowman and a partner founded the Monongahela Bank and Bowman served as president until 1843.

It was not only his influence in the community that grew, his family also grew to include nine children. In the early 1800s Bowman built a substantial mansion, now the center section of the house, while retaining the original trading post.

Visitors to Nemacolin Castle are amazed to see goods that Jacob Bowman brought with him when he settled in Brownsville. There are chairs, kitchenware and other items that have been in the trading post since 1789. Standing against the wall is his postmaster's desk.

As you tour the second section of the house, added by Jacob Bowman in the early 1800s, you'll see two bedrooms. An original Franklin-style stove is still in place in the fireplace. There is also a collection of vintage clothes displayed on a rotating basis throughout the house.

The second generation added the tower and formal Victorian wing. The Bowmans never called their home a castle, they called it Nemacolin Tower. It was local residents who referred to it as the castle. There was a bedroom in the tower, and an observatory on the top, used by Charles Bowman as his architectural work room, and in later generations as a children's playroom. This was a very sophisticated house for this region and even included a conservatory beneath the Victorian balcony. One of the bedrooms was called the Bishop's room, because when the Bishop visited Brownsville he stayed with the Bowmans. The family donated land for Christ Episcopal Church. The entrance way has pulpit chairs from the church altar.

Four generations of Bowmans lived at Nemacolin Castle and each left their impact on the house. It was used as a home as late as 1959. Currently, Nemacolin Castle is operated by the Brownsville Historical Society. Forty-five minute guided tours include 20 furnished rooms. It is open Easter weekend 1:00 P.M. to 5:00 P.M., then weekends through mid-October 10:00 A.M. to 4:30 P.M. Also, Tuesday through Friday 11:00 A.M. to 4:30 P.M. during June, July and August. **Christmas Candelight tours** are given for ten evenings, beginning the day after Thanksgiving from 4:00 P.M. to 9:00 P.M. Admission is charged.

Directions: From I-76, take the New Stanton exit south on I-70 to Exit 15. Go south on Route 43 (a toll road) to Exit 40 east. Then travel east on Route 40 for two miles to the high-level bridge over Monongahela River at Brownsville. You can see the castle as you cross the bridge. Once across the river, turn right at the first traffic light. Go one block and turn right again on Brashear Street which ends at the castle parking lot.

Ohiopyle State Park and White-water Rafting

First Class, Class Fives

The Delaware, Shawnee and Iroquois who hunted the area called it Ohiopehhle meaning "white frothy water," and the Youghiogheny River certainly is that. The river drops 90 feet in the first two miles and 13 feet per mile for the next five miles as it flows through the Youghiogheny Gorge. There are 22 rapids in $7^1/_2$ miles.

The 1,700 foot gorge is the heart of the 18,719 acre park. The spectacular scenery can be enjoyed by white-water enthusiasts, hikers and bicyclists. It undoubtedly was viewed with more mixed emotions by George Washington, who explored the area in 1754 seeking a water route to Fort Duquesne, where Pittsburgh now stands. When Washington saw the tumbling water of the **Ohiopyle Falls** he abandoned hope for this route.

The 20-foot falls are the main lure for most visitors, and the overlook platforms provide excellent vantage points. This was the first area to be accessible to the public when the state acquired the area for a park in the mid-1960s. A great many visitors who come to view the scenic splendor of the Youghiogheny River return to test their mettle on its swift currents.

The first commercial white-water rafting east of the Mississippi River was on Ohiopyle's Youghiogheny (pronounced Yock-a-GEN-ee) in 1964. Today it's the most recreationally rafted river in the world with four guided raft trip companies. It is estimated that close to 2,000 rafters, canoeists and kayakers use the Yough each day.

White-water rafters in the Youghiogheny gorge tackle 22 rapids in 7¹/₂ miles.

The original guided rafting outfitter on the Youghiogheny is **Wilderness Voyageurs Inc.** Owner Lance Martin took the first trip. (P.O.Box 97, Ohiopyle, PA 15470, 800-272-4141) Their **Lower Yough** trip, with Class III and IV rapids, is their most popular trip but they run other rivers in Maryland, West Virginia and further afield. Rafters 12 years or older can tackle the 7.5 mile Lower Yough adventure which takes between three and five hours. For family groups who don't want to experience quite this much excitement, there is the **Middle Yough**, a quieter section of water ideal for participants from 4 to 84. Here there are only Class I and II rapids, but the scenery is splendid as the river winds around the base of Sugarloaf Mountain, the second highest point in the state. In addition to running guided raft trips, Wilderness Voyageurs rents single or double duckies, two-person rafts, canoes and kayaks. They also offer guided fishing trips, rappelling sessions, overnight trips, float runs and family peddle and paddle trips. Call as early as possible to book these trips which run from April through October, rain or shine.

Before setting out to experience the thrills of white-water rafting do remember that you will get wet, so dress accordingly. Bring along a change of clothes. Also if you want to take pictures, your best bet is to tie one of the disposable underwater cameras around your wrist or belt. Don't bring an expensive camera; it is likely to get wet, if not lost. You will be expected to paddle and you may want to bone up on your left and right, in the excitement of the moment a surprising number of rafters forget this basic concept. The average raft holds three to five rafters, although in high water companies often use rafts that hold eight visitors and a guide.

Mountain Streams is another popular outfitter offering trips on the Lower and Middle Yough as well as West Virginia's Cheat, Gauley, Tygart and Big Sandy Rivers, the Upper Yough in Maryland and the Russell Fork River that runs between Virginia and Kentucky. A unique feature of their rafts are foot stirrups to provide greater stability. Call (800) 245-4090 for white water rafting details, or write P.O. Box 106, Ohiopyle, PA 15470.

White Water Adventurers, Inc. offers guided raft trips on the Ohiopyle and other rivers, call (800) WVA-RAFT for details (P.O. Box 31, Ohiopyle). **Laurel Highlands River Tours** is another Ohiopyle outfitter that offers a wide range of recreational options; call (800)-4-RAFTIN (P.O. Box 107, Ohiopyle) for information.

Hiking and biking are also popular along the Yough, 28-miles of abandoned railroad right-of-way is now part of the "**Rails- to- Trails**" network. The smooth, hard surface of this trail is ideal for bicycling. There is also an off-road mountain bike trail. The 70-mile long **Laurel Highlands Hiking Trail** ends at Ohiopyle, and within the park there are 41 miles of trails. One of the most scenic is **Cucumber Run Trail** that winds along the stream past waterfalls, including the tall, narrow falls from which the trail get its name, **Cucumber Run Ravine** has a wildflower bedecked area particularly scenic in the spring when the rhododendron blooms. Another habitat so floriferous it's listed as a National Natural Landmark is **Ferncliff Peninsula**, a horseshoe bend in the river, where numerous botanical treasures grow along four miles of easy hiking trails.

Ohiopyle State Park also offers wilderness trout fishing, picnicking, camping, hunting and a wide range of winter activities including snowmobiling, tobogganing, cross-country skiing and sledding. Much of Ohiopyle is a wilderness area and there are steep banks, slippery rocks and fast water. Caution and watchfulness should be observed, particularly with young children.

Directions: From I-76, the Pennsylvania Turnpike, take Exit 9, Donegal, and head east on Route 31 to Route 381/711, which takes you to Mill Run and past the entrance to Fallingwater to Ohiopyle State Park.

Old Bedford Village and Fort Bedford Museum

Legacy of 1795

Pioneer living in the southern Allegheny Mountains comes alive at Old Bedford Village. More than 40 centuries-old log structures relocated here serve as the backdrop for cottage industries and oral interpretation as costumed staff members recreate daily life in post-colonial America.

The village of **Bedford**, like Brownsville (see Nemacolin Castle selection) to the west, served as a point of departure for those traveling to Pittsburgh and the frontier wilderness. Men under the command of General John Forbes charted the route from Bedford to Pittsburgh. By 1795, numerous businesses met the needs of nearby settlers and western travelers. Bedford had blacksmiths, innkeepers, attorneys, a doctor, tanner, distillers and brewers, carpenters, sawmill owner and operators, farmers, soldiers and a constable.

The 72-acre village shows how settlers lived and how they made their living. As you stroll the paths of this small community, you're aware of a barrage of sensory impressions. Individual sounds stand out: the banging of the blacksmith hammer, barnyard noises, even the sweep of a straw broom across a wooden floor. Then there are the smells: bread baking, the smell of freshly cut grasses and aromatic flowers. Finally, the sights: the old church steeple, the rustic simplicity of the cabins and the beauty of the handcrafted quilts and pottery.

Old Bedford Village is open daily from the second Sunday in April through the last Sunday in October from 9:00 A.M. to 5:00 P.M. Admission is charged; there is a discount for AAA members. The walkways are not paved so wear comfortable shoes. This is a picturesque spot, so bring your camera. Most visitors spend approximately three hours touring the village. Light meals are served at **Pendergrass Tavern** and the restaurant in the Visitor Center. Twenty different crafts are practiced in the village, and the artisans' work is sold at the gift shop. Theatrical productions are mounted in the village's **Log Opera House**; call the box office for prices and performances, (814) 623-3335. There is also a full schedule of special events including a June crafts festival, bluegrass in July, gospel music in August, pioneer days and Civil War re-enactments in September, pumpkin festivals and mystery evenings in October and an old-fashioned Christmas celebration in December.

After a look at village life, take a walk along the historic streets of the town of Bedford. At the Tourist Information Center, in the **1815 Anderson House** at Pitt and Richard Streets, you can pick up a map with the historic sites pinpointed. From 1815 to 1832, the east room of the Anderson House served as Bedford's first bank, the Allegheny Bank of Pennsylvania. Adjacent to this house is where **Fraser Tavern** once operated; now it's an antique shop and gallery. John Fraser and his wife operated an inn and trading post for travelers and army officers stationed at Fort Raystown, as the Bedford fort was called. Fraser served as guide and interpreter for Colonel Washington during the French and Indian War.

Farther west on Pitt Street is the **1771 Espy House**, which served as President Washington's headquarters in October, 1794 while he reviewed the troops assigned to quell the Whiskey Rebellion. The military focal point of Bedford is **Fort Bedford Museum**, known as Fort Raystown when it was built by Colonel Henry Bouquet's men in three months during the summer of 1758. The British used the fort as a rendezvous point along the Forbes Road as they pursued the objective of capturing Fort Duquesne from the French (see Fort Pitt Museum selection). The village of Bedford grew up around the fort during the decade the fort stood along the banks of the Raystown River.

The fort is not standing, nor is there a full-scale reconstruction of the fort. The museum is in a blockhouse structure that suggests a fortification and there is a scale model of the fort. Displays include Native American artifacts, weapons and uniforms from the country's early military struggles and a wide range of articles from the pioneer period from the large Conestoga wagon to children's toys. The museum is open daily May through October from 10:00 A.M. to 5:00 P.M. In May, September and October it does close on Tuesdays. Admission is charged.

Your walking tour of historic Bedford includes two additional sites along Penn Street. The first is an area called **The Squares**, indicated on a 1761 survey as land set aside by William Penn's family, as property of the town of Bedford. Finally, there is the **1816 Georgian-style Russell House**, built for the first burgess of Bedford, James Russell.

Directions: From I-76, the Pennsylvania Turnpike, take Exit 11, Bedford. Turn right on Business Route 220, you will pass Old Bedford Village on your right. For the community of Bedford, continue for two miles to the second light, turn right onto Pitt Street and continue to the intersection with Richards Street for the Tourist Information Center.

Shawnee State Park and Gravity Hill

Non-indigenous Flora and Fauna

Bedford County has scenic parks such as Shawnee and Blue Knob, but a number of its attractions are non-indigenous. In the latter category you will find Reynoldsdale Fish Hatchery, sheep and buffalo farms, sprawling orchards and picturesque covered bridges.

Within **Shawnee State Park**'s 3,983 acres is the 451-acre Shawnee Lake, where boating, fishing and swimming are popular activities. The lake is stocked with warm water game fish. Anglers can be spotted from sunrise to the last light of day. Twelve miles of trails lead into the state's Ridge and Valley Region. Remnants of the historic **Forbes Trail** can be followed within the park. General Forbes's men blazed this trail in 1759 during the French and Indian War, as the British marched against the French at Fort Duquesne. The park itself is named for the Shawnee Indians who camped in this area in the early 1700s.

There are 265 camp sites in the park. If you prefer less rustic accommodations, the Covered Bridge Inn is just outside the park's boundaries on the Forbes Road. It is a six-room B&B operated by Greg and Martha Lau. Call (814) 733-4093 for information. This comfortable farmhouse along a trout stream sits beside the **1894 Colvin Covered Bridge**. The inn's smokehouse serves as a warming hut where skiers who have enjoyed the park's cross-country trails can sit before a roaring fire and toast both themselves and marshmallows.

Shawnee State Park has 11 miles of snowmobiling trails, toboggan and sledding hills, ice skating and ice fishing.

The inn has arranged packages with nearby Blue Knob Ski Resort, located within **Blue Knob State Park** in northwestern Bedford County. This park has roughly 12 feet of annual snowfall. At the end of hunting season, eight miles of snowmobiling trails are open. Blue Knob is the second highest peak in the state, roughly 67 feet less than Mount Davis in Somerset County. On clear days photographers can get excellent shots from the 3,146-foot crest overlooking the ridges and valleys to the east. The park has 17 miles of hiking trails, horseback riding trails, a guarded swimming pool, picnicking, camping, hunting and fishing.

Colvin Covered Bridge is number seven out of 14 covered bridges on the Bedford County Tourist Promotion Agency's self-guided map. It is also near a farm where buffalo roam. You can see these massive animals grazing in the field as you drive slowly along Route 30 just a half mile from the Covered Bridge Inn.

Cuppett's and Ryot Bridges (#8 & 9) are near a curious spot called **Gravity Hill**. There is a hilly spot on a country road (2.2 miles along State Route 4016) where you put your car in neutral, release the brake, and your car will move uphill instead of down. If you have a jug of water in the car, pour the water onto the road and watch it run uphill. Some curious visitors even bring beach balls and marvel as they roll slowly up the road. It's a phenomenon that interests young and old.

Following the covered bridge map along Route 56 to #10 Dr. **Knisely Bridge** across Dunnings Creek, you will pass the Reynoldsdale Fish Hatchery Visitor Center, open 8:00 A.M. to 3:45 P.M. One intriguing exhibit is called "Gourmet's Delight," as seen through the eyes of a trout. Fish specimen are exhibited in dry tanks, while live specimens swim in outdoor holding tanks. This is one of Pennsylvania's 14 hatcheries. The hatcheries decided how many fish various streams will support. The Reynoldsdale facility raises 400,000 adult trout annually.

Not far from here on State Route 936 is **Monsour Sheep Farm**. They have over a 1,000 head of ewes and lambs grazing the rolling Allegheny foothills. Jack Monsour works the sheep with the help of his award-winning border collies and Great Pyrenees guard dogs who stay in the fields with the lamb night and day. Jack and Kathy Monsour sell their lamb as well as both breeds of dogs. They also train dogs and sell sheepskin slippers, car seat covers, blankets, shawls and other products. Call (814) 623-8243 for additional information.

Another option is to explore Bedford County's orchards. The **Orchard Trail** directs you to six spots in the fruit growing region. The rewards of this drive change with the seasons. From April through June the fields are a visual delight with the delicate-hued blossoms. By late July you can hand-pick fruit and vegetables or purchase them at roadside stands.

Anyone who has ever traveled the turnpike around Bedford has seen the **Jean Bonnet Tavern** from the car window. While exploring this area, take the time to sample lunch or dinner at this historic tavern. Travelers have been stopping here since the 1760s. First documentation of a transaction involving this land was when an agent of William Penn transferred 690 acres to land speculator Hans Ireland. Robert Callender, Indian trader and scout for George Washington, acquired the property in 1762. Callender had the native-stone and chestnut-beamed structure built as a plantation home when he was in his eighties. After his death, in 1779, the house was purchased by Jean Bonnet, who ran it as an inn until 1815.

On October 1780 Jean Bonnet obtained a license, it read: "Petitioner lives at the Fork of roads leading to Fort Pitt and the Glades with everything necessary for keeping Public House . . ." The tavern was on Forbes Trail, the only road connecting the eastern sections of the state with the western territories. The tavern is on the National Register of Historic Places, and lodging is still available. Call (814) 623-2250 for additional information.

Directions: From I-76, the Pennsylvania Turnpike, take Exit 11, Bedford. Turn right on Business Route 220 and continue for two miles to the second light; turn right onto Pitt Street, Route 30 west. For Shawnee State Park take Route 30 into the village of Schellsburg and turn left on Route 96 which will take you to Shawnee Lake; the park can also be reached off Route 30. For the Covered Bridge Inn when you get to Schellsburg, turn left one block past the traffic light at the Colvin Covered Bridge sign. The inn is a half mile on the right. For Gravity Hill at Schellsburg, take Route 96 north toward New Paris for approximately four miles; you will see Fix's Country Way Restaurant on the right. After passing the restaurant, take the first paved road on the left, you will see a small marker reading State Route 4016. When you pass a brown stone house on your right, start clocking your mileage and travel 2.2 miles farther. There will be a white house on the right back off the road, and an old brown barn a little bit farther up on the left and a small white house on the right across from the barn. Between the points of the first white house and the brown barn there is a slight dip in the road—this is gravity point where you can conduct your experiment. (For a printed map call the Bedford County Tourist Promotion agency at (800) 765-3331, they also will send covered bridge and orchard trail maps.) If you continue north on Route 96 and then north on Route 869 you will reach Blue Knob State Park. For the Reynoldsdale Fish Hatchery take Route 96, turn right on Route 56 at Pleasantville and head south. The hatchery will be on your left. For Jean Bonnet Tavern take Route 30 west; the tavern is four miles from historic Bedford at the intersection of Routes 30 and 31.

Somerset Historical Center and Georgian Place

Rural Heritage and Urban Shopping Mecca

Somerset Historical Center is undergoing profound, though slow-moving changes. Ultimately the center will have three farmsteads presenting an in-depth look at farming in the late 18th, mid-19th and early 20th centuries. The Visitor Center identifies the changes in farming and explains why they occurred. Themes that are investigated include: women's work, war, medicine, communication, transportation, technology and entertainment. These concepts are introduced in a orientation video, examined in Visitor Center exhibits and brought to life on the farmsteads.

The Allegheny Mountains served as a barrier to settlement. In the early 18th century while eastern communities expanded, it was primarily fur trappers and hunters who found their way

382

over the mountains by following Forbes Road (see Bushy Run selection) and Braddock's Trail (see Fort Necessity selection).

A few hearty pioneers settled in this part of western Pennsylvania as early as the 1760s. They had to produce all the necessities of life on their rural homesteads. These pioneers produced little that could be sold for profit. The farmstead representing this pioneer era is simple, with hand tools for field work. Crops and livestock reflect the period. True to the time the gardens are fenced and the livestock runs free.

Plans are on the drawing board for a mid-19th-century farmstead to represent the change from hand-power to horsepower. This farmhouse will be bigger and more comfortable and the kitchen moved to a dependency. Agricultural education pursued at land-grant colleges introduced the concepts of crop rotation and fertilization and yield per acre improved. Furnishings will represent the 1850s. The stable and smokehouse currently at the site will be part of this farmstead.

The third planned farmstead will depict the 1920s and reflect changes made by the Industrial Revolution, which introduced steam power and internal combustion engines. By this time roads and railroads made it possible to transport surplus produce to city markets.

The historical center also has a maple sugar camp that is operational from late February through April. Using techniques that extend back to the Native Americans who once hunted this area, the maple trees are tapped. The process of extracting syrup from sap is as labor intensive as it was for the early settlers. It still takes roughly 50 gallons of sap to make one gallon of syrup—the sap is 97 percent water. The water is boiled off, leaving the syrup which is 95 percent sugar.

More antique equipment is found in the **Hoffman Exhibition Hall** and **Agricultural Exhibit Hall**. Hoffman is entered through a turn-of-the-century kitchen, filled with gadgets popular at the time such as a coffer grinder, butter churn and cherry seeder. Unlike kitchens from earlier periods, everything here is bought or bartered, nothing is handmade. Next is a cooper's shop where buckets and barrels were made. There's also a print shop, tin shop and general store, circa 1910 to 1915, with the produce still on the shelves. The floor of the hall is filled with vehicles from a Conestoga wagon to fire engines and mail wagons.

In **Fluck Hall** there is a wide array of agricultural machinery: steam engines, threshing machines, harvesters, tractors, corn huskers, reapers, binders, cultivators and more. Visitors interested in genealogical research can use the center's research library.

The Somerset Historical Center is open Tuesday through Saturday 9:00 A.M. to 5:00 P.M. and Sunday NOON to 5:00 P.M. It is closed Mondays and holidays except Memorial Day, July 4th and Labor Day. Each year the center hosts **Mountain Craft Days** on the Friday, Saturday and Sunday following Labor Day. It is the big event of the year with over 125 craftspersons demonstrating and selling their work.

Heading from the turnpike to Somerset Historical Center you will pass **The Inn at Georgian Place**, a 22-room Georgian mansion built in 1915 for D.B. Zimmerman, a local coal and cattle baron. Zimmerman was born in Somerset County but left as a teenager to work on a cattle ranch in North Dakota. He eventually acquired the largest cattle ranch in the country, selling entire train loads of cattle. When he returned to this part of Pennsylvania he became the largest independent coal operator in the area. His success is reflected in his opulent mansion, which utilized 65 sets of architectural drawings, took ten years to build and cost $300,000. It is startling to discover that the house and 45 acres were sold in a sheriff's sale in 1949 for $30,500. In 1989 the house was acquired by RSB Corporation who restored it as an elegant bed and breakfast inn. The inn overlooks Lake Somerset. Tours of the inn are given at 1:30 P.M. each day at a nominal cost. The public is also welcome to partake of afternoon tea between 1:00 P.M. and 4:00 P.M., a delightful lunch menu served in a gracious setting. Call (814) 443-1043 for reservations and information.

Down a flight of stairs from the inn is **Georgian Place Outlet Center** with 60 stores offering discounts of 30 to 70 percent off regular retail prices. Stores include Bass, Boston Traders, Casual Corner, Guess, Izod, Cape Isle Knitters, Brooks Brothers, Nine West, Polo, S&K Menswear, Stone Mountain Handbags, Westport, Swank, Van Heusen and many more. Stores are open Monday through Saturday from 10:00 A.M. to 8:00 P.M. and Sunday 11:00 A.M. to 6:00 P.M. Closed Easter, Thanksgiving and Christmas Day.

If you continue on Route 985 a half mile past the intersection with Route 30 you will reach the **Mountain Playhouse** and **Green Gables Restaurant**. The theater season runs from mid-May to mid-October; call (814) 629-9201 for current schedule and prices. The theater, an 1805 log gristmill built in 1805, was moved to this site in 1939. Plays have been presented here for 54 years except during World War II, making it one of the country's oldest summer stock companies.

The restaurant's wooden beams and stone floors blend with the rustic setting. Each room offers a bucolic view of the mountain stream that feeds Stoughton Lake. There are often ducks and geese on the mountain lake. The restaurant is open from mid-March through January 1; call (814) 629-9411 for lunch or dinner reservations.

Directions: From I-76, the Pennsylvania Turnpike, take Somerset Exit 10 and follow Route 601 north. At the intersection with Route 985 veer left onto Route 985 and the Somerset Historical Center will be on your left in approximately 500 feet.

Swigart Museum

Country's Oldest Automobile Museum

Henry Ford organized his motor company in 1903, so the automotive industry was still young in 1920 when the late W. Emmert Swigart began collecting cars. Although Ford himself said, "the past is more or less bunk," Swigart disagreed and made it his advocational quest to preserve cars by manufacturers that appeared only briefly on America's industrial horizon.

In the earliest days of automobile production, small companies turned out their own models. Between 1923 and 1927 the smaller companies lost the competitive war and the total number of companies was reduced from 108 to 44. Cars made by the defunct companies were called orphans. By 1930 three companies virtually controlled the market, nine out of ten cars were made by Ford, Chrysler and General Motors.

Swigart Museum's collection of orphans is quite impressive, there are models here unknown to all but the most enthusiastic automotive buff. Who else would know about the 1920 Carroll? The one in the museum is the only Carroll in existence, it was kept by Carroll, its Ohio manufacturer. He shipped the other 50 he built to California and when the train was side-tracked due to inclement weather the cars froze and the engines broke.

There are other rare orphans including a 1906 Firestone Columbus with buggy-type wheels that was called a Highwheeler; a 1907 one-cylinder, two-cycle engine Jewel; a 1909 Mora designed as the French Renault; and the 1914 Grant, one of eight cars named after U.S. presidents.

Between 40 and 48 automobiles are exhibited at a time from the approximately 200 car collection; among the cars that you are likely to see is the striking 1930 Duesenberg Model J with a style all its own. This is the only existing 1930 model built with a Murphy body, there were two but the other was destroyed by fire. Another car sure to be on view is the 1937 Cord Phaeton, with hide-away headlights and front wheel drive. It was years ahead of its time.

There are stories connected with many of the cars, like the 1916 Scripps-Booth Town Car. Current museum owner William E. Swigart, Jr. spoke with builder Scripps Booth decades after

The Swigart Museum specializes in rare orphan cars made by early manufacturers who by 1930 had lost out in the competition with Ford, Chrysler and General Motors.

the car was crafted and he couldn't remember ever building the car for tennis star Eleanor Sears. He visited the Swigart Museum and when he saw the Mercedes-style V radiator, the small Model T size and the elegant quality of the Rolls Royce with imported hand-carved ivory door handles he remembered it well.

The museum has the country's most diverse collection of one- and two-cylinder cars. It also has the world's largest display of name plates—the crests and emblems found on the front of automobiles. A comprehensive array of license plates extends from the very first year they were issued to the present.

Automobiles are also one of the focuses of the museum's antique toy collection along with trains and dolls. The display cases are filled with a wide array of automobile memorabilia. The walls are hung with horns, lights, emblems, tools and other displays. There are scrapbooks with postcards and pictures of a wide range of automobiles available to the public over the years.

The Swigart Museum is open daily June, July and August and weekends only in May, September and October. Hours are 9:00 A.M. to 5:00 P.M. Admission is charged.

Directions: From I-76 the Pennsylvania Turnpike take the Fort Littleton Exit 13 and head north to Mount Union on Route 522 then take Route 22 to the Huntingdon area. The Swigart Museum is on the right four miles east of Huntingdon.

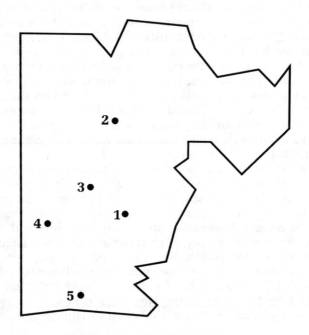

PITTSBURGH REGION

1. *Pittsburgh*
   Andy Warhol Museum
   Carnegie Museums of Art and
     Natural History
   Carnegie Science Center and
     USS *Requin*
   Clayton
   Duquesne and Monongahela
     Inclines
   Fort Pitt Museum
   Hartwood Acres
   Kennywood and Sandcastle
   Nationality Classrooms at the
     University of Pittsburgh
   Phipps Conservatory
   Pittsburgh Children's
     Museum
   Pittsburgh Zoo and National
     Aviary in Pittsburgh
   Station Square
   Strip District and Senator
     John Heinz Pittsburgh
     Regional History Center
   Tour Ed Mine

2. *Portersville*
   McConnell's Mill State Park
     and Moraine State Park

3. *Ambridge*
   Old Economy Village

4. *Franklin Springs*
   Wildflower Preserve Raccoon
     State Park

5. *Washington*
   David Bradford House and
     Century Inn
   LeMoyne House and Duncan
     & Miller Glass Museum
   Pennsylvania Trolley
     Museum and Meadowcroft
     Village

Pittsburgh
Region

Seen from atop the city's two inclined planes or exiting the Fort Pitt Tunnel, Pittsburgh's dazzling skyline is a dramatic surprise. But the skyscrapers and high-tech industries fortunately have not robbed the city of its traditional ethnic spirit and friendliness. To grasp the complex web of roughly 81 distinct ethnic communities that compose this polyglot city, visit the Nationality Rooms at the University of Pittsburgh's Cathedral of Learning.

Titans of industry who made their fortunes in Pittsburgh made contributions that enrich the city: Andrew Carnegie's Carnegie Institute includes the Museums of Art and Natural History, the Science Center and the new Andy Warhol Museum. Henry Frick's house, Clayton, is now a museum. Adjacent to it is the Frick Art Museum. Henry Phipps gave Pittsburgh its glass-domed Victorian Conservatory. On a different order, the legacy of George Rapp and his Harmonist sect endures at Old Economy Village.

Recreational opportunities abound from the beauty of the Wildflower Preserve at Raccoon State Park to the rocky gorge cut through McConnell's Mill State Park. Kennywood, Sandcastle, the Pittsburgh Zoo and the Pittsburgh Children's Museum beckon families with endless delights.

Andy Warhol Museum

A Legend in His Own Mind

Few viewers are neutral when it comes to Andy Warhol: they either love his work or loathe it. For some, his most successful creative work was himself and for others Warhol was one of the 20th century's defining figures. The place to form your own opinion is **The Andy Warhol Museum**, the most comprehensive single-artist museum in the country.

Located in an industrial building in the heart of Pittsburgh just a few miles from Warhol's boyhood home, the museum's six floors of gallery space delve into the man and his art. More than 500 works of art and countless mementoes saved by Warhol during his life reveal the private and public figure. Warhol was a painter, sculptor, graphic artist, filmmaker, music producer, author, publisher and media celebrity.

The ground floor explores Warhol's heritage. His parents, Andrej and Julia Warhola, immigrated to America from the Carpathian Mountains—the area that is now part of Slovakia. Andy was born in 1928. He was a frail youngster who spent much of his time alone. He grew up on Dawson Street in Oakland. His mother recognized his artistic leanings, although when Warhol was asked when he started painting, he answered, "When I was nine years old I had St. Vitus Dance. I painted a picture of Hedy Lamarr from a Maybelline ad. It was no good, and I threw it away. I realized I couldn't paint." (This is just one of many snippets pinned within the cases of memorabilia on each floor of the gallery.) Andy took art classes at Carnegie Institute beginning in the fourth grade and later at Schenley High School. Then he studied painting and design at Carnegie Institute of Technology (now Carnegie Mellon University). He graduated in 1949 and went to New York with fellow student Philip Pearlstein to further their art careers.

From the ground floor, the museum directs visitors to the seventh floor which focuses on three members of Warhol's extended family: Diana Vreeland, Frederick W. Hughes and Halston. The theme on this level is "**Fame, Fortune and Fashion.**" *Harper's Bazaar* and *Vogue* editor Diana Vreeland was Warhol's ideal, representing both the creative and the celebrated. Vreeland was fashion editor of *Harper's Bazaar* from 1936 to 1962, and an editor at *Vogue* from 1963 to 1971. Warhol's business manager Frederick Hughes represents the fortune phase of the theme. Warhol called Hughes "his beautiful amanuensis" and named him executor of his estate. Designer Halston was a close associate of Warhol's throughout his artistic career. This floor also is used for temporary exhibitions.

Moving to the sixth floor, visitors begin to get a chronological glimpse of Warhol's work. The themes here are "**Success: 1950s**" and "**Early Pop.**" During his first years in New York, Warhol achieved success in the commercial art field. His drawings of shoes for I. Miller created a sensation in the industry. Displayed in galleries on this floor are his student work, personal drawings, sketch books and a series of silkscreen portraits of movie stars. Stars given the Warhol treatment and exhibited here include Marilyn Monroe, Natalie Wood, Elvis, Troy Donahue, Tuesday Weld and others. His famous pop paintings of Campbell's soup cans and Coca-Cola bottles also hang here. The sixth floor also has a small gallery where Warhol's silent films are shown.

Don't miss the postcards in the display cases. Warhol's mother had joined him in New York three years after he left Pittsburgh (his father had died) and was a tremendous influence on his work, in effect serving as his assistant. Warhol sent his mother postcards when he traveled around the world in 1956. One has to wonder at the brevity of the messages. They read: "Hi, Im (sic) alright im in Rome now its real nice here. Bye" Each has the same message with the substitution of Bangkok or Japan or elsewhere.

"**The Silver Factory, The 1960s**" is the theme of the fifth floor galleries. In 1963, Warhol moved from the Hook & Ladder, Company 13 building on the Upper East Side to a new studio at 231 East 47th Street. Fellow artist Billy Name painted the entire place with silver metallic paint and it became known as "The Silver Factory." By this time Warhol had branched out into filmmaking and was a rock music entrepreneur producing The Velvet Underground. He also collaborated on a modern dance called *Rainforest* with Merce Cunningham. The silver theme is captured in the gallery where the mylar *Silver Clouds* float. This floor also has the *Cow* wallpaper and the *Rain Machine*, made for the Osaka Expo in 1970. A key series in Warhol's career were his *Disaster* paintings also exhibited here.

The fourth floor focuses on "**Enterprise, The 1970s**." After Warhol was shot and seriously wounded in 1968 by a young actress, Valerie Solanas, who was reputedly rejected for a role in one of Warhol's films, the art world assumed that he had given up painting and filmmaking to devote himself to socializing and publishing *Interview* magazine. Confounding expectations as usual, Warhol in fact created some of his largest and most ambitious paintings during the 1970s. They include portraits of Chinese leader Mao, a series of *Skull* paintings and works based on religious images. The last works Warhol did, based on Leonardo da Vinci's *The Last Supper*, were exhibited in Milan just before he died in February 1987.

On the third floor are covers from *Interview* magazine that Warhol began publishing in 1969. In his magazine he combined all his loves: fashion, art, high society, film and modeling. The **Archives Study Center** on this floor has stacks of cardboard boxes that Warhol assembled (the museum has 608 of these "time capsules"). His "time capsules" are filled with a wide variety of material ranging from items he collected while traveling to clothing, correspondence and eclectic odds and ends. A changing display from these boxes is exhibited in the Archives Study Center.

The last exhibit space is on the second floor where the artist's late "abstract" paintings are showcased. Here are works Warhol did in collaboration with Jean-Michel Basquiat and Francesco Clemente. There are also paintings and drawings based on advertisements. The first director of the museum, Tom Armstrong, said, "Interestingly, these paintings based on advertisements return in an almost mystical way to the work of the late '50s. To some extent, Andy's work is a closed circle."

The museum has an attractive coffee shop on the lower level. At the bottom of the staircase is a vintage photo booth such as you might have found in a arcade in the 1960s. Here, you can take multiple pictures of yourself in the same format as Warhol's early portraits. The lower level also has an education department which conducts programs for adults and children. Special symposia, lectures and gallery talks are scheduled; call (412) 237-8300 for details. On the ground floor there is a museum shop with prints, T-shirts, posters, books, videos and other Warhol-related merchandise and a theater space where Warhol's films are screened.

The Andy Warhol Museum is one of the museums of Carnegie Institute and is a collaborative project with Dia Center for the Arts and The Andy Warhol Foundation for the Visual Arts, Inc. The museum, on Pittsburgh's north side, is open Wednesday and Sunday from 11:00 A.M. to 6:00 P.M. On Thursday, Friday and Saturday, hours are 11:00 A.M. to 8:00 P.M.

Directions: From I-76, the Pennsylvania Turnpike, take Exit 6, the Parkway West, I-376 E inbound. Follow signs for Three Rivers Stadium. Exit onto Reedsdale Street. Turn left onto Allegheny Avenue, which becomes North Shore Drive, which then becomes Stadium Drive East. Take the first right onto West General Robinson, go three blocks and turn left onto Sandusky Street. Parking lots are located under the expressway on the left and right. If you are traveling from the south, take I-279 South inbound and follow signs to Three Rivers Stadium and Fort Duquesne Bridge. Exit Reedsdale Street and follow directions above. If you are traveling from the north, take I-279 north inbound to East Street, Route 28 exit. Turn right onto East North Avenue. Continue to Federal Street and turn left. Turn right onto North Commons (one way circle) which becomes West Commons and South Commons. Turn right onto Federal Street, left onto General Robinson and then left onto Sandusky Street.

The Carnegie Museums of Art and Natural History

What's in a Name?

Carnegie libraries are found in far flung towns across America and Great Britain, testaments to the philanthropic vision of Andrew Carnegie. But it is in Pittsburgh, that the Carnegie name graces a score of cultural offerings dedicated to the understanding and enjoyment of literature, art, science and music. Carnegie called these the "noble quartet," and The Carnegie makes these disciplines available to all through the Library of Pittsburgh, Music Hall, Museum of Natural History, Museum of Art, The Carnegie Science Center (see selection) and the new Andy Warhol Museum (see selection).

In 1848, 13-year-old Andrew Carnegie moved with his family from Scotland to Allegheny City (which later became part of Pittsburgh). Carnegie immediately went to work in a cotton factory earning 20 cents a day, but from this modest beginning he quickly worked his way up to jobs with better pay. In 1853 he began a 12-year stint with the Pennsylvania Railroad where he gained ever more responsible positions.

Carnegie gained an appreciation of the importance of iron and steel while working with the railroad. In 1873, he acquired the Edgar Thompson Steel Mill and began concentrating on steel. In 15 years Carnegie's steel companies were served by tributary coal and iron fields, a 425-mile railroad system and a line of steamships. In 1901, Carnegie's companies were sold to J.P. Morgan and incorporated as the U.S. Steel Corporation.

In 1889 Carnegie's *Gospel of Wealth* was published, setting forth his idea that surplus wealth should be used for the public benefit. Carnegie's actions spoke as loud as his words and Pittsburgh was only one of the beneficiaries of his largesse. Other major trusts include the Carnegie Corporation of New York, the Carnegie Institution of Washington, D.C., The Carnegie Hero Fund, the Carnegie Foundation for the Advancement of Teaching and the Carnegie Endowment for International Peace.

Carnegie's forward thrust was exemplified in the art museum he founded. Museums in Carnegie's day featured Old Masters, but Carnegie said, "The field for which the gallery is designed begins with the year 1896," and he encouraged collecting the "Old Masters of Tomorrow." Many art historians consider **The Carnegie Museum of Art**, the country's first modern art museum.

The collection includes an impressive array of Impressionist and Post-Impressionist paintings by Monet, Matisse, Bonnard, Degas, van Gogh, Cassatt and others. Paintings are exhibited in galleries in combination with sculpture and decorative arts creating a felicitous blending of the arts. The marble **Hall of Sculpture** continues to awe visitors, as it has for almost a century. The hall is designed like the enclosed interior of the Temple of Athena on the Acropolis in Athens using Pentelic marble, from the same quarries used to build the Parthenon. Ancient Greece is also recalled in the **Hall of Architecture**, which contains the largest collection of plaster casts in the country, and one of the three largest such collections in the world. A history of world architecture is revealed in these casts of architectural masterpieces from ancient Egypt, Greece, Rome and from three periods of European design: Romanesque, Gothic and Renaissance. The Hall of Architecture is based on the Mausoleum at Halicarnassus, one of the seven wonders of the ancient world.

The Carnegie Museum of Natural History rivals the Smithsonian Institution with its extensive dinosaur collection. The museum has bones from 36 different species. In **Dinosaur Hall** are full skeletons of 11 species including *Diplodocus carnegii*, one of the very first dinosaurs ever mounted, as well as a *Tyrannosaurus rex*, the most renowned of all dinosaurs. The skeletons are displayed in chronological order with the oldest at the entrance. Most of the bones displayed are real, while the majority of skulls are casts. Specimens were found predominantly in the western United States.

Another crowd pleaser is the **Hillman Hall of Minerals and Gems** with a staggering array of mineral specimens. Some of the specimens are the finest examples of their kind exhibited anywhere in the world. This is certainly true of the rhodochrosite from Colorado and the hemimorphite after calcite from Missouri. The exhibit includes displays of fluorescent minerals, microminerals, Pennsylvania mineralogy and the art of lapidary.

Soapstone is exhibited in the **Polar World: Wyckoff Hall of Arctic Life exhibit**, though not in its natural state. It is shown as part of the Inuit exhibit because native carvers excel at carving this pliable stone. The cultural history of the Inuit is traced over a 4,500 year period. By 1996, this cultural history will be expanded with the addition of the **Alcoa Foundation Hall of Native Americans**, which will explore Native American relationships with the natural world. On display will be more than 2,000 artifacts from the museum's Plains, Southwest, Northwest Coast, Northeast and Urban collection. Most of these objects have never been exhibited before. Another must see exhibit is **The Walton Hall of Ancient Egypt** which uses dioramas, videos, interactive computer programs and artifacts to reveal details of daily life in ancient Egyptian society.

There is no way to see all of the museum's life sciences collections which include 11 million specimens of insects, a world-class bird specimen collection with more than 10,000 eggs, a butterfly collection that includes 95 percent of all known species and 92,000 mammal specimens. Only a small portion of these massive collections are displayed.

The acoustically perfect **Carnegie Music Hall** was the last hall of its kind built in the United States. Carnegie's self-described "dream" opened in 1895 to give Pittsburghers an elegant ceremonial hall in which to enjoy symphonic music and classical entertainment.

The gilt and marble Music Hall foyer evokes the Edwardian Age. Marble from six nations is used in the foyer, including red Verona and Siena from Italy, green Connemara from Ireland and white marble from England. Twenty-four ceiling-high pillars of green "vert tinos" stone surround the foyer. The ceiling is enhanced with a gold Baroque design and the walls are of French eschallion with fine patterned inlays. All in all it is a breathtaking chamber.

There are approximately 2,500 Carnegie libraries worldwide. The grandest is the **Main Library of the Carnegie Library of Pittsburgh**, the mother of the city's system of 19 libraries. Andrew Carnegie's hometown library has 4.5 million books, periodicals and audiovisual items. In 1989 a major restoration of the lobby and main reading rooms returned the Main Library to its original appearance and the rose-colored marble again gleams. Ornamentation on the staircase walls and ceiling was regilded.

The library is a public trust, while the other four components are a private corporation known collectively as Carnegie Institute. All of the components, excepting The Carnegie Science Center and The Andy Warhol Museum (see selections), are located in adjoining buildings in the heart of Oakland, Pittsburgh's university area. They are directly across the street from the Cathedral of Learning (see selection). The hours of The Carnegie are 10:00 A.M. to 5:00 P.M. Tuesday through Saturday, Sunday 1:00 P.M. to 5:00 P.M., and Mondays in July and August from 10:00 A.M. to 5:00 P.M. They are closed on Mondays from September through June and major holidays. There is a suggested contribution, not a fixed admission price. Be sure to stop at the well-stocked museum shops and you can lunch at The Museum Cafe or the cafeteria.

Directions: From the Pennsylvania Turnpike, I-76, take Exit 6, Monroeville exit, to I-376. Take I-376 through the Squirrel Hill Tunnels to the Oakland exit, Bates Street. Follow Bates Street to Bouquet Street. Turn left and follow Bouquet Street to Forbes Avenue. Turn right and follow Forbes Avenue to South Craig Street. At South Craig Street, turn right to enter The Carnegie's parking garage. From I-79, take I-279 into downtown Pittsburgh. Follow signs for I-376 East (Monroeville). From I-376 take Exit 5, Forbes Avenue/Oakland, and follow Forbes Avenue to South Craig Street, then turn right to enter parking garage.

The Carnegie Science Center and USS *Requin*

Participatory Fun House

Plan to spend the entire day at **The Carnegie Science Center** since there are four distinct points of interest and all are absorbing, entertaining and enlightening. There are science center exhibits, an OMNIMAX theater, a planetarium and a decommissioned World War II submarine.

The center sprawls across five floors. The ground floor area has a cafe and access to the submarine and four other exhibit floors. On the first floor at the entrance to the OMNIMAX is aquabatics, a popular interactive water sculpture. Cylinders of water suspended from the ceiling generate vertical streams that hit a clear panel on the second floor, then flow farther down to the first floor. Simultaneously, water shoots up from the basin on the first floor with enough force to balance colorful balls on the tip of the water spout. An explanation board outlines Bernoulli's Theorem which accounts for the balls being held aloft.

On the river side of the center's first floor is **Science Way**, a fun house area where everyday objects are altered and used to illustrate scientific principles. A red wagon with square wheels demonstrates how to get a smooth ride on a bumpy surface. Psychedelic black wavy patterns on a cabinet door teach lessons about sound waves, while a marble spiraling down a drain reveals the laws of gravity. Also on this floor there's a small gallery with short-term exhibits leading to the health science theater where live programs and videos explore numerous science topics.

The second floor has major traveling exhibits. **The Great Miniature Railroad & Village**, a Pittsburgh tradition since 1954 when Charles Bowdish created the first Christmastown Railroad, appears from just before Thanksgiving to late April. Originally the railroad was only displayed during the holiday season but it proved so popular that it now runs for almost five months to accommodate more than 125,000 annual visitors.

The 83 by 30-foot "O" gauge miniature railroad presents an amazingly complete recreation of western Pennsylvania in the 1920s. Technology was ushering in the industrial age during this decade, a turning point for this area and the country. One section is the world's most complete miniature depiction of a steel mill. The replica of the Sharon Steel Mill actually has smoke billowing out of the mill's four smokestacks. There's also a nearby coal mining operation and a stone quarry. Some elements of the layout are more light-hearted, including a number of the more than 93 animations. A circus parade winds through the city streets, where numerous historical landmarks have been recreated. A ferris wheel reflects the fact that this amusement park staple was the brainchild of Pittsburgh-based engineer George Washington Gale Ferris. His invention debuted at the 1893 World's Columbian Exposition in Chicago. Each year new elements are added to the layout, which moves from night to day at least once while you explore its wonders. Eight Lionel trains cover the more than 1,203 feet of track.

The seasonal Great Miniature Railroad and Village at The Carnegie Science Center was called "the best in the country" by Model Railroading *magazine.*   Photo by Clyde Hare

Young visitors have two special areas of interest on the third floor. For children three-to-six there is **Ports of Discovery** where water games teach science lessons. There is room to crawl, climb, build and give rein to a variety of artistic expressions. Next to this is Science Pier for children 7-to-13 years old. Here the interactive water table teaches more complex concepts like how canal locks operate. There is also a live beehive, lasers, computers, a microscope and an assortment of live specimens that only kids could enjoy like Madagascar hissing cockroaches. At the entrance to these children-oriented discovery areas is a sea life aquarium, a completely self-sustaining ecosystem, with a fore reef, back reef and lagoon section.

Exhibits on the top floor include an intriguing look at eating, the human body, and **The Works** area—five exhibits on robotics, cryogenics, lasers, molten metal and artificial lighting.

All of the above can be explored with an exhibits ticket; to see any of the additional offerings requires a combination ticket. Planetarium tickets are only sold in combination with the general exhibit admission. **The Henry Buhl, Jr. Planetarium** is a 150-seat audiovisual environmental theater that presents a series of interdisciplinary programs throughout the year. As you wait in line the frequently asked question is "Where is the best seat?" Most visitors prefer center back for the best view and it is certainly easier on the neck. There is no bad seat and all the seats are wired for programs that invite audience response. The planetarium also simulates realistic three-dimensional flight through space in some of its programs.

Offering a different, but equally exciting visual experience is the **OMNIMAX** theater, for which separate admission tickets can be purchased or they can be combined with the exhibits and the planetarium at a reduced rate. This is one of roughly a dozen OMNIMAX theaters in the country showing films over ten times the size of regular films. These oversize movies are projected with a 180-degree lens that fills the theater's vast dome as well as the viewer's peripheral vision. This creates an all-encompassing film experience that lets you feel the sense of plummeting off a cliff, floating weightlessly in outer space, skimming over fields in a low-flying plane, shooting the whitewater rapids or other wondrous feats. The sense of sound is also so intense it seems to fill the air. Again the best seats are center back.

When you arrive at The Carnegie Science Center check the schedule for the OMNIMAX and planetarium (neither are recommended for children under four). Sometimes the shows sell out. On busy summer weekends it is advisable to plan ahead and purchase tickets through Ticketmaster; call (412) 323-1919.

There is a separate admission to visit the USS *Requin*, docked in the Ohio River at the foot of The Carnegie Science Center. Guided submarine tours are given every half hour throughout the day. This 312-foot long, 27-foot wide Trench class submarine was built in Portsmouth, New Hampshire at a cost of $4 million and launched in 1945. The *Requin*, which means sand shark in French, carried a crew of 81. She joined the Pacific Fleet and reached Pearl Harbor in July, 1945. She was there when World War II ended. The following year the *Requin* was converted to a radar picket submarine. In 1948 the submarine was reclassified and joined the Sixth Fleet. Her last conversion came in 1959 when the *Requin* became a Fleet Snorkel submarine. She was decommissioned in 1968, although she served as a Naval Reserve Training ship until struck from the Navy list in 1971.

Full physical mobility is required for the roughly hour long tour. If you are claustrophobic you may want to skip the confined quarters. You enter the forward torpedo room via a flight of steep stairs. It seems impossible that 18 enlisted men slept in the narrow, tight "racks" or beds stacked over, under and around the six loaded torpedo tubes and 8-to-12 spare torpedoes. There hardly seems room for an average-size individual to squeeze into some of the racks. It's also amazing to contemplate the crew loading the 3,200-pound torpedoes by hand. While in this compartment the guide points out the single flare gun. There's one both port and starboard so that if the sub ever went down on its side, one of the flares would be pointing up. Whether the gun could fire a flare that would travel the distance from the bottom to the top was fortunately something the *Requin* crew never had to test.

Essentially all the activity aboard the sub was on a single level with the exception of the sonar and pump room, neither of which are included on the tour. The tour next passes the officers' shower, which was not used often since water was a scarce and valuable commodity aboard subs. At best the men showered once a week but it could extend as long as two or three months between showers. The forward battery is the officers' quarters where ten officers ate, slept and planned. You'll see several state-rooms, an office, wardroom and pantry.

Next you'll see the control room with equipment necessary for steering, navigating and submerging the submarine. Although the sonar room is not accessible, a screen shows car movements on the Fort Pitt Bridge. Most visitors think the red lights glowing in the control room indicated battle stations or danger but instead they were used to preserve the seamen's night vision. The Navy has now switched to blue lights, because the red lights had a negative impact on the men's disposition. They tended to make the men angry and this was not advisable for crews like the *Requin* who spent one to three months in these tight quarters (nuclear submarines now stay at sea for up to six months).

Next is the crew's mess and quarters. The men ate their four meals a day in three shifts, which left little time to enjoy the checkers and chess games laminated on the surface of the four tables. It was said that the crew literally ate their way into having living space. Canned goods and dried stores were kept in the showers and any available space. The crew's sleeping quarters had racks, also called coffins or bed pans, for 32 men. In all there were racks for two thirds of the crew, there was always one shift on duty and so beds were shared. No linen was used, the men used their shirt as a pillow, then as a rag to wipe off the vinyl bed. It's hard to imagine what it must have been like, especially when you learn the temperature ranged from 80-to-125 degrees. The only private space the enlisted men could call their own was a small cubbyhole in the submarine's side. Additionally, the 70 crewmen only had three toilets, and those were decidedly temperamental.

The tour continues through another hatch to the forward engine room with its massive diesel engines and electrical generators. Next comes the smaller compartment, the maneuvering room. Here controls distribute electrical power throughout the submarine. The last compartment is the after torpedo room, or stern room. Once a torpedo chamber, as well as sleeping space for 22 men, this area became a radar compartment when the

Requin went through its first conversion in 1946. Most visitors thankfully gulp the fresh air as they exit the submarine, relieved that their stay aboard the *Requin* was a brief, albeit fascinating, one.

The Carnegie Science Center is open Monday through Thursday 10:00 A.M. to 5:00 P.M. On Friday, Saturday and Sunday it remains open until 6:00 P.M. During the summer, hours are daily 10:00 A.M. to 6:00 P.M. OMNIMAX shows are given Friday and Saturday evenings at 7:00 P.M. and 8:00 P.M. A cafe and gift shop are open during the same hours. The cafeteria offerings are reasonably priced and there are vending machines and tables available on the third floor as well. A per car parking rate is also charged. For additional information call (412) 237-3400.

Directions: From I-76, the Pennsylvania Turnpike, take Exit 6, the Parkway East, Route 376/22, across the Fort Duquesne Bridge past the Three Rivers Stadium to Allegheny Avenue and make a left. Allegheny Avenue will take you to The Carnegie Science Center parking lot.

Clayton

Pittsburgh's Best Preserved House Museum

Henry Clay Frick, one of Pittsburgh's most influential industrial giants, lived at **Clayton** from 1882 to 1905. His exquisite 19th century mansion, along what was called Millionaires' Row in Point Breeze, is the city's best preserved example of the luxurious life styles of its legendary tycoons. It was built in 1866 by Benjamin Vandervort who called his two-story Italianate 11-room house "Homewood". The Fricks purchased it from his widow in 1881.

It took a six million dollar restoration to return the house to its appearance during the Frick years. The project was undertaken in 1984 at the death of 96-year old Helen Clay Frick, the daughter of Adelaide and Henry Clay Frick. Helen moved back into her girlhood home in 1981 and envisioned Clayton as a house museum. Her will provided the funds to carry out her dream. Had her parents remained in this Pittsburgh house instead of moving to New York in 1905, Clayton would probably have been greatly expanded. The Fricks built a 104-room Georgian summer home in Prides Crossing, Massachusetts. Frick died in 1919 and his wife in 1931. The Fricks are buried in Pittsburgh's Homewood Cemetery on a knoll surrounded by a yew hedge.

Henry Clay Frick is remembered in Pittsburgh as the man who broke the bloody Homestead steel strike. His determination stifled the formation of a union for more than 40 years. Frick was shot and stabbed by anarchist Alexander Berman during the strike because of his resistance to organized labor. After Frick's coke company was consolidated with Carnegie's steel company, the two men were for a time partners. Frick was acting for Carnegie when he stood against the strikers.

Although Clayton's architecture is considered Victorian, it does mix other styles, perhaps because the Fricks commissioned four remodelings while living here. When Frick first purchased the house he had the interior completely remodeled. Then ten years later the house was enlarged in a French chateau style. You enter Clayton through an elaborate porte-cochere, a covered carriage entrance. It's the only visible reminder of the original house. Once inside you find yourself in a small hallway with rich-looking embossed walls and ceiling coverings. On one side of the corridor is the parlor and dining room. On the other side is the reception and breakfast room. A kitchen, butler's pantry and scullery is at the rear on the first floor. Family journals, accounts and photographs help fill the room with authentic furnishings and bibelots. Great effort was expended to preserve existing furnishings and fixtures. Indeed, 95 percent of its furnishings, textiles, china and crystal are original. The grand scarlet curtains in the music room are only slightly frayed around the edges. The dining room still has its original Honduran mahogany beamed ceiling, built-in china cabinets and matching sideboards. It also has P.A.J. Dagnan-Bouveret's 1899 wall-size (11 by 6 feet) painting *Consoler of the Suffering of the Madonna and Child*. On July 4, 1902 President Theodore Roosevelt joined 19 other influential males for dinner at Clayton.

Henry Clay Frick's bedroom and bath chamber is on the second floor connected by a dressing room with his wife's bedroom. The original bird's-eye maple paneling can still be seen in Henry's bedroom but it is Adelaide's that is perhaps least changed. Combs and brushes still rest on the bureau in her rose-and-silver bedroom giving the impression that she could return momentarily. Her large carved bed with brilliant scarlet pillows is the room's focal point. Family portraits are scattered around the room.

Clayton was on the cutting edge of new technology. The house had telephones and flush toilets as soon as they became available. The silver-plated lighting fixtures installed in the 1880s were fitted for both gas and electricity. By 1902, electricity was a more reliable source of power and the fixtures were no longer dual.

Also on the second floor is a guest bedroom and the peach-colored children's room last used by Helen. A favorite with visitors is the sitting room at the rear of the second floor. It's a room book lovers appreciate with cubbyholes, deeply cushioned chairs and an abundance of books and art, including a charming landscape by Monet and another by Childe Hassam.

Docents do not simply lead tours of the house, they encourage visitors to become part of an earlier era. Docents share the family history as well as information on Victorian housewifery, decorative and fine arts and special interests such as flower arranging and architecture.

Also on the six-acre grounds is the **Frick Art Museum** open without charge. The Greenhouse is once again filled with flowers. Vintage automobiles, 13 carriages and 2 sleighs sit in the **Carriage House**. Conducted tours of the house begin in the Visitors Reception Center, formerly Helen's playhouse. Here she played with her dolls and entertained guests on child-size furniture. At the back of the playhouse her brother Childs had his own bowling alley. Tours include 13 of Clayton's 23 rooms. The top two floors have not been restored. Hour-long tours are given Tuesdays through Saturday 10:00 A.M. to 5:30 P.M. and Sundays NOON to 6:00 P.M. by reservation. Clayton is closed on major holidays. An admission is charged for the house tours. For reservations call (412) 371-0600.

Directions: Clayton is located at Penn and South Homewood Avenues in Point Breeze. Parking is available at no charge in The Frick Art Museum lot off Reynolds Street.

David Bradford House and Century Inn

Lawyer and Rebel

Sometimes when exploring historic houses you encounter an individual you wish you could have met. David Bradford is such a person. On two occasions, in Washington, PA and New Orleans, he successfully established himself in a new community and quickly gained both reputation and wealth.

Twenty-year old Bradford arrived in Washington in 1780 from Maryland's Upper Chesapeake Bay region. Within six years he had established himself as a prominent attorney, the youngest admitted to the county bar, and successful businessman. He owned a grist and sawmill, and shipped flour down the Chartiers Creek to Ohio and New Orleans.

In 1786 he started construction on the Georgian mansion that still stands on Main Street. It was to this home that Bradford brought his bride, Elizabeth Porter of Bucks County. Their home was considered the most magnificent in the county. It cost $4,500 to build and Bradford often remarked that it cost him a guinea (about 21 shillings) a step—there are 43 steps. No expense was spared with the interior appointments. West Indian mahogany for the imposing staircase was hauled over the mountains from

Philadelphia. Additions were made to the townhouse as the Bradfords' five children were born. Bradford also had a country house at his farm a few miles from town.

By 1783 Bradford was Deputy Attorney General of Pennsylvania. In 1792, he was elected to the state legislature. But legislation passed the preceding year was to be his temporary downfall. The excise tax on whiskey was extremely unpopular with the farmers in western Pennsylvania. These farmers' cash crop was rye. Transported as grain, only four bushels could be carried by each horse. Distilled into alcohol, six times that amount could be transported. But with the new seven cents per gallon tax, to be paid outright before the whiskey was sold, this was no longer profitable. Unless rescinded the whiskey tax threatened their livelihood. Six western counties (one in what is now West Virginia) opposed the whiskey tax. Liberty poles with slogans expressing the farmer's viewpoint were soon supplanted by more direct action. Tax collectors were tarred and feathered, farmers who complied with the law were harassed and frontier vigilantes stole the mail from the post rider.

Bradford was a prominent figure in the rebellion, heading up the Democratic Society that argued for violent measures against the whiskey tax. The exact extent of his involvement is still argued by historians but he was involved sufficiently in clandestine actions to justify the arrest warrant issued in 1794 by George Washington. The president, as commander-in-chief, rode with the 13,000-man federal army under General "Lighthorse" Harry Lee as far as Bedford. Washington wanted to be personally involved in the action against this first challenge to the power of the federal government. From Bedford, General Lee continued west with the army.

According to local lore, Bradford was packing to escape his arrest when he heard troops approaching on Main Street. He then jumped from a window of the master bedroom onto the roof of the cistern, then onto his saddled horse. In McKees Rock, Bradford traded his horse for a canoe and made his way down the Ohio. He eventually settled in the Louisiana territory, still under Spanish domain.

Bradford practiced law and established a wealthy cotton plantation, "The Myrtles." His wife and children remained in Washington until President Adams pardoned Bradford in 1799. Bradford returned briefly to sell the Pennsylvania house. Mrs. Bradford stayed until 1803 when she bartered her passage to Louisiana for a shipment of flour. She and the children moved to Bradford's southern plantation. Bradford fathered four more children before he died in 1810 at age 49. He's buried on the plantation grounds.

Over the years the Washington County house passed through a number of hands, serving for a time first as a doctor's home and office, then as a funeral parlor and finally the location of several commercial establishments. In 1959 the Pennsylvania Historical and Museum Commission acquired the house and supervised its restoration. It is now run by the Bradford House Historical Association.

Both interior and exterior again reflect the 18th century. Period furnishings befitting the style enjoyed by the Bradfords fill the rooms. The old well in the back is restored and a small garden planted. The David Bradford House is open May through December Wednesday through Saturday from 11:00 A.M. to 4:00 P.M. and Sunday 1:00 P.M. to 4:00 P.M.

The same year that David Bradford left Washington an inn was built not far from town (in what is now the village of Scenery Hill) on the Nemacolin Indian Trail. This route became the National Road linking the eastern seaboard with the western frontier. **Century Inn**, a National Landmark of Historic Places site, is the oldest continuously operated inn along this historic road. The inn's front parlor displays a rare surviving flag used by Whiskey Rebellion insurgents.

You can join a distinguished list of clientele when you enjoy a meal or stay at the inn. Andrew Jackson was a guest at the inn in 1824; he stopped again on his way to his inauguration on February 2, 1826. General LaFayette had breakfast here on May 26, 1825 as he toured the emerging country on his triumphal return visit.

Dr. and Mrs. Gordon Harrington acquired the inn in 1945. They restored it and filled the rooms with an amazing array of antiques. There are five historic dining rooms and they never look lovelier than they do at Christmas time when festive holiday decorations are added to the already appealing decor. The cuisine has garnered awards and continues to delight repeat visitors. Overnight accommodations are available as well; call (412) 945-6600 for information or reservations.

Not only is Washington County crossed by the National Road, but side roads offer their own appeal. The county has 25 covered bridges and a county map provides directions and a colored drawing of each. When asked why bridges were covered, a Pennsylvania carpenter answered, "Keeps 'em dry." He was not talking about travelers, their carriages or the horses but rather the bridges' supporting timbers that would rot if exposed to the elements. You have to chuckle at the response of a Southerner to the same question, "Our bridges were covered, my dear Sir, for the same reason that our belles wore hoop skirts and crinolines—to protect the structural beauty that is seldom seen, but nevertheless appreciated."

Each year the third weekend in September, Washington and Greene Counties host a **Covered Bridge Festival**. Crafters demonstrate and sell their wares at designated bridges. The festival also includes entertainment and homestyle food. For details on the festival or to obtain a copy of the covered bridges map call (800) 531-4114.

Directions: From I-70 take Exit 7A, Murtland Avenue into Washington. Turn left on Locust Avenue and continue to Main Street. Turn left on Main Street to 175 South Main Street. The David Bradford House will be on the right. There is parking behind the house. For Century Inn take Route 40 out of Washington to Scenery Hill.

Duquesne and Monongahela Inclines

Things are Looking Up

When company comes to town, Pittsburghers head for the **Duquesne Incline**. Its overlook atop Mt. Washington offers the best view of the city, night or day. This is not a new phenomenon as the **Monongahela Incline**, the first passenger incline in the country, was built in 1870. The *Street Railway Journal* of October 1891 stated, "Of the many engineering features that are offered by Pittsburgh, there is no one that is likely to have more interest for a stranger than the inclined planes which afford access to the high lands that surround the city."

Mt. Washington was first called Coal Hill, supplying fuel for early settlers, the garrisons at Fort Pitt and for local industries that developed along the river. The coal hoists that moved the coal cars foreshadowed the more elaborate cars of the inclines.

Inclines predated electric streetcars and automobiles, providing a quick, safe way to climb a hill. Inclines operated even on the snowiest days carrying passengers, freight and even horse-drawn wagons up and down Pittsburgh's steep hills. Before 1900, 30 companies were chartered to build inclines. Of these, 17 were actually built and two survive.

In the early 1870s horse-drawn vehicles were the main means of transit, including horse-drawn streetcars. But a new mode of transport was inaugurated on May 28, 1870 when the Monongahela Incline began operation. A freight incline was added at the Mon Incline in 1884 to haul horses, buggies, furniture and coal. It continued in operation until 1935. The Mon Incline was extensively reconstructed in 1982-83. The Mon Incline is 635 feet in length and rises to an elevation of 367.39 feet. It travels at a rate of six miles-per-hour. One car ascends while the other descends.

The Monongahela Incline runs Monday through Saturday 5:30 A.M. to 12:45 A.M. On Sunday and holidays hours are 8:45 A.M. to Midnight. The fare is a dollar each way. (Rates on the first inclines ranged from 1 to 5 cents.) In 1994, a $3 million reconstruction included the addition of two different color lights along the track. The tracks of the nearby Duquesne Incline have been bedecked with lights for years.

The **Duquesne Incline**, which opened in May 1877, was built by Samuel Diescher, who went on to become the country's foremost incline builder. Diescher positioned the Duquesne Incline in the tracks of a 1854 coal hoist operated by Kirk Lewis. The Duquesne Incline rises 400 feet between its stations at the bottom and the top. The slope distance between stations is 800 feet; the angle of track is 30 degrees. The cars were run by a steam engine for the first 50 years, then were converted to electricity.

In November 1962 the Duquesne Incline was closed for repairs and the owners decided it was bringing in too little revenue to warrant the costly repairs. It was a case of not realizing the value of a handy convenience until it is eliminated. Faced with the threatened loss, residents of Duquesne Heights decided to try to save their incline. A community-wide effort paid for the repairs. The incline is now operated by the Society for the Preservation of the Duquesne Heights Incline.

Community support has continued and resulted in the restoration of the cars and station to their original appearance. Layers of gray paint were removed to reveal the hand-carved cherry panels trimmed with oak and bird's-eye maple. The cable drum and unique wooden-toothed drive gear are as good as they were in 1877. The station waiting rooms have been preserved and the upper station has incline exhibits and mementoes. In 1987, an observation deck was added providing the definitive view of the **Three Rivers and the Golden Triangle**.

The Duquesne Incline runs Monday through Saturday 5:30 A.M. to 12:45 A.M. On Sundays and holidays it doesn't start service until 7:00 A.M. The fare is $1.00 each way.

Directions: From the Pennsylvania Turnpike, I-76, take Exit 6, the Parkway East to downtown Pittsburgh. Cross the Fort Pitt Bridge and make a right turn onto West Carson Street. Signs will indicate parking area for the Duquesne Incline. For the Monongahela Incline take the Parkway East to the Smithfield Bridge (which is before the Fort Pitt Bridge) and then make a left on West Carson and enter the parking lot for the incline.

Fort Pitt Museum

Commanding Prize

The Forks of the Ohio meet at The Point in present day Pittsburgh. This land was hotly contested during the French and

Indian War, the mid-18th century conflict between Britain and France for control of North America. The conflict's name is misleading, as Native Americans fought with both the French and the British.

In western Pennsylvania control of the American frontier rested with whomever commanded the **Forks of the Ohio**. The first to fortify The Point were settlers from Virginia. It was this group that George Washington was planning to reinforce before he was stopped near Jumonville Glen and forced to build Fort Necessity in hopes of protecting his small military force from the French and their Native American allies (see selection). The French seized the British outpost at the Point, Fort Prince George, then attacked and defeated Washington and his men at Fort Necessity. Following these victories, the French erected **Fort Duquesne** and were able to control the Forks and the Ohio Valley until 1758.

In 1758, six thousand British and Colonial soldiers under General John Forbes marched against Fort Duquesne. Rather than surrender Fort Duquesne to a superior force, the French blew up the fort two days before the British arrived, burned the barracks and retreated. (A bronze marker at Point State Park indicates the location of the Fort Duquesne.) The following spring the British began constructing **Fort Pitt**, the most elaborate and largest British fortress in the American colonies. Virtually upon the heels of its completion, the French surrendered their territory in the New World to the British. Fort Pitt was used by the British as a base of operations during their negotiations and for trade with the Indians. It was attacked and under siege for six weeks during the Indian uprising known as Pontiac's Rebellion in 1763 (see Bushy Run Battlefield selection).

The British were stationed at Fort Pitt until 1772. With the American Revolution looming on the horizon, patriot forces occupied the fort while attempting to wrest control of British outposts in Illinois. Fort Pitt was abandoned in 1792, by which time the town of Pittsburgh had grown up around the former frontier outpost.

The **Fort Pitt Museum** has exhibits, dioramas, reconstructed rooms and models that reveal the turbulent story of the frontier years leading to the founding of modern day Pittsburgh. The main gallery hall of the museum extends into the fort's original Monongahela Bastion. In the center of this hall is a scale model of Fort Pitt, where visitors can listen to a taped explanation of the fort. Living history presentations are offered by the Royal American Regiment, a modern volunteer group. It recreates the British 60th Regiment of Foote that helped build and garrison Fort Pitt. On summer Sunday afternoons the regiment brings to life the sights and sounds of the 18th-century British army. Call

(412) 281-9284 for performance dates and times. Around the museum are excavations of the fort's earthworks and bastions. The fort's Blockhouse now serves as a welcome center and gift shop.

The Fort Pitt Museum is open Tuesday through Saturday 10:00 A.M. to 4:30 P.M.; on Sunday it opens at NOON. The museum is closed Monday and some major holidays (during the winter it is also closes on Tuesday; it is a good idea to call for correct hours). Admission is charged.

Point State Park is a popular congregating spot for visitors and residents. Throughout the year festivals and celebrations are held at the park, including fireworks on the 4th of July and on Holiday Light-Up Night in late November. During the summer a 200-foot fountain at the tip of the point provides a refreshing focal spot.

Directions: From the Pennsylvania Turnpike, I-76, take Exit 6, the Parkway, Route 376, to downtown Pittsburgh. Exit on Stanwick Street. Fort Pitt is located in Point State Park in the city's Golden Triangle.

Hartwood Acres

A Little Bit of England

If the stately Tudor **Hartwood Acres Mansion** reminds you of England's Cotswold region, the resemblance is deliberate. Built on a crest overlooking the gently undulating foothills of the Allegheny Mountain, this 649-acre equestrian estate combined design elements from several English estates admired by John and Mary Flinn Lawrence. Not only was architect Alfred Hopkins instructed to borrow architectural details, but the Lawrences purchased wall panelling, a living room fireplace and furniture from "Lee Hall," a 1620 English castle. Other furnishings were acquired at "Braemar," the English family home of William Flinn.

It was Mary Flinn Lawrence's two-million-dollar inheritance from her father, U.S. Senator William Flinn, that paid for the construction of this lavish mansion. Flinn's construction company grossed over four million dollars a year, but it was his political career that made his reputation. An influential Republican, Flinn directed his party's activities in Pittsburgh for nearly 20 years. His daughter Mary was one of six children. She, too, was politically active. She worked for women's suffrage, the British War Relief (her father was born in England) and aid for crippled children, among other causes. The Lawrences adopted two young English boys, William and John.

John Lawrence had a successful insurance business. He, too, worked for numerous social causes and served in both World Wars. He and Mary were both enthusiastic horsemen. They competed in equestrian events and rode to the hunt. John was Master of the Fox Chapel Hunt.

John Lawrence died in 1945 at age 54. Mrs. Lawrence died in 1974, but in 1969 she sold the estate and its contents to Allegheny County for $1.3 million (with subsequent additions it totaled $1.7 million). When you tour 18 of the mansions 32 rooms, you will see all of the family furnishings, photographs and decorative pieces still in place. This provides a provocative look at their lifestyle in the early 20th century. Time seems to have stood still, and you expect the family to return momentarily.

The hour-long guided tour starts in the cottage, where the family lived while the main house was built. Eventually the cottage served as the guest wing. Next, you move to the library. Architectural details to note here are the random-width oak floors, the Renaissance-style plaster ceiling and the 15th-century stone mantlepiece. The floor simulates the butterfly wedges and wooden pegs used in England to secure the floor boards. Once in place, they were saturated with water, so they expanded and held the planks in place. Here the use is decorative since hidden nails hold down the boards. The wooden molds for all the plaster ceiling patterns were made at Hartwood. Like the ceiling the library table is of Italian Renaissance style. The books belonged to the Lawrences and reflect their interests: horses, conservation and politics. The silver trophies are a testament to their equestrian success.

Moving to the gallery, used by Mrs. Lawrence as a solarium, you will see portraits of the Lawrences, their children and the Flinn family. The huge living room, or music room, is designed in a Jacobean style. Rich wood paneling covers the walls. One side is covered with an elaborate Flemish tapestry. Mrs. Lawrence was an accomplished musician and the room has a 1901 Steinway piano and one of only three **Eolian organs** in the country. The organ was purchased in 1908 for Braemar, her girlhood home. The pipes are beneath the floor and the sound travels through wall passages and into the room through tilted wall panels. The panels also conceal a secret compartment used to haul wood from the basement for the massive fireplace. The elaborately carved oak firemantle was done in 1620. A 1650 cast iron fireback protected the stones at the back of the fireplace. Enhancing the English look are the diamond-pane bay windows with inset stained-glass sections.

Along with the lavish architectural appointments, the Jacobean style employed more lavish furnishings. This is certainly apparent in this stylish room. The 1870 Bijar Persian carpet with its still vibrant colors has two stags, or harts, embroidered in the design to denote Hartwood. There is also needlework motifs on the rare early Georgian gaming tables.

In the green and gold dining room a Georgian style is employed. A gold decorative border pulls the eye up to the ceiling from which hangs a delicate Czechoslovakian glass chandelier. Gold also tops the decorative pillars flanking the green and white marble fireplace. The table is set with dishes from one of the 15 sets of china the Lawrences received as wedding gifts (more china can be seen in the pantry). China also fills the lighted built-in cabinet. Another cabinet holds hammered silver weddings gifts.

Like the popular English television series that revealed upstairs and downstairs, at Hartwood you will see the butler's pantry, the warming kitchen and a servant's dining room. On the second floor there's a linen press room and the butler's bedroom. As you move down the upstairs corridor you'll peek in the cedar room. It's a large storage closet where you can get a sense of the Lawrences' avocational pursuits: tennis rackets hang from the wall, ski gear is lined up and suitcases perch atop the shelves. You'll also see the side-saddle riding outfit Mrs. Lawrence wore until she was 74 and Mr. Lawrence's bearskin parachute jumping suit from World War I.

Their interests are also readily apparent in their bedrooms. Mr. Lawrence's suite, with his easel standing in the windowed-alcove overlooking the Allegheny foothills, seems to lack only the artist. The art hanging in the room speaks of his love of horses, as does the sporting art throughout the house. The bedroom suite is very masculine with dark wood and 18th-century English country furniture. A fine example is the fireside chair made of yew and elm.

In complete contrast is Mrs. Lawrence's light and flowery suite done in the French Empire style. The walls are hung with Chinese rice paper painted with a non-repeated pattern of flowering trees and birds. The white bedroom set came from Mrs. Lawrence's girlhood bedroom in Bryn Mawr. Even the doorknobs and keyhole covers are white porcelain painted with delicate flowers.

These are the highlights of the mansion tour, but that is just the beginning. There is more to see and do at Hartwood Acres. Don't miss seeing the stable complex, nestled in the valley, and totally hidden from the house on the hill. Again architect Alfred Hopkins utilized design elements from the Cotswolds. The vine-covered stone stables, barns, silo (masked as a tower) and other elements are laid out in an appealing asymmetrical fashion. The stables are wood panelled with polished brass hardware.

Riding is still done on the 25 miles of bridle paths. Enthusiasts must supply their own mounts, since horses are not available. You can make reservations for a horse-drawn hayride by calling (412) 767-9200. Fifty-minute rides are given daily except holidays and during March. These are done primarily for groups; the wagon holds 16 passengers.

Even if you can't ride the grounds, don't miss the chance to explore the gardens and woods. The formal gardens around Hartwood Mansion were designed by Rose Greely, while Alfred Hopkins and Ralph Griswold planned the original landscaping. Mrs. Lawrence had 96,000 pine trees planted on the grounds to augment the 400 acres of virgin timberland and meadow. The woodland trails are delightful for hiking or cross-country skiing. You can pick up a guide to the **mile-long primitive nature trail** through the forest at Hartwood. It highlights 27 points of interest. The trail is particularly appealing in the spring when the wildflowers bloom.

In the summer, the evenings come alive with sparkling tent theater on the mansion lawn. Free music and dance performances are also given at **Hartwood's Middle Road performance area**, still part of the park but two miles from the mansion.

To arrange a tour of the mansion call (412) 767-9200. Tours are given Wednesday through Saturday from 10:00 A.M. to 3:00 P.M. and Sunday NOON to 4:00 P.M. From mid-November through mid-January the house is decorated for the holidays and is even more enticing than usual. Admission is reasonable, costing less than an evening at the movies.

Directions: From I-76 traveling west, the Pennsylvania Turnpike, take Exit 5, Allegheny Valley. Bear right onto Route 910 west at the intersection by Ames. Take Route 910 for $4^1/_2$ miles and turn left onto Saxonburg Boulevard at the blinking red light. Follow this for about $2^1/_2$ miles; the Hartwood Park entrance is on the right. Enter park and follow signs for the mansion parking lot. Traveling east on I-76, take Exit 4, Butler Valley. Turn left and head south on Route 8 toward Pittsburgh. Make a left onto Harts Run Road and travel approximately $2^1/_2$ miles to Saxonburg Boulevard. Make a left onto Saxonburg and travel approximately one mile. Hartwood Park entrance is on the left.

Kennywood and Sandcastle

Park Yourself in Pittsburgh

During the first battle of the Civil War, Washingtonians packed a picnic lunch and headed out to the rolling hills of Virginia to watch the battle being fought along Bull Run. On that same sunny July day in the 1860s, it wouldn't have been surprising to see Pittsburgh picnickers relaxing along the tree-shaded stream on Charles Kenny's farm, having arrived by horse-and-buggy or ferry. In 1898 Andrew Mellon's Monongahela Street Railway Company opened a small trolley park beside this stream and Kennywood's history began. As early as 1906 the McSwigan and Henninger families obtained the lease to run the park and descendants still run the park.

It's the excitement of the rides that interests the crowds thronging to **Kennywood**, not the fact that this is one of only two parks that are National Historic Landmarks. But the past is reflected in the present and sets the mood for good-spirited family fun. There's plenty of excitement but it's tempered with good manners and good taste. The park looks like it has a history: the trees are towering, the plantings lush and the design evokes memories of old-fashioned days. The original carousel building and the restaurant building date from 1900. In 1994, for the eighth straight year, National Amusement Park Historical Association members voted Kennywood their favorite traditional amusement park. The **Thunderbolt** got members' vote as their second favorite wooden roller coaster, after the Texas Giant at Six Flags over Texas. The **Steel Phantom** was the second favorite steel coaster, after Ohio's Cedar Point's Magnum XL200.

Kennywood's roller coasters have made the park a hit since its early years. The first coaster, a figure eight toboggan coaster, was built in 1902. Even most coaster enthusiasts don't realize that the world's first coaster was built in St. Petersburg, Russia in the 16th century. Thrill-seekers rode sleds down a 70-foot wooden-frame ice slide. Since those prototype roller coasters, rides have become high-tech and high-speed. That is certainly true of the Steel Phantom. At 80 mph it's the world's fastest coaster with the longest drop, 225 feet. The park also has **The Racer**, a twin or racing coaster and the **1921 Jack Rabbit**, the oldest coaster in the park.

It's hard to imagine any ride being more exciting—more terrifying—than a roller coaster, but the **Skycoaster** really tests the mettle of its riders. Actually, it isn't a ride, it's a flight. Hearty souls lie down in a full body flight harness, then two support cables raise the flyer—hanging face down with arms fluttering in the wind—a breathtaking 200 feet in the air. From this tree-top position, the flyer pulls a rip cord and free falls 60 feet, then swings in an arc over the lagoon at speeds of 60 to 70 mph. Even watching the flyers is heart-stopping. If you want to experience this, sign up when you arrive at the park, because it does sell out when the park is crowded.

Generations of youngsters growing up in the Pittsburgh area have their favorite Kennywood rides, from the gaily painted

Families can spend a fun-filled day enjoying rides like the Wave Swinger at Kennywood or tackling the 15 water slides at Sand-castle.

horses on the Dentzel carousel to the miniature railroad and the scaled-down rides in Kiddieland. Other popular rides are the Auto Race, the Whip, Turtle and trip through the Old Mill.

Kennywood opens daily from mid-May through Labor Day weekend, and on weekends only in late April and early May. The park opens at NOON and closes at 10:00 P.M. There is a general admission option or a ride-all-day fee; the Skycoaster is a separate fee. Throughout the summer there are musical performances at the Garden and Lagoon stages and special event days at the park.

While you will certainly get wet riding Kennywood's Raging Rapids, for a full-day of wet fun head for **Sandcastle**, just six miles away along the Monongahela River. It's the next best thing to being at the ocean, with a quarter-mile wooden boardwalk complete with shops, snacks and video arcade. There are 15 water slides (one is an 82 foot speed slide), two pools, a waterland for children, a quarter-mile lazy river where you can float along on inner tubes, three hot tubs (one is the world's largest), miniature golf, a Formula 1 speedway and a kids go-cart track.

Sandcastle transformed the land used during World War II by the USX Homestead Works, part of the "Arsenal of Democracy." This rolling greensward was once a railroad yard. But Kennywood General Manager Harry Henninger saw beyond the overgrown foliage and seven miles of track, envisioning instead a water playground. His vision began to take shape in May 1989 and the park opened July 1990.

After the Action Park closes, **Club Wet** opens from 7:00 P.M. to 1:00 A.M. Wednesday through Saturday, and 8:00 P.M. to Midnight on Sunday. Food, drinks and music are available on the riverside deck.

Sandcastle is open during the summer months from 11:00 A.M. to 6:00 P.M.; on weekends it stays open until 7:00 P.M. There is a pool pass admission and a slide-all-day fee. The miniature golf and speedways charge additional fees. For information call (412) 462-6666. Boaters can dock at Sandcastle at no charge.

Directions: From I-76, the Pennsylvania Turnpike, take Exit 6, Route 376 west to Exit 9, Swissvale exit and follow the Kennywood signs. Turn left on Route 837 for Kennywood. For Sandcastle turn right on Route 837 after crossing the Mon River and follow blue Sandcastle signs.

LeMoyne House and Duncan & Miller Glass Museum

Triply Blessed

The Washington County Historical Society is the envy of other Pennsylvania counties for three reasons. When they acquired the **LeMoyne House**, the historical property that serves as their headquarters, they also obtained most of the household furnishings.

The closets and attic were crammed with pertinent documents and other material. Secondly, the Society was founded in 1900 by a group of attorneys, many veterans of the Civil War. From their founders the Society has an impressive collection of Civil War weapons as well as munitions from later conflicts. Thirdly, the Society has the contents of a time capsule impeded in the town hall by President Grant.

The LeMoyne House's rich history has its roots in the French Revolution. Five hundred French families, fleeing the depredations of the new order, purchased land in America. They arrived and discovered their land was a swamp in Ohio. The newly formed Congress, rectified this by providing land for the defrauded Frenchmen to purchase on the banks of the Ohio River. Dr. John Julius LeMoyne made his way through Pennsylvania toward this Ohio land in 1790. (Another settlement established by French aristocrats was Azilum, see selection.)

Six years later, Dr. John LeMoyne left the French settlement in Ohio and returned to establish a home in the area he passed through on his way west. He married Nancy McCully, set up his medical practice and opened a tavern in Washington.

In 1812, the doctor built one of the largest and finest stone homes west of the Alleghenies. It was also the first in the region to add Greek Revival features to a post-Colonial design. Some details had a practical explanation. The two front entrances were needed because one served the doctor's office while the more formal doorway flanked by large columns was the family entrance. The LeMoynes had only one child, Francis Julius, who followed his father into the medical profession and eventually joined his practice. Their former office now contains medical instruments, apothecary items like they once prepared and information on the first crematorium in the country. It was established by Doctor Francis LeMoyne just a few blocks from their office. (Although no longer operational it still stands.)

The family never discarded anything, so letters, bills of sale, ledgers, appointment books as well as family furniture and decorative items are all original. The last descendant, Dr. Francis's youngest daughter Madeleine lived from 1843 to 1943. At her death the house was acquired by the historical society along with most of the LeMoyne furnishings and memorabilia.

Dr. Francis LeMoyne was a progressive thinker. In addition to the first crematorium, he established the first free public library, was one of the founders of the first women's seminary west of the Alleghenies and ardently supported the abolitionist cause. The LeMoyne house was a stop on the **Underground Railroad**. While touring the master bedroom, you will hear the story of how Dr. Francis's wife, Madelaine Bureau LeMoyne, hid six runaway slaves under her bed while the house was searched.

415

Another upstairs room houses the military collection but long range plans are to exhibit these at another location. The cases now filled primarily with Civil War weapons, are only a small part of the military items in the possession of the Washington County Historical Society.

There is also a museum case containing personal effects of Ulysses S. Grant who had a cousin living in Washington, Pennsylvania. In 1869, Grant came to town to place a time capsule in the town hall. He was called back to the capital because of Black Friday, the financial crisis created by Fisk and Gould. Grant averted disaster by releasing the gold in Fort Knox. When the town hall was torn down in 1991, the capsule was removed and its contents became part of the Historical Society's collection.

The society has a research library and a gift shop. The LeMoyne House is open for tours February through mid-December Wednesday through Friday NOON to 4:00 P.M. and Sunday 2:00 P.M. to 4:00 P.M. Admission is charged. The research library is open Tuesday through Friday from NOON to 4:00 P.M.

Among the lovely decorative pieces in the LeMoyne dining room are two Duncan Miller three-face compotes. This local glass plant produced glass now treasured by collectors. For an overview of the glass made by this company visit the **Duncan & Miller Glass Museum**. Rooms on two floors of this private home converted to a museum display 1500 pieces of glass.

George Duncan & Sons established a glass company in Pittsburgh in 1874. In 1891 the company was merged into U.S. Glass Company, but a year later the entire plant was destroyed by fire. **Duncan & Miller Glass Company** relocated to Washington and opened a factory in 1900. This remained operational until the summer of 1955. The museum has photographs of the factory along with some glass-making tools and molds.

The major thrust of the museum is to display the glass made by both the Pittsburgh plant and the Washington facility. Few of these pieces are marked with the company name; they are recognized by the glass color and patterns. The glassware handcrafted by the first plant were cut with more complex designs than the latter pieces.

The Duncan & Miller Glass Museum is open mid-April through mid-October Thursday through Sunday from 1:00 P.M. to 4:00 P.M. Admission is charged.

Directions: From I-79 take Exit 7, Murtland Avenue, Route 19 S. into Washington. Continue on Route 19 to N. College. Take N. College to Route 40, E. Maiden Street, and turn right. The LeMoyne House is on the right at 49 East Maiden Street. For the Duncan & Miller Glass Museum turn off Main Street onto West Chestnut Street and then make a right on Jefferson Avenue. The museum is on the left at 525 Jefferson Avenue. There is parking behind the museum.

McConnell's Mill State Park and Moraine State Park

Tumbling and Quiet Water

In 1852, at a sharp bend in the tumbling waters of Slippery Rock Creek where the creek bed drops, Daniel Kennedy built a gristmill. Hand-hewn oak timbers support the walls, and the floor rests on a huge stone block foundation. These roughly cut blocks seem a part of the rocky gorge slope.

Fire destroyed the first mill, but Kennedy rebuilt in 1868. Seven years later Thomas McConnell purchased the mill. He modernized, replacing the water wheel with water turbines and adding rolling mills instead of grinding stones. This was one of the country's earliest rolling mills. Local customers were able to process corn, oats, wheat and buckwheat faster and more efficiently than before. The mill operated until 1928.

Mechanical engineering students at the University of Pittsburgh are involved in a challenging long-term project to restore the mill and make it operational. Complicating this project are environmental regulations that require innovative adaptions of the milling process. Free guided tours of the mill are given from 10:00 A.M. to 6:00 P.M. Memorial Day through Labor Day.

One of the best vantage points to photograph the mill is from across the creek. Your route is through a picturesque covered bridge built in 1874. It's a Howe Truss bridge; it was covered to protect it from rotting and rusting.

Interesting though these are, it's the scenic beauty of the 2,512-acre park that brings visitors back. Slippery Rock gorge was formed by the southern tip of the Wisconsin Ice Sheet that covered this area tens of thousands of years ago. As the ice receded, a 400-foot gorge was cut and huge house-size sandstone boulders slid partway down the gorge. An excellent spot from which to view the gorge is the **Cleland Rock** area, off Breakneck Bridge Road, a short distance by car from the historic site where the mill and bridge are located.

There are seven miles of rugged trails in the park. One of the easiest is the two-mile self-guided portion of the **Kildoo Nature Trail**. The serpentine trail to the **Hell's Hollow** area is spectacular in the spring because wildflowers bloom in profusion in the hemlock-lined valley along Slippery Rock Creek. The Hell's Hollow trail leads to a cascading waterfall and the remains of the 1846 Lawrence Furnace. This is one of only two remaining iron furnaces in the area; the other is on private land. Guided nature walks are given on summer weekends. There are also two areas designated for climbing and rappeling. Beginners can tackle the **Rim Road** climbing area across the creek from the mill, while more advanced enthusiasts can head for the rugged area at **Breakneck Bridge**.

Another group of adventurers, ardent kayakers and whitewater canoe buffs, also frequent the park, and enjoy the challenging swift water that rushes through the gorge. On summer weekends there is plenty of colorful action in the water around the dam, providing yet another photo opportunity. It's about a 2.5-mile run through the gorge to the dam area, where boaters portage around the dam. It's possible to extend the run to six miles for those who want the full experience. No rafts or other equipment is rented, so boaters must have the appropriate gear including personal floatation devices. The water is swift and dangerous and there is absolutely no swimming permitted in Slippery Creek. Exercise caution when viewing the creek from the rocks along its banks. These are often damp and slippery and there are deep pools and rapids that are extremely hazardous.

Hunting and fishing are permitted in the park in designated areas with the proper licenses. There are two picnic areas and a playing field.

A few miles to the east on Route 422 is **Moraine State Park**, named for the ground moraine deposits left by the Wisconsin glacier. The lake that was created here in the late 1960s covers terrain that eons ago was covered by glacial lakes. The restoration of this parkland involved sealing deep mines, filling and grading strip mines and damming the tributary streams flowing into Muddy Creek to form the 3,225-acre **Lake Arthur**.

The best ways to enjoy the park are by boat or bike. There are 11 boat launching areas and two rental concessions for motorboats, pontoons and sailboats. Sometimes on breezy summer days the lake seems alive with brilliant skimming birds, as the small, single-man windsurfers tack to the wind. Fishermen can try their luck for muskellunge, northern pike, striper, bass, walleyes, catfish, crappies and bluegills from boats and from shore. Fishing is not allowed at the beach area and boat docks, moorings or launching area. For landlubbers, there's a seven-mile paved bicycle trail along the north shore of Lake Arthur; bikes can be rented. There's also a nine-mile trail from the Jennings Environmental Education Center to the northwest corner of the park. The short mile-long **Sunken Garden Trail** begins at the Pleasant Valley picnic area. There is also the two-mile **Hilltop Nature Trail** and the 4.2-mile **Wyggeston Trail**.

On hot summer days the two beaches along the lake are packed with visitors. There is a 1,200-foot turf beach at the **Pleasant Valley Day-Use Area** and a sand beach at the **Lakeview Day-Use Area**. Lifeguards are on duty from 11:00 A.M. to 7:00 P.M. daily from Memorial to Labor Day. Picnicking is not permitted on the beaches themselves but there are 1,200 tables in nearby picnic areas and other areas throughout the park. There are ten modern cabins for rent within the park; call (412) 368-8811.

Hunting and trapping is permitted in season in designated areas with a proper permit. During the cold winter months, you can ice skate, cross-country ski, ice boat, ice fish, snowmobile, sled or take winter hikes.

Directions: From I-79 take Exit 29, Route 422 west for 1.6 miles, then take Route 19 south to Kildoo Road which leads to the parking area for McConnell's Mill where you can pick up park and trail maps. For Moraine State Park take Exit 29, and follow Route 422 east for three miles; take the first exit and turn left at end of the ramp for the park.

Nationality Classrooms at the University of Pittsburgh

World-Wide, World-Wind Tour

Pittsburgh has more than 80 distinct ethnic communities. Immigrants settled this area generations ago, forming tightly knit villages that have in many cases survived to this day. Eastern Europeans gathered on the city's South Side, Italians came to Bloomfield, Polish settlers developed Polish Hill, Germans settled in Mount Troy and Mount Oliver and Jewish immigrants claimed Squirrel Hill.

You don't have to travel all over the city to enjoy the atmosphere of these diverse cultures. Within the University of Pittsburgh's 42-story Cathedral of Learning, 23 unique **Nationality Classrooms** offer visitors an intellectual United Nations.

This Gothic cathedral, one of the tallest academic buildings in the world, was completed in 1938. Contributions came from many sources including 17,000 men and women plus 97,000 area school children, each giving ten cents to the building fund.

The Cathedral Commons Room is four stories high, with soaring arches and towering columns. Encircling the Commons Room on the first and third floors are the Nationality Classrooms, each designed to represent a creative period in the countries from which Pittsburghers draw their ethnic heritage.

The Irish Classroom, one of 23 unique Nationality Classrooms at the University of Pittsburgh's 42-story Cathedral of Learning, suggests a 6th-century oratory from the west coast of Ireland.

Visiting these dramatically different classrooms lets you glimpse the art, architecture and history of each country. An information desk, near the 5th Avenue entrance, rents tour cassettes for a nominal fee. The tapes provide details about each classroom.

Inspiration for these classrooms was found in diverse spots around the globe: Pericles' 5th-century Athens, a palace hall in Beijing's Forbidden City, a 6th-century oratory from Ireland's Golden Age, the 16th-century Polish castle of Wawel and London's House of Commons. The English classroom has a stone fireplace salvaged in 1941 from the bomb-damaged Parliament. Antique tables near the classroom's bay were gifts to the University of Pittsburgh from the late Queen Mary.

It's difficult to single out rooms because each has its own appealing elements. However, one of the most popular, and the only one that was transported intact from the country of origin, is the **Syria-Lebanon room**, originally a library from a palatial home in Damascus. The gold satin cushions on the mosaic-patterned marble built-in sofas contribute to the room's luminous glow. The linden-wood wall panels are decorated in a Byzantine style called gesso painting. This is one of the few rooms that is not a classroom. Another is the **Early American room**, a kitchen-living room of 17th-century America. Two-hundred-year-old bricks are used for the nine-foot fireplace. There is a secret staircase to the upper loft.

A folkloric style is captured in classrooms representing Czechoslovakia, Hungary, Lithuania, Norway, Sweden, Russia and Yugoslavia. Additions made within the last ten years include an African temple courtyard and a replica of a 10th-century Armenian stone library chamber in the Sanahin Monastery. An **Israel Heritage classroom**, where major components are based on a 2nd- and 3rd-century Capernaum synagogue on the Sea of Galilee and a reception room in a 17th-century Ukraninian gentry residence can also be seen. Plans are in place to add an Austrian, Japanese and Indian classroom. The Austrian room is modeled after the music salon in the Esterhazy Palace near Vienna, the Japanese recreates a traditional garden and the Indian is based on the Gupta period, 3rd to 7th centuries A.D., the height of the Indian Renaissance.

From several of the Nationality Classrooms windows you will glimpse the **Heinz Chapel** with its French Gothic design suggesting the Church of Ste. Chappelle in Paris. When the sun streams through the chapel's 73-foot-high stained-glass windows, its interior glows with an ethereal beauty. The chapel is open 9:00 A.M. to 4:00 P.M. during the week with a NOON mass each day. Saturdays are reserved for weddings. There are services on Sunday and the chapel is open from 1:30 P.M. to 5:30 P.M.

The Nationality Classrooms, Visitor Information and Gift Center are open Monday through Saturday from 9:00 A.M. to 4:30 P.M., Sundays and holidays 11:00 A.M. to 4:30 P.M. Guided hour-and-a-half tours are given until one hour before closing. A nominal fee is charged. Only groups need tour reservations, which should be made two weeks in advance by calling (412) 624-6000. If you are in town the first Sunday in December that is the very best day of the year to visit the Nationality Classrooms because docents in national dress talk about the festive traditions of each homeland; many indigenous crafts and ornaments are on sale. During December many of the rooms are decorated in traditional holiday style.

There are two additional buildings of interest on the University of Pittsburgh's campus: the **Stephen Foster Memorial** and the **Frick Fine Arts Building**. Another impressive Gothic stone building, the Stephen Foster Memorial auditorium is used for theatrical performances and lectures. There is also an extensive collection of Foster memorabilia and books. Hours are weekdays 9:00 A.M. to 4:30 P.M. The Italian Renaissance Frick Fine Arts Building has an art gallery, fine arts reference library, studios and a cloistered garden. Exhibit hours are Tuesday through Saturday 10:00 A.M. to 4:00 P.M. and Sunday 2:00 P.M. to 5:00 P.M.

Directions: From the Pennsylvania Turnpike, I-76, take Exit 6 to Route 376 west, then Exit 7A into Oakland on Bouquet Street. Make a right on Forbes Avenue and take that down to Bellefield Avenue, make a left and then another left on 5th Avenue. The Nationality Classrooms Information Desk is at the 5th Avenue entrance.

Old Economy Village

Abide With Me

George Rapp and his Harmonist followers laid out their settlement with the certainty that the Second Coming was imminent. They believed with absolute certainty that Jesus Christ would walk in their gardens and be made welcome in their homes.

Old Economy Village ends a story that began in 1785 near Stuttgart, Germany when 28-year old George Rapp had a religious vision. Believing that he was a prophet who would lead his followers into heaven, Rapp separated from the Lutheran Church and established his own prayer group. Within ten years he attracted 2,000 followers.

The Rappites, as they were called, interpreted the Bible literally. Closely following the New Testament Book of Revelation, they immigrated to America, believing that they, like Jesus Christ, were called to wander in the wilderness. The ten year cycles of the two Harmonist communities reflect the passage in Revelations 12:14, "into the wilderness, for a time, and times, and half a time."

The cycle began in 1804 shortly after their arrival in America when they moved to 9,000 acres in Butler County. Here they drew up articles of agreement, which legally created the Harmony Society. The main thrust of the document was that all property was held in common for the common good, just as had been done in the Early Christian Church.

Three years later the men and women of the Society adopted celibacy. Perpetuating their group was not a concern because they believed that the Millennium would occur in 1829, signaling the end of the world as they knew it. The Harmonists were confident that they were among the select and would travel with Jesus Christ to Jerusalem to rebuilt the temple as foretold in Revelation.

During this first decade, the Harmonists began moving from an agrarian and craft economy toward a manufacturing one. They established a domestic cloth industry at a time when the country was anxious, because of the War of 1812, to end its dependence on European goods. Hard work and clear vision enabled the Harmonists to become self-sufficient, although throughout the group's existence items were purchased to improve the quality of life of its members.

In 1814, the Harmonists moved to their second settlement, nearly 30,000 acres along the Wabash River in Indiana. Unlike other pietistic groups such as Ephrata Cloister's Seventh-Day Baptists and Lancaster County's Amish, the Harmonists took part in the economic and political activities of the region in which they lived.

The third and last community was established in 1824, on the banks of the Ohio River in southwestern Pennsylvania. Unlike the others this was not called Harmony, but Oekonomie, Greek for divine economy. Architectural changes were also made, the most significant was replacing the town square with a formal garden. This step may have been taken because the members were aging and it was more convenient for them to live closer to the community center. As in the past, Frederick Rapp, the adopted son of the group's leader, laid out the town in a grid pattern with clapboard and brick houses along the streets. Two hundred buildings were constructed in 18 months, many out of bricks. This was at a time when 75 percent of the people in the Pittsburgh region lived in one-room log houses.

The astonishing range of Harmonist interest can be seen in **Old Economy Village's Museum Building**, currently also serving as the Visitor Center. The village has more than 16,000 Harmonist objects and 335 manuscript pages, more than anywhere else in the world. This makes it possible to interpret the Harmonists in the original buildings using the original artifacts. The museum is the country's second oldest building, constructed and continuously used as a museum. (Baltimore's Peale Museum is the oldest.) When it was built in 1827 one side of the first floor displayed fine arts and the other natural sciences. Plans are to return it to its 19th-century appearance. Some items have never left the museum. The elk, whose head looms over the exhibit cases, once lived in the village deer park and ate out of Father Rapp's hand. The Harmonist Feast Hall was on the second floor because the Bible states the Last Supper was held in a large upper chamber. At 100 by 50 feet this was the largest room of this type in America.

After exploring the museum, you can take a guided tour of six original buildings, then with a self-guiding map do a walking tour of the six-acre National Historic Landmark village which will cover six other buildings and the gardens. Exiting the museum, you will see the community kitchen with 12 original cauldrons used for preparing food for festivals in the feast hall.

The cabinet shop, and the clock and lock shops have all original Harmonist tools. The operational cooper's and blacksmith's shop have tools of the period, the actual tools are cataloged and not in use. One of the Society's three granaries still stands and it is being converted into an exhibit area covering the industrial side of the Society. Preparing for the Millennium, the Society stored a two-year supply of grain. They also secreted a half million dollars in gold and silver in a vault beneath George Rapp's house. These earmarked "Church Funds" would be used to finance the journey members would make with Jesus Christ to Jerusalem.

A massive stone-arched cellar was carved out beneath the brick **Mechanics Building**. Being Germans, the Harmonists enjoyed both wine and beer, though never to excess, and the original barrels are still in the cellar. Above this are the tailor and hat shop, the shoe shop and print shop. The craftsman took care of member's needs, the tailor and shoemaker watched members arrive for Sunday service. Replacements were provided for worn shoes and shabby clothes. Members often hesitated to request replacements because they did not want to deplete the Society's supplies. The print shop has the country's oldest flat-bed printing press still sitting in its original shop.

The store was one of the few places the Harmonists met outsiders, but since most members spoke only Swabian German they couldn't communicate. On the store counter is an 1827 listing, complete with prices charged, for all merchandise. The shelves reveal the scope of goods for sale in the village. Behind the store is the 19th century post office with mail slots still containing magazines sent to Society members. Across the hall is the doctor's office, an indication of the success of the community, since few wilderness communities retained the services of a doctor.

The **Baker House**, the only family household open to the public, contains furnishings that reflect an inventory taken for an 1847 court case. Storekeeper and second Harmonist leader Romelius Baker, lived here with his wife (although following the Society's celibacy requirements) and his biological sister. In 1832, the Hungarian poet Nicholas Lenau spent six months with the Baker household. Like many households after 1858 a shed was added to provide additional downstairs bedrooms so that older members did not have to climb the stairs.

Behind the house is the family shed which had multiple uses: outhouse, root cellar, cowshed, plus a wood, tool and drying shed. Illustrating their concern for economy of labor, the Harmonists trained the cows to come to the shed to be milked, rather than following the customary tradition of having the worker go to the field. Each household also had a garden plot for vegetables, herbs and flowers.

Across the street, behind a stone wall is the **1825 George Rapp Garden**, one of the first in the country. It symbolizes the Garden of Eden, while the water in the pond symbolizes baptism. Paths form a cross, the grape vines in the northwest quadrant are reminders of the Last Supper and the southwest quadrant represents the wilderness. The statue of Harmony in the pavilion harkens back to Revelation 12:1, "a woman clothed with the sun." The garden grotto's rough-stoned, thatched-roof exterior yields to a harmonious classical Greek and Roman interior. This symbolizes the concept that while harmony might not seem worthwhile when viewed from outside, once it is achieved within it is beautiful.

Off the garden are the houses of Frederick and George Rapp. Their homes contain treasures from around the world and finely crafted furnishings from Pittsburgh and Philadelphia. George Rapp's bedroom still has the bed in which he died.

Throughout your visit of Old Economy Village you will not see any hint of denial or self-sacrifice. There is a joyous sense of a community working with a full heart for the greater glory of God. The Harmonists did not endure because they neither propagated nor proselytized, but the flourishing religious community they created still has much to teach us.

Old Economy Village is open Tuesday through Saturday 9:00 A.M. to 4:00 P.M., on Sunday it opens at NOON. Admission is charged.

Directions: From I-76, the Pennsylvania Turnpike, take Exit 3, Cranberry, and follow I-79 south. At Ambridge take Route 65 north for six miles and turn at the sign for Old Economy Village. The Museum Building is at 14th and Church Streets.

Pennsylvania Trolley Museum and Meadowcroft Village

Streetcars You'll Desire

Only one person is paid to work at the **Pennsylvania Trolley Museum**—for the approximately 90 volunteers who devote roughly 19,000 hours annually—it is a labor of love. That proves significant to visitors because the enthusiastic volunteers share their fascination with trolleys with all who stop by.

The museum was started in Washington County more than 40 years ago by a group of rail fans. Dismayed at the prospect of trolleys heading for the scrap yards, the group, then Pittsburgh Electric Railway Club, acquired first one and then additional cars. The museum they established in 1954 was originally called the Arden Trolley Museum, named after the stop on the Pittsburgh Railways Company's Washington interurban line. It opened to the public in 1963.

As you park in the museum lot, you'll see three interurban passenger shelters. Step inside the first shelter to see photographs of the interurban system that once ran in this area. More photographs can be seen in the Visitor Education Center. These tell the story of trolleys from their development to their decline. For most of the year, they show old trolley movies in the back room, but during December the room has a Lionel train layout. It's the only layout in the state where visitors can run the trains.

Visitors are welcome to roam through the car restoration shop where you will see part of the museum's 40-car collection. Almost all of the cars are from Pennsylvania; one exception is the car that once ran on New Orleans's Desire line. A photograph of this car appeared in a 1947 *Life* magazine feature on Tennessee William's play *Streetcar Named Desire*. At Halloween the museum has a haunted ride called "**Streetcar Named Expire**."

The restoration shop has cars in varying degrees of repair. Volunteers do all the work restoring the cars and along the side of the shop are an assortment of tools and equipment they use. Some of the tools, such as the World War I band saw called the Defiance, are older than the trolleys.

Seeing the cars that are still being worked on, you notice various features not readily apparent when they are fully restored. One thing to note is the canvas roof on some of the older trolleys. Canvas was a good insulator, if the electric connection disengaged repairmen could touch them without harm. This would not have been the case with a metal roof.

Many of the cars are work cars; notice the rattan brushes on the snow sweeper. There is also a side-dump car that carried stone and dirt, a hopper car and a bottom-dump car that dropped gravel on the track to support the wooden crossties. Once restored, the cars are moved to the operating carbarn across the tracks. Outside on a railroad siding are a few railroad cars, including the oldest operating Diesel locomotive in the country. Made in 1930 in Philadelphia and East Pittsburgh, this 400-horsepower car was used by the Armco Steel Company in Butler.

To bring the trolley era to life, the museum operates several of their restored trolleys. You can take a $2^1/_2$-mile ride into the past. When the Washington County Fair is in progress you can park at the museum and ride the trolley to the fairgrounds.

The Pennsylvania Trolley Museum is open NOON to 5:00 P.M. on weekends and holidays during May, June, September, October, November and December. It is open daily in July and August. The admission charge includes trolley rides, a guided tour and entry to museum displays. A museum shop has a wide array of trolley memorabilia. There is a shaded picnic grove on the museum grounds.

The museum is planning a major expansion to include a new facility, the **Pennsylvania Transportation Heritage Center**. This will include exhibits previously seen in the Transportation and Technology Museum at Pittsburgh's Station Square. The new building will be linked with the current museum by a trolley line.

The development of trolleys, beginning in the 1890s, helped American cities to grow. Another spot in Washington County looks back to the era when settlers were carving communities out of the wilderness. **Meadowcroft Museum of Rural Life** in Avella brings to life the 1800s complete with log house, one-room school, blacksmith's shop, country store, a covered bridge and other buildings.

Albert and Delvin Miller established this village, moving structures into this woodsy setting from different parts of the state. The log house of George Miller Sr., one of their Scotch-Irish ancestors, was one of the original structures on the homestead he built in 1795. The Miller Museum traces the family history and the career of Delvin Miller, Harness Horse Hall of Famer and one of the co-founders of the Meadows Race Track. Another exhibit is on **Dan Patch**, the famous pacer who never lost a race. Dan Patch's time of 1:55 minutes to run a mile stood until 1960. The horse's owner, Marion Savage, used his pacer to sell his International Feed Company products.

An archeological dig on the Meadowcroft Village grounds uncovered evidence of the earliest human occupation of this hemisphere. The Smithsonian Institution carbon dated the artifacts back to 16,000 B.C. The site is not open to the public but a display shows how these prehistoric people lived.

Meadowcroft Museum of Rural Life is open May through October Wednesday through Saturday 10:00 A.M. to 5:00 P.M., and on Sunday 1:00 P.M. to 6:00 P.M. Admission is charged. There is a gift shop and snack shop. The Village hosts a number of special events ranging from Civil War re-enactments to concerts and festivals. Call (412) 587-3412 for a schedule.

Directions: From I-79 and I-70, take I-79 north to Exit 8A, the Meadow Lands. Turn left onto Pike Street and go to the light. Make a left turn (after crossing railroad tracks), onto Country Club Road. Go to stop sign and make a right turn onto N. Main Street Extension. Follow the road around to the left and make a left turn into the Trolley Museum at North Main Street and Museum Road. For Meadowcroft take Exit 11, Bridgeville. Take Route 50 west. Continue on Route 50 west for approximately 18 miles. After you pass the town of Avella, you will come to a "Y" in the road, bear right onto Fallen Timber Road. Continue on Fallen Timber Road until you come to Meadowcroft Road. Make a left onto Meadowcroft Road. It is about 1.5 miles to the entrance of Meadowcroft Museum of Rural Life on the left.

Phipps Conservatory

Petals Under Glass

In the not-too-distant past, Pittsburgh was called Steel City, Smoke Town and the Soot Capital of America. Only vestiges of that time remain, but the industrial barons who made a fortune during that era left a legacy of art and culture. Andrew Carnegie endowed an art and natural history museum (see Carnegie Institute selections), Henry Clay Frick's Clayton is now a house museum and his Frick Art Museum delights visitors (see selection). In 1893, Henry Phipps built an exotic glass-domed conservatory as his gift to the city. It is one of the country's few remaining Victorian conservatories.

The two-and-a-half acres under glass are luxuriously planted year-round. It's worth remembering in mid-winter when the snow lingers on the frozen ground and the sky remains a leaden gray that a world of color awaits amid the lush tropical foliage at **Phipps Conservatory**. You can get a jump on spring when you stroll through the 13 display rooms during the annual Spring Flower Show.

With the arrival of spring you can enjoy Phipps outdoor garden. So visitors can take the time to savor this floriferous setting, there are benches beside sparkling fountains. Just listening to the dancing water is relaxing, which explains why so much of New Age music includes the sound of water. Brick paths wind through a medieval herb garden, one of six small gardens. Both the perennial and annual gardens change with the season. In the spring, the semi-shade garden is particularly appealing with its flowering rhododendrons and azaleas in a series of woodland glades. The dwarf conifer collection provides a year-round appeal with its unusual forms, textures and colors that range from gold to emerald to deep blue.

The origin of design elements found in current landscaping are traced in the Conservatory's French and Japanese gardens. Other indoor specialty areas include a desert room, orchid room and a tropical palm court, the mainstay of Victorian conservatories. Chrysanthemums showcase autumn's riotous colors in the annual autumn show and the year ends with the December winter flower show.

Phipps Conservatory is open year-round, Tuesday through Sunday from 9:00 A.M. to 5:00 P.M. Admission is charged. There is no charge to stroll through the outdoor garden, which stays open until dusk from April to September. For additional information on a visitor information tape call (412) 622-6914.

Directions: From the Pennsylvania Turnpike, I-76, take Exit 6 to Route 376 west, then Exit 7A into Oakland on Bates Street. Make a right on Forbes Avenue, then make a right in front of the Carnegie Library on Bigelow Street (there is no sign indicating the name of the street, but you can't miss the library on the corner). Cross the Schenley Park Bridge and the Phipps Conservatory is on the right.

Pittsburgh Children's Museum

A Maze-ing Puppets

By definition, most museum exhibits require visitors to come to see them. Stuffee, the **Pittsburgh Children's Museum**'s mascot, has wanderlust. Not only does the seven-foot soft sculpture doll travel to local schools and community groups, he also opens his heart, and other vital organs, to teach children about health, nutrition and how their bodies work. **Stuffee** is so popular, he's been cloned. More than 12 smaller copies have been sold to museums across the country and to international museums like Northern Ireland's Ulster Museum.

Actually, the Pittsburgh Children's Museum (PCM) is not a static collection. Instead it offers interactive, hands-on exhibits and live performances in the historic Old Post Office Building at Allegheny Center. **Luckey's Climber**, a two-story maze in the rotunda, combines art and activity. The name is not misspelled and doesn't refer to the climber's chances of success. The creator of this amazing maze is Tom Luckey. His whimsical creation features randomly placed, colorful carpeted platforms linked by tunnels and openings through which kids wiggle, jump, squirm, climb and crawl as they make their way up this mesh-enclosed, tree-like configuration. Going down is easy, since there is an 11-foot sliding board from the seventh level.

Christopher Priore's Sky hangs in the center dome of the rotunda above Luckey's illusionary tree. This suspended mixed-media sculpture is a whimsical interpretation of the universe. Children have fun identifying celestial fixtures like the Big Dipper, represented by a giant soup ladle, and Pisces, a colorful fish.

Whimsy is a reoccurring motif at PCM, and it's certainly apparent in the **Andy Warhol Myths gallery** featuring a 1981 series of childhood fantasy figures—Mickey Mouse, Superman and Santa Claus—captured on silkscreen prints. A collection of toys, gadgets and memorabilia attest to the popularity of the icons of American culture depicted by Pittsburgh-native Andy Warhol (see Andy Warhol Museum selection). In an adjacent hands-on silkscreen printing studio visitors to the Warhol exhibit can learn how he worked while they create their silkscreen prints using pre-cut screens.

The PCM has its own celebrities. In the collection of puppets through the ages there are cultural icons, like the puppets from Mister Rogers' Neighborhood of Make-Believe and Jim Henson's whimsical creatures from *Dark Crystal* and the *Labyrinth*. On loan are such stars as Henson's Grover, the Swedish Chef and Animal. A short video shows how the Muppet television programs were produced and there are excerpts from several Jim Henson programs. The permanent puppet gallery showcases the international collection of Pittsburgh puppeteer Margo Lovelace. The oldest item in the more than 650-piece collection is a 1850 Belgium monk rod puppet. There's a Punch and Judy booth, Turkish shadow puppets, a 40-pound armored Sicilian rod puppet and a myriad of other colorful puppets from around the world.

The museum's **Riverscape**, the 1920s wharf area may be geographically on the lower level, but it's high on the list of fun spots for young visitors. Activity here includes loading the packet boat's cargo and taking it to market. Other areas include **Playpath**, a five-and-under playspace, and the **Limb Bender** where intrepid explorers climb to the ceiling and back while enjoying a series of ramps and slides.

Finally, the rotunda is also the scene of thematic programs. The programs include live performance and puppet shows, storytelling and crafts. Winter time's "**Magic of the Season**" lets families play in the snow without getting cold in its indoor snowscape. During the summer it becomes "**Summer in the City**"; fall brings "**Haunts, Hoots and Howls**." Call (412) 322-5062 for scheduling details. The museum takes many of their programs on the road including an award-winning musical comedy about good health habits.

The Pittsburgh Children's Museum's activities are designed for children 12 and younger to enjoy with their family and friends. Summer hours are Monday through Saturday 10:00 A.M. to 5:00 P.M. and Sunday 1:00 P.M. to 5:00 P.M.. The rest of the year hours are Tuesday through Saturday 10:00 A.M. to 5:00 P.M. and Sunday NOON to 5:00 P.M. Admission is charged. The museum shop carries a wide array of educational games, puzzles, books, craft kits and other gift items.

Directions: Take the Pennsylvania Turnpike, I-76, to Exit 5, proceed south on Route 28, the Allegheny Valley Expressway south; exit at the sign that reads Interstate 279. You will be on East Ohio Street, stay on that street and do not get on I-279. When you come to East Commons you must turn right. Follow the street around to North Commons and down the West Commons. After you pass the light on the West Commons turn left where you see the sign on the building marked "Apartment Manager" and an arrow pointing left. You may park on the street next to the museum or in the lot behind the museum. The Pittsburgh Children's Museum is at 10 Children's Way in Allegheny Center.

Pittsburgh Zoo and National Aviary in Pittsburgh

How do you Zoo?

The Pittsburgh Zoo is no longer in transition. It fully reflects the concept of natural habitats. Animals are not confined in cages, but roam free. Moats, rock enclosures, streams and vegetation provide natural and protective screens separating visitors from the animal.

This is an incredible turn-around since the **Pittsburgh Zoo** is an old-school zoo that opened on June 14, 1898. It was the third zoo in the city. Small collections existed in Riverview Park, now the North Side, and in Schenley Park in Oakland. The Pittsburgh Zoo, established in Highland Park, was described as a curiosity shop—one large building with cages inside, each with a door to an outside enclosure. Additions were made over the years: the bear and hoofed animal exhibit in the 1930s, a children's zoo in the 40s, and a nocturnal animals and aqua zoo in the 60s. It was not until 1980 that a ten-year plan was developed to reflect the new philosophy of zoo design, landscape immersion.

Animals and visitors are immersed in a landscape that recreates the natural habitat of each species. These expansive enclosures allow animals to interact as they would in the wild. Since fences and barriers are concealed as much as possible, this gives visitors a sense of adventure, of being a voyeur not a jailor. In keeping with this new trend, the Pittsburgh Zoo is also part of a program to preserve and propagate endangered species.

The Asian Forest and the African Savanna areas were the first habitats to reflect this new approach. Their objective was to give exotic, endangered species the chance to live and breed in a wilderness-like setting approximating their natural environment. At the same time, visitors see these animals as they would on safaris to far-flung spots on the globe.

Visitors in the **Asian Forest** glimpse Siberian tigers pacing the rocky promontory at the edge of a sharp precipice that falls in a sheer drop to the moat below. Only 200 to 400 of these largest

Habitats at the Pittsburgh Zoo recreate natural environments for animals like the snow leopard. A new $3.5 million Kid's Kingdom creates a stimulating seven-acre interactive environment for young visitors. PHOTO BY RAYMOND E. BAMRICK

of all cats exist in the wild. Now these rare Siberian tigers are breeding in zoos, including the Pittsburgh Zoo. The path leads from the tigers to a quiet pond with Asian waterfowl such as the demoiselle crane and Mandarin ducks. A few paces farther another pond with brilliant flamingos is shaded by lush marsh grasses and tropical trees. Don't settle for just a cursory glance, stay awhile and watch the long-legged birds' behavior. These social creatures engage in several unusual patterns of courtship like "head flagging" during which all move their heads in one direction and "marching" when the entire flock seems to be on parade.

The flamingos mark a transition to another continent and the land and plant life changes. The **African Savanna** is rough, arid terrain where lions, leopards and white rhinoceros thrive. Another glassy pond with floating plants is enjoyed by Egyptian geese, sacred ibises, crowned cranes and lesser flamingos. The leopards are often spotted in the branches of a 45-foot tree either sleeping or keeping an eye on nearby zebras and gazelles, their natural prey. An early morning visit may give you a chance to catch the massive elephants bathing in their 100,000 gallon pool. Springtime is particularly appealing because the abundant yellow iris surrounding the pool are in bloom. The elephants' terrain is bare sandy soil but, nearby, the giraffes enjoy a grassland spotted with locust trees.

Completing the ten year plan was the **Tropical Forest** exhibit that opened in April 1991. These unique ecosystems are disappearing at a rate of 50 to 100 acres per minute. If the world loses the tropical forests, half of the plants and animals that exist on this planet will also be extinct. Consider that several acres of forested Pennsylvania has perhaps 10 species of trees and a tropical forest has 200, and you will have some idea of the magnitude of these threatened forests. Pittsburgh Zoo's Tropical Forest shelters 16 species of endangered primates and 2,000 specimens of over 90 species of tropical plants. Visitors enter a misty 5-acre indoor/outdoor jungle divided into four geographic regions—Madagascar, South America, Asia and Africa—to reflect the animals exhibited. Family groups of the Western lowland gorilla are a popular hit in this habitat. There are also lemurs, spider monkeys, sloths, howler monkeys, pacas, saki monkeys, gibbons, orangutans, DeBrazza's monkeys, Colobus monkeys and mandrills.

The zoo also has a bear exhibit, herpetairum, aqua zoo and children's zoo where youngsters can have a hands-on experience. Young children also enjoy the merry-go-round and train ride.

The zoo is open daily year round. Winter hours are 9:00 A.M. to 5:00 P.M. Summer hours are 10:00 A.M. to 6:00 P.M. The zoo is closed only on Christmas Day. Admission is charged.

It should also be noted that Pittsburgh has the only indoor zoo in the country devoted entirely to birds. The **National Aviary** is Pittsburgh's collection of over 450 birds, representing 175 species, one of the largest in the country. Here too, the hope is to preserve and breed endangered species. The collection includes 15 endangered and 25 threatened species. The National Aviary opened in 1952; it was called the Pittsburgh Aviary until 1993. Popular areas include the marsh room that simulates tropical wetlands with egrets, herons, ibis and spoonbills and a tropical jungle. After wandering through the conservatory, stroll around the exterior to see additional specimens. The aviary is open daily 9:00 A.M. to 4:30 P.M. Closed on Christmas Day. Admission is charged.

Directions: Take the Pennsylvania Turnpike, I-76, to Exit 5, proceed south on Route 28, the Allegheny Valley Expressway south and take that to the Highland Park Bridge. Cross the bridge, then turn right on Butler Street and the zoo will be just ahead on the left in Highland Park. For the National Aviary, don't cross the bridge. Instead, continue on the Allegheny Valley Expressway onto East Ohio Street to Allegheny Center Mall; this runs into East Commons, which you will follow around the Allegheny Mall Square as it becomes North Commons, then West Commons. The Aviary is in West Park off Allegheny Commons West.

Station Square

Plane Geometry: Square, Point, Triangle

The Allegheny, Monongahela and Ohio Rivers converge in Pittsburgh. In the early 19th century the city was a terminus for flatboats, packets, towboats, rafts and canal boats moving goods and people east and west, north and south. By the mid-19th century, railroads were added to this transportation hub. Steam trains, electric interurbans, trolleys and inclines put the city on the cutting edge of transit.

It is claimed that the first automobile in the country, the 1898 Panhard was imported from France to Pittsburgh by H.J. Heinz. The presence of iron, steel, glass, aluminum and oil industries—all the components of automobile manufacturing—created an ideal environment in which to build cars. Pittsburgh was producing automobiles *before* Detroit. Within a 60-mile radius there were 23 automobile and truck manufacturers in the first four decades of the 20th century.

Station Square's Bessemer Court has rail and trolley cars as well as a paddlewheel and a ten-ton Bessemer converter. Along the Monongahela River there is an **Industrial Riverwalk**, an outdoor walking museum, with displays revealing artifacts from the region's industrial heritage.

The boilerhouse, now the **Station Square Playhouse**, is only one of numerous buildings remaining from the time when this was a 40-acre complex of railroad yards and buildings used by the Pittsburgh & Lake Erie Railroad. This station was the terminus for 76 passenger trains a day and thousands of tons of freight and mail.

The 1897 Freight House now houses The Shops at Station Square with over 70 boutiques and shops and more than a dozen dining spots. Shop hours Monday through Saturday 10:00 A.M. to 9:00 P.M. and Sundays NOON to 5:00 P.M. Restaurant hours vary. There are also four antique rail cars, converted to the Bessemer Court Car Shops, that are open April through December. The Shovel Warehouse has been converted to Commerce Court with more shops and office space.

To evoke the heyday of the railroad era when passengers wore bowler hats, spotless spats, boas and bustles, you can enjoy the award-winning cuisine at the **Grand Concourse Restaurant** and **Gandy Dancer Saloon** in the 1901 railroad terminal under the original 60-foot stained-glass vaulted ceiling. The waiting room is the main dining area, while the former ladies waiting room and station dining room serve as small intimate dining areas. A former walkway is the glass-enclosed River Room and the baggage chamber is the Gandy Dancer Saloon and Oyster Bar. Both restaurant and saloon are decorated with vintage railroad photographs and artifacts. Outside the Gandy Dancer, there's an open-air Garden Cafe.

As you might expect, the term Gandy Dancer comes from the early railroad days. In the early 1800s there was an Irish boss named Gandy overseeing immigrants who were laying track. He sang old tunes while the workers swung their picks and hammers in tune to his songs. The workers became known as Gandy's Dancers. A less colorful tale traces the term to workers using tools produced by the Gandy Manufacturing Company.

East of the Smithfield Street Bridge and along the river, is an open-air amphitheater, the site of ethnic festivals, musical performances and arts and crafts festivals. If you stroll a bit farther on this side of the bridge, you will be able to take a ride on the Monongahela Incline (see selection).

At the other end of the Station Square complex along the Riverwalk, a new riverfront restaurant is projected. Just past this is the parking lot for the Duquesne Incline (see selection).

Heading back toward the main Station Square action, directly on the river, is the dock for the **Gateway Clipper Fleet**, the largest and most successful passenger sightseeing vessel fleet in the United States. Gateway Clipper riverboats explore all three rivers, including a narrated lock-and-dam cruise, fall foliage

The Gateway Clipper Fleet, the largest and most successful passenger sightseeing vessel fleet in the country, provides some of the best views of Pittsburgh.

---

trips, moonlight dinner-dance cruises and special ethnic cruises. For times and fares call (412) 355-7980.

Directions: From the Pennsylvania Turnpike, I-76, take Exit 6, the Parkway East to downtown Pittsburgh. Cross the Fort Pitt Bridge and make a right turn into the Station Square parking area.

Strip District and Senator John Heinz Pittsburgh Regional History Center

Regional Smorgasbord

Grandfathers, fathers and sons have worked as wholesale and retail food vendors in Pittsburgh's **Strip District**. Penn Avenue and Smallman Street encompass the district, which now extends west of the 16th Street bridge to include The Boardwalk, an entertainment complex on the Allegheny River.

The Strip has something for everyone—fresh baked specialty breads and pastries, chicken feet, mountain oysters, wood ears, cuttlefish, shitake mushrooms, nearly a dozen varieties of paprika, roughly 25 varieties of olives, 64 types of coffee, fresh figs, lemongrass plus the area's best selection of fresh fish (Wholey's and Benkovitz are must stops when at the Strip) and produce.

Scattered among these food vendors, who literally spill over into sidewalk stands, are quaint shops selling a variety of merchandise from pottery to potted plants. There's an ethnic mix as well with vendors offering southern and eastern European specialties along with Hispanic and Asian restaurants and groceries.

The City of Pittsburgh is committed to preserving this wholesale food district and has purchased the produce terminal using Urban Renewal Authority and Community Development Block grants. Unlike some cities, here the old world and the new is thriving. Since the market has generations of history behind it, there is little fear that it will become too yuppified. Here the shops have character. You can still see establishments with copper-stamped ceilings and many have buckled plank floors. The air is pungent with a mix of spices, fish, flowers, fresh baked bread, chocolate and enticing aromas from the vendors cooking tasty treats at the sidewalk carts.

Shipments of produce arrive Wednesday, so the freshest supplies are available on Thursday. The best bargains are to be had on Saturday afternoons because vendors lower prices so they won't have to carry perishables over the weekend. The majority of the stores open Monday through Saturday from 8:00 A.M. to 5:00 P.M. Saturday morning is the busiest time to browse.

In the early 1900s there were 17 churches in the Strip District. Four remain and one is open to the public. **St. Patrick's Roman Catholic Church**, Liberty Avenue and 17th Street, has a piece of Ireland's Blarney Stone in the steeple. The courtyard sanctuary is a replica of France's Grotto of Lourdes. Another not-to-be-missed spot is the **Society for Art in Crafts**, 2100 Smallman Street, which has permanent art exhibits and juried work that is available for purchase.

The Adelman Lumber Company's 1880s warehouse on Smallman Street is being converted into the **Senator John Heinz Pittsburgh Regional History Center**. The museum's interactive exhibits and audio visual programs will interpret the local history of the ethnic groups who settled around Pittsburgh. It will focus on the workers and industrial and political leaders. Pulitzer Prize-winning author and historian David McCullough says the center, which is scheduled to open in 1996, "will be unlike that of any city in the nation, if not anywhere in the world."

There are numerous delicatessens and eateries in the Strip plus several restaurants, Crewser's, River Watch and Buster's Crab. For entertainment there is Donzi's, a dance club in the Down by the Riverside complex. Metropol is the late night spot for modern rock enthusiasts. This converted warehouse at 1600 Smallman Street has a regular weekend crowd. Adjacent to the Metropol is Rosebud, a coffeehouse with international and domestic coffees and desserts plus a few other light menu selections.

Directions: From I-76 take Exit 5, which will put you on Route 28 South. Turn at sign for Route 28 Expressway south to Pittsburgh. Cross the 16th Street Bridge and turn left on Liberty Avenue. Go up several blocks and make a left which will take you over to Penn Avenue, which is the Strip District's main street.

Tour-Ed Mine

Light at the End of the Tunnel

There is no substitute for first-hand experience and no written description of mining can convey what it was like for coal miners in Pennsylvania in the 1800s. But when you take the miner's train a half mile down into the **Tour-Ed Mine** and listen to a retired miner talk about his work, you will begin to sense what it was like to work the coal mines. You'll also see the impressive improvements in mine equipment and mine safety.

There were once over a hundred coal mining operations beneath Allegheny County, employing 40,000 to 50,000 men. Tour-Ed is the only mine in the area that provides a glimpse of this once thriving industry. Allegheny Steel (now Allegheny Ludlum) built this mine in the early 1900s to supply coal needed to fuel the steel-making operation, essential until electrical power supplanted coal. Several other mining companies worked these shafts, before they were acquired by Ira Wood in 1965. Wood owns and works several mines in the area, and he operated this mine for 15 years, then switched to operating it as an educational venture. Wood wanted to show visitors how mining had progressed since 1932 when he dug coal with a pick and shovel for $2.36 a day.

Safety is a continuing concern. In all the years the mine operated there was never a fatality or serious injury. Each day before tours begin, a safety inspection is conducted. Before visitors go down into the mine the guides provide background on this mine, mining in general and mining equipment. Lighting equipment is shown from early candles, through oil lights, carbide lights and modern lights operated by power packs.

Visitors, like the 200 miners who once worked this vein, enter through a tunnel-like portal called a drift entry. Even small kids have to bend way down to get into what were called "man-trip" cars. Once inside, you sit on the low benches in one of the five compartments. In the early days of mining, the cars entering the mines had neither seats nor roof. They rolled down on a gravity incline and were pulled back up by mules. Now the cars are powered by an electric locomotive. Another significant improvement is the illumination in the tunnel. In the beginning the miners worked in inky darkness, relieved only by the flickering light of the candles on their cloth caps.

When you reach the main shaft, you'll be 164 feet beneath the surface (under the town of Hunting Hills), with a temperature around 52 degrees. The low ceiling makes you glad you were issued a hardhat with your ticket. Guides demonstrate how the ceilings are tested and how support bolts are drilled. Display tunnels have working examples of equipment that span the decades and chart the course of mine improvement.

The main tool in the first area, representing the years 1800 to 1860, is the pick. The first thing a miner would do when he began his shift was check the solidity of the roof and make sure the air in the shaft was safe. Then the miner would lie down on his side and dig at the bottom of the coal vein with his pick, clearing a slot or "kerf" so that when the dyanmite exploded the coal would shoot down into the slot. Dynamite holes were hand-drilled with an auger. From his meager wages, the miner had to purchase his tools and dynamite. After the coal was blasted out, it was shoveled onto a wooden cart like the one on display. Miners called their shovels "banjoes."

Next, in the display covering 1860 to 1900, you'll see the pick's replacement, a punching machine that ran like a jackhammer. Although part of the work was done by machines, the miner still had to dynamite the coal and load it into wagons.

After 1900, electric tools such as drills and cutting machines made the work easier. While it took hours to hack out a slot with a pick, the cutting machine did the job in 15 minutes. Later models took only three minutes. Concurrent with the cutting machine, the shaker conveyor belt was introduced, the first mechanical method of loading coal. The noise of these unyielding machines seems even louder in the confines of the mine's tunnels.

The final display area has modern equipment, from 1942 to the present. There is a Joy loader, with two arms that scoop up the coal like a giant robot. The earliest models scooped six tons a minute, recent models load 25 tons a minute. A Joy shuttle car carries the coal to the intermediate or main haulage, thus eliminating the need for track. Finally, there is a Joy continuous miner, which eliminated drilling, blasting and loading. This behemoth starts digging into the coal at the floor level and rips a 24-inch path to the roof. After cutting the coal, it proceeds to load it onto a carrier. Such improvements have increased the daily output of coal per miner from $2^1/_2$ tons in 1890 to 20 tons today.

After riding back to the surface, you can compare underground mining with a strip mining operation. Equipment is in place that shows you the basics of this operation. Also on the surface is an oil shed, hardware shed, blacksmith's shop, 1785 pioneer cabin, wagon barn and a working sawmill.

Also interesting is the museum display of **Ira's artifact collection** from early mining days. Shelves have merchandise sold at a typical company store where miners spent their scrip, distributed by some companies instead of money. There are hundreds of old bottles, many still filled with their medicinal tonics. The collection also includes mining lamps, caps and other tools. A parlor, kitchen and bedrooms have been set up to suggest a miner's home. There is also a 1918 barber shop, with equipment obtained from the Allegheny County Workhouse. One wall-long display cabinet contains Ira and his wife's collection of dogs and donkeys.

The Tour-Ed Mine is open daily from 1:00 P.M. to 4:00 P.M. from Memorial Day to Labor Day; it is closed Tuesdays. Admission is charged for the tour that takes approximately two hours. On the third Sunday of the month from May through September an **Antique Flea Market** is held on the grounds. For additional information call (412) 224-4720.

Directions: From I-76, the Pennsylvania Turnpike, take Exit 5, the Allegheny Valley Interchange. Take the Allegheny Valley Expressway, Route 28, north to Exit 14, Tarentum, and follow the Red Belt West signs for one-half mile. The mine is opposite Woodlawn Golf Course on Bull Creek Road and is visible from the expressway.

Wildflower Reserve Raccoon Creek State Park

Dainty But Wild

At one of the largest and most beautiful parks in the state (7,323 acres), you'll discover unique stands of wildflowers. A 314-acre wildflower preserve is carved out of **Raccoon Creek State Park** along its eastern boundary. Eight trails covering 5.5 miles wind through the preserve where more than 500 species of flowering plants can be spotted in a variety of habitats. You'll hike through oak-hickory forests and past pine plantations, abandoned fields and into flood plain forests.

The widest selection of wildflowers is seen from late April through mid-May. The earliest wildflowers bloom in late March when the snow trillium begin peeking out. They continue into mid-April when they are joined by skunk cabbage, coltsfoot and trailing arbutus. Interestingly, skunk cabbage is in the same family as jack-in-the-pulpit, which doesn't bloom until mid-May.

In late April along Raccoon's trails you will see hepatica,

bluets, trout lily, wild ginger, spicebush and roughly ten additional blooming plants. Early May brings another 15 wildflowers into bloom including trillium, woodland phlox, goldenseal, violets, wood anemone and bluebells. If you've never hiked the wildflower trails, mid-May is probably your best bet because whether spring is early or late you are sure to see a wide variety of blooms including marsh marigold, wild geranium, buttercups, columbine, spring larkspur, yellow lady's slipper and a host of others. Coming into bloom in late May are fire pink, bedstraw, May apple, green dragon, celandine and others.

June and July are slower months, but by late July the forest will be blooming with evening primrose, sunflowers, cardinal flower, flowering spurge, virgin's bower and roughly 20 other wildflowers. Fewer flowers bloom in August and September but you will see the colorful coneflower, blue lobelia and closed blue gentian.

All of the trails within the preserve are pedestrian only, but within Raccoon Creek State Park there are three miles of bridle trails. The park at large also has four self-guided nature trails and exhibits at the interpretative building. One of the trails leads past the old **Frankfort Mineral Springs**, a nationally renown health spa in the 1800s. Visitors once sought the healing power of these mineral springs. Now hikers can appreciate their scenic appeal, particularly in the winter months when spectacular ice formations appear. Park personnel lead wildflower walks, night hikes and other interpretive programs from April through December. Roughly 4,000 acres of the park are open for hunting, trapping and dog training from the beginning of archery season through March. Game found in the park include deer, wild turkey, grouse, squirrel and rabbit.

The park's most popular feature is the 101-acre **Raccoon Creek Lake**. Non-powered and electric-powered boats are permitted on the lake. There is a boat launch area and rowboats and canoes can be rented during the summer months. Fishermen try their luck at catching bluegills, sunfish, bullheads, catfish, yellow perch, walleye, crappies, largemouth and smallmouth bass. The lake and its feeder streams also have brook and rainbow trout. During the summer months there is a guarded turf beach open 11:00 A.M. to 7:00 P.M. Picnicking and camping are also popular. Winter is slower but hearty outdoor enthusiasts can enjoy ice fishing and skating on the lake. Sledding, snowmobiling and cross-country skiing is also permitted in the park.

Directions: From the Pennsylvania Turnpike, I-76, take I-376 to I-279. Then continue south on Route 22/30 where they split, follow Route 30 west. Raccoon Creek State Park's wildflower preserve is just off Route 30. The park entrance is well-marked. There is a second park entrance off Route 18.

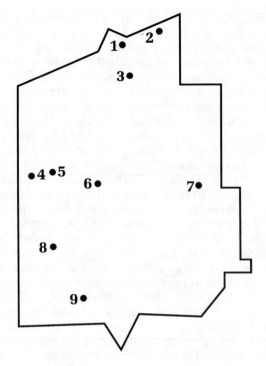

LAKE ERIE REGION

1. *Erie*
   Discovery Square and Erie
     Zoo
   Presque Isle State Park
   United States Brig *Niagara*
   Watson/Curtze Mansion and
     Firefighters Historical
     Museum

2. *North East*

3. *Waterford*
   Waterford and Fort LeBoeuf

4. *Linesville*
   Pymatuning Lake

5. *Conneaut Lake*

6. *Meadville*
   Baldwin Reynolds House and
     Market House

7. *Titusville*
   Drake Well and Oil City
   Otto Coupler Torpedo Mu-
     seum and Oil Creek and
     Titusville RR

8. *Greenville*
   Brucker Great Blue Heron
     Sanctuary and Mercer
     County

9. *Mercer*
   Mercer County Historical So-
     ciety

Lake Erie
Region

Pennsylvania is the only state both on the Canadian border and the Mason-Dixon Line. It owes the first distinction to Lake Erie, part of the 32,000 acres of lakes that make up this water lover's recreational paradise. Lake Erie may be the state's only "Great" lake, but others in the region are noteworthy. The region's largest man-made lake is Pymatuning, the largest and deepest natural lake is Conneaut.

Presque Isle State Park, the 3,200-acre sandy peninsula that juts seven miles into Lake Erie, is one of the top five places in the world for birdwatching according to *Bird Watcher's Digest* and the second best in the world for sunsets according to the *National Geographic Traveler*.

During the War of 1812, one of the most famous battles in American naval history took place on Lake Erie. Commodore Oliver Hazard Perry, aboard the U.S. Brig *Niagara*, one of the last remaining early 19th-century warships now renovated and docked in Erie, issued his triumphant claim: "We have met the enemy and they are ours."

This region changed the world when Edwin Drake drilled America's first oil well in 1859 near Titusville. Drake Well, Oil City, the Otto Cupler Torpedo Museum and other sites have combined as the Oil Region Heritage Park to reveal the complete story of this remarkable era.

Baldwin-Reynolds House
and Market House

Meadville Memories

Secret compartments, hidden doors, a disguised safe and stories that go back to the region's earliest inhabitants await at Meadville's **Baldwin-Reynolds House**.

In 1789, in return for his service to the Continental Army,

Squire Samuel Lord was given 403 acres of land in what was then Allegheny County, and later Crawford County. He built a log cabin overlooking French Creek and the Venango Indian Trail, over which George Washington trekked in 1753 on his way to Fort LeBouef.

Henry Baldwin purchased the Lord property at the Squire's death in 1840. Baldwin, one of the county's first two attorneys, moved to the area after graduating from Yale Law School. He lived for many years in Pittsburgh and pursued a political career, serving in Congress, becoming a staunch supporter and developer of the protective tariff and an influential backer of Andrew Jackson. Repaying his political supporter, Jackson appointed Baldwin to the Supreme Court. Many years ago Ripley's "Believe It or Not" column had a story about Baldwin's youthful duel in 1805. It claims he was shot over the heart by his opponent but survived because he was carrying a silver dollar in his breast pocket.

About the time Baldwin acquired land in Meadville, he visited his son at Hunter's Hill plantation, outside Nashville, Tennessee. Baldwin was so impressed with the Greek Revival houses in this area that he gave his builder a drawing of one of the mansions and said, "Build this for me." Less than a year after moving into his new home, Baldwin died, leaving his widow Sarah Baldwin with huge debts. She leased the house to a female boarding school and after three years, in 1847, sold the property to her nephew William Reynolds, who became the first mayor of Meadville. Over the next 60 years William did much to beautify the house including adding gas chandeliers, parquet floors and a solarium. His interest extended to the lawns and gardens.

The last family to inhabit the house was William's son John Earle, and his wife Katherine Shryock. John Earle inherited the house at the death of his parents in 1911. He too was town mayor, serving three terms. He also wrote a history of the region.

William Reynolds expanded the first floor library, adding ornate paneling with many hidden storage areas and secret compartments. The area was used for theatrical tableaus popular at the time; the two library doors served as stage entrances. Family members and guests acted out scenes from plays and dramatic readings. William also had a hidden in-house vault in the dining room.

William died in the bedroom where he was born. At his widow's death in 1963 the house was acquired by the Crawford County Historical Society. Seventeen of the rooms are filled with period and family furniture as well as historical displays.

Young visitors appreciate the toys and dolls in the upstairs nursery. There is also exhibit space in the basement area, including cases filled with Native American artifacts and a collection of delightful songbird carvings done by Ulysses Reynolds. There is also the office equipment from John Reynolds's land office. A later of-

444

fice acquisition is the old Franklin typewriter with the keys organized in a different manner than the standard typewriter.

The Baldwin-Reynolds House is on the National Register of Historic Places, but so too is the small **country office of Dr. J. Russell Mosier** that was moved to the estate grounds from Littles Corner. Mosier graduated from the Baltimore campus of the University of Maryland Medical School in 1883 at age 28. He purchased this office six years later from his wife's uncle for $325.00. Mosier carried out daily medical examinations and performed surgery in this office. When he died in 1938, his office was locked with everything intact. In 1976, the office and equipment was acquired by the Crawford County Historical Society and moved to this location, although there is no connection between these two properties.

Dr. Mosier showcased his collection of shells and historical memorabilia in his waiting room, and even in 1938 the doctor's office had magazines. A 1909 rural postal delivery map helped the doctor with directions for his house calls, which he made by horseback, although later he did have a car. In the examination room there is a chair that pulls into a table, two electric shock machines, his desk, ledgers and correspondence. He charged between 50 cents and $1.50 depending on the problem, and the ledger shows he was often paid in produce. Dr. Mosier delivered 2,300 babies and saved so many lives during the flu epidemic in 1918-1919 he was invited to join the staff at the Meadville hospital. He, however, preferred to continue his rural practice. There's also a small pharmacy in Mosier's office since he mixed his own pills and nostrums. Mosier had one of the first crank telephones in the county (1901), but it was only connected to his adjacent house so that his wife could call him to dinner. Dr. Mosier saved a skeleton from his medical schools days in Baltimore. He called it "Uncle Billy"; legend claims it was the body of an executed convict. It's missing a few teeth and bones because his children enjoyed playing with it.

Tours are given of Baldwin-Reynolds from Memorial Day through Labor Day on Wednesdays through Sundays from 1:00 P.M. and 5:00 P.M. and by appointment after Labor Day through October, call (814) 724-6080. There is a nominal charge. Bi-annually the house museum is open for "Trees of Christmas" a holiday celebration. For details on this event call (814) 333-2689.

The **Market House** was built about a decade before Dr. Mosier arrived in the Meadville area. It is the oldest continuously operated market in the state. Offering fresh produce in season and a host of homemade items year-round including pasta, maple sugar products, coffees, baked goods and a butcher shop. The market, at 910 Market Street, opens Tuesday through Saturday at 7:00 A.M. and closes at 3:00 P.M. The Meadville Council of the Arts has gallery space, art classrooms, a small theater and a dance

445

studio on the second floor. Browsers are welcome Tuesday through Friday 12:30 P.M. to 4:00 P.M. and Saturdays 9:30 A.M. to NOON.

There are two additional spots of interest in town. One is the **David Mead Log Cabin**, a replica of the cabin David and his brother built on the east bank of French Creek in 1787. This was the beginning of the first settlement in northwestern Pennsylvania. This was actually two cabins with a breezeway connecting them, called a dog trot. One side suggests Mead's home while the other represents a schoolhouse since his second wife was a teacher. The cabin, across French Creek from Meadville's downtown area, is open Memorial Day through August on weekends from 1:00 P.M. to 4:00 P.M.

Finally, there is the **1885 Academy Theater**, designed to be a Temple of Amusement for the citizens of Meadville. Community theater, films, recitals and special events take place at the theatre at 275 Chestnut Avenue. For a schedule call (814) 337-8000.

Ten miles east of Meadville (7 miles on Route 27 east and 3 miles on State Route 2032; in Guys Mills continue east on State Route 198 for .8 miles) is the **Erie National Wildlife Refuge**. This 4,967-acre habitat provides a temporary home for migratory waterfowl. Spring migration is in March and early April while the fall season is September to November. Frequently-seen species include black duck, wood duck, hooded merganser, blue-winged teal and mallard. Also sighted in the varied habitats are great blue heron, woodcock and bald eagle. There is a second section of the refuge, the 3,027-acre **Seneca Unit**, ten miles north near Cambridge Springs. Habitats at the refuge include forests, swamps, beaver ponds, impoundments, grasslands and croplands. These diverse areas have attracted more than 236 species, with 15 more sighted on only one or two occasions. There is a small Visitor Center, nature trails (these are closed during hunting season), a wildlife drive and an observation blind overlooking Reit's Pond. For additional information on the refuge call (814) 789-3585.

Directions: From I-79 take Exit 36-A Route 6/19/322 across the French Creek Bridge. Head north on the French Creek Parkway and exit on Reynolds Avenue for the Baldwin-Reynolds House at the corner of Reynolds and Terrace Street. Continue down Terrace Street and turn right to 910 Market Street for Market House.

Brucker Great Blue Heron
Sanctuary and Mercer County

On the Wing and Hot Wings

Mercer County makes good on its boasts. The first boast: the **Brucker Great Blue Heron Sanctuary** of Thiel College has the largest colony of breeding blue herons in the state with over 210 nests. The 45-acre sanctuary is three miles south of Greenville on Route 18. Approximately 400 great blue herons live in the colony at this sanctuary.

Herons are one of the largest birds native to western Pennsylvania. Most are over four feet tall with a seven foot wingspan. They can fly as fast as 35 mph. Their nests are usually three-to-four-feet across and around 70 to 90 feet above the ground.

The entire sanctuary is open September through January. During the rest of the year the herons nest and visitors are restricted to the observation shelter. A number of the nests can be seen from the shelter, particularly with the aid of binoculars. March, April and May are the best times to see nesting herons, the earlier the better, since it is easier to see them before the trees leaf out. Herons fly in and out of the woods through July. In the fall they leave for their winter migration to Mexico, Cuba, the West Indies and South America.

Superlatives are also used when it comes to shopping. Whether you stay in the Mercer area or travel east or west of it, there are interesting and unique shopping spots. Just one mile outside town on Route 62 is **Old Timber Farm** with a Victorian farmhouse, a centuries-old barn with antique tools, craft shops and a restaurant.

Southeast of Mercer, over the county line is **Volant**, a quaint community with an old mill, covered bridge and 50 unique craft, antique and country shops. The New Wilmington area is home to Old Order Amish families and their home-crafted items are available for sale in and around Volant.

In the west around **Sharon** there is a trio of shops with impressive credentials. Reyers Shoes claims to be "The World's Largest Shoe Store," with more than 175,000 shoes and 300 name brands. All shoes are at least 15 percent off regular retail price (800-245-1550). Just down State Street is The Winner that purports to be "The World's Largest Off-Price Ladies Fashion Store." They have four floors of fashion at up to 70 percent off retail prices. Continuing down State Street you'll come to Daffin's Candies with a unique Chocolate Kingdom. Children love the 700 pound rabbit, the 400 pound turtle and the 175 pound elephant. There is even a chocolate castle. To reach this delectable kingdom you have to pass through a tempting array of candy made at the Daffin chocolate plant.

If you want to enjoy lunch while shopping in Sharon you can't beat Quaker Steak & Lube. They boast: "The World's Most Famous Wings." These award-winning wings are delicious and the setting is fun as the former gasoline station now has cars hanging upside down from the ceiling. There's also a 1936 Chevrolet on the garage rack. There are Classic cars, an Indy 500 race car and a '57 T-Bird. Their license plate collection runs from

1910 to the present, plus there is a great deal more automobile memorabilia. It's open every day of the year for lunch and dinner.

Just southeast of the juncture of I-79 and I-80 in Grove City is **Wendell August Forge.** Free tours of the plant are given Monday through Friday between 8:00 A.M. and NOON and 12:30 P.M. to 4:00 P.M. Wendell August is noted for its unique hand-forged gifts. They boast they are the country's oldest and largest operating forge.

In Greenville, near the heron sanctuary, there are two transportation museums. At the **Greenville Railroad Museum** they have the only surviving engine from a group of the nine largest switch engines ever built. Engine 604, built in 1936 by the Baldwin works in Philadelphia, weighs 322 tons. This engine was used in the steel industry on the Union Railroad. On display with this historic engine is a coal tender, hopper car and caboose. The stationmaster's quarters and dispatcher's office are reconstructed. Railroad exhibits include old train schedules and railroad uniforms.

Visitors are especially interested in the exhibit on **Stefan Banic,** born in Slovakia. Banic emigrated to America and lived in Greenville from 1907 to 1921. While he worked as a coal miner, he invented the parachute. He patented it in 1914 and donated the concept to the United States government in return for honorary membership in the Army Air Corps.

The Greenville Railroad Museum, on Route 358, is open Friday, Saturday and Sunday from NOON to 5:00 P.M. from the first weekend in May through the first weekend in June and on Memorial Day. It is open daily from the second week in June through Labor Day. The weekend schedule is in effect during September and October. There is no admission charged.

At Lock 22 on Alan Avenue in Greenville, you'll find the **Canal Museum** with a full-size replica of the 40-foot *Rufus S. Reed.* This canal freighter hauled coal and supplies in the 1840s. There are also dioramas, canal tools, equipment and old photographs of the Erie Extension Canal. The museum is open daily 1:00 P.M. to 5:00 P.M. from Memorial Day through Labor Day and on weekends in the fall. Admission is charged.

For those staying overnight in the area, the most atmospheric place is Tara, a plantation house inspired by *Gone With The Wind.* Guest rooms and gourmet dining combine to make this a memorable experience; call (412) 962-3535 for information and reservations. Tara is north of Hermitage, outside of Clark off Route 258.

Directions: From I-79 take the I-80 exit west; at Exit 2 follow Route 19 north to Mercer. For Hermitage and Sharon take Route 62 south from Mercer. To reach the Brucker Great Blue Heron Sanctuary in Greenville take Route 18 north from Hermitage. For Volant take Route 158 south to New Wilmington then Route 208 east to Volant. For additional information on Mercer County attractions call (800) 637-2370.

Conneaut Lake

Resort Strong Century Later

By the 1870s, when Aaron Lynce established a boat launch and picnic area on **Conneaut Lake**, passenger steamboats had been plying the waters for over a decade. The recreational appeal of Pennsylvania's largest natural lake expanded in the 1870s when the lake was lowered nine feet to its present level and a railroad line was added. Conneaut Lake became more accessible from nearby towns. During the heyday of steam navigation more than seven passenger boats operated simultaneously.

In 1892, a group of investors who purchased and expanded Lynce's Landing, opened the **Conneaut Lake Exposition Park** with amusement rides and a music pavilion. They envisioned this as a Pennsylvania Chautauqua. The park expanded the popularity of Conneaut Lake and in the first two decades of the 20th century more luxurious steamboats were introduced and the strains of dance music drifted across the quiet water. Conneaut's Golden Age crashed with the stock market in 1929. The empty boats fell into disrepair and were dismantled, burned or sunk. Many of these sunken vessels still lie beneath the waters of Lake Conneaut. At least three old steamboats lie in **Ice House Bay** just south of Mosquito Point. You can wreck dive in the lake but anything you recover belongs to the state.

This certainly wasn't the end of water traffic on the lake. Smaller passenger boats maintained a ferry service until 1982 and small sightseeing vessels also operated. In 1972 Conneaut Lake Cruises launched a 65-foot sternwheeler, the *Barbara J*, the only working paddle boat in the state. Forty-five minute narrated cruises depart from the dock at Conneaut Lake Park hourly from NOON to 8:00 P.M. (Note: When you enter the park to board the cruise boat you are not charged the park admission, and you can stroll around the park after your cruise. To enjoy the rides you have to pay a park admission fee.) If you want to get out on the lake on your own, you can rent motor boats and pontoons from 10:00 A.M. to dusk. For details call (814) 382-7472. Conneaut is one of the few lakes in the area that has no horsepower limit for boats.

The century-old **Conneaut Lake Park** is an old-fashioned amusement park with rides (including a 1938 wooden roller coaster), water attractions, midway arcade, kiddieland and picnicking. The park has a sandy beach for swimming and a boardwalk along an eighth- of-a-mile of the nine-mile shoreline. Weekend concerts and special events like polka fests and vintage car shows add to the fun.

You can camp at the park or stay at the Hotel Conneaut, a comfortable old property that opened in 1909 and has a loyal following who return year after year and generation after generation. The hotel restaurant overlooks the lake and rocking chairs on the wide porch offer a cool respite on hot summer days.

The small **Lakeland Museum** in the old firehall on the park grounds has photographs from the steamboat era, musical advertisements from the Big Bands who once played at the Beach Club and the 1922 speedboat *Liberty the Second*. This experimental prototype, powered by a World War I plane engine, set a world speed record before it sank in the lake. The boat was recovered in 1985 and ran again in 1987.

If you want to enjoy a swim head for **Firemen's Beach** on the southern shore. There is a parking fee charged. This end of the lake is where you'll find Conneaut Cellars Winery, which had its first commercial crush in the fall of 1982. This small country-style winery makes 1,500 gallons of wine a year, with 17 varieties from sweet to dry. The winery is open daily for tours. Although they have contracts with local growers, they do have some grapes growing behind the winery. On your tour you'll also see the old-fashioned vertical press and the American oak barrels in which the wine is fermented and aged. Be sure to taste some of these award-winning wines including their Cabernet Sauvignon. Inquire about the hand-painted labels that can be special ordered for holidays, birthdays, weddings and other events. The winery is open 10:00 A.M. to 6:00 P.M. From January through April they are closed on Mondays.

Across the highway from the winery is Silver Shores Restaurant. Wide windows provide a panoramic view of the lake and is a scenic spot for lunch or dinner.

Directions: From I-79 take Exit 36-B, and head west six miles on Route 322. Make a right on Route 18 to circle the lake. For Conneaut Cellars Winery continue on Route 322 and the winery will be on your left.

Discovery Square and Erie Zoo

Simply Eriesistible

In the historic Bayfront District of downtown Erie there is a collection of cultural, historical and educational attractions that provide a multi-focused glimpse of Erie's past and present. **Discovery Square** includes the Erie History Center and Cashiers House, the Erie Art Museum and the new expERIEnce Children's Museum.

Local history, industry and architecture are the focus of changing exhibits in the 1840 commercial building renovated to serve as the headquarters for the **Erie County Historical Society**. The society has an excellent library and archives facility, including 11,495 glass plate negatives from the Francis J. Bassett Collection taken in Waterford and Erie at the end of the 19th and beginning of the 20th century. They also have an extensive collection of maps of the region.

You can step from the History Center into the adjacent **Cashiers House**, an 1839 Greek Revival townhouse designed by Philadelphia architect, William Kelly. The house served as the residence of Peter Benson, the Cashier or chief executive officer, of the Erie Branch of the U.S. Bank of Pennsylvania (located right next door). Benson died in 1843, the same year the bank failed, and since that time the house has served many purposes. It is now a house museum whose elegant interior is in sharp contrast with the plain stucco-covered brick exterior. The carved woodwork interior and the marble fireplaces are original but the furnishings span the years 1830 to 1900, American Empire to true Victorian. The focus of the house is to interpret life in Erie during the antebellum period.

The History Center is open Tuesday through Saturday 9:00 A.M. to 5:00 P.M. Tours of the Cashiers House are given on those days from 1:00 P.M. to 4:00 P.M. Donations are requested.

After the Erie Branch of the U.S. Bank failed, its building became a customs house in 1849 and is now known as the Old Custom House. The imposing marble building with fluted columns and Greek fretwork is now the **Erie Art Museum**. Permanent collections include American and European painting, drawing and sculpture, Western and Asian graphics, photography, Indian bronze and stone sculptures, Chinese porcelains and American ceramics.

One of the most popular pieces in the museum's collection is Lisa Lichtenfel's *The Avalon Restaurant*. Twenty-one soft sculpture figures, scaled down a third, can be seen on both sides of the counter at the Avalon, a now-defunct downtown diner where the artist once worked as a waitress. Long-time Erie residents can put names to the various figures—the former owners are behind the counter and the waitress is a self-portrait. The museum galleries has both permanent and changing exhibits. Each spring there is a juried exhibition open to local artists. The museum conducts classes and workshops and presents lectures, concerts and special events.

The Erie Art Museum is open Tuesday through Saturday 11:00 A.M. to 5:00 P.M. and Sunday 1:00 P.M. to 5:00 P.M. A nominal admission is charged. Supplemental gallery and classroom space is utilized three doors down at 423 State Street at the Erie Art Museum Frame Shop and Gallery. The shop does museum-quality framing.

The **expERIEnce Children's Museum** is located directly behind the History Center. It opened in early 1995 as an educational and recreational center for children ages 2 to 12. The museum's focus is expressed in the Chinese proverb: "I hear and I forget. I see and I remember. I do and I understand." Children with their adult companions participate in hands-on exhibits that explore natural, social and physical science. Call (814) 870-4025 for hours and admission fees.

Having partaken of this entertaining and educational history and art mix, add another dimension to your day with a visit to the **Erie Zoo**. It's not a huge facility—only 15 acres—but still well worth a visit that can easily be done in a couple hours. The main building has recently been renovated to suggest an African experience with specimens such as the family of meerkats and grivet monkeys. Another new exhibit area is the dual river otter habitat. The collection includes 300 animals, representing nearly 100 species from six continents, plus a children's zoo, train ride and carousel. There are picnic areas and concession stands. The zoo is open 10:00 A.M. to 5:00 P.M. year-round. On summer Sundays and holidays it stays open until 6:00 P.M. Admission is charged.

After exploring these major points of interest, you may want to expand your exposure by taking one of the six driving tours of Erie County. Routes for each are available from the Erie County Historical Society. Booklets with map, directions and descriptions of historic and other sites of interest can be purchased for a nominal amount at the Erie History Center or by calling (814) 454-1813. They also have walking tour maps of Erie and some of the boroughs of Erie County available at no charge.

The Historical Society manages the **Battles Museums of Rural Life** in Girard, an additional site that is well worth exploring. A 130-acre museum complex interprets life in Erie County from 1840 to the present. There are two residences, both built by Rush Battles, plus the old R. S. Battles Bank building and the First Universalist Church of Girard. The latter is used for special programs and group orientation.

Rush Battles built his steel, brick and stone bank on Main Street in 1893, just after the railroad came through town. This was the only bank in Pennsylvania to remain open during President Roosevelt's moratorium on banking in the Great Depression. In 1946 the bank merged with the National Bank of Girard. This is now one of the few Bank Museums in the country, and it still contains much of the original teller's caging and the safes in the vault. Each summer special exhibits examine a different theme of rural life.

The complex includes a second museum, the **Charlotte Elizabeth Battles Memorial Museum**, which also addresses different themes dealing with rural life as well as telling the Battles family story. This museum is in the Battles family residence. Rush Battles built this house in 1861 for his young bride Charlotte Webster. Their daughter, Charlotte Elizabeth, lived here until her death in 1952. Family furnishings still fill all the rooms so the house accurately reflects Miss Battles' lifestyle. Charlotte's ornamental garden has also been restored.

The **Yellow House**, located just a short way down Walnut Street, was built by Rush Battles in 1857-58 for his mother and two unmarried sisters. Now renovated, the first floor depicts farm life with changing exhibits. The farmland around the house shows agricultural processes common in the period being represented by the exhibitions. Long range plans call for a demonstration farm showing commercial agriculture in the region from the 1840s to the present.

Reflecting the fact that man's history is formed by his environment, the complex includes several **Ecology Trails** to teach visitors about the native inhabitants and the indigenous plants and animals. These trails wind through nearly 40 acres of woodlands.

The Battles Museums of Rural Life are open from May through September. Call the Erie County Historical Society (814) 454-1813 for hours and information about upcoming special events.

Directions: Take I-79 north to Erie; it becomes the new Bayfront Parkway. Turn right on State Street. The Erie History Center is at 417-422 State Street. The Erie Art Museum is 411 State Street. For the Erie Zoo, from downtown, take State Street south to 26th Street, turn right one block to Peach Street, Route 19, and turn left at 38th Street. From Route I-90, take Exit 7 and head north for three miles on Route 19, turn right on 38th Street. The zoo is at 423 West 38th Street. For the Battles Museums of Rural Life take Route 20 exit off I-79 and head west passing through Fairview to Main Street in Girard. The Battles Bank Museum will be on your right just past Walnut Street. After touring the museum take Walnut Street out to the C.E. Battles Memorial Museum, the Yellow House and ecology trails. Backtrack north on Walnut Street and turn left on Locust Street for the Universalist Church at Locust and Myrtle Street.

Drake Well Museum and Oil City

Founder of Modern Petroleum Industry

On August 27, 1859 Edwin L. Drake's perserverance made Oil Creek "The Valley that Changed the World" when he drilled the world's first oil well. Drake proved that petroleum could be obtained in substantial quantities by drilling through rock into the earth.

Even Drake's crew did not believe they would succeed. The men who raised the derrick called it "Drake's yoke." No one in the region believed drilling was the way to obtain oil and they thought the notion "wild and woolly." In 1858, when Drake hired his first driller, the man didn't report for work. When he was later asked about this he responded that he thought Drake was "crazy." He signed on with Drake just to get rid of him.

Petroleum deposits are thought to be created from the bodies of tiny sea plants and animals that lived millions of years ago. Natural oil springs have been written about since before the time of Christ, and notations of their existence have been recorded since European explorers traveled to North America. The first recorded notation of oil in Pennsylvania was on a 1755 map. Like the Native Americans, white settlers in the state skimmed petroleum from the streams and springs in northwestern Pennsylvania. Originally petroleum was used as a medicine to heal burns and cuts.

By 1850 there were in excess of 50 companies in the United States manufacturing oil from coal. Oil was becoming popular as a lighting fluid. The first commercial refinery of petroleum was in Pittsburgh, making use of the petroleum produced by salt wells in Tarentum. It was to Tarentum that Drake went to find equipment and drillers for his well outside Titusville. In the spring of 1859, Drake hired William Smith to come to Oil Creek and build a derrick and engine house for his well. They built the largest standard rig ever used in Pennsylvania up to that time. Drilling began in late June or early July but there were problems with gravel caving in the hole. To solve this problem Drake drove a pipe down to bedrock and drilled inside the pipe. This procedure worked and drilling went smoothly. On Saturday, August 27, the drill bit reached a depth of 69 feet and then slipped down another six inches into a crevice. The next day when "Uncle Billy" Smith checked the well he discovered oil floating on top of the water close to the derrick floor. A pump was attached and Drake's well was soon producing roughly 20 barrels of oil each day. That was twice the amount produced by any other source at that time.

By the next month a *New York Times'* correspondent was reporting, "The excitement attendant on the discovery of this vast source of oil was fully equal to what I ever saw in California when a large lump of gold was accidently turned out." A year after Drake's success, wells lined Oil Creek and the Allegheny. In three years, there were so many producing wells that the oil price dropped precipitously and drove Drake and his partners out of business.

Drake speculated unsuccessfully in oil stocks and died in dire

The replica of Edwin Drake's derrick and engine house stands at the exact spot where he drilled the world's first oil well.

straits, but his remarkable discovery was never forgotten. In the 1930's the American Petroleum Institute purchased the site of Drake's first well and built a small museum that was subsequently turned over to the state.

Drake Well Museum provides a comprehensive exposure to the early Pennsylvania oil companies and Drake's pioneer efforts. Your first stop is the main museum building where you pay the admission fee. The museum has over 70 exhibits detailing the story of oil. There are drawings and models of various types of drilling rigs: spring pole, standard rig, wood and steel rigs and a modern rotary drilling rig. A nitroglycerine wagon introduces the hazardous occupation of "shooting wells" (see Otto Cupler Torpedo Museum selection). The "Colonel Drake" steam fire engine, purchased by the Titusville Fire Department in 1868, reminds us of another hazard of the early oil towns. There is also a working oil pump and you can hear the sound it makes as it runs. Each power house had a unique sound.

The museum has an extensive collection of period photographs including some sobering shots of the **Great Flood and Fire of 1892.** On June 4, 1892 a heavy rainfall caused the dam in Spartansburg to give way and a 20-foot wall of water raced down the valley, hitting oil storage tanks and igniting them. The oil refineries in Titusville and Oil City ignited, causing explosions at the refineries. In all there was one-and-half million dollars of damage done and 132 lives lost. If time permits before leaving the museum, watch the 30-minute movie on Drake's discovery.

The grounds have ten additional sites of interest, the first being the Daughters of the American Revolution Monument erected on the well site to commemorate the 50th anniversary of Drake's oil well. The sandstone monument was moved to its present location when a replica of Drake's derrick and engine house was built. The original had burned two months after the well came in; a second derrick and power house stood until 1876. Photographs of the second structure were used to build the replica. While Drake's original steam engine and boiler were purchased from an Erie company, the other equipment was made by Uncle Billy Smith. The working steam engine in the replica pumps oil at the exact spot as the original. The well was recased to the original $69^1/_2$ feet. The oil is recirculated and has the consistency and color of chocolate milk.

Next you'll see a spring pole drilling rig, the kind used by a substantial number of salt well drillers in the early 19th century and adapted to drill oil wells. It did not take much capital to build this simple rig. A drill bit was hung from a limber sapling above the site of the well. The operator would "kick down" the well with their feet, drilling roughly a yard a day.

Capital was also saved by the practice of pumping more than one well with a single power source. Thus central power houses were built with wells connected by rod lines. Some oil leases in Pennsylvania still operate by this method. Natural gas was often drawn off the wells, then the gas was used to run the engine. The remainder was pumped back into the ground to help the oil flow (see Allegheny National Forest selection).

Early oil derricks were locally crafted in slightly individual styles, but by 1875 the Pennsylvania standard rig could be seen in oil fields around the world. These 65-to-85-foot wooden derricks were built to drill to 2,000 feet. The museum's standard rig is a cable tool rig that could drill to over 5,000 feet.

Another problem was moving oil over long distances. This was resolved in 1865 through the use of pipelines. First steam pumps were used to move the oil, then gas engines were used as you will see in the museum's **National Transit Pipeline Station**.

Another outdoor exhibit you'll see is the Sanderson Cyclone Drilling rig, a portable rig that could drill shallow oil wells. It turned out to be used primarily for water wells and boring holes for coal mines. Before leaving walk down to Oil Creek to see the mystery pits, perhaps dug by prehistoric people to obtain oil.

The grounds have several picnic spots, a wildflower walk, a great trout stream and a museum gift shop. The Drake Well Museum is open Tuesday through Saturday 9:00 A.M. to 5:00 P.M.; on Sunday it opens at NOON. Closed Monday and holidays except Memorial Day, July 4th and Labor Day. Admission is charged.

Adjoining the Drake Well Museum is **Oil Creek State Park**, which includes 13.5 miles of scenic Oil Creek Gorge. The park's Visitor Center at Petroleum Center (toward the southern end of the park) has historic and environmental programs in spring, summer and fall. A popular feature of the park is the 9.5-mile paved bicycle trail through Oil Creek Gorge. You can get on the trail at Drake Well Museum and Petroleum Center. Bikes can be rented during the summer at a concession at the latter site. There are also 52 miles of hiking and interpretive trails. Canoeing, fishing, hunting, picnicking and cross-country skiing can also be enjoyed at the park.

The park extends within four miles of **Oil City** at its southernmost point. The Venago Museum of Arts, Science and Industry, 270 Seneca Street in Oil City, is mounting a new permanent exhibit on the origins of the oil industry. Oil City was the "Hub of Oildom," the site of industries involved in the production, shipping and refining of oil. Just north of Oil City is the terminus for the Oil Creek and Titusville Railroad (see selection), that runs north to Titusville, passing many sites that are significant to the oil industry in this valley.

Directions: From I-79 take the Meadville exit and follow Route 27 east to Titusville. The Drake Well Museum is just south of Titusville off Route 8. From I-80 take Exit 3, Barkeyville, and follow Route 8 north.

Mercer County Historical Society

Settlers and Native Americans

In 1803 the village of Mercer was established, taking its name from Revolutionary War hero, Brigadier General Hugh Mercer, who lived here for many years. He later moved to Fredericksburg, Virginia where he practiced medicine. His apothecary shop in this quaint Virginia town still stands just as he left it when he went off to fight the British.

Equally well-preserved are the Victorian homes you'll see in Mercer's historic district. They were built at the turn of the century by prosperous local businessmen. Mercer's most prominent landmark is the town's second courthouse, a Gothic-style building with a domed clocktower, finished in 1911. The dome is a reproduction of St. Peter's Basilica in Rome.

The Mercer County Historical Society has a complex that includes the Magoffin House Museum and the Henderson Historic area with the Helen Black Miller Memorial Chapel and McClain Print Shop. Elsewhere in the county stands the Caldwell One-Room School, Frederick J. Raisch Log Cabin and Indian Cemetery.

The 1821 Magoffin House was the home of Dr. James Magoffin who, after obtaining a medical degree from the University of Glasgow, immigrated to Pennsylvania. His wife, the daughter of a Dublin doctor, was a leader in Mercer society and the mother of ten children. Within their home is the historical society museum and library. The former has more than 100,000 items including pioneer tools and furnishings as well as Native American artifacts. The library has genealogical research material and an extensive collection of early medical books.

The Henderson Historic area adjoins the Magoffin House and contains the **Helen Black Miller Memorial Chapel**. Built in 1883 for the Mercer Episcopal Congregation, it was an active church until 1964. Concerts have been held in the chapel since its move to the historic complex.

Also part of the complex is the **McClain Print Shop**. The building, relocated on this site, served as a dental office, law office, barber shop and Thomas McClain's print shop. The shop has old printing equipment.

The Mercer County Historical Society complex is open Tuesday through Saturday from 1:00 P.M. to 4:30 P.M. and Friday evenings from September through May. During the summer months it is open from 10:00 A.M. to 4:30 P.M. The complex is at 119 South Pitt Street in Mercer. Just across the street is the **Magoffin Inn**, built in 1884 as the home and office of Dr. Montrose Magoffin, son of James Magoffin. The home now has five guestrooms and a restaurant serving lunch Tuesday through Friday from 11:00 A.M. to 2:00 P.M., April through December. Dinner is served year- round on Thursday, Friday and Saturday from 5:00 P.M. to 8:30 P.M. Call (800) 841-0824 for additional information.

At one time Mercer County had more than 200 one-room schoolhouses, though few survive. The **Caldwell One-Room School** remained operational until the late 1950s. To insure its preservation it was eventually given to the historical society. The school museum has original school equipment and desks, some marked with initials carved by students decades ago. Photographs and books recall the era of the one-room school. Hours are Sundays and holidays 1:30 P.M. to 5:30 P.M. from Memorial Day through the second week of October. The school is on Route 58 midway between Mercer and Greenville.

The Frederick J. Raisch Log Cabin was discovered in 1977 within a white clapboard house in Sharon. Research by the Mercer County Historical Society, to whom the cabin was deeded, indicated it was built between 1790 and 1810. The cabin was dismantled log by log and reassembled and restored at Buhl Park, on 10th Street in Hermitage. The log cabin is open Sundays and holidays between 2:00 P.M. and 5:00 P.M. from Memorial Day to Labor Day.

The Historical Society is also custodian of an **Indian Cemetery** seven miles east of Milledgeville in the northeast corner of the county. This area was once known as Custologa Town, a contested area during the French and Indian War. Although disputed, it is claimed that Guyasutha, an important Native American chief, is buried in this small cemetery.

Directions: From I-70 take the I 80 exit west, at Exit 2 follow Route 19 north to Mercer.

North East

History and Horticulture

Pennsylvania is the only state that has one border on the Mason-Dixon line and another with Canada, albeit out on the lake. The Erie area is the only part of Pennsylvania on the Great Lakes. Just 15 minutes outside the city near the New York border is **North East**, a historic lakeside community, where they claim the waters yield more fish than any other area along the Great Lakes. North East is noted for its acres of chrysanthemums, its rolling fields of grapes and its historic district.

There are more than 14 acres and 150 varieties of chrysanthemums at the Paschke family farm. From mid-September through October the carpet of bright flowers is a photographic delight. For a very nominal cost you can pick yourself a bouquet from a special garden. The Paschke family began planting mums in the front yard as a hobby in 1932. Over the next decades the seven children worked with their parents to make the farm an autumnal showcase. While the Paschkes sell their plants wholesale, visitors can also purchase plants, including many seldom-seen varieties (you can also order plants from a catalog). A display building has over 1,200 chrysanthemums. In the fall you can also purchase pumpkins, gourds, Indian corn and apples. Throughout the year they sell local fruit in season, much of which is grown on their farm, and a wide array of flowering plants. Families enjoy the horse and buggy rides offered on pleasant Sunday afternoons. There are also Sunday afternoon concerts in the pagoda. **Mums by Paschke** is open from mid-August to mid-November Monday through Saturday 9:00 A.M. to 8:00 P.M., on Sundays it opens at 1:00 P.M. The greenhouse is open during those hours from May to July 4th.

Like a number of his neighbors D.C. Paschke planted an experimental vineyard. This vast stretch of concord grapes grown by Welch's is the largest vineyard east of the Mississippi River. There are also four wineries in North East, a concentration matched by only four other towns in the United States.

Five generations of the Bostwick family are responsible for the award-winning success of **Heritage Wine Cellars**. In addition to family effort, the climatic conditions of this Lake Erie wine region contribute to the fine tasting wines produced here. Along the lake shoreline there is a frost-free growing season up to 30 days longer than inland areas just a few miles south. The winery is open Monday through Thursday from 9:00 A.M. to 6:00 P.M., Fridays and Saturdays until 8:00 P.M. and Sundays 10:00 A.M. to 6:00 P.M. The winery also sells Homemade Heritage Jellies.

Mazza Vineyards overlooks Lake Erie, along scenic East Lake Road. Before you reach the winery, you will see mile after mile of French hybrid and native American vines. The tour of the winery takes you through each step from grape selection through crushing, pressing, fermentation, aging, bottling and tasting. After tasting, purchasing and enjoying Mazza wines from the vineyard, you can later purchase them at your local state store. Mazza Vineyards is noted for its Labor Day weekend festival, Noon to 5:00 P.M., which features grape stomping, hayrides, wine tasting and other activity. The winery is open Monday through Saturday 9:00 A.M. to 8:00 P.M. in July and August. From September to June it closes at 5:30 P.M. Sunday hours are always 11:00 A.M. to 4:30 P.M. Other wineries in the area include **Penn Shore Winery** and **Presque Isle Wine Cellars**. The latter sells home winemaking supplies.

North East, incorporated in 1834, is on the National Register of Historic Districts. You can pick up a self-guided walking tour, at the wineries, local stores and area museums and begin exploring on the corner of Main and Lake Streets. North East is noted for its octagon barn, a refurbished 1873 one-room schoolhouse and the **Lake Shore Railway Museum**. Within the former New York Central passenger depot you will see vintage black and white photographs, calendars, models, signal lanterns and an assortment of railroad equipment and memorabilia. Attention focuses on the 1943 Centralized Traffic Control Board upon which a single dispatcher controlled a large stretch of track. This museum is on a busy railroad corridor and more than 60 trains a day pass on the track outside the station. Several pieces of rolling stock are of interest including a fireless steam locomotive, dining and sleeping cars, a 1922 tank car, three refrigerator cars and others. The museum is open 1:00 P.M. to 5:00 P.M. Wednesday through Sunday from Memorial Day through Labor Day weekends and on weekends in September. No admission is charged.

Directions: From I-79 north, take I-90 east and take Exit 12, Route 20. If you turn right on Route 20, Mums by Paschke will be on your immediate right. For Heritage Wine Cellars when you take Exit 12 go west, or left on Route 20 and the winery will be on your right. Take Route 89 north of Route 20, then connect with Route 5, East Lake Road and turn right. Mazza Vineyards is well marked at 11815 East Lake Road. For Penn Shore Winery take a left on Route 5 for two miles and the winery will be on your left. For Presque Isle Wine Cellars take Route 20 through North East. Outside of town on your right you will see the winery. For the Lake Shore Railway Museum take Route 20 into North East and turn left at Mill Street, then left again at Wall Street. The museum is along the tracks at 31 Wall Street.

Otto Cupler Torpedo Company Museum and Oil Creek & Titusville Railroad

It's A Blast!

Few visitors to the **Otto Cupler Torpedo Company Museum** know anything about oil well shooting. Even the background of this dangerous business is fascinating. The story begins with Walter and Edward Roberts, brothers who were wealthy New York city dentists. Walter B. Roberts invested in Pennsylvania oil wells and learned about the oil business, including the fact that wells frequently clogged up with paraffin. The paraffin build up slowed production of oil to a mere dribble.

Walter's brother, Edward, also took an interest in the oil industry. While serving as a colonel in the Union Army at Fredericksburg in 1862, he saw Confederate shells exploding in a canal. The energy from the shell blew out the side of the canal and it occurred to Colonel Roberts that torpedoes could be used to clean out oil wells.

In 1865 the Roberts brothers established the Roberts Petroleum Torpedo Company. Colonel Roberts found a kindred soul in Captain Mills, who also served in the Civil War, and so the torpedo concept was demonstrated at Mills Ladies' Well along Watson Flats on January 21, 1865. In shooting the well, the torpedo caused an explosion in the oil bearing sand that cracked the sand and rock, letting the oil flow through the cracks into the well where it was pumped to the surface. On wells with a paraffin buildup this explosion brought the well back to its original output.

The Roberts patented their invention in 1864 but others also filed applications for torpedoing oil wells. The Roberts filed suit against all those attempting to use their concept without paying them a percentage. From 1866 to 1883 there was such intensive litigation and hostilities that the era was called the Nitroglycerin, or Torpedo, Wars. The Roberts hired 200 Pinkerton detectives to fight infringements of patent by a group soon called "moonlighters," who "shot" wells secretly at night. Since this was a dangerous process, working at night was extremely hazardous and many moonlighters lost their lives. Oil well owners, incensed at the monopoly the Roberts had on the process of oil well shooting, frequently preferred to pay the moonlighters the lower rates. Whenever the detectives discovered this, litigation followed. The Torpedo Wars claimed 110 lives. In June 1880 the court ruled in Edward Roberts favor, but he did not have long to enjoy his victory since Colonel Roberts died in 1881. His brother continued the business until 1883. From 1883 to 1893, the business was called the High Explosives Company and from 1893 to 1937, A. Cupler Jr. and Company. It became the **Otto Cupler Torpedo Company** in 1937.

After hearing fascinating stories about the Torpedo Wars, visitors to the museum will see Colonel Roberts' first torpedo and learn exactly how to shoot a well with nitroglycerin. At one time there were hundreds of companies in the country shooting oil wells. Now the Otto Cupler Torpedo Company is the only oil well shooting company in existence. This is not a process abandoned decades ago as wells are still shot to this day.

The explanation of the process starts with the original methods and equipment and moves to more modern technology. The museum has a moonlighters' shack, where they used primitive and highly volatile techniques for making a torpedo. The moonlighters operated in two ways—they either sold the oil men a torpedo and let them blow their own wells or they would come out and shoot the well. Moonlighters made their torpedoes by putting a stone crock inside a wooden tub of water, then mixing nitric acid and sulfuric acid. Next, with a rubber hose, they slowly added glycerin, a drip at a time. The mixture had to stay between 75 and 80 degrees.

At the museum in the company's Quonset hut, you'll watch a guide prepare a torpedo and load it into a replica oil well. The first step is to lower a dummy torpedo into the well to check that it is free of obstruction. Second, a setter is lowered below the deepest sand to be shot, this forms a platform where the torpedo rests. Next, the first torpedo is filled with nitroglycerin and lowered into the well. Enough torpedoes are used to fill the space from the setter at the deepest oil bearing sand to the top of the oil bearing sand. The process is continued until each level of oil bearing sand has its proper number of torpedoes. The last step is to add water, or other fluid, to hold the explosion inside the well as long as possible. Once these steps are completed, the well is detonated with a squib, a metal tube filled with dynamite with a fuse and cap, that is dropped into the well. Or a "go devil" is dropped onto percussion caps that were lowered on the last torpedo. This is when the shooter yells, "fire in the hole," and goes like the devil. After this explanation, it's fascinating to see a movie showing an oil well being shot in Oil Creek Valley in 1991.

This museum would be well worth visiting if that was the extent of your introduction to oil well shooting but they offer an additional incentive in a special effects play given twice each day on weekends (once on Wednesday). This living history reenactment about moonlighters and oil well shooters culminates in a real oil well shooter loading and firing four oil wells in a dazzling burst of flame that shoots over forty-feet into the sky. This tour is not given during inclement weather.

Tours are given June and September Monday through Friday at 9:30 A.M., 11:00 A.M., 12:30 P.M., 2:00 P.M. and 3:30 P.M. On Saturdays there's a tour at 9:30 A.M., it is closed Sundays. In July, August and October tours are on Monday, Tuesday and Thursday at the same weekday times, Wednesday at 9:30 A.M., 2:00 P.M. and 3:30 P.M. and Fridays and Saturdays at 9:30 P.M. only. The special effects tour is given at 12:30 P.M. and 2:30 P.M. on Friday, Saturday and Sunday; on Wednesdays it is only offered at NOON.

Admission is charged to the museum and there is an added fee for the special effects tour. For additional information call (814) 827-2921 or 966-3277.

This unique museum is scheduled to operate on a schedule similar to that of the nearby **Oil Creek & Titusville Railroad**, whose northern terminus is in the Perry Street Station in Titusville. This restored 1892 station has displays of railroad memorabilia, a craft and souvenir area and snack shop. The train rolls through "the valley that changed the world" stopping at Drake Well Park (see selection), and ending at Rynd Farm, the southern terminus just four miles north of Oil City. This farm is the location of **Jonathan Watson's well**. Watson was one of the first oil millionaires. Guides on the train regale visitors with historical information on the oil rush boom days in the valley. The train has the only **working railway Post Office car** in the country and you can have your postcards and letters cancelled as you watch. The rear gondola car is an ideal place for photographers.

Trains run on weekends from mid-to-late June and again in September. In July, August and October Wednesday and Friday runs are added. Call (814) 676-1733 for specific times. You can order tickets using your credit card, or write the railroad at P.O. Box 68, Oil City, PA 16301. Tickets may also be purchased at all the stations. The fall runs are among the most popular, and reservations are all but a must in October. The railroad also hosts special events including holiday runs, mystery dinner excursions and a moonlight honky tonk trip.

Directions: From I-79 take Exit 36-A, Route 6/19/322 east to Meadville, then pick up Route 27 east past Titusville. When you see Wolfiel's Garage on the left, turn on Enterprise Road, State Route 2028 and continue for one mile to the Otto Cupler Torpedo Company Quonset hut for the museum. The special effects tour takes place just a bit up the road on Dottyville Road. The Oil Creek & Titusville Railroad Perry Street Station is off Truck Route 8 south in downtown Titusville. The Rynd Farm Station is on Route 8N By-Pass north of Oil City.

Presque Isle State Park

Almost an Island, Definitely a Paradise

Eighteenth-century French explorers named the seven mile sandy peninsula jutting into Lake Erie, **Presque Isle**, meaning almost an island. More recently the National Geographic Society named Presque Isle sunsets the second best in the world. Presque Isle, designated a National Natural Landmark, is a place where recreation and an ecological preserve uniquely co-exist.

The peninsula, a remnant of the last glacial age, is the state's youngest single large-scale geological feature. The sand and gravel deposits were left when glacial ice retreated. The widest section, at the eastern end, is roughly 2.5 miles and lagoons stretch across the sandy terrain. Along the 14-mile loop drive you'll see an amazing diversity of habitats: beaches, dunes, grasslands, savannas, mature forests, marshes, swamps, ponds and lagoons. These habitats support 320 bird species, 47 mammals species and 30 varieties of amphibian and reptiles. Presque Isle is one of the top birding spots in the country. A sanctuary on the peninsula's eastern tip is a significant feeding and resting area for migratory waterfowl, shore and water birds. Migration peaks occur from mid-to-late May and during September.

Pennsylvania's most visited state park, Presque Isle averages about four million visitors a year, over a million more than Yel-

Pennsylvania's most visited state park, Presque Isle, is noted for its beaches, sunsets and bird watching. The 1873 Peninsula Lighthouse is just one of its scenic spots.

lowstone National Park in a typical year. Yet, on busy days, the park never seems crowded because of its large size and abundant beaches. The lakeside beaches often resemble the ocean shore, the lake has a tide that gets rough during heavy storms. At other times the calm, fresh water beckons. *Conde Nast Traveler* magazine ranked these beaches among America's "top 100" swimming places. It is on the lakeside of the peninsula that the sunsets beckon. Like in Key West, sunsets are a major draw on Presque Isle. A drive past Beach 11 will bring you to the houseboats on Horseshoe Pond, the Coast Guard Station, and the North Pier, where you can watch sailboats, speedboats, yachts and even an occasional ocean-going freighter travel through the channel between Lake Erie and Presque Isle Bay.

Hiking and running trails wind along the bayside. There is a seven-mile network of trails. One of the most popular is a 5.8 multi-use trail for hikers, bikers, joggers and skaters. This trail ends at the **Perry Monument on Misery Bay**. The monument to Commodore Oliver Hazard Perry looks out over a bay that is the final resting place for at least 12 wrecked ships. **Dobbins Landing**, Erie's public dock and terminus for the ferry that runs to Presque Isle during the summer months, is named for Daniel Dobbins, the shipbuilder who helped construct Perry's Lake Erie fleet during the War of 1812. Between March and July, 1813 Perry, then a young naval officer, had a fleet of six ships built to eliminate the threat England posed on the Great Lakes. The struggle for supremacy lasted nine weeks before Perry defeated the British (see US Brig *Niagara* selection).

At the Visitor Center, located near Barracks Beach, you'll see exhibits on the history and the natural wonders of Presque Isle. You can pick up a bird checklist, information on day-use cabins and pavilions, and details on all the park's recreational options. Swimming is permitted only at guarded beaches open 10:00 A.M. to 8:00 P.M. Memorial Day weekend to Labor Day. During this same time, lagoon pontoon tours leave at scheduled intervals from the Watercraft Concession. Lake Erie and Presque Isle Bay both lure fishermen. An accessible fishing wharf on the bay side and a unique boardwalk at Beach 7 on the lake side permit wheelchair-bound visitors to get right down to the water and make Presque Isle an accessible place for the physically-challenged. The park is also popular with winter sports enthusiasts: ice fishing, cross-country skiing, ice boating and ice skating.

Just before the park entrance you'll pass **Waldameer Park & Water World** a family park with slides, pools and 43 rides, including a giant ferris wheel rising 100 feet above the bluff overlooking Presque Isle. There are special rides and pools for very young children. The park opens at 11:00 A.M. Tuesday through Sunday.

Directions: From I-90 take Exit 5 to Route 832 north, Sterrettania Road. It becomes Peninsula Drive, which will lead to Presque Isle State Park. From downtown Erie, take Route 5A to Route 832, then turn right.

Pymatuning Lake

Spillway Bottleneck

Pennsylvania Governor Gifford Pinchot dedicated the Pymatuning Dam on August 17, 1934 stating, "All human accomplishments begin with a dream." **Pymatuning** began with the dream of reclaiming the swamp land and ended with a recreational treasure, the state's largest manmade lake.

Although much of the land has been utilized for recreational needs, there are still wilderness areas. The Iroquois called the area Pymatuning, meaning "the crooked-mouthed man's dwelling place." The name refers to the time when the area was inhabited by an Erie tribe ruled by a cunning and devious queen. The earliest inhabitants were the Mound Builders, prehistoric people who erected great ceremonial mounds that still stand in North Carolina, Georgia and a few other states.

The easternmost part of the lake is the **Pymatuning Waterfowl Area**, a refuge for migrating waterfowl. The Linesville spillway is one of the most interesting spots on the lake because this is where visitors feed the fish and there is a heavy concentration of carp. Ducks and geese literally walk on the fishes' backs. It is almost unsettling to see so many fish. They don't even have enough room to swim. Fish are so tightly packed that many are tilted sideways. Concessionaires sell bread and food to feed the fish.

Just up the road from the spillway is the **Pennsylvania State Wildlife Museum** with mounted specimens of many of the waterfowl that migrate along the Atlantic Flyway. There are cases filled with eggs and others with weasels, ermine, mink, muskrat and beaver all common to this area. A nature walk leads from the museum to lakeside overlooks. Be sure to bring high-powered binoculars to see the state's largest colony of bald eagles. Rangers provide directions for driving tours of the area.

Continuing north just a bit, you'll reach the **Linesville Fish Cultural Center**, the world's largest inland hatchery. The facility raises warm water fish to stock state streams, plus two cold water species for Lake Erie. An aquarium gives you a close look at native fish. Mounted on the wall is a record setting 54 pound muskellunge caught in Pennsylvania on September 30, 1924 by Louis Walker Jr. of Meadville. The hatchery tanks for small fish are inside. As they grow the fish are moved to outdoor pools.

Fishing is a popular sport on Pymatuning. The catch includes walleye, muskellunge, carp, crappies, largemouth and smallmouth bass and others. Sportsmen try their luck summer and winter. Non-powered boats and those with up to 10 horsepower engines are permitted (if you have a more powerful motor, you are still allowed on the lake, you just can't use your motor). Three locations on the lake rent boats.

The **Pymatuning State Park** is located 1.5 miles north of Jamestown, at the foot of the lake just above the dam. The park has boat moorings, launchings and rentals, picnic areas and a playground. Within the park are three campgrounds offering 657 family camping sites in three areas: Jamestown, Tuttle and Pymatuning. There are four protected beaches open Memorial Day through Labor Day.

During the winter months in addition to ice fishing, visitors can enjoy cross-country skiing, ice boating, skating, snowmobiling and sledding. A winter concession rents ski equipment, skates and snowmobiles.

Directions: From I-79 take Route 6/322 east. To reach the northern end where you'll find Linesville, the spillway, hatchery and museum stay on Route 6 when they split. To reach the park office outside Jamestown veer left on Route 322. For more information on the park call (412) 932-3141.

United States Brig *Niagara*

Don't Give Up the Ship

A coast guard station was built on Presque Isle in 1876, three years after the first lighthouse on the peninsula began operating. Until the War of 1812, the waters of Lake Erie were peaceful, although alliances between the Indians, French and English fur traders in the area were volatile. No incidents occurred to mar the tranquility of this Great Lakes region.

When the fledgling nation became embroiled with England, the Great Lakes region was contested and the British and Americans improvised naval squadrons on Lake Erie. This was a significant accomplishment since the remote Erie settlement had only about 500 inhabitants, few skilled boatbuilders, and few of the necessary supplies. From Pennsylvania's ports and cities came shipwrights, blockmakers, blacksmiths, caulkers, boat builders and laborers. Iron was sent from Pittsburgh and Meadville, sail canvas from Philadelphia, rigging, cannon shot and anchors from Pittsburgh and cannon from Washington, D.C. Local timber was cut, hewed and squared by hand since there were no sawmills in the Erie region. The formidable task of building six vessels was first overseen by Daniel Dobbins, a Great Lakes shipmaster who lived in Erie. In February 1813, New York shipbuilder Noah Brown arrived to supervise the construction. Commodore Oliver Hazard Perry, who commanded the fleet of two brigs, the **Lawrence** and **Niagara**, and four schooners, arrived on the scene in March.

While construction was underway a British squadron effectively controlled the waters around Erie, but when these ships withdrew on August 1, the newly completed American ships emerged from Erie harbor and began training sessions. The British and American squadrons met on September 10, 1813 near Put-in-Bay, Ohio. Perry's flagship the *Lawrence*, engaged the 19-gun brig *Detroit*, whose long guns had a range of about a mile.

US Brig Niagara, *one of six vessels constructed on Lake Erie during the War of 1812, was the ship from which Commodore Perry ultimately won an epic victory over the British.*

This was farther than the twelve pounders and carronades on the American ships could reach.

Perry, directing the battle from the deck of the *Lawrence*, endured the British fire until he could get his ship close enough to inflict damage on the *Detroit*. The *Niagara*, under the command of Captain Jesse Duncan Elliot, did not close on the enemy with expected speed (after the war there was a court of inquiry regarding the action of Elliot and the *Niagara*). By the time the *Niagara* arrived beside the *Lawrence*, the latter was a shattered hulk, with all her officers except Perry either wounded or dead. A small boat delivered Perry to the *Niagara* and he took command, hoisting his battle flag which read: Don't Give Up the Ship. Perry proceeded to lead another vigorous attack and British Commodore Barclay was severely wounded and his ships defeated.

Following the battle Perry wrote to General William Henry Harrison: "We have met the enemy and they are ours: two ships, two brigs, one schooner, and one sloop." Historians consider this an epic victory. No other American commander has ever shifted his flag in the middle of battle, or forced an entire enemy squadron to surrender and brought back every ship as a prize of war. Perry's victory ended British power west of the Niagara gateway.

The *Niagara* patrolled Lake Erie and was involved in several minor actions before the war ended, then was used as a service ship until 1820 when she was scuttled in Misery Bay to reserve its hull. The *Niagara* was raised and rebuilt using some of the old timbers in 1913 to celebrate the centennial of the Battle of Lake Erie. The *Lawrence* was raised, cut in half and shipped by railroad to Philadelphia and reconstructed for Philadelphia's 200th anniversary, but she was destroyed by fire. In late 1987 the *Niagara* was again dismembered and a historically accurate major reconstruction undertaken, again using some original timbers. On September 10, 1988, the 175th anniversary of Perry's epic battle, the *Niagara* was again launched.

The *Niagara* is the centerpiece of a maritime museum on Erie's Bayfront. Construction began in 1994 and it is scheduled to open in 1996. It is fascinating to step aboard the *Niagara*, now the official flagship of Pennsylvania, and see exactly how this frontier ship was designed. She had approximately 200 oars, and was steered with a tiller instead of a wheel, making her hard to control in rough seas. During the Battle of Lake Erie the *Niagara* had a crew of 142 and 13 officers. Beneath the deck the junior officers slept on bunks and there was a small wardroom for senior officers. The captain's cabin was in the very forward section of the ship.

The *Niagara* sails as a historical ambassador visiting ports along the East Coast and the Great Lakes. When in port the *Ni-*

agara can be boarded and toured Monday through Saturday 9:00 A.M. to 5:00 P.M. and Sundays NOON to 5:00 P.M. Admission is charged. It is advisable to call before visiting, (814) 871-4596. When the *Niagara* is at sea, the site and gift shop remain open.

Directions: Take I-79 north, it will eventually turn into the Bayfront Parkway. Follow Bayfront Parkway across State Street. The *Niagara* is moored at the foot of Holland Street, the first road on your left. The Bayfront area has interesting shops and restaurants beside Dobbins Landings, the pier at the foot of State Street. This is a gathering spot for Erie residents and tourists alike.

Waterford and Fort LeBoeuf

Wayfarers in the Wilderness

Western Pennsylvania's mountainous terrain made land travel difficult for representatives and armies of the colonial powers. The French built a series of forts to control the water routes needed for their fur trade with the Native Americans. Their most important fort was at the Forks of the Ohio, where the Allegheny and Mongongahela join to form the Ohio (see Fort Pitt selection). Controlling the rivers enabled the French to move back and forth between Canada and their domain in Louisiana.

The French began the task of securing control of the Ohio in 1753. New France Governor Ange de Menneville, the Marquis de Duquesne, started building forts at strategic points along the waterways. The French first built Fort de la Presqu'isle (see Presque Isle selection), then tortuously carried materials 21 miles overland to **Fort LeBoeuf** on French Creek which emptied into the Allegheny River. Winter halted their southward momentum. Leaving only a small garrison, the French withdrew to Montreal.

During that winter 21-year-old Major George Washington undertook a hazardous thousand mile mission to Fort LeBoeuf with a message from Virginia Governor Robert Dinwiddie. The governor asked, "By whose authority [have the French] invaded the King of Great Britain's territories? It becomes my duty to require your peaceable departure." The commander of the French fort replied, "As to the summons you send me to retire, I do not think myself obliged to obey."

If this casual dismissal seems offhand, the actions of the French indicated more concern. Braving the dismal weather the French renewed their efforts to stake their claim at the Forks of the Ohio, and so they began construction on Fort Duquesne.

For seven years Fort LeBoeuf served as a way station along the French defensive line from the Great Lakes to the Forks of the Ohio. After the British captured Fort Duquesne, the French could no longer successfully defend Fort LeBoeuf from attack. In 1759 they burned the fort and withdrew. A year later the English erected a fort on the same spot; it too was burned in a conflict with the Native Americans in 1763 during Pontiac's Rebellion (see Bushy Run Battlefield selection). A third fort was built in 1794 to protect settlers from Indian attacks. The story of these three forts is told at the **Fort LeBoeuf Museum**, 123 High Street. There is a model of the French fort, a movie on Washington's mission to the fort (across the street from the museum is the only statue of George Washington in a British uniform, commemorating his 1753 visit), exhibits on the Indians who moved through this area, the fur trade plus artifacts from archaeological excavations of this site. The museum does not have regular tour hours. Call (814) 732-2573 for information on public openings.

In 1794, United States troops built huts and a stockade at the fort and within a year the town of **Waterford** was laid out by Andrew Ellicot, General William Irvine and Albert Gallatin (see Friendship Hill selection). Waterford quickly became a major stopping point for travelers between Pittsburgh and the Great Lakes. One of the early settlers was Amos Judson. His successful general store soon enabled him to build the Greek Revival home that still stands in Waterford. It's now a house museum showcasing antique furnishings and paintings. You can tour the **Judson House** the third weekend in July and the third weekend in November. There is a research library that can be used the second Saturday of each month from 1:00 P.M. to 4:00 P.M.

Also across from Fort LeBoeuf Museum is the **Eagle Hotel**, built of local stone by Thomas King in 1826. This was one of the few stone buildings in this frontier area and it soon became the center of social and civic life. By the 1860s this was a resort area and the Eagle was noted for its fine accommodations. The Eagle Hotel has been in use for all but one year of its existence. It closed for repairs after a fire in 1845. Today it is a restaurant that is open daily.

In 1885, the **Riverside Inn** opened in nearby Cambridge Springs. The popularity of mineral water therapy in the late 19th and early 20th century ensured the community's success. At one time there were 40 hotels. Of these rambling resort meccas only the Riverside Inn remains situated on the banks of French Creek.

The discovery of the mineral springs was entwined with the discovery of oil. After Colonel Edwin L. Drake discovered oil in Titusville (see Drake's Well selection) in 1859, people in the area got "black gold fever." Dr. John Gray, seeking to find oil on his farm along French Creek discovered a crystal spring instead. Local gossip soon held that farm workers who were drinking from the spring were enjoying extremely good health. Dr. Gray had been involved with treatments at Hot Springs, Arkansas and soon realized his own water had similar properties. He successfully treated various ailments with the mineral spring water, then began selling it for a nominal fee. It was at this point that the Riverside Inn was built. In 1895 the hotel acquired a new owner who also purchased the mineral springs and the hotel became a health spa.

The springs are no longer a part of the hotel operation, but the slow pace of this old-fashioned Victorian-style resort certainly relaxes the vacationing guests. There are attractive gardens, shuffleboard, a putting green, tennis courts, a swimming pool and canoeing on French Creek. In addition to a spacious dining room there is also a dinner theater. For additional information call (800) 964-5173 or (814) 398-4546.

Directions: From I-90 take Exit 6, onto Route 19 south to Waterford. From I-79 take Exit 38 to Edinboro, then take Route 6N to Route 19 north which will becomes High Street in Waterford. If you turn right on E. 1st Street and then right again on East Street you will come to Waterford's covered bridge. To reach Cambridge Springs and the Riverside Inn just continue south on Route 19.

Watson/Curtze Mansion and Firefighters Historical Museum

Delight in Details

Among the mansions on Erie's West Sixth Street's historic "Millionaires' Row" is the **Watson/Curtze Mansion**. It is an architectural delight, filled with charming decorative touches like hand-painted friezes, coffered ceilings, stained-glass windows, marble mosaic floors and exotic marble fireplaces. The mansion houses the Erie Historical Museum so although some rooms have period furnishings others contain exhibit cases filled with artifacts detailing regional and maritime history. The mansion's carriage house now serves as a planetarium.

The mansion reflects the life style of Erie's affluent industrial barons during the 1890s. Paper manufacturer Harrison F. Watson built the Richardsonian Romanesque house between 1889 and 1891. This style features massive geometric shapes, with the effect of the house depending on mass, volume and scale rather than individual details. Following the Watson family years, Erie Trust Company president Felix F. Curtze purchased the house in 1923. The Curtze family offered the house to the local school district as a museum and it is now operated by Gannon University.

Visitors, like guests in bygone days, first enter the main hall or foyer. If details are not the main thrust of the exterior design, they certainly are significant in the splendid interior. In the foyer alone there are numerous features to note including the Italian Breccia fireplace with carved woodwork and glass Celtic-motif mosaics, the white quartered oak with cherry-stained woodwork, the stained glass windows, marble mosaic floor and the hand-painted friezes on the coffered ceiling, above the wall panelling and in the alcoves. A few original family pieces remain in the foyer: an 1890 Durfee clock, stair lamp and an Italian marble statute entitled "Blinded by Love."

The drawing room is furnished with 1880 reproductions of Louis XV and Louis XVI revival-style furniture. These pieces and the decorative items are from the Taylor-Winder estate in Erie. Architectural details abound here too. There is a Mexican onyx fireplace, pine-lacquered white woodwork, gesso-duro ceiling and fabric-covered walls made from synthetic rayon that suggests silk brocade.

The stained glass in the dining room is decorated with cherubs. This motif is picked up in the friezes which also are highlighted with putti, the name given to children in classical times. Here the fireplace is yellow African marble while the woodwork is Mexican frontier mahogany. The built-in china cabinets showcase Mrs. Watson's collection of art glass and her Meissen and Dresden china. The mahogany Aesthetic Movement style dining room pieces are original to the house.

From the 1879s the decor moves to the 1900s in the warm, sunny solarium with its marble mosaic floor, decorative stone work and the original wrought iron lighting fixtures. In his den, Harrison Watson, had shallow-drawer cabinets built to hold his butterfly collection. This masculine room also has a brown tile fireplace, hazelwood woodwork, a quadruple vaulted ceiling and Arabic-motif friezes on the ceiling and wall.

Upstairs in the sitting room there is an exhibit on the house with photographs and portraits of the Curtze family. The bedrooms now contain exhibit cases, but the fine architectural details of the house are still captivating, especially the round stained glass windows made of small florets in Winifred Watson's bedroom. The master bedroom has a lovely carved wood mantle above the Lisbon marble fireplace.

An expansive ballroom takes up much of the third floor. The ceiling and walls are stenciled with a rose trellis design. Additional exhibits are mounted in the basement. This intriquing house museum can be toured Tuesday through Sunday from 1:00

P.M. to 5:00 P.M. During the summer months on Tuesday through Friday the house opens at 10:00 A.M. The planetarium has shows on Thursday, Friday and Saturday at 2:00 P.M. and on Sunday at 2:00 P.M. and 3:00 P.M. A nominal admission is charged.

Just a half block away is the **Firefighters Historical Museum** in the old #4 Erie Firehouse. Here you'll find a treasure-trove of firefighting memorabilia. They have over 1,300 items on display. Antique fire apparatus, an extensive collection of uniforms, badges, ribbons, helmets, masks and fire extinguishers fill the museum. Youngsters will be intrigued by the demonstration of how fire call boxes relayed word of a fire. Individual pieces of note include an 1823 hand tub, an 1830 hand pumper, an 1886 hand-pulled hose cart (this was the first piece of equipment in nearby North East), a 1920 LaFrance pumper and a 1927 LaFrance fire-truck. This is the only museum to have an 1889 Remington horse-drawn fire engine.

From May through August the Firefighters Historical Museum is open Saturdays 10:00 A.M. to 5:00 P.M. On Sundays it opens at 1:00 P.M. In September and October weekend hours are 1:00 P.M. to 5:00 P.M. A nominal admission is charged.

Directions: Take I-79 to Erie, turn right on Route 5 (12th Street), then make a left on Cherry Street and a right on Sixth Street (Route 5A). While driving the two blocks to Chestnut Street, notice the beautiful mansions on the way to the Erie Historical Museum and Planetarium of Gannon University at 356 West Sixth Street, on the left corner of Chestnut. The Firefighters Historical Museum is at 428 Chestnut Street. For a more scenic route than Route 5, stay on I-79 as it become the Bayfront Parkway, taking that past the marinas and the historic waterworks buildings to State Street. Turn left and drive several blocks through Perry Square, with its water fountain and gazebo on either side, turning right on South Park Row. Then right again and immediately left onto West Sixth Street, with the Gannon Univeristy historic "Old Main" administration building on the left and the Erie County Court House on the right. Drive three blocks to Chestnut Street.

Calendar of Events

PHILADELPHIA AND THE COUNTRYSIDE

JANUARY

Early:
Mummers Parade, Broad & Snyder Streets, Philadelphia, (215) 336-3050
Mid:
Martin Luther King, Jr. Celebration, Afro-American Historical & Cultural Museum, (215) 574-0380
Late:
Welcome Spring Display, Longwood Gardens, (through April), (215) 388-6741

FEBRUARY

Early:
Black History Month, Afro-American Historical & Cultural Museum, (215) 574-0380
Mid:
President's Day Weekend, Valley Forge National Historical Park, (215) 783-1077
Gen. Washington's B-day Celebration, Brandywine Battlefield Park, (215) 459-3342

MARCH

Early:
Maple Sugar Festival, Springton Manor Farm, (215) 344-6415
Philadelphia Flower Show, Civic Center, (215) 625-8253
Mid:
Charter Day, PA Historical & Museum Sites Statewide, (717) 783-1990

APRIL

Early:
Easter Egg Hunt, Quarry Valley Farm, (215) 794-5882
Acres of Spring, Longwood Gardens Outdoor Display, (through May), (610) 388-1000
Late:
Penn Relays, Franklin Field, Univ. of PA, (215) 898-6145
Historic Yellow Springs Art Show, Village of Yellow Springs, (215) 827-7414
Philadelphia Open House, House & Garden Tours, (through mid-May), (215) 928-1188

MAY

Early:
Spring Fling Festival, Lock Ridge Furnace Museum, (215) 435-4664
Shad Festival, Bethlehem's 18th-Century Industrial Area, (215) 691-5300
Celebration of Spring, Pennsbury Manor, (215) 946-0400
Sidewalk Art Show, Historic Bethlehem, (215) 866-1177 or 868-1513
Wildflower Plant & Seed Sale, Brandywine River Museum, (215) 388-2700
French Alliance Day, Valley Forge National Historical Park, (215) 783-0535
Mid:
Bethlehem Bach Festival, Packer Memorial Church, Lehigh Univ., (215) 866-4382
Traditional Craft Show & Colonial Fair, Colonial PA Plantation, Ridley Creek State Park, (215) 566-1725
Outdoor Mummers String Band Concerts, Mummers Museum Parking Courtyard, (Tuesdays through September), (215) 336-3050
Late:
Tyler Springfest, Tyler State Park, (215) 860-0731
Philadelphia International Theater Festival for Children, Annenberg Center, Univ. of PA, (215) 898-6791 or 898-6683
Mayfair, Allentown Parks System, (215) 437-6900
Antique Show, Brandywine River Museum, (215) 388-2700
Chadds Ford Winery Mayfest, Chaddsford Winery, (215) 388-6221
USAIR Jambalaya Jam, Penn's Landing, (800) 321-WKND, (215) 636-1666
Commemoration Day: Valley Forge Pk., Valley Forge Natl. Hist. Pk., (215) 783-4356
Festival of Fountains, Longwood Gardens, (through September), (610) 388-1000

JUNE

Early:
Bucks County Classic Arts & Crafts Fair, Bucks County Fairgrounds, (215) 493-0706

Mid:
Delco Scottish Games, Delaware County Horse Show Grounds, (215) 825-7286
Departure of the Continental Army, Valley Forge National Historical Park,
(215) 783-1077
Frontier Day, Warwick County Park, (215) 344-6415
Yellow Springs Craft Festival, Village of Yellow Springs, (215) 827-7414
Head House Craft & Fine Arts Fair, Head House Square, Society Hill, (through
early September on weekends), (215) 790-0782
Late:
Victorian Tyme Art & Craft Show, Skippack Village, (215) 584-1438

JULY
Early:
Phila. Freedom Fest., Independence Hall, Penn's Lnd. & elsewhere, (215) 636-1666
Freedom of Expression Wknd., Phila. Zoo, (800) 321-WKND or (215) 636-1666
Mid:
Canal Festival, Hugh Moore Park, (215) 250-6700
All-American Teddy Bears' Picnic, Peddler's Village, (215) 794-4000
Easton Area Heritage Day, Center City, (215) 250-6610
Late:
Civil War Reenactment, Colonial PA Plantation, (215) 566-1725
River Blues Festival, Penn's Landing, (800) 321-WKND or (215) 636-1666

AUGUST
Mid:
Old Fiddlers' Picnic, Hibernia County Park, (215) 344-6415
Musikfest, Historic Downtown Bethlehem, (215) 861-0678
Late:
Hispanic Fiesta at Penn's Landing, Penn's Landing Plaza (215) 627-3100 or 923-4992
Great Allentown Fair, Fairgrounds, (215) 433-7541

SEPTEMBER
Early:
National Mushroom Festival, Kennett Square, (month long), (215) 444-4951
Chadds Ford Winery Jazz Festival, Chaddsford Winery, (215) 388-6221
Mid:
Chadds Ford Days, Chadds Ford, (215) 388-7376
Pennsburg Manor Fair, Pennsbury Manor, (215) 946-0400
Tyler Fallfest, Tyler State Park, (215) 860-0731
Peddler's Village Scarecrow Weekend, Peddler's Village, (215) 794-4000
Revolutionary Times at Brandywine, Brandywine Battlefield Park, (215) 459-3342
Children's Fest., Fonthill & Moravian Tileworks Grnds, (215) 757-0571 or 348-6114
Franklin Mint Antique Automobile Festival, Franklin Mint Museum, (215) 459-6168
Late:
Penns Landing In-Water Boat Show, Penn's Landing, (215) 449-9910
Chevrolet Celtic Classic Highland Games & Festival, Historic Downtown Bethle-
hem, (215) 868-9599
German-American Steuben Parade, 20th & Benjamin Franklin Pkwy to Indepen-
dence Hall, (215) 742-3587 or 663-9655
Harvest Show, Fairmount Park Horticulture Center, (215) 625-8263

OCTOBER
Early:
Battle of Germantown Reenactment, Cliveden, (215) 848-1777
Skippack Days Arts & Crafts Show, Skippack Village, (215) 584-3074
Down on Farm Autumn Leaves Fest., Lock Ridge Furn. Mus., (215) 435-4664
Mid:
Historic Fallsington Day, Village of Fallsington, (215) 295-6567
Columbus Day Parade, Downtown Philadelphia, (215) 636-1666
Fest-O-Fall, Pool Wildlife Sanctuary, (215) 965-4397
Apple Wine Weekend, Chaddsford Winery, (215) 388-6221
Yellow Springs Antique Show & Sale, Village of Yellow Springs, (215) 827-7414
Late:
Haunted Halloween Farm, Quarry Valley Farm, (215) 794-5882
Chrysanthemum Festival, Longwood Gardens, (though November), (610) 388-1000

NOVEMBER

Early:
Whitemarsh Encampment, Hope Lodge, (215) 646-1595
Mid:
Handweaver of Bucks County Show & Sale, Washington Crossing State Park, (215) 448-0764 or 883-1366
Late:
Channel 6 Thanksgiving Day Parade, Downtown Philadelphia, (215) 581-4529
A Brandywine Christmas, Brandywine River Mus., (thru early Jan.), (215) 388-2700
Christmas City Night Light Tours, Bethlehem Vis. Ctr., (thru Dec.), (215) 868-1513
Moravian Christmas Putz, Bethlehem's Christian Education Building, (through December), (215) 866-5661 or 867-0173

DECEMBER

Early:
Park House Christmas Tours, Fairmount Park, (215) 787-5449
Christmas Festival, Peddler's Village, (215) 794-4000
Illuminaire Nites, Skippack Village, (215) 584-3074
Christmas Conservatory Display & Outdoor Lighting, Longwood Gardens, (through early January), (610) 388-1000
Mid:
Holly Night, Pennsburg Manor, (215) 946-0400
Live Bethlehem Christmas Pageant, Bethlehem's Comm. Arts Pav., (215) 867-2893
Washington's March into Valley Forge, Valley Forge Nat. Hist. Park, (215) 783-1077
Late:
Reenactment of Washington Crossing the Delaware, Washington Crossing Historic Park, (215) 493-4076

POCONO MOUNTAINS REGION

JANUARY

Mid:
Ice Carving Festival, Mountain Laurel Resort & Conference Center, White Haven, (717) 443-8411
Late:
Greater Pottsville Winter Carnival, Pottsville, (717) 682-2702

FEBRUARY

Early:
Ice Tee Golf Tournament, Lake Wallenpaupack, Hawley, (717) 226-3191
Mid:
Sullivan County Sleigh Rally, Forksville Fairgrounds, (717) 928-9550
Late:
Keystone State Games, Montage Ski Area, Scranton, (717) 969-7669

MARCH

Early:
St. Patrick's Day Parade, Scranton, (717) 348-3412
Mid:
Spring Carnival, Elk Mountain Ski Resort, Union Dale, (717) 679-2611
Charter Day, PA Historical & Museum Sites Statewide, (717) 783-1990

APRIL

Late:
Maple Syrup Festival, Alparon Park, Troy, (717) 297-2791

MAY

Early:
Jazz Fest at Cherry Blossom Time, Wilkes-Barre, (717) 823-3165
Tour Du Pont, Pocono Mountains, (800) POCONOS or (717) 421-5791
Mid:
Pocono Mts. Dog Show & Obed. Trial, West End Fairgrnds, Gilbert, (717) 424-9511
Late:
Animal Frolic, Quiet Valley Living Historical Farm, Stroudsburg, (717) 992-6161
Pocono's Greatest Irish Fest., Jack Frost Mtn. Ski Area, Blakeslee, (717) 443-8425

JUNE

Early:
Heritage Days Festival, French Azilum, Towanda, (717) 265-3376
Lackawanna Arts Festival, Courthouse Square, Scranton, (717) 347-1151

Mid:
Arts & Crafts Fair, Bingham Park & Main Street, Hawley, (717) 226-3191
Champion Spark Plug 500, Pocono International Raceway, (800) RACEWAY or
  (717) 646-2300
Laurel Blossom Festival, Railroad Station, Jim Thorpe, (717) 325-3673

Late:
Patch Town Days, Eckley Miners' Village, Eckley, (717) 636-2070
PA Wine and Food Festival, Split Rock Resort, Lake Harmony, (800) 255-ROCK or
  (717) 722-9111

JULY

Early:
Old Fashion 4th Celebration, Kirby Park, Wilkes-Barre, (717) 823-3165
Wyoming County Historical Society's Arts & Craft Fair, Wyoming County Fair
  Grounds, Meshoppen, (717) 836-5303
Summer Madness, Mauch Chunk Historic District, Jim Thorpe, (717) 325-2224

Mid:
Big Boulder Chili Cook-Off, Big Boulder Ski Area, Blakeslee, (717) 722-0101
Wilkes-Barre/Scranton Fair, Pocono Downs Race Track, (800) 749-3247
Outdoor Antique Market, Village Green, Eagles Mere, (717) 525-3503

AUGUST

Early:
Stroudsmoor's Italian Festival, Stroudsmoor Country Inn, (717) 421-6431

Mid:
Eagles Mere Arts & Crafts Festival, Village Green, (717) 525-3503

Late:
Bradford County Old-Timers Show, V.F.W. Grounds, E. Smithfield, (717) 596-2527
Pocono Mountainfest, Sun Mountain Resort, Shawnee-on-Delaware, (215) 860-0731
Armed Forces Airshow, Wilkes-Baree/Scranton Int'l Airport, (717) 655-3077
Civil War Encampment, Eckley Miners' Village, Eckley, (717) 636-2070
Big Pond Bluegrass Festival, Big Pond, (717) 297-2900

SEPTEMBER

Early:
Celebration of the Arts, Delaware Water Gap, (717) 476-8265
Early Fall Antique Market, Village Green, Eagles Mere, (717) 525-3503
Farewell to Summer Fireworks, Camelback Ski Area, Tannersville, (717) 629-1661

Mid:
Arts & Crafts Street Fair, Bingham Park & Main Street, Hawley, (717) 226-3191
PA National Arts & Crafts Autumn Fest, Lackawanna County Stadium, Scranton,
  (717) 763-1254

Late:
Heritage Days/Civil War Encampment, Orwigsburg, (717) 366-3925 or 366-0165
Oktoberfest, Jack Frost Mountain, Blakeslee, (717) 443-8425

OCTOBER

Early:
Fall Foliage Festival, Towanda Airport Grounds, (717) 265-6156 or 265-2732
Fall Festival, Elk Mountain Ski Resort, Union Dale, (717) 679-2611
Fall Foliage Festival, Railroad Station, Jim Thorpe, (717) 325-3673
Harvest Festival, Quiet Valley Living Historical Farm, Stroudsburg, (717) 992-6161
Shawnee Mountain Lumberjack Festival, Shawnee-on-Delaware, (717) 421-7231
Arts & Crafts Show, Jack Frost Mtn., White Haven, (717) 443-8425

Mid:
Shawnee Autumn Balloon Festival, Shawnee Inn, (717) 421-1500 x 1742
Octoberfest, Stroudsmoor Country Inn, Stroudsburg, (717) 421-6431

Late:
Oktoberfest, Shawnee Mountain Ski Area, Shawnee-on-Delware, (717) 421-7231

Late:
Christmas in the Country Craft & Antique Fair, Stroudsmoor Country Inn, Strousburg, (717) 421-6431
Santa's Snowtime Express Stourbridge Line Rail Excursion, Honesdale Train Station, (through early December), (717) 253-1960

DECEMBER
Early:
Old-Time Christmas Celebration, RR. Sta., Jim Thorpe, (717) 325-2224 or 325-3673
Tree Lighting Celebration, Marketplace at Stroudsmoor, Stroudsburg (717) 424-1199

HERSHEY/DUTCH COUNTRY REGION
JANUARY
Early:
PA Farm Show, Farm Show Complex, Harrisburg, (717) 787-5373

FEBRUARY
Early:
Eastern Sports Boat, Camping, Travel & Outdoor Show, Farm Show Complex, Harrisburg, (717) 536-8152
Mid:
Valentine's Day Craft Show, York Fairgrounds, (717) 764-1155
Late:
Maple Sugaring Demonstrations, Central Park, Lancaster, (717) 299-8215

MARCH
Mid:
Charter Day, PA Historical & Museum Sites Statewide, (717) 783-1990
Late:
Quilters Heritage Celebration, Lancaster Host Resort, (717) 854-9323

APRIL
Early:
Easter Bunny Express, Temple & South Hamburg Stations, Reading, (215) 562-4083
Mid:
Tulip Display, Hershey Gardens, (through early May), (717) 534-3492 or 534-3439
Spring Craft Show, York Fairgrounds, (717) 764-1155
Late:
Spring Antique Extravaganza, Black Angus Antique Mall, Adamstown, (215) 484-4385 or (717) 569-3536
Spring Carlisle Collector Car Flea Mkt. & Corral, Carlisle Fairgrnds, (717) 243-7855
Renninger's Antique Extravaganza, Renninger's Antique Auction, Kutztown, (717) 385-0104 or (215) 683-6848
York Show Country Crossroads, York Fairgrounds, (717) 776-6988

MAY
Early:
Apple Blossom Fest., S. Mtn. Fairgrnds, Arendtsville, (717) 677-7444 or 334-6274
Union Canal Tunnel Fair, Union Canal Tunnel Park, Lebanon, (717) 272-1473
Hershey in the Spring, Hersheypark, (800) HERSHEY or (717) 534-3900
Herb Faire, Landis Valley Museum, Lancaster, (717) 569-0402
Olde York Street Fair, York, (717) 854-1587
Mid:
Gettysburg Bluegrass Camporee, Granite Hill Campgrounds, (800) 642-TENT or (717) 642-8749
Rhubarb Festival, Kitchen Kettle Village, Intercourse, (717) 768-8261
Late:
Gettysburg Outdoor Antique Show, Gettysburg, (717) 334-6274
Corn Festival, Shippensburg, (717) 530-1390
Greater Harrisburg Arts Festival, Capitol Complex, (717) 238-5180
Memorial Day Parade & National Cemetery Service, Gettysburg, (717) 334-6274

JUNE
Early:
Lancaster Designer Spring Art & Craft Mkt., Lancaster Cty. Cent. Pk., (717) 295-1500

Foundry Day Arts & Craft Festival, Boiling Springs, (717) 240-8048
International Food Festival, Chambersburg, (717) 261-0072
Ephrata Community Hospital Day, Ephrata, (717) 738-6692
Landis Valley Fair, Landis Valley Museum, Lancaster, (717) 569-0401
Mid:
Rose Display, Hershey Gardens, (through late September), (717) 534-3492 or 534-3439
Middletown Colonial Arts & Crafts Fair, Hoffer Park, Middletown, (717) 944-4435
Berks Cty. Civil War Living Hist., Berks Cty. Heritage Ctr., Reading, (215) 374-8839
Cloister Classic Vintage Automobile Show, Ephrata, (717) 738-6692
Late:
Gettysburg Civil War Heritage Days, Gettysburg, (717) 334-6274
Kutztown Folk Fest., Kutztown Fairgrnds, (thru Aug.) (800) 447-9269/(215) 683-8707

JULY

Early:
PA Renaissance Faire, Mt. Hope Estate and Winery, Cornwall, (717) 665-7021
Harrisburg Independence Wknd. Fest., Riverfront Pk. & City Isl., (717) 255-3020
Reading RR. Wknd, Railroad Museum of PA, Strasburg, (717) 687-8628
4th of July Fireworks Spectacle, York Fairgrounds, (717) 751-3162
Mid:
Shippensburg Community Fair, Fairgrounds, (717) 532-5509
Late:
Chambersfest, Chambersburg, (717) 264-7101
Lancaster Summerfest, Franklin and Marshall College, (215) 860-0731
Scenic River Days, Riverfront Park, Reading, (215) 375-6508
Hanover Dutch Festival, Center Square & Wirt Park, Hanover, (717) 637-6130
Bavarian Beer Fest, Black Angus Complex, Adamstown, (weekends through early
   September), (215) 484-4385

AUGUST

Early:
Quilt Auction, Brethren Home, New Oxford, (717) 624-2161
Mid:
Lebanon Bolgona Fest, Lebanon Fairgrounds, (717) 272-8555
Reading Aerofest, Reading Regional Airport, (215) 372-4666
Circus Week, Railroad Museum of Pennsylvania, Strasburg, (717) 687-8628
Late:
Corn Festival, Shippensburg, (717) 530-1390
Riverwalk Art Festival & Exhibition, York County Colonial *Courthouse & Codorus
   Bike Path*, (717) 854-1587

SEPTEMBER

Early:
Family Oktoberfest, Mill Bridge Village, Strasburg, (wknds thru Oct.), (717) 687-6521
Kipona Celebration, Riverfront Park & City Island, Harrisburg, (717) 255-3020
Labor Day Arts & Crafts Mkt., Renfrew Mus. & Pk., Waynesboro, (717) 264-9425
Mid:
Hay Creek Valley Fall Festival, Historic Joanna Furnace, Morgantown, (215) 286-0388
Colonial Day, East Berlin, (717) 259-7198
Fall Fiddle Festival, Lyons Park, Lyons, (215) 682-6103
Hispanic Heritage Month, York Spanish American Ctr., (thru mid-Oct.), (717) 846-9434
Harvest Festival, Kitchen Kettle Village, Intercourse, (717) 768-8261
Fort Hunter Day, Fort Hunter Mansion, Harrisburg, (717) 599-5751
Pagoda Festival, Tower on Mt. Penn, Reading, (215) 929-0234
Late:
Ephrata Fair, Main Street, (717) 733-8132
Wrightsville Heritage Day, Constitution Square, Wrightsville, (717) 252-3304
Pippinfest, Fairfield, (717) 642-5640

OCTOBER

Early:
Apple Harvest Festival, South Mountain Fairgrounds, Arendtsville, (717) 334-6274
Heritage Celebration, Berks County Heritage Center, Reading, (215) 374-8839
Harrisburg Harvest Fest., Broad St. Farmer's Mkt. & Mid. Harrisburg, (717) 233-4646
Arts Festival & Octubafest, High Street, Carlisle, (717) 245-2548
Harvest Days, Landis Valley Museum, Lancaster, (717) 569-0401

Mid:
PA National Horse Show, Farm Show Complex, Harrisburg, (717) 236-1600
Late:
Creatures of the Night, ZooAmerica North American Wildlife Park, Hershey, (800)
   HERSHEY or (717) 534-3860
Pumpkin Patch Weekend, Landis Valley Museum, Lancaster, (717) 569-0402
Edgar Allan Poe Halloween, Mount Hope Estate & Winery, Cornwall, (through
   early November), (717) 665-7021
Halloween Lantern Tours, Railroad Museum of PA/Strasburg Railroad, Strasburg,
   (717) 687-8628 or 687-7522
York Halloween Parade, York, (717) 854-1587

NOVEMBER
Early:
Lancaster Designer Craft Market, Lancaster, (717) 295-1500
Mid:
York Yulefest, York Fairgrounds, (215) 860-0731
Anniversary Celebration of the Gettysburg Address, Gettysburg, (717) 334-6274
Hersheypark Christmas Candylane, Hersheypark, (through December),
   (800) HERSHEY or (717) 534-3900
Late:
Harrisburg Holiday Parade, Harrisburg, (717) 255-3020
Christmas Parade, Penn Street, Reading, (215) 376-6424
Crafts & Trains Show, Stoy Museum, Lebanon, (717) 272-1473
Crystal Cave Candlelight Tours, Kutztown, (215) 683-6765
Belsnickel Craft Show, Boyertown, (215) 367-9843
Charles Dickens Christmas Past, Mount Hope Estate & Winery, Cornwall, (through
   December), (717) 665-7021
Savor the Season, Kitchen Kettle Village, Intercourse, (thru Dec.), (717) 768-8261
Santa Claus Special Railroad Ride, Blue Mountain & Reading Railroad, Hamburg,
   (through mid-December), (215) 562-4083
Ride the Train with Santa, Middletown & Hummelstown Railroad, Middletown,
   (717) 944-4435
Model Railroad Exhibit & Open House, York, (through December), (717) 767-4998

DECEMBER
Early:
Christmas at Fort Hunter, Fort Hunter Mansion, Harrisburg, (through December,
   closed Monday), (717) 599-5751
Christmas Magic—A Festival of Lights, Rocky Ridge Park, York, (through Decem-
   ber), (717) 771-9440
PA Christmas & Gift Show, Farm Show Complex, Harrisburg, (717) 233-5100
Christmas Craft Show, York Fairgrounds, (717) 764-1155
Mid:
An Eisenhower Christmas, Eisenhower National Historic Site, Gettysburg, (through
   December), (717) 334-1124
Gettysburg Yuletide Festival, Gettysburg, (717) 334-6274
Late:
Christmas at Landis Valley, Landis Valley Museum, Lancaster, (717) 569-0401
New Year's Eve Celebration, Market Square, Harrisburg, (717) 255-3020

VALLEYS OF THE SUSQUEHANNA
FEBRUARY
Mid:
Victorian Valentine (Trolley) Venture, Williamsport, (800) 358-9900 or (717) 321-1200

MARCH
Early:
Maple Syrup Sunday, Montour Preserve Visitor Center, (717) 437-3131
Charter Day, PA Historical & Museum Sites Statewide, (717) 783-1990

APRIL
Early:
Easter Bunny Express, Delta Place Station, Lewisburg, (717) 524-4337
Arts Festival, Packwood House Mus., Lewisburg, (thru early May), (717) 524-0320

Late:
  Festival of the Arts, Lewisburg, (800) 458-4748 or (717) 524-7234

MAY
Late:
  Memorial Day in Boalsburg, Boalsburg, (814) 466-6210 or 466-6263

JUNE
Early:
  Nittany Antique Machinery Show Spring Warm Up, Penn's Cave, Centre Hall, (814) 364-1664
Mid:
  Strawberry Festival, Historic Warrior Run Church, Turbotville, (717) 649-5363
  Historic Cruise, Bellefonte, (814) 355-2761
Late:
  Perry Cty. Auto. Meet, Lupfers' Grove, Shermans Dale, (717) 582-4935 or 582-2922

JULY
Early:
  Central PA Festival of the Arts, State College & Penn State, (814) 237-3682
Mid:
  Frontier Days & Rodeo, Benton Airport Grounds, (717) 925-6181
  Olde Tymers' Day, Selinsgrove, (717) 374-2929

AUGUST
Early:
  Antiques at Bloomsburg, Bloomsburg Fairgrounds, (717) 784-8279
Mid:
  Walnut Acres Open House & Cty. Fair, Walnut Acres, Penns Creek, (717) 837-0601
Late:
  Bellefonte Arts & Crafts Fair, Bellefonte, (814) 355-2917
  Anthracite Heritage Memorial Parade, Shamokin, (717) 648-4675
  Little League Baseball World Series, Lamade Stad., S. Williamsport, (717) 326-1921
  New Berlin Heritage Day, New Berlin, (717) 966-3674

SEPTEMBER
Early:
  Labor Day Regatta, Susquehanna Riverbank, Lock Haven, (717) 893-4037
  Nittany Antique Machinery Steam Engine Days, Penns Cave, Centre Hall, (814) 364-1664
Mid:
  Black Arts Fest., Penn State, State College, (thru mid-October), (814) 865-1779
Late:
  Bloomsburg Fair, Fairgrounds, (717) 784-4949 or 784-5728

OCTOBER
Early:
  PA State Flaming Foliage Festival, Renovo, (717) 923-2411
  Buffalo Valley Antique Machinery Show, Delta Pl. Sta., Lewisburg, (717) 524-4337
  Boalsburg Culture Heritage Festival, Columbus Chapel and Boal Mansion Museum, (814) 466-6210
  Apple Butter Day, Curtin Village, Bellefonte, (814) 355-1982
Mid:
  Covered Bridge & Arts Fest., Knoebel's Amusement Res., Elysburg, (717) 784-8279
  Oktoberfest, Shamokin, (717) 648-4675

NOVEMBER
Late:
  Run for Diamonds, Berwick, (717) 759-1300

DECEMBER
Early:
  Selinsgove White Christmas, Market Street, Selinsgrove, (717) 374-0466 or 374-2929
  Mifflinburg Christkindl Mkt., Market St., Mifflinburg, (800) 45-VISIT or (717) 743-7234
  Victorian Holiday Weekend, Downtown Victorian Lewisburg, (800) 458-4748 or (717) 743-7234

Bellefonte Victorian Christmas, Bellefonte, (814) 355-2917 or 231-4658
Santa Claus Express, Delta Place Station, Mifflinburg, (717) 524-4337
Anthracite Model Railroad Club & Railroad Museum Open House, Shamokin,
   (Weekends throughout month) (717) 648-5674
Mid:
Little Buffalo Christmas Program, Little Buffalo State Park, Newport, (717) 567-9255

ALLEGHENY NATIONAL FOREST REGION

JANUARY
Early:
Rodeo in the Snow, Potter County Snowmobile Club House, Coudersport,
   (814) 667-2528 or (717) 867-5588
Late:
PA Cross-Country Sled Dog Championship, Allegheny National Forest, (814) 778-9944
Chapman Winter Carnival, Chapman State Park, (814) 723-5030

FEBRUARY
Early:
Groundhog Day, Gobbler's Knob, Punxsutawney, (814) 938-7700
Wellsboro Winter Weekend, Wellsboro, (717) 724-1926
Winter Family Festival, Parker Dam State Park, (814) 765-0630
PA SLed Dog Races, Chapman State Park, (814) 723-5030
Mid:
Tionesta President's Day Winterfest, Tionesta, (800) 222-1706 or (814) 927-8818

MARCH
Early:
Charter Day, PA Historical & Museum Sites Statewide, (717) 783-1990

APRIL
Mid:
Cameron County Canoe Classic, River Park, (814) 486-1691

MAY
Late:
Clarion River Country Days, Clarion Memorial Park, (814) 226-9161

JUNE
Early:
Susquehanna Trail Pro Rally, Wellsboro, (717) 724-1926
Mid:
Western PA Laurel Festival, Brookville, (814) 849-2024
PA State Laurel Festival, Wellsboro, (717) 724-1926
Late:
Punxsutawney Groundhog Festival, Punxsutawney, (814) 938-7687
Forest Fest, Allegheny National Forest, (814) 772-5502
Snake Hunt & Rattlesnake Sacking Contest, Cross Fork Fire Company Grounds,
   (717) 923-1428

JULY
Early:
Brockway's Old-Fashioned Fourth Celebration, Brockway, (814) 268-8621
Bark Peelers Convention, PA Lumber Museum, (814) 435-2652
Mid:
Sawmill Woodcarving Show & All-Wood Festival, Sawmill Center for the Arts,
   Cook Forest State Park, (814) 927-6655
Tom Mix Roundup, Tom Mix Birthplace Park, (814) 546-2044 or 546-2628
Late:
Allegheny Mountain Championship Rodeo, Flying W Ranch, (814) 463-7663

AUGUST
Early:
Galeton Rotary Woodman's Show, Cherry Springs State Park, (814) 435-2907
Mid:
American Indian Pow Wow, Flying W Ranch, (814) 463-7663
Tionesta Indian Festival, Tionesta Recreation Field, (814) 755-4362

Late:
 Sawmill Summerfest & Quilt Show, Sawmill Center for the Arts, Cook Forest State
  Park, (814) 927-6655
 Crook Farm Country Fair, Crook Farm, (814) 778-9944

SEPTEMBER
Mid:
 PA Trappers, Hunters & Outdoorsmen's Show, Clearfield Cty. Fairgrnds, (814) 328-2065

OCTOBER
Mid:
 Heritage Days Antique Show & Sale, PA Lumber Museum, (814) 435-2652

DECEMBER
Early:
 Historic Brookville Victorian Christmas Celebration, Brookville, (814) 849-8448
 Dickens of a Christmas, Wellsboro, (717) 724-1926

LAUREL HIGHLANDS REGION

FEBRUARY
Early:
 Winter Carnival, Hidden Valley Resort, Somerset, (814) 443-6454

MARCH
Early:
 Spring Carnival, Hidden Valley Resort, Somerset, (814) 443-6454
Mid:
 Charter Day, PA Historical & Museum Sites Statewide, (717) 783-1990
Late:
 PA Maple Festival, Meyersdale, (814) 634-0213

APRIL
Late:
 Raystown Country Sports Show, Huntingdon County Fairgrounds, (814) 669-4170

MAY
Early:
 In-Water Boat & RV Show, Lake Raystown Resort & Lodge, (800) 628-4262 or (814)
  658-3500
 Flea-tique at Old Hanna's Town, Greensburg, (First Monday of the month through
  September), (412) 836-1800
Late:
 Blair County Arts Festival, Altoona, (814) 949-2787
 Albert Gallatin Regatta, Point Marion City Park, (412) 725-5205 or 725-5245
 Memorial Day Wknd. Polka Fest., Seven Springs Mtn. Res., Champion, (412) 274-5440

JUNE
Early:
 Strawberry Festival, McConnell Park, McConnellsburg, (717) 485-4064
 Founders Day Antique Auto Show, Altoona, (814) 684-5369
Mid:
 Antique Car Show, Lake Raystown Resort & Lodge, Entriken, (800) 628-4262 or
  (814) 658-3500
 Monessen Cultural Heritage Festival, Monessen, (412) 684-3200
Late:
 Arts & Crafts Festival, Old Bedford Village, (814) 623-1156

JULY
Early:
 Westmoreland Arts & Heritage Festival, Twin Lakes Park, Greensburg, (412) 830-3950
 Nemacolin Community Festival, Nemacolin Woodlands Resort, Farmington,
  (800) 422-2736 or (412) 941-8497
 Settlers Day American Indian Pow Wow, Old Bedford Village, (814) 623-1156
 Somerfest, Philip Dressler Center for the Arts, Somerset, (814) 443-2433

Late:
Bluegrass Festival, Old Bedford Village, (814) 623-1156

AUGUST
Early:
Shade Gap Picnic, Harpers Memorial Park, (814) 259-3279
Anniversary of the Battle of Bushy Run, Bushy Run Battlefield, Jeanette, (412) 527-5584
Bedford County Fair, Bedford, (814) 623-9011
Mid:
PA St. Gospel Singing Conv., Morrisons Cove Mem. Pk., Martinsburg, (814) 695-9356
Late:
Westmoreland Agricultural Fair, Westmoreland Fairgrounds, Mutual (412) 423-5005

SEPTEMBER
Early:
Johnstown Folk Festival, Johnstown, (814) 539-1889
Mid:
Mountain Craft Days, Somerset Historical Center, Somerset, (814) 445-6077
Ligonier Highland Games, Idlewild Park, (412) 833-6995
Polka Day, Bland's Park, Tipton, (814) 684-5369
Scottdale Coke & Coal Heritage Festival, Scottdale, (412) 887-5700
Late:
Carmichael's Covered Bridge Festival, Greene Academy, (412) 966-7996
Italian Food Festival, Bland's Park, Tipton, (814) 684-5369
Jazz in the Mountains, Hidden Valley Resort, (814) 443-2433
Wildlife & Sporting Art: The Master's Show in Ligonier, Wildlife Club & National Guard Armory, (412) 238-7560
Harvestfest, Bland's Park, Tipton, (814) 684-5369
Friendship Hill Festifall, Friendship Hill National Historic Site, Point Marion, (412) 725-9190

OCTOBER
Early:
Ghosts & Goblins Tour, Lincoln Caverns, Huntingdon, (814) 643-0268
Springs Folk Festival, Festival Grounds, Springs, (814) 662-4158
Pioneer Days, Perryopolis, (412) 736-4383
Fall Foliage Festival, Bedford, (814) 623-2121
Octoberfest Polka Wknd., Seven Springs Mtn. Res., Champion, (412) 274-5440
Fort Ligonier Days, Fort Ligonier & Downtown Ligonier, (412) 238-4200
East Broad Top Fall Spectacular, Rockhill Furnace, (814) 447-3011
Mid:
Antique Tractor, Small Engine & Farm Machinery Show, Fulton County Fairgrounds, McConnellsburg, (717) 485-5386
Dollhouse & Miniature Show, Mountain View Inn, Greensburg, (412) 837-1494
Fulton County Quilt Show, Fulton Cty. Fairgrnds, McConnellsburg, (717) 485-5386
Late:
Great Pumpkin Festival, Old Bedford Village, (814) 623-1156

DECEMBER
Early:
Christmas at Mt. Vernon Tavern, Fort Necessity, Farmington, (412) 329-5512
Christmas Parade, Waynesburg, (412) 627-5926
Old-Fashioned Christmas Celebration, Old Bedford Village, (814) 623-1156

PITTSBURGH REGION
JANUARY
Late:
Pittsburgh Boat Show, David L. Lawrence Convention Center, (412) 244-1505

FEBRUARY
Early:
Greenberg's Great Train, Dollhouse & Toy Show, Pittsburgh Expo Mart, Monroeville, (412) 795-7447

MARCH
Mid:
Pittsburgh Home & Garden Show, David L. Lawrence Conv. Ctr., (412) 922-4900
Charter Day, PA Historic & Museum Sites Statewide, (717) 783-1990

MAY
Early:
Pittsburgh Marathon, Highland Park Zoo to Point State Park, (412) 765-3773
Greek Food Festival, St. Nicholas Cathedral, Pittsburgh, (412) 682-3866
Mid:
Pittsburgh Children's Fest., North Side, Allegheny Ctr. & West Pk., (412) 321-5520
May Market, Mellon Park, Pittsburgh, (412) 441-4442
Nationality Days Festival, Ambridge, (412) 266-3040
National Pike Festival, Washington, (800) 531-4114 or (412) 222-8130
Late:
Pittsburgh Folk Festival, Station Square, (412) 281-5173
Bluegrass & Old Time Music Fest., Brady's Run Pk., Beaver, (412) 457-7091/457-7980
Balloon Quest, Scotland Meadows Park, New Castle, (412) 667-1188 or 656-1200
Hartwood Music & Dance Festival, Hartwood Acres, Pittsburgh, (Sundays through August), (412) 392-8411
South Park Summer Concert Series, Pittsburgh's South Park, (Friday evenings through August), (412) 392-8411

JUNE
Early:
Summer Flower Show, Phipps Conservatory, Schenley Park, (through early September), (412) 622-6915
Summer Sounds at the Carnegie, Carnegie's Sculpture Court, Pittsburgh, (Friday evenings through August), (412) 622-3131
Three Rivers Arts Festival, Downtown Pittsburgh, (412) 481-7040
Mid:
Mellon Jazz Festival, Pittsburgh, (412) 496-9000
Butler Rodeo, Butler Farm Show Grounds, Meridian, (412) 865-9337
Late:
Ford City Area Heritage Days, Ford City Borough Park, (412) 763-1966 or 763-7667

JULY
Early:
Station Square Food & Music Festival, Pittsburgh, (412) 471-5808
Ellwood City Arts, Crafts & Food Festival, Ewing Park, (412) 758-5630
Southside Summer Street Spectacular, E. Carson Street, (412) 481-0651
Kunstfest (Craft Festival), Old Economy Village, Ambridge, (412) 266-1803
Mid:
Apollo Moon Landing, Apollo, (412) 478-1492

AUGUST
Early:
Fort Armstrong Folk Festival, Riverfront Park, Kittanning, (412) 543-6363
Pittsburgh Three Rivers Regatta, Point State Park, (412) 261-7055
Butler Farm Show, Butler, (412) 482-4000
Mid:
Beaver County River Regatta, Bridgewater, (412) 843-6645
San Rocco Festa, Sheffield Terrace, Aliquippa, (412) 728-7655
Shadyside Summer Arts Festival, Walnut Street, Pittsburgh, (412) 681-2809
Washington County Agricultural Fair, Fairgrounds, (412) 225-7718
International Village, Renziehausen Park, McKeesport, (412) 675-5033
North Washington Fireman's Rodeo, Washington, (412) 894-2596
Late:
Big Knob Grange Fair, Big Knob Fairgrounds, Rochester, (412) 843-7863

SEPTEMBER
Early:
Fall Flower Show, Phipps Conservatory, Schenley Pk., (thru mid-Oct.), (412) 622-6915
Tour De Strongland Bicycle Race, Northmoreland Park, Apollo, (412) 727-2553
Allegheny County Rib Cook-Off, South Park Fairgrounds, Library, (412) 678-1727
Italian Fest at Station Square, Pittsburgh, (412) 471-5808

Mid:
Fair in the Park, Mellon Park, Pittsburgh, (412) 361-8287
Pittsburgh Irish Festival, Station Square, (412) 422-5642
Kit-Han-Ne Native American Indian Mkt., West Kittaning, (412) 548-8823/548-8575
Oktoberfest, New Castle, (412) 656-1200
Covered Bridge Fest., Washington & Greene Counties, (800) 531-4114/(412) 222-8130
Penn's Colony Festival, North Park, Pittsburgh, (412) 241-8006
Oktoberfest, Station Square, Pittsburgh, (412) 471-5808
Late:
Ukranian Festival, Cathedral of Learning, Pittsburgh, (412) 624-6000
Great Race (Foot Race), Frick Park to Point State Park, (412) 255-2493

OCTOBER
Early:
Lapic Wine Festival, Lapic Winery, New Brighton, (412) 846-2031
Mid:
Erntefest, Old Economy Village, Ambridge, (412) 266-1803
Fright Night, Phipps Conservatory, Schenley Park, (thru end of Oct.), (412) 622-6915

NOVEMBER
Mid:
Polishfest, Soldiers & Sailors Memorial Hall, Pittsburgh, (412) 231-1493
Light-Up Night, Pittsburgh, (412) 261-2887
Late:
Greenberg's Great Train, Dollhouse & Toy Show, Pittsburgh Expo Mart, Monroeville, (412) 795-7447
Festival of Trees, Scottish Rite Cathedral, New Castle, (412) 654-5323
Winter Flower Show, Phipps Conservatory, Schenley Pk., (thru mid-Jan.), (412) 622-6915
Celebrate Season Holiday Parade, Civic Arena to Pt. St. Pk., Pitt., (412) 232-2177

DECEMBER
Early:
Holiday Adventure, Pittsburgh Civic Garden Center, (412) 441-4442
McKeesports' Festival of Trees, Renziehausen Park, (412) 675-5033
Holiday Open House, Univ. of Pittsburgh's Nationality Rooms, (412) 624-6000
Mid:
Candlelight Christmas, Old Economy Village, Ambridge, (412) 266-1803

LAKE ERIE REGION
FEBRUARY
Early:
Meadville Area Winter Carnival, Meadville, (814) 724-6006
Pymatuning Snow Fun Days, Pymatuning State Park, (412) 927-2162
Penn's Woods West Folk & Art Festival, Mercer, (412) 662-1490

MARCH
Mid:
Charter Day, PA Historical & Museum Sites Statewide, (717) 783-1990

MAY
Late:
Conneaut Lake Antiques Market, Pioneer Show Grounds, Saegertown, (814) 333-9738

JUNE
Early:
Great Lakes Rib Cook-Off, Gravel Pit Park, North East, (814) 725-4262
Penn-Ohio Polka Festival, Conneaut Lake Park, (800) 828-9619 or (814) 382-5115
Mid:
Thurston Classic Hot Air Balloon Event, Colonel Crawford Park, Meadville, (800) 332-2338 or (814) 333-1258
Late:
Erie Summer Festival of the Arts, Gannon University, (814) 864-0191

JULY

Early:
Small Ships Revue, Sharon, (412) 981-3123
Firemen's Cherry Festival, North East, (814) 725-1537
Classic Cars & Classic Rock & Roll Show, Conneaut Lake Park, (800) 828-9619 or
  (814) 382-5115
Mid:
Heritage Days Fest., Greenville Riverside Pk. & Hist. Main Street, (412) 588-7150
Oil Heritage Week, Oil City, (814) 676-8521
Late:
Bavarian Fun Fest, Sharon, (412) 981-3123
Mercer Victorian Weekend, Historic Courthouse Square, (412) 662-1490

AUGUST

Early:
Conneaut Lake Antiques Market, Pioneer Show Grounds, Saegertown, (through
  mid-August), (814) 333-9738
Harborfest/Harborflyte, Harborcreek Community Park, Erie, (814) 899-9173
Mid:
Oil Festival, Titusville, (814) 827-2941
We Love Erie Days, State Street at Dock, (814) 454-7191
Late:
Penn-Ohio Polka Festival, Conneaut Lake Park, (814) 382-5115
Pymatuning Lake Festival, Pymatuning Lake, (412) 927-2571
Crawford County Fair, Meadville, (814) 336-1151
Conneaut Lake Jazz Party, Conneaut Lake Park, (814) 724-2163

SEPTEMBER

Early:
Great Stoneboro Fair, Stoneboro Fairgrounds, (412) 372-2852
Mid:
Pymatuning Waterfowl Expo, Linesville, (814) 683-5839 or 683-4793
Late:
Wine Country Harvest Festival, Gibson Park, North East, (814) 725-4262
Applefest, West & South Parks, Franklin, (814) 432-5823

OCTOBER

Early:
Fall Pumpkin Fest/Hot Air Balloon Rally, Conneaut Lake, (814) 382-5115
Mid:
Zoo-Boo, Erie Zoo, (814) 864-4091

NOVEMBER

Late:
Festival of Trees, Erie Plaza Hotel, (814) 452-5312

DECEMBER

Early:
Journey to Bethlehem, Greenfield Baptist Church, North East, (814) 725-4160

INDEX

About the Author

Jane Ockershausen became a best-selling author by concentrating on the popular weekend travel market. She has written nine One-Day Trip Books covering sights in Washington, D. C., Philadelphia, Virginia, Maryland, North Carolina and Georgia. She also wrote the popular Washington area guide to historic sites, *One-Day Trips Through History*.

Jane was a correspondent for *The National Geographic Traveler* for several years. Her byline has appeared in *The Washington Post*, *The Chicago Tribune* and *The Pittsburgh Post Gazette*. She has written for numerous other newspapers and magazines.

She is a member of the Women's Press Club of Pittsburgh and the PA Speakers Association. She is on the Board of Directors of the Society of American Travel Writers and is a member of the American Society of Journalists and Authors. Active on the lecture circuit, Jane has addressed numerous state-wide conferences on travel and tourism and lectured at the Smithsonian Institution.